A Companion to Roman Britain

In Honorem

Francis Haverfield
Robin Collingwood
Ian Richmond
Sheppard Frere

A COMPANION TO ROMAN BRITAIN

Edited by
Malcolm Todd

THE
HISTORICAL
ASSOCIATION
THE VOICE FOR HISTORY

Blackwell
Publishing

© 2004, 2007 by Blackwell Publishing Ltd

BLACKWELL PUBLISHING
350 Main Street, Malden, MA 02148-5020, USA
9600 Garsington Road, Oxford OX4 2DQ, UK
550 Swanston Street, Carlton, Victoria 3053, Australia

First published 2004 by Blackwell Publishing Ltd
First published in paperback 2007 by Blackwell Publishing Ltd

1 2007

Library of Congress Cataloging-in-Publication Data

A companion to Roman Britain / edited by Malcolm Todd.
p. cm. – (Blackwell companions to British history)
Includes bibliographical references (p.) and index.
ISBN-13: 978-0-631-21823-4 (alk. paper)
1. Great Britain–History–Roman period, 55 B.C.-449 A.D. 2. Great Britain–Antiquities,
Roman. 3. Romans–Great Britain. I. Todd, Malcolm, FSA. II. Series

DA145.C586 2004
936.1′04–dc21   2003051821

ISBN-13: 978-1-4051-5681-3 (paperback : alk. paper)

A catalogue record for this title is available from the British Library.

The publisher's policy is to use permanent paper from mills that operate a sustainable forestry policy, and which has been manufactured from pulp processed using acid-free and elementary chlorine-free practices. Furthermore, the publisher ensures that the text paper and cover board used have met acceptable environmental accreditation standards.

For further information on
Blackwell Publishing, visit our website:
www.blackwellpublishing.com

BLACKWELL COMPANIONS TO BRITISH HISTORY

Published in association with The Historical Association

This series provides sophisticated and authoritative overviews of the scholarship that has shaped our current understanding of British History. Each volume comprises up to forty concise essays written by individual scholars within their area of specialization. The aim of each contribution is to synthesize the current state of scholarship from a variety of historical perspectives and to provide a statement on where the field is heading. The essays are written in a clear, provocative and lively manner, designed for an international audience of scholars, students and general readers.

The *Blackwell Companions to British History* is a cornerstone of Blackwell's overarching Companions to History series, covering European, American and World History.

Published

A Companion to Roman Britain
Edited by Malcolm Todd

A Companion to Britain in the Later Middle Ages
Edited by S. H. Rigby

A Companion to Tudor Britain
Edited by Robert Tittler and Norman Jones

A Companion to Stuart Britain
Edited by Barry Coward

A Companion to Eighteenth-Century Britain
Edited by H. T. Dickinson

A Companion to Nineteenth-Century Britain
Edited by Chris Williams

A Companion to Early Twentieth-Century Britain
Edited by Chris Wrigley

A Companion to Contemporary Britain
Edited by Paul Addison and Harriet Jones

In preparation

A Companion to the Early Middle Ages: Britain and Ireland
Edited by Pauline Stafford

The Historical Association is the voice for history. Since 1906 it has been bringing together people who share an interest in, and love for, the past. It aims to further the study of teaching of history at all levels. Membership is open to everyone: teacher and student, amateur and professional. Membership offers a range of journals, activities and other benefits. Full details are available from The Historical Association, 59a Kennington Park Road, London SE11 4JH, enquiry@history.org.uk, www.history.org.uk.

Contents

Figures

Contributors

Miranda Aldhouse-Green, Professor and Director of the SCARAB Research Centre (Study of Culture, Archaeology, Religions and Biogeography), University of Wales College Newport.

Lindsay Allason-Jones, Director of University Museums, University of Newcastle upon Tyne.

Margaret Cox, Professor of Forensic Archaeology and Anthropology, University of Bournemouth.

Alexandra Croom, Curator, Arbeia Roman Fort and Museum, South Shields.

James Crow, Senior Lecturer in Roman and Byzantine Archaeology, University of Newcastle upon Tyne.

Barry Cunliffe, Professor of European Archaeology, University of Oxford, and former President of the Society of Antiquaries.

Jeffrey Davies, Senior Lecturer in Archaeology, Prifysgol Cymru Aberystwyth, University of Wales.

Simon Esmonde Cleary, Reader in Roman Archaeology, University of Birmingham.

Michael Fulford, Professor of Archaeology and Deputy Vice-Chancellor, University of Reading.

Annie Grant, Director of Educational Development and Support, University of Leicester.

William Hanson, Professor of Roman Archaeology, University of Glasgow.

Colin Haselgrove, Professor of Prehistoric Archaeology, University of Durham.

Martin Henig, Fellow of Wolfson College, University of Oxford.

Richard Hingley, Lecturer in Roman Archaeology, University of Durham.

Michael Jones, Lincoln City Archaeologist and Special Lecturer in Roman and Early Christian Archaeology, University of Nottingham.

Anthony King, Professor of Archaeology, King Alfred's College, Winchester.

William Manning, Professor Emeritus of Archaeology, University of Cardiff.

Gordon Maxwell, former Head of Archaeology, Royal Commission on Ancient and Historical Monuments in Scotland.

Rosalind Niblett, District Archaeologist, St Albans District Council.

Charlotte Roberts, Reader in Archaeology, University of Durham.

Pat Southern, Librarian of Trafford Borough Council, and author of *Domitian* (1997), *Augustus* (1998) and *The Roman Empire from Severus to Constantine* (2001).

Malcolm Todd, Professor Emeritus of Archaeology and former Principal of Trevelyan College, University of Durham.

John Peter Wild, Reader in Archaeology, University of Manchester.

Ian Wood, Professor of History, University of Leeds.

Abbreviations

BAR	British Archaeological Reports.
CBA	Council for British Archaeology.
CIL	*Corpus Inscriptionum Latinarum*, Berlin.
CSIR	*Corpus Signorum Imperii Romani.*
Gallic Chronicle	*Chronica Minora*, volume I, ed. T. Mommsen, Berlin, 1892 (= *Monumenta Germaniae Historica*, AA9).
ILS	*Inscriptiones Latinae Selectae*, ed. H. Dessau. 3 vols, Berlin, 1892–1916.
RCAHMS	Royal Commission on Ancient and Historical Monuments in Scotland.
RCAHMW	Royal Commission on Ancient and Historical Monuments in Wales.
RCHM(E)	Royal Commission on Historical Monuments (England).
RIB	*The Roman Inscriptions of Britain I. Inscriptions on Stone*, ed. R. G. Collingwood and R. P. Wright. Oxford, 1965. Revised edition, with addenda and corrigenda, by R. S. O. Tomlin. Stroud, 1995. *The Roman Inscriptions of Britain II. Inscriptions on Other Objects*, ed. S. S. Frere and R. S. O. Tomlin. Fascicules 1–8, Stroud, 1990–5.
Tab.Sul.	The curse tablets, by R. S. O. Tomlin. In B. Cunliffe, *The Temple of Sulis Minerva at Bath. 2. The Finds from the Sacred Spring.* Oxford, 1988, 59–277.

Introduction

MALCOLM TODD

For four centuries Britain was part of an empire the centre of which was Rome. Although in later centuries Britain, and especially southern Britain, was intimately engaged politically and culturally with the adjacent Continent, it was never again so closely bound up with a European power for so long a time. The involvement of Britain with the world of Rome was by no means confined to the long period during which the island was directly subject to the rule of Rome. For a century and a half before the army of Claudius invaded Britain in AD 43, the island had been drawn by political and commercial forces into relationships with the western provinces of Rome. And for long after the end of Roman rule the literate inhabitants of Britain still looked to Rome as the fount of culture and knowledge in a world utterly changed from that of Claudius and Hadrian.

Despite this long association of Britain with Rome, the study of Roman Britain for long enjoyed a somewhat equivocal status. The reasons are complex and they are involved with the character of university education in Britain. Down to the 1950s, Roman Britain played a relatively minor role in the curriculum of universities. The subject was taught in a number of centres, including London, Durham, Newcastle, Exeter and Reading, but few lectureships were reserved for Romano-British and related studies. After about 1960, there was steady development in this direction elsewhere, notably at Leicester, Manchester, Nottingham, Cardiff and Bristol. Some of the specialists appointed then moved on to university chairs and, as many of them had been trained in the study of the Empire as a whole, Roman Britain was given an increasingly firm basis within the historical, Classical and archaeological curriculum.

It is a central fact that several academic disciplines contribute to the study of Britannia and these are deployed in this volume. They include the interpretation of Greek and Roman texts, the study of inscriptions, the excavation of Roman sites, and more recently the investigation of biological and environmental data. No one scholar could aspire to master all of these exacting fields, hence the large number of specialists represented here. Excavation has tended to dominate the subject; fresh discoveries continue to add to the record, and in some cases to transform it. The excavation of Roman sites in Britain reaches back to the seventeenth century at least and the record of this activity is as good or better than that of any other part of the Empire. Yet the organized study of Britannia made slow progress until the mid-nineteenth century. Work on individual sites and monuments such as the frontier walls (see p. 114) made significant advances, but these efforts were severely constrained by the lack of reliable dating media, notably pottery. Stratigraphic investigation was, at best, inchoate and usually non-existent before 1880. Another obvious gap was the inadequate record of inscriptions, Emil Huebner's collection published in 1872 having many weaknesses (see p. 457). This lacuna was recognized by Francis Haverfield, who took steps to remedy the situation. Progress was slow, and the first successor volume to that of Huebner did not appear until 1965.

The quality of excavation on Roman sites in Britain remained at a low level until after the First World War. To take only one example, the work at Corbridge was very loosely supervised before 1914; the rich haul of finds was taken to justify the means. The record of work at Richborough and Wroxeter tells its own story. R. E. M. Wheeler commented on the fact that the ordered record of work in the 1880s and 1890s was not followed up in the following thirty years. While Wheeler tended to overstate his own contribution to the development of field archaeology in the 1920s and 1930s, there is no doubt that he did much to promote exacting practice in excavation and recording, and to train a new generation in field techniques, notably through his work in Wales and later at Verulamium. There was still much to do, and progress before 1939 was slow, largely for economic reasons. The outbreak of war brought many projects to an abrupt conclusion, but its aftermath was to provide a much-needed stimulus. The destruction of several historic city centres offered an opportunity for the examination of the early history of such cities as London, Exeter and Canterbury. Numerous opportunities were missed elsewhere, partly for lack of funds, partly because no local organization existed to supervise the necessary work. But there was a major advance in research on Romano-British cities, which was to provide a basis for more deliberate research programmes at, for example, Verulamium, Silchester, Wroxeter and Leicester.

It is a curious fact that a major history of Roman Britain did not appear until 1967. R. G. Collingwood's contribution to the first volume of the *Oxford History of England* in 1936, following his *Archaeology of Roman Britain* in 1930, for long served as the basic textbook on the province. This brilliantly written work of a moral philosopher held the field for thirty years, but it left many areas unexplored. No major competitor appeared before Sheppard Frere's *Britannia* in 1967. Thereafter, several general histories have made the history and culture of Roman Britain more accessible and familiar to a wide public.

Several approaches to the study of Roman Britain have developed over the past century. For long the dominant approach was from Rome down to this distant island. Those who studied and exposed the Roman past of Britain down to the mid-twentieth century were inclined to emphasize the Roman aspects of Britannia. Given the prevailing Classical education and cultural ethos of the time, this is no surprise. Francis Haverfield was the first major scholar to raise the matter of the degree of Romanization in Britain in a paper of 1905, later expanded into an influential volume which went through several editions and which accompanied his Ford Lectures of 1907, eventually brought to the press by George Macdonald in 1924. Seen as a whole, Haverfield's publications presented a clear and distinctive picture of a Roman frontier province and, in its essentially pre-1914 context, it probably could not have been bettered. But a firm and full basis for the study of Roman Britain still did not exist, a fact which Haverfield clearly recognized. Not only had few major sites been well excavated and published before 1914. The record of inscriptions was inadequate, and a major project conceived and begun by Haverfield, *The Roman Inscriptions of Britain*, was designed to set this to rights. Ninety years later this enterprise continues in an expanded form.

As a frontier province which contains the remains of two massive frontier works and a multitude of forts and camps of varied date, Britain has naturally figured prominently in the study of the Roman army and its operations. Research on Hadrian's Wall and the Antonine frontier in Scotland occupied a distinguished series of observers and investigators from the eighteenth century onward, chief among them John Horsley and William Roy, and opened a rich vein of information on the organization and practice of the Imperial army. The inseparable association of the army with its frontier works placed Roman Britain at the centre of the study of the Roman provinces in the twentieth century, leading roles being taken by George Macdonald, F. G. Simpson, I. A. Richmond, E. B. Birley and Kenneth St Joseph among others. This work was perhaps more seriously appreciated outside Britain than at home; and tension between *Limesforscher* and those more closely concerned with other aspects of Britain has taken many years to dissipate. But no one can seriously doubt the importance of the British evidence to knowledge of Roman military affairs in the widest sense. If there were any doubts, they were dispelled by the discovery of the astonishingly informative texts at Vindolanda, superbly read and interpreted by Professor A. K. Bowman and J. D. Thomas. Before the early 1970s, no one would have predicted that such documents would be recovered from northern Britain. It is likely that there is more to come.

In counterpoint to the study of military works, and partly in reaction to it, the contribution of the Britons to Romano-British culture has been increasingly highlighted over the past half-century. Although this field was entered by both Haverfield and Collingwood, the basis for examination of the Romanization of Britannia has been greatly expanded since 1950. The destruction of several historic city centres in 1940–5 provided an opportunity for investigation on an unprecedented scale, although available funding remained at a modest level. But the foundations for study of urban and rural communities were laid and quickly built upon. As 'rescue archaeology' developed in the 1960s, excavation of multi-period settlements enlarged knowledge of the native population of Britain and its relations with the cultures of the western provinces in particular. Urban archaeology came into its own after 1950, with major programmes at Verulamium, Wroxeter, Winchester, Silchester and York. Study of rural sites and their environmental evidence began to contribute hugely to knowledge of Britain over time. No longer was the emphasis upon villas, though investigation of many continued and illuminated the gradations from luxurious estates to modest farmsteads, to all of which the term villa might be applied.

Other approaches have been opened up over the past twenty years, partly in reaction to long-established themes, partly in response to post-modern approaches and partly also reflecting the general decline of traditional Classical scholarship. The application of theoretical archaeology has lain at the centre of important reassessments of the evidence provided by the four centuries of Roman Britain. Not all of the results are likely to be enduring, but at the very least these interventions have stirred debate about major issues. More traditionalist observers may wonder at the passing over of inconvenient evidence in silence.

What is undeniable is the fact that public interest in the Roman past of Britain is higher than it has ever been. Anyone admitting to an interest in Roman Britain is at risk of a bombardment of questions and opinions, many of them well informed. This interest has been fed and nurtured by a wide range of accessible books, many of high quality. The surviving and visible monuments of Roman Britain have been displayed and promoted with much greater effectiveness than ever before. The fragmentation of the heritage between a variety of official and private bodies was far from ideal, but the resulting basis for conservation and public education is sustainable and sound.

No single volume can now encompass all aspects of Roman Britain and, in consequence, several subjects do not receive direct coverage here. Thus, Roman art in Britain and Romano-British art are not given specific treatment, though they appear in Henig's chapter and have been extensively discussed by him elsewhere. Likewise, burial and memorial of the dead are not directly discussed, though they figure in several chapters. The Christian religion and its impact appear in the chapters by Henig, Esmonde Cleary and Wood. The complex subject of Romanization could have come in for separate treatment, but it has been well aired in numerous recent works; and study of this volume as a whole should allow the reader to arrive at a balanced, independent judgement.

The editor's particular thanks go to all contributors for their prompt responses and their forbearance of inevitable delays. Equal or greater debts are owed to Tessa Harvey, Angela Cohen and Tamsin Smith for their kindness, guidance and above all patience over the past three years. It has been a pleasure and a reward to work with these members of staff of Blackwell Publishing.

CHAPTER ONE

Britain and the Continent: Networks of Interaction

BARRY CUNLIFFE

The Channel which has divided Britain from the Continent for the last 8000 years or so has seldom been a barrier to the movement of people and goods. Indeed the sea, to those who understood its ways, could provide easier access and speedier travel than a journey of equivalent length on land and it is a reasonable supposition that sea-going vessels had developed already in the Mesolithic period. From the latter part of the fourth millennium BC there is direct archaeological evidence of a flow of commodities to and from the island, and by the beginning of the first millennium BC Britain was part of an exchange system which bound the peoples of Atlantic Europe together in a complex network of maritime interactions.

Some pale reflection of the shipping plying the Channel can be glimpsed in a few invaluable Classical texts. The earliest reliable account, transmitted by Diodorus Siculus, evidently comes from an earlier source, quite possibly originating in the now lost book written by the Massalliot, Pytheas, following his journey to Britain in about 320 BC (Cunliffe 2001). Diodorus (*Bibliotheca historica*, 5.1–4) describes a trading port called Ictis sited on an island just off the coast of south-western Britain, where merchants buy tin from the friendly natives and sail with it to Gaul, from where it is taken overland on a thirty-day journey to the mouth of the Rhône. In a rather more obscure text Pliny, probably describing the same system, refers to the Britons' use of hide boats (*Nat. Hist.* 4.104). There is no suggestion in either text that the carriers were other than people from the south-west of Britain and Armorica, and what was described may have been simply one of a series of frequently used routes linking the coasts of Gaul and Britain.

That trade was a norm is certainly implied by Caesar's famous account of the Veneti and their fleet. 'They have a great many ships,' he writes, 'and regularly sail to and from Britain' (*De Bello Gallico*, III.8). He goes on to say that since they control the few harbours they are able to extract tolls from others who sail in these waters. The same general point is reiterated a little later by Strabo (*Geography*, 4.4.1). Elsewhere Strabo provides details of the routes in frequent use. There were four, from the Rhine, Seine, Loire and Garonne, though vessels coming from the Rhine sailed down the coast to the territory of the Morini before making the crossing (*Geography*,

4.5.2). Elsewhere he tells us that from the territory of the Lexobii and Caleti, coastal tribes on either side of the Seine estuary, it is less than a day's run to Britain (*Geography*, 4.1.14). Later on he writes that 'people sailing on the ebb tide in the evening land on the island about the eighth hour on the following day' (*Geography*, 4.3.4).

Clearly, at the time that Strabo was writing, probably at the end of the first century BC, communication between Britain and the Continent was well established. What we are probably seeing here are long-used routes now invigorated by the Roman presence in Gaul. Strabo provides lists of exports from the island, noting hides, slaves and hunting dogs as well as grain, cattle, gold, silver and iron (*Geography*, 4.5.2). In exchange the Britons received 'ivory chains, necklaces, amber gems, glass vessels and other pretty wares of that sort' (*Geography*, 4.5.3). In other words, in exchange for consumer durables the Roman world acquired raw materials, exotic animals and manpower.

Of the ships involved in these cross-Channel exchanges there is some evidence. Substantial plank-built vessels have a long pedigree in Britain going back to the beginning of the second millennium BC (McGrail 2001: 184–94). The earliest so far known is the Ferriby boat now radiocarbon-dated to *c*.2000–1800 BC (Wright et al. 2001) and such is the quality of the carpentry and of the boat-building skills that there can be little doubt of the deep antiquity of the tradition. The robust high-prowed sea-going ships of the Veneti with their massive timbers nailed together, their raw-hide sails and iron anchors and anchor chains, so vividly described by Caesar (*De Bello Gallico*, III.13), clearly belong to this Atlantic plank-boat tradition. No vessels of this kind have yet been found, but a schematic depiction on a coin of Cunobelin (Muckelroy, Haselgrove and Nash 1978) and an iron anchor and chain from a Late Iron Age context in the Dorset hillfort of Bulbury (Cunliffe 1972) are tangible indicators of the Channel-going vessels of the first century BC. Nor should we forget the hide boats mentioned by the Classical writers, carrying tin from the south-west. There is a long tradition of hide-boat construction in Atlantic waters (McGrail 2001: 181–3) and there can be little reasonable doubt that substantial craft capable of long open-sea journeys were in operation in the first millennium BC. The famous gold model from Broighter in the north of Ireland was evidently a square-rigged craft accommodating seven rowers. Light vessels of this kind were well able to ride the Atlantic weather as their modern equivalents still do (MacCullagh 1992).

To what extent Mediterranean vessels ventured into British waters in the later first millennium BC is a matter of debate, but the discovery of a lead anchor stock of Mediterranean type, dating to possibly as early as the second century BC, off the north Welsh coast at Porth Felen, Aberdaron, is an indication that some vessels were exploring these distant lands, though whether they were reconnoitring or trading is difficult to judge (Boon 1977). Until the conquest of Gaul it is probable that the Channel traffic was in the hands of local communities of sailors, and even after Gaul was fully incorporated into the Roman world there is unlikely to have been any significant change. The Blackfriars boat found in the Thames (Marsden 1994) and the wreck in St Peter Port harbour, Guernsey (Rule and Monaghan 1993), both of the later Roman period, were built in the 'Romano-Celtic' tradition and were probably little different in design from those three or four centuries earlier.

In the Early and Middle Iron Age (*c*.600–100 BC) it may reasonably be assumed that the entire Channel, from Cornwall to the Thames estuary, was frequently crossed by shipping using a number of preferred routes. The shortest, from east Kent to north-east Gaul, would have been the simplest to follow. A middle route from the Cotentin to the Solent would have served the Gaulish coast from Tregor to the Seine, with a western route linking the north coast of Finistère to the south coast of Devon and Cornwall (McGrail 1983).

Direct archaeological evidence for these contacts is not particularly profuse. Two pyramidal iron ingots found at Portland probably come from Armorica (Grinsell 1958: 137), a small collection of fibulae from Harlyn Bay, Cornwall, and Mount Batten, Devon are of western French type (Boudet 1988) and a sherd of haematite painted pottery from Poundbury, Dorset, is of an Armorican fabric (Cunliffe 1987b). Further east there are close similarities between certain pottery found in Kent and the adjacent Continent, and some at least of the very large number of early Mediterranean coins found in southern Britain must have arrived at this time (Cunliffe 1991: 431). These archaeological scraps are only a pale reflection of the volume of cross-Channel contact that must have gone on (Cunliffe 1982: 1990). How much of this contact can fairly be regarded as 'trade' is a debatable point. In all probability metal exportation from the south-west was on an appropriate scale, as the Classical authors' interest in tin implies, and there is a wreck site producing ingots of tin in the Erme estuary in southern Devon which, though undated, could belong to this early period (Fox 1997). One of the main ports of trade at this time was Mount Batten, a promontory jutting into Plymouth Sound, where casual discoveries and excavations have produced ample evidence of copper ingots and copper scrap in contexts dating from the Late Bronze Age to the Middle Iron Age. Mount Batten is well sited to serve as a collecting base for a range of metals, copper, tin, gold and silver, from the fringes of the Dartmoor massif (Cunliffe 1988).

Towards the end of the Middle Iron Age, about 150 BC, archaeological evidence for contact between Britain and the Continent begins to increase quite dramatically, though whether this is because of an intensification of contact or simply greater archaeological visibility it is difficult to say.

The earliest evidence comes from the south-east and is reflected in an increasing number of Gallo-Belgic coins found widely in south-eastern Britain but centred mainly on the Thames estuary and to a lesser extent the coast of Sussex. These issues, Gallo-Belgic A, B and C, were made in Belgic Gaul and copies of them were minted in Britain (for a summary, see Cunliffe 1991: 110–18). The context for the movement of the coins no doubt lies in the complex social relationships which must have existed between tribes on the two sides of the Channel. The gold coins would have featured in the cycles of gift-giving by means of which the different groups maintained harmonious relationships. Some hint of this is given by Caesar when he describes Diviciacus, king of the Suessiones, as 'the most powerful ruler in the whole of Gaul who had control not only over a large area of this region but also of Britain' (*De Bello Gallico*, II.4). The implication here is that Diviciacus had probably gained recognition among some of the British tribes as some kind of over-king. In such situations tribute and gifts could be expected to flow (Nash 1984).

It was about this time, or soon after, that a trading network linking the north coast of Armorica and the Solent becomes apparent. In Britain the main, and possibly only, port of entry was Hengistbury Head, a dominant promontory of sandstone separating the open sea from a well-protected harbour (now Christchurch harbour) sheltering in its lee (Cunliffe 1987a). Hengistbury Head has many advantages as a port of trade. Of prime importance was the comparative ease with which it could be approached from Armorica. By sailing on a northerly bearing a navigator would be able to position himself with little difficulty by reference to the two landmarks of Durlston Head on Purbeck and the Needles at the western extremity of the Isle of Wight. Sailing on, midway between the two, he would soon have recognized the profile of Hengistbury Head and would then have been able to steer on a bearing to take his vessel safely around the headland and into the harbour, beaching his ship on the sloping gravel of the north shore. The attraction of the harbour was not only the protection afforded by the headland but the convenient routes provided by the rivers Avon and Stour, leading deep into the densely occupied parts of Wessex.

Hengistbury lay in the centre of a productive region. Near at hand, on the headland itself, was a convenient source of high-grade ironstone, while the Isle of Purbeck to the west provided salt, Kimmeridge shale, favoured for armlets, and good potting clay. Inland, along the river routes, it was possible to reach the rich farmlands of the Wessex chalk downs. A further advantage lay in its coastal position, easily linked by cabotage to the south-west peninsula productive of metals and hides.

The archaeological evidence, extracted from Hengistbury as the result of several excavations during the course of the last century, is rich (Cunliffe 1987a: 14–20). It shows that around 100 BC or soon after a major trading axis developed with the northern coast of Armorica, probably in the region of the Baie de Saint Brieuc, with the island of Guernsey serving as a port of call en route (Cunliffe 1996, 1997: 40–7).

Evidence of the Armorican link is plentiful, consisting in the main of quantities of Armorican pottery found in the excavations at Hengistbury. Three basic types are represented – black cordoned ware, graphite-coated ware and micaceous wares – all produced around the Baie de Saint Brieuc. At Hengistbury these imports dominate, in some of the stratified contexts amounting to between 45 and 65 per cent of the total pottery recovered (Cunliffe 1997: 47–51). Similarly, among the 27 Armorican coins found at Hengistbury 20 are of the Coriosolites – the tribe controlling the north-eastern coast of the peninsula (Sellwood 1987; de Jersey 1997). The implication seems to be that the trading axis reflects a monopoly held by the Coriosolites with the port of Hengistbury. This raises interesting questions about the status of Hengistbury, which would appear to lie in the borderland between the Durotriges and the Atrebates. One possibility is that the headland was extra-tribal, a status appropriate to a port of trade. As such it may well have housed a small population of Armorican traders, if not on a permanent basis at least seasonally. Some such explanation would account for the high percentage of imported pottery and coins.

Through Hengistbury the movement of a wide range of commodities was articulated. Imports included north Italian wine, mainly in Dressel 1A amphorae, metalwork, purple and yellow glass, and figs, as well as the Armorican coins and the Armorican pottery (or more probably its contents). All this is attested in the archaeological record. The commodities stockpiled and worked at Hengistbury, presumably for export, included grain, probably hides, silver, gold, copper alloy, Kimmeridge shale and possibly iron. The metals and hides were probably transported to the site from the south-west of Britain by coastal vessels which brought with them local decorated pottery from Cornwall, Devon and Somerset.

How long this cross-Channel exchange system was maintained and at what intensity it is difficult to say with any degree of precision, but there is some evidence to suggest that the activities may have spanned several decades and, judging by the quantity of imported pottery, estimated to have amounted to 12–13,000 vessels and to have included more than 1000 amphorae (Cunliffe 1997: 47), the volume of the exchanges must have been considerable. We are, of course, seeing only the archaeologically visible commodities: other imports could have included fabrics, spices and perhaps barrels of fish sauce, while exports may have numbered the slaves and hunting dogs mentioned some decades later by Strabo. There can be little doubt that trade on this level would have had a significant impact on the social dynamics of central southern Britain. Changes evident in settlement systems and technology in the area in the first century BC may have been caused, or at least exacerbated, by this new imperative.

The possibility that other axes of intensified trade may have developed at this time remains, but if so none has the visibility of the Armorican–west Solent axis. Further west, however, traditional links seem to have been maintained between western Armorica and south-west Britain. The promontory settlement of Le Yaudet, at the mouth of the Léguer on the north Breton coast, has produced a few sherds of British pottery including decorated wares from Devon, as well as a few items of Kimmeridge shale, while the port of Mount Batten has yielded a sherd of Armorican black cordoned ware. Several Dressel 1 amphorae also found their way into Cornish settlements (Cunliffe 1982: figure 12) but the quantity of traded goods is minute compared to Hengistbury and such exchanges as there were must have been on a limited scale.

Further to the east, along the coast of the eastern Solent and West Sussex, there is a suggestion of contact with Lower Normandy and the Seine estuary. It was in this region that new pottery forms and cremation rites similar to those of Belgic Gaul make an appearance by the early first century BC (Fitzpatrick 1997) and it is possible that some local coin types develop from imports from that region (de Jersey 1997: 85–91). The link is evident but its direct cause is not. One possibility, however, is that we may be seeing here the reflection of an actual incursion of people from Gaul. In one of his more often quoted statements, Caesar tells us that the coastal areas of Britain were 'inhabited by invaders who crossed from Belgica to plunder and then when the fighting was over, settled down and began to till the land' (*De Bello Gallico*, V.12). He gives no further geographical precision. However, the fact that following the invasion of AD 43 the region of Hampshire and West Sussex was ascribed by Roman administrators to the canton of the Belgae, with its capital at *Venta Belgarum* (Winchester), lends some credence to the idea that Belgic immigrants may have landed in the harbours of the east Solent and spread into the hinterland (Cunliffe 1984: 19–20). Some further support for this suggestion comes from an event some decades later when in 51–50 BC the Atrebatic king, Commius, who had served Caesar as an ambassador to Britain in the prelude to his invasion of the island, fell foul of Rome and fled to Britain to 'join his people already here'. He reappears in the British archaeological record minting coins, the distribution of which suggests that he settled immediately to the north of the earlier Belgic enclaves with his capital at *Calleva Atrebatum* (Silchester). A landing among kinsmen in the east Solent, before moving north to establish a territory of his own, would have made good sense.

Caesar's expeditions to Britain in 55 and 54 BC introduced an entirely new dynamic into the relationship between Britain and Gaul. The details of the campaigns need not detain us here except to note that the landings were made in the east of Kent and the military activity was restricted largely to the Thames estuary region, more particularly to the present counties of Kent, Surrey and Essex, during which time Caesar engaged four kings of Kent and the Catuvellauni and Trinovantes to the north of the Thames.

In an interesting aside, in his description of the preparations for the 55 BC expedition, Caesar notes that the Gauls knew practically nothing of Britain. 'In the normal way no one goes to Britain except traders, and even they know only the sea coast and the areas opposite Gaul' (*De Bello Gallico*, IV.20). Even the traders rounded up for interview were uninformative, though one may suspect that this may have been reticence rather than ignorance.

The main tangible results of Caesar's intervention in Britain were the treaty relationships he established with British rulers. The Trinovantes and their king Mandubracius (who had fled to Caesar's protection and was now restored) were put under Roman protection and their hostile neighbours (presumably the Catuvellauni) led by Cassivellaunus were ordered not to molest the Trinovantes. With these agreements, and others of lesser significance, firmly in place Caesar could depart, claiming to have brought the two most powerful tribes of the south-east under submission. From now on this northern side of the Thames estuary provided a safe point of entry for Roman merchants.

Caesar's campaigns in Gaul and Britain completely changed the political geography of the region. The Armorican tribes, who previously had played a significant part in the maritime exchange systems, had been severely mauled in Caesar's devastating attack on them in 56 BC following their rebellion. During this time he had destroyed the Venetic navy and there can be little doubt that traditional trading systems were totally disrupted. His political activities in the Thames region, on the other hand, had established a new friendly interface conveniently close to the north coast of Gaul, which was now firmly and finally in Roman hands. It was not long before a network of new roads fanned out northwards from the hub of *Lugdunum* (Lyons) to bring the Channel ports and the Rhine frontier into easy reach of the Mediterranean and thus to make these distant ports directly accessible to its merchants (Drinkwater 1983: 238). In two brief decades in the middle of the first century BC the political map had been transformed and with it the whole economic infrastructure of the region.

In the ninety years or so following the Caesarian raids extensive contacts were maintained between Roman Gaul and Britain, but the pattern of interaction had changed quite dramatically.

At Hengistbury there seems to have been a marked diminution in the volume of trade. This is reflected in the number and type of amphorae recovered (Williams 1987). Two different types of Dressel 1 amphora were found on the site, Dressel 1A and Dressel 1B. The 1A variety circulated quite widely in the period *c*.150–50 BC while the 1B type dated mainly to the later part of the first century BC, though there was an overlap of one or two decades when both types appear to have been in circulation (Fitzpatrick 1985). If one accepts the rough approximation that the majority of 1A amphorae were pre-Caesarian and most of 1B were post-Caesarian, then the ratio of 1A:1B found at Hengistbury – a ratio of 6:1 – suggests a significant fall-off in the amount of imported Italian wine reaching the port after Caesar's campaigns. That similar figures also apply to Armorica shows that the decline in the transport of Italian wine affected the entire Atlantic seaboard and was not simply specific to the fortunes of Hengistbury. That said, some Italian wine was still being trans-shipped along the Atlantic routes and to this small quantities of Catalan wine in distinctive Dressel 1–Pascual 1 amphorae – a type current until about AD 20 – were now being added. A further indication of Atlantic coastal trade was the appearance at Hengistbury of small quantities of fine pottery imported from Aquitania.

The relative decline in the importance of Hengistbury in the post-Caesarian period seems to be compensated for by the increasing importance of Poole harbour as a port of entry (Cox and Hearne 1991). Late Iron Age occupation focuses on the Ower peninsula, on the south side of the harbour and on the adjacent Green Island and Furzey Island, which may at that time have been part of the mainland. Furzey Island and Green Island both produced small quantities of Armorican imports typical of Hengistbury in its 100–50 BC phase and were therefore part of the same trading network. After about 50 BC the Poole harbour sites begin to yield more imports. At Ower Catalan wine in Dressel 1–Pascual 1 amphorae is comparatively common, amounting to 83 per cent of the total number of amphorae, and a wide range of Gallo-Belgic tablewares now make an appearance, including platters, pedestal beakers, butt beakers and tazze. The earliest of these could be as early as c.15 BC though most probably date to the first half of the first century AD (Fitzpatrick 1991). In contrast, Hengistbury has produced practically nothing of this period. The inescapable conclusion must be that, after the disruption caused by Caesar's campaigns in Gaul and Britain, the trading network previously focused on Hengistbury declined dramatically, but Atlantic coastal trade continued at a reduced volume now favouring the southern shores of Poole harbour. The prominence of the harbour continued up to the time of the Roman conquest, when a Roman military base was established on the north shore at Hamworthy.

Why the shift of focus took place is not clear but the decline in the pre-eminence of Hengistbury may well be embedded in local power struggles and political readjustments following Caesar's interventions. It could simply be that the Armorican trading monopoly, disrupted during the Caesarian campaign, was never re-established and what emerged after the chaos was a wider network of contacts affecting a more extensive swathe of the south coast. It would not be surprising to find evidence of exchanges taking place at other nodes in, for example, Southampton Water, Chichester harbour and the Arun estuary, where some pre-conquest imports have been identified at Bitterne, Fishbourne/Chichester and Arundel Park.

While cross-Channel trade with the south coast appears to have been on a comparatively modest level, the Thames estuary developed as a major axis in the post-Caesarian period, a development no doubt involving trading monopolies between Roman merchants and the Trinovantes and Catuvellauni with whom Caesar had negotiated settlement deals. Through direct mechanisms such as these, very large quantities of wine, in Dressel 1B amphorae, entered eastern Britain via the ports of

Essex, together with Gallo-Belgic ceramics appropriate to the tables of the local elites wishing to embrace Roman manners.

But other systems of contact were also in operation. At a more general level the estuary zone (roughly Kent, Essex and Hertfordshire), including the North Downs to the south and the Chilterns to the west, adopted the Gallo-Belgic rite of cremation burial together with an assemblage of wheel-turned pottery closely reminiscent of Gallo-Belgic wares. Although it is likely that these developments had begun before c.50 BC, as the result of social relationships between northern Gaul and south-eastern Britain, it was only after that date that what has been called the Aylesford–Swarling culture of the south-east became fully developed (Cunliffe 1991: 130–41). The implication of this is that the native elites on the two sides of the Channel developed closer relationships, the British communities emulating their Gallo-Belgic neighbours. The nature of the relationships is likely to have been complex and multifaceted and must have been deeply embedded in binding social systems. At the very least we may envisage a constant flow of people crossing the Channel.

While these social networks will have accounted for a parallel development of culture, they will also have encouraged a flow of goods embedded in systems of gift exchange and reciprocity. In this way small personal items such as brooches and the like, as well as more elaborate gifts of wine and feasting furniture, will have been introduced into the island.

Yet over and above this there is evidence suggestive of directed trade articulated by Roman entrepreneurs resident in Britain. Enclaves of this kind are known to have existed in Gaul before the conquest. Indeed Caesar specifically mentions the Roman merchants who had settled in the native oppidum of *Cabillonum* (*De Bello Gallico*, VII.42). In Britain there is archaeological evidence to suggest just such a group residing in the settlement of Braughing–Puckeridge (Potter and Trow 1988: 158–9). The list of exotic material recovered here is impressive: a variety of amphorae implying the importation of wine, olive oil and fish sauce, a range of Gallo-Belgic and north Italian tableware, polychrome glass bowls, mortaria for preparing food in the Roman manner, together with bronze toilet instruments and other small items. Most telling, perhaps, are two iron styli and a number of graffiti scratched on a variety of pottery vessels, together demonstrating literacy in the pre-conquest period. Although the evidence could all be explained as an accumulation of traded items arriving through a variety of mechanisms, it is simpler to see it in the context of a community of Roman, or Gallo-Roman, traders who had settled among the local community to organize imports and exports.

Other likely places for enclaves of traders are the two major tribal oppida of Verulamium and Camulodunum. Verulamium occupies a very similar location to Braughing–Puckeridge, both settlements commanding river valleys on the lower slopes of the Chilterns. Camulodunum, close to the estuary of the river Colne, controls a significant point of entry from the sea. It may be significant that the three sites lie at the foci of the dense distributions of imported wine amphorae – the commodity most likely to have been among the principal bulk trade imports at the time. Yet another possibility for the establishment of a Gallo-Belgic enclave towards the end of the first century BC is *Calleva* (Silchester) where a regular layout of buildings and roads and a wide range of imports hint at an alien presence (Fulford and Timby 2000: 545–64). *Calleva* occupies a 'frontier' position in relation to the

Wessex chalkland not unlike that of Verulamium and Braughing–Puckeridge in relation to the Chiltern ridge. All three sites could be regarded as convenient 'gateway communities' between the Thames estuary zone and the rest of Britain beyond.

In addition to what might be regarded as normal trade goods a range of more exotic items were brought to Britain in the period 50 BC–AD 50. These include Italian metal tableware like the silver cups from burials at Welwyn Garden City (Stead 1967) and Welwyn (Smith 1912), the bronze oenochoe (jug) and patella (pan) from burial Y at Aylesford, Kent (Evans 1890), the bronze jugs and patera from Welwyn (Smith 1912), the bronze patella from Stanfordbury (Dryden 1845) and possibly the bronze strainer and dish from Welwyn Garden City (Stead 1967: 23–7). An even more exotic range of imports, including ivory-mounted furniture, ornamented mail armour and the famous medallion of Augustus, were recovered from a small group of extremely rich burials – Folly Lane, Stanway and Lexden (see below, pp. 32–4). While it is possible that these items were introduced through the normal social networks, or by entrepreneurial traders, another possibility is that some, if not all, were diplomatic gifts brought to Britain by ambassadors of Rome intent on cementing fresh political relationships with the local elites. Some such explanation surely lies behind the symbols of 'kingly' status found at Folly Lane and Lexden.

These considerations, which reflect on the personalities and the power of the British paramounts, are also a reminder of political mobility: kings could be installed and deposed during local factional rivalries and in all this the patronage of Rome was now a significant factor. In one possible scenario, if a paramount maintained his position and power by dispersing elite goods, acquired through the auspices of Rome, to his clients, then it would have been a simple matter for Rome to topple him by bringing the supply to an end or by favouring a rival. There is no direct evidence that this was done, but the likelihood is that manipulation of this kind would not have been uncommon in Rome's treatment of her cross-Channel neighbours.

In the inter-tribal rivalries that seem to have pervaded the polities of the south-east, Roman patronage and protection was evidently a significant factor. A number of cases are recorded of British leaders fleeing to Rome. The *Monumentum Ancyranum*, dating to around AD 7, records the flight of two British leaders, Tincomarus and Dubnovellaunus, who put themselves under the protection of Augustus, probably at the end of the first century BC. It is about this time that Strabo could record 'certain of the British dynasts have obtained the friendship of Caesar Augustus by embassies and courtesies and set up offerings in the Capitol' (*Geography*, 4.5.3). Taken together the evidence might suggest a phase of particular instability in the south-east of Britain consequent on dynastic changes. Forty years later there were further departures. In AD 39 Adminius fled the country to seek the help of Gaius, having fallen out with his father, and three years later Verica, a ruler of the Atrebates, left Britain for the protection of Claudius, possibly because his kingdom was coming under pressure from the Catuvellauni to the north. Some would argue that it was this event that provided Claudius with the resolve to send an army of conquest in AD 43. Mobility of this kind among barbarian elites would have been quite normal in frontier zones and it is well known that Rome made good political use of it by welcoming and educating the children of the paramount families and sending them back when the occasion arose to rule in their own right (Creighton 2000). It is quite possible that

Togidubnus, who ruled as a client king in Hampshire and West Sussex, in the early decades of the occupation, is an example of this policy in action.

In the ninety years following the campaigns of Julius Caesar the south-east of Britain was drawn closer and closer into the Roman sphere. Beneath it all lay the long-established social networks which bound the native communities on either side of the Channel together and enabled a common culture to develop. On this was laid a new system of direct trade articulated by Roman entrepreneurs for their own commercial interests, and over the top was a system of elite patronage serving a Roman political agenda. The escalation of Roman involvement was such that many living in south-eastern Britain would have regarded the invasion of AD 43 as a wished-for inevitability.

REFERENCES

Boon, G. C. 1977. A Graeco-Roman anchor stock from North Wales. *Antiquaries' Journal*, 57, 10–30.

Boudet, R. 1988. Iberian type brooches [from Mount Batten, Plymouth]. In B. Cunliffe, *Mount Batten, Plymouth*. Oxford, 64.

Cox, P. W. and Hearne, C. M. 1991. *Redeemed from the Heath: The Archaeology of the Wytch Farm Oilfield 1987–90*. Dorchester.

Creighton, J. 2000. *Coins and Power in Late Iron Age Britain*. Cambridge.

Cunliffe, B. 1972. The Late Iron Age metalwork from Bulbury, Dorset. *Antiquaries' Journal*, 52, 293–308.

—— 1982. Britain, the Veneti and beyond. *Oxford Journal of Archaeology*, 1, 39–68.

—— 1984. Relations between Britain and Gaul in the first century BC and early first century AD. In S. Macready and F. H. Thompson (eds), *Cross-Channel Trade*. London, 3–23.

—— 1987a. *Hengistbury Head, Dorset*. Volume 1. *The Prehistoric and Roman Settlement, 3500 BC–AD 500*. Oxford.

—— 1987b. The Iron Age fineware import [from Poundbury, Dorset]. In C. S. Green, *Excavations at Poundbury*. Volume 1. *The Settlements*. Dorchester, 117, mf B13–14.

—— 1988. *Mount Batten, Plymouth: A Prehistoric and Roman Port*. Oxford.

—— 1990. Social and economic contacts between western France and Britain in the Early and Middle La Tène Period. In *La Bretagne et l'Europe préhistorique* (*Revue Archéologique de l'Ouest*: Supplément 2), 245–51.

—— 1991. *Iron Age Communities in Britain*, 3rd edn. London.

—— 1996. Guernsey and the Channel Islands in the first millennium BC. In B. Burns, B. Cunliffe and H. Sebire, *Guernsey: An Island Community of the Atlantic Iron Age*. Oxford, 125–7.

—— 1997. Armorica and Britain: The Ceramic Evidence. In B. Cunliffe and P. de Jersey, *Armorica and Britain*. Oxford, 2–71.

—— 2001. *The Extraordinary Voyage of Pytheas the Greek*. London.

Cunliffe, B. and de Jersey, P. 1997. *Armorica and Britain: Cross-Channel Relationships in the Late First Millennium BC*. Oxford.

de Jersey, P. 1997. Armorica and Britain: the numismatic evidence. In B. Cunliffe and P. de Jersey, *Armorica and Britain*. Oxford, 72–103.

Drinkwater, J. F. 1983. *Roman Gaul*. London.

Dryden, H. 1845. Roman and Romano-British remains at and near Shefford, Co. Beds. *Proceedings of the Cambridgeshire Antiquaries' Society*, 1, no. 8.

Evans, A. J. 1890. On a Late-Celtic urn-field of Aylesford, Kent. *Archaeologia*, 52, 315–88.

Fitzpatrick, A. 1985. The distribution of Dressel 1 amphorae in north-west Europe. *Oxford Journal of Archaeology*, 4, 305–40.

—— 1991. Poole harbour and Hengistbury Head. In P. W. Cox and C. M. Hearne, *Redeemed from the Heath*. Dorchester, 230–1.

—— 1997. *Archaeological Excavations on the Route of the A27 Westhampnett Bypass, West Sussex 1992. Volume 2. The Cemeteries*. Salisbury.

Fox, A. 1997. Tin ingots from Bigbury Bay. *Proceedings of the Devon Archaeological Society*, 53, 11–24.

Fulford, M. and Timby, J. 2000. *Late Iron Age and Roman Silchester: Excavations on the site of the Forum-Basilica 1977, 1980–86*. London.

Grinsell, L. V. 1958. *The Archaeology of Wessex*. London.

MacCullagh, R. 1992. *The Irish Currach Folk*. Dublin.

McGrail, S. 1983. Cross-Channel seamanship and navigation in the late 1st millennium BC. *Oxford Journal of Archaeology*, 2, 299–337.

—— 2001. *Boats of the World*. Oxford.

Macready, S. and Thompson, F. H. (eds) 1984. *Cross-Channel Trade between Gaul and Britain in the Pre-Roman Iron Age*. London.

Marsden, P. 1994. *Ships of the Port of London*. London.

Muckelroy, K., Haselgrove, C. and Nash, D. 1978. Pre-Roman coin from Canterbury and the ship represented on it. *Proceedings of the Prehistoric Society*, 44, 439–44.

Nash, D. 1984. The basis of contact between Britain and Gaul in the late pre-Roman Iron Age. In S. Macready and F. H. Thompson (eds), *Cross-Channel Trade*. London, 92–107.

Potter, T. W. and Trow, S. D. 1988. Puckeridge–Braughing, Herts.: The Ermine Street Excavations, 1971–1972. The Late Roman and Iron Age Settlement. *Hertfordshire Archaeology*, 10.

Rule, M. and Monaghan, J. 1993. *Gallo-Roman Trading Vessel from Guernsey*. St Peter Port.

Sellwood, L. 1987. The non-Durotrigian Celtic coins [from Hengistbury]. In B. Cunliffe, *Hengistbury Head*. Oxford, 138–40.

Smith, R. A. 1912. On Late-Celtic antiquities discovered at Welwyn, Herts. *Archaeologia*, 63, 1–30.

Stead, I. M. 1967. A La Tène III burial at Welwyn Garden City. *Archaeologia*, 101, 1–62.

Williams, D. 1987. Amphorae [from Hengistbury]. In B. Cunliffe, *Hengistbury Head*. Oxford, 271–5.

Wright, E. V., Hedges, R. E. M., Bayliss, A. and Van de Noort, R. 2001. New AMS radiocarbon dates for the North Ferriby boats – a contribution to dating prehistoric seafaring in north-western Europe. *Antiquity*, 75, 726–34.

CHAPTER TWO

Society and Polity in Late Iron Age Britain

COLIN HASELGROVE

We know surprisingly little about social and political organization in Late Iron Age Britain. Most previous discussions have started from the few contemporary Classical sources and so tend to be couched in terms of Roman social and political categories, and their perceived modern equivalents. In many cases, we can doubt whether terms like *rex* (king) or *civitas* (tribe) were appropriate, while in other situations their use probably says more about the relationship of a specific community with Rome than it does about native institutions (Wells 2002). This is equally true of some of the inscriptions found on Late Iron Age coins, the only significant written evidence we possess from pre-Roman Britain itself.

The archaeological evidence poses further problems. Even basic questions about social or political organization are difficult to answer by archaeological means alone and crucial evidence is all too easily read in different ways according to the preconceptions of the interpreter. It is, however, clear from the considerable regional differences in the archaeological record that Iron Age Britain was not a uniform cultural or ethnic entity (Gwilt and Haselgrove 1997; Bevan 1999). As a result, the idea that the Britons and other north-west European peoples shared a common Celtic identity, customs and institutions has been challenged (James 1999), and archaeologists have become wary of invoking textual evidence from Iron Age Gaul or early medieval Ireland to fill in gaps in the insular material. The borrowing of supposedly general anthropological models of society such as chiefdoms or prestige-goods economies – many of which have already passed their 'use-by' date in the parent discipline – is open to similar criticism, but as yet archaeologists have done little to develop social and political categories of their own with which to analyse the material.

These factors make it difficult to offer an overview of later Iron Age social and political organization across the whole of Britain. This chapter will focus on the relative scale and complexity of Late Iron Age communities in different regions and the processes of change which they were undergoing; it will seek to go into greater detail where this is possible. First, however, we need to assess the nature of the various sources of evidence for Late Iron Age societies, first textual and numismatic, and then archaeological.

Literary and Numismatic Sources

Although late Iron Age Britain was described by a number of contemporary authors, including Caesar (*De Bello Gallico*, especially V. 12–14), Strabo (IV. 5), and Diodorus Siculus (V, 21–2), only Caesar actually visited the island, and then only the extreme south-east. His commentaries were written mainly for self-promotion, and the accuracy of his account of the Britons will have been of little importance either to the author or his readership. His claim that peoples in the 'interior' mostly did not grow corn (*De Bello Gallico*, V. 14), for instance, is contradicted by the ample evidence now available for later Iron Age cereal cultivation in northern and western Britain (Haselgrove 2001). The comment that the Britons considered it unlawful to eat hare, fowl or geese (*De Bello Gallico*, V. 12) also seems to run counter to excavated evidence.

We ought therefore to be equally cautious on the rare occasions when Caesar mentions ethnicity or social structure, notably his oft-quoted remarks about the continental ancestry of the peoples of the 'maritime' zone; or their apparently polygamous, patrilineal and, perhaps, patrilocal, kinship structure (*De Bello Gallico*, V. 12, 14; Fitzpatrick 1992: 18). Ironically, while the division which Caesar drew between different parts of Britain probably stems from the contemporary Classical attitude to 'barbarians', whereby the further a territory from the Mediterranean centre of civilization, the more savage its inhabitants (Webster 1999), there are valid archaeological reasons for differentiating between the north and west of the island on the one hand and the south and east on the other, as we shall see.

Similar qualifications apply to Caesar's mentions of specific individuals or identity groups, not least that they represent a mere snapshot in time of a society which the Roman invasion had put under exceptional stress. Some interesting points do emerge. Both rulers and named groups are linked to territories (*De Bello Gallico*, V. 11, 20–2), but only the Trinovantes definitely reappear a century later, suggesting that significant changes occurred in the interim. There were evidently mechanisms for bringing normally independent units together to discuss matters of common interest, as in 54 BC when Cassivellaunus was chosen as war leader. One individual, Lugotorix, is singled out as being of high birth (*nobilis*); another, Mandubracius, whose father had been 'king' of the Trinovantes, was himself confirmed in this role by Caesar. It would be wrong to read this episode as evidence for hereditary succession, but it does suggest that lineage was important. This episode was also a portent for the future; from the mid first century BC onward, numerous rulers in south-east England evidently obtained their appointment through Roman backing (Creighton 2000).

The two other significant pre-Conquest sources, Strabo and Diodorus, derived much of their information about Britain from Caesar, but add some useful insights of their own. The most notable of these is Strabo's account of political and economic dealing between British rulers and the Roman world during the Augustan period (IV. 5, 2–3), although his comments on Ireland (IV. 5, 4) reflect the same prejudices as Caesar – in an even more extreme form (Webster 1999). After this, the next major source is Tacitus, writing at the end of the first century AD; by then, however, the presence of the Roman army and administration must have affected certain aspects of indigenous social and political structure, even beyond the frontier, while his depiction of the pre-Roman Britons (*Agricola*, 11–12) must be treated with additional caution on account of his evident intention to moralize. Elsewhere, Tacitus does provide significant insights, particularly on the important leadership roles played by women as rulers (e.g. Cartimandua) or war leaders (Boudicca).

Many of the individuals and places mentioned in the different sources for the Conquest period can be linked directly to the archaeological record, through the medium of inscribed coinage. The practice of putting legends on coins first emerged north and south of the Thames in the later first century BC and quickly spread. Many regional coinages actually employ hybrid Gallo-Latin alphabets – like those which came into use in northern Gaul in the second and third quarters of the first century BC – rather than fully Roman lettering. It is an interesting question whether knowledge of writing reached Britain independent of the arrival of the Romans in Gaul and, if so, to what use it was initially put (Williams 2001). Coins bearing fully Roman legends are essentially confined to the areas where we also find heavily Roman-influenced styles of coin design, suggesting that they were the work of rulers who had been officially recognized by the Romans as 'friendly kings', most notably Eppillus, Tincomaros and Verica south of the Thames, and Tasciovanus and Cunobelinus in eastern England. It has even recently been suggested that many client rulers had a Roman upbringing, as *obsides* (hostages) taken by Caesar and his successors (Creighton 2000).

More generally, the inscribed British coinages provide valuable insights into the geographical origins and status (at least in Roman eyes) of their issuers, and the extent of the territory over which their position was apparently recognized. Descent from a previous ruler – whether real or claimed – continues to be an important theme; the Latin term *filius* (son of) appears in abbreviation on many of the Romanized coinages. There are, however, many aspects of the coin evidence that we do not understand. Paired names, for example, are reasonably common and, as well as indicating lineage, could be those of paramount and subordinate ruler; of ruler and moneyer; or of co-rulers. Often, the chronology is too imprecise to determine whether individuals minting coinages in the same region succeeded one another or were contemporary. The fact that the number of names on coinage increases in the late stages of both Tasciovanus' and Cunobelinus' reigns does however imply some kind of subdivision or fragmentation of domains that were apparently previously under their sole control, a pointer perhaps to the essentially personal and transitory nature of their power (Haselgrove 1989)

Nor is the relationship between the issuers of coinage and the identity group to which they belonged always very clear. In general, the conservative coin types found in an outer arc of territories stretching from Dorset and the Severn–Cotswolds region to Lincolnshire and East Anglia seem to suggest greater stress on shared cultural identity. In south-east England, the emphasis is much more on individual issuers, rulers like Tasciovanus and Cunobelinus whose influence evidently extended beyond the boundary of their own identity group. However, as soon as we analyse regional coin distributions within either zone in more detail, it becomes clear that they are far from homogeneous in either space or time. Some coinages seem to have circulated in more than one region, and it is common to find zones around the main regional coin distributions where only gold seems to have been accepted (Haselgrove 1987). In general, the findspots of struck bronze coinage are more clustered than either gold or silver, implying that base metal issues were used only where their value was guaranteed by the issuing authority. Such observations would be consistent with the view that even the most powerful British rulers exercised direct control only over relatively small areas and that the degree of political centralization suggested by the extensive coin distributions may be illusory.

The most significant distinction of all, however, is that between the part of Britain where Iron Age coinage was regularly used – essentially south and east of a line drawn from Humberside to the Devon border – and the rest of the island, where coinage never caught on (Haselgrove 1987). This is not due to ignorance of the idea, since isolated finds occur throughout northern and western Britain from an early date; nor can low population densities be the explanation, since many of the areas that failed to adopt coinage are as densely settled as their coin-using neighbours.

A similar division in fact exists in the Low Countries, where the northern limit of the diffusion of Iron Age coinage broadly coincides with the southern limit of the north European byre-house tradition, where people and cattle shared the same dwelling. Roymans (1999) suggests that the reason why coinage failed to penetrate the north-west European plain was the deeply rooted position of cattle in the cultural value system of these peoples. In these areas, possession of cattle was an indicator of wealth and prestige, and social relations like marriage or clientage were given shape by exchanging cattle, thus imbuing them with an ideological significance over and above their strict economic value. In turn, the central place of cattle – as opposed to other valuables – in the ideology and exchange systems of these peoples presented a powerful barrier to the introduction of coinage as an alternative way of building social relations.

There is nothing to indicate that cattle in the part of Britain that rejected coinage possessed a symbolic importance comparable to those of the north-west European plain – although they do seem to have been more important in the agricultural economies of these regions than in many lowland areas (Haselgrove 2001) – and I do not wish to imply that identical circumstances obtained in Britain and northern Gaul. On the other hand, a basic difference in cultural values or the nature of the exchange system does seem to provide one of the simpler explanations for why the inhabitants of one zone adopted coinage while those of the other rejected it.

Archaeological Framework

Coinage apart, three main categories of archaeological evidence are normally used as indicators of Late Iron Age social and political organization: burials, prestige goods and settlements (Champion 1995). Burials are often privileged, because they seem to give the most direct insights into social identities (as interpreted by the mourners), but in Iron Age Britain, archaeologically visible burial rites are the exception rather than the norm. The quantity of mortuary evidence does increase in the Late Iron Age, although this is offset by the disappearance in East Yorkshire of a well-established Middle Iron Age tradition of burying the dead in barrow cemeteries, which died away almost completely in the first century BC.

The principal Late Iron Age burial traditions include the use of cist graves in Cornwall (where they had earlier origins) and south-east Scotland; inhumation cemeteries (accompanied as in Dorset, and unaccompanied as in East Anglia); and the widespread adoption of cremation in south-eastern England. In addition, Late Iron Age graves containing weapons or mirrors occur sporadically throughout southern

Britain, from Kent to the Isles of Scilly, and from Anglesey to East Yorkshire, both in apparent isolation and as founder graves for small cemeteries (Haselgrove 2001).

Nowhere is the total number of known burials especially large, and only in south-east England do they exhibit significant variations in form and content, ranging from simple unurned cremations to the extremely wealthy burials of the Welwyn and Folly Lane series (discussed by Rosalind Niblett in chapter 3). Even here, however, the archaeologically visible graves probably represent a fairly small fraction of the total population, albeit one that included the leading sections of Late Iron Age society. Elsewhere, apart from the occasional weapon or mirror burial, most burial grounds tend to be small and relatively homogeneous, while analysis of basic age or gender differences is often impeded by poor preservation. Where investigation has been carried out, for instance, at Trethellan Farm, Newquay (Cornwall) or Dunbar (East Lothian), they seem to be the burial grounds for isolated communities, with adults of both sexes and children all present.

The study of decorative metalwork and other valuables suffers from similar problems. As well as being largely absent from the burial record outside south-east England, such items were rarely deposited in settlements, so that our knowledge of their incidence is heavily conditioned by patterns of ritual deposition in contexts like rivers, bogs and dryland shrines. As with burial, such practices were regionally specific (Hunter 1997) and the resultant picture is decidedly uneven. For example, a practice of 'hoarding' gold torcs, probably as offerings, developed in the second century BC in East Anglia, but elsewhere such items occur at best sporadically. Similarly, iron bars were frequently deposited at boundaries and at other symbolically charged locations in a region stretching from Dorset and Hampshire up through the Cotswolds into the East Midlands, but only occasionally beyond this zone (Hingley forthcoming). Does this indicate that torcs were never worn outside East Anglia or that iron was exchanged as standard bars only in this one area? It seems far more likely that the present-day distributions above all reflect the incorporation of such objects into culturally determined depositional practices and not the original area of use. Certain regional metalwork styles can nevertheless be discerned, such as the massive armlet tradition of north-east Scotland or the distinctive Late Iron Age sword scabbard and hilt-guards found in northern England and southern Scotland.

The deposition of weaponry, horse harness and chariot fittings, and other prestige goods (including coinage) rose significantly in most parts of Britain during the Late Iron Age, both in wetland and in dryland contexts (Haselgrove 1989; Hunter 1997). South and east of the Humber–Severn line, this increase extends to Late Iron Age settlements, where a greater range and quantity of all kinds of object is found, especially small items like brooches and toilet instruments (Hill 1997), whereas these continue to be rare on sites in most areas of northern and western Britain. Rather than indicating greater poverty on the part of their inhabitants – as was once widely thought – this particular distinction seems likely to be due to the operation of cultural filters like those discussed above.

Some other differences in material culture between the two broad zones characterized by the presence or absence of coinage do seem to be real: beyond southern and eastern England, the use of decorated pottery is confined to the south-west peninsula and the Scottish islands. Over most of central, northern and western Britain, pottery was used only in small quantities and never played the same role in differentiating individual identity groups as it did in the south-eastern third of the island. Again, with the exception of Cornwall, the Late Iron Age adoption of wheel-made pottery and the importation of Roman wine amphorae and finewares – and the practice of imitating the latter locally – are more or less confined to the south and east.

Despite the gaps in the modern distributions, it seems on balance that broadly similar types of decorative metalwork were available to Late Iron Age societies throughout Britain, which could have used them to express differences in social rank. On its own, this brings us no nearer to knowing whether (and if so, on what basis) there was unequal access to wealth within different communities, nor indeed whether there were significant regional variations in the relative quantities of such material in circulation. What is clear is that all over Britain, certain individuals or groups possessed the means to maintain long-distance ties – albeit possibly through intermediaries – with their counterparts elsewhere in the island and even in mainland Europe.

This is apparent both from the general stylistic similarities in certain widely distributed types of metalwork, and from the discovery of individual objects far from their territory of origin: a north British spiral 'snake-headed' armlet in a rich burial at Snailwell, Cambridge; a Roman Haltern 70 amphora from Gurness, Orkney; the Netherurd hoard of Gaulish gold coins and East Anglian torcs from southern Scotland; an enamelled harness fitting from Paillart, France; or the decorated British mirror from Nijmegen, Netherlands (Collis 1994). There were two main axes of continental contact: between south-east England and the near continent, using the short sea crossings over the Channel and the North Sea; and along the Irish Sea corridor and down the Atlantic seaboard of France (Cunliffe 1991). A scatter of finds of Iron Age date along the coasts of western Britain and Ireland testifies to the enduring nature of this latter network, most notably the early first century BC barbary ape from Navan, County Antrim.

Settlements are the only form of archaeological evidence for the later Iron Age to occur practically everywhere, and thus they ultimately offer our best means for investigating social and political organization in different parts of Britain. Only a few areas, like the Lake District, are still virtually blank (Haselgrove et al. 2001), probably due either to the difficulty of locating open settlements or to problems in dating sites. This does not mean that the settlement evidence elsewhere is unproblematic. For instance, the positioning or decoration of roundhouses could have been used to display social differences, but this is difficult to assess from ground plans alone. At some sites, the porches of certain buildings seem to have been particularly elaborate, which may well be significant.

The construction and repeated rebuilding of imposing earthworks around settlements of all sizes, sometimes out of all keeping with the likely number of inhabitants, has led many Iron Age archaeologists to argue that such projects were undertaken primarily as a means of social display and conspicuous consumption rather than for defence (Sharples 1991; Collis 1996; Hill 1996). At many sites, the earthworks are noticeably more elaborate immediately beside the entrance, precisely where they would be visible to people approaching the site (Haselgrove 2001). However, while testifying to the ability of groups or individuals to mobilize the necessary labour and resources for such projects, this brings us no nearer to understanding the social mechanisms at work. The necessary numbers could have been collected, for example, as a form of reciprocity between groups of equal status, each of whom would help their kin or neighbours when the occasion demanded; through an obligation to provide labour to social superiors or to the community as a whole; or through the coercion of individuals or groups, for instance, those who had been defeated in warfare. It is almost impossible to differentiate between such possibilities by purely archaeological means.

No simple rules govern how social and political relations between individuals or groups can be translated into specific forms of settlement pattern. We should be wary of the idea that settlement hierarchies inferred from traits we have ourselves selected, such as the number of inhabitants, the scale of enclosure or the presence of a range of craft activities, correspond in any meaningful way with social or political hegemony. During the Late Iron Age, a number of prominent ringworks such as Arbury Camp and Stonea Camp were built in East Anglia, but the lack of internal occupation suggests that they were used only intermittently.

This underlines the danger of assuming that the largest and most prominent sites necessarily formed the apex of the regional settlement hierarchy; in the Fenlands, this role may well have been performed by much smaller but comparatively rich enclosed settlements like Wardy Hill on the Isle of Ely (Haselgrove 2001). The Meare lake village in Somerset is thought to have housed one of the principal workshops for Iron Age glass production in north-west Europe, but was probably the site of a seasonal fair and may not have been permanently occupied. At the other extreme, some individuals of higher rank or political authority may have resided at sites which cannot be differentiated archaeologically from those of lower rank; in such contexts, the absence of any overt settlement hierarchy does not imply an egalitarian society.

It is now generally thought that the universal insular preference for living in circular houses stems from an adherence to a common set of beliefs or principles, which transcended more localized ethnic or cultural distinctions. This would help explain the remarkable stability in time and space of the later prehistoric roundhouse trad-ition (particularly when other types of building structure, such as above-ground storage structures, were rectangular). Evidence that the preferred orientation of Iron Age roundhouse entrances (either due east or south-east towards the midwinter sunrise) is of cosmological rather than practical significance has been accumulating for some time (Hill 1996; Parker Pearson 1996; Oswald 1997), while more recently Fitzpatrick (1997) has argued persuasively that if Iron Age societies had a cyclical conception of time – as seems highly likely – the very circularity of the roundhouse itself may have been used to count the passage of time.

A number of better-preserved Iron Age roundhouses, mostly in northern Britain but including some in southern England, exhibit a bipartite division around an east–west axis aligned on the entrance. Evidence for everyday activities like food preparation and eating, and spinning and weaving, is confined to the southern half of buildings, that for storage and sleeping to the northern half. The orientation of the entrance towards the rising sun marks the passing of night and of the seasons, while the 'sunwise' organization of daily and seasonally referenced activities around a central hearth mimics both the diurnal movement of the sun around the southern half of the house and the unfolding of the annual agricultural cycle (Fitzpatrick 1997; Giles and Parker Pearson 1999).

The idea that the symbolic and ideological concerns of insular societies were intimately linked to the agricultural cycle gains additional support from the nature of the ritual deposits found on Iron Age domestic sites. These involved the sacrifice of agricultural or household objects, domestic animals and sometimes even people, and they tend to be placed in liminal locations like house entrances, enclosure ditches and grain storage pits (Hill 1995), suggesting a link with concerns like fertility and regeneration. On smaller farmsteads, such rituals probably took place only once every few years, but on larger sites like hillforts, they were more frequent, and may have played a role in integrating the wider community. The phenomenon is most marked in southern and eastern England – partly because it was first recognized here, and partly because the use of grain storage pits is confined to this region – but it is now clear that broadly similar practices were enacted on Iron Age settlements throughout the length and breath of Britain (e.g. Hingley 1992).

Less is known about other key aspects of domestic organization, such as the composition of households (those who lived together in a single building or cluster of related buildings), their relationship to families, or the division of labour between the sexes. The only detailed study, Clarke's (1972) influential analysis of the Glastonbury lake village, is now seen to be deeply flawed in its handling and interpretation of the archaeological data. Various regional and temporal trends are apparent, however, indicating that whatever shared ideas ultimately lay behind the circular building tradition, there were significant social and cultural differences between communities (Haselgrove 2001). In southern Britain, for instance, average house size seems to decrease markedly during the Iron Age, while in northern Britain the trend is more varied. In some areas, most circular buildings seem to have been houses, while in others they had a wider range of functions, including use as animal byres and storage structures, and even as shrines The stone broch towers and some of the other substantial timber building types found in Scotland evidently had upper floors and could thus be used to overwinter animals, while the people lived above.

There were also important regional variations at the level of the settlement as a whole, some of which echo distinctions noted above in relation to the material culture and mortuary evidence. The practice of defining settlement territories with linear earthworks is essentially confined to southern and eastern England, as indeed are the majority of developed hillforts of Middle Iron Age date. This area also saw an increasing separation between ritual and domestic activity, with the construction for the first time in the Late Iron Age of purpose-built shrines. Perhaps significantly, this change coincided with the widespread appearance of rectangular residential buildings of sill-beam construction on settlements in south-east England. Certain other architectural forms – such as souterrains – are only found to the north and west of the line between the Humber and Severn estuaries.

It will be convenient then to adopt a similar geographical split in considering what settlement evidence – in conjunction with other archaeological material – can tell us about the changing scale and complexity of later Iron Age communities in different parts of Britain. Most surveys begin with southern and eastern England on account of the literary and numismatic evidence relating to these regions, but I shall start with the zone to the north and west, which after all accounts for nearly three-quarters of the overall land area.

Central and Atlantic Britain

The area beyond the Humber–Severn line can usefully be further divided into unequal halves, the first comprising the mainly upland regions of south-west England, Wales, north-west England, south-west Scotland and the Scottish highlands and islands; the second, the west and north Midlands, north-east England and eastern Scotland (Haselgrove 2001). The Atlantic zone endures a wetter and less favourable climate, whereas what I will term 'central Britain' has more low-lying land and better quality soils for agriculture, which is reflected in generally higher settlement densities. The Irish Sea acted as a unifying factor for the Atlantic zone by creating a corridor of communication extending from Cornwall in the south to Orkney and Shetland in the far north (Cunliffe 1991). Drystone architecture predominated throughout most of this zone, while timber was the main building material on settlements in central Britain.

Throughout both zones, there was a significant increase in settlement density during the later Iron Age. This involved settlement expansion into previously thinly occupied areas and was not simply a consequence of the greater visibility of sites due to the more frequent use of enclosure. In many upland areas of northern England and southern Scotland, for example, the pollen evidence indicates a dramatic increase in woodland clearance during the later Iron Age, particularly from c.200–100 BC onwards (Tipping 1997). The rapidity and scale of this clearance leaves little doubt that its purpose was to increase the land available for agriculture. In central Britain south of the Tyne valley, this agricultural expansion was accompanied by the adoption of less labour-intensive crop husbandry methods and a switch from emmer to spelt wheat (Haselgrove 2002), whereas further to the north and west crop husbandry methods remained labour-intensive and more of the newly cleared land seems to have been used for livestock. Although population increase is thought ultimately to have been the driving force behind this agricultural intensification, social competition and the consequent need for a disposable surplus, whether of animals or crops, may have contributed.

Although enclosures predominated throughout central Britain, these varied significantly from one region to another: the Welsh Marches had substantial hillforts; in the Midlands and north-east England rectangular enclosures are the commonest later Iron Age settlement form, although other types do occur; while in the Borders and eastern Scotland, curvilinear enclosures ranging in size from a single homestead to substantial communities are most frequent. In a rank–size analysis of settlement north and south of the Tyne, Ferrell (1997) detected significant differences between the Tees lowlands – where sites display a greater size range and a higher level of integration, potentially symptomatic of a more developed social hierarchy – and upland Northumberland, where the picture is reversed. Here, individual sites were larger, but they were often isolated and lower levels of interdependence prevail. Ferrell suggests this contrast reflects different kinds of social structure, one consisting of small, competitive household groups with a strong emphasis on individual ownership and status; the other focused on larger residential groups, for whom communal ownership of resources and group identity were more important.

The Tees valley is one of several lowland areas from south-east Scotland to the Trent valley, where similar clusters of enclosures can be recognized. In the middle

Tweed valley, for example, these 'neighbourhood groups' average about two square kilometres in extent and are generally focused on a body of water such as a river or loch (Wise 2000). Their stability over long periods of time implies close social ties between the constituent households, presumably kin-based. Such a pattern could well have its roots in the nature of the colonization process, with the initial settlements in sparsely inhabited land being gradually augmented by secondary infilling as the population increased.

Over time, competition between different descent-based groups may have led to the development of regional mechanisms for regulating conflict and settling disputes, but the potential for common action by these larger social groupings is likely to have remained weak. Many rectilinear enclosures in north-east England are attached to linear ditches indicative of large-scale partitioning of the landscape (Haselgrove 2002), while the later Iron Age pit alignments in the East Lothian coastal plain presumably served a similar purpose, dividing up territories between competing groups (Armit 1999). Groups of individual Late Iron Age houses set among their fields, found in adjacent upland areas like the Peak District or the North York Moors, probably represent a form of social grouping closer to Ferrell's (1997) communal type.

In Atlantic Britain, the overall picture is more diverse. A broad distinction can nevertheless be drawn between Wales and south-west England – where many larger settlement types, such as multiple-enclosure forts and 'cliff castles' were certainly occupied in the later Iron Age – and Atlantic Scotland, where individual stone-built homesteads of various forms (including those classified as brochs and duns) predominate, sometimes set within enclosures. The enclosure-dominated landscape of south-west Scotland resembles the rest of southern Scotland, but also includes isolated houses in the form of crannogs and duns (Hingley 1992; Armit 1997).

Although recent excavations have pushed back the date at which the monumental free-standing brochs first appeared, their main period of use dates from the second century BC onward. It remains a matter of debate whether – at least at this stage – brochs represented the dwellings of an elite within a hierarchical social system, or were built to project the unity and isolation of individual households (Armit 1997; Sharples and Parker Pearson 1997). In many ways, this is a matter of semantics – what is clear is that their owners were able to mobilize the resources needed to build elaborate dwellings and had contacts with other groups throughout the Atlantic region. In many areas, the distributions of brochs can be shown to correspond to that of the better-quality land, for instance, in Skye, where they are apparently confined to the northern half of the island (Armit 1997). Possibly the answer lies in the difficulty in finding contemporary open settlements. In north-east England, for instance, it is clear that the rectilinear enclosures discussed above coexisted with smaller open settlements, implying status differences within neighbourhood groups (Haselgrove 2002). It would not be at all surprising if this were eventually to prove to be the case in many other areas of central and Atlantic Britain.

With the exception of the Welsh Marches hillforts and the larger forts of south-west England and southern Scotland, there is little evidence throughout most central and Atlantic Britain of dominant settlements which acted as foci for a wider region. It is conceivable that some abandoned hillforts, like Eildon Hill or Traprain Law, were still used for periodic gatherings (Hingley 1992; Armit 1999), while in other areas, votive sites might have played this role. The important votive site at Llyn Cerrig Bach in Anglesey is now believed to have been in use throughout the later Iron Age (Haselgrove et al. 2001), but it is the exception. Most votive sites are less obvious, but the frequent discovery of bog butter and items like votive ploughs in wet areas implies they did exist elsewhere. The widespread evidence for Iron Age reuse of older ritual monuments (Hingley 1999) may also be relevant, while we should not overlook the possibility that certain types of enclosures which resemble settlements, like the Cornish cliff castles, or the low-lying site at Over Rig in Annandale (Hingley 1992), were in fact periodic gathering places for dispersed communities.

In the first centuries BC and AD, there are indications of increasingly widespread changes in both zones, although the dating evidence is generally too poor to determine to what extent they were contemporary across wider regions. In the Welsh Marches, the intensive occupation of major hillforts like Croft Ambrey and Credenhill (Herefordshire) ceased in the Late Iron Age (Haselgrove 1997) and their populations appear to have moved into smaller settlements in the surrounding lowlands. In south-west England, a similar process seems to have occurred with the gradual abandonment of multiple enclosure forts for smaller enclosed settlements known as rounds (Cunliffe 1991). In Wales, too, the emphasis appears increasingly to be on smaller but prominent types of enclosure.

In southern and eastern Scotland, the trend is the reverse. Although enclosures continued to be built, many more ceased to be maintained (Armit 1999), with houses being built over the infilled ditches, especially at larger sites such as Broxmouth (East Lothian). North of the Forth, open settlements with souterrains became common (Hingley 1992), as at Newmill (Perthshire). In the highlands and islands, events took a divergent course, with nucleated settlements developing in Orkney and Caithness – the so-called broch villages like Gurness and Howe – while a new building form known as the wheelhouse appeared in the Western Isles and in Shetland.[1]

Armit (1997) has suggested that these Scottish developments indicate the assertion of social and political power at a level higher than the individual household. Certainly in the case of the broch villages, analysis of the layout leads to the conclusion that a significant gulf in social rank existed between the broch dwellers and the rest of the community (Foster 1989). More stable political authority would also help explain the declining importance of enclosure in southern Scotland, especially if this was linked to the spread of new forms of social display, which placed greater emphasis on individual status and ranking than on the identity and membership of particular groups. It is significant that metalwork deposits on votive sites seem to increase at much the same time as enclosures ceased to be built or renewed (Hunter 1997). A new emphasis on individual status is equally apparent in the Welsh Marches and the other hillfort-dominated areas of southern Britain, where the partitioning of the landscape around many abandoned hillforts into separate farms may even indicate the passing of land that was formerly under communal control into individual hands (Sharples 1991).

There were also changes which perhaps point to increased political centralization in the intervening areas of central Britain. These include the laying out of large coaxial field systems in the Trent Valley and the even larger 'brickwork' systems of Nottinghamshire and South Yorkshire, while in north-east England long-established enclosed farms gave way to extended open settlements (Haselgrove 2001). The mid-first

---

1   In Shetland, this may not be until the second century AD.

century AD construction of massive earthworks around an existing open settlement and ritual focus at Stanwick (North Yorkshire) is quite exceptional, however, and must be viewed in the context of increased Roman involvement in the region following the conquest of the south (Haselgrove 2002).[2]

Standing back from this material, we would have to conclude that some degree of social ranking existed throughout most of central and Atlantic Britain. Not surprisingly, however, there were differences in the way that such ranking was constituted and expressed over such a vast area, and the Romans will almost certainly have had more difficulty assimilating some of the groups and households who held status and authority locally to their own category of *nobiles* than others (cf. Wells 2002). At this stage, few of these local leaders can have had access to the Roman imports which might have marked them out, and those that did may have rejected some and adapted others – as happened with brass imported into northern England, which was rapidly transformed into traditional valuables such as horse harness.

It is worth pausing briefly to follow this process into the Roman Iron Age. As soon as goods like samian, which fitted with existing arenas of social display such as feasting or wearing personal ornaments, started penetrating Scotland, the leading sections of society became more visible archaeologically, and social differences can be mapped geographically (Hunter 2001). In south-east and eastern Scotland, for example, both areas where Roman goods were readily available, Hunter's analysis indicates a clear hierarchy of access to imports. This implies a strongly hierarchical society, where control over Roman imports may even have helped those of high rank to increase their social distance from other members of society.

In south-west Scotland, on the other hand, Roman imports are distributed across a wider spectrum of society, suggesting control by many lesser leaders rather than fewer, more powerful individuals. In Atlantic Scotland, there is a general dearth of Roman goods, but two areas stand out as having a wider range of finds and marked variation between sites: these are Orkney and Caithness, with their strongly hierarchical broch villages; and Argyll and the inner Hebrides, where differential occurrence of imports at architecturally similar sites could imply that status differences within the leading group were now being expressed through material culture (Hunter 2001).

Prior to the Roman conquest, there were undoubtedly differences in the degree of political authority wielded by people of higher social rank in our two major zones. The continued emphasis on enclosed settlements and substantial houses in Atlantic Britain implies that decentralized political conditions persisted there down to the Roman period. In central Britain, on the other hand, there are some signs of increased political centralization by the first century AD, as we saw above. It cannot be coincidental that these changes were focused on those lowland areas with better quality soils, where the agricultural improvements of the later Iron Age had permitted population and settlement to expand dramatically in a short space of time.

Southern and Eastern England

Like central and Atlantic Britain, southern and eastern England is usefully subdivided into two zones: one comprising the territories bordering the Thames and the coastal

---

2   The site may be compared to the 'royal' sites such as Colchester discussed below.

areas of south-east England, the other consisting of an outer ring extending from Wessex to East Yorkshire, and into East Anglia (Haselgrove 1989). In the Middle Iron Age, this second zone encompassed what were probably the most densely populated and socially developed areas in Britain – Wessex itself or the East Midlands river valleys – but in the Late Iron Age, the balance shifted dramatically to south-east England (Hill forthcoming).

Until the end of the second century BC, the inhabitants of developed hillforts like Danebury and Maiden Castle each controlled well-defined territories which they had gradually enlarged over the centuries (Sharples 1991; Cunliffe 1991). Whatever their precise composition, these dominant communities are usually viewed as strongly hierarchical in character, although this view has been challenged (Hill 1996). Individual social differences were generally muted in terms of material culture distinctions, the main exception being East Yorkshire, where the burial tradition provides insights into the complexities of individual social ranking (Parker Pearson 1999).

In the first century BC, however, major changes occurred, some of which recall developments in central and Atlantic Britain. A marked restructuring of the settlement pattern is apparent almost everywhere: the developed hillforts in the south were abandoned for a range of smaller enclosure types, while in East Yorkshire, settlement territories defined by linear earthworks gave way to 'ladder' settlement complexes in a process which seems to parallel developments in Wessex (Collis 1994) and the existing burial tradition disappeared. In eastern England, nucleated settlements like Fengate (Cambridgeshire) declined in size, and display more evidence of internal differentiation. In yet other areas such as Northamptonshire, small but prominent enclosures proliferated (Haselgrove 2001). New types of focal sites appeared throughout southern and eastern England, among them Gussage–Cow Down (Dorset), Bagendon–North Cerney (Gloucestershire) and Fison Way–-Thetford (Norfolk). As a class these are rather diffuse, but they generally included cult foci and often had zones defined by linear dykes. As I noted earlier, the quantity of material culture deposited on settlements and in votive contexts increased significantly, particularly items which could be used to define individual social identities and hierarchies, such as brooches or decorative metalwork.

As in central Britain, settlement expansion into thinly settled areas – and the social processes underlying this phenomenon – are increasingly emerging as some of the key features of the later Iron Age in southern and eastern England (Haselgrove et al. 2001). Frequently, the expansion process is linked with developing craft specialization – for example, in the working of iron, pottery or glass in areas as far apart as Kent, Somerset and East Yorkshire (Haselgrove 1989, 2001) – and with production for non-local exchange. Arguably, control of these industries and their exchange networks might have provided emerging groups with the means to challenge the traditional power structures of the developed hillfort communities, which were founded on control of agricultural production (Sharples 1991).

The process of expansion is particularly clear in south-east England, where material culture allows us to differentiate between the long-established occupants of densely populated regions such as the chalk downland of Sussex and Kent, some of whom retained their 'Middle Iron Age' cultural traditions into the first century AD; and incoming groups in hitherto thinly settled areas, who were much quicker to adopt 'Late Iron Age' innovations such as wheelmade pottery and coinage (Hill 2002, forthcoming). This probably happened partly because the incomers lacked the deep-rooted social relationships between households which characterized areas that were already densely inhabited, and partly on account of their need to build up new social networks through exchange. Hill (forthcoming) plausibly suggests that one reason for increased use of gold coinage in the second and first centuries BC is that it provided a way of establishing relations with other groups, while the adoption of new, continentally influenced funeral rites could equally relate to the building up of new marriage and alliance networks.

Throughout the areas where 'Late Iron Age' material culture made its appearance, we also find new settlement forms in new locations, and new uses of space (including rectangular dwellings). Other breaks with the past include the greater emphasis on individual identities and personal grooming (Hill 1997);[3] a clearer separation of domestic and ritual activity, with more of the latter conducted at formal temples and cult enclosures (Haselgrove 2001); and new ways of preparing and serving food (Hill 2002). It is clear from the character of the material that more intensive contact with Gaul was among the main factors shaping these changes. While older ideas about large-scale immigration from Belgic Gaul have fallen out of favour, it is now widely accepted that small-scale settlement and the movement of individual leaders such as Commios – who may have been granted territory in Britain as part of the Caesarian settlement (Creighton 2000) – played a part in fostering closer social and cultural links between the peoples on either side of the Channel (Haselgrove 2001). This would also explain the suggestion of Belgic political hegemony in both numismatic and literary sources (*De Bello Gallico*, II. 4).

Creighton (2000) has recently discussed the character of the changes which accompanied the subsequent growth of Roman cultural and political influence in the parts of south-east England closest to the continent. The promotion of various Britons to client kingship under Augustus and Tiberius in effect precipitated a process of state formation, as rulers sought to consolidate and expand polities inherited from their predecessors. The legends on their coins show that dynasty building became a preoccupation, while the burial evidence implies that this centralization of political power was accompanied by more absolute forms of social ranking. This contrasts with the regions closer to the Severn and the Humber, where the coinages lay greater stress on shared cultural identity and less on the attributes of individual leaders (Haselgrove 1989).

Another facet of political centralization in south-east England was the foundation by British client kings of new seats of power – including Colchester, Silchester and St Albans – on the margins of existing settlement and coin distributions, evidently intended to unify previously distinct groups. Analysis of the King Harry Lane cemetery at St Albans, in use *c*.10 BC–AD 45, implies that as the settlement grew, social networks created through day-to-day interaction became more important than kinship links (Millett 1993). These 'royal' sites were all major religious foci – indeed, if they were already periodic meeting-places, this could well have been a factor in their choice as permanent centres – and their rulers may have derived some of their authority from acting as religious leaders (Creighton 2000). The length of the

3   Personal grooming was not confined to the south-east, as the manicured fingernails of the first century AD Lindow Man bog body from Cheshire demonstrate.

earthworks around these sites leaves little doubt that they were erected as a statement of power and social exclusion, rather than for defence.

In conclusion, we can see that Roman influence is behind the much greater degree of political centralization and social stratification apparent in south-east England. In turn, the overt degree of social differentiation in areas of southern and eastern England nearer the Severn and the Humber is much greater than anywhere in central or Atlantic Britain, although the level of political centralization in the territories just beyond the Severn–Humber line may not have been much less than among their coin-using neighbours. Even in south-east England, however, the political changes that had taken place by the Claudian invasion were far from irreversible (Haselgrove 1989), as the apparent disintegration of the polity formerly ruled by Cunobelinus seems to indicate. Social power in Late Iron Age societies was still, to a large extent, personal, and whether the polities fashioned by particular rulers through dynastic alliance or military conquest were passed on intact to their blood relations will have depended on various factors, although Creighton (2000) is surely right to argue that in areas of south-east England which had been regarded as Roman territory since Caesar's day, Roman backing was what mattered.

FURTHER READING

For a comprehensive account of the British Iron Age, see B. W. Cunliffe, *Iron Age Communities in Britain* (London, 1991) with a bibliography of major sites; the latter is updated by Haselgrove (2001), which provides more detail on many of the topics explored here. Shorter surveys include Armit (1997) for Scotland; J. D. Hill (1995), who takes a different approach to Cunliffe on many aspects of Iron Age society; and Haselgrove (1989), which discusses the later Iron Age in southern Britain. Hingley (1992) provides a valuable overview of Iron Age settlement and society in Scotland.

The problems of reconstructing Iron Age social and political organization in a European context are discussed in Champion (1995). Simon James' *The Atlantic Celts* (1999) reviews the controversies surrounding the identification of the Iron Age Britons as Celts. The collective works edited by Gwilt and Haselgrove (1997), and Bevan (1999) contain several other important articles about Iron Age cultural practices other than those cited in my article. Practical measures to help elucidate the issues and research questions currently occupying Iron Age specialists are put forward by Haselgrove et al. (2001).

A full critique of David Clarke's pioneering study of Iron Age social organization, which set the agenda for much subsequent work, is provided by J. M. Coles and S. Minnitt (1995); their own interpretation offers important new insights on this exceptional site.

John Creighton's *Coins and Power* (2000) contains a host of stimulating, if often controversial, ideas on the nature of Roman influence on south-east England in the decades before the invasion, and shows that even familiar material has many surprises in store if only we ask the right questions.

REFERENCES

Armit, I. 1997. *Celtic Scotland*. London.
—— 1999. Life after Hownam: the Iron Age in south-east Scotland. In B. Bevan (ed.), *Northern Exposure*. Leicester, 65–79.

Bevan, B. (ed.) 1999. *Northern Exposure: Interpretative Devolution and the Iron Ages in Britain*. Leicester Archaeology Monograph 4. Leicester.

Champion, T. 1995. Power, politics and status. In M. J. Green (ed.), *The Celtic World*. London, 85–94.

Champion, T. C. and Collis, J. R. (eds) 1996. *The Iron Age in Britain and Ireland: Recent Trends*. Sheffield.

Clarke, D. L. 1972. A provisional model of an Iron Age society and its settlement system. In D. L. Clarke (ed.), *Models in Archaeology*. London, 801–69.

Coles, J. M. and Minnitt, S. 1995. *Industrious and Fairly Civilised: The Glastonbury Lake Village*. Taunton.

Collis, J. R. 1994. The Iron Age. In B. Vyner (ed.), *Building the Past*. London, 123–48.

—— 1996. Hillforts, enclosures and boundaries, in T. C. Champion and J. R. Collis (eds), *The Iron Age in Britain and Ireland*. Sheffield, 87–94.

Creighton, J. 2000. *Coins and Power in Late Iron Age Britain*. Cambridge.

Cunliffe, B. 1991. *Iron Age Communities in Britain*, 3rd edn. London.

Ferrell, G. 1997. Space and society in the Iron Age of north-east England. In A. Gwilt and C. C. Haselgrove (eds), *Reconstructing Iron Age Societies*. Oxford, 228–38.

Fitzpatrick, A. 1992. The roles of Celtic coinage in south-east England. In M. Mays (ed.), *Celtic Coinage: Britain and Beyond; The Eleventh Oxford Symposium on Coinage and Monetary History*. BAR 222. Oxford, 1–32.

—— 1997. Everyday life in Iron Age Wessex. In A. Gwilt and C. C. Haselgrove (eds), *Reconstructing Iron Age Societies*. Oxford, 73–86.

Foster, S. 1989. Analysis of spatial patterns in buildings (gamma analysis) as an insight into social structure: examples from the Scottish Atlantic Iron Age. *Antiquity*, 63, 40–50.

Giles, M. and Parker Pearson, M. 1999. Learning to live in the Iron Age; dwelling and praxis. In B. Bevan (ed.), *Northern Exposure*. Leicester, 217–31.

Gwilt, A. and Haselgrove, C. C. (eds) 1997. *Reconstructing Iron Age Societies*. Oxbow Monograph 71. Oxford.

Haselgrove, C. C. 1987. *Iron Age Coinage in South-east England: The Archaeological Context*. BAR (British Series) 174. Oxford.

—— 1989. The later Iron Age in southern Britain and beyond. In M. Todd (ed.), *Research on Roman Britain 1960–89*. Britannia Monograph 11. London, 1–18.

—— 1997. Iron Age brooch deposition and chronology. In A. Gwilt and C. C. Haselgrove (eds), *Reconstructing Iron Age Societies*. Oxford, 51–72.

—— 2001. Iron Age Britain and its European setting. In J. R. Collis (ed.), *Society and Settlement in Iron Age Europe: Actes du XVIIIe Colloque de l'AFEAF, Winchester*. Sheffield Archaeological Monograph 11. Sheffield, 37–72.

—— 2002. The later Bronze Age and the Iron Age in the Lowlands. In C. Brooks, R. Daniels and A. Harding (eds), *Past, Present and Future: The Archaeology of Northern England*. Architectural and Archaeological Society of Durham and Northumberland Research Report 5. Durham, 49–69.

Haselgrove, C. C., Armit, I., Champion, T. C., Creighton, J., Gwilt, A., Hill, J. D., Hunter, F. and Woodward, A. 2001. *Understanding the British Iron Age: An Agenda for Action*. Salisbury.

Hill, J. D. 1995. *Ritual and Rubbish in the Iron Age of Wessex*. BAR (British Series) 242. Oxford.

—— 1995. The Iron Age in Britain and Ireland (*c*.800 BC–AD 100). *Journal of World Prehistory*, 9, 47–98.

—— 1996. Hillforts and the Iron Age of Wessex. In T. C. Champion and J. R. Collis (eds), *The Iron Age in Britain and Ireland*. Sheffield, 95–116.

Hill, J. D. 1997. 'The end of one kind of body and the beginning of another kind of body?' Toilet instruments and 'Romanization' in southern England during the first century AD. In A. Gwilt and C. C. Haselgrove (eds), *Reconstructing Iron Age Societies*. Oxford, 96–107.

—— 2002. Just about the potter's wheel: using, making and depositing Middle and Later Iron Age pots in East Anglia. In A. Woodward and J. D. Hill (eds), *Prehistoric Britain: The Ceramic Basis*. Oxford, 143–60.

—— (forthcoming). Was the core really a periphery? Indigenous changes in late Iron Age eastern England. In C. Haselgrove and T. Moore (eds), *The Later Iron Age in Britain and Beyond*. Oxford.

Hingley, R. 1992. Society in Scotland from 700 BC to AD 200, *Proceedings of the Society of Antiquaries of Scotland*, 122, 7–53.

—— 1999. The creation of later prehistoric landscapes and the context of reuse of Neolithic and early Bronze Age monuments in Britain and Ireland. In B. Bevan (ed.), *Northern Exposure*. Leicester, 233–51.

—— (forthcoming) Iron Age 'currency bars' in Britain: items of exchange in liminal contexts? In C. Haselgrove and D. Wigg (eds), *Ritual and Iron Age Coinage*. Studien zu Fundmünzen der Antike. Mainz.

Hunter, F. 1997. Iron Age hoarding in Scotland and northern England. In A. Gwilt and C. C. Haselgrove (eds), *Reconstructing Iron Age Societies*. Oxford, 108–33.

—— 2001. Roman and native in Scotland: new approaches. *Journal of Roman Archaeology*, 14, 289–309.

James, S. T. 1999. *The Atlantic Celts. Ancient People or Modern Invention?* London.

Millett. M. 1993. A cemetery in an age of transition: King Harry Lane reconsidered. In M. Strück (ed.) *Römerzeitliche Gräber als Quellen zu Religion, Bevölkerungsstruktur und Sozialgeschichte*. Archäologische Schriften des Instituts für Vor- und Frühgeschichte der Johannes Gutenberg-Universität Mainz 3. Mainz, 255–82.

Oswald, A. 1997. A doorway on the past: practical and mystic concerns in the orientation of roundhouse doorways. In A. Gwilt and C. C. Haselgrove (eds), *Reconstructing Iron Age Societies*. Oxford, 87–95.

Parker Pearson, M. 1996. Food, fertility and front doors in the first millennium BC. In T. C. Champion and J. R. Collis (eds), *The Iron Age in Britain and Ireland*. Sheffield, 117–32.

—— 1999. Food, sex and death: cosmologies in the British Iron Age with particular reference to East Yorkshire. *Cambridge Archaeological Journal*, 9, 43–69.

Roymans, N. 1999. Man, cattle and the supernatural in the Northwest European Plain. In C. Fabech and J. Ringtved (eds), *Settlement and Landscape: Proceedings of a Conference in Aarhus, Denmark, May 4–7 1998*. Mooesgård, 291–300.

Sharples, N. M. 1991. *Maiden Castle: Excavation and Field Survey 1985–6*. English Heritage Archaeological Report 19. London.

Sharples, N. M. and Parker Pearson, M. 1997. Why were brochs built? Recent studies in the Iron Age of Atlantic Scotland. In A. Gwilt and C. C. Haselgrove (eds), *Reconstructing Iron Age Societies*. Oxford, 254–65.

Tipping, R. 1997. Pollen analysis and the impact of Rome on native agriculture around Hadrian's Wall. In A. Gwilt and C. C. Haselgrove (eds), *Reconstructing Iron Age Societies*. Oxford, 239–47.

Webster, J. 1999. Here be dragons! the continuing influence of Roman attitudes to northern Britain. In B. Bevan (ed.), *Northern Exposure*. Leicester. 21–31.

Wells, P. S. 2002. Perspectives on changes in early Roman Gaul. *Archaeological Dialogues*, 9, 47–51.

Williams, J. H. C. (2001). Coin inscriptions and the origins of writing in pre-Roman Britain. *British Numismatic Journal*, 71, 1–17.

Wise, A. 2000. Late prehistoric settlement and society: recent research in the central Tweed valley. In J. Harding and R. Johnson (eds), *Northern Pasts: Interpretation in the Later Prehistory of Northern England and Southern Scotland*. BAR (British Series) 302. Oxford, 93–9.

CHAPTER THREE

The Native Elite and their Funerary Practices from the First Century BC to Nero

ROSALIND NIBLETT

The difficulties of using material deposited in graves to determine social status are well known. Differential preservation of grave goods may give a false impression of the wealth or variety of the material originally deposited, while ignorance of the motives determining the choice of particular objects further distorts our perception. In reality, rites preceding the cremation or burial may well have been of greater significance than the grave itself or any offerings placed within it. Such rites will not necessarily be detectable in the archaeological record and may not have been conducted on, or even close to, the site of the final burial. At the important Late Iron Age site at Elms Farm, Heybridge (Essex) 19 pyre sites were excavated together with pits in which broken pottery and pyre debris had been buried, but only two cremation burials were found (personal communication from the excavator, Mark Atkinson).

In the first century BC the previously sparse burial record was significantly augmented. Inhumation cemeteries developed, particularly in the Dorset region (Whimster 1981: 39–55), but also in parts of eastern Britain (for instance at Fisons Way, Thetford; Gregory 1991: 169). In the south-east cremation burials in the Aylesford tradition had become established by the time of Caesar's expeditions, and may have already appeared by the end of the second century BC (Haselgrove 1997). Typically Aylesford graves comprised cremated ashes, generally in a ceramic container, and often accompanied by other, usually intact, grave goods. Aylesford cemeteries rarely exceeded 30 graves; the cemeteries at Westhampnett, 3 kilometres east of Chichester (Fitzpatrick 1997a), and King Harry Lane, Verlamion (Stead and Rigby, 1989) were exceptional with 161 and 455 cremations respectively. It is clear therefore that the Aylesford rite was confined to a specific social group.

In a small proportion of Late Iron Age graves the presence of exceptionally rich grave goods has made the burial of a high-status individual a reasonable assumption. Inhumations in the south were occasionally accompanied by mirrors (as at Portesham, Dorset (Fitzpatrick 1997b) or 'warrior' equipment, for example, by a sword, shield and spear at Great Braxted (Kelvedon) Essex (personal communication from

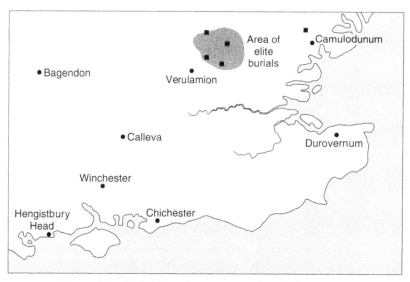

Figure 3.1 Major Iron Age concentrations before AD 43.

Paul Sealey) and a sword and 'helmet' at Deal, Kent (Parfitt 1995). At Owslebury, Hampshire, an adult male was buried with a sword, shield and spear within one of two ditched burial enclosures in the early first century BC; later cremation burials were grouped around it (Collis 1994). Two inhumations, both within ditched enclosures and accompanied by swords, have been excavated recently at Brisley Farm, Ashford, Kent, and provisionally dated to the first half of the first century AD (personal communication from Casper Johnson).

The so-called Welwyn-type graves in south-east England, north of the Thames, are characterized by (generally unurned) cremations accompanied by 'feasting equipment', such as wine amphorae or firedogs, together with local and imported pottery and metalwork. The burials usually occupied large, rectangular pits, often with traces of timber linings or coverings, suggesting the presence of a burial chamber or vault in which the grave offerings could be carefully laid out. These were deposited intact; amphorae might be placed upright against the wall of the vault, and tableware arranged on the grave floor. Pyre debris was not included. The earliest Welwyn-type grave so far recorded, at Baldock (Hertfordshire), dates from the first half of the first century BC. Here the grave goods included a Dressel 1A amphora, a bronze and iron cauldron, a bronze bowl, two firedogs and two bronze-bound buckets, but lacked the rectangular, timber-lined grave pit and pottery characteristic of later Welwyn-type burials (Stead and Rigby 1986). The burial in the large, timber-lined vault from Welwyn Garden City was accompanied by five Dressel IB amphorae, an Italian silver cup, three bronze- or iron-bound wooden containers, a bronze bowl and strainer, an iron knife, 24 glass gaming counters and 36 pottery vessels, including three Gaulish imports. Dating from the second half of the first century BC, it represents the fully developed rite (Stead 1967).

Until the early 1990s Welwyn-type graves were generally regarded as representing the pinnacle of late pre-Roman Iron Age funerary practices in this country. Their classification as aristocratic burials, however, rested on the perceived value of the grave offerings combined with the range of objects represented. Little attention was paid to rites preceding or succeeding the actual cremation and burial. However, all burials, whether cremations or inhumations and including those simply placed in a pit without any grave offerings, would have been part of some sort of funerary process. The significance of a particular individual's death to the living may be evidenced more by the scale and complexity of the funerary rites and the position afforded to the funerary site in the landscape than simply by the number and range of the objects placed in the grave. A small number of graves, first appearing at the end of the pre-Roman Iron Age, have produced evidence for protracted and elaborate rites. These rites, combined with the scale of the monuments, their position in the contemporary landscape and the range and value of the associated offerings, imply the presence of individuals whose status surpassed even that of the occupants of Welwyn-type graves.

At Folly Lane, on the northern edge of the territorial *oppidum* of Verlamion, evidence for the funerary rituals was unusually well preserved (Niblett 1999). Like the majority of burials in Late Iron Age Verlamion, that at Folly Lane lay in a rectilinear ditched enclosure. Covering an area of nearly two hectares, however, this enclosure was nearly ten times larger than the largest of the seven other complete funerary enclosures known from the area, while its position on a prominent slope, close to a main route into the *oppidum*, appears to have been deliberately chosen to overlook the centre of the pre-Flavian settlement.

The burial, dating from the early fifties of the first century AD, lay in a shallow pit near the centre of the enclosure and was accompanied by the remnants of an exceptionally rich collection of material. This material had been broken and burnt on the funeral pyre and included remains of ivory-mounted furniture, bronze-bound caskets or chests, iron mail and over 2.5 kg of solidified molten droplets of silver. The burial lay on the north edge of a rectangular, timber-revetted shaft, measuring 8×11 m and cut nearly 3 m into the natural gravel. Traces of an inner mortuary chamber, surrounded by a raised walkway, survived on the floor of the shaft. Scattered across its floor and in the lower levels of the material over it were unburnt sherds from nearly 40 vessels, including amphorae, samian and imported Gallo-Belgic wares, together with fragments of metal objects and occasional crumbs of cremated bone. The timber revetment had been deliberately destroyed, and the shaft filled with soil brought from a variety of different locations. This deposit had almost certainly continued above ground to form a barrow over both the burial and the shaft. In the centre of the enclosure, a few metres to the west, were traces of a pyre, subsequently marked by a post, and later still, by a Romano-Celtic temple. Some idea of the value of the combined burial and shaft assemblages can be gained by comparing the material from them with that from other high-status sites. The number of imported ceramic vessels at Folly Lane is comparable to that at the contemporary settlement site at Gorhambury (Neal et al. 1990: 192–201), while the number of samian vessels in the shaft is more than three times the total from the entire King Harry Lane cemetery.[1] The weight of molten silver from the burial is nearly three times that of the three silver cups from the Welwyn Garden City and Welwyn graves which are estimated to represent the annual pay of a Roman legionary (Rigby 1995: 255–6).

1 Rigby, The Pottery from the Funerary Shaft and Burial Pit, in Niblett 1999: 190.

Four very similar timber-revetted pits within ditched enclosures have been excavated at Stanway, on the western limit of the Camulodunum *oppidum* (Crummy 1995). The Stanway pits were significantly smaller than that at Folly Lane and had been dug only about a metre into the subsoil. The enclosures themselves were also smaller; the largest covered 1.2 ha. Like the Folly Lane shaft, however, the Stanway pits contained unburnt sherds from up to 30 vessels, all connected with the serving or consumption of food and drink. Other parallels included the deliberate demolition of the revetments, the infilling of the pits and the presence of pyre sites within three of the four enclosures. In spite of extensive excavation within the Stanway enclosures, no graves were found that were obviously associated with the timber-revetted pits. As in the case of the Folly Lane burial, however, these may have been relatively shallow, and could well have been destroyed by ploughing. Three of the enclosures also contained secondary cremation burials dating from between the first century BC and the Neronian period; these contained prestige objects, including, in one case, a set of medical instruments, but this material had been deposited intact, making the burials closer to the warrior or Welwyn-type graves than to Folly Lane.

Many of the features of the Folly Lane burial are paralleled in the Late Iron Age burial at Lexden, nearly 2 km east of Stanway. It was excavated in 1924 by Henry Laver, and published by his brother, Philip (Laver 1927). Reassessment of the excavation by Jennifer Foster showed that the burial had lain in a pit, approximately 8 m square and 1.8 m deep; it was covered by a barrow 30 m in diameter (Foster 1986: 47). In addition to 346 gr of cremated human bone, the pit contained a remarkably rich collection of material. This included sherds from at least 16 amphorae, fragments of gold thread, silver mounts in the form of trefoils and 'corn ears', remains of iron- and bronze-bound chests, statuettes and cut-up sections of iron mail. A silver medallion of Augustus provided a *terminus post quem* of 17 BC for the deposit. Much of the material was broken and incomplete, a fact originally explained in terms of later robbing. In the light of the deliberately broken and unburnt material from the timber-revetted pits at Stanway and Folly Lane, however, a more tenable explanation is that these objects had been deliberately broken, and fragments removed, as part of the funerary ritual.

Foster suggested that the large pit had contained a mortuary chamber. She identified four iron ferrules as bases for timber uprights supporting a substantial structure. All four had been broken at similar points, suggesting deliberate demolition. Their exact position was not recorded in the original report, but at least one came from an area on the north side of the pit where Laver had noticed a marked change in the character of the fill. It was in this same area that the majority of the amphorae sherds were found. It is possible therefore that a mortuary chamber stood in the northern part of the pit in which rites culminating in the destruction of large numbers of amphorae were performed. In the south-east sector of the pit Foster tentatively identified five globe-headed iron pins as evidence of another, slighter, timber structure. This structure would have separated the cremated bone and most of the iron mail from the other material and from the putative chamber in the north end of the pit.

The most notable feature of all these sites is the presence of timber structures in large pits. Unlike the timber-lined vaults in Welwyn-type graves, these had been deliberately destroyed and buried. Since neither the Folly Lane nor Stanway structures contained burials (apart from tiny amounts of cremated bone in their filling) they are best interpreted as mortuary pits in which the corpse was stored or exposed prior to cremation. Many of the unburnt fragments found on the floor and in the filling of the mortuary pits, however, are from types of objects that were deposited intact in Welwyn-type graves. As well as fragments of high-status metalwork, sherds of amphorae and other tableware are well represented, but the latter include a high proportion of platters rather than the drinking vessels that predominate in the Welwyn graves. It is likely that this material was used in the funeral feast prior to the cremation and that the mortuary pits were the places in which (or in the case of Stanway around which) the feast took place. It is noteworthy that at Lexden the area of the putative mortuary chamber coincides with the area in which the broken amphorae sherds were concentrated. No doubt other rites were also performed. The raised walkway around the mortuary chamber in the base of the Folly Lane pit showed signs of trampling, perhaps resulting from repeated processions (or dancing). A similar explanation has been advanced for a trampled area on the important funerary site at Clemency (Luxembourg) (Metzler et al. 1991: 47).

However prolonged the rites may have been, once completed all traces of them were systematically destroyed together with the structures and objects they contained. The 'shrines' on the periphery of the Westhampnett cemetery may have been used as mortuary chambers for the exposure of the dead, and similar structures may have existed on other Aylesford cemeteries. One of the features that distinguish the Folly Lane/Stanway rite, however, is the careful demolition of these structures as part of the funerary ritual.

At both Folly Lane and Stanway the pyre site itself seems to have had a particular significance. Enclosure 3 at Stanway contained a 'sub' enclosure centrally placed in its southern half and surrounding the pyre site. In enclosure 4 the pyre site lay in the centre of the enclosure, just as at Folly Lane where its importance was further underlined by the erection over it, first of a large post, and later of a Romano-Celtic temple. At Westhampnett bases of seven pyres were identified, concentrated at the margins of the cemetery. Here pots were apparently smashed over the pyre at the conclusion of the cremation, but otherwise there was no clear indication of continued veneration of the pyre site. Similar rites presumably took place round the pyre bases and pits at Elms Farm. It is also worth noting that, although no pyre sites were found in the King Harry Lane cemetery, central burials within enclosures or groups of burials were distinguished by the presence of small quantities of pyre offerings or pyre debris, suggesting that here too the pyre had a particular significance (Niblett 2000: 101).

Compared to the significance that was clearly attached to the mortuary pit and the pyre, the site of the burial was apparently of lesser importance. This is very much in line with Caesar's description of aristocratic Gallic funerals, which focused on the act of cremation rather than the disposal of the ashes.[2] At Folly Lane the burial had been simply dumped in a comparatively small grave adjacent to the mortuary pit, while at Stanway the absence of graves clearly linked with the mortuary pits may be due to their shallow depth. The burial of only a proportion of the ashes was a common feature of the Aylesford burial tradition, but at Folly Lane only a token amount of

---

2 Caesar, *De Bello Gallico*, VI. 19.

ashes and pyre debris was buried. Nevertheless, there are indications of the careful selection of material for burial. Burnt amphorae sherds were well represented and were almost certainly derived from the same vessels represented by unburnt sherds in the mortuary pit. Other pottery was virtually absent, and in view of the number of vessels represented by unburnt sherds in the mortuary pit it is difficult to see this as anything other than deliberate selection. Pottery sherds were also absent from the burial area at Lexden but were concentrated in the area of the putative mortuary chamber. Other feasting equipment also was curiously lacking from the burial deposits at both Folly Lane and Lexden. A fragment of a firedog was found in the mortuary chamber at Folly Lane, but there was no sign of it among the iron fragments in the burial pit itself. This absence is in marked contrast to the Welwyn-type graves, one of whose chief characteristics was the presence of feasting equipment and which often included substantial quantities of other pottery as well as amphorae. Instead items of ceremonial insignia were chosen. At Lexden, the coin of Augustus, mounted in bronze, has been seen as a diplomatic gift, and Creighton has suggested that iron fragments in the same deposit derive from a *sella curulis* (Creighton 2000: 183). The objects cremated at Folly Lane included an ivory-mounted couch or chair (perhaps another *sella curulis*) and bronze tubes which were initially identified as being part of a carynx, but which should more probably be seen as from a ceremonial sceptre. A tiny fragment of a bronze bird from the pyre site has been tentatively identified as part of a priestly head-dress (Niblett 1999: 171).

Neither at Folly Lane nor Stanway did the burial signal the end of the ritual activities. The revetments were removed from the mortuary pits, which were then carefully filled in, a process that itself seems to have been subject to specific rites. Handfuls of cremated and crushed bone were scattered at intervals in the filling, and at Folly Lane analysis of the earth filling the pit showed that it had been brought from different locations. What became of the cremated ashes and the remains of pyre goods not included in the burial is unknown. They may have been retained as mementoes, they may have been scattered, or they may have been deposited on sacred sites. At Lexden, Folly Lane and (probably) Stanway mounds were constructed over the destroyed mortuary pits, and it is possible that, as at Clemency, these became foci of commemorative rites (Metzler et al. 1991: 39).

At present funerary sites like that at Folly Lane are rare, but no doubt further examples will be discovered. It now seems more than likely that the religious complex at Gosbecks, 0.5 km east of Stanway, originated as a funerary site. In the Roman period the complex focused on a large Romano-Celtic temple in one corner of what was initially a Late Iron Age ditched enclosure covering 1.5 ha. The off-centre position of the temple has long been explained in terms of an earlier, presumably Late Iron Age feature (Hull 1958: 257–64). On analogy with Folly Lane, it now seems likely that this later Iron Age feature was the remnant of a demolished mortuary structure and funeral pyre.

Folly Lane, Stanway and Lexden date from between the second half of the first century BC and the Neronian period. What may be an earlier form of the rite was excavated at Baldock, approximately 200 m north-east of the early Welwyn-type grave described above, and roughly contemporary with it. The burial lay in a 33 m square, ditched enclosure at the centre of which was a pit containing the unburnt remains of three pigs and an intact bronze-bound bucket. Slightly off-centre to the enclosure was a smaller pit containing a cremation accompanied by cut-up iron mail, molten bronze fragments, one with traces of gilt, and sherds from a pedestal urn. These pits appear to mirror the evidence from Folly Lane and Lexden for the separation of the cremated remains from the unburnt remains in the mortuary pits. Outside the Baldock enclosure, but contemporary with its use, were two inhumations, both sealed by the floor of a small timber structure which had possibly served as a mortuary chamber (Burleigh 1984: 12–14).

At the mid-first-century BC site at Hayling Island, 14 km south-west of the *oppidum* of the southern Atrebates at Chichester, a square, palisaded enclosure surrounding an inner, fenced enclosure was focused on a pit. Early in the first century AD the inner enclosure was replaced by a circular timber building centred on the same pit, which itself remained open (King and Soffe 1994: 114–16). Coins, broken weapons, fragments of iron mail and occasional, disarticulated human remains were deposited in the south corner of the outer enclosure and bronze objects, mainly brooches, were deposited in the pit. The circular building was replaced in the early Roman period by a circular Romano-Celtic temple and the site continued in use until the later second century. Although no burial was found at Hayling Island, it is possible that the inner enclosure originated as a mortuary enclosure (Forcey 1998: 196). Initially Hayling Island may have been a cult centre associated with the funerary and inauguration rites of the southern Atrebatic dynasty of Commios. There is no way of knowing whether other Late Iron Age 'shrines' such as those at Lancing Down and Heathrow also originated as mortuary structures, but the possibility should not be ignored (Black 1986: 203–4).

Away from south-eastern England there is less evidence for social hierarchy in the Late Iron Age. In response to contact with Rome after AD 43, however, the centralization of authority tended to increase in those areas also, as it had earlier in the south-east. With it came a greater emphasis on personal prestige, a trend which may have been reflected in funerary rites.

At Fisons Lane (Thetford) a circular timber building within a square enclosure has been interpreted as the cult centre for the Iceni. It was built shortly after the Roman conquest on a site previously occupied by a high-status settlement site (Gregory 1991: 41–118). Adjacent to the enclosure on the west, approximately 60 unaccompanied inhumation burials were grouped within ring-ditches or rectilinear enclosures. The excavator suggested that these may have been high-status graves placed close to the main Icenian cult centre. In the fifties of the first century AD the main enclosure was enlarged and elaborated. Additional ritual structures were put up within it, although no burials were associated with them. Nevertheless it is clear that this was a major cult centre and as such it was no doubt closely associated with the local paramount authority; quite possibly it was the place where inauguration, and perhaps funerary rites, took place. The site was deliberately demolished, probably in the aftermath of the defeat of Boudicca in 61.

Further north a deposit of metalwork found in the nineteenth century at Melsonby, adjacent to the Brigantian centre at Stanwick, has recently been reassessed (Fitts et al. 1999). The metalwork appears to have lain in a deep pit. It included four horse harnesses, fragments of iron mail, a bucket and at least one iron-bound chest. Much of the material was found in a fragmentary state and had clearly been burnt. Although no burial was recorded, fragments of cremated bone could well have been missed in the circumstances of the nineteenth-century discovery. The presence, close to a major tribal settlement, of a large pit containing heavily burnt metalwork with no associated pottery, has obvious similarities to the burial at Folly Lane.

It is clear from the above that the rites at Folly Lane and Stanway were protracted and complex. In such circumstances significant variations were likely to develop both regionally and chronologically. This makes the whole question of where and when the rites originated a particularly difficult one. They display certain affinities with funerary practices in the territory of the Treveri, implying links between the elites in Hertford-shire and Essex and those in north-east Gaul. Parallels with Clemency have already been noted, and there is also dramatic evidence for the practice of excarnation and exposure in elaborate mortuary structures at La Croizette, Acy-Romance (Ardennes) (Lambot et al. 1994: 252–7, 287–303). The rich burials at Vieux-les-Asfeld, also in the Ardennes, could also be interpreted as including mortuary chambers destroyed at the time of burial (Niblett 1999: 397–8).

The apparent links with the Treveri may result at least in part from accidents of preservation, or may simply reflect areas where field work has been concentrated. It is quite possible that the ideas behind the Folly Lane and Stanway rites were widespread among those Late Iron Age communities in which power was becoming centralized. At Navan (County Armagh) a ditched enclosure, probably constructed early in the first century BC, surrounded an enormous setting of timber uprights, undoubtedly ritual in character and dated by dendrochronology to 94 BC. The timber structure had been deliberately burnt, soon after completion, and then buried beneath an enormous mound incorporating earth brought to the site from elsewhere. As C. J. Lynn has pointed out, the deliberate destruction of a ritual timber structure, and its burial beneath a mound containing imported soil have clear connotations with the destruction of the mortuary chamber at Folly Lane.[3] No burial was found associated with the mound, but little excavation was carried out on the enclosure itself, and as Lynn remarked, the possibility of one or more burials existing close by cannot be ruled out. It is also particularly interesting to note the reference in early Irish literature portraying the site as a royal centre,[4] where (possibly) the kings of Ulster were inaugurated.[5]

This discussion has largely focused on the Late Iron Age rites in south-east England, where two distinct elite burial rites developed: rich Welwyn-type graves and burials of the Folly Lane type. In the former the dead were accompanied by high-status and exotic grave goods, normally deposited intact. In many instances the volume of material and the need to arrange it carefully led to the construction of timber-lined vaults holding both the grave goods and the ashes of the deceased. Pyre offerings or pyre debris were not usually included; occasional small fragments of molten metal probably derive from clothing in which the dead were cremated. In contrast, Folly Lane type burials demanded the construction of a mortuary pit and chamber used only for funerary rites prior to the cremation and immediately demol-ished. Grave goods were not deposited in the grave intact. Instead, prestige equip-ment was cremated with the deceased and a token amount buried close to the site of

3 Lynn, in Waterman, 1997: 221.
4 Mallory, Emain Macha and Navan Fort, in Waterman 1997: 197–206.
5 Lynn, in Waterman, 1997: 229.

the mortuary pit in a simple, and probably shallow, grave pit. All this suggests a very different attitude towards the deceased and objects associated with them, compared to those in Welwyn or Aylesford rites.

The beliefs driving these differences can only be guessed at. If the cremation process was seen as liberating the dead person's spirit, perhaps leading to reincarnation, or to the transfer of potency to a successor, it may have been important to ensure that the insignia of power was also destroyed, enabling its potency to be similarly 'liberated' and transferred.[6] The presence of intact material in the Welwyn graves would suggest that here transference of power was not so crucial.

As noted above, the appearance of the Folly Lane rites coincides chronologically with the centralization of personal authority in the later first century BC. No doubt this importance increased following exposure of the native aristocracy to the concept of dynastic succession established by Augustus. It is likely that tribal societies saw the strength of the chieftain as vital to the welfare of the tribe as a whole. On his death, rites transferring his power and authority to a successor would have been enormously important to the tribe as a whole. In the Late Iron Age such rites may well have necessitated a considerable delay, either to allow time to assemble all the participants or to coincide with an appropriate time in the calendar. In the case of formal treaty arrangements with Rome, there was probably a need to involve the Roman authorities in approving a successor. All this could have necessitated lengthy delays and there would have been obvious advantages in having a mortuary chamber in which the dead chieftain could 'lie in state'.

Burials of the Folly Lane type remain rare but appear to be associated with major tribal centres, either ritual sites or territorial *oppida*. This alone strongly suggests that the individuals buried with these rites were closely connected with the centre, presumably either the paramount chieftain or at least a member of the ruling dynasty. The rich but less complex burials represented by the Welwyn-type graves and warrior burials no doubt represent high-status individuals, but are best seen as lesser chieftains, whose death did not affect the tribal group as a whole.

In England the origin of the Folly Lane/Stanway rite lies in the first century BC, but it survives at least until the early Neronian period, and elements of it can still be seen in some early Romano-British elite graves. At Holborough, Kent, for instance, a late first-century AD burial beneath a tumulus contained a folding chair and other high-status material, all of which was broken when buried, while the timber chamber in which the material lay had been deliberately destroyed before the tumulus was constructed (Jessup 1954).

By the second century both Folly Lane and Gosbecks had become the focus of extensive cult centres. At Folly Lane the pyre site was marked by a Romano-Celtic temple and the ditch levelled and marked out with chalk nodules so as to be clearly visible from the centre of Verulamium. The temple was linked to a wider complex including a bath-house, a second Romano-Celtic temple and a theatre, the last two structures being within the town itself. It is difficult to avoid the conclusion that by the Antonine period the burial site had become the focus of an important local cult. A similar process can be seen at Gosbecks where the Late Iron Age enclosure was converted into a large colonnaded precinct with a Romano-Celtic temple in its

6   As discussed by Creighton, *Coins and Power in Late Iron Age Britain*, 188–97.

southern corner. Here again the temple became the focus of an extensive complex including a theatre, aqueduct and probably also a bath-house. The second-century statuette of Mercury from the site no doubt represents the god in his role as conductor of the dead. It demonstrates the continuing importance to a Romano-British community of what must surely have originated as an aristocratic funerary site at the end of the Iron Age.

ACKNOWLEDGEMENTS

I am grateful to Mark Atkinson, Philip Crummy, Casper Johnson and David Rudling for information on their excavations, and I have greatly benefited from discussions with John Creighton and Paul Sealey. I am also indebted to Colin Haselgrove for drawing my attention to the Melsonby material.

FURTHER READING

For a survey of Iron Age burial practices with a full bibliography up to 1980, see R. Whimster, *Burial Practices in Iron Age Britain* (1981). Detailed reports of the excavation of the large cemeteries at Westhampnett and King Harry Lane are contained in I. M. Stead and V. Rigby, *Verulamium: The King Harry Lane Site* (1989), and A. P. Fitzpatrick, *Archaeological Excavations on the Route of the A27, Westhampnett Bypass, West Sussex*. Volume 2: *The Cemeteries* (1997). For Welwyn-type graves see I. M. Stead, 'A La Tène burial at Welwyn Garden City', *Archaeologia*, 109 (1967), 1–63. For the Folly Lane site see R. Niblett, *The Excavation of a Ceremonial Site at Folly Lane, St Albans* (1999) which also includes a discussion of the funerary rituals. J. Foster, *The Lexden Tumulus*, BAR (British Series) 156 (1986), is the reassessment of the Lavers' excavation of the Lexden burial. The Stanway burials have yet to be fully published, but for a summary see P. J. Crummy, *City of Victory* (1997), 23–8. For a discussion of late Iron Age funerary rituals in northern Gaul see A. P. Fitzpatrick, 'Sequence, Ritual and Structure: Late Iron Age Mortuary Practice in North-West Europe' (2000). The important sites in the Ardennes are comprehensively discussed in J. Metzler et al., *Clemency et les tombes de l'aristocratie en Gaule-Belgique* (1991) and B. Lambot et al., *Le site protohistorique d'Acy-Romance (Ardennes) II: Les necropoles dans leur contexte régional* (1994).

Some of the difficulties encountered in interpreting data from burials are summarized by J. Pearce, in Pearce et al., *Burial, Society and Context in the Provincial Roman World* (2000), while particular issues are addressed in M. Millet, 'A cemetery in the age of transition; the King Harry Lane cemetery reconsidered' (1993) and A. P. Fitzpatrick, 'Death in a material world' (1991). For a discussion of high-status burials in the context of the centralization of power in south-east England at the end of the Iron Age see J. Creighton, *Coins and Power in Iron Age Britain* (2000), particularly chapter 7.

REFERENCES

Black, E. W. 1986. Romano-British burial customs and religious beliefs in south-east England. *Archaeological Journal*, 143, 203–4.

Burleigh, G. 1984. Excavations at Baldock. *Herts Past*, 12, 1–18.

Collis, J. R. 1994: The Iron Age and Roman Cemetery at Owslebury, Hampshire. In A. P. Fitzpatrick and E. Morris (eds), *The Iron Age in Wessex: Recent Work*. Salisbury, 106–8.

Creighton, J. 2000. *Coins and Power in Late Iron Age Britain*. Cambridge.

Crummy, P. J. 1995. Late Iron Age burials at Stanway, Colchester. In J. Swaddling, S. Walker, and P. Roberts (eds), *Italy and Europe: Economic Relations 700 BC–AD 50*. British Museum Occasional Paper 97. London, 264–6.

—— 1997. *City of Victory*. Colchester.

Fitts, R. L., Haselgrove, C., Lowther, P. C. and Willis, S. H. 1999. Melsonby reconsidered: survey and excavations 1992–5 at the site of the discovery of the 'Stanwick' North Yorkshire Hoard of 1843. *Durham Archaeological Journal*, 14–15, 1–52.

Fitzpatrick, A. P. 1991. Death in a material world. The Late Iron Age and early Romano-British cemetery at King Harry Lane cemetery, St Albans, Hertfordshire. *Britannia* 23, 323–7.

—— 1997a. *Archaeological Excavations on the Route of the A27, Westhampnett Bypass, West Sussex*. Volume 2. *The Cemeteries*. Wessex Archaeological Report 12. Salisbury.

—— 1997b. A 1st-century AD 'Durotrigian' inhumation burial with a decorated Iron Age mirror from Portesham, Dorset. *Proceedings of the Dorset Natural History and Archaeological Society*, 118, 51–70.

—— 2000. Ritual, sequence and structure in Late Iron Age mortuary practices in north-west Europe. In J. Pearce, M. Millett and M. Struck (eds), *Burial, Society and Context in the Roman World*. Oxford, 15–29.

Forcey, C. 1998. Whatever happened to the heroes? In *Theoretical Roman Archaeology Conference Proceedings 1997*. Oxford, 87–98.

Foster, J. 1986. *The Lexden Tumulus*. BAR (British Series) 156. Oxford.

Gregory, A. K. 1991. *Excavations at Thetford, 1980–82, Fisons Way*. East Anglian Archaeological Report 53. Norwich.

Haselgrove, C. 1997. Iron Age brooch deposition and chronology. In A. Gwilt and C. C. Haselgrove (eds), *Reconstructing Iron Age Societies*. Oxbow Monographs 71. Oxford, 51–72.

Hull, M. R. 1958. *Roman Colchester*. Society of Antiquaries Research Report XX. Oxford.

Jessup, R. F. 1954. The excavation of a Roman barrow at Holborough, Snodland. *Archaeologia Cantiana*, 68, 1–61.

King, A. and Soffe, G. 1994. The Iron Age and Roman temple at Hayling Island. In A. P. Fitzpatrick and E. Morris (eds), *The Iron Age in Wessex: Recent Work*. Salisbury, 114–16.

Lambot, B., Fribulet, A. and Méniel, P. 1994. *Le site protohistorique d'Acy-Romance (Ardennes) II: Les necropoles dans leur contexte régional*. Mémoires de la Société Archéologique Champenoise 8. Reims.

Laver, P. G. 1927. The excavation of a tumulus at Lexden, Colchester. *Archaeologia*, 26, 241–54.

Lynn, C. J. 1997. Excavations at Navan Fort, 1961–71. In D. M. Waterman (ed.), *Excavations at Navan Fort*. Northern Ireland Archaeological Monographs 3. Belfast.

Mallory, J. P. 1997. Emain Macha and Navan Fort. In D. M. Waterman (ed.), *Excavations at Navan Fort*. Belfast, 197–206.

Metzler, J., Waringo, R., Bis, R. and Metzler-Zens, N. 1991. *Clemency et les tombes de l'aristocratie en Gaule-Belgique*. Dossiers d'Archéologie du Museé National d'Histoire et d'Art 1. Luxembourg.

Neal, D. S., Wardle, H. and Hunn, J. 1990: *The Excavation of an Iron Age, Roman and Medieval Settlement at Gorhambury, St Albans*. English Heritage Archaeological Report 14. London.

Millett, M., 1993. A cemetery in the age of transition; the King Harry Lane cemetery reconsidered. *Archäologische Schriften des Instituts für Vor- und Frühgeschichte der Johannes*

Gutenberg-Universität Mainz. Band 3. *Römerzeitliche Gräber als Quellen zu Religion, Bevölkerungsstruktur und Sozialgeschichte,* 255–82.

Niblett, R. 1999. *The Excavation of a Ceremonial Site at Folly Lane, St Albans.* Britannia Monograph 14. London.

—— 2000. Funerary rites at Verulamium during the early Roman period. In J. Pearce, M. Millett and M. Struck (eds), *Burial, Society, and Context in the Provincial Roman World.* Oxford, 97–104.

Parfitt, K. 1995. *Iron Age Burials from Mill Hill, Kent.* London.

Pearce, J., Millett, M. and Struck, M. (eds) 2000. *Burial, Society, and Context in the Provincial Roman World.* Oxford, 1–12.

Rigby, V. 1995. Italic imports in late Iron Age Britain: a summary of the evidence from 'chieftains' burials. In J. Swaddling, S. Walker and P. Roberts (eds), *Italy and Europe: Economic Relations 700 BC–AD 50.* British Museum Occasional Paper 97. London, 235–64.

Stead, I. M. 1967. A La Tène burial at Welwyn Garden City. *Archaeologia,* 109, 1–63.

—— 1989. The earliest burials of the Aylesford Culture. In G. de G. Sieveking, I. M. Longworth and K. E. Wilson (eds), *Problems in Economic and Social Archaeology.* London, 401–16.

Stead, I. M. and Rigby, V. 1986. *Baldock: The Excavation of a Roman and Pre-Roman Settlement, 1968–73.* Britannia Monograph 7. London.

—— 1989. *Verulamium: The King Harry Lane Site.* English Heritage Archaeological Report 12. London.

Waterman, D. M. 1997. *Excavations at Navan Fort, 1961–71.* Northern Ireland Archaeology Monographs 3. Belfast.

Whimster, R. 1981. *Burial Practices in Iron Age Britain.* BAR (British Series) 90. Oxford.

CHAPTER FOUR

The Claudian Conquest and its Consequences

MALCOLM TODD

Caesar to Claudius

Julius Caesar's two invasions of Britain, in 55 and 54 BC, enjoyed immense *réclame* in Rome at the time. This island beyond the stream of Ocean and little known to the general public, its very existence still doubted by some, was a place at the limits of the known world, a land fruitful in legends. But Britain had already presented itself in another guise to the expanding world of Rome, as a source of mineral wealth, a perennial attraction to Mediterranean powers. This did not provide the main reason for Caesar's interventions in Britain. Caesar's own account of his motives for his assault on the island is manifestly selective and inadequate (Mitchell 1983). He was fully aware of the long-standing relationships between southern Britain and northern Gaul, which went back at least to the rule exercised by Diviciacus on both sides of the Channel in the earlier first century BC. He would also have known about trade connections between the continent and the island, which were not confined to the Channel narrows (see p. 2–5). He admitted to seeking intelligence from traders about the peoples of Britain, their institutions, warfare, and ports which might accommodate an invasion fleet, but claimed that he found little of use from this source. This is disingenuous, to put it mildly. Caesar's Gaulish informants could have told him much about the southern British tribes; traders would have known a good deal about about markets and harbours. Caesar was intent on portraying his expedition of 55 as a venture into an unknown and dangerous land. Bold as his enterprise was, Caesar was probably as well informed about Britain as any Roman could have been at the time.

Major reconnaissance in 55 almost ended in disaster and achieved little. The greater enterprise of 54 exposed more fully the difficulties of operating so far from Gaul when that province was still not completely conquered. Caesar's object in 54 was to add Britain to Rome's domain in north-western Europe, but he overreached himself. He was in no position to leave Roman troops in Britain and seems to have hoped that the British rulers who had surrendered to him would guarantee the payment of tribute in following years. There is no evidence that such tribute was ever paid. It is possible, but not certain, that Caesar had it in mind to return to Britain in 53; equally, his mind may have been turning elsewhere, perhaps to the northern Balkans. In any event, 53 was absorbed by operations against the Treveri in north-eastern Gaul and a crossing of the Rhine. In the following year, central Gaul was engulfed in the revolt led by Vercingetorix. Britain slipped from the forefront of Roman interest in the West, without disappearing entirely (*Gallic War*, IV.20–36; V.8–23)

The immediate consequences of Caesar's acts in 54 have been much discussed and remain debatable. In an influential paper, C. E. Stevens (1951) argued that Caesar had effectively made some of the peoples of south-eastern Britain subject to Rome, having imposed tribute on them (but see also Brunt 1963). This does not mean that a permanent treaty relationship was established in 54. As Strabo reports, writing thirty years later, the tribute was not paid; and agreements between Caesar and the Britons were breached in other ways (*Geography*, 115–16, 200). Whatever Caesar had in mind in 54 therefore did not survive for long, if at all. For the next twenty years, the sources we possess are silent on the subject of Britain, scarcely a surprise given the circumstances of the time. The next indication that Britain was again catching imperial attention occurs a decade after Caesar's murder.

In 34, 27 and 26 BC there were poetic references to conquest of the Britons by Augustus (Stevens 1951; more importantly, Griffin 1984). How are these comments to be interpreted? Was there any real basis to them in the form of a military plan? Was this no more than propaganda by Augustus or his confidants to conceal his true intentions or to control the Britons from afar by veiled threats? Or was it merely a rhapsodic fantasy on the part of Horace in particular? It must be noted that the Britons figure on an unlikely list of potential military targets, along with Parthians and Indians. The real fighting of the day, in Spain, attracted virtually no attention from the Augustan poets. It is hard to interpret the poetic references to Britain, singly or combined, as issuing from a plan of conquest. Early in his reign Augustus was cautious in his external policies. After 16 BC his focus was on the peoples beyond the Rhine and Danube. Britain was a minor concern and its dynasties could be kept in check by non-military means. Strabo's summary of the view of Rome on Britain may have been close to Augustus' own sentiments (*Geography*, IV.5.1–3). Britain had been made virtually a part of the Roman realm by British rulers who had sent embassies to Augustus and gained his friendship; the cost of occupation would outweigh tribute from the island; customs dues on trade goods entering Britain would be reduced if tribute was imposed. Strabo also called Britain remote and offering no aggressive threat. It is not certain to what date Strabo's comments refer. A likely context is the late twenties BC, when references to the conquest of Britain fade away.

After about 23 BC, and certainly before 16, Britain was no longer a serious objective of Roman policy or even a subject for propaganda. But diplomatic relations were maintained, if only to make secure the Channel coast of Gaul. The recorded embassy of the British rulers Tincommius and Dubnovellaunus (*Res Gestae*, 32) probably belongs to the years after 16, though the relationship of these kings with Rome could have begun earlier. Nominally at least, some of the British tribes could be viewed as subjects of Rome following the events of 54. This was scarcely a realistic view, but it could be used, along with economic arguments along the lines of those advanced by Strabo, to justify a policy of non-intervention in the island. There followed what Tacitus much later called the *longa oblivio* of Britain, sanctioned by Augustus and extended by Tiberius in accord with his overall strategy of containment.

Support of British rulers is likely to have extended to subsidies of one kind or another. Coins of several rulers in the late first century BC, including Verica, Tincomarus and Eppillus, reveal designs based on and close to Roman coin-types and engraved gems. Further, some coins of Tincomarus were struck from the same metal alloy as Roman denarii, or from denarii which were melted down for the purpose. It is at least plausible that the dies which produced these issues were engraved by Roman craftsmen under a diplomatic agreement which may have included recognition as an allied king. Later, Cunobelin's large coinage also portrayed designs based on classical prototypes, and a further hint of high-level connection with Rome lies in the abundance of the gold coins of this ruler. Britain was not notably rich in gold, but Rome could have made over supplies of the metal as a subsidy (in general, see Creighton 2000).

Roman diplomatic relations with Britain were quiet in the reign of Tiberius, perhaps even dormant, while commercial activity flourished, especially in the south-east of the island. With the accession of Gaius in 37 and the death of Cunobelin shortly afterwards, there was a distinct quickening of interest in western conquest. The unstable mind of Gaius fixed first on Germany and then turned to Britain. Across the Channel two of Cunobelin's sons, Caratacus and Togodumnus, emerging from the shadow of their long-lived father, struck a more aggressive pose towards the Empire, possibly detecting a change in Roman intentions. Gaius' plans for invasion famously came to naught, though the intention to invade should be taken seriously. The flight of Adminius, another son of Cunobelin, to Gaul was an encouragement. In 40 a force was assembled in northern Gaul and grouped at Boulogne. The ensuing events are difficult to reconstruct, but it is clear that there was no stomach among the troops for an expedition to Britain. Gaius was losing his tenuous grip on reality by this time and was unable to provide any authoritative direction to an operation on this scale. The project was shelved, but two years later Claudius had reason to return to it.

The Claudian Achievement

The Claudian plan for the conquest of Britain was not an aberration (Levick 1990: 137–44).

Claudius' motivation was not simple, but the very fact that this was a project which Julius Caesar had not been able to bring to fruition will have weighed with this admirer of the dictator. There were subsidiary but substantial reasons. A major military success would do much to secure the position of an emperor who had only recently come to power against the expectations of many. There were also more local imperatives. The long-lasting and stable relations between Rome and the dynasties was breaking down, following the death of Cunobelin about 40. It is unlikely that the threat to the security of Gaul was serious, but the diplomatic breach may have presented an affront to Roman authority in north-western Europe. Among the more material attractions of Britain were minerals, always of interest to the Roman state, particularly if precious metals were involved. This aspect of Britain had been discounted by some authorities in the first century BC, but their views were unduly pessimistic. The overriding consideration, however, was political and closely related to the position of Claudius in the first two years of his reign.

The planning of the Claudian invasion was of a different order from anything which had gone before, but it was not free of problems. The invading force was led by Aulus Plautius, a kinsman and associate of Claudius, legate of Pannonia and a safe, though not brilliant, military commander. There were more experienced generals, such as Domitius Corbulo and Hosidius Geta, but the regime was still young and the accent was on the avoidance of risk. Hosidius Geta was included as a corps commander, as was the later emperor Sulpicius Galba. Flavius Sabinus was also given a command, as was his younger brother Flavius Vespasianus, later emperor, but now commanding the Second Legion Augusta. Others were involved, either in the initial invasion or in the emperor's entourage at a later stage, because they could not safely be left behind in Rome. Claudius was mindful of the fact that at the time of his accession several voices called for the restoration of the Republic and his own removal. Relatives, mainly by marriage, were also drawn in, though none is known to have received a major command. In Rome, Lucius Vitellius was entrusted with the conduct of affairs and Domitius Corbulo was left behind to add substance to military counsels.

The role of Gnaeus Sentius Saturninus in the invasion force has attracted much attention. He had been consul at the time of the assassination of Gaius and the elevation of Claudius. His views on the Principate are far from clear and his support for Claudius need not have been total (Levick 1990: 31). He has been credited with a leading role in the command of the expeditionary force, but this is not certain (Frere 1987: 52–3). He may have been included to secure his loyalty rather than for any other reason.

After another episode of mutiny, defused by Narcissus, one of the emperor's trusted freedmen, the invading force sailed, somewhat later than had been planned. Their landing was not opposed and the army quickly established itself and consolidated its position. Nothing further is heard of Verica and it is unlikely that he was restored to a position of authority, even under a regime which was fully prepared to employ friendly rulers in areas recently acquired. The earlier refugee Adminius likewise does not figure in early Roman Britain. After the landing, Roman diplomacy was quickly at work and had probably been active in the previous weeks or months.

Four legions formed the core of the invasion force: the Second Legion Augusta (from Strasbourg), the Ninth Legion Hispana (from Pannonia), the Fourteenth Legion Gemina (from Mainz) and the Twentieth Legion Valeria (from Neuss). The size and composition of the auxiliary forces is not easily computed; the record is incomplete and may always remain so. The discharge diplomata of the period 43–70 present a limited register of auxiliary units in Britain, and the surviving inscriptions on stone, though informative, are not an extensive source. The units which were certainly or probably in Britain in the Claudio–Neronian period include a number earlier based in northern Gaul and the Rhine; some of these may have been earmarked for Gaius' aborted invasion.

The build-up to the invasion may have occupied much of the late year of 42 and the winter of 42/3. Roman knowledge of the major harbours of south-eastern Britain will have greatly increased over the previous century; recent intelligence will have come in from traders and exiles. The much-ridiculed preparations for invasion by Gaius included at least the building of a lighthouse at Boulogne (*Gesoriacum*), an

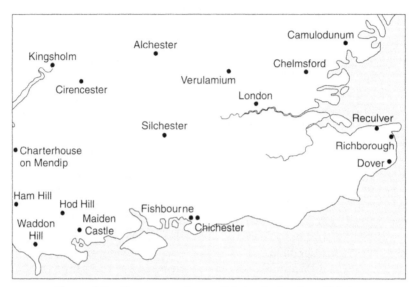

Figure 4.1   Conquest and consolidation in Southern Britain.

obvious assembly–point for a cross-Channel force. After a delay occasioned by the reluctance of the Roman force to embark upon a hazardous crossing across an arm of Ocean to a still mysterious island, the fleet sailed. Where did it make landfall?

The site of Richborough (Cunliffe 1968) has long dominated discussion of the landing-sites chosen by the invading force, with good reason. An early beach-head protected by a bank and ditch was quickly succeeded by the construction of a major supply-depot containing numerous granaries and other store-buildings. This base continued to serve as the main entrepôt for supplies reaching Britain for several decades. At the end of the first century a triumphal *quadrifons* was placed at the centre of the site, underlining the importance of the port in the phase of conquest.

It is unlikely that Richborough was the sole landing-place of the expeditionary force. There were other good harbours on the south-east coast, including Dover, Reculver and Lympne. None of these, however, has yet produced secure evidence for use by the Claudian army. It might have been expected that the estuary of the Thames, with its access deep into the island, caught the attention of Roman commanders, but the only surviving account of the advance through the south-east speaks only of a land campaign towards the Thames. It has been argued that the invasion army landed well to the west, in the anchorages between Chichester and Southampton (Hind 1989). This is unlikely, as the lines of communication northward were poorer than those through Kent. Dio Cassius' account suggests that the army was held together and moved on to the Thames in the later summer of 43. There it paused to allow Claudius to join his troops in taking control of the great oppidum at Camulodunum. The role of London and its region in the phase of invasion has long been debatable and is still shadowy. The strategic position of London might seem to mark it out as a potential nodal point in the military network. Military equipment has been recovered from several sites in London and from the Thames;

Claudian pottery and coinage has been recorded in a variety of locations; but indubitable structural evidence for a Claudian fort has yet to appear. Nevertheless, the number of mid-first century military objects clearly points to the presence of Roman troops on this stretch of the Thames. While a fort could yet be found beneath the later city, there are other possibilities. A crossing of the Thames existed upstream at Fulham, as is demonstrated by finds of Iron Age and early Roman coins; this passage may have been easier to negotiate than a crossing at Londinium itself. If there was a military base at or near Londinium, it is unlikely to have existed for long after 43. As the advance gained momentum, the military significance of the lower Thames was reduced, though its importance as a port was greatly enhanced (Milne 1985: Brigham 1998).

The thesis here adopted is that the invasion force came ashore in Kent, probably with a main landing at Richborough supported by subsidiary landings in east Kent. Another view espouses a landing or landings in west Sussex, on slender evidence and heavy supposition (Hind 1989). The transport of a large expeditionary force of four legions and an unknown number of auxiliary units would have been directed to the nearest area of Britain which offered useful harbours: that area was Kent. Roman commanders would also have been intent on neutralizing British opposition and taking possession of the major centres of power as soon as possible. Camulodunum and Verulamium could be more easily taken from the lower Thames valley than from further up-river. No direct route led from west Sussex to the Thames. The oppidum at Silchester could be bypassed without evident danger. In any case, aside from the depot at Fishbourne, no certain Claudian base has been identified on the Sussex harbours. The Great Harbour (*megas limen*) of Ptolemy remains unlocated and could well relate to a much later situation in the history of Roman Britain. To return to Richborough, if this port played so minor a part in the invasion of AD 43, why were so many store-buildings erected here and why was it considered an appropriate setting for a triumphal monument half a century later? The Sussex thesis depends heavily upon the existence of a pro-Roman enclave in Sussex and Hampshire, arguably the realm left by Verica/Berikos shortly before the Claudian invasion. While there had long been links between this region, with a power centre at Silchester and possibly another in the area of Chichester, there is no shred of evidence that pro-Roman sentiment was still alive in the area after Verica's flight to Rome. The weightiest objection, however, is that which relates to the unlikelihood of any Roman commander, especially one conveying a large force across a sea known to be dangerous and who had just been confronted by mutinous troops, preferring a long sea-crossing to the shortest possible passage of the Channel (Frere and Fulford 2001).

Discussion of the friendly kings of Britain has been dominated by the figure of the ruler earlier known as Cogidubnus, not least as he appears in the *Agricola* of Tacitus and also on a surviving inscription found at Chichester. Yet much remains unknown about this ruler. The dates of his career are not precisely definable, though he is much more likely to have figured in the Claudian scheme of administration than in that of Nero. Allied rulers within provinces were not favoured instruments of Roman policy after about 60. Even the exact form of his name is not certain. The first two letters of his cognomen on the Chichester stone are lost and may be To or Ti rather than Co, giving the name Togidubnus or Tigidubnus. As to the date of his rule, all that Tacitus reports is that he maintained his loyalty 'down to our own day', which may mean Agricola's governorship, or even his earlier service in Britain, an obvious chronological possibility. His origins are unknown, but it is a fair assumption that he was a member of a British élite who quickly threw in his hand with Rome. His jurisdiction over several tribes is redolent of Claudian practice but it is not known which tribes these were; presumably they lay between the Thames and the Channel (*RIB* 91; see also Corrigenda, p. 758).

After the occupation of Camulodunum part of the site was taken over by Roman troops, partly reusing the Iron Age defences in the Sheepen area. A timber-fronted rampart and gate were constructed, probably providing winter quarters in the first months after invasion (Todd 1985). This work was only briefly occupied and was succeeded by a regularly planned legionary fortress designed to house a single legion. This base was probably built in 44–45; only four years later it made way for a colonia, the *Colonia Victrix Camuloduni*. The legion in garrison is not known for certain but may have been the Twentieth Valeria Victrix. Whichever unit it was, it was soon to be deployed to the north-west (Hawkes and Crummy 1995: 55–65).

The British élite at Camulodunum continued to observe at least some elements of their traditional culture, as revealed by burials. Outside the oppidum dykes at Stanway a series of funerary enclosures contained timber-lined mortuary chambers dating to the years immediately after the conquest. One of the finest burials of a leading Briton contained shield and spear, imported Roman bronzes, glass and pottery vessels, a central Italian amphora, a gridiron for cooking and a gaming board. The Stanway graves continue to about 60 and then abruptly ceased, probably because the connections between the leading families of the colonia and their Roman masters made them targets for the rebels led by Boudicca (see above, p. 33).

By the winter of 43 it was clear that the invasion force had achieved major objectives: a firm foothold in the island, the seizure of the British centre at Camulodunum and an initial dispersal of opposing forces. What followed was a familiar mixture of collusive diplomacy and main force. On departing from Britain, Claudius left instructions with Aulus Plautius to conquer 'the rest'. How this order was interpreted at the time is no clearer than it is in the accounts of modern commentators. It may have meant the entire island or only those areas which could be held by a combination of the available Roman forces and allied tribes.

With an impressive victory fairly easily won, Claudius could take his time over his return to Rome. Having sent his sons-in-law on ahead to deliver the news, he crossed Gaul, probably travelled up the Rhine and on through the Alps to Ravenna and thence to Rome with a senatorial entourage. He had been away for over five months, of which sixteen days had been spent in Britain. In 44 he could celebrate his British triumph, safe in the knowledge that his army had won the most resounding success for decades and that his own position was immeasurably strengthened (Levick 1990: 142–4).

After the seizure of Camulodunum and the adjacent territory, several tribes may have come to terms or been recognized as allies. The Iceni of Norfolk were one of the allied peoples, retaining their land, their own ruler and the right to issue silver coins (Allen 1975; Davies 1996). Their king at the time of the invasion cannot be identified with certainty, but may not have been Prasutagus whose death about 60 precipitated the complete absorption of the kingdom into the Empire and the subsequent rebellion led by his widow Boudicca. Nothing is heard of the attitude of the Corieltauvi to the Roman arrival, nor that of other groups to the south-west of them.

The middle Thames basin was both a strategic and tactically important area following the invasion. The valley provided an obvious route to the west. Equally important may have been the relations between the tribes quickly overrun by Roman arms and those to the west. A significant recent discovery seems to find its context here. This is a large military base at Alchester, near Bicester, a site with no evident tactical meaning, but with great potential in a role which might have combined forward military movement with diplomatic activity. The Alchester site is early, probably established by 45 or even in the previous year, as a tree-ring date suggests. Of the possible routes of approach into this area, that running west through the Thames valley seems the most obvious. The site was occupied for some time, as at least two phases of construction are in evidence. Although not tactically strong, Alchester was an important nodal position from which routes led across the Cotswolds to the Vale of Severn and northward to the line of Watling Street, crossing the Midland plain towards the Welsh uplands (Sauer 2000).

Resistance by the Britons crumbled quickly after their initial reverses. After the Roman crossing of the Thames, nothing is heard of fighting in the south-east of the island. Togodumnus is not further mentioned; Caratacus withdrew to the west to lead peoples who had yet to face an enemy of a kind not encountered before. The mere fact that it was possible for a leader from the south-east to direct warfare so far to the west illustrates the lack of cohesion among the western tribes. For the following six or seven years, Caratacus was the acknowledged leader of British opposition to the invaders. In the early years he was able to hold a front which may have extended from the upper Wye to the upper Severn but, as Roman control of the land and its resources strengthened, he was forced on to the defensive. Eventually, in 51, he had no recourse but to confront a Roman force in a defensive battle; the outcome was not long in doubt. The most effective leader of the Britons in the first years of occupation was removed from the scene (Webster 1982).

Famously, the Claudian triumphal arch erected in Rome in celebration of the triumph over Britain in AD 51 boasted the subjection of eleven British kings without loss to the Empire. By that date, most of southern Britain had been secured and the list of kings no doubt included any ruler who might be regarded as a king. Caratacus was an obvious focus of attention in Rome; Cartimandua will have had special appeal as a barbarian queen. Presumably Togidubnus was included, along with the ruler of the Iceni. Others were no doubt drawn from the western and midland peoples, but their names are unknown (*CIL* VI, 920; cf. *CIL* III, Supplement 7061, VI, 841).

Working Out a Strategy

The role of the Fosse Way in the early years of occupation has been much discussed over the past forty years. There is little doubt that this road, running transversely from south Devon to central Lincolnshire, was laid out in the mid-first century. Much more controversial is its role as a line of lateral communication within a temporary frontier system. There have been influential proponents of this view, but the objections to it are weighty. One of the most substantial is the fact that a frontier system of this kind played no part in Roman military strategy at this date. Strategic roads linking series of forts on a linear alignment are not known at this time. In the context of Claudian Britain, a temporary frontier behind the Trent and Severn makes

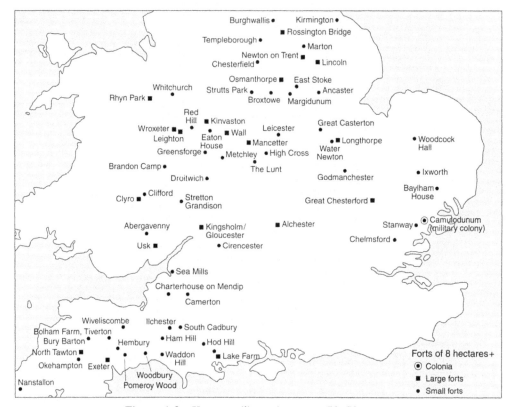

Figure 4.2   Known military sites *c*. AD 58–70.

neither strategic nor tactical sense. Ostorius Scapula was clearly intent on extending control beyond the Severn–Trent basin in the face of continuing resistance (Tacitus, *Annals*, XII, 31). The episodic account of Tacitus for the period AD 47–58 is notoriously inadequate, his geographical notices being particularly weak and uninformative. His report that Ostorius disarmed those who were disaffected and consolidated the Roman hold on areas already acquired does not shed clear light on the military situation in Britain about AD 50. Still less does it indicate that a frontier, however inchoate or temporary, was envisaged at this stage, or at any stage before the later Flavian period.

Early in the governorship of Ostorius Scapula came the first serious setbacks to Roman occupation. Late in the year 47 hostile forces attacked the lands of allied tribes, possibly on the Welsh borderlands. The invaders were promptly driven out by the auxiliary forces sent against them. Shortly afterwards, revolt broke out among the Iceni of East Anglia and their neighbours. The rebels briefly held out against Roman troops in a rural fortification before being overwhelmed. It is not entirely clear why the eastern tribes rose at this time. The Iceni, or some of them, may now have realized that alliance with Rome gave no guarantee of any degree of independence. The centre of the rebellion may have lain at Stonea Camp in Cambridgeshire (Jackson and Potter 1996), an island in the Fens which was abruptly abandoned about this date, its ditch filled with rampart material in a manner suggestive of Roman military practice. Interestingly, the major Icenian ceremonial site at Thetford (Gregory 1991) was substantially rebuilt after 50 and was in use for some time later, indicating that not all the tribe was involved in the disturbance. From the late forties, however, a firmer military hold was exercised on the territory of the Iceni, forts being sited at Saham Toney and possibly at Caister-by-Norwich. Resentment continued to rankle and was exacerbated by events a decade or so later.

The remarkably large number of forts covering at least 8 hectares (or 20 acres) is a feature of Claudio-Neronian Britain which is seemingly not paralleled in Gaul and the German commands. Nearly twenty such forts are now known, though few have been examined on a scale which might reveal their internal layout. The most extensively studied, Longthorpe, does not seem to have housed closely built structures (Frere and St Joseph 1974). The point is relevant to any discussion of the likely garrisons of these bases. On a priori grounds it is dangerous and wrong to treat all sites of this size as a homogeneous category. Some may have been short-lived garrison posts and campaign bases, others were probably supply depots. The blanket terms which have so far been applied, half-legionary or vexillation fortresses, have no secure foundation and judgment must be reserved. Legions were not usually divided in the early Empire, and when they were they were quickly reunited, after a limited operation in the field. Legions going into winter quarters normally did so at full strength or as close to their full complement as was possible. Vexillations were drawn from single units, or from several units and deployed as a field force for a specific campaign, but there is no indication that this was normal practice.

The clearest indication of the speed of the Roman sweep across southern Britain is the fact that by AD 49 Roman troops were overseeing the extraction of silver and lead from the Mendip mineral deposits, only a few kilometres from the Bristol Channel (*RIB* II, 2404, 1; 2404, 2). This implies that the south-western peninsula was effectively sealed off by this date and that Roman control had been established in the previous year or so. Given normal practice, it must be assumed that legionaries (perhaps of the Second Legion Augusta) were engaged in this work – in any case deducible from one inscribed ingot (*RIB* II, 2404, 2). This not only represented a significant seizure of mineral assets. It also implies a measure of firm control over the south-western peninsula which released forces for action elsewhere, not least in Wales. A legionary base established at Exeter by about 50, or 55 at the latest, secured the peninsula and was well placed to keep a watch on the peoples to the east. Various dates have been put forward for the foundation of the Exeter base: AD 50 or shortly afterwards seems the most probable on the evidence so far published. Some of the earliest material, however, may be referable to a pre-fortress installation (Bidwell 1979; Holbrook and Bidwell 1991).

An especially notable feature of the Roman occupation of south-western Britain was the use of existing Iron Age forts, either as they stood or as bases for more conventional forts. For the latter the *locus classicus* is Hod Hill (Dorset), within one corner of which was sited a carefully planned Claudian fort some 2.5 hectares in area (Richmond 1968). Several other hill-forts in the region are also known to have housed Roman troops in the Julio-Claudian period (Todd 1985). The two largest south-western forts, Ham Hill (Somerset) and Maiden Castle (Dorset), appear to fall into the former category on the basis of finds from their interior, strikingly so at Ham

Hill. South Cadbury (Somerset) has produced convincing evidence of early Roman military buildings, though possibly not of the earliest phase of occupation. A clearer case is that of Hembury (Devon), where military structures, including a *fabrica*, are associated with Claudian pottery and coins. It is fairly certain that Hembury had been abandoned well before the Roman advance and the same may be true of Ham Hill, Hod Hill and South Cadbury. The excavators of Hod Hill and Maiden Castle argued for resistance and sieges at both sites, but the available evidence is capable of more than one interpretation. Use of these pre-existing defended sites, which may also have included Chalbury (Dorset) and Bilbury Rings (Wiltshire), may explain in part the scarcity of temporary camps in southern Britain, despite favourable conditions for their discovery from the air.

A relic of the fighting in these early years may be the deposition of Iron Age and Roman equipment and human remains in a ditch of the hill-fort at Spetisbury (Dorset), perhaps the result of a cleaning-up operation. The well known 'war cemetery' at Maiden Castle has long been associated with early Roman campaigns among the Durotriges, but the dating evidence is far from secure and may relate to an episode a decade or more later. Another disturbance is attested at South Cadbury, again years later than the invasion period.

The eastern Midlands, between the Nene and the Trent basin, were certainly occupied within a few years of the invasion and may have posed few or no military problems. The campaign base at Longthorpe, near Peterborough (Frere and St Joseph 1974), was garrisoned by the late forties at the latest, and several auxiliary forts were operational by the same time. The well-planned fort at Great Casterton (Todd 1968) was one of these; so was, probably, the unpublished site at Ancaster. Most of the smaller forts, including the unexcavated example at Water Newton, secured communications and river crossings. Penetration of the broad vale of the Trent certainly began in the Claudian period and quite possibly by 50. A campaign base at Newton-on-Trent may represent early intrusion, though it is not yet closely dated. Troops were in occupation at Margidunum, close to a Trent crossing at Gunthorpe, by about 50 and this may also be true of the small fort at Thorpe-by-Newark. Newark itself has produced pre-Flavian material but no structural evidence.

It is most unlikely that the tactically strong and strategically important site of Lincoln was overlooked in the early years. A major Iron Age site lay around the Brayford Pool at the foot of the steep-sided hill on which the later Roman complex was developed, and this may have remained in being after 43. The known legionary fortress lay on the height but it appears to date from the late fifties or about 60 (Darling and Jones 1988; *RIB* 254, 255, 257). There are, however, at Lincoln three tombstones of three soldiers of the Ninth Legion, all without cognomina and thus unlikely to date after 55 at the latest. All three inscriptions were found a kilometre or more south of the known fortress. Their location suggests strongly that an early legionary base lay on this low ground, perhaps from about 50; a decade later this was replaced by the fortress on the hill, possibly in the aftermath of the Boudiccan revolt. It is worth noting that in the early Roman period the sea-coast lay much closer to Lincoln than it does today; the early military sites could thus have been supplied from the sea like their contemporaries at Gloucester and Exeter and the later bases at Chester and York.

The low-lying land around the Humber estuary has yielded little in the way of evidence for Claudian activity, though forts have been mooted at Kirmington and Old Winteringham at the southern end of a crossing. The broken country of the Lincolnshire Wolds was no doubt policed, and both Caistor and Horncastle have produced Claudian coinage.

Further south, the site of Leicester fairly certainly housed a Roman unit within its later Iron Age settlement, certainly by the fifties. On and beyond the middle Trent, forts were established at Broxtowe on the northern outskirts of Nottingham and at Strutt's Park, north-west of Derby. The latter site covered an extensive area and may have supported early operations in the southern Pennines, possibly in the later fifties. Units were also occupying the broken country around Sherwood Forest and the broad plain to the north. A large fort lay at Osmanthorpe near Southwell, and another at Rossington Bridge near Doncaster. Both are undated but may have been connected with operations in support of Cartimandua or probing of southern Brigantian territory or both (Hartley and Fitts 1988: 16).

The broad rolling country between the middle Trent and the Welsh uplands offered little of a geographical basis for strategic control. The line of the Fosse Way, running from the Devon coast to Lincoln, was long seen as an embryonic frontier line in the period from 47 to the sixties, but this is not a tenable hypothesis. Although it was a strategically important route, the Fosse Way did not define or service a *limes*. Its course does, however, imply a firm grasp of the geographical realities of southern Britain, and it was clearly designed to support the forward units to the west and north-west. The wide gap between the middle Trent and middle Severn could not have been closed without the establishment of tactical forward positions, and the indications are that this was done. A large base at Wall and another at Kinvaston lie on a route running west from the Fosse Way towards the Severn, a line almost certainly taken by a legionary force, plausibly the Fourteenth legion. The line was continued to Leighton, near Wroxeter, and on to Rhyn Park at the edge of the North Wales massif. None of these sites is well dated, but there is a fair presumption that they were related to the encirclement of the Ordovices in the late fifties. Other large forts extended from the lower Severn into the valleys of the Usk and Wye (see pp. 63–4).

The importance of naval support for the advance after 43 is often underrated. Roman command of the seas around Britain was effectively total. The supply network depended heavily upon the fleet, and the fleet depended in turn on the south coast harbours. The evidence for the port and supply depot at Richborough is fully established (Cunliffe 1968; see also p. 46); other depots were no doubt used along the south coast, of which Fishbourne was only one. The rapid advance through the south of the island could have been facilitated by the transport of troops by sea, accompanied or closely followed by their supplies. Once the Isle of Wight was secured by the Second Legion under Vespasian, movement along the coast of Dorset and Devon would have been straightforward. Several large natural harbours were at the disposal of Roman forces, including Poole Harbour (possibly the *megas limen*), Portland, several smaller anchorages on Lyme Bay and the Exe estuary. Roman forces were certainly operating in Dorset by the late forties and could have penetrated as far as east Devon by the same date. Although lying 10 kilometres inland, the large fort at Lake Farm, unpublished as yet, could have provided support to naval operations in

Poole Harbour. To the west, forward movement may be marked by the fort at Shapwick, military occupation within the hill-fort of Maiden Castle, the irregularly planned fort at Waddon Hill and usage of the empty hill-fort at Hembury. Dates require further definition, but Lake Farm and Hembury were probably occupied from the late forties to the later fifties at least.

The main route into the further south-west was clearly the one that ran from the lower Exe north of Dartmoor to the Tamar in the vicinity of Launceston. The key site, representing repeated use by forces on campaign, is that at North Tawton. Here, at least two temporary camps were succeeded by a large fort, into one corner of which a small post of two phases was later inserted. This sequence was completed by a fort with an attached annexe. The overall picture is of a nodal point in the phase of initial conquest and possibly in the later system of control (Griffith 1984: 20–4).

Forward Movement

The further conquest of the south-western peninsula proceeded in the fifties and sixties in campaigns which receive no mention in the surviving accounts. Communications were crucial in a region which possessed few obvious routes through a landscape in which valleys were probably heavily wooded and in which extensive uplands intruded major obstructions to movement. The major routes into and across the peninsula, as they do today, led from the Somerset lowlands into east Devon, through the broken country north of Dartmoor, and possibly across the South Hams from the lower Exe to the Tamar valley. From the Exe another route ran along the Yeo and Taw valleys towards the north Devon coast. Forts on all of these lines are known. The route from the Taunton area towards the Exe is marked by a fort near Cullompton. Those north of the lower Exe were covered by forts at Bolham, near Tiverton, and Bury Barton, near Lapford. North Devon is largely a blank at present, though a military presence is to be presumed in the area of Barnstaple and Bideford, perhaps in conjunction with a port. The region around Exmoor, rich in minerals, especially iron, is likely to have attracted Roman interest, and a possible fort has been noted at Rainsbury, east of the moor on the Brendon Hills. A few small forts, including Woodbury near Axminster, Okehampton and possibly Topsham, are to be related to policing duties on major routes.

West of the Tamar the record of military activity is remarkably thin. The fort at Nanstallon, near Bodmin, is the only base thus far identified, though it dates from no earlier than the later fifties and is very small (Fox and Ravenhill 1972). Communications across Cornwall have been notoriously difficult until modern times. In antiquity and later, a route north of Bodmin Moor would have provided the most direct east–west route, but the heads of estuaries were strategically crucial locations and some may have been secured. Further east, movement by sea, taking advantage of the deep indentations provided by estuaries, could have played a major role. The inhabitants of the far south-west lacked cohesion and may have been easily brought under control. Some of the numerous enclosed sites in Cornwall offered possible bases in the short term. One at Carvossa, near Probus, has produced Claudio-Neronian pottery and military equipment and was possibly linked with westward probing along the south coast. As yet there is no clear evidence for military involvement in the exploitation of the tin deposits of Devon and Cornwall. The conquest of Cornwall is unlikely to have been protracted or difficult. By the early sixties the peninsula was secured and units could be withdrawn for service elsewhere, leaving small units behind to keep the peace and protect communications. A legion, or a legionary detachment, was retained at Exeter until the early seventies, but greater imperatives then took over.

Ostorius Scapula was now able to turn his attention to an attack on the territory of the Degeangli, or Decangi, in north-east Wales, possibly influenced by the presence of silver, lead and copper in their land. There may also have been a strategic objective, as possession of this area and the Cheshire plain would insert a wedge between the western tribes and those of the western Pennines. The silver and lead deposits were certainly being worked by the late fifties, but exploitation could have began a decade earlier. The central uplands of Wales could best be penetrated by way of the middle and upper Severn valley. Several forts are known on this route, but excavation has been limited, except at Wroxeter. A large base, covering 8 hectares at Leighton, seems to mark early activity by a campaigning force on the middle Severn, as does an auxiliary fort at Wroxeter, but both are undated. The foundation of the full-sized legionary fortress at Wroxeter is also not closely dated, but it is likely to have been the work of Didius Gallus in the mid-fifties. The Fourteenth Legion Gemina played a role here, possibly from the beginning. Auxiliary cavalry, an *ala* of Thracians, may also have been in garrison for a time. A *beneficiarius* of the Twentieth Legion is also attested, but the nature of this post associates him with the governor's staff and not necessarily directly with his own regiment. The size and detailed layout of the fortress are not clear; the internal plan will always be difficult to recover, as the base lies beneath the later city of Viroconium. The Fourteenth Legion seems to have remained in garrison here until the mid-sixties, when it was withdrawn for service in the eastern provinces.

Ostorius Scapula enjoyed a measure of success, though his arduous campaigns may have shortened his life. Operations against the tribes of Wales continued until 60 under his successors, when a successful outcome was in sight and Suetonius Paullinus could attempt the subjection of the northern peoples of Wales and the occupation of the fertile island of Anglesey. Had not the revolt led by Boudicca broken out, the conquest of all of Wales might have been achieved in the early sixties. As it turned out, another fifteen years were to elapse before this front was secure (see p. 69).

The events of the revolt in 60–1, substantially relayed by Tacitus, have been fully discussed by modern writers and need not be repeated here (Frere 1987: 70–4; Webster 1993; Sealey 1997). Revolts against Roman authority in the early Empire were rare, so that the rebellion of the Iceni and Trinovantes was all the more disturbing, even though it was of Rome's own making. Tacitus gives heavy emphasis to the adverse effects of insensitive treatment, amounting to brutality, on the part of Roman officials, which no doubt played its part. But equally influential may have been the insidious effect of debt interest on loans advanced by Roman financiers, who included Nero's adviser Seneca (Cassius Dio 62, 2,1; Tacitus, *Annals* 13, 42,4 on Seneca's loan activities elsewhere in the Empire). Shattering as it was (the destruction of a colonia and two other cities in a single episode is without parallel in the early Empire), the revolt did not disrupt long-term Roman aims, though it clearly slowed further advances to the west and north. For the time being, the tribes of Wales were contained (see pp. 69–70). The more urgent problem lay beyond the Trent basin on the front facing the unstable Brigantian confederacy.

The reaction of the western tribes to a changed world was obviously a critical factor in determining Roman strategy. Much has been made of the early capitulation of a part of the Dobunni, the Bodunni of Dio's account. This could quickly have provided the invaders with a foothold in the Cotswolds and lower Severn, and may also have led to the seizure of the Mendip mineral deposits. A succession of forts at Cirencester was occupied by auxiliary units, among them two *alae*, the *ala* Indiana and an *ala* of Thracians, pointing to wide-ranging activity by cavalry. Military material at Bath implies a unit here, though no evidence of structures has appeared. A key strategic site was Gloucester, at the head of the Severn estuary. The first base at Kingsholm (Hurst 1985) was occupied from about 48 to 50, a large fort which most probably housed legionaries (perhaps of the Twentieth), though an auxiliary unit, the Sixth Cohort of Thracians, is also attested by a tombstone and may also have been in garrison, unless this unit was housed in a separate fort. The base at Gloucester was linked with Wroxeter by a road east of the Severn via forts at Greensforge, Droitwich and probably Worcester. Kingsholm was retained for nearly twenty years and was then supplanted by a new fortress below the later Roman city of Glevum. The foundation of this base is unusually well dated by coins in primary deposits to 67–8. This is later than might have been expected, and the strategic context is far from clear. The date falls in the governorship of Trebellius Maximus, a period of sedition within the highest military ranks in Britain. The commander of the Twentieth Legion, Roscius Coelius, led a mutinous movement against Trebellius, driving him from his post and from Britain. If the Twentieth was indeed stationed at Gloucester, its commander may have become restive at the cautious policy of consolidation espoused by Trebellius and taken matters into his own hands. There is a further complication, which involves Gloucester and other western legionary bases. A legion remained in station at Exeter until 73–4 (Bidwell 1979), which meant that for a time three legionary bases in the west were held for some years at the same time, while Wroxeter had seemingly been empty since 66, when the Fourteenth Legion was withdrawn from Britain. But that legion returned to Britain in 69 and remained until the following year. Clearly, all these fortresses were not held in anything like full strength during these years. Detachments and auxiliary forces could have been brought into play.

Delay and Retrenchment

From an early date Roman governors faced one of their most difficult problems, the security of the north beyond the Trent basin. The large tribe of the Brigantes was a fissile confederacy presided over by Cartimandua, but containing elements which were hostile to her pro-Roman stance. Precisely when she was recognized as an allied ruler is not known but this probably came about in the mid to late forties, when Roman units first arrived in the Trent basin. Her handover of Caratacus to Rome in 51 cemented the alliance, but her hold on the Brigantes remained shaky. The chronology of the next twenty years is difficult to reconstruct. Cartimandua's husband Venutius may have become restive at her pro-Roman policy shortly after the delivery of Caratacus, but he could make no decisive move then or at the time of the Boudiccan revolt. His opportunity seemed to present itself eight years later, when the Empire was engulfed in civil war. Cartimandua had received support from Roman troops in the mid-fifties, and later from a legionary force. Venutius struck in either 68 or 69, and the Brigantian leader had to be rescued by a Roman intervention, leaving Venutius in control for a time. An effective Roman response was not possible for the next two or three years. When it came it was decisive.

Archaeological evidence for this phase of transition from a divided allied kingdom to outright conquest is not easily identified or interpreted. The territory of the Parisi north of the Humber could have provided a base for operations to the north. The large forts at Rossington Bridge and Templeborough (see p. 53) may have existed from the sixties and may have been garrisoned by units responsible for the provision of support for the pro-Roman party among the Brigantes. Vettius Bolanus, the governor from 69, given no credit by Tacitus, had a difficult path to tread, faced by civil strife at the heart of the Empire and by a policy void on the northern flank of his province. He may have been more adventurous than Tacitus alleged. A large base of 12.5 hectares at Malton in east Yorkshire may have been established by him on the eastern side of Brigantian territory. An impressive series of Claudio-Neronian coins at York (RCHM 1962: xxx) hints at a military presence there before 70, as these issues did not circulate in quantity after that date, but no supporting evidence has been reported. On strategic grounds, an early seizure of the Vale of York makes excellent sense, but this has not yet been demonstrated. A complex site which might earn attention in connection with early campaigns in east Yorkshire is Cawthorn, north of the Vale of Pickering (Richmond 1933). Here a sequence of temporary camps has long been identified as practice works thrown up by the legion based at York, 45 kilometres away to the south-west. One of the works at Cawthorn, 'Camp D', is clearly a fort and one which has its closest analogies in the Claudian forts at Hod Hill and Great Casterton. The planning of the defences of this fort has no parallel in Neronian or Flavian Britain. The case for more detailed investigation of the interior is underlined.

The military situation in Britain as a whole remained fluid during the civil war of 68–70. Detachments from three legions in Britain went to support Vitellius, while the Fourteenth came out for Otho. The resumption of conquest in the west and north after the appointment of Petillius Cerealis in 71 brought major changes to legionary dispositions. In the west, Gloucester was given up early in the seventies and Exeter by 74, when the Second Legion Augusta moved to Caerleon. Chester was shortly to be chosen as a base to control North Wales and later the western Pennines. Lincoln remained the base for the Ninth Legion, which was much engaged with the collapsing alliance with the Brigantes, and later, from 71, housed the newly raised Second Legion Adiutrix. The stage was now set for a succession of energetic governors to reopen operations towards the Claudian goal of conquest of 'the rest' (Dio Cassius 60, 25).

REFERENCES

Allen, D. F. 1975. Cunobelin's Gold. *Britannia*, 6, 1–19.
Aurelius Victor. 1975. *De Caesaribus*, ed. P. Dufraigne. Paris.
Bidwell, P. T. 1979. *The Legionary Bath-House and Forum and Basilica at Exeter.* Exeter.

Brigham, T. 1998. The port of Roman London. In B. Watson, *Roman London: Recent Archaeological Work*. Portsmouth, 23–34.

Brunt, P. A. 1963. Review of H. D. Meyer, *Die Aussenpolitik des Augustus und die augusteische Dichtung* (Cologne 1961). *Journal of Roman Studies*, 53, 170–6.

Cassius Dio. 1898–1931. *Cassius Dio*. ed. U. P. Boissevin. 5 vols. Berlin.

Creighton, J. 2000. *Coins and Power in Late Iron Age Britain*. Cambridge.

Cunliffe, B. W. (ed.) 1968. *Fifth Report on the Excavations of the Roman Fort at Richborough, Kent*. Oxford

Darling, M. J. and Jones, M. J. 1988. Early settlement at Lincoln. *Britannia*, 19, 1–57.

Davies, J. A. 1996. Where eagles dare: the Iron Age of Norfolk. *Proceedings of the Prehistoric Society*, 62, 63–92.

Eutropius. 1999. *Breviarium*, ed. J. Mellegovarc'h. Paris.

Fox, A. and Ravenhill, W. 1972. The Roman fort at Nanstallon, Cornwall. *Britannia*, 3, 56–111.

Frere, S. S. 1987. *Britannia*, 3rd edn. London.

Frere, S. S. and Fulford, M. 2001. The Roman invasion of AD 43. *Britannia*, 32, 45–56.

Frere, S. S. and St Joseph, J. K. 1974. The Roman fortress at Longthorpe. *Britannia*, 5, 1–129.

Gregory, T. 1991. *Excavations in Thetford, 1980–1982*. Dereham.

Griffin, J. 1984. Augustus and the poets: Caesar qui cogere posset. In F. Millar and E. Segal (eds), *Caesar Augustus: Seven Aspects*. Oxford, 189–218.

Griffith, F. M. 1984. Roman military sites in Devon: some recent discoveries. *Proceedings of the Devon Archaeological Society*, 42, 11–32.

Hartley, B. and Fitts, L. 1988. *The Brigantes*. Gloucester.

Hawkes, C. F. C. and Crummy, P. 1995. *Camulodunum 2*. Colchester.

Hind, J. G. F. 1989 The invasion of Britain in AD 43 – an alternative strategy. *Britannia*, 20, 1–21.

Holbrook, N. and Bidwell, P. T. 1991. *Roman Finds from Exeter*. Exeter.

Hurst, H. R. 1985. *Kingsholm, Gloucester*. Cambridge.

Jackson, R. P. J. and Potter, T. W. 1996. *Excavations at Stonea Cambridgeshire 1980–85*. London.

Josephus. 1980. *Bellum Judaicum*, ed. A. Pelletier. Paris.

Levick, B. 1990. *Claudius*. London.

Manning, W. H. 1988. *Early Roman Campaigns in the South-West of Britain*. Cardiff.

Maxfield, V. A. 1991. Tiverton Roman Fort (Bolham): Excavations 1981–86. *Proceedings of the Devon Archaeological Society*, 49, 25–98.

Milne, G. 1985. *The Port of Roman London*. London.

Mitchell, S. 1983. Cornish tin, Iulius Caesar and the invasion of Britain. *Studies in Latin Literature and Roman History*. Collection Latomus 180. Paris, 80–99.

Orosius. 1990–1. *Historia adversus Paganos*, ed. M.-P. Arnaud-Lindet. Paris.

Richmond, I. A. 1933. The four Roman camps of Cawthorn. *Archaeological Journal*, 89, 17–78.

—— 1968. *Hod Hill II*. London.

Royal Commission on Historical Monuments. 1962. *Eboracum: Roman York*. London

Sauer, E. 2000. Excavations at Alchester, Oxon. *Archaeological Journal*, 157, 1–78.

Sealey, P. R. 1997. *The Boudican Revolt against Rome*. Princes Risborough.

Stevens, C. E. 1951. Britain between the Invasions (54 BC–AD 43). In W. F. Grimes (ed.), *Aspects of Archaeology, in Britain and Beyond*. London, 332–44.

Suetonius. 1927. *Divus Vespasianus*, ed. A. W. Braithwaite. Oxford.

—— 1959. *Divus Claudius*, ed. J. C. Rolfe. London and Cambridge, MA.

—— 1959. *Galba*, ed. J. C. Rolfe. London and Cambridge, MA.

Todd, M. 1968. *The Roman Fort at Great Casterton*. Oxford.

—— 1985. Oppida and the Roman army. *Oxford Journal of Archaeology*, 4, 187–99.

—— 1996. Pretia Victoriae? Roman lead and silver mining on the Mendip Hills, Somerset. *Münstersche Beitrage zur Antiken Handelsgeschichte*, 15, 1–18.

—— 1999. *Roman Britain*. Oxford.

Tacitus. 1967. *Agricola*, ed. R. M. Ogilvie and I. A. Richmond. Oxford.

Wacher, J. and Mc Whirr, A. 1982. *Early Roman Occupation at Cirencester*. Cirencester.

Webster, G. 1980. *The Roman Invasion of Britain*. London.

—— 1982. *Rome against Caratacus*. London.

—— 1993. *Boudica*, 2nd edn. London.

Webster, G. (ed.) 1988. *Fortress into City*. London.

CHAPTER FIVE

The Conquest of Wales

WILLIAM MANNING

The Conquest Begins

The Romans did not recognize Wales as a separate country; to them it was a part of western Britain which was occupied by two major and two minor tribes. The major tribes were the Silures of south-eastern Wales and the Ordovices, who probably occupied most of mid-Wales but extended to the north-east as far as Anglesey. The minor tribes were the Deceangli of the north-western Marches and the Demetae in the south-west. We do not know where the exact boundaries lay between these tribes, or where the frontiers were between them and their neighbours in western England, the Cornovii in the north and the Dobunni in the south. It is this lack of precise information which helps to give an element of uncertainty to our interpretation of the historical evidence. We are fortunate in having a relatively complete historical account of the opening stages of the conquest of Wales in Tacitus' *Annals* and, in a more cursory form, in the biography of his father-in-law, Agricola.

The Roman army came into direct contact with the Welsh tribes at about the time when Aulus Plautius' term of office came to an end in 47, and it is at this point that Tacitus' narrative in the *Annals*, lost for the earlier years of the conquest, begins. By comparison with the other literary sources for Roman Britain, the *Annals* is exceptionally detailed, but it is also frustratingly generalized, and the accounts of the Welsh campaigns are almost completely lacking in geographical information. Indeed, it is not until we reach the attack on Anglesey in 60 that we can be sure of the location of any of the events which Tacitus describes. The last forty years have seen a considerable increase in the archaeological information available for this period in Wales, mainly in the form of newly discovered forts, but even where these have been excavated, and the majority have not, few can be dated with the degree of precision required for them to be correlated with Tacitus' text. Nonetheless, the advance in our knowledge has been considerable, and while future work may prove some of the details wrong, the general picture is likely to be correct.

By 47, when Plautius left Britain, he had brought most of England to the south of the client kingdom of Brigantia under Roman control, by either military conquest or

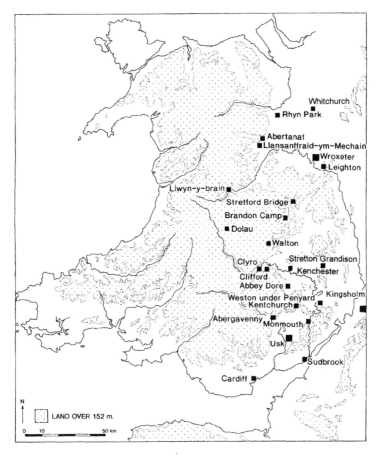

Figure 5.1 The early occupation of Wales.

the creation of client kingdoms. The conquest of the south-western peninsula was probably still incomplete, but the occupation of Somerset and Wiltshire meant that the Dumnonii were largely isolated from other tribes which might still be hostile to Rome. Only in the Welsh Marches were there likely to be major problems (see p. 69).

The few ancient references which we have to the inhabitants of Wales at this time are less than helpful, but there is no reason to suppose that they differed very much from the other tribes found in the less Romanized parts of western England. The distribution of hill-forts, which are the main type of settlement found in much of Wales, suggests that the population was concentrated in the coastal lowlands of the south and west and in the river valleys of the interior, which in some areas, such as that around Brecon, widened out to form large areas of high but fertile land. The material culture was probably similar to that of the adjacent parts of England, save for an almost universal rejection of the use of pottery, a considerable inconvenience for the archaeologist. It is perhaps significant that Tacitus never refers to the rulers of the Welsh tribes, and it is possible that the physical nature of much of the country, with its ranges of barren hills separating the more fertile valleys, had produced a less centralized society than that found in eastern England. The evidence suggests that the traditional way of life changed little before the end of the first century AD.

We know little of the earlier career of Plautius' successor, Ostorius Scapula, but there is no doubt that he was an experienced and competent general (Birley, 1981: 41ff.). Tacitus tells us that he arrived to find that a tribe, which he does not name, had attacked a Roman ally, which he also fails to identify, but which was probably a client kingdom. This action is usually placed in the west country on or near the borders of Wales, largely because Scapula's reaction was to disarm suspect tribes, including the Iceni, and garrison the country between the Trent and Severn (*Annals*, XII, 31), before attacking the 'Decangi', as Tacitus calls them. This tribe can almost certainly be identified with the Deceangli of north-east Wales, an identification which is confirmed by Tacitus' observation that this campaign took the Roman army almost as far as the Irish sea. Tacitus does not provide a date for this war, but it must have been in 48 or 49. It was followed by an attack on the Silures of south-eastern Wales, who, Tacitus says, were turned neither by brutality nor by clemency from pursuing the war and required the establishment of a legionary fortress to keep them down (*Annals*, XII, 32). His phraseology makes it clear that this cannot have been their first contact with the Roman army, and the decision to move a legion into the area must have been the consequence of experiences which are not described in the surviving sections of the *Annals*. The fact that a colony was founded at Camulodunum to release the required legion indicates that it was Legio XX which had been based there. Unfortunately, Tacitus does not say where the new fortress was built.

At this point in his narrative Tacitus introduces, or, since we have lost his earlier references to Britain, more probably reintroduces, Caratacus, the hero of the resistance. We do not know how Caratacus, whose own kingdom had been in south-eastern England, became the leader first of the Silures and then of the Ordovices; no doubt the answer lay in the complex pattern of client/patron relationships which were fundamental to Iron Age society. His wars against the Romans involved both the Silures and Ordovices, and it was in Ordovician territory that he risked and lost all in a pitched battle. But this victory was not to be the end of the war and Tacitus records a series of Roman setbacks, none catastrophic but some, such as the defeat of two auxiliary cohorts, sufficient to embarrass Scapula and encourage his enemies who, Tacitus makes clear, included the Silures (*Annals*, XII.38). A measure of their success is provided by the fact that an exasperated Claudius threatened to extirpate the entire tribe, a threat which only served to strengthen their resistance (*Annals*, XII, 39; Manning 1981: 29). In 52, in the midst of these problems, Scapula died, and before his successor, Didius Gallus, could arrive, the Silures succeeded in defeating a legion, probably Legio XX, although Tacitus, rather maliciously, only records the name of its commander, Manlius Valens (*Annals*, XII. 39).

The Consolidation of the Southern Frontier

Tacitus did not like Gallus, and damns him with faint praise – he was inactive and failed to expand the area under Roman control – although in the *Agricola* (14) he does admit that he built a number of forts in new areas, which presupposes some advances. However, it is clear that Gallus had little difficulty in restoring the chaotic military situation left by Scapula, and since he remained in post until 57, he must have been regarded as competent by the authorities in Rome. The details of his career confirm that he was an older man who had been highly successful both as a soldier and administrator (Birley 1981: 44). For Tacitus action in the field was the prime, indeed almost the only, requirement of a successful governor, but in reality major campaigns could not be undertaken without imperial approval. Once Gallus had restored order on the Welsh front, which may have taken some time, the death of the emperor Claudius late in 54, and the accession of the young Nero, may have led to a reassessment of the situation in Britain, resulting in the conclusion that the new province required a period of consolidation before major campaigns were resumed. The impression given by Tacitus is that for the latter part of his governorship Ostorius Scapula had been reacting to events rather than following a planned course of action, and by the time of his death the army may have needed regrouping in new forts before major campaigns could be resumed.

With the exception of Legio XX, which had been kept as a reserve in a fortress at Camulodunum, none of the other three legions appears to have constructed a fortress large enough to house the entire legion before the mid-fifties, a fact which must reflect the military situation in Britain at this stage in the conquest. Instead we find a number of half-sized fortresses, usually called vexillation fortresses, of around 8 hectares rather than the 20 hectares of a full fortress (Frere 1987a: 57 and map, 58; but see above, p. 51). We assume that their garrisons included legionary detachments, possibly with some auxiliaries, although the bulk of the auxiliaries must have been in forts of their own on or near the frontiers, or garrisoning the newly occupied territory. At some time in the mid-fifties this arrangement was changed and we find the legions building full-sized fortresses. This must be the result of a decision to undertake a major rearrangement of the military forces in the province. Two of these fortresses lay on the Welsh front in positions designed to defend what the Romans already held and to act as springboards for fresh advances. Both the archaeological and historical evidence suggests that Didius Gallus is the person most likely to have been responsible for this rearrangement. The fact that Scapula had fought campaigns against the Deceangli, the Silures and the Ordovices indicates that he must have been active along the whole of the Welsh border, but how far these campaigns extended into Wales itself remains uncertain, although the Roman army probably fought over a wider area than it garrisoned. What is certain is that the new legionary fortresses will have lain some way behind the frontier, and that they will have been part of a series of garrisons, most of which will have been auxiliary forts.

The new fortresses were at Usk (Burrium) on the river Usk, and Wroxeter (Viroconium), to the east of Shrewsbury, on the River Severn. Tombstones from Wroxeter make it fairly certain that the legion there was Legio XIV Gemina (Collingwood and Wright 1965: 98, nos 292 and 294), but the evidence for the legion at Usk is largely circumstantial. It is virtually certain that the legion brought against the Silures by Scapula about 49 was Legio XX Valeria, but it cannot have been based at Usk as early as that. Not only do the pottery and coins from the fortress leave little doubt that the fortress was not constructed until the mid-fifties (Manning 1981: 31ff.), but Usk lies well within Silurian territory rather than on its eastern edge. The original legionary base was probably at Kingsholm, where a large but rather ill-defined site of the right date lies on the edge of modern Gloucester, a strategically important point where the River Severn could be crossed relatively easily (Hurst 1985, 1988: 49). The relatively early date for the foundation of Kingsholm suggests that it was probably a vexillation fortress housing part rather than the whole of the legion. The discovery of a tombstone of a soldier of the Legio XX at Wotton, to the north-east of Gloucester (Collingwood and Wright 1965: 36, no. 122), provides evidence that men from that legion were based in the area, but the fact that it was found with the tombstone of a Thracian cavalryman (Collingwood and Wright 1965: 36, no. 121) may indicate a mixed garrison. It is unfortunate that we have no certain knowledge of where the eastern edge of Siluria lay. The River Wye has been suggested in the past, but there is some evidence that it could have been as far east as the Severn, in which case Kingsholm lay very close to Silurian territory (Manning 1981: 20).

There are two obvious routes into south Wales from Gloucester. The modern road runs along the River Severn to Chepstow and then through the coastal lowlands of Monmouthshire and Glamorgan. But such evidence as we have suggests that this was not the route preferred during the conquest. This was the road which became Iter XIII in the Antonine Itinerary (Rivet and Smith 1979: 175) and which ran to the north of the Forest of Dean as far as Ross-on-Wye, where it entered the valley of the Wye, from where it went south along the valley before turning along a minor valley to enter the Usk valley at Usk. Although no certain Roman forts are known on the first part of this route, early material from Weston-under-Penyard, the Roman town of *Ariconium*, just to the east of Ross-on-Wye, may indicate a fort there (G. Webster 1960: 66; Manning 1976: 31). Further south a fort is now known under the centre of Monmouth (Clarke, Jackson and Jackson 1992: 1). Once in the Usk valley the Roman army was able to move south towards the coastal plain or to follow the river to the north-west to Abergavenny, where there was a fort which was contemporary with Usk (Blockley et al. 1993), and the uplands of Breconshire. No forts of this early date are known to the west of Abergavenny.

From Monmouth the valley of the River Monnow leads north-west towards the mouth of the Golden Valley, which runs through the eastern edge of the Black Mountains to meet the Wye valley near Hay-on-Wye. Two forts are known near the mouth of the Golden Valley, one at Kentchurch (Frere 1987c: 323; Musson 1989: 56), the other at Abbey Dore in the valley itself (Musson 1989: 56). The fact that these two sites are less than four miles apart indicates they cannot be contemporary, although both are likely to date from the fifties or sixties. Their presence confirms that this was a significant route between the Usk and Wye valleys, the more so as it enters the Wye valley at the point where it emerges from the hills of Breconshire. We know of no fewer than three large forts or vexillation forts in this area, two at Clifford (St Joseph 1973: 338–9; Frere 1992: 283) and another at Clyro (Nash-Williams 1969: 77). None of these has been extensively excavated – most have not been excavated at all – but the material from Clyro would agree with its being pre-Flavian, and it is extremely difficult to imagine at what other stage in the conquest such large forts would have been needed in this area. Given the relatively early date of the legionary fortress at Usk (Manning 1981: 24ff.) it seems unlikely that all three forts in the Wye valley predated it; rather, we must suppose that vexillations of the legion, perhaps with some auxiliaries, continued to be based in the Wye Valley even after the construction of the fortress at Usk. The Wye Valley is one of the great river valleys running into the hills of Wales from the Marches, and the forts at Clifford and Clyro were clearly designed to control movement along it. In the early stages of the conquest it would have been sensible to have had a relatively large force of legionaries in this area, for it was two days march from Usk, too far for a rapid response in an emergency.

The Golden Valley was not the only route into the Wye valley from England; indeed, it may have come into use only after the construction of the fortress at Usk had brought the XX Legion into Monmouthshire. Before that the Wye valley was probably approached by a route which ran north-west from Gloucester to a fort at Stretton Grandison, 8 miles east of Hereford (G. Webster 1970: 189), from where a road runs due west to the Roman town of Kenchester (*Magnis*), which lies almost exactly midway between Stretton Grandison and Clyro, and which *may* have been the site of another early fort (G. Webster 1981: 73). Such forts must represent the phase which followed the initial conquest, although in the *Annals* (XII.38) Tacitus makes it clear that this was sufficiently well advanced for Scapula to have been building forts in Siluria before his death in 52. Nor is a fort as large as Clyro likely to have been built on what was then the front line, although if there were forts in front of it they have yet to be discovered. Nor can we have discovered all the forts to the south of the fortress at Usk. Two are known at present, an unusually large one at Cardiff (P. V. Webster 1990: 35ff.) and one on the shore of the Severn estuary at Sudbrook (Nash-Williams 1939; Manning 1981: 41f.) which was created by occupying an existing Iron Age fort, something which we now know the Roman army to have done on a number of occasions. The fort at Cardiff will have given the Romans control both of the point at which the rivers Ely and Taff run from the hills into the coastal plain and of movement along that plain. The River Taff, on which the new fort lay, will have provided a harbour for the fleet which we must assume operated in the Severn estuary. The occupation of the Iron Age fort at Sudbrook almost certainly reflects the existence of a ferry across the Severn from England, and a road ran from Sudbrook to meet the main east–west road at Caerwent. This crossing continued to be of importance throughout the Roman period and appears in the Antonine Itinerary as part of Iter XIV, a route from Caerleon to Silchester (Rivet and Smith 1979: 176). A fort at or near the city of Caerwent is not impossible, although a recent reassessment of the early material from the site (P. V. Webster, forthcoming) would accord with a roadside settlement at the junction of the road from Sudbrook and the main road rather than a fort. If so, it would suggest that the main east–west road was in existence from a relatively early date.

Whether there are any other forts in this area remains uncertain. A fort between Usk and Cardiff would not have been surprising, although an earthwork at Coed-y-Caerau, on the east side of the Usk valley opposite Caerleon, which has been suggested as a Roman fort, is more likely to be of Iron Age date (Manning 1981: 41). No sign of an early fort has been found at Caerleon, and at 8 miles it is probably too close to Usk in any case. It has also been suggested that a fort may have been built at Chepstow where that road must have crossed the estuary of the River Wye, but again positive evidence is lacking (Jarrett 1994: 25).

The Roman aim seems to have been to use auxiliary forts to block the major valleys leading into the hills of south Wales, and in particular to those areas where concentrations of hill-forts and other settlements suggest that the bulk of the native population lived. This will have severely limited the ability of the Silures to raid the territory already under Roman control, while providing bases for the further advances which were surely intended. A small fort in the valley of the Hindwell Brook at Walton, to the east of New Radnor, must have been placed there to command the route into mid-Wales which is still followed by the A44 road (St Joseph 1973: 239f.; Frere 1977: 360).

The Consolidation of the Northern Frontier

The north of Wales fell within a different command, that of Legio XIV, but many of the same principles appear to have applied as in the south. The River Severn has always been an important route into the central Marches, and from the mid-sixties it was controlled by a legionary fortress at Wroxeter, a few miles to the east of Shrewsbury, which was founded at about the same time as that at Usk, almost certainly as part of the same programme of military reorganization. In this case we can see rather more of the stages which led to the construction of the fortress, for it lies at the end of a series of vexillation fortresses – all on or near the line of Watling Street – which must mark the progress of the Roman army across the west Midlands. The first is at Mancetter, followed by Wall, Kinvaston and, finally Leighton, an 8-hectare fortress which is only four miles from Wroxeter, and which must have preceded the fortress there (Frere 1987a: 65). We do not know their precise dates, but they were probably the work of Scapula rather than Gallus; those furthest east could have been built by Aulus Plautius (see p. 51).

We know less about the auxiliary forts which will have screened the fortress at Wroxeter than we do about those in south Wales. The southern end of the command of the Legio XIV may have been near Leintwardine, an area which the army appears to have held more or less throughout the Roman period, probably because it controlled a major route into mid-Wales. The first fort was probably that at Brandon Camp, just south of Leintwardine itself, where the army occupied an Iron Age hill-fort (Frere 1987b: 49ff.). This in turn was replaced by a fort at Jay Lane at Leintwardine itself (Nash-Williams 1969: 93). Further north, another fort at Stretford Bridge is probably of this general date (St Joseph 1973: 235).

The largest fort to the north of Wroxeter is at Rhyn Park near Chirk, a complex site known from air photographs and excavation, where a vexillation fortress is replaced by an auxiliary fort (Frere 1977: 394; Goodburn 1978: 436, 1979: 296). It lies near the mouth of one of the valleys running into the mountains of north Wales, a route still followed by the A5 road. The fact that the first military post there was a vexillation fortress suggests that it was constructed at an early stage in the conquest, and, as Sheppard Frere has pointed out, it is well placed to have been involved in Scapula's early attack on the Deceangli (Frere 1987a: 65). However, it is over twenty miles from Wroxeter in a position which will have retained its strategic importance throughout the conquest period, and it is not surprising that when the vexillation fortress was closed, an auxiliary garrison replaced it.

A number of forts are known in the northern Marches, all probably for auxiliaries, and others must have existed. Twenty miles north of Wroxeter there is a fort at Whitchurch, Shropshire (Mediolanum) (Jones and Webster 1968), now well outside Wales but, if the evidence of Ptolemy's *Geography* is accepted, within the territory of the Ordovices (Rivet and Smith 1979: 415). The distance between Whitchurch and the Dee estuary is too great and too strategically important for it to have been left unguarded, and a fort in the area of Chester has been postulated though not as yet located. Another lies further to the west at Lwyn-y-Brain, near Caersws in the Severn Valley (Nash-Williams 1969: 66), a critical point where several major valleys meet and which is within striking distance of the west coast. As with so many of these early forts, it is assigned to this period on the grounds that it is too close to a known Flavian fort (in this case Caersws) for the two to be contemporary. Unfortunately, at what point in the twenty-five years of campaigns in Wales it was built cannot be decided without excavation. The fact that it lies so far to the west suggests that it cannot predate Gallus, and it is perhaps more likely to have been constructed after the campaigns of one of his successors. However, it is certain that there must have been at least one fort, and possibly more than one, in the Severn valley between Wroxeter and Llwyn-y-Brain. Two forts are known to the north-west of Wroxeter at Llansanffraid-ym-Mechain (Frere 1987c: 304, 1988: 417ff.; 1989: 260) and Abertanat (Frere 1987a: 259, 1988: 417, 1991: 223, 1992: 257); both guarded the mouths of minor river valleys leading to the west, but they lie within a couple of miles of one another, too close to be contemporary. Forts of this period, with defences of turf and earth and timber buildings, did not involve the same investment of time and resources as a stone fort, and the Roman army had little hesitation in replacing them with other forts, either because a new position was felt to be better or because a new garrison had different requirements.

Without the discovery of more of the forts which must have existed in the north of Wales and extensive excavations within those which are known, we cannot hope to assign most of these forts to specific governors, and even then this may be impossible. Tacitus' account shows that both north and south Wales saw repeated campaigns throughout the fourteen years between the arrival of Scapula and the Boudiccan revolt. With each of those campaigns the military situation will have changed, and with it the need to construct new forts and abandon old ones. As we know it today, the overall arrangement of these early forts would seem to be part of a system designed to give the Roman army control of the major and some of the minor routes into the uplands of south, mid and north Wales.

The Conquest Resumed

Gallus' successor in 57 was an able general, Quintus Veranius, whose orders were to resume the conquest. He began with a campaign against the Silures only to die within a year of his arrival. In his will he claimed that had he lived for another two years he would have brought the whole province under Roman control (*Annals*, XIV.29). Tacitus' reaction was one of contempt, but we should note that, if Tacitus' record is accurate, Veranius referred to the province, not to the whole of Britain. In 57 Brigantia effectively formed the northern limit of the Roman province, and the only areas to the south of it which were not under Roman control were Wales and probably parts of Devon and Cornwall. In reality, Veranius was claiming that he could have conquered those areas in three years, a not impossible aim and one which his successor almost achieved.

We hear of no more campaigns against the Silures until their final reduction in the seventies, but it is unlikely that they were left in peace until then. A small fort at Dolau (Nantmel) in Radnorshire (Nash-Williams 1969: 138), on a route west from

Leintwardine, is only a few miles from the Flavian fort at Castell Collen, near Llandrindod Wells, and so is likely to predate it. Its position suggests that it is part of a system extending into mid-Wales, but at present we lack the information to tell whether such a system was ever completed or was abandoned when circumstances changed with the Boudiccan revolt.

Tacitus' reference to Veranius' campaign – 'trifling raids' – is slighting, but the fact that his successor, Suetonius Paulinus, did not find it necessary to campaign in south Wales but was able to move the war to the north suggests that his success was more than superficial. Tacitus presents Paulinus' campaign as an attack on Anglesey (*Annals*, XIV, 29), but this could only have come after the Ordovices had been defeated and the Roman supply routes secured. He must have arrived in Britain in 58 after the death of his predecessor, and was in North Wales when the Boudiccan revolt broke out, probably in 60 (Syme 1958: 765). This means that he will have had at least one campaigning season in Britain before the attack on Anglesey in 59, and, if Veranius died fairly early in 58, he could have had much of a second; all facts which confirm that the attack on Anglesey was the culmination of more than one campaign. This is largely confirmed in Tacitus' *Agricola* (14), where he states that 'Suetonius Paulinus enjoyed two years of success, conquering tribes and establishing strong forts' before he attacked Anglesey. Tacitus records that the already large population of Anglesey (Mona) was swollen with refugees, and it appears to have been a centre of the Druids, whom the Romans particularly disliked. It is often assumed that it was this latter fact which led to Paulinus to attack the island, but if he had already campaigned through much of North Wales an attack on Anglesey would have been inevitable. The Druids and their followers add greatly to the drama of Tacitus' account, but they may have had less military significance.

There are a number of routes by which Paulinus could have reached the Menai Straits from the northern Marches. The most obvious is by way of the valley of the River Dee, a route which offers a number of possible approaches to the north coast; the forts at Rhyn Park confirm a Roman interest in this valley. From the Dee valley Paulinus' army could have struck north into the Vale of Clwyd to reach the sea near Rhyl, continued further west to the Vale of Conwy, or moved through Snowdonia to reach the Menai Straits at Bangor or Caernarfon. If the aim was to subdue the northern Ordovices, as it surely was, the army may have been divided and used more than one route. Exactly where they crossed the Menai Straits is not recorded, but the obvious point will have been near Bangor, where the water is relatively shallow, and this suggestion is strengthened by Tacitus' observation that the boats used to carry the infantry across the strait had to be flat-bottomed to cope with the shallows. The cavalry part waded, part swam across, a feat which suggests that they were Batavians, famous for their ability to swim alongside their horses in this way. Tacitus tells how the Romans were faced with a howling mob of warriors, black-clad women with their hair loose and blazing torches in their hands – resembling the Furies, he says – and Druids uttering curses, clearly rather ineffectually, as, after a moment's hesitation, the Roman soldiers cut them down. Suetonius' victory was complete and he was able to install a garrison on the island. Subsequent events reveal that the army used in this campaign included Legio XIV, as one would expect, since it was the legion stationed in the northern Marches, together with vexillations from Legio XX, as well as auxiliaries who, as we have seen, almost certainly included Batavian cavalry. The garrison which Tacitus records being installed after this victory

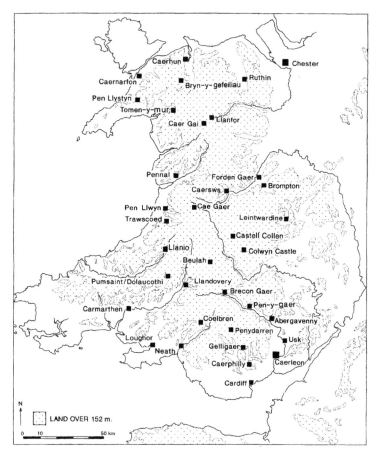

Figure 5.2 The occupation of Wales *c.* AD 74.

cannot have been the only one in north-west Wales, and we must remember Tacitus' reference in the *Agricola* (14) to Paulinus establishing forts in the area, although, as yet, we lack any archaeological evidence for these.

The Boudiccan revolt, which followed hot on the heels of the victory on Anglesey, forced the Roman authorities to rethink their entire strategy for Britain, and while we are not specifically told that the recent conquests in Wales were abandoned, the fact that both the Silures and Ordovices had to be reconquered in the seventies makes it clear that this is what happened. No doubt the need for the troops in the east of England after the suppression of the revolt meant that some were withdrawn from Wales, but it must have been clear that to spread the existing resources even further by garrisoning west and north Wales would have invited trouble. Presumably the forts in the east of Wales and the Marches, which have been discussed above, were maintained, but the details remain obscure. One side-effect of the revolt was the conferment of the title *Victrix* on the two legions involved in suppressing it, the Fourteenth and Twentieth.

The few references we have to events in Britain in the remaining eight years of Nero's reign do not mention Wales; they are either generalized references to the inaction of Roman governors (*Agricola*, 16), or to the marital problems of

Cartimandua, the Queen of the Brigantes, which eventually escalated into a civil war within the tribe (*Annals*, XII.40). It seems unlikely that the Romans and the Welsh tribes spent the whole of the sixties in an amicable peace, but any conflicts which arose were not sufficiently dramatic to excite the interest of Tacitus. However, there was another reason for the Romans not resuming the conquest of Wales, the removal from Britain in 66 of Legio XIV, together with its auxiliaries, as part of the troop movements which preceded Nero's plan for a war with Parthia. Although the removal of a quarter of the British garrison confirms that order had been restored in Britain, the departure of Legio XIV from Wroxeter will have left the northern Marches undefended and the north-west of the province open to incursions from an increasingly unstable Brigantia. The chosen solution was to move Legio XX from Usk to Wroxeter and build a new fortress at Gloucester for the Legio II Augusta, which had been based at Exeter since the mid-fifties (Manning 1981: 50). Neither of the older fortresses was demolished, but they can have had no more than holding garrisons, perhaps vexillations from the legion at Gloucester, or auxiliary units, or perhaps both. The apparent conversion of a barrack block into stables at Usk at about this time may support the latter idea (Marvell 1996). These legionary movements must have been accompanied by the movement of their associated auxiliaries, and this may account for some of the cases where two early forts are found within a few miles of each other, as at Kentchurch and Abbey Dore in the south of Wales, and Llansanffraid-ym-Muallt and Abertanat in the north. It is also probably the explanation of the fact that the fort at Abergavenny was rebuilt at about this time (Ponsford 1999).

The Conquest Completed

The accession of Vespasian, victor in the vicious civil war which divided the Empire in 68–9, led to a reassessment of the military situation in Britain and the decision to resume the conquest of the island. The collapse of the client kingdom in Brigantia, which had occurred during the civil war (Tacitus, *Histories*, III.45), meant that the first objective of Petillius Cerealis, the new governor, was the forcible incorporation of the former kingdom into the province. It fell to his successor, Julius Frontinus, who arrived in 74, to resume the conquest of Wales. The only account of his campaigns is the terse comment in the *Agricola* (17) that Frontinus subdued the Silures, although Tacitus' account of the opening campaign of Agricola, who succeeded Frontinus in 78, makes it clear that Frontinus had brought part, perhaps a large part, of the Ordovices under Roman control. We know few details of Frontinus' campaigns. Presumably he used Legio II Augusta, then still based at Gloucester, and part rather than all of Legio XIV from Wroxeter; the rest of the legion will have been needed to watch the Ordovices and guard the southern Pennines. With the legions will have come their auxiliaries. The fact that forts were built on some of the more important estuaries on the south Welsh coast in the Flavian period has led to the suggestion that Frontinus probably used his fleet to outflank the enemy. But this ignores the fact that such forts will have been built after the Romans had gained control of the area and so must reflect the arrangements made to hold rather than conquer it.

In theory the best evidence for these various campaigns are the temporary or 'marching' camps which were built by the armies in the field. Unfortunately, although quite large numbers are known in Wales, it is extremely difficult to assign any of them to a specific campaign (Frere 1987a: map, p. 175; Arnold and Davies 2000: 7, fig.1.1A). Since the size of a camp probably reflects the size of the army involved in a campaign, it should be possible, at least in theory, to discover the route taken in that campaign by linking camps of the same size. Unfortunately, although this principle works in Scotland, attempts to apply it in Wales have not proved successful. A number of concentrations are known, some of which are early, one of the largest and probably earliest being around Wroxeter, with others near Clifford (Arnold and Davies 2000: 7). However, it is notable that a high proportion lie close to Roman roads in areas which are unlikely to have been occupied by the Romans before the seventies. Such camps are largely absent from the south-west and south-east of Wales. The former may be a genuine absence and reflect the fact that this area was brought under Roman control without difficulty, a possibility which is strengthened by a lack of forts to the west of Carmarthen. Their absence from south-east Wales is less easily explained, although the intensive agriculture of the Vales of Glamorgan and the Usk valley may in part account for it.

Gnaeus Julius Agricola, who succeeded Frontinus in 78, had served in Britain on two previous occasions, as a junior officer under Suetonius Paulinus and as commander of Legio XX under Cerealis. The military achievements which were so lauded by Tacitus, his son-in-law, were mainly in Scotland, but before he moved north he completed the conquest of the Ordovices. Tacitus attributes only the conquest of the Silures to Frontinus, but the fact that the provocation which led Agricola to take the field as soon as he arrived in Britain was an attack by the Ordovices on a cavalry unit stationed in their territory indicates that at least part of their land was already occupied by the Romans. This is confirmed by Tacitus' remark that Agricola's modesty after his victory was because 'he had kept a conquered people under control' rather than extending his province (*Agricola*, 18). Although we do not know the exact extent of Ordovician territory, it must have been considerable. Clearly it reached Anglesey, while Jarrett and Mann (1969) have shown that it included much of mid-Wales, which it must have done if Ptolemy's *Brannogenium* is *Bravonium*, the modern Leintwardine (Rivet and Smith 1979: 142), while, if we accept Ptolemy's attribution of Whitchurch in Shropshire (reading *Mediolanum* for Ptolemy's *Mediolanium*) (Rivet and Smith 1979: 415) to the Ordovices, their territory extended well to the east of the modern border of Wales.

Tacitus' account of Agricola's actions in north-west Wales is typically dramatic and characteristically imprecise; only when Agricola reaches the shore opposite Anglesey do we have any real idea of where he is. He launched his attack on Anglesey by having his cavalry swim across the strait with their horses, an idea which he may have learned from Paulinus' attack on the island twenty years before. Tacitus claims that this manoeuvre was so brilliantly successful that the islanders surrendered at once, which was probably fortunate as Agricola had not bothered to wait for the boats necessary if he was to move his infantry across to support the cavalry (*Agricola*, 18).

The Flavian Forts

The completion of the conquest of Wales was accompanied by a total reorganization of the military system which involved not only the replacement of almost all of the auxiliary forts, but the foundation of new fortresses for the two legions which guarded Wales. Excavations in many of the Flavian forts of Wales have shown that the majority originated in the seventies, and it is assumed that they were the work of Frontinus. The obvious exceptions are those in the north-west of Wales which, as we have seen, was not fully conquered until Agricola became governor. Whether work on any of them had begun before Frontinus arrived must remain uncertain – if only because the nature of archaeological evidence rarely allows the degree of precision required to differentiate between the early and mid-seventies – but it seems unlikely. Cerealis was fully occupied in the north, and his predecessors had been too busy trying to control an army made restive by the civil war to start reorganizing the western frontier.

Wales was to remain under military control for the rest of the first century. Excavations at Caerwent (Venta Silurum), the Roman capital of the Silures, have shown that the forum and basilica there were built early in the second century and this is likely to have followed fairly soon after the tribe was granted a degree of self-government (Brewer 1993: 11). The Ordovices never received a similar grant, but the eastern part of their territory may have been merged with that of the Cornovii whose capital was at Wroxeter (Viroconium), where a forum and basilica were built under Hadrian (Collingwood and Wright 1965: 97, no. 288). Before these areas were granted self-government they will have been administered by the army, presumably through the commanders of the legions at Caerleon and Chester, with financial matters being handled by the officers of the provincial procurator.

Incomplete though our knowledge of it is, it is clear that the system of military control created by Frontinus and Agricola will have kept the inhabitants of the newly conquered areas under very firm control. At first sight the Roman army might seem an improbable agent of Romanization, but it proved sufficiently effective to allow the closure of most of these forts early in the second century, when their garrisons were required on Hadrian's Wall. Even so, Romanization was not wholly successful and the normal forms of civilian government, based on the *civitates*, never developed in the central and northern parts of the country, which must have remained under some form of military control.

FURTHER READING

The conquest period in Wales is discussed in the most of the standard studies of Roman Britain, of which the most recent and detailed is Frere 1987a. More specific accounts can be found in two recent books on Roman Wales (Arnold and Davies 2000 and Manning 2001), and two of the annual Caerleon Lectures of the National Museum of Wales (Manning 1988 and Jarrett 1994). The most important ancient literary texts are Tacitus' *Annals* and, to a lesser extent, the *Agricola* and the *Histories*, and many translations exist of all three. A series of books and papers by Graham Webster deal with all aspects of the Roman conquest; the most relevant to Wales being Webster 1960, 1970 and 1981. The main excavation reports are those on the fortress at Usk (Manning 1981, 1989; Marvell 1996) and the fort at Brandon Camp (Frere 1987b). Summary accounts of recent discoveries and excavations appear annually in *Britannia* and *Archaeology in Wales*, published by the Council for British Archaeology: Wales, the latter usually providing the most detail, and these are the only published sources for many sites.

Many of the sites discussed in this chapter were discovered by aerial photography and were reported in the annual summaries referred to above; a particularly important paper is St Joseph 1973. All ancient geographic references to Wales, including Ptolemy and the *Antonine Itinerary*, are discussed in detail in Rivet and Smith 1979. The most important discussion of the Flavian forts and their later history remains M. G. Jarrett's revision of Nash-Williams' *Roman Frontier in Wales* (1969).

REFERENCES

Arnold, C. J. and Davies, J. L. 2000. *Roman and Early Medieval Wales*. Stroud.

Birley, A. R. 1981. *The* Fasti *of Roman Britain*. Oxford.

Blockley, K., Ashmore, F. and Ashmore, P. J. 1993. Excavations on the Roman fort at Abergavenny, Orchard Site, 1972–73. *Archaeological Journal*, 150, 169–242.

Brewer, R. J. 1993. *Caerwent Roman Town*. Cardiff.

Clarke, S., Jackson, R. and Jackson, P. 1992. Archaeological evidence for Monmouth's Roman and early medieval defences. *Archaeology in Wales*, 32, 1–2.

Collingwood, R. G. and Wright, R. P. 1965. *The Roman Inscriptions of Britain I: Inscriptions on Stone*. Oxford.

Frere, S. S. 1977. Roman Britain in 1976. I. Sites explored. *Britannia*, 8, 356–425.

—— 1987a. *Britannia: A History of Roman Britain*, 3rd edn. London.

—— 1987b. Brandon Camp, Herefordshire. *Britannia*, 19, 49–92.

—— 1987c. Roman Britain in 1986. I. Sites explored. *Britannia*, 18, 301–59.

—— 1988. Roman Britain in 1987. I. Sites explored. *Britannia*, 19, 416–84.

—— 1989. Roman Britain in 1988. I. Sites explored. *Britannia*, 20, 258–326.

—— 1991. Roman Britain in 1990. I. Sites explored. *Britannia*, 22, 222–92.

—— 1992. Roman Britain in 1991. I. Sites explored. *Britannia*, 23, 256–308.

Frere, S. S. and Tomlin, R. S. O. (eds) 1991. *The Roman Inscriptions of Britain* II.3. Stroud.

Goodburn, R. 1978. Roman Britain in 1977. I. Sites explored. *Britannia*, 9, 404–72.

—— 1979. Roman Britain in 1978. I. Sites explored. *Britannia*, 10, 268–338.

Hurst, H. R. 1985. *Kingsholm, Gloucester*. Cambridge.

—— 1988. Gloucester (*Glevum*). In G. Webster, *Fortress into City*. London.

Jarrett, M. G. 1994. *Early Roman Campaigns in Wales. The Seventh Annual Caerleon Lecture*. Cardiff.

Jarrett, M. G. and Mann, J. C. 1969. The tribes of Wales. *Welsh Historical Review*, 4, 161–71.

Jones, G. D. B. and Webster, P. V. 1968. Mediolanum: excavations at Whitchurch 1965–6. *Archaeological Journal*, 125, 193–254.

Manning, W. H. 1976. The conquest of the West Country. In K. Branigan and P. J. Fowler (eds), *The Roman West Country*. Newton Abbot, 15–41.

—— 1981. *Report on the Excavations at Usk 1965–1976: The Fortress Excavations 1968–1971*. Cardiff.

—— 1988. *Early Roman Campaigns in the South-west of Britain. The First Annual Caerleon Lecture*. Cardiff.

—— 1989. *Report on the Excavations at Usk 1965–76: The Fortress Excavations 1972–1974 and Minor Excavations on the Fortress and Flavian Fort*. Cardiff.

—— 2001. *A Pocket Guide to Roman Wales*. Cardiff.

Marvell, A. 1996. Excavations at Usk 1986–1988. *Britannia*, 27, 51–110.

Musson, C. 1989. Air-photography and Roman forts, summer 1989. *Archaeology in Wales*, 29, 56.

Nash-Williams, V. E. 1939. An Iron Age coastal camp at Sudbrook near the Severn Tunnel, Monmouthshire. *Archaeologia Cambrensis*, 94, 42–79.

—— 1969. *The Roman Frontier in Wales*, rev. M. G. Jarrett. Cardiff.

Ponsford, M. 1999. Abergavenny, Castle Street Car Park. *Archaeology in Wales*, 39, 98–9.

Ptolemy. 1881. *Geographia*, ed. C. F. A. Nobbe. Leipzig.

Rivet, A. L. F. and Smith, C. 1979. *The Place-Names of Roman Britain*. London.

St Joseph, J. K. 1973. Air reconnaissance in Roman Britain, 1969–72. *Journal of Roman Studies*, 63, 214–46.

Syme, R. 1958. *Tacitus*. Oxford.

Tacitus. 1967. *De Vita Agricolae*, ed. R. M. Ogilvie and I. A. Richmond. Oxford.

—— 1967. *Historiarvm Libri*, ed. C. D. Fisher, Oxford.

—— 1973. *Annalivm*, ed. C. D. Fisher, Oxford.

Webster, G. 1960. The Roman military advance under Ostorius Scapula. *Archaeological Journal*, 115, 49–98.

—— 1970. Military situations in Britain A.D. 43–71. *Britannia*, 1, 179–97.

—— 1981. *Rome Against Caratacus*. London.

Webster, G. (ed.) 1988. *Fortress into City: The Consolidation of Roman Britain, First Century AD*. London.

Webster, P. V. 1990. The first Roman fort at Cardiff. In B. C. Burnham and J. L. Davies, *Conquest, Co-existence & Change: Recent Work in Roman Wales*. Trivium 25. Lampeter, 35–9.

CHAPTER SIX

The Roman Penetration of the North in the Late First Century AD

GORDON MAXWELL

Writing an account of the earliest Roman penetration of what is now Scotland has never been an easy matter – not since we began to distinguish between history and archaeology. In early days, the difficulty lay in identifying the relevant archaeological material, which seemed all too sparse or elusive compared with the apparent richness of the literary account. More recently the positions have been reversed, and we now struggle to find a suitable place in a somewhat spindly historical framework for the burgeoning quantities of data relating to mid and late first-century Roman artefacts and military structures. It is rather like trying to follow the thread of a conversation at a crowded cocktail party, where the voices of adjacent guests intrude alarmingly upon one's thoughts, occasionally because of their loudness, but more often through having an equally interesting story to tell.

Just as earplugs would be an inappropriate solution at a party (as would talking loudly in response), it is probably unwise to deal with such diversity by devising some kind of 'unifying' narrative, or concentrating on the discrepancies between the conclusions being drawn from different fields of study. What follows, therefore, is mainly a selective consideration of certain Roman sites and structures, or classes of structures, in the hope that more sharply focused examination or (re)interpretation may reveal more clearly their role in the Flavian penetration of the North. As we shall see, the abundant presence in Scotland of many, or indeed all, of these selected structures provides an opportunity, scarcely equalled throughout the Empire, to recognize not just spatial correlations but also complementary functions.

It may help, therefore, to indicate the various respects in which the Flavian advance into Scotland led the Romans both literally and metaphorically into new territory and, at the same time, to define what is meant by 'new'. The historian Tacitus, writing of the achievements of his father-in-law, Julius Agricola, who governed Britain from AD 77/8 to 83/4, refers on several occasions to the novelty of Agricola's policies or operations: the circumnavigation of Britain by way of the Orkneys and Shetlands was a first for the Roman fleet (*Agricola*, 10.4); the mopping-up operation which tied up the Brigantes and presumably their northern neighbours was unprecedentedly successful (*Agricola*, 20.3); the advances of the fourth and fifth campaigns extended Roman power over entirely new tribal areas (*Agricola*, 22.1 and 24.1); and the final overwhelming victory at *Mons Graupius* planted the flag in new tribal areas, far beyond the conquests of previous governors. Even without the trimmings of adulation for soldierly or diplomatic qualities which should have been the stock-in-trade of any staff-officer and commander in the field, Tacitus' account leaves the reader in no doubt that Agricola, in his opinion, was a star performer. It should not surprise us, therefore, particularly in an age when public reputations are so precarious, that this high opinion is not shared by all modern scholars (Breeze 1980; Hanson 1987) and is considered by some to be nothing more than Tacitean 'spin'.

In consequence, it may be helpful not only to examine how the currently available archaeological evidence supports or contradicts the picture drawn by Tacitus, but also to review the ways in which the territories opened up by Flavian campaigning in the North differed from the lands already overrun. The physical characteristics of the terrain are the most obvious difference; the upland landscapes that predominate north of York and Chester created a wide range of difficulties, distorting lines of access and communication and imposing more restricted patterns of land-use. On the other hand, by the early seventies AD the Roman army had already experienced campaigning in Wales and the southern Pennines, where comparable conditions prevailed; and still further afield, from Armenia or Africa to Dacia or Rhaetia, natural obstacles of much greater extent and severity had been seen and overcome. The point is amply demonstrated by reference to the varying fortunes of more modern armies which have attempted to operate in the same area. It is, of course, the combination and interaction of land, climate and human settlement which should concern us.

Fortunately, recent decades have witnessed an appreciable increase in the amount and quality of palaeo-environmental and ecological data relating to the North in Roman times. Much of it has been gathered with specific archaeological or geographical objectives in mind, and its collation is gradually producing an outline picture of land-use patterns over selected areas of the country (Van der Veen 1992; Smout 1993; Whittington and Edwards 1993; Mercer and Tipping 1994; Armit and Ralston 1997; Hanson 1987; RCAHMS 1997: 13–25; Tipping 1999). Although the evidence is too scanty to apply in detail to any given type of site or narrowly defined period, we can be sure that the countryside through which the first Roman columns were deployed was quite rigorously managed and that in southern Scotland pastoralism will have been the main support of rural communities; but this need not imply a slacker tempo of economic life or wealth accumulation, although much of this will have gravitated to wealthier families, many of whom owned the 'substantial houses' of the area.

North of the Forth and Clyde, however, it is less easy to offer structural evidence to demonstrate the working of the economy. Much of the population apparently lived in unenclosed villages and clachans of round, timber-built, or occasionally stone-founded, houses; many, perhaps most, of these settlements were associated with curving, underground storage chambers, now known as souterrains (Watkins 1981; RCAHMS 1994: 41–50 and 59–75; Armit 1999). In addition to these settlements and occasionally enclosed by ditch or palisade, but often situated at their centre, there were substantial round or subcircular dwellings which appear to have been of greater size or had loftier architectural pretensions (Hingley 1992: 26–53).

Usually interpreted as the evidence of a family of above average wealth and considerable local influence, possibly representing the estate centre of a magnate with wider responsibilities, 'substantial houses' of the North may be over-represented in the archaeological record, by reason of their ability more successfully to survive as recognizable structures. Nevertheless, their recognition allows us to posit a distinguishing characteristic of native communities in North Britain, demonstrating that even in kin-based social networks, economic relationships were as significant as the ties of family or politics. Seeking a parallel to this somewhat 'flattened' profile of contemporary society, one might compare the situation to that obtaining in Scotland a millennium and a half later, when the introduction of heritable feu-farm tenures by the Church and major magnates led to the emergence of 'bonnet lairds', a distinctive class of small landowners. Before they were swallowed up by more powerful proprietors, the 'substantial houses' of these lairds caught the eye of foreign (that is, English) visitors, as much by reason of their numbers as by their appearing more like castles than houses. If the comparison is apt, it may provide a useful pointer to the character of the native society which the Romans faced at the start of their northward advance in the seventies of the first century AD.

There is little in the literary evidence to suggest that this character differed in any way from that of their more southerly neighbours; Tacitus' remarks about the physical characteristics of the people of Caledonia (*Agricola*, 11.2) point at the best, not social distinctions, although they may underline the possibility of long-lasting cultural traditions. On the other hand, his observation (*Agricola*, 12.1) that kingship in the Britain of his days was a thing of the past, with each *civitas* subject to the whims of the local chieftain, may indicate that, in Roman eyes, the unconquered part of Britain, including the recently abandoned areas, traditionally enjoyed a different kind of social order.

Political coherence, however, did not need to be underwritten by kingship. Fissile though Iron Age society might seem to Tacitus, judging by Roman imperial values, there are good reasons to believe that the boundaries of native political or cultural jurisdictions were extremely durable on both the large and the small scale. Thus, tenth-century Alba, the kernel of historic Scotland, was coextensive with Pictland, which was in turn the equivalent of Tacitus' Caledonia – all the (eastern) mainland north of the Clyde–Forth isthmus. Our knowledge of the political subdivisions of North Britain, in the Roman period, both within Caledonia and to the south, depend on the evidence presented by Ptolemy, whose main source, the writings of Marinus of Tyre, was largely composed of data collected during the late first century AD, presumably during the earliest military operation; it is therefore highly relevant to our theme.

Although the defects of his sources and the specialist nature of his ambitions (Maxwell 1995) put the validity of Ptolemy's evidence in question, what we know of the post-Roman situation may help to fill out the picture of northern Britain in the late Iron Age. Just as Caledonia/Pictland/Alba represents a comprehensible spatial continuum, even so we can perceive a similar continuity in the smaller constituent provinces there and south of the Forth: the Votadini occupied the same rich coastal lowlands of the Lothians as their forerunners, the early historic Gododdin, although they did not extend as far south as the Tyne or even the Coquet; a precursor of Anglian Bernicia may have vanished from the map south of St Abb's Head; the Damnonii probably occupied territories coextensive with later Strathclyde, and not unlike the medieval archdeaconry of Glasgow, extending from the district (deanery) of Lennox in the north-west to Carrick in the south and Lanark in the east, but excluding Peebles; the latter probably represents the heartland of the Selgovae, who most likely also controlled Teviotdale (another deanery of Glasgow). The remaining deaneries of the diocese of Glasgow, lying to the south-west of Teviotdale, fell in Roman times within a north-westward extension of Brigantian territory. Beyond them, to the west, the lands of the Dark Age kingdom of Galloway (also a medieval diocese in its own right) then belonged to the Novantae.

The situation to the north of the Forth and Clyde is more complex. If the Damnonii did not extend further north than Lennox, that is, beyond the high ground separating the upper Forth from the lower course of the River Clyde, a tribal vacuum appears in the area occupied by the Ptolemaic sites of Alauna, Lindum and Victoria, locations most probably including the forts of Ardoch in Strathallan and Drumquhassle near the end of Loch Lomond. While the problem might be solved by assuming that Ptolemy had located the Vacomagi and the Caledonii too far north, in a recent edition of the Dark Age work, the *Gododdin* of Aneirin, it is convincingly argued (Koch 1997: 184) that the homeland of the Venicones lay to the north of *Bannauc*, that is, in the district once known as Menteith, to the west of Stirling. Fife, which is as yet innocent of indisputable evidence for Roman military penetration in the Flavian period, may not have figured largely in the initial surveys of Caledonia (and it is certainly poorly depicted in Ptolemy).

If we assume that the limit of Roman conquest or campaigning by land is indicated in Ptolemy by the most northerly named *polis*, elements of the army advanced to the shore of the Moray Firth, some way to the west of the River Spey. Whether the 'Winged Camp', *Pinnata Castra*, located there, is a Roman work or a reference to a native stronghold cannot be determined, though the precursor of the important Pictish stronghold on the promontory of Burghead must be a strong candidate. What is more significant is the reasonable presumption that to reach this goal the legions appear to have traversed, or touched on, the territories of three separate tribal groups lying beyond the Venicones: first the Vacomagi; beyond them the Caledonii; and lastly the Taexali. Of these, only the Taexali can be located with any degree of safety since they gave their name to the promontory which marks the north-easternmost point of Buchan. However, as the final element of the tribal name Vacomagi bears the connotation of 'field, plain', it would not be unreasonable to accept the link that many scholars have advocated with Strathmore, 'the great valley'. With the Caledonii the problem is slightly different, in that *all* the inhabitants of Caledonia, as defined by Tacitus, might justly be called Caledonians. In this case, a more specific identification of the tribal heartland would seem to be required.

In all probability the question admits of no definitive answer, but once again a comparison with the situation in post-Roman times proves instructive, even though the evidence derives from late ninth-century documents. There is good reason to accept that the Pictish provinces there described were of considerable antiquity and probably corresponded to Late Iron Age tribal territories, and more specifically that four of the southernmost can be identified more or less precisely: thus the lands of the Taexali became the province of Mar and Buchan (each Pictish entity apparently comprising two subregions), while those of the Vacomagi were reborn as Circinn or Angus and the Mearns, while the successors of the Caledonii held sway over Atholl and Gowrie, or the entire length of the Tay, from its many headwaters to its broad estuary; lastly, from the territory of the Venicones, as here relocated, arose the province of Fortrenn, or Strathearn and Menteith. Such continuity may seem remarkable, but the truth is that, given the innate conservatism of rural communities, it would have been more surprising if the settlement pattern had altered significantly over the few hundred years that are here in question. Persistence over much longer periods is amply attested by the archaeological evidence.

By the late first century AD, however, these regional communities, though still politically coherent, no longer undertook such great public works as had embellished the landscape in the Neolithic. Furthermore, as we have seen, the great majority of their dwellings and settlements, even if enclosed, were not ostentatiously defensive in character. And yet it is precisely in these northern parts that one finds an immense flowering of the Roman military engineer's art; its most prominent manifestation was the temporary camp, apparently produced, and certainly surviving, in numbers that are unequalled in comparable sectors of the Imperial frontiers, and only palely reflected in other regions of Britannia. In asking ourselves why this should be, we are perhaps really considering the reverse of another, more basic problem that has exercised scholars (e.g. Sargent 2002), the explanation of the cultural divide which separated the north and west of Roman Britain from the south and east – the latter with its urban development, villas, temples and substantial rural buildings, the former with the ubiquity of military fortifications and the prevalence of garrison-related civil settlements. Just as it is not enough to appeal to the traditional cleavage between Highland and Lowland zones, it is also inappropriate to refer solely to cultural fault-lines fully attested in the Late Pre-Roman Iron Age (Cunliffe 1991). Clarification may be provided by the testimony of other indicators, for example, the widespread presence in the south and east of coin-mints, pottery- and glass-making centres, as well as elaborate public buildings, in other words, all the trappings of a money-based market economy, which had been developing along such lines for decades before the Roman invasion, and had long enjoyed close contacts with Roman producers. It is interesting, too, that among the common place-names applied to settlements in these parts (and rarely, if ever, elsewhere) one finds *venta* and -*magus*, both elements probably referring to marketing functions, and recognized as *Forum* in Roman toponymy.

When the invasion came, the impact of Rome on native societies of this level of economic sophistication is bound to have caused more massive dislocation than would have been experienced in less highly structured communities; conversely, once a *modus vivendi* had been agreed or imposed, the redevelopment of the infrastructure could have proceeded more swiftly. It would be strange if an appreciation of this had not modified the tactics and strategy of military commanders in the field. Beneath the Claudian claims of sweeping victories in southern England, totally bloodless in the official account (ILS 216), but not unstrenuous in the eyes of those more closely involved (Suetonius, *Divus Vespasianus*, 4), one may perhaps glimpse both the process at work and its effect: a series of short, sharp shocks, and then total submission. For a decade and more after AD 43, short-range operations and, for the most part, piecemeal absorption of territory, were the rule, interrupted by the occasional flaring of resistance. Army groups in transit could live off the land – possibly by negotiated agreement with the local population, who found it an opportunity to sell off surplus produce. In such a pattern of operations, it might seem appropriate for each legion to adopt a fluid arrangement, spreading its force between a home base and an outstation, as the situation demanded. It is not surprising, therefore, that such tactics produced what till recently were classified as vexillation fortresses, semi-permanent bases of mixed legionary and auxiliary brigades, some twenty of which are scattered across these Lowland areas.

Clearly, by the time that the Romans began to involve themselves in the affairs of the north, first by entering into a treaty relationship with the ruler of the Brigantes, and then having to deal with a collapse in that relationship, the situation had changed out of all recognition. Doubtless military practices had evolved in the meantime; quite probably the regional preferences of senior officers for different policies and practices, perhaps imported from distant theatres of war, also played a part. It is difficult, however, to discount the possibility that the distribution of Roman temporary works appearing north of a line drawn from Preston to Bridlington, and growing ever more dense the further north one looks, derives in part from the need to deal with a more intransigent foe. This need not mean that the local population was more belligerent or less soft than southern *civitates*, but rather that the structure of northern society was more resilient. It is thus possible that the widespread existence of families owning and occupying 'substantial houses' produced a network of independent settlements capable of absorbing and resisting adverse conditions without losing their functional effectiveness. To borrow a term from the mathematics of engineering, they formed a geodesic network, a structure whose exceptional strength springs from its being composed of numerous identically shaped elements. A further clue to the distinctive character and narrower social compass of northern communities is a toponymic one, corresponding to the presence of -*magus* and *venta* place-names of the south; instead one finds curia or *coria* names, signifying the meeting-places of the *pagi* forming the subdistrict of each *civitas*. This distinctive clue to the structure of local social units is found in only one example to the south of Hadrian's Wall (Rivet and Smith 1979). Similar conclusions might be drawn from the complementary distribution in the north and west of *pagus* names ending in -*vices* (= warriors), or of place-names ending in -*vicium* (i.e. Gabrantovices, *Delgovices, *Longovices, *Vercovices, and of course Ordovices).

The need to deal with this problem may have strengthened the incentive for Roman armies on the march to reintroduce the practice of constructing a defended enclosure at the end of each day's progress, but another consideration may have been the additional security sought by troops operating at an appreciable distance from the relevant legionary base. In northern England, for example, distribution of camps marking the routes north and north-east of York begins to thicken some 70 Roman miles from the fortress. This is to assume, of course, that York was already in existence when the camps in question were built – which is to beg the whole question of dating, a difficult problem and one for which there is as yet no simple solution. In general, the dates assigned to the camps have depended either on external relationships –

proximity to a permanent site of a known date, or to a road, for example – or on some subjective assessment of an essential characteristic of the camp itself, mainly shape, proportions and gate defence; the problem is made slightly easier when the example belongs to a series of marching-camps, whose strategic objective is easily identifiable. However, there are relatively few series whose line of march is plainly obvious, and fewer still that are accurately datable. In short, about the vast majority we can make only the most tentative guesses.

Some of these guesses, however, are based upon premises that appear at present to be eminently reasonable, and one is consequently tempted to adopt an intuitive approach, the main thrust of which is to view most examples of the marching-camp class as belonging to the mid to late first century or the early second century.

Given this approximate contemporaneity, it seems worthwhile exploring more minutely what we have already called the internal characteristics displayed by camps in Britain, on the assumption that the basic parameters affecting their use, specifically the size and internal organization of the army units that constructed them, will not have altered significantly over the period in question. It is possible, therefore, that such differences as are detected may lead to a better understanding of the class, providing not just a clue to the identity of the camp's builders, but insights into such aspects as function and capacity.

The raw material for this study has been accumulating for more than two and a half centuries, the first review of its significance being produced, not surprisingly, by a senior officer in the British army (Roy 1793) with personal field experience of operations in North Britain. In the second half of the twentieth century, refinement of aerial reconnaissance, particularly the Cambridge University programme conducted by J. K. S. St Joseph and D. R. Wilson, has enormously increased the quantity and quality of the evidence (St Joseph 1976; Frere and St Joseph 1983). Most of the evaluation and interpretation of this material, however, has taken the form of specialist studies of selected problems or individual sites (e.g. St Joseph 1978 – the Mons Graupius campaign; Pitts and St Joseph 1985: 223–46 – the Inchtuthil labour-camps). Various attempts have also been made to assign dates to specific classes or series of camp, especially in Wales and its approaches, and in Scotland (St Joseph 1973, 1976, 1978; Maxwell 1981), while the capacity of different sizes of camp has been, since Roy's time, a constant object of enquiry (e.g. Richmond and McIntyre 1934; Hanson 1978). Beyond doubt, the most significant addition to the literature is the most recent, a handsome inventory of temporary camps in England illustrated by accurate plans of both earthwork and crop-mark sites at standard scales (Welfare and Swan 1995).

The evaluation of this rich, deeply stratified mass of record and commentary is a long-term task. Ongoing assessment of the Scottish material (Maxwell forthcoming) suggests, however, that in addition to the approaches already explored – size, shape and internal characteristics – there are four areas which may justify particularly close examination: the microtopography of sites for which accurate plans exist, by which is meant the rigorous interrogation of a camp's physical structure; a statistical analysis of the attributes of camps compared with those in different parts of Britain; the superficial evidence for structural relationships within complex sites; and evidence that may indicate, on the one hand, the identity of the camp's builders, and on the other, the reason for its construction, including the political objectives it might serve. As one might guess, the same concerns are appropriate to the study of most classes of Roman military work.

The particular importance of microtopography may be judged after consideration of two widely separated temporary camps. At the first, the 13-hectare camp of Little Clyde in Lanarkshire (RCHAMS 1978: no. 258), field survey recorded axial dimensions within its rampart of 440 by 290 metres, verified on the ground to within 15 centimetres. Not until after publication was it realized that overall this approximated very closely to 1500 by 1000 Roman feet; the overall area was thus 1,500,000 square feet. However, the area *within* the rampart, now some 3 metres thick, so narrowly approaches 100 square *actus* (or 50 *jugera*) that there seemed equally good reason for assuming that the inner capacity of the camp was uppermost in its builders' minds.

The second example is the site of Y Pigwn in Brecknock (RCAHMW 1986: 150–3), where a 10.5-hectare camp overlies another almost half as big again, so carefully placed as to make it seem that one had been designed to fit snugly, but at an angle, inside the other. Since the gates of each had been defended by internal *claviculae*, it would be easy to believe both were built by the same unit, operating at different strengths. What is remarkable is that, despite the appreciable difference in size, both are of precisely the same proportions, 5:6. What this meant in practice is that, where the sides of the larger camp were 10 *actus* (1200 Roman feet) and 12 *actus* (1444 feet), the smaller, to fit within the larger, had to be 10 *actus* by $8\frac{1}{3}$ *actus* (1000 feet), but oriented with great precision. The reasons for this almost pedantic exactness elude us, but the accuracy and the modules employed (the 120-foot *actus*) are most evident.

Naturally, convincing proof of camps being planned and built to standard *actus* measurements will not be available at every site. It seems possible that some surveyors used the overall dimensions as their starting-point, others the inside face of the rampart, and so forth. Likewise, errors or misunderstandings will have crept in during the construction process. Nevertheless, at this stage of enquiry, a good case can be made out for measurement within the rampart, which would provide a more uniform reckoning of usable space. With this in mind, it is interesting to note that at what is perhaps the best-known indubitably Flavian example, the large labour-camp at Inchtuthil, measurement *within* the established line of the rampart (from a computer-rectified air-photograph plot of the site) produces a total internal area of 149.8 square *actus*. At Dalginross and Glenlochar, which are comparably well endowed with crop-mark evidence, the rectified air-photograph plots show interiors of about 75 and 100 square *actus* respectively. The extrapolation of these figures to camps known only from their outlines, whether as crop-marks or intermittently preserved earthworks, suggests an interesting continuum with not only the above, but also the series of large camps which extend from Newstead on the Tweed to Kair House at the north-eastern end of Strathmore and which are assigned to the Severan period. More significantly, the numerical pattern to which all these belong harmonizes acceptably with that observed in the peak frequencies of sites in England (Welfare and Swan 1995: 10–11). Thus, the groupings of sites at about 8.7, 12.5 and 16 hectares have their parallels in Scotland (and Wales), with internal area equivalents of about 75, 100, and 125 *actus* respectively. The next stage of 150 square *actus* is represented in Scotland by camps at Inchtuthil, Newstead and Inveresk, which have no close analogies elsewhere in Britain, while the series of about 24-hectare camps exploiting the natural corridors of Annan, Nith and Clyde at Lochmaben, Dalswinton and Castle-dykes have a capacity of 175 square *actus*. The 200 square *actus* class in Scotland is comprised solely of the 25-hectare camps of Severan date, measured *over* the rampart, as are the members of the Severan 52-hectare group which covered 400 square *actus*. The only equivalents to the smaller of these groups in the south are Brampton Bryan, Herefordshire, and Blaen-cum-Bach in Glamorgan, the latter being a particularly informative example, as it was evidently planned to measure 3000 feet by 1000 feet over a 15-foot rampart, covering 208.3 square *actus* from which the rampart took up 8000 × 15 square feet, or precisely 8.3 square *actus*; the parallel with the method-ology employed at Little Clyde is absolute.

There are no camps in England and Wales of greater size than this, but in the north, from the very start, the use of larger battle-groups appears to have been a vital part of the tactics, as occasionally happened on the Continent. Though the northern examples are relatively few, they are instructive, providing a harmonious interpolation in the series already outlined. Interestingly, they all appear to have been based on overall measurement, possibly because the area occupied by the rampart represented less than 2 per cent of the total. In these sites, an irregularity of plan occasionally makes it difficult to be sure of the areas involved, but the estimates in each case are more than mere conjecture. Thus, the massive army that advanced eastward along Strathearn to the Tay was accommodated in camps of 350 square *actus* in area, and a similar capacity was provided by the camps of roughly 45 hectares which indicate an avenue of advance from the Dee towards the doorway into Moray. The unusually irregular site at Raedykes, which probably marks the halting place of the same battle-group when still in the process of formation, extended over 300 square *actus*. At Durno, beneath the towering summit of Bennachie, near Inverurie, that process was completed and, at its maximum strength, the army required a colossal 55 hectares or 450 square *actus*. No mightier force sought to dictate Rome's terms to Caledonia until an Imperial expedition in the early third century advanced up Lauderdale from Newstead to the Forth in camps that attained 66.7 hectares or 500 square *actus*.

Against the noticeable bunching of the size of larger temporary camps, at intervals of 25 square *actus* (3.15 hectares), one must set the observation that these bunches represent a minority of the measurable sites. Between them there lies what appears to be a random distribution of sites, indicating that the number of occupants, and therefore the sizes of the marching unit, might be infinitely variable. The desire to ascertain the size of forces deployed in the field has, for centuries, led to scholars suggesting a density of occupation that varied between 192 men per acre (Roy 1793: 52) to a calculation of 495, based on the manual composed by Hyginus (Lenoir 1979). Applying the latter estimate to the 144-acre camp at Durno produces a total of about 70,000 troops, which is impossibly big, calling for a force appreciably larger than the entire garrison of Britain in the first century. Similarly exorbitant figures were produced by an assessment of Rey Cross in County Durham, which seemed to suggest that a legionary quingenary cohort needed no more than 1.7 square *actus* of camp-ground (Richmond and McIntyre 1934) and that a legion with its complement of *auxilia* might occupy only 7 or 8 hectares. On that assessment, Durno was designed for almost 80,000 men.

It is possible that these overestimates were an inevitable consequence of starting at the wrong end of the size scale, looking at the larger camps and comparing them with the dimensions of better-known permanent fortresses (where, incidentally, the variation in overall size from legion to legion should have alerted us to the dangers of seeking universally applicable standards). Two discoveries, in particular, have directed attention to the opposite end of the scale: the first was the recording during an aerial survey of an attached camp at the north-eastern extremity of the 16.8-hectare camp at Carlops in Lothian (Keppie 1997: 408–9). The second was the publication of the survey of a number of small Roman camps lying to the north-west of the legionary fortress at Chester (Philpott 1998). The curiously elongated proportions of the former and its area (about 0.9 hectare), assumed major significance when it was realized that until then only Severan 25-hectare camps were known to display such annexes (all of which were also closely comparable in size at about 1.05 hectares). It was at this point that the group's shared characteristics indicated that they had accommodated a similarly sized unit.

Since there are no comparable annexes attached to large camps in England, it seemed prudent to examine examples of small independent camps (0.5–5.0 hectares), which abound especially in north-east England, but are also found in Wales, where they form a class distinct from the so-called practice-camps (Davies and Jones forthcoming). The results have been most encouraging, for it is already apparent that, of the 72 English examples considered by the Royal Commission in England (Welfare and Swan 1995), 63 are found in northern England, roughly half of these in the Hadrian's Wall/Stanegate zone. The major bunching as regards size, occurs at about 0.55, 1.0 and 1.6 hectares, and significantly the axial dimensions often approximate to *actus* modules, producing the area bunches already mentioned, at 4, 8 and 12½ square *actus*. Now, although this type is found most frequently on the Tyne/Solway corridor, the densest single concentration is at Upton, Chester, where the sites must constitute legionary labour-camps or training-camps; the 13 examples whose dimensions have been exactly assessed may be divided into four subgroups which mirror the three identified above, together with a 2-hectare group (16 square *actus*). By more than a coincidence, the two small camps long known at Bootham Stray on the outskirts of York, and doubtless also the work of legionary builders, belong to the 8 square *actus* category; at both Chester and York the appearance of *claviculae* argues strongly for an early period of use. More important, however, the repetition of the different sizes (based on the 4-*actus* module) suggests that each was intended to accommodate a different size of legionary unit. On the basis of various assumptions, but especially the inadequacy of the suggested Rey Cross *pedaturae*, it seems most likely that the 1.0 hectare (8 square *actus*) sites housed the six *centuriae of* a quingenary legionary cohort. If that was so, allowing for a 10- to 15-foot rampart, the internal space would have been almost exactly 6 square *actus*, the equivalent of 1 square *actus* per century.

Before applying this allocation of camp space to any larger sites, three points must be made: first, that the smaller the camp, the smaller the proportion of the overall area available for the accommodation of troops; secondly, the larger the camp, the greater the likelihood of it containing auxiliary units who received a more restricted allocation; and thirdly, as documents recovered from Vindolanda record (Bowman and Thomas 1991), detachment of parties for outposted duties might considerably decrease the strength of a unit, and though these records related to an auxiliary regiment, the same reductions must be assumed for legions. In other words, it may be necessary to expect that, like *castella*, camps were planned for paper-strength units, and estimates of capacity therefore represent a maximum. A review of the larger camps in Scotland (and their equivalents elsewhere) would thus rate their *maximum* capacity as follows: Dalginross (Rey Cross/Malham) 9.7 hectares = 5600; Glenlochar 1, or Ythan Wells 1 (Birdhope 1, Greensforge 5) 13.4 hectares = 8000; Carlops 1 and Newstead 2 (Bellshill, Uffington 2) 1618 hectares = 10,000; Newstead 1, or Inchtuthil 1 (no precise equivalent) 20 hectares = 12,000; Castledykes 1 or Dal-swinton (Brampton Bryan, Blaen-cwm-bach) 24 hectares = 15,000; Raedykes, 38 hectares = 24,000; Dunning or Ythan Wells 2, 45 hectares = 28,000; Durno, 58.1 hectares = 36.000.

Although, for the reasons given above, the figures are probably still on the high side, the results are promising. Dalginross and its analogues remain as the likeliest candidates for a single-legion force, while at the top end Durno provides a more acceptable figure for a maximum-effort operation in a situation of critical import-ance. In the former case, if we assume that the 'legion' in occupation represents between 70 and 80 per cent of its full establishment (the recruit-heavy cohorts, for example, being mostly absent), the number actually enclosed might have been closer to 4000, a similar revision of Durno, where the army was, however, presumably comprised of equal numbers of legionaries and auxiliaries, reducing its total to 24,000. Although we are now still a long way from being able to deal confidently with such equations, the archaeological evidence for the initial penetration of North Britain can now be viewed in a somewhat clearer light. Consequently, if we were to attempt to dispense with the literary evidence – an almost impossible feat – what kind of narrative (which is to say, what kind of analysis of the material evidence) might we then construct?

First of all, comparison with similar material elsewhere in Britain would lead us to suspect that the tactics and methodology practised by the Romans in Scotland differed significantly from those of earlier commanders; and what points us towards this conclusion is not just the density of temporary sites, the greater expanse of country over which they are dispersed, and the more frequent occurrence of very large camps, but the more richly varied character of the structures themselves, which often provide a clue to the identity of their builders or the role they played in the strategy of invasion. In Wales or the English approaches to Wales the picture is very much more uniform: in the former area there are very few square camps – most are rectangular, and in most the gates are defended by *claviculae*, all of them internal; in the Welsh Marches, however, although the square plan form is similarly uncommon, the *clavicula* is totally absent, gates being defended by a *titulus*. The camps of each area nevertheless differ in choice of size, only a fifth of those in the Marches being of single-legion type or smaller, against more than half in the Welsh examples. Such local uniformity might be the result of operations in each region being dominated by one particular legion – in the southern half of Wales this might point to the part played by the Second Legion Augusta in the course of Frontinus' campaign against the Silures between AD 74 and 77; the English sites cover a much longer period of operations, but it would be strange if there the Twentieth Legion had not been a leading participant.

In Scotland and the north generally, the numbers of square and rectilinear camps of presumed late first-century date are evenly divided; the square examples, some 24 in number, display *clavicula*-defended gates, and of these half again favour the gateway known as the 'Stracathro' type (where clavicular terminals are complemented by an oblique external traverse). The distribution of Stracathro camps is markedly western in southern Scotland, extending from Beattock in Annandale and Dalswinton in Nithsdale to Camelon on the Forth; the simple type of *clavicula*, on the other hand, is most numerous in the south-eastern borders and Redesdale, areas which lie athwart the axis of northward advance from the Flavian vexillation base at Red House, near Corbridge, and were therefore the operational responsibility of the Ninth Legion, based at York. The exotic Stracathro gates of the former, by contrast, have been assigned to the Second Legion Adiutrix (Maxwell 1998), which was introduced to Britain from Lower Germany early in the Flavian period; by the end of the eighth decade it was based at Chester and well placed to conduct operations beyond the Solway. The handiwork of this legion is thereby attested in the 24-hectare camps located at important river crossings or the like at Lochmaben, Dalswinton, Beattock and Castledykes, at each of which they probably served as bases for a force of between 10,000 and 15,000 troops or springboards for local operations, rather than halts en route; Girvan on the Ayrshire coast may be another member of the group. At Dalswinton, where the camp was eventually succeeded by a semi-permanent fort garrisoned by legionary troops, and later by a large auxiliary fort, also perhaps the work of the Second *Adiutrix* (Maxwell 1998), the sheer structural complexity of the site illustrates the ultimate potential of all such 24-hectare locations in the mind of the military planner. Remarkably, in addition to all this, Dalswinton also exhibits an extremely small Stracathro camp, perhaps 3.0 hectares in area; its relationship to the large camp indicates that it must be the earliest structure on the site, capable, on the modular rate described above, of housing some 2000 troops. Its role at so early a stage can only be guessed, but the recognition of similar structures at other major campaigning bases in Scotland hints at a process about which we can only guess – exploration, intelligence gathering, diplomacy? Whatever the purpose, examples can be identified at Castledykes and Inchtuthil (both 1 hectare in size, with the former also demonstrably early), and at Lochlands, near Camelon (2.0 hectares). The recognition of such possibilities raises intriguing questions about the 70 or so examples known in northern England, especially on the Stanegate corridor and Stainmore route, where they form the vast majority of temporary works.

But they are not alone in those sectors; it has long been recognized that the series of three comparable camps at Rey Cross, Crackenthorpe and Plumpton Head indicate very early troop movements indeed. Between 8 and 10 hectares in size and, with one exception, of square plan (hence comparable with Dalginross), they mark the advance of a force some 5000 strong, presumably from York to Carlisle. Their most interesting structural characteristics are the provision of multiple *titulus*-guarded gates and a relationship to the adjacent Roman road which indicates that the road is later. Their location and character amply support the proposition that they were built during the campaigns of Petillius Cerealis against the Brigantes; more than that, they suggest by their overall appearance, which is unlike virtually any other set of northern camps, that they represent really early essays at camp building. It has recently been proposed (Maxwell 1998) that the series may have continued beyond Carlisle, the evidence being the early phases of two curiously disposed, multi-gated camps at Burnswark, near the foot of Annandale, whose conjoined area and proportions approximate to those of the Stainmore sites. The objective at Burnswark being the hilltop position that dominates lower Annandale, one may imagine that the tactical purpose in this case was the neutralization of a tribal rallying-point in the north-western extension of Brigantia.

Returning to the later Flavian campaigns in the south-west of Scotland, one must remark that the capacity of the 24-hectare bases implies the involvement of more than one legion within the occupying force (and one's conjecture would be that the companions of II Adiutrix would be XX Victrix, for whose presence at Carlisle there is documentary evidence). Yet the chain of 16-hectare camps extending from Upper Clydesdale via Biggar, along the southern Pentland edge to Midlothian, totally eschews the Stracathro *clavicula*, favouring instead the more elongated shape exhibited by similarly sized English examples at Swindon, Uffington and Burlington. It is quite possible that this marks the advance of the Twentieth Legion and its auxiliary complement operating on its own during a drive towards the Forth, where it could unite with the field-force directed by the Ninth Legion. The operations of the latter are much less easy to detect as a coherent pattern, but the equivalent springboard bases on that side of the country, of 20-hectare extent, may be tentatively identified at Newstead and Inveresk, where an 8000-strong force may have been based. In addition to all these, reinterpretation of aerial data has suggested that there were at least three expeditions of legionary strength traversing the lateral route from Tweedsdale through Clydesdale and Avondale to the western sea. Clearly, the operations in southern Scotland must have involved more than one or two legionary brigades for more than one campaigning season. Traces of similar operations are also to be found in the valleys of south-west Scotland, extending Rome's control within the area defined by the major bases. Significantly, of all the tribal groupings recorded in these parts, only the Votadini remained untouched by large-scale, or possibly by any, troop movements.

Of the campaigning activity which must have secured the central valley of Scotland we have no evidence – unless the series of smaller camps adjoining the second-century frontier, the Antonine Wall, includes examples of the associated early 'exploratory' camps referred to above (which is entirely possible). It is only at the crossing of the Carron Water, north-west of Falkirk, that we renew contact with the Flavian field forces in the form of Stracathro-gated camps of legionary strength, lying within an apparently early enclosure perhaps as much as 25 hectares in area, and amidst a complex of variously sized camps that includes a 2-hectare example of the 'exploratory' class. The dense assemblage of structures provides one of the best illustrations of a springboard site in Roman military archaeology – a gathering ground or rendezvous for the disparate elements of a Flavian field-army, prior to the launching of the assault – in this case against Caledonia. Northward of this point the pattern changes: in lower Strathearn lie the 45-hectare camps that must, with their potential capacity of 20,000 to 25,000 men, have sheltered the two armies of the south combined. Apart from these, there are a few possible candidates for the bivouacs of individual vexillations on the march, while in the furthest north, between the Dee and the Spey, consecutive halting-places of a truly massive army must have drawn deeply on the reserves of the army in Britain, putting forth perhaps almost a third of its total military strength. Intermediate between these widely differing activities in space and time was a scattering of semi-permanent bases of differing strength – Dalginross, Malling, Stracathro itself and Bochastle – in total representing some 55 hectares of fortified space and theoretically engrossing much of the field-army's reserves in probing or guarding the margins of the Highland massif. It is barely conceivable that these three phases of operation could have been practically attempted in a single year, since it would have involved the assembling, dispersal and reconstitution of the individual elements over a wider area than many early commanders had struggled to reduce to order within the limits of a three-year governorship.

From the above account it will be seen that the precise order and tenor of Tacitus' version of the Roman penetration of the north cannot be constructed solely from the archaeological evidence of legionary activity in the field. Nevertheless, several conclusions may safely be drawn: first, that the material bears ample testimony to the vast and innovative strides made by the military machine in the later first century AD; secondly, that the planning and practice evident in the construction of these structures were the products of a rigorous adherence to practised discipline; thirdly, that the closest interrogation of the surviving remains will handsomely repay the time and effort spent; and finally, that when Tacitus justified embarking on a description of Britain by the observation *quia tum primum perdomita est*, 'because that is when it was completely conquered', the material evidence thoroughly supports his claim for the completeness of the conquest.

REFERENCES

Armit, I. 1999. The abandonment of souterrains: evolution, catastrophe or dislocation. *Proceedings of the Society of Antiquaries of Scotland*, 129, 577–96.

Armit, I. and Ralston, I. B. M. 1997. The Iron Age. In K. J. Edwards and I. B. M. Ralston (eds), *Scotland: Environment and Archaeology, 8000 BC–AD 1000*. Chichester, 169–94.

Bowman, A. K. and Thomas, J. D. 1991. A military strength report from Vindolanda. *Journal of Roman Studies*, 81, 62–73.

Breeze, D. J. 1981. Agricola the Builder. In J. Kenworthy (ed.), *Agricola's Campaigns in Scotland*. Scottish Archaeological Forum 127, 14–24.

Cunliffe, B. 1991. *Iron Age Communities in Britain: An Account of England, Scotland and Wales from the Seventh Century BC until the Roman Conquest*, 3rd edn. London.

Davies, J. L. and Jones, R. H. (forthcoming). Recent research on Roman camps in Wales. In *Roman Frontier Studies 2001*. Papers presented to the 18th International Congress of Roman Frontier Studies.

Edwards, K. J. and Ralston, I. B. M. (eds) 1997. *Scotland: Environment and Archaeology, 8000 BC–AD 1000*. Chichester.

Frere, S. S. and St Joseph, J. K. S. 1983. *Roman Britain from the Air*. Cambridge.

Hanson, W. S. 1978. Roman campaigns north of the Forth–Clyde isthmus: the evidence of the temporary camps. *Proceedings of the Society of Antiquaries of Scotland*, 109, 140–50.

—— 1987. *Agricola and the Conquest of the North*. London.

Henig, M. 2002. *The Heirs of King Verica: Culture and Politics in Roman Britain*. Stroud.

Hingley, R. 1992. Society in Scotland from 700 BC to AD 200. *Proceedings of the Society of Antiquaries of Scotland*, 122, 7–53.

ILS 1892–1916. *Inscriptiones Latinae Selectae*, ed. H. Dessau. 3 vols. Berlin.

Keppie, L. J. F. 1997. Roman Britain in 1996: Scotland. *Britannia*, 28, 405–14.

Koch, J. T. 1997. *The Gododdin of Aneirin: Text and Context from Dark Age Britain*. Cardiff.

Lenoir, M. 1979. *Pseudo-Hygin*. Paris.

Maxwell, G. S. 1981. Agricola's campaigns: the evidence of the temporary camps. In J. Kenworthy (ed.), *Agricola's Campaigns in Scotland*. Scottish Archaeological Forum XII. Edinburgh, 25–54.

—— 1995. Map-making in Roman Scotland: from Marinus to the military survey. *Proceedings of the Society of Antiquaries of Scotland*, 125, 1199.

—— 1998. *A Gathering of Eagles*. Edinburgh.

—— 2003. Size matters: a review of small camps and temporary camp annexes in Scotland and northern England. In G. B. Dannell (ed.), *Papers Presented to K. F. Hartley*.

Mercer, R. J. and Tipping, R. 1994. The prehistory of soil erosion in the northern and eastern Cheviot hills, Anglo-Scottish borders. In S. Foster and T. C. Smout (eds), *The History of Soils and Field Systems*. Aberdeen, 1–25.

Philpott, R. A. 1998. New evidence from aerial reconnaissance for Roman military sites in Cheshire. *Britannia*, 29, 341–53.

Pitts, L. F. and St Joseph, J. K. S. 1985. *Inchtuthil*. Britannia Monograph Series 6. London.

Richmond, I. A. and McIntyre, J. 1934. The Roman camps at Rey Cross and Crackenthorpe. *Transactions of the Cumberland and Westmorland Antiquarian and Archaeological Society*, ser. 2, 34, 50–61.

Rivet, A. L. F. and Smith, C. 1979. *The Place-names of Roman Britain*. London.

Roy, W. 1793. *The Military Antiquities of the Romans in North Britain*. London.

Royal Commission on the Ancient and Historical Monuments of Scotland. 1978. *Lanarkshire: An Inventory of the Prehistoric and Roman Monuments*. Edinburgh.

—— 1994. *South-east Perth: An Archaeological Landscape*. Edinburgh.

—— 1997. *Eastern Dumfriesshire: An Archaeological Landscape*. Edinburgh.

Royal Commission on Ancient and Historical Monuments in Wales. 1986. *An Inventory of the Ancient Monuments in Brecknock (Brycheiniog): The Prehistoric and Roman Monuments, Part II: Hill-forts and Roman Remains*. Cardiff.

St Joseph, J. K. S. 1973. Air reconnaissance in Roman Britain, 1969–72. *Journal of Roman Studies*, 63, 214–46.

—— 1976. Air reconnaissance in Roman Scotland, 1939–75. *Glasgow Archaeological Journal*, 4, 1–28.

—— 1977. Air reconnaissance in Roman Britain, 1973–76. *Journal of Roman Studies*, 67, 125–61.

—— 1978. The camp at Durno and Mons Graupius. *Britannia*, 9, 271–88.

Sargent, A. 2002. The north–south divide revisited: thoughts on the character of Roman Britain. *Britannia*, 33, 219–26.

Smout, T. C. (ed.) 1993. *Scotland since Prehistory: Natural Change and Human Impact*. Aberdeen.

Tipping, R. 1999. Towards an environmental history of the Bowmont valley and the northern Cheviot Hills. *Landscape History*, 20, 41–50.

Van der Veen, M. 1992. *Crop Husbandry Regimes: An Archaeological Study of Farming in Northern England, 1000 BC–AD 5000*. Sheffield Archaeological Monographs 3. Sheffield.

Watkins, T. 1981. Excavation of a settlement and a souterrain at Newmill, near Bankfoot, Perthshire. *Proceedings of the Society of Antiquaries of Scotland*, 110, 165–208.

Welfare, H. and Swan, V. 1995. *Roman Camps in England: The Field Archaeology*. London.

Whittington, G. and Edwards, K. J. 1993. *Ubi solitudinem faciunt, pacem appellant*: the Romans in Scotland, a palaeo-environmental solution. *Britannia*, 24, 13–25.

CHAPTER SEVEN

Soldier and Civilian in Wales

JEFFREY DAVIES

The frontier in the west, dormant since the early sixties, suddenly awoke with the launching of a series of campaigns which within the span of three or four years was to bring about the conquest of the whole of Wales. Tacitus' account of these operations is eulogistic: 'But when Vespasian in the course of his general triumph, restored stable government to Britain, there came a succession of great generals and splendid armies, and the hopes of our enemies dwindled' (*Agricola*, 17).

Certainly the situation in Britain as a whole was transformed. For the first time since Claudius' reign we have undisputed evidence that an emperor planned for a total rather than a limited conquest of Britain (Jarrett 1994a: 8). While we cannot entirely rule out late Neronian military activity in Wales, other factors – specifically the withdrawal of Legio XIV in 66/7 – militated against a resumption of large-scale operations, and the quiescence of the Welsh tribes was probably achieved by a combination of diplomacy and threat. Nero's suicide was followed by civil war, and the outbreak of hostilities with the Brigantes delayed matters still further. Wales had to wait until their subjugation by Petillius Cerealis (71–73/4), the first of Tacitus' 'great generals'. His successor, Julius Frontinus (73/4–77) was certainly mandated to resolve unfinished business in Wales. The fuller account of his operations in the *Histories* is, unfortunately, lost. We are merely informed that, 'He subdued by force of arms the strong and warlike tribe of the Silures, after a hard struggle, not only against the valour of his enemy, but against the difficulties of the terrain.' Behind Tacitus' hyperbole lies the harsh reality of a conquest which had eluded Rome for a generation; the seizure or destruction of crops and livestock and the imposition of harsh penalties on those communities whose resistance was either too protracted or successful. Though only the Silures are recorded as having been conquered by him, a reference to the stationing of a cavalry regiment among the Ordovices and the appearance of forts in the far south-west – Demetian lands – indicates that the geographical extent of operations was much wider. Tacitus' focus upon the Silures simply serves to indicate that these, among the most famous of British tribes – their name being frequently applied to south Wales in general – were Frontinus' principal foes. He would have undoubtedly recognized the necessity of attempting total conquest if possible.

The role of Julius Agricola (77–83) is more problematic and the subject of extensive debate (Hanson 1987: 46–54). The Tacitean account (*Agricola*, 18) is detailed but rhetorical; a punitive campaign, utilizing a scratch force, against Ordovician rebels in the autumn of 77, followed by an equally hastily planned but successful seizure of Anglesey. Hanson warns us against overestimating the magnitude of the Ordovician problem just because Tacitus makes much of the situation. The Ordovices' fate was near annihilation, but whether this refers to their fighting men or the community at large is impossible to tell. The location and the extent of Ordovician territory has figured large in the debate since it has been said that the unpremeditated extension of operations to the far north-west of Wales would hardly have been justified, or even feasible, unless Ordovician territory lay close to Anglesey (Hanson 1987: 46–7). Other evidence suggests a mid-Wales location for the tribe (Jarrett and Mann 1969). Certainly, the capture of Anglesey was a prerequisite for the control of Snowdonia, since it functioned as the local granary and a refuge for dissidents, while its mineral deposits may also have been an influential factor. The campaign appears to have brought operations in Wales to a close, and represents the last record of resistance by the native population. If there were subsequent operations they are unrecorded. There can be little doubt that some of the Snowdonia forts – Caernarfon, Pen Llystyn and Caerhun in particular – must be attributed to Agricola, since their coexistence with an unassailed Anglesey is scarcely credible. As for the remainder of the Flavian forts in mid and north Wales, none have produced material which is sufficiently diagnostic to differentiate between a foundation under Frontinus or Agricola. Dendrochronology may hold the key to their dating.

A precondition of successful campaigning was the gathering of forces and supplies at key points, and the building of strategic bases both to project military power into hostile territory and to retain effective control over that which had been won. To this end, legionary fortresses had been established in the fifties at Wroxeter and Usk. Overwhelming force was now brought to bear on the Welsh front in the early seventies; no fewer than three of the British legions, XX, II Augusta and II Adiutrix, the last recently arrived in Britain, participated in the campaigns. Strategic concerns dictated that a new fortress be established by II Adiutrix at Chester in the lower Dee valley, thereby facilitating operations into north Wales or along the western margin of the Pennines and newly annexed Brigantia. Usk, bereft of its legion since about 67, though not apparently abandoned (Manning 1981: 50), was replaced by a new fortress for II Augusta within the tidal reach of the river at Caerleon. Dendrochronology indicates the felling of timber for its building in the winter of 73/4.

These events represent part of some complex legionary movements in the two decades following the withdrawal of Legio XIV from Britain, and its short-lived return in 69, involving the movement of Legio XX, II Augusta and II Adiutrix, together with the foundation and closure of fortresses from south-western England to Scotland, including Exeter, Gloucester, Usk, Caerleon, Chester and Inchtuthil. Scholarly opinion is still sharply divided as to the precise movement of these units since archaeological evidence can be manipulated to fit a number of theories (Hassall 2000). Indeed, the more evidence that is unearthed then the more complex the picture becomes, as is illustrated by the sequence at Gloucester which seemingly perpetuates activity by Legio XX into the mid-eighties. On balance Wroxeter (perhaps occupied by Legio XX) is unlikely to have been abandoned until campaigning was over, while Chester and Caerleon were certainly in building in the mid-seventies.

Reconstructing the course of Flavian campaigning in Wales is a difficult and tentative exercise in the absence of literary evidence. It is dependent upon the recognition and interpretation of archaeological data: the temporary camps and the operational bases. The fact that the army had been campaigning intermittently in Wales for a generation meant that they must have accumulated a considerable body of geographical knowledge and details of the strengths and weaknesses of the opposition. Real and potential campaigning routes must have been mapped out and the practicalities of combined operations – the use of the fleet, if only for the supply of the army in the field – must have been considered. The coastal/estuarine position of forts such as Neath, Loughor and Carmarthen may be significant in this respect. When operations were launched between 73/4 and 77 the Roman columns utilized routes reconnoitred and even used before – the Usk valley, the upper Wye, upper Severn, Dee and the north and south coasts – though the evidence of marching-camps signifies new routes being exploited by forces thrusting into the interior via the difficult terrain posed by the south and mid-Wales valleys. The camps survive as earthworks in the uplands, or they are seen as lowland crop-marks, but they are relatively few in number and probably unrepresentative of the total built. The majority have been destroyed by agriculture or other developments, and new camps are likely to be found only in conditions favourable to crop-mark formation and the application of intensive aerial reconnaissance. Distinguishing between camps of the pre-Flavian and Flavian era is fraught with difficulty, though it is a reasonable supposition that those in close proximity to Flavian forts are likely to be contemporary: for example, at Coelbren and Caerau in the south and Tomen y Mur in the north (Arnold and Davies 2000: 13–15).

Reconstructing the course of operations on the basis of such scanty evidence is difficult, though a comparison of camp size and spatial relationships can prove instructive. For example; three camps in close proximity to one another in the upper reaches of the Wye – Cwm Nant, Esgairperfedd and Trefal – and of similar size (15.6–18 acres) suggest the passage of battle-groups of approximately 5000 men north, or south along a hitherto unsuspected route linking the upper Wye and the Severn. In Snowdonia Pen y Gwryd and Derwin-bach may also be linked on grounds of size (10 acres), such modest-sized camps being in keeping with the forces that could be effectively deployed in difficult terrain. While it is tempting to assign them to Agricola's autumnal campaign, such an association must be entirely speculative. It is notable that there is a distinct lack of camps exceeding about 40 acres in Wales (Blaen-cwm-bach at 62acres being the largest) in contrast to the sometimes much larger Flavian camps in Scotland. The differential probably reflects the topography and also the nature of resistance, expected as well as real.

As soon as field operations were over the army set about consolidating its hold on the newly conquered territory, establishing a network of auxiliary forts and ancillary structures at key points, on average 17 to 20 kilometres apart. While pre-Flavian forts had been designed to block egress from the uplands, the new network was designed to control the native population. The majority were thus situated in key valley positions, or to supervise a shadowy upland population and at the same time control vital communication routes between the coast and the interior. Others encircled as

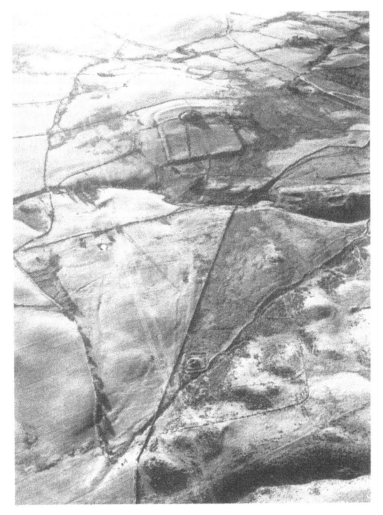

Figure 7.1   Tomen-y-Mur (Merioneth) from the south-west. The corners of two successive marching-camps are visible in the foreground. The medieval earthwork castle straddles the site of the north-west gate of the reduced fort (© RCAHMW).

well as penetrating mountain fastnesses such as Snowdonia. While the majority were new foundations, some existing sites were retained, as at Cardiff, Abergavenny and Hindwell Farm. Those irrelevant to the new strategic requirements were either soon closed or replaced, sometimes demonstrating site-shift as, for example, Jay Lane/ Leintwardine/Buckton. There is some evidence to suggest that some forts had larger precursors, sometimes of unknown size, as at Neath (Marvell and Heywood 1992) and Llandovery, while Llanfor and Llwyn y brain may be the precursors of standard *castella* at Caer Gai and Caersws. This early phase of fort building may be broadly contemporary with campaigning, when large forts housing a number of units, or mixed garrisons, may have been built in preference to the classic *castellum*. There is

Figure 7.2 Caerau (Beulah)(Brecon) from the north-east. The circuit of the original fort defences and reducing defences, visible immediately before the outbuildings of the farm, highlighted in low sunlight (© RCAHMW).

little evidence that the fort builders actually displaced indigenous communities, though at Caernarfon, Pen Llystyn (Hogg 1969: 107–9) and Brithdir there is evidence for late prehistoric occupation, but whether that continued to the seventies is not known.

Wherever necessary, fortlets were built instead of forts, sometimes controlling vital river crossings as at Pen-min-cae. There is also some evidence that timber towers set within semicircular or squarish emplacements – hitherto known only in Flavian contexts in northern England and Scotland – were used to observe traffic and signal the nearest garrison, as at Carreg y Bwci (J. L. Davies 1986). They are difficult to detect and their frequency remains to be determined.

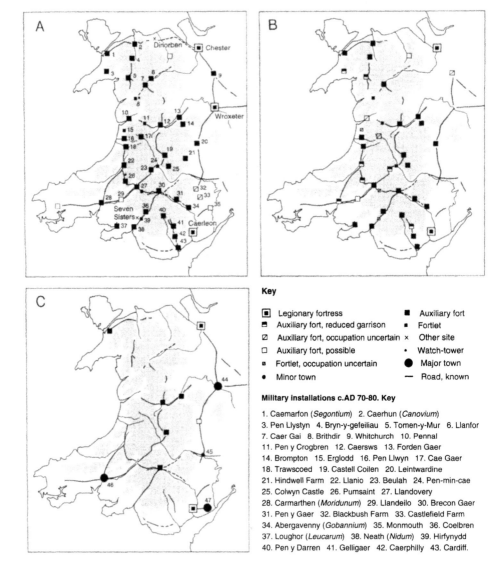

Key

▣	Legionary fortress	■	Auxiliary fort
▣	Auxiliary fort, reduced garrison	▪	Fortlet
▨	Auxiliary fort, occupation uncertain	×	Other site
▢	Auxiliary fort, possible	∙	Watch-tower
▫	Fortlet, occupation uncertain	●	Major town
●	Minor town	—	Road, known

Military installations c.AD 70-80. Key

1. Caernarfon (*Segontium*) 2. Caerhun (*Canovium*)
3. Pen Llystyn 4. Bryn-y-gefeiliau 5. Tomen-y-Mur 6. Llanfor
7. Caer Gai 8. Brithdir 9. Whitchurch 10. Pennal
11. Pen y Crogbren 12. Caersws 13. Forden Gaer
14. Brompton 15. Erglodd 16. Pen Llwyn 17. Cae Gaer
18. Trawscoed 19. Castell Coilen 20. Leintwardine
21. Hindwell Farm 22. Llanio 23. Beulah 24. Pen-min-cae
25. Colwyn Castle 26. Pumsaint 27. Llandovery
28. Carmarthen (*Moridunum*) 29. Llandeilo 30. Brecon Gaer
31. Pen y Gaer 32. Blackbush Farm 33. Castlefield Farm
34. Abergavenny (*Gobannium*) 35. Monmouth 36. Coelbren
37. Loughor (*Leucarum*) 38. Neath (*Nidum*) 39. Hirfynydd
40. Pen y Darren 41. Gelligaer 42. Caerphilly 43. Cardiff.

Figure 7.3 **a** Military installations *c.* AD 70–80. **b** Military installations *c.* AD 100–120.
c Military installations *c.* AD 160.

While the distribution of garrison posts clearly maps out the areas deemed trouble-some, areas hitherto regarded as occupied by communities well disposed towards Rome, such as the Demetae, have produced forts; for example, Carmarthen and possibly Llandeilo, while the discovery of a road running forty kilometres west of the former suggests that at least one other remains to be discovered in west Wales. The situation among the Deceangli is more problematical since, despite hints of such a building at Ruthin, no certain forts are known between the Dee and the Conwy. Whether they remain to be discovered, or the area had been pacified between the fifties and seventies, is open to question.

We can sum up the situation in early Flavian Wales as it presents itself to the archaeologist in the following terms. An army of occupation of three legions and about thirty-five auxiliary units was ingeniously deployed about those areas that had either offered resistance or were deemed potentially troublesome. However, this intensive phase of garrisoning was relatively short-lived.

Surprisingly little is known of the internal arrangements, and hence the garrisons, of the earth and timber forts of Flavian era. It is only when their buildings were converted into 'stone' that we gain some insight into their planning. Excavations at Caernarfon (Casey and Davies 1993) and Loughor (Marvell and Owen-John 1997) detected primary timber buildings, but work was limited and no comprehensive timber fort plans have appeared since rescue work at Pen Llystyn in the sixties. Nevertheless, a rich corpus of information is available concerning the siting and planning of forts of the Conquest era. Attempting to identify garrison types by simply matching the number of men in a unit to the size of the fort is a risky exercise, since it is quite possible that similar units may not have built forts of equal size. Caernarfon, the largest fort in north-west Wales at 5.6 acres(2.27 hectares), seems to have housed a milliary cohort. Pen Llystyn at 4.5 acres seems to have been occupied by two brigaded quingenary cohorts (Hassall 1983: 119), whereas on grounds of size a single equitate cohort might be deemed a more suitable garrison. With its 'parrot's beak' type gates (ditches incurving and uniting on either side of the entrance to create a funnelled approach), this fort may the handiwork of Legio II Adiutrix (Maxwell 1998: 40). It remains the only example in a region where this legion, based at Chester, might be expected to operate. Brecon Gaer, Caersws and Forden, at about 8 acres, are much larger than the norm and were probably designed to house composite garrisons. Thereafter, their garrisons could change. Brecon Gaer accommodated the 500-strong Ala Hispanorum Vettonum at the turn of the century. It is also unique among Welsh forts in the possession of a forehall spanning the *via principalis*, though not symmetrical about the axis of the *principia* as is normally the case. Common in forts along the German frontier from the later first century, though much less so in Britain, forehalls can be shown to have been connected either with *alae* or with equitate regiments (Johnson 1983: 120–6; Bidwell 1999: 89), but whether the Vettonians were at Brecon when the forehall was built is impossible to say. Two of the Welsh forts, Gelligaer II and Caerhun, have long been considered as type-sites (that is, a correlation between fort plan with unit type has been acknowledged) and this has given rise to a lively debate as to the veracity of the exercise (Hassall 1983). Recent work at Wallsend (Bidwell 1999: 85–8), clarifying the requirements of stabling, has almost certainly vindicated Caerhun's claim to have housed a *cohors quingenaria equitata*, though not necessarily in the Flavian period. It is only when epigraphic material becomes available in the second century that garrison identities emerge, for example, Coh I Nerviorum at Caer Gai and Coh II Asturum at Llanio. Curiously, the only cavalry regiment certainly known in Wales in the Flavian period, Ala I Thracum, is attested at Caerleon (*RIB* II, 2145.39), where it may have been conceivably brigaded with the legion. It had certainly left south Wales by 124 (Jarrett 1994b: 44).

All forts had external garrison bath-houses, the most complete excavated examples being those at Castell Collen, Caerhun and Gelligaer (Nash-Williams 1969: 165–72). Many forts had annexes, sometimes housing complex, stone courtyard buildings termed *mansiones*, almost certainly linked to the operation of the *cursus publicus*. Tomen y Mur is unique among Welsh forts in the possession of a *ludus*, an earthen amphitheatre (Nash-Williams 1969: 174), an amenity now increasingly recognized in northern Britain, and also a levelled area probably functioning as a parade-ground (Nash-Williams 1969: 111–13), thereby echoing facilities outside the legionary fortresses (Boon 1987: 16).

The total number of forts occupied in the aftermath of campaigning is of the order of thirty-two to thirty-five, and second-century 'diploma' evidence (Nash-Williams 1969: 14–16) suggest that they fell under the administrative control of the legionary legates, reduced to two following the closure of Wroxeter. Legionary brick-stamps (*RIB* II 2459.1–71; 24631–64) indicate that Chester 'command' (also embracing north-west England) extended as far west as Caernarfon and south to Caersws in the upper Severn; Caerleon command to Brecon Gaer, though epigraphic evidence indicates its extension north to Castell Collen. There were thus 8000 auxiliaries in the Caerleon command in AD 103, somewhat fewer in Chester command in AD 98–105. These are too few to have garrisoned all the known forts, and the implication is that either the Welsh garrison had been substantially reduced by then, or forts housed detachments rather than complete units.

The backbone of the strategic system was the legionary fortresses at Wroxeter, Chester and Caerleon. Wroxeter, useful in the context of the campaigning phase, was destined for replacement by Chester, closure being delayed only for as long as Legio XX was operating in Scotland. Unequivocal evidence of pre-Flavian occupation has still to be found at Chester, current work indicating only that a possible temporary camp and a few timber buildings occupied its site (Mason 2001: 31–3). At 60.9acres, the fortress is 20 per cent larger than either Caerleon or York, and Mason suggests that it had a special function, demonstrable by special buildings, including a stone elliptical structure and another with a huge courtyard arrangement, which added a complete range to the *latera praetorii* of the fortress. These, he suggests, formed part of an administrative and cult quarter possibly linked with the person of the governor of the province (Mason 2000: 76–80; 2001, 93–8). Work on the elliptical building was still in progress in 79, but stopped with the advance into Scotland, only being revived and completed, though to a different plan, in the third century. The baths, granaries and possibly the fortress' walls and gates, were of stone from an early date, though the majority of its buildings, including the barracks and the external amphitheatre, were initially of timber. Some evidence of building renewal has been assigned to the handover of the base to Legio XX in the late eighties (Mason 2001: 128ff.).

Caerleon, like Chester on the banks of a navigable river, replaced Usk, and was built by Legio II Augusta (Boon 1987). Its primary defences were in earthwork and timber, and the majority of its buildings were of wood, though, as at Chester, some of the principal buildings, the *principia*, baths and a *fabrica*, were in stone from the outset. Where primary occupation has been claimed, for example, barracks with cobble footings, these can now be shown to be not earlier than *c.*85–100 (Brewer 2000: 33). An officer's house, datable to *c.*75, on the Museum site, was entirely of timber.

Just as significant from the point of view of exercising control over the conquered was the construction of an all-weather communication system. Although a road

Figure 7.4 Caerleon (Monmouthshire) from the south showing the site of the legionary fortress wall, south corner, and amphitheatre and the Prysg Field barracks near the west corner. The area occupied by modern housing (top right) and the Afon Lwyd (in trees) was occupied by part of the *canabae*, as was a large area between the R. Usk (bottom right) and the southern and south-western defences (© RCAHMW).

network had already linked the legionary fortresses and forts of the pre-Flavian era, one of the most dramatic repercussions of the conquest was the building of a minimum of some 1100 to 1200 kilometres of roads and numerous bridges linking the newly established garrison bases with those already in existence. They were designed to allow the rapid movement not so much of troops as of supplies, since only some 25 per cent of the bases could be supplied by sea. It was a formidable task and a long-drawn-out process, pushed through despite some atrocious terrain, as illustrated north of Caersws and south-east of Caer Gai, where two converging roads head towards a fort yet to be discovered in this wild country, possibly in the Banwy valley. Elsewhere, and contrary to received wisdom, roads were raised on an embank-ment (*agger*) in the flood plains of the major river valleys such as the Severn and Tywi. There are obvious gaps in the network, some of which, as in the case of the isolated small fort of Cae Gaer, may relate to unfinished schemes resulting from the abandon-ment of some forts after a brief occupation. However, it is through diligent fieldwork tracing their course that 'missing' installations may be discovered, thereby determin-ing whether some parts of Wales really were devoid of a military presence. As for their dating, our earliest milestone, from near Caerhun, is of 121 (*RIB* II, 2265), though this is more likely to relate to repair than construction. Outside the fort at Llanio the road overlies some of the earliest *vicus* buildings, though others, still Flavian in date, are aligned upon it (Davies 1994: 305).

While they may have seen much military traffic up to the Hadrianic period, usage may have declined rapidly thereafter, though the transportation of minerals and civilian traffic ensured the upkeep of some, particularly the north and south coastal routes, the Severn and Usk valley roads, and those linking Caerleon to Gloucester and Chester, long thereafter. By this time their upkeep will have become the responsibility of the civilian *civitates. Mansiones*, frequently forming part of military complexes, may well have remained in use long after the abandonment of a fort, possibly accommo-dating outposted soldiers – *stationarii* – in supervisory or administrative duties along some of the key routes (Arnold and Davies 2000: 28). This may account for the presence of later material on some forts. Certainly the road network is perhaps the most eloquent and certainly the most enduring product of the Flavian conquest, surviving long after the army had relinquished its hold over the country, as testified by third- or fourth-century milestones and roadside burials of the Early Christian period.

The Flavian military network represents the apogee of the Roman system for controlling newly conquered territory. But the impression conveyed is of an over-garrisoned region that required reduction as soon as conditions allowed. Once the situation had stabilized there were minimal changes in the overall location of the garrisons, Bryn y Gefeiliau in Snowdonia, founded about 90, being an exception. But once the decision had been taken to advance into Scotland, a policy of gradual garrison reduction was initiated, continuing well into the second century and beyond. Wales soon ceased to house the largest element of the British garrison. That distinc-tion was to pass to northern Britain in the eighties.

The great offensive against the peoples north of the Tyne–Solway line, which dominated the scene between 79 and about 86/7, necessitated the withdrawal of troops from Welsh bases, sometimes for good, since not only was there a need to field an army but also to garrison northern territories. The bulk of Legio XX and certainly detachments of II Adiutrix and II Augusta must have accompanied Agricola in the northern advance. With auxiliaries it was normal to remove the whole unit. But with Wales only recently conquered, such a move would have been risky, so redeployment north may have been accomplished by selective withdrawals or the division of some regiments and their posting as detachments to garrison other forts, as is attested at Chesterholm at the turn of the century (Bowman 1994: 22–3). This would have maintained an effective military presence in key areas without the high-risk strategy involved in the abandonment of forts so soon after the conquest. The abandonment of most of Scotland by about 90 will have released a number of units – less those which accompanied Legio II Adiutrix to the Danube – to return to their Welsh bases, and archaeological traces of demolition and replacement of barrack accommodation within forts at Caernarfon, Trawscoed and Caersws, or even the replacement of one fort by another on a different axis, as at Neath, could be interpreted as a result of this activity. On the other hand, forts such as Hindwell Farm could be given up for good, having outlived their usefulness. Wroxeter too was abandoned soon after 87; Legio XX replacing II Adiutrix at Chester.

The subsequent story is of the steady decrease in the size of the Welsh auxiliary garrison as conditions permitted, until it ceased to represent a heavily militarized zone by the second quarter of the second century. The legionary presence was still substantial to the mid-third century, if not beyond, but as we shall see, legionary bases had a function beyond their immediate region or even province.

The process of thinning out the auxiliary garrison accelerated in response to the need of redeploying manpower to participate in Trajan's Dacian Wars of 101–2 and 105–6, and also to northern Britain now that the frontier region was itself being stripped of troops. Thereafter the outbreak of war in northern Britain at the beginning of Hadrian's reign, coupled with the start of Wall-building operations, themselves possibly halted by another war about 125–6, provide significant contexts for the movement of auxiliary regiments out of Wales. Historical episodes such as these are probably reflected in the histories of individual Welsh forts, though chronological precision, let alone specific contexts, remain elusive. It was certainly within the earlier part of Hadrian's reign that the process of disengagement reached its climax, and though the dates at which individual forts were abandoned must have varied there are hints that some may have been synchronous, probably the result of a decision to disengage on a regional basis. It was not only military factors that came into play. The granting of *civitas* status to the Silures by about 120 (Brewer 1993: 65), and to the Demetae not long thereafter (James 1992: 15), must have been a critical factor in explaining, at least in part, the decision to abandon forts in south Wales. In the south-west, the abandonment sequences seem to be Trajanic at Carmarthen, early Hadrianic at Trawscoed, Llanio, Llandovery and Pumsaint, with the latest archaeological deposits frequently indicative of demolition and orderly withdrawal. In the south-east Loughor, Neath, Pen y Darren, Gelligaer, Caerphilly and Pen y Gaer were all abandoned by about 130 at latest, and those sites that remained, Neath, Abergavenny and Cardiff, though yielding later Hadrianic and Antonine material, do not produce the quantities that one might expect of a full or long-term occupation.

The process of thinning out the auxiliary garrison was achieved in a number of ways, ranging from outright closure to a reduction in the size of a fort's garrison, a process that may be archaeologically reflected in the most graphic form by a reduction in the size of the defended perimeter, normally involving the abandonment of the *retentura* and the construction of a new defence perimeter as at Tomen y Mur (Nash-Williams 1969: 11–13) and Caerau (Nash-Williams 1969: 46–8), or reduction to a fortlet as at Pumsaint and Pen Llystyn (Hogg 1968: 148–55), or by means of an internal rearrangement as at Caernarfon (Casey and Davies 1993: 12). Uniquely, the sequence at Gelligaer involved the construction of a brand new, smaller fort close to the old, in the period 103–11 (Nash-Williams 1969: 88–91). While reduction to a fortlet allowed a much greater dispersal of men through outposting small detachments, the same result could be achieved by retaining the original perimeter but accommodating a smaller unit or part of a unit, as at Caernarfon. The history of the fort at Chesterholm, which at the beginning of the second century had its garrison split unequally between it and *Coria*, should serve as a salutary warning against assuming that forts always accommodated complete units (Bowman 1994: 22–3). However, some forts, such as the one at Castell Collen, appear to have been held in strength and it may well be that certain areas were regarded as potential or real trouble-spots.

The whole issue of dating garrison reduction and abandonment in the second century is fraught with problems, and while there need be no coincidence in size reduction or modifications to defences, since such events are most likely specific to the site in question, we tend to look to events outside Wales for answers. Very few Welsh forts were occupied after Hadrian's reign, and these were geographically restricted to mid- and north-west Wales, presumably retaining a policing cum administrative role. The fact that the majority could be abandoned, normally for good, makes it abundantly clear that, by the latter part of Hadrian's reign, the Welsh tribes had accepted Roman rule. But the greater part of Wales lacked the normal administrative framework based upon the tribal *civitas*, even allowing for an inordinate extension of the *civitas* boundaries of the Cornovii, Demetae and Silures. The remaining forts may thus have provided a number of foci for an administrative framework vested in the army, such as that recorded for part of north-western England early in the second century: a system dependent upon the judico-administrative role of the *centurio regionarius*, such as Annius Equester, a senior legionary centurion, based upon Carlisle, a fort, not a town (Bowman 1994: 28). One might be permitted to speculate that the unparalleled sequence of buildings succeeding barracks, and culminating in a stone courtyard house of Hadrianic–Antonine date, within the fort at Caernarfon, may have been the residence of such an official rather than a *procurator metallum* as suggested by Casey and Davies (1993: 13–14).

Clearly, unlocking the secret of Trajanic–Hadrianic and later occupation on Welsh fort sites is going to be realized only by large-scale excavation and rigorous analysis of the finds assemblages. Small-scale work, while useful in providing a chronological snapshot, cannot reveal detailed information in respect of alterations to the internal arrangement of forts, particularly extreme changes involving the construction of non-standard buildings, as at Caernarfon.

It has long been recognized that prior to abandonment the defences and principal buildings of a number of forts had been replaced in stone, a process considered as having been initiated at the legionary fortresses. This was erroneously interpreted as 'confirming' the decision to maintain them, reflecting that 'permanence' hitherto considered lacking. This rebuilding was initially dated to the first decades of the second century on the basis of associated epigraphic and ceramic evidence. Following a recension it was assigned to the later Hadrianic/Antonine period (Simpson 1964). Since then the publication of excavations at Loughor (Marvell and Owen-John 1997), Penydarren and Neath has reset the chronological clock once more. Stone rebuilds of both defences and selected internal buildings can occur any time from the Trajanic period onwards, and quite independently of one another. As far as the fortresses are concerned, we have already seen that some of their buildings were of stone from the outset. Moreover, rebuilding in stone was a piecemeal affair; stone defences could well have been initiated in the late first century and completed early under Trajan, though the *principia* at Caerleon may not have been completed until the late second century. Some of the stone barracks at Caerleon, formerly dated to the Antonine period, may also be earlier than previously thought (Brewer 2000: 33). At Chester some of the barracks had already been replaced in stone in the Trajanic era, but elsewhere, as in the *retentura*, rebuilding seems to have been halted, or at least postponed, until after about 160, the product of the absence of much of the legion from its base.

The history of the fortresses is at variance with those of the auxiliary forts, being retained long after the areas they were designed to watch were pacified. Certainly as far as II Augusta is concerned, its presence in south Wales after the Antonine period was an anachronism, since by then it was remote from any serious threat. Its continued existence is best explained partly by the forces of military inertia and by the fact that it formed a strategic reserve. In the aftermath of the division of Britain under Caracalla, as one of the legions in Britannia Superior it also represented a key piece in the balance of power. Chester and Caerleon remained as their units' administrative headquarters, supply and maintenance depots, the base for legionary craftsmen and engineers whose skills could be used in a variety of capacities, particularly building away from base, but also as bases for detachments (vexillations) serving away from the parent body, normally for the duration of a campaign, sometimes for extended periods. We know that detachments of II Augusta and XX VV were serving in Domitian's German campaign of 82/3 (*ILS* 9200); a pattern of overseas service that was to continue to the third century, when a brigade of the two legions was serving in Gallienus' field army at Mainz and then Sirmium in 258 (*CIL* XIII 6780; III 3228). More significant from a British standpoint is the evidence for the large-scale deployment of these legionaries in northern Britain (Breeze 1989). Epigraphy demonstrates that men from II Augusta and XX VV played a key role in the building of the Hadrianic and Antonine Walls, and in campaigning preceding and post-dating the construction of these frontier works. After participating in Septimius Severus' operations in Scotland (208–11) II Augusta was involved in the construction of the fortress at Carpow on the Tay. Thereafter brigaded vexillations of the two legions formed a quasi-independent unit in Britannia Inferior for much of the third century. In addition to vexillation duties, individual officers and men served in a variety of capacities, as temporary commanding officers of auxiliary units and on the staff of the governor at London. Archaeological evidence from Chester and Caerleon provides a solid body of data attesting to the effects of frequent, long-term absences of large bodies of men. The halting or postponement of rebuilding barracks in stone in the *retentura* at Chester is attested from the 120s, while the production of legionary tiles at Tarbock in 167 and their discovery within the fortress suggests a project to reroof individual barracks in readiness for the return of absent detachments (Swan and Philpott 2000). At Caerleon too there is minimal evidence of occupation in some so-called Antonine barracks (Brewer 2000: 33 n. 80).

The second half of the second century undoubtedly saw a further diminution in the already slim auxiliary garrison. Only Caernarfon, Caersws, Forden, Castell Collen, Brecon Gaer and possibly Leintwardine continued in occupation into the reign of Marcus and beyond, and though their individual histories vary considerably, one fact that they seem to share in common is a smaller garrison. For example, at Brecon Gaer

Figure 7.5 Castell Collen (Radnorshire) from the north. The excavated remains of the stone *praetorium, principia* and a granary can still be seen in the central portion of a fort which has been reduced in size. The two circular feeding-troughs (extreme right) mark the line of the earlier defences (© RCAHMW).

a small, internal bath replaced the external bath-house and served a smaller unit to the 260s (Wheeler 1926: 49–51). But not all were run down. The defences at Forden were massively refurbished sometime after 150, while at Castell Collen an intensive phase of occupation continued to the third century (Britnell et al. 1999), and the fort may have been in receipt of reinforcements in the form of Sarmatian horsemen, historically attested as having been settled in Britain by Marcus about 175. The retention of these forts, even if only on a spasmodic and lightly manned basis, is difficult to explain in the context of the crises – Continental and British – that periodically affected the Welsh garrison. It indicates a real concern for security, but it remains unclear as to whether this was on the grounds of an incipient threat to more peaceable communities such as the Cornovii, or the necessity of policing a region prone to inter-clan feuding or brigandage, coupled with the need to provide security for the storage of taxes in kind with the institution of the *annona militaris* in the third century. Soldiers, probably legionary *beneficiarii*, were stationed at certain key points to fulfil these duties, and where else in upland districts but at forts or *mansiones?* As for those southern forts that produce a little Antonine material, such as Gelligaer and Neath, occupation, already attenuated, certainly ended before the middle of the century.

Figure 7.6   Caersws (Montgomery) from the south. Parch-marks show part of the street-grid within the fort. The wider parch-mark issuing out of the east gate represents one of the main streets within the *vicus* (see fig 7.8) (© RCAHMW).

The third century represents a watershed in the history of the Welsh garrison. The return of troops to base after the Severan campaigns is represented by considerable rebuilding, particularly of barracks, within Chester and Caerleon in the first quarter of the third century, commencing with the production of bricks bearing *ANTO* stamps of the period 212–22 (*RIB* II 2459.54–60; 2463.51–3). Extensive building work at Caerleon is also attested at the amphitheatre and riverside quay, but at the same time some barracks in the *retentura* were apparently no longer occupied, attesting to the absence of two full cohorts (Casey and Hoffmann 1995). Certainly, rebuilding and repair continued as and where necessary. Two barracks at Myrtle Cottage, Caerleon, showed signs of refurbishment and occupation continuing into the fourth century, while an inscription of 255–8 records the restoration of barracks of the Seventh Cohort (*RIB* I, 334). But in contrast, the diminution in the strength of the legion is graphically illustrated by the closure of the legionary baths about 230 (Zienkiewicz 1986: 49). Doubtless bathing facilities continued to be provided, but probably at the so-called Castle Baths or some other facility outside the defences. Chester also provides evidence of similarly intensive earlier third-century rebuilding, including that of the *principia, fabrica*, and bath-house as well as numerous barracks. Vacant plots were now occupied for the first time, and the enigmatic elliptical building and associated structures completed (Mason 2001: 160–92). The reopening of the

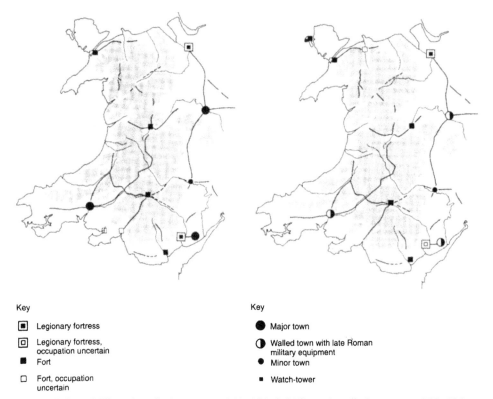

Key

▣	Legionary fortress
▢	Legionary fortress, occupation uncertain
■	Fort
□	Fort, occupation uncertain

Key

●	Major town
◑	Walled town with late Roman military equipment
●	Minor town
▪	Watch-tower

Figure 7.7 **a** Military installations *c.* AD 260–300. **b** Military installations *c.* AD 350–390.

legion's brick and tile works at Holt, inactive since the early Antonine period, is itself indicative of the scale of refurbishment at Chester (Grimes 1930; Swan and Philpott 2000: 62). However, a marked change had come over the military establishment in the later third century, with a dramatic reduction in the garrison caused by the withdrawal of troops from the quiet backwaters of the two British provinces for service on the Continent, the years 233–76 representing a potentially disastrous period of wars against 'new' peoples, Franks, Alamanni and Goths, exacerbated by dynastic struggles.

There was a dramatic decline in the strength of military units in this period, a legion eventually shrinking to 400 to 1000 men (Tomlin 2000: 169–73), auxiliary units to a few hundred at best. Castell Collen had certainly been abandoned by about the close of the third century, Forden certainly before the middle, while at Caernarfon, Caersws and Brecon the garrisons were very small. Again, the military input may have been largely focused on administrative duties rather than upon an incipient threat.

These changes, paralleling those in northern Britain, resulted in a dramatic decline in military strength and effectiveness at a time when internal strife and cross-frontier intrusions on the Continent were threatening irreparable fractures in the Imperial fabric, and when the British provinces, including western regions, were themselves coming under external threat for the first time. Prior to the last quarter of the century, there is no suggestion that military bases in Wales were designed for anything other than internal policing. It is only from the 270s that we have indications that the role of some, including sites possibly reactivated after long abandonment, changed to that of bases concerned with warding off external threats, specifically that of the *Hiberni* (Irish), now recorded as among the principal enemies of the Britons. At Caernarfon a scheme to revamp a fort showing all the signs of neglect was implemented, but not fully realized until about 330 or later, when the garrison was apparently increased (Casey and Davies 1993: 129). A further concern for littoral defence may be signalled at two old, estuarine fort sites, Neath (Marvell and Heywood 1992: 292) and Loughor (Marvell and Owen-John 1997: 227–8), which produce evidence of occupation from about 260 to 320, but whether that was military is unclear. The building of a 3.6-hectare fort, embodying the new architectural features of the later third century, massively thickened walls and bastions, at Cardiff sometime after about 260, might be considered proof positive of a reaction to an Irish sea-borne threat, mirroring contemporary activity on the south and southeast coasts of England, the late forts at Portchester and Lympne being close comparators. Recent discussion has emphasized their role within the context of military supply and the maintenance of communications, at the expense of their function as bases for soldiers and ships charged with the interception of cross-Channel raiders (Cotterill 1993). If, however, Cardiff did play a defensive role, blocking access to the rich urban and villa-dominated belt of the lower Severn region, then the system it represents could not have functioned effectively without some form of observation system on the sea-cliffs from the Gower peninsula to Cardiff Bay, a coastline which has, unfortunately, suffered severe erosion.

This period saw sweeping changes to military dispositions. Two inland forts, Caersws and Castell Collen, were abandoned, but more significant and problematical is what happened to the old legionary fortresses, Caerleon in particular. Numismatic and archaeological evidence combine to show a base in an advanced state of dereliction, the abandonment and dismantling of buildings, including the *principia*, being interpreted as signalling the virtual closure of the fortress under the usurper Carausius (286–93) (Boon 1987: 43–5), part of a long overdue reorganization, including the transfer of its surviving elements elsewhere, as already argued by Frere (1987: 175) in the case of a vexillation moved to Richborough under Probus (276–82). Other evidence has been interpreted as indicating the continuing use of some buildings (Evans and Metcalf 1992). While it is clear that the fortress had experienced drastic change (the abandonment of the Bulmore settlement being symptomatic), the debate revolves around the question of whether we are witnessing a rationalization of building usage within an enclosure vastly too large for a late legion, or abandonment by the military and a partial takeover by civilians, some of whom were engaged in demolition and salvage. The demolition of redundant structures, however, need not be inconsistent with the continued use of others, including barracks, to the fourth century. Numismatic evidence suggests that activity had ceased on virtually all sites after about 350, and final evacuation under Magnentius is possible. As for the fate of what remained of the legion we have to turn to the *Notitia Dignitatum*, where two components can be traced; one of limitatensian status at Richborough and the *Secundiani Iuniores* in the army of the *Comes Britanniarum*.

The Chester sequence post 300 (Mason 2001: 193–204) contrasts sharply with that at Caerleon. While some barracks had been demolished before the close of the third century, a large number, together with the major buildings, apparently continued in use. Part of the defences also shows signs of rebuilding about 300. After 350 the contrast with Caerleon is even more marked. Major buildings, including the baths, continued to be maintained, and Valentinianic coinage, virtually unknown at Caerleon, continued to circulate, the latest coins apparently being of the early 390s. However, Legio XX is not listed in the *Notitia* and its fate remains unknown.

Writing a coherent account of fourth-century military activity in Wales is difficult (R. W. Davies 1989: 55–6). What are we to make of the reoccupation of Forden, presumably by a unit of *limitanei* in the 360s? The answer must lie in the specific needs of certain critical areas, as at Caernarfon, which has the distinction of being one of the latest, if not the last, purpose-built garrison post to be occupied. Why was this? Was it simply the Irish threat? Certainly the mineral wealth of the north-west may have been a factor, while the construction of a 0.4-hectare walled enclosure, probably a stores depot, outside the fort sometime in the fourth century, testifies to its importance as a collection point for supplies.

Caernarfon did not stand in isolation. It is numismatically linked with a stone watchtower on Holyhead Mountain, the 'eyes' of the 0.32-hectare beach-head fortlet at Caer Gybi (Holyhead), possibly representing elements of an integrated, and perhaps more extensive system of coastal defences extending as far as Chester (Mason 2001: 208–9). Its abandonment can be linked to the withdrawal of troops by the usurper Eugenius in 392–3, which explains the non-appearance of Caernarfon and Chester in the *Notitia*, itself datable to *c.*395 (Casey and Davies 1993: 16).

Whether any elements of the British field-army were thereafter based upon the towns, as might be suggested by the extensive post-394 coinage from Caerwent, and items of military equipment (including *plumbatae*, the characteristic disarming weapon of the late army) from Caerwent and Wroxeter (Barker et al. 1997: 202–5), is unclear, but such a transient presence should occasion no surprise, since this was common practice. These units, billeted upon the townsfolk, drawing supplies from urban magazines, represent mobility rather than static defence and could operate with the same effectiveness as their early imperial forebears. It is these shadowy soldiers who represent the last stages in a military presence that had lasted for 350 years.

Though present in strength only to the reign of Hadrian, the army was omnipresent in some areas for a protracted period. Even in areas subjected to Romanizing influences in respect of urban development and rural lifestyles, there were major bases, such as Caerleon. Consequently, there existed a long-lasting and fruitful inter-relationship, amounting to a symbiosis, between military personnel and civilians at large, particularly in respect of those whose livelihood was dependent upon the army. While it is manifest that soldiers did not represent a Romanized community in terms of the cultural values and norms of the Mediterranean world, representing a distinct caste with their own codes of behaviour and set of values, their social and economic impact was nevertheless considerable, local recruitment leavening cultural distinctions in some areas.

In some respects that impact was enduring, the requirements of supplying the garrison being paramount. As an upland zone, Wales has never been noted for its propensity towards the production of food surpluses, least of all grain. Yet the Flavian–Trajanic garrison would have required about 7300 tonnes of wheat, the produce of 9830 or 21,000 acres, depending upon the calculated yield, and the Imperial administration aimed at local supply whenever possible. The impact upon the agricultural regime must therefore have been considerable, almost certainly involving bringing new land under cultivation, together with new crops such as bread wheat, whose presence is unknown before the Conquest. The army may then have indirectly accelerated certain trends within the Welsh agricultural regime. The grain requirement would have eventually fallen dramatically with the shrinkage of the garrison, and by the third century a local rather than a regional or provincial supply network may have prevailed. While the provision of animal products may not have tested the economy to the same extent, the trend towards beef consumption may have affected some local economies, with some producers raising cattle principally for their meat (J. L. Davies 1997).

The economic impact of the army is also manifest in other ways, for example, in respect of industrial processes and the marketing of consumer goods. While there is little evidence that the army was directly involved in the extraction of Welsh minerals, except for its own use, the incidence of brick-stamps of Legio XX on lead-silver processing settlements in north-east Wales is probably indicative of its responsibility for the provision of the infrastructure for such activity (Arnold and Davies 2000: 100–3), while a supervisory role, as perhaps at the Dolaucothi gold mines, may also have been prominent. As a consumer, the army attracted a vast range of commodities to its bases, and none so prominent as ceramics, which as both a container and a good represents the durable remains of a much more extensive trade in other commodities. As a good it was required in a variety of forms and in quantities that could not be obtained locally, most of Wales being aceramic prior to the Conquest (Lynch et al. 2000: 199–202). The genesis of pottery production in Wales can thus be traced to the needs of military supply, initially met by direct military production or the activity of immigrant potters working in the *vici* satisfying the needs of individual bases in the first century (Arnold and Davies 2000: 109–10). The genesis of the South Wales Grey Ware industry, a dominant second- to third-century product, together with other coarseware types, can be traced back to this military-inspired influx.

Nowhere is the military impact more graphically displayed than upon the settlement pattern. Dependants – merchants, craftsmen, the unofficial wives and children of serving soldiers, and increasingly veterans – formed an almost invariable adjunct to a military establishment. These extramural settlements, *canabae* in a legionary and a *vicus* in an auxiliary context, housed folk who earned a living by virtue of the spending power of the soldiers. While some *vici* represent little more than a ribbon development of rectangular buildings flanking extramural roads, others developed complex street-grids, as at Caersws, where it eventually encompassed an area twice the size of the fort (N. W. Jones 1993). A symbiotic existence meant that a reduction in the size of a garrison or the closure of a fort could prove deleterious, and the majority of *vici* were abandoned in Hadrian's reign. None survived beyond the third century, a feature that Welsh *vici* share with those on the northern frontier. While *vici* appear to have relatively brief lives, the settlements associated with the fortresses were more durable and undoubtedly had a proportionately greater impact upon the regional environment by virtue of size and longevity. At Caerleon (Evans 2000) and Chester

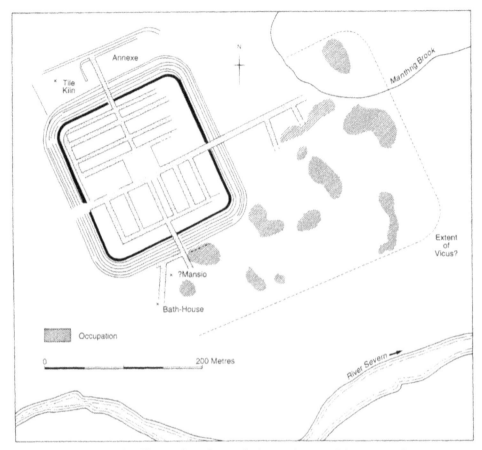

Figure 7.8   The auxiliary fort and *vicus* at Caersws (Montgomery).

(Mason 2001: 118–22) the *canabae* embraced the fortress on three sides, while satellite, roadside settlements developed some two kilometres distant at Bulmore and Heronbridge respectively. At about 35 hectares, the *canabae* at Caerleon dwarfed the 18-hectare tribal town of the Silures at Caerwent, while Chester's was probably of equivalent size and seems to have possessed a larger proportion of sophisticated 'public' and private buildings than Caerleon. The eastern part may have even been walled in the third century. While excavations have revealed much, there is a great deal to learn about the *canabae* and the satellites. If they were functionally towns, did they ever attain charted status, as is the case with some comparable Continental sites? What was the status of the apparently officially constituted satellite settlements at Bulmore and Heronbridge? Why was Bulmore apparently abandoned about 290 but occupation continued in the *canabae*? Was this a purely civilian settlement after 300?

We may close with reference to the tribal towns of the Silures and Demetae at Caerwent (*Venta Silurum*) and Carmarthen respectively, and to 'small towns' such as Cowbridge (Parkhouse and Evans 1996), since the army may have been indirectly responsible for their establishment. A military style bath-house and stamped bricks of II Augusta at Cowbridge could indicate a short-lived post in the heart of the Vale of

Glamorgan, followed by a classic ribbon-development of strip-buildings occupied to the fourth century. Caerwent (Brewer 1993) straddled the military road to Caerleon, fifteen kilometres distant, and a possible intersection with another to a ferry across the Severn at Sudbrook. Carmarthen developed next the site of a fort and *vicus*. While there need be no causal link between occupation continuing in the *vicus* following the abandonment of the fort and the foundation of the *civitas*, it is difficult to escape the conclusion that the military input in terms of infrastructure must have been a potent factor in the choice of site for the tribal town of *Moridunum* sometime after about 130 (James 1992). Such appears to have been the case at many other Romano-British urban settlements, though more graphically emphasized in a Welsh context by virtue of the sparsity of the phenomenon.

FURTHER READING

A comprehensive treatment of Wales in the Roman period has recently been published: C. J. Arnold and J. L. Davies, *Roman and Early Medieval Wales* (2000), whilst the late prehistoric background is reviewed in Lynch, *Prehistoric Wales* (2000). V. E. Nash-Williams, *The Roman Frontier in Wales*, revised by M. G. Jarrett (1969), remains the standard work on the garrison and its bases, though now well out of date, especially in respect of chronology and its treatment of the pre- and early Flavian period. However, the legionary fortresses have been the subjects of recent treatment. The definitive report on G. Webster's excavations at Wroxeter is imminent. Chester has a comprehensive volume of its own: D. J. P. Mason's *Roman Chester: City of the Eagles* (2001), while monographs treat the legionary defences and the elliptical building in detail. See C. LeQuesne, *Excavations at Chester. The Roman and Later Defences. Part 1* (1999) and D. J. P. Mason, *Excavations at Chester. The Elliptical Building* (2000). Unfortunately, no comparable discussion is available at present for Caerleon. G. C. Boon's guides, *Isca: The Roman Legionary Fortress at Caerleon, Monmouthshire* (1972) and *The Legionary Fortress of Caerleon-Isca* (1987) remain the standard, and complementary, works. For reports on individual components of the fortress, see: D. R. Evans and V. M. Metcalf, *Roman Gates: Caerleon* (1992); J. D. Zienkiewicz *The Legionary Fortress Baths at Caerleon* (1986). There are numerous reports on small-scale excavations at auxiliary forts and other installations, but A. G. Marvell and H. S. Owen-John, *Leucarum. Excavations at the Roman Auxiliary Fort at Loughor, West Glamorgan 1982–84 & 1987–88* (1997), and P. J. Casey and J. L. Davies, *Excavations at Segontium (Caernarfon) Roman Fort, 1975–79* (1993) are particularly noteworthy, the latter specifically in respect of the late Roman occupation. For a discussion of the significance of *vici*, see J. L. Davies, 'Military vici: recent research and its significance', in B. C. Burnham and J. L. Davies (eds), *Conquest, Coexistence and Change: Recent Work in Roman Wales*, Trivium 25 (1990), 65–74.

REFERENCES

Arnold, C. J. and Davies, J. L. 2000. *Roman and Early Medieval Wales*. Stroud.

Barker, P., White, R., Pretty, K., Bird, H. and Corbishley, M. 1997. *The Baths Basilica Wroxeter. Excavations 1966–90*. London.

Bidwell, P. (ed.) 1999. *Hadrian's Wall 1989–1999*. Kendal.

Boon, G. C. 1972. *Isca: The Roman Legionary Fortress at Caerleon, Monmouthshire*. Cardiff.

—— 1987. *The Legionary Fortress of Caerleon-Isca*. Cardiff.

Bowman, A. K. 1994. *Life and Letters on the Roman Frontier*. London.

Breeze, D. J. 1989. *The Second Augustan Legion in North Britain. The Second Annual Caerleon Lecture*. Cardiff.

Brewer, R. J. 1993. Venta Silurum: a civitas capital. In S. J. Greep (ed.), *Roman Towns: The Wheeler Inheritance*. London, 56–65.

—— 2000. Caerleon and the archaeologists: changing ideas on the Roman fortress, *Monmouthshire Antiquary*, 17, 9–33.

Britnell, J. E., Cool, H. E. M., Davies, J. L., Manning, W. H. and Walters, M. J. 1999. Recent discoveries in the vicinity of Castell Collen Roman fort, Radnorshire. *Studia Celtica*, 33, 33–90.

Casey, P. J. and Davies, J. L., with Evans, J. 1993. *Excavations at Segontium (Caernarfon) Roman Fort, 1975–79*. London.

Casey, P. J. and Hoffmann, B. 1995. Excavations at Alstone Cottage, Caerleon, 1970. *Britannia*, 26, 63–106.

Cotterill, J. 1993. Saxon raiding and the role of the Late Roman coastal forts of Britain. *Britannia*, 24, 227–39.

Davies, J. L. 1986. Carreg y Bwci: a Roman watch-tower? *Archaeologia Cambrensis*, 135, 147–53.

—— 1990. Military *vici*: recent research and its significance. In B. C. Burnham and J. L. Davies (eds), *Conquest, Coexistence and Change: Recent Work in Roman Wales*. Trivium 25. Lampeter, 65–74.

—— 1991. Roman military deployment in Wales and the Marches from Pius to Theodosius I. In V. A. Maxfield and M. J. Dobson (eds), *Roman Frontier Studies 1989. Proceedings of the XVth International Congress of Roman Frontier Studies*. Exeter, 52–7.

—— 1994. The Roman period. In J. L. Davies and D. P. Kirby (eds), *Cardiganshire County History*. Volume I. Cardiff, 275–317.

—— 1997. Native producers and Roman consumers: the mechanisms of military supply in Wales from Claudius to Theodosius. In W. Groenman-van Waateringe, B. L. van Beek, W. J. H. Willems and S. L. Wynia (eds), *Roman Frontier Studies 1995. Proceedings of the XVIth International Congress of Roman Frontier Studies*. Oxford, 267–72.

Davies, R. W. 1989. *Service in the Roman Army*. Edinburgh.

Evans, D. R. and Metcalf, V. M. 1992. *Roman Gates: Caerleon*. Oxford.

Evans, E. 2000. *The Caerleon Canabae. Excavations in the Civil Settlement 1984–90*. London.

Frere, S. 1987. *Britannia*, 3rd edn. London.

Grimes, W. F. 1930. *Holt, Denbighshire: The Works Depot of the Twentieth Legion at Castle Lyons*. London.

Hanson, W. S. 1987. *Agricola and the Conquest of the North*. London.

Hassall, M. 1983. The internal planning of Roman auxiliary forts. In B. Hartley and J. Wacher (eds), *Rome and her Northern Provinces*. Gloucester, 96–131.

—— 2000. Pre-Hadrianic legionary dispositions in Britain. In R. J. Brewer (ed.), *Roman Fortresses and their Legions*. London, 51–67.

Hogg, A. H. A. 1968. Pen Llystyn: a Roman fort and other remains. *Archaeological Journal*, 125, 101–92.

James, H. 1992, Excavations in Roman Carmarthen 1978–1990. *Carmarthenshire Antiquary*, 37, 5–36.

Jarrett, M. G. 1994a. *Early Roman Campaigns in Wales. The Seventh Annual Caerleon Lecture*. Cardiff.

—— 1994b. Non-legionary troops in Roman Britain: Part 1: the units. *Britannia*, 25, 35–78.

Jarrett, M. G. and Mann, J. C. 1969. The tribes of Wales. *Welsh History Review*, 4, 161–71.

Johnson, A. 1983. *Roman Forts of the 1st and 2nd Centuries* AD *in Britain and the German Provinces*. London.

Jones, N. W. 1993. Caersws Roman fort and *vicus*, Montgomeryshire, Powys, 1984–92. *Montgomeryshire Collections*, 81, 15–96.

Le Quesne, C. 1999. *Excavations at Chester. The Roman and Later Defences. Part I*. Chester.

Lynch, F., Aldhouse-Green, S. and Davies, J. L. 2000. *Prehistoric Wales*. Stroud.

Manning, W. H. 1981. *Report on the Excavations at Usk, 1965–1976: The Fortress Excavations, 1968–1971*. Cardiff.

Marvell, A. G. and Heywood, B. 1992. Excavations at Neath. *Bulletin of the Board of Celtic Studies*, 39, 171–298.

Marvell, A. G. and Owen-John, H. S. 1997. *Leucarum. Excavations at the Roman Auxiliary Fort at Loughor, West Glamorgan 1982–94 and 1987–88*. London.

Mason, D. J. P. 2000. *Excavations at Chester: The Elliptical Building*. Chester.

—— 2001. *Roman Chester: City of the Eagles*. Stroud.

Maxwell, G. 1998. *A Gathering of Eagles. Scenes from Roman Scotland*. Edinburgh.

Nash-Williams, V. E. 1969. *The Roman Frontier in Wales*, rev. M. G. Jarrett. Cardiff.

Parkhouse, J. and Evans, E. 1996. *Excavations in Cowbridge, South Glamorgan, 1977–88*. Oxford.

Simpson, G. 1964. *Britons and the Roman Army*. London.

Swan, V. G. and Philpott, R. A. 2000. Legio XX VV and tile production at Tarbock, Merseyside. *Britannia*, 31, 55–67.

Tomlin, R. S. O. 2000. The legions in the Late Empire. In R. J. Brewer (ed.), *Roman Fortresses and their Legions*. London, 159–78.

Wheeler, R. E. M. 1926. The Roman fort at Brecon. *Y Cymmrodor*, 36.

Zienkiewicz, J. D. 1986. *The Legionary Fortress Baths at Caerleon*. Cardiff.

CHAPTER EIGHT

The Northern Frontier of Britain from Trajan to Antoninus Pius: Roman Builders and Native Britons

JAMES CROW

The dominant events in the history of Roman Britain from the end of Domitian's reign until the accession of Marcus were the construction of the two barrier walls across the island: the walls of Hadrian and Antoninus Pius. Both these works were major structural enterprises and although, on one hand, they declare the failure of Rome to dominate the whole island, the two walls and their garrisons represent a clear commitment to maintaining the security of the northern frontier of the province. The last classical writer to mention the Roman province of Britain was Procopius of Caesarea whose account of Justinian's wars in Italy, written in Constantinople in the 540s, includes a short digression concerning an island he calls *Brittia*. His account reports that this was an island where men of ancient time had built a long wall (*to makron teichos*) cutting off a great portion of the island (*Wars*, VIII. xx. 42–6: Rivet and Smith 1979: 82–3). Procopius here used the technical term of 'the long wall', a feature of the late Roman defences in central and eastern Europe within the frontiers of the Empire (Crow 1986; Napoli 1997). At first reading, the Britannia he describes appears to us as a land of fable and little more than a setting for travellers' tales (Cameron 1996: 214–15). According to Procopius, one part of the island was well populated and fertile, no different from any other part of the populated world, but beyond 'the long wall' the air was deadly and the land occupied by dangerous beasts and snakes. To cap these sinister details, he adds that 'they say that the souls of the dead are always led to this place' (beyond the wall). While it may seem surprising that less than 150 years after the withdrawal of imperial authority from Britain, to the cultured élite of the eastern Roman empire the island had become so remote and distant, one memory still endured: the wall (of Hadrian) cutting across the island. And it is fitting that in a chapter concerned with the period in which the building of Hadrian's Wall was the most significant event, we should begin by recalling the last reference in classical literature to Roman Britain. It also serves to remind us that the wall was not an isolated phenomenon in the Roman world, a theme to be considered later in more detail.

Returning to Procopius' account, the real contrast he presents is between the habitable and uninhabitable parts of the island separated by the long wall. Elsewhere in his writings he wrote about the army of the Principate, often taking some pride in explaining Latin words and military terms to his Greek audience, and it is quite clear he had access to and used a number of earlier sources which are no longer extant. Indeed, it is Procopius who provides the evidence that Trajan's bridge across the Danube was designed by Apollodorus of Damascus. So what of the island of *Brittia* and its long wall? This chapter will consider the northern frontier of Britain from the withdrawal of Roman armies in central Scotland to the reoccupation and final abandonment of the Antonine Wall. In a sense it begins and ends with moments of Roman failure to control and conquer the northern part of the island. Tacitus' melancholy phrase, *perdomita Britannia et statim omissa* (*Histories*, I.2) written in the early second century, echoes throughout much of later commentaries, but it is radically different from Procopius' later interpretation. The latter sets the wall as a barrier which allowed the areas within it to flourish and as a protection against the dangerous and evil land outside and beyond it. While his source is unknown, it may be seen to represent a view of Roman frontiers closer to the attitudes expressed in the fourth-century biography of Hadrian in the Augustan History, where the Wall was described as a measure to divide the Romans from the barbarians (A. R. Birley 1997). Procopius' source appears to reflect a later time when the lands beyond the Wall were not just 'barbarian', but had become in a sense demonized, perhaps as a way of explaining Roman losses and the failure of imperial ambition.

Sources

The period from the withdrawal of Legio II Adiutrix and the demolition of the legionary fortress at Inchtuthil coincides with a significant change in the available sources for the history of Roman Britain. With the end of Tacitus' *Agricola* and the *Histories*, little is known in the written sources after about AD 85. In effect a detailed narrative history of Roman Britain ends, and for Trajan's reign there are no historical accounts relating to Britain. While it is not always possible to reconcile the written sources with the structural and material evidence for the period of Agricola's governorship, the ensuing debate can provide a fuller and more nuanced understanding of the events and the process of conquest. In contrast, the following decades were overshadowed by what in Roman terms were the 'glorious' events of Trajan's conquests on the lower Danube and the east (Bennett 2001). There is no mention of Britain in any of the surviving written accounts, in itself perhaps a reflection of the relatively stable conditions prevailing throughout the province, and in northern Britain in particular. Although this period witnessed the first construction of fort walls and buildings in stone, very few stone inscriptions survive, with the exception of a few tombstones, such as the impressive equestrian relief of Flavinus now in Hexham Abbey, but presumed to come from one of the Roman forts at Corbridge. The consequence of the dearth of written sources, narrative or otherwise, is that any account of the military occupation relies essentially on the chronology of pottery and coins from excavated sites (Hartley 1972; Hobley 1989). One exception is the remarkable discovery of an archive of writing tablets from Vindolanda excavated and studied over the past twenty-five years (Bowman 1998; A. R. Birley 2002). It is unique in providing a vast range of documents for the economic and social history of the garrisons in the years from AD 90 to 105, even if they can contribute little to the narrative military history of the period. One reviewer of the detailed publication of this corpus observed that they provide 'a galaxy of pinpoints of light' (A. R. Birley 1997: especially 123 ff.; Tomlin 1996: 463). And the overall picture gained so far from the tablets is one of a series of literate Roman military communities, monetized and fully integrated by regular communications with the rest of the province. Of the native population there is hardly any note apart from a disparaging reference to the *Brituncu^li* or 'little Brits' who in any case are more likely to be native levies than hostile Britons.

The transition to stone construction from the time of Hadrian onwards as the essential construction material of fort defences and buildings ensured the survival of a wide range of stone inscriptions. These are vital not just for dating structures but also for providing evidence of garrisons and the communities of soldiers and civilians which developed around the forts of the Hadrianic frontier. Surviving literary sources remain limited throughout the second century, and the main account of Hadrian's reign is the biography compiled in the later fourth century, which is more likely to reflect the contemporary conditions and attitudes of that time than the circumstances and ambitions of the early second century (A. R. Birley 1997: especially 123ff.). Whatever these limitations, the combination of well-preserved stone buildings and extensive epigraphic evidence allows a much fuller and clearer picture of the structural events and activities of the building of the new frontier, even if our understanding of the motives and purpose for the Wall remains a continuing question for modern enquiry.

Inchtuthil to the Stanegate: Nerva and Trajan

Most modern accounts of this period characterize it as one of military withdrawal while the wider imperial concerns lay elsewhere in the Empire, especially in the upper and lower Danube, a consequence of either the pressures of predatory tribes or the demands of imperial conquests (Maxwell 1989; Breeze and Dobson 2000). In Britain the high tide of expansion and military presence had been reached beyond the river Tay under Agricola, and that over next the three decades, in the reigns of Domitian, Nerva and Trajan, the purpose and location of Roman armies remains uncertain until the construction of the monumental linear boundary of Hadrian's Wall. After about AD 87 Roman garrisons relinquished their control over the approaches to the Highlands and were moved south into the Scottish lowlands. The real problem in interpreting the very limited evidence for this period is to establish whether the Roman commanders envisaged northern Britain either as a zone of military garrisons linked by a network of roads, similar to the dispositions known in the Pennines from the time of Hadrian onwards, or as a sequence of what today might be termed 'stop lines', recognized lines of advance or withdrawal, often interpreted by Roman archaeologists as formal frontiers. It could be argued that the military history of Roman Britain has been bedevilled by this notion of frontiers. An extreme view is exemplified by one recent general book on Roman Britain which includes a map showing a sequence of Flavian and Trajanic frontiers throughout the north with a caption stating: 'At each stage the frontier was defended by a line of forts, probably with watch towers, certainly with regular patrols, but without any continuous linear barrier' (Faulkner 2001: figure 18). The first of these lines is located on the Gask Ridge in Scotland, a second on the Forth–Clyde isthmus, a third in southern Scotland from Newstead across to Broomholm, and finally the Stanegate between the Tyne and the Solway, correctly shown extending from Carlisle to Corbridge. This preoccupation with Roman linear frontiers has even influenced two leading experts on the British Iron Age. Thus Barry Cunliffe (1991) in his authoritative account of Iron Age Britain, explains that the line of the so-called Roman frontier along the Fosse Way followed the pre-existing line of an Iron Age tribal boundary, although since the concept of an early frontier is now rejected by Roman military archaeologists, the otherwise unattested tribal boundary must surely be questioned. In turn, a leading Iron Age scholar in northern England has summoned up a Roman frontier on the Humber, something most Roman archaeologists have not suspected before and a view mistakenly predicated on the interpretation of the distribution of Roman pottery in the first century AD (Haselgrove 1999: 272–3, based on an interpretation of Willis 1996). These two examples demonstrate the extent to which at best the notion of 'frontiers' pervades much current scholarship about the Roman conquest of Britain, and at worst show how the habit of joining dots on a small-scale map pervades many historical and archaeological interpretations of Britain in the first and second centuries AD.

One objection to such views is that they are simply not supported by any ancient text concerning Britain in the decades before the reign of Hadrian, although, given the paucity of written sources after the *Agricola*, this might not be surprising. A more serious concern is the extent to which such interpretations derive either by analogy with near-contemporary Roman frontiers in Germany, or retrospectively from the Hadrianic decision to construct a barrier wall across northern England. The latter issue will be considered more fully below, but so far as the comparative evidence from Germany is concerned, it is important to at least note a very significant revision of the chronology of the German system. Analysis of the dendrochronological evidence from the frontier structures has recently questioned the Domitianic dates for the earliest system of watch-towers and roads, instead dating the primary structures to Trajan's reign between 105 and 115, less than a decade before the building of Hadrian's Wall (Sommer 1999: 177–8). Excluding the two interventions by Iron Age scholars, all the other four examples cited above may either be rejected or subjected to very different interpretations. Thus the Gask Ridge, which was probably abandoned about AD 90, comprised a road and timber towers between the forts of Ardoch and Strageath. One recent publication recognizes this as a frontier line created as part of the gradual withdrawal of Roman armies after the departure of the legion from Inchtuthil (Jones and Wooliscroft 2001). Other recent assessments are altogether more circumspect, recognizing the Gask line as a road with towers, but certainly not stressing the road's importance as a *frontier line* (Maxwell 1998: 32–4). Throughout the military zone in northern England and in Scotland, roads were on occasion provided with watch-towers used as observation posts and in some instance for signalling. Indeed, on Trajan's Column towers are shown with lit torches along the line of the Danube bank, but although a regular system of towers is a feature of the so-called *limes* in Germany from the time of Trajan onwards, not all roads with towers and fortlets are by definition frontier lines and many, such as the road over the Stainmore pass linking York with the Eden valley in Cumbria, are most definitely not.

Moving southwards in Scotland, the narrow isthmus between the Forth and Clyde later formed the line of the Antonine Wall, but although earlier occupation can be demonstrated at some of the later forts, this is not enough to constitute a distinct frontier during the period of the withdrawal of garrisons under Nerva or Trajan (Breeze 1996: 58). Further south, the large fort of Newstead in the shadow of the Eildon Hills and at the crossing of the Tweed was certainly maintained in occupation throughout much of this period, but once again there is little to commend the notion of a 'frontier' running south-westwards towards Broomholm in Eskdale, which in any case does not account for the large late Flavian fort at Dalswinton in Dumfriesshire (RCAHMS 1997).

In North Britain, if we set aside this model for a formal strategic withdrawal, the evidence during the reigns of Nerva and Trajan may indicate a continued, and to some extent flexible, military presence throughout the Scottish lowlands until at least about 105, focused around a series of large forts such as Newstead or High Rochester. These in turn controlled former centres of the native population such as the Eildons or Burnswark, although from that date onwards there appears to be greater emphasis on the forts located on the Tyne–Solway isthmus between Corbridge, Vindolanda and Carlisle, the so-called 'Stanegate frontier'. For the majority of forts of this period, with the exceptions of Newstead, Vindolanda, Carlisle and Corbridge, excavations have been limited in their extent and are often restricted to later periods. The model proposed by Hartley's study of samian stamps (published in 1972) has established the chronology for both for the Flavian and Trajanic forts in south Scotland and northern England, although with the inevitable exception of Newstead, the size of the sample is very small, especially when contrasted with the numbers available from the Antonine period forts. Because of this discrepancy, it is possible to question whether the absence of this material accurately reflects the total withdrawal after about AD 105 to the Tyne–Solway line. Two pieces of evidence can demonstrate, at the very least, the continuing concern and interest of the Romans in the region. First, a well-known inscription recording a census of Annandale in south-west Scotland by a *censitor Brittonum Anavio(nensium)* probably dated to AD 112 (Rivet and Smith 1979: 249–50), possibly to levy troops for service in Germany. The second piece of evidence is the identification of the name *Bremenium* (High Rochester) on a writing tablet from Vindolanda dated from a late Trajanic context, thus indicating that the fort north on Dere Street remained in occupation at this time (A. R. Birley 2002). Further evidence for Roman activity along this road can be suggested from an exceptional brooch of early second-century date from Risingham, a fort normally considered to date from the Antonine period.[1]

While there is evidence for activity in southern Scotland and north Northumberland from about AD 105 onwards, there appears to be greater emphasis on the forts located on the Tyne–Solway isthmus between Corbridge, Vindolanda and Carlisle (Bidwell 1999: 11–14). This is the line of the Roman road known as the Stanegate, which in turn has formed the basis for theories relating to the so-called

---

1   The fibula from Risingham is in the Museum of Antiquities. University of Newcastle upon Tyne. It was discovered in mint condition, suggesting very little use (Lindsay Allason-Jones, personal communication).

'Stanegate Frontier'. These were most fully developed by Eric Birley, who clearly modelled his interpretation on the available evidence from the frontiers of upper Germany and Raetia. More recent discussion and fieldwork has cast doubt on this view (Breeze and Dobson 2000: 16–24), although it is apparent that some scholars still perceive this line as a direct precursor to the later Hadrianic frontier, a view with considerable implications for our understanding of the situation at the time that Hadrian's Wall was designed and built (Jones and Wooliscroft 2001: 21ff.).

Perhaps the most persuasive observations on the early 'Tyne–Solway frontier' are to be found in Bowman's recent commentary and discussion of a selection of the Vindolanda writing tablets. Among the most significant of these was a strength report for the First Cohort of Tungrians dating to *c*. AD 92–7 from the large, period two fort at Vindolanda. Elements of the unit were dispersed not just in the north at Corbridge (noted in the text by its Roman name of *Coria*) and elsewhere but as far afield as London. Bowman (1998: 24) concludes about Roman dispositions before Hadrian:

> This means that the spread is rather thinner, the communications more embracing and coherent, the psychology is completely different from something based on the relatively rare need to confront in battle. The frontier line is not so much a system of continuous perimeter defence, nor even a symbolic division between Roman and non-Roman, but the basis for a continuous and active process of policing, organisation and control involving intensive exchange of information in the frontier zone itself and in the regional infrastructure to the rear.

A more enduring contribution that Eric Birley made to the study of the Stanegate and the pre-Hadrianic period was the commitment of himself and his family to the long-term excavations at Vindolanda. The results over the past twenty-five years have revealed not only a wealth of textual and material evidence for this period but have also demonstrated a complex sequence of timber forts constructed between about AD 85 and 112. The plans of these forts display a remarkable variety in size, and it is suggested that the large fort at Vindolanda forms part of a sequence of forts across the isthmus, providing garrisons for the armies withdrawn from the lowlands of Scotland and north Northumberland after AD 105. The evidence from both Carlisle (Caruana 1997) and Vindolanda (A. R. Birley 2002) derives from dendrochronology and provides dating independent from ceramic chronologies, which underpin much of the chronology from elsewhere.

Hadrian's Wall: Setting and Introduction

The physical setting of Hadrian's new frontier work follows the northern rim of the Tyne–Solway isthmus, the narrowest line across northern England. The line of the wall began in the east at Wallsend 7 kilometres from the mouth of the Tyne, follows a direct line westwards to the bridgehead at Newcastle and then climbs to the west to follow the high ground north of the river. From there to the river crossing of the north Tyne at Chesters, the wall takes a direct course, occupying the ridge and often incorporating hilltops along its length. A determining feature of the wall line seems to have been the Romans' desire to incorporate the imposing natural escarpment of the Whinsill crags as part of the new frontier. By contrast, in the west beyond the crossing of the river Irthing, the line of the wall frequently appears to avoid a tactically advantageous situation and in a number of places seems to be overlooked by higher ground to the north. This is probably a pragmatic response to the more broken country north of the Irthing valley, although whether this reflects different concerns for security from the builders in this sector to those to the east has not been investigated. Beyond the Cam Beck the wall crosses the north Cumbrian plain, heading for the major river crossing of the Eden north of Carlisle, from where the wall follows the south shore of the Solway estuary as far as Bowness. The wall line stops at this point, but a sequence of frontier works, including a possible palisade, continues south for a further 42 kilometres to Maryport.

When it was first constructed, the mural barrier of Hadrian's Wall comprised two quite different structures: in the east the wall was initially built of stone and ran from Newcastle upon Tyne to the river Irthing in Cumbria, a distance of 45 Roman miles (67 kilometres). Beyond that for 31 Roman miles (45 kilometres) to the west as far Bowness-on-Solway, the wall was constructed of cut turf or clay with, in places, a stone foundation. Later (but probably before the end of Hadrian's reign) this turf wall was replaced by a stone wall. In both the stone-wall and turf-wall sectors the wall was provided from the outset with a regular sequence of small forts or milecastles located approximately a Roman mile apart (1472 metres). These defined the wall into fixed lengths and are conventionally numbered from the east to facilitate identification. Between each of these fortlets were two towers, normally described as turrets, spaced at a third of a Roman mile apart. To the front of the wall was a ditch 9 metres wide, and in places close to Newcastle recent excavations have revealed traces of closely spaced pits situated on the berm (6 metres wide). These are thought to have concealed sharpened stakes as an additional defensive feature for the wall (Bidwell 1999: 95–7; further examples have recently been excavated at Byker and west of Newcastle towards Heddon).

Evidence for the construction of the wall derives from a combination of the epigraphic sources for the building of the wall with observations of the wall-structures made by antiquarians and archaeologists over the past three centuries. Between Newcastle and the north Tyne the wall was laid out and built at a broad gauge (3 metres) referred to as the Broad Wall. Beyond the crossing of the north Tyne the foundations of the wall were laid out to the broad gauge, and most of the turrets and milecastles were also constructed with 'wing-walls' in anticipation that the curtain wall would be of a similar width. In the event the stone wall that was constructed from the north Tyne to the Irthing and beyond as far as the Burtholme Beck (wall-mile 54) was completed at a narrowed gauge of 2.4 metres; this is known as the Narrow Wall. Beyond this point to the west as far as Bowness, the turf wall was later replaced by a stone wall 2.70 metres wide, known as the Intermediate Wall.

It is normally assumed that construction began from Newcastle, where the first traces of the Broad Wall are found, and are associated with the bridge across the Tyne: Pons Aelius (*RIB* 1319, 1320) where two inscriptions of Ocean and Neptune were set up by Legio VI Victrix. Recently Breeze and Hill (2001) have made the intriguing suggestion that rather than starting close to the mouth of the Tyne, the building of the stone wall commenced at the point where the main road, Dere Street, crossed the line of the wall at the Port Gate, due north of the main river crossing of the Tyne at Corbridge and half a mile west of the fort at Halton Chesters. They suggest that one

Milecastles and turrets	Inscriptions from milecastles	Dating
Construction of Broad Wall and Broad foundations	MC 37 – *RIB* 1634 MC 38 – *RIB* 1637/1638	122/126
Turf Wall	MC 42 – *RIB* 1666 MC 47 – *RIB* 1852 MC 50 TW – *RIB* 1935	122/126
Forts constructed over Broad Wall	Inscriptions from forts Benwell – *RIB* 1340 Halton – *RIB* 1427	122/126
Fort constructed over Broad foundation	Greatchesters – *RIB* 1736	128/138
Forts later than the Vallum	Carrawburgh – *RIB* 1550 Carvoran – *RIB* 1818–1820	130/133 136/138

Figure 8.1 Building inscriptions from milecastles and forts (after Napoli 1997: 154).

legionary team worked in the direction of Newcastle, with a second working away towards the west. At the western end of the wall it is not known whether the turf wall was either constructed before or contemporary with the stone wall: following the Breeze and Hill model, building work may have commenced at the bridgehead across the Eden north of Carlisle. The main evidence for the builders of the wall derives from the building inscriptions from the milecastles and forts, as well as the centurial stones set up by the individual centuries. The three British legions were involved in the building: II Augusta from Caerleon, XX Valeria Victrix from Chester and VI Victrix recently arrived from lower Germany, possibly at the same time as the new governor Platorius Nepos. In addition, an inscription from Benwell records construction by detachments from the British Fleet (Classis Britannica).

The Structure of the Wall

First impressions can be misleading: the regularity of the major elements of the Hadrianic frontier often belie significant variations between similar structures, for example, milecastles, as well as the complex evolution of the system within a relatively short period. Study over the past century has revealed the overall pattern of the wall and its structures, which indicate a clear vision in the ordering of the system, while at the same time showing very significant variations and major changes in the execution of the project. All this is not surprising, given the scale of the undertaking, since the work of building the wall and the forts probably lasted for over a decade and involved a workforce of more than 15,000 men.

A quotation from Sir Ian Richmond's tenth edition of the *Handbook for the Roman Wall* (1947: 187–8) will give some idea of the complexity of the mural structures and how they have been interpreted:

The ditch of the Wall will be observed swinging northwards and taking the bottom of the northward slope. This is a secondary ditch. The older one, still outlined by certain conditions of growth, followed the Wall to turret 54a, excavated in 1933, when reason for the change became plain. There had been two turrets. The first one, a Clay-Wall turret, had collapsed into the ditch, owing to unstable subsoil, after a measure of use. A new Wall, this time of turf, was then built further north, with the secondary ditch, whilst the new turret was built behind the old one as an isolated tower. Later came the Stone Wall which was run up to the new turret. Finally, when the Stone Wall was destroyed in the disaster of A.D. 197, the Severan Stone Wall was built without any turret across the ruins of the earlier building. This complicated story provides ample proof that the Turf Wall here lasted for some time: its replacement is stone, but not immediate.

With the exception of the supposed 'disaster of A.D. 197', this interpretation continues to be accepted, and Richmond's account provides not only an example of the complexities which excavation can reveal about the wall and minor structures such as the turrets, but also shows how the evidence can be presented as a structural narrative for the building of the wall throughout Hadrian's reign.

From Wallsend to Burtholme Beck in Cumbria, the stone wall was built from grey sandstone common throughout south Northumberland and south-east Cumbria. The Burtholme Beck corresponds with the Red Sandstone fault, and from there westwards the mural barrier was initially constructed as a turf or clay wall, probably because of the limited availability of good sandstone for building and of limestone for making mortar. The Broad Wall, known from Newcastle to the north Tyne, was built with sandstone facings with a clay-bonded core. The only mortar employed was in the plaster render of the wall face known from the excavations at West Denton in 1987 (Bidwell 1999: 18). Construction of the Narrow Wall differed since the core was not clay-bonded, but some evidence survives for mortar pointing in the joints of the facing stones and possibly the core. What is clear is that the mortars for the Hadrianic Narrow Wall lacked the durability found in the later rebuilding, which followed after the withdrawal from the Antonine Wall (Crow 1991: 55–7). The facing stones were generally uniform in shape with a square face, although they tend to be larger in size in the Broad Wall sectors than for the Narrow Wall lengths on the crags and elsewhere. In all cases the modules used for the wall-stones can all be handled by one or two men, and this size was adopted to simplify construction. This style of building is correctly styled 'coursed rubble', since the blocks were only roughly dressed (Woodside and Crow 1999: figures 20, 21). The decision to change the gauge of the wall from Broad (3 metres) to Narrow (2.4 metres), a reduction of 2 Roman feet, probably arose from a need to speed the work by reducing the quantity of core materials used. This change would not have affected the number of facings needed unless the height was altered, although Hill and Dobson (1992: 28) have argued that this reduction could imply a change in use.

The construction of the Turf Wall from regular cut turfs followed a standard pattern of Roman military building. The turfs were cut from the ground immediately adjacent to the wall, and this has an important implication for the contemporary land-use, which must have been open pasture before construction began. Recent excavations near Birdoswald have shown that in places the available turf must have been brought in from sites adjacent to the wall and not from the line itself. In some areas the wall was built of clay with turf revetting, and west of Carlisle the wall was found to have a stone foundation similar to those more commonly attested on the later Antonine Wall. The overall width of the Turf Wall was 6 metres and recent recon-

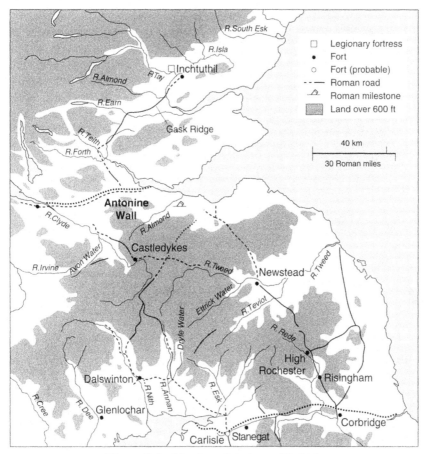

Figure 8.2 Northern Britain AD 85–145.

structions assume a height of 4.4 metres with a parapet of hurdles on the north side (Wilmott 2001: 41–5).

Estimates for the height of the Turf Wall derive from projections of the slope of the exterior face of the turfs: for the Stone Wall a number of differing sources of structural evidence survive. It is generally accepted that the wall (both Narrow and Broad) was about 4.4 metres (15 Roman feet) high, which was supplemented on the north side by a parapet, attested by the presence of chamfered stones known from a number of contexts to have marked the boundary between the wall-top and the parapet (see figure 8.5). There is no evidence whether this parapet was crenellated, although good evidence exists from the forts, turrets and milecastles (Crow 1991: 59–61). Seen from the north, the total height of the curtain wall would have been 6 metres, an imposing structure to scramble over. The overall impact of the wall would have been raised by the whitewashing and rendering noted from recent excavations (Bidwell 1999: 18).

Immediately to the north of the wall was a level space (termed the berm) 6 metres wide, and then a broad V-shaped ditch with an average width of about 9 metres and a

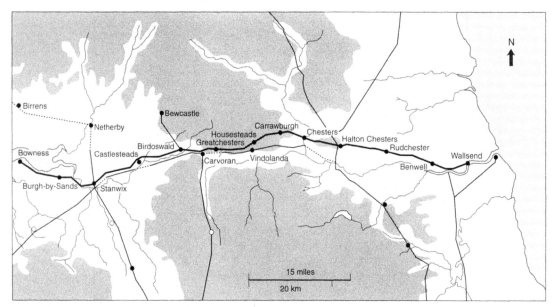

Figure 8.3   Map of Hadrian's Wall at the time of Hadrian's death.

maximum depth of 3.35 metres, although in some places it is as little as 2.3 metres deep. Beyond the ditch there was normally a mound of upcast material probably derived from cleaning and recutting the ditch. In the central sector the ditch was unnecessary along the crags and is only found in the gaps of the Whinsill. South of the wall was another great earthwork known as the Vallum, a Latin term more correctly attributed to the wall itself. The Vallum comprises a wide, flat-bottomed ditch 6 metres across and 3 metres deep; the ditch was flanked to the north and south by two parallel mounds 6 metres wide forming a broad zone 36 metres across. In many places a second mound survives on the south edge of the ditch (the marginal mound) and this has recently been shown to be contemporary with the two outer mounds. The Vallum is not known east of Newcastle, probably because the proximity of the River Tyne limited access towards the south side of the wall. Elsewhere the Vallum was a continuous feature normally set out in long straight lengths over 3 kilometres long. It ran approximately parallel to the wall at a distance of about 60 metres. As far as turret 33b, where the line of the crags begins, the ditch was often cut through the bedrock of sandstone and in places the hard dolerite of the Whinsill. Faced with Whinstone bedrock close to milecastle 30 (Limestone Corner) the wall-builders left the wall-ditch unfinished, whereas the Vallum was completed. As the 1947 *Handbook* reports, 'for the Vallum the ditch was the essential thing, while for the Wall it was an accessory' (Richmond 1947: 99).

The wall ditch and Vallum, to north and south of the curtain wall, were not, however, contemporary. Cutting of the ditch appears to have followed the building of the wall, although there have been too few excavations of the wall curtain and ditch as a single unit to be certain that was always the case. At Halton Chesters fort the wall ditch was deliberately filled in with massive foundations below the west and east gates when the fort was added to the line of the wall (figure 8.3), whereas the Vallum can be seen from recent geophysical survey to divert south of the fort, a clear indicator that it is later in date (Taylor et al. 1998: figure 4).

Milecastles and Turrets

With the exception of some lengths of wall in the central sector, construction of the milecastles and turrets preceded the building of the curtain wall or the forts, and it is likely that the surveying of these elements was the first stage in creating the mural system. The milecastles were small forts attached to the inner face of the wall, about 15 metres by 18 metres square with entrances to the north and south. Significant differences have been noted in the layouts and size of many of the stone milecastles, and these factors have helped to attribute specific buildings to particular legions (Breeze and Dobson 2000: 66–72). Turf Wall milecastles were constructed with turf walls and timber gates, but they are somewhat larger with overall dimensions of 18 by 21 metres. Within the milecastles there was a central open space, flanked by small barracks capable of housing 8 to 16 men. There were gates to the north and south.

The turrets were approximately 6 metres square and were built integrally with the curtain wall (Hill 1997). There was a single doorway on the south side and normally a raised platform against one of the interior walls. Unlike the Turf Wall milecastles, the turrets on this sector were also constructed in stone. Although the curtain wall did not extend any further than Bowness, the regular system of mile fortlets and towers continued down the Cumbrian coast as far as Maryport. These did not differ greatly from the wall structures except that they were free-standing and the mile fortlets were not reconstructed of stone (Bidwell 1999: 184–5, Swarthy Hill mile fortlet).

Forts

In the early part of the building programme there were only eleven forts attached or built adjacent to the wall located at distances of between 6 and 9 miles (9.6 to 14.4 kilometres) (Bidwell 1999: 21; Breeze and Dobson 2000: 47–56). Carrawburgh was added during Nepos' governorship, but the evidence for Burgh-by-Sands remains very uncertain. Newcastle and Drumburgh forts were not constructed before about 200. The stone fort at South Shields, located at the mouth of the Tyne, is mid-Antonine in date but traces of earlier material and structures have been found (Bidwell 1999: 73). The garrisons varied from normal-sized infantry or mixed cavalry and infantry cohorts of about 500 men to the larger *cohortes milliariae* of 800 infantry, or the very large cavalry regiment of 1000 stationed at Stanwix. Fort sizes in general seem to have reflected the size of the initial garrison. East of the river Irthing, with the exception of Carvoran, all forts were attached to the wall and built of stone. The majority were laid out so that one third of the fort and three of the main gates projected north of the wall. The exceptions are Housesteads, where the north wall follows the edge of the crags, Carrawburgh, which is clearly an addition since the Vallum was filled in to allow for its construction, and Great Chesters, which overlies a Broad Wall milecastle and length of foundation but does not project north of the wall curtain. Carvoran fort was part of the earlier Stanegate forts and, for reasons which remain obscure, was separated from the wall by the Vallum.

West of the Irthing the earliest phases known from forts such as Birdoswald were constructed with turf ramparts and projected beyond the wall. When the fort was rebuilt in stone later in Hadrian's reign, the north wall was then aligned with the Narrow Wall curtain (Wilmott 2001). Stanwix and Bowness were constructed on the line of the wall, but both Castlesteads and Burgh II (Jones and Wooliscroft 2001: 62–5) were set back from the wall line. Although the overall image remains unclear and some sites remain poorly investigated, it is apparent that where possible the primary Hadrianic forts were expected to project beyond the line of the wall. This disposition has been understood to reflect the essentially offensive character of the original auxiliary garrisons. However, as with other aspects of the primary building, such as the over-provision of both milecastles and fort gates, the initial design of the forts included somewhat impractical almost bombastic elements indicative of a design conceived away from the realities of the frontier.

North of the wall two major roads led into Scotland. To the west outpost forts were built at Birrens and Netherby, on the line of the west road into Dumfriesshire, and another at Bewcastle, north of Birdoswald. These served to provide forward bases to gain intelligence and control the lands immediately to the north. On Dere Street to the east, it has normally been argued that the outposts at High Rochester and Risingham were not occupied until the Antonine occupation of Scotland. However, as noted above, there is good reason to suggest occupation of both forts in the first decade of the second century, evidence which merely draws attention to how little is actually known from many of these sites.

'The Fort Decision'

The structural developments of Hadrian's Wall outlined in the previous section were largely understood by the outbreak of the Second World War. In 1937 Richmond had rather gleefully written: 'The Wall-question, indeed, moves so fast as to excite the mirth even of those who work upon it: and excavations published in these pages (*Archaeologia Aeliana*) now show that not only the Wall but its forts were modified during building,' although in the same year the excavators of Halton Chesters noted with rather more reserve that the construction of the fort was 'an afterthought in the same design, not an afterthought of someone new to the work' (Simpson and Richmond 1937: 162). Subsequently a limited programme of fieldwork was undertaken by Simpson and Richmond during the war years to establish the regular spacing of turrets built at Housesteads, Chesters and Birdoswald before the construction of the forts. By 1950 Richmond was confident enough to be able to write: 'The principal periods in the history of the monument were firmly fixed and the complicated relationship between its component parts was securely defined' (Richmond 1950: 43). Critical for an understanding of these changes was the recognition of a 'thorough revision of the design' involving 'the construction of forts on the Wall itself' (cf. Crow 1991: 51). This process has been termed 'the fort decision', an interpretation of the evidence which envisaged that the wall, turrets and milecastles were originally designed and built to be a single line of stone or turf, supported by main garrisons set back on the line of the Stanegate. Subsequently it was decided to advance these garrisons from forts, such as Vindolanda, onto the wall itself, a move involving the demolition of at least three turrets, one milecastle and the massive additional foundations for the forts' gates, such as were found at the main west and east gates of Halton Chesters, constructed over the pre-existing wall ditch (figures 8.4 and 8.5).

This hypothesis was based on direct observations of the structural evidence. Subsequently, however, it became the basis for historical speculation which imagined that the decision was a response to specific, but historically unattested, events, such as a revolt of the North British tribes indignant at the construction of the wall across their territories (see, however, the comments of Jarrett 1976: 150–1). It is certainly clear from the limited ancient sources for Hadrian's reign that there was a major tribal revolt in Britain involving significant Roman military losses, comparable to those suffered during the Bar Kochba revolt in Judaea (A. R. Birley 1997: 123–4). Further support for barbarian agitation has been sought from a memorial slab of a centurion recorded to have died *in bello*, found at Vindolanda, although if he died in a major war, it is still not certain which it was. Over the past half-century some of the more elaborate speculations have been set aside, but the force of the hypothesis remains (Bidwell 1999: 14) despite a number of reservations by wall scholars, including Richmond himself.

A major reservation in accepting this hypothesis is that it does not fully consider some of the major discontinuities apparent from the structural record. Between Newcastle and the north Tyne, construction of the Broad Wall clearly preceded the building of the forts, and the same process probably occurred in the Turf Wall sector, only here excavation has been much more limited. For much of the sector from the

Figure 8.4 Halton Chesters: west gate built over the ditch of Hadrian's Wall.

Figure 8.5 Chamfered blocks from the parapet of Hadrian's Wall.

north Tyne to Carvoran (19 wall-miles), however, the Broad Wall phase is represented only as a foundation, absent completely along the line of the crags from milecastle 39 westwards (Woodside and Crow 1999: 36–40). The Broad Wall resumes west of Carvoran as far as Birdoswald (3.5 wall-miles). Not only did the wall remain incomplete, but so also were some of the milecastles and turrets. Yet ironically this is the classic sector for the 'fort decision' hypothesis, where the Stanegate and the wall are most closely spaced. Beyond the Irthing the river separates the garrisons and the wall. Returning to the east, where the Broad Wall is known to have been completed, there as yet no secure evidence that the Stanegate ever extended east from Corbridge towards the mouth of the Tyne, on either the north or south bank of the river. This remains a matter of speculation, informed by the assumption that there was a pre-Hadrianic frontier across the isthmus.[2] Only west of Carlisle, along so-called western Stanegate, is there evidence from forts such as Burgh-by-Sands I–II which might support the twin lines (Austen and McCarthy in Bidwell 1999: 177–9: Jones and Wooliscroft 2001: 62–5).

The close contact between German and British archaeologists working on Roman frontiers since the late nineteenth century has ensured there have been a number of fruitful comparative studies which have tended to stress the similarities between the two frontiers, as, for example, Birley's comparison of the so-called Stanegate frontier with contemporary works in upper Germany. It is equally helpful to consider the differences between the two land frontier lines. In practice the two systems were significantly different, especially in terms of the development and complexity of Roman civil settlements successfully established within the frontier zone of Germany and Raetia. The sequence of ditch, wall and vallum found in Britain was altogether a much more comprehensive barrier than the timber palisade found in Germany. This complexity was of course much easier to achieve, since the line from coast to coast was considerably shorter than the contemporary *limes* in upper Germany and Raetia. However we interpret some of the detailed evidence for the function of Hadrian's Wall, it was quite clearly the most exclusive frontier line the Romans ever built, itself a reflection not just of the shorter distance the line crossed but also of the perceived threat that was faced in northern Britain. The long stone barrier that Hadrian constructed was unique until the late Roman period. Precedent can be found in the long siege works constructed by Roman armies from the late Republic onwards, and in particular in the 19-mile barrier Caesar constructed against the Helvetii between the Jura Mountains and the shore of Lake Geneva (Napoli 1997). Like the late Antonine Wall in Britain, this wall was constructed of soil, turf and timber whereas more than two-thirds of Hadrian's Wall from the outset was constructed in stone.

The tradition of stone 'long walls' was known from the Greek world, including the famous long walls connecting Athens to the Piraeus (the term in Greek is the same as that used by Procopius in his account of the British wall). Many of these were located at narrow isthmuses, such as at Corinth and across the Gallipoli peninsula in Turkey. Although they were originally constructed in the sixth and fifth centuries BC, many either survived into Roman times or were reported by historians or writers contemporary with Hadrian. It is possibly significant that the emperor's friend, Platorius Nepos, was first a governor in Thrace, a province extending from European Turkey into modern Bulgaria and which included the site of the Gallipoli wall. He subsequently moved on to lower Germany, where the military garrisons were located on the bank of the Rhine, before coming to Britain in AD 122 to start the new frontier of Hadrian's Wall. Hadrian's military commanders and governors, such as Nepos and his contemporary Arrian, governor of Cappadocia and historian of Alexander the Great, were highly educated and cultivated men, who like the emperor himself formed part of the revival of Greek culture known as the second Sophistic. When assessing the form and location of the stone barrier wall in Britain, we need to be aware of this tradition since it may have been a more significant influence on Hadrian and his

2 See the cautious comments of Bidwell 1999: 14; for the fort at Washing Well/Whickham see Jones and Wooliscroft 2001: 38, figure 10.

planners than the timber palisade in Germany or an existing pattern of garrisons on the Stanegate (Crow 1986; A. R. Birley 1997: 133).

The Purpose and Function of the Wall

Throughout the nineteenth century the wall was seen as a military barrier: John Hodgson, the first antiquarian to recognize that Hadrian was the builder of the wall, perceived it as protection against 'poor and predatory neighbours' (cf. Crow 1986: 724), while at the end of that century Haverfield wrote that 'The object of the Wall is plain, like the Great Wall of China it is a fortification to bar ingress and resist armed attack' (Crow 1991: 53). The First World War and the tragic experience of fixed lines and trench warfare seems to have radically altered this consensus, so that in 1922 R. G. Collingwood dismissed this military interpretation and established a new orthodoxy which envisaged that the mural barrier was intended to control peaceful movements across the 'frontier' and to prevent limited, small-scale raiding. The wall itself was considered to be ineffective as a fighting platform. This view has been maintained and developed by many scholars throughout the twentieth century, and most recently John Mann insisted that the wall was 'merely a piece of rhetoric'.[3] This latter view not only underestimates the structure and physical presence of the wall but also assumes that Roman armies were able to control and dominate the military zone beyond and behind the wall, making it, as the quotation might suggest, in effect redundant. Although a variation of Collingwood's view continues to be expressed in Breeze and Dobson's standard work on the wall, an alternative interpretation stressing the military significance of the wall was maintained by Daniels and continues to be advanced by Bidwell and others. Most of those who maintain the military significance of the wall have been involved in excavations of the wall itself.

Any student of the wall needs to realize that what is known of the purpose and function of Hadrian's Wall is essentially derived from an interpretation of the physical remains. At a strategic level this includes the disposition of forts and their garrisons, the provision of communications as well as other factors. On a tactical level the debate revolves around the character of the curtain itself: how high it was; was there a fighting platform; what was the access to the wall-top? It now seems generally accepted that the wall was in places a high, vertical barrier up to 5 metres in height. The wall-top was flat with a parapet on the north side signified by a chamfered string course, but without evidence for crenellations. Access up to the wall-walk seems to have been restricted to the turrets, milecastles and perhaps forts as well, although the exact function of the turrets seems to be disputed. The next main issue is concerned with the problem of crossing the wall and to what extent the barrier was permeable. Recent excavations of the Vallum have reminded archaeologists that it constituted a very significant obstacle to movement, and, as completed, the horizontal barrier of the ditch, wall and Vallum was over 100 metres wide. Access through the wall was limited to the milecastles, but at only one

---

3 For Collingwood's views and references see Breeze and Dobson 2000: 42–3, 310: see also Bidwell 1999: 31–3 and Crow 1986: 728 n. 4.

instance (milecastle 50) is there certain evidence for a gateway through the Vallum opposite a milecastle. Otherwise access through the barrier was limited to the forts where there were Vallum crossings, or on the two points where main roads passed through the wall, such as the Port Gate for Dere Street north of Corbridge. Like other frontiers, it is quite possible that the main access points were limited to these places and not through the forts, so that the wall system initially must have made a very significant impact on any local tribes of the Brigantes and the Votadini by limiting movement in the frontier zone.

The role of the wall as a military barrier is more difficult to assess. Recent excavations near Newcastle have revealed evidence for additional protection on the berm, where a series of pits have been uncovered. Probably filled with sharpened stakes, they represent a common practice in the ancient world, similar to modern barbed wire. It is difficult to understand why these additional defences were provided if the Romans did not perceive a real military threat to the wall, rather than merely a formal barrier with customs posts. Assessing the military threat to the wall, however, is rather like watching shadow-boxing; it is only possible to recognize the response from one side: the Roman. The scale of the construction of the Hadrianic frontier can be interpreted as a response to a real military threat, but in turn that remains anonymous. The success of Agricola's campaigns in northern Scotland was to bring the northern tribes to a formal battle, where Roman military superiority could be exploited. In later campaigns, such as those of Septimius Severus, the Romans were unable to exploit this advantage and the British tribes could benefit from what is now termed 'asymmetrical warfare'. The tribes could use their knowledge of the terrain and avoid direct confrontation, thus denying the Romans the opportunity for any clear victories, but at the same time provoking Roman armies into small-scale local conflicts where the northern British tribes had at least an equal advantage.

This interpretation can explain the Roman failure to control the whole island, but in itself it does not address the question of why the Romans constructed two linear barriers across Britain and maintained Hadrian's Wall into the fourth century. Military unrest and raids among the northern tribes are reported in the ancient sources from the time of Hadrian onwards, although it is often very difficult to be sure where the threat was based and to assess what impact these raids may have had. Before the fourth century AD a common element in the accounts of barbarian warfare against Rome was their inability to engage in siege warfare. Analogies with the better documented campaigns in the Balkans suggest that fortifications and barrier walls within the frontiers could help resist barbarian attack. The invaders lacked a formal logistical support and they were forced to live off the land which they passed through. This made them more mobile, as they were not restricted to lines of communication and supply but, in common with many pre-industrial armies, they required a constant and relentless foraging for supplies. The siege of any fortification, whether a fort or a barrier wall, imposed a logistical strain and could have delayed any raid sufficiently to ensure an effective response from the defending garrisons. Analyses of the wall as a military structure often stress the weaknesses and difficulties in manning the structure and controlling an enemy, but at the same time assume great confidence and abilities in the wall's attackers.

The Roman Iron Age Population

With the possible exception of the Vindolanda Britunculi, the indigenous population of North Britain remains anonymous in the textual records. In attempting to study the relations between Roman and native a key problem remains the incompatibility of their relative chronologies: in some instances it is possible to date Roman actions within a year or even closer, while the dating of the structures and artefacts of the Roman Iron Age peoples relies on either radiocarbon dates or their reuse of Roman artefacts. The construction of Hadrian's Wall provides, for the archaeologist at least, a welcome intrusion of Roman and therefore datable actions on the pre-existing landscapes (Hodgson 2001). From a number of excavations along the wall archaeologists have recognized earlier agricultural activities sealed by the wall-builders. It is not yet possible to be certain whether this ploughing was disrupted by the arrival of the Romans or represents an agricultural activity several generations earlier in date. The overall impression, however, especially in Northumberland from the Whin Sill elsewhere crags eastwards, is of extensive arable cultivation before the building of the mural barrier. To these peoples at least, the wall would have made a significant impact on their daily lives in the same way that the building of a motorway can disrupt isolated rural communities. A more general impact throughout the north was the need for timber for the construction of forts and internal buildings (Hanson 1996), although it is now clear the deforestation of the northern centuries began millennia before the arrival of the Romans (Tipping 1997). Previous studies of the Roman Iron Age have stressed the extensive available evidence for settlement preserved throughout the uplands of northern Britain (e.g. RCAHMS 1997); however, recent studies have considered Roman interaction with the local peoples, including the circulation and deposition of artefacts (Hunter 1997: 2001).

An Antonine Postscript

By the end of Hadrian's reign the whole system was complete, the most complex frontier system in the Roman world, but in the following reign of Antoninus Pius, a new wall was constructed in Scotland, 100 kilometres north on the Forth–Clyde isthmus. The barrier was half the length of Hadrian's Wall (60 kilometres) and was constructed of turf, two-thirds of the width of Hadrian's turf wall but constructed throughout on a solid stone footing. Initially there were six forts, and building of the forts preceded work on the turf rampart. It seems that between the forts was a regular system of fortlets, but before the rampart was completed at least ten additional forts were added on to the line, so that some of the forts were only 3.2 kilometres apart. This created a barrier much more intensively manned than Hadrian's Wall, but at the same time it seems that some at least of the forts on the earlier wall remained garrisoned and there was a provision for more forts and watch-towers in the zone between the two walls (Maxwell 1989; Breeze 1996; Breeze and Dobson 2000). The decision to advance into Scotland appears to have partly motivated by the need for military conquest, but it also reflects an attempt to address the continuing problems of security in North Britain. Construction began in 142 and the wall was occupied at least until 158 (Hodgson 1995), although from that date inscriptions record reconstruction work on Hadrian's Wall and within a few years the more northerly frontier line was abandoned (see below, pp. 136–8).

FURTHER READING

Hadrian's Wall by Breeze and Dobson (2000) provides an accessible but authoritative general account of the northern frontier. It is now in its fourth edition, but for a more detailed discussion of individual sites see the *Handbook to the Roman Wall* (Daniels 1978). It can be updated by reference to Bidwell (1999) with a comprehensive recent bibliography. A new edition of the *Handbook* is in preparation by David Breeze. Eric Birley's *Research on Hadrian's Wall* (1960) remains an essential guide to the historiography of the wall. A recent development in the bibliography of the wall is a series of popular but detailed and informed studies of sites, including Housesteads (Crow 1995), Birdoswald (Wilmott 2001), Vindolanda (A. R. Birley 2002) and Carlisle (McCarthy 2002). Napoli (1997) provides a detailed summary in French of current work to 1991 in the context of a unique study on the archaeology of Roman frontiers. A number of studies give accessible and detailed accounts of Roman Scotland (see Maxwell 1989 and Breeze 1996).

REFERENCES

Bennett, J. 2001. *Trajan: Optimus Princeps*. London.

Bidwell, P. 1997. *Roman Forts in Britain*. London.

—— 1999. *Hadrian's Wall 1989–99: A Summary of Recent Excavations and Research*. Kendal.

Birley, A. R. 1997. *Hadrian: The Restless Emperor*. London.

—— 2002. *Garrison Life at Vindolanda: A Band of Brothers*. Stroud.

Birley, E. 1961. *Research on Hadrian's Wall*. Kendal.

Bowman, A. K. 1998. *Life and Letters on Hadrian's Wall*. London.

Bowman, A. K. and Thomas, J. D. 1996. New writing tablets from Vindolanda. *Britannia*, 27, 299–328.

Breeze, D. J. 1996. *Roman Scotland*. London.

Breeze, D. J. and Dobson, B. 2000. *Hadrian's Wall*, 4th edn. London.

Breeze, D. J. and Hill, P. R. 2002. Hadrian's Wall began here. *Archaeologia Aeliana*, 5th ser. 29, 1–2.

Cameron, A. 1985. *Procopius and the Sixth Century*. London.

Caruana, I. 1997. Maryport and the Flavian conquest of North Britain. In R. J. A. Wilson (ed.), *Roman Maryport and its Setting: Essays in Memory of Michael G. Jarrett*. Carlisle, 40–51.

Creighton, J. D. and Wilson, R. J. A. (eds) 1999. *Roman Germany: Studies in Cultural Interaction*. Journal of Roman Archaeology, Supplementary Series 32. Portsmouth, RI.

Crow, J. G. 1986. The function of Hadrian's Wall and the comparative evidence of Late Roman long walls. In *Studien zur Militärgrenzen Roms III (13 Internationaler Limes Kongress Aalen 1983)*. Stuttgart, 724–9.

—— 1991. A review of current research on the turrets and curtain of Hadrian's Wall. *Britannia*, 22, 51–63.

—— 1995. *English Heritage Book of Housesteads*. London.

Cunliffe, B. 1991. *Iron Age Communities in Britain*, 3rd edn. London and New York.

Daniels, C. M. 1978. *Handbook to the Roman Wall*, 13th edn. Newcastle upon Tyne.

Faulkner, N. 2000. *The Decline and Fall of Roman Britain*. Stroud.

Gwilt, A. and Haselgrove, C. C. (eds) 1997. *Reconstructing Iron Age Societies: New Approaches to the British Iron Age*. Oxford.

Hanson, W. S. 1996. Forest clearance and the Roman army. *Britannia*, 27, 354–8.

Hartley, B. R. 1972. The Roman occupation of Scotland: the evidence of Samian Ware. *Britannia*, 3, 4–15.

Haselgrove, C. 1999. Iron Age societies in Central Britain: retrospect and prospect. In B. Bevan (ed.), *Northern Exposure: Interpretation, Devolution and the Iron Ages in Britain*. Leicester Archaeology Monographs 4. Leicester, 253–73.

Hill, P. R. 1997. The stone wall turrets of Hadrian's Wall. *Archaeologia Aeliana*, 5th ser. 25, 27–49.

Hill, P. R. and Dobson, B. 1992. The design of Hadrian's Wall and its implications. *Archaeologia Aeliana*, 5th ser. 20, 27–52.

Hobley, A. S. 1989. The numismatic evidence for the post-Agricolan abandonment of the Roman frontier in northern Scotland. *Britannia*, 20, 69–74.

Hodgson, N. 1995. Were there two Antonine occupations of Scotland? *Britannia*, 26, 29–49.

Hodgson, N., Stobbs, G. and Van der Veen, M. 2001. An Iron Age settlement of earlier prehistoric date beneath South Shields Roman fort. *Archaeological Journal*, 158, 62–160.

Hunter, Fraser. 1997. Iron Age hoarding in Scotland and northern England. In A. Gwilt and C. C. Haselgrove (eds), *Reconstructing Iron Age Societies*. Oxford, 108–33.

—— 2001. Roman and native in Scotland: new approaches. *Journal of Roman Archaeology*, 14, 289–309.

Jarrett, M. G. 1976. An unnecessary war. *Britannia*, 7, 145–51.

Jones, G. B. D. and Wooliscroft, D. 2001. *Hadrian's Wall from the Air*. Stroud.

Kendal, R. 1996. Transport logistics associated with the building of Hadrian's Wall. *Britannia*, 27, 129–52.

McCarthy, M. 2002. *Roman Carlisle and Lands of the Solway*. London.

Maxwell, G. S. 1989. *The Romans in Scotland*. Edinburgh.

—— 1998. *A Gathering of the Eagles: Scenes from Roman Scotland*. Edinburgh.

Napoli, J. 1997 *Recherches sur les fortifications linéaires romaines*. Collection de l'École Français de Rome 229.

Richmond, I. A. 1937. Review of R. G. Collingwood and J. N. L. Myres, *Roman Britain and the English Settlements*. *Archaeologia Aeliana*, 4th ser. 14, 258–67.

—— 1947. *Handbook to the Roman Wall*, 10th edn. Newcastle upon Tyne.

—— 1950. Hadrian's Wall 1939–49, *Journal of Roman Studies*, 40, 43–56.

Rivet, A. L. F. and Smith, C. 1979. *The Place-names of Roman Britain*. London.

Royal Commission on Ancient and Historical Monuments in Scotland. 1997. *Eastern Dumfriesshire: An Archaeological Landscape*. Edinburgh.

Simpson, F. G. and Richmond, I. A. 1937. The Roman fort on Hadrian's Wall at Halton, *Archaeologia Aeliana*, 4th ser. 19, 151–71.

Sommer, C. S. 1999. From conquered territory to Roman province: recent discoveries and debates on the Roman occupation of south-west Germany. In J. D. Creighton and R. J. A. Wilson (eds), *Roman Germany*. Portsmouth, RI, 160–98.

Taylor, D. J. A., Robinson, J. and Biggins, J. A. 2000. A report on a geophysical survey of the Roman fort and *vicus* at Halton Chesters. *Archaeologia Aeliana*, 5th ser. 28, 37–46.

Tipping, R. 1997. Pollen analysis and the impact of Rome on native agriculture around Hadrian's Wall. In A. Gwilt and C. C. Haselgrove (eds), *Reconstructing Iron Age Societies*. Oxford, 239–47.

Tomlin, R. S. O. 1996. The Vindolanda writing tablets. *Britannia*, 27, 459–63.

Welfare, H. and Swan, V. 1995. *Roman Camps in England: The Field Archaeology*. London.

Whittaker, C. R. 2000. Frontiers. In A. K. Bowman, P. Garnsey and D. Rathbone (eds), *The High Empire*, A.D. *70–192. The Cambridge Ancient History*, volume XI, 2nd edn. Cambridge, 293–319.

Willis, S. 1996. The Romanization of pottery assemblages in the east and north-east of England during the first century A.D.: a comparative analysis. *Britannia*, 27, 223–82.

Wilmott, Tony. 2001. *Birdoswald Roman Fort: 1800 Years on Hadrian's Wall*. Stroud.

Woodside, R. and Crow, J. 1999. *Hadrian's Wall: An Historic Landscape*. London.

CHAPTER NINE

Scotland[1] and the Northern Frontier: Second to Fourth Centuries AD

W. S. HANSON

The Chronology and Extent of Roman Control

The Romans did not return to occupy Scotland until the reign of Antoninus Pius, the conquest stimulated more by political necessity than frontier strategy. Reconquest probably began in AD 139, shortly after the accession of the new emperor. The limited objective, the reoccupation of the Lowlands, seems to have been completed by AD 142, culminating in the construction of a turf rampart and ditch, the Antonine Wall, across the Forth–Clyde isthmus, with outpost forts extending north as far as Bertha on the Tay (figure 9.1). The new wall was modelled on Hadrian's Wall in its developed form, with forts at intervals of approximately 8 miles, and fortlets every mile, though indisputable evidence of a system of watch-towers has yet to be recovered. Before construction of the wall had been completed, however, a major change of plan was introduced, involving the construction of an additional series of generally smaller forts along the line. This brought the spacing between them to about 2 miles, closer than on any other imperial frontier (figure 9.2).

Debates about the chronology of the northern frontier in the later second century have a long history. For some time a consensus view seemed to have been reached, which placed the end of the Antonine occupation of Scotland in about AD 164, though some scholars continued to maintain, on the basis of the epigraphic and numismatic evidence, that occupation continued almost to the end of the century after a lengthy period of return to Hadrian's Wall. But the archaeological data will not sustain a lengthy hiatus in the Antonine occupation of Scotland. Indeed, a cogent case has been put forward for bringing forward its end to AD 158 and dismissing the existence of a second period of occupation entirely. It is suggested that where two phases can be demonstrated, they reflect changes of garrison as a result of the change

---

1   The use of the term Scotland in this paper should be taken as a convenient shorthand for Britain north of the Tyne–Solway isthmus, rather than the contemporary political entity, which has no geographical relevance to the period under consideration.

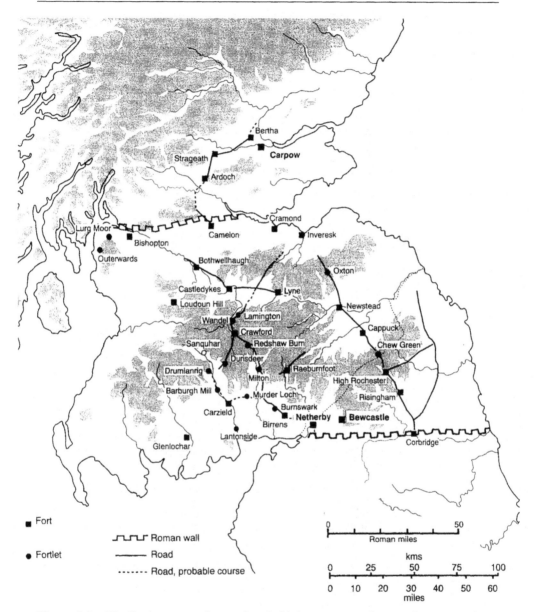

Figure 9.1 Distribution map of second and third century AD Roman forts in northern Britain (after Breeze et al. 1997, 41, 43 and 44).

of plan, or simply piecemeal alterations and repairs (Hodgson 1995). The scattering of artefacts of slightly later date recovered from some Antonine Wall forts is explained as either a phased withdrawal or the occasional use of certain sites as outposts of the more southerly frontier line.

The abandonment of the Antonine Wall and the return to the frontier on the Tyne–Solway isthmus did not see the complete cessation of Roman contact with

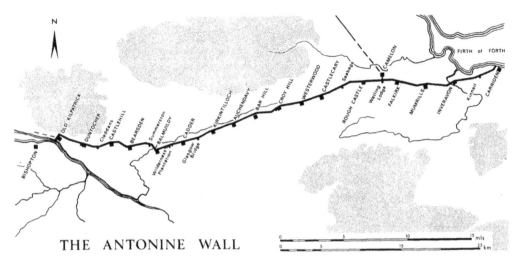

THE ANTONINE WALL

Figure 9.2 Plan of the Antonine Wall as completed (after Breeze and Dobson 2000, 106).

Scotland, though the Roman presence thereafter was restricted to its southern periphery. In the west, outpost forts were maintained immediately north of Hadrian's Wall as they had been earlier, though in the east they extended as far north as Newstead (Melrose) for a further twenty years or so.

The third and final Roman occupation of Scotland was even more short-lived. Between AD 208 and 211 the emperor Septimius Severus conducted major campaigns in Scotland, either personally or through his elder son Caracalla. Only two garrison posts are known definitely to have been occupied at this time, at Cramond on the Forth and Carpow on the Tay (figure 9.1), but neither seems to have continued in use for more than a year or two after Severus' death in AD 211. Thereafter the Roman frontier reverted to Hadrian's Wall and its outposts in northern England, though some still argue that Rome maintained political control through the supervision of tribal meeting-places within the Scottish Lowlands (Mann 1992). Although the Romans did campaign into Scotland on several occasions thereafter, these were solely punitive exercises and did not result in any further attempt to occupy territory. Thus, for most of the Roman period Scotland lay on the periphery of the Empire, explored and within reach, but mainly beyond any formally defined boundary.

The Local Population: Resistance

The most obvious primary contact between the indigenous population and Rome came in the form of armed resistance. Given the failure of Rome to complete the conquest and occupation of Scotland, it is not infrequently suggested that the local population was too warlike to be easily contained, and that they successfully ejected the occupying forces more than once. Certainly, the northern tribes must have been construed by Rome as a potential threat to local security, since there seems to have been a fairly consistent need to maintain substantial military forces within or on the borders of their territory. Indeed, the need to increase the density of troop dispositions during the construction of the Antonine Wall referred to above suggests an unprecedented concern for the strength of potential local opposition. This view appears to be supported by the limited Roman literary accounts available, occasionally hinted at in epigraphic sources, but only rarely attested archaeologically. Supposedly, the Britons could not be kept under control in the reign of Hadrian and war was threatening again early in the reign of Marcus Aurelius (*Scriptores Historiae Augustae*: Hadrian, 5.2; Marcus, 8.7). In the 180s AD unnamed tribes crossed Hadrian's Wall, inflicting a serious defeat on Roman troops (Cassius Dio 72.8.2) and three adjacent sites, Haltonchesters, Rudchester and Corbridge, show sufficiently extensive destruction to suggest that it resulted from such hostilities (Gillam 1974: 7–10). An altar from Kirksteads at the western end of Hadrian's Wall, erected by the commander of the sixth legion, probably in the late second century, gives thanks for 'the successful outcome of action conducted beyond the Wall' (*RIB* 2034). Similarly, the commander of an auxiliary unit at Corbridge records the slaughtering of a band of Corionototae, an otherwise unattested group of tribesmen presumably from beyond the wall, again probably in the second century (*RIB* 1142). A reassessment of the evidence from the hill-fort at Burnswark in Dumfriesshire suggests that it was indeed subject to siege by Roman forces later in the second or early in the third century AD (information from D. B. Campbell). In 208 AD the tribes were again laying waste the frontier area, the situation requiring the presence of the emperor, Severus (Herodian 3.14.1). After his campaigns, however, the frontier seems to have remained peaceful for some time. The peoples further north began to cause trouble again in the fourth century, and punitive campaigns had to be undertaken against the Picts in AD 305, 360, 367, 382 and in the late 390s (*Pan. Lat. Vet.* vi (vii) 7.1–2; Ammianus Marcellinus 20.1; 26.4.5; 27.8; *Chron. Gall.* 452; Claudian, *De consolatu Stilichonis*, 2.247–55). The Traprain Treasure may represent loot from associated native raiding. Dating to the late fourth/early fifth century, it contains at least 120 fine silver objects which had all been broken or cut up, presumably with the intention of melting them down for reuse, indicating that they were not prized as objects but as bullion.

Although the above records confirm that armed hostility remained a feature of Roman and native relations in northern Britain, they are not sufficiently frequent or severe to indicate that the problems involved were greater than elsewhere in the Empire. Nor do they suggest that the intensity of native opposition was responsible for Roman failure to bring the conquest of Scotland to its natural geographical termination or to maintain a hold on that territory which they did bring under their sway. There is little sign in the archaeological evidence that the withdrawal of Roman forces was ever brought about by hostile pressure from local peoples. The fluctuations in the occupation of Scotland can be most readily explained in terms of Roman political necessity and actions on the wider imperial stage, rather than the unprecedented strength of the opposition.

During occupation, resistance to Rome might manifest itself in different and subtler ways. Post-colonial perspectives on the interpretation of archaeological data suggest that material culture may have been used to express resistance of a more passive nature. For example, the continued construction of round houses through into the late Roman period within settlements across much of the province has been taken as a potential symbol of the rejection of Roman values by some segments of the indigenous population (Hingley 1997). Similarly, the absence of Roman artefacts from native sites may reflect a positive rejection of such material, as has been suggested to explain their exclusion from hoards in north-east Scotland (Hunter 1997: 121 and see p. 142 below). Even where Roman artefacts are found in non-Roman contexts, they may sometimes be shown to have been used in entirely different ways. A few sherds of decorated samian from Traprain Law had been converted into spindle whorls or circular gaming counters, while others show forms of intentional secondary cutting to create rectangular pieces of uncertain purpose (Erdrich et al. 2000: 449). Such reuse of Roman pottery is not uncommon on native sites in northern Britain, but only rarely attested in Roman forts. Such interpretations of the significance of material culture can be difficult to prove, but it should always be borne in mind that the adoption of Roman or the retention of native material symbols was to a large extent a matter of deliberate choice.

The Local Population: Diplomacy

Contact between Rome and the indigenous population was by no means all hostile in nature. It was Roman practice to make frequent use of diplomacy when attempting conquest of an area, playing one tribal group off against another. The giving of gifts or payment of financial subsidies as part of an agreement between Rome and peoples along the frontiers of her Empire was a common practice and proved an efficient and cost-effective method of frontier control. It was designed to purchase active military assistance, to buy immunity from attack and to foster dissension among Rome's enemies. After the withdrawal of military forces and the abandonment of most of the forts in Scotland, Roman control over the peoples now living beyond the Imperial borders once more was largely restricted to such contacts. Thus, the Maeatae were bought off by the governor Virius Lupus prior to the campaigns of Severus, and the reference further implies that the Caledonians were in some sort of treaty relationship with Rome at the time (Cassius Dio 75.5.4). At the end of those campaigns, after the death of Severus, Caracalla made further treaties with the Caledonians and withdrew from their territory (Cassius Dio 77.1.1; Herodian 15.6). Whatever reservations there may be about the opportunity that the Romans lost to complete the conquest, this diplomatic conclusion to the hostilities seems to have resulted in peace on the frontier for almost a century. The Ravenna Cosmography, an eighth-century listing of Roman place-names, identifies a number of places (*diversa loca*) in northern Britain which were long thought to have had some special significance in terms of the maintenance of Roman control beyond the frontier in the later third and the fourth century. The list includes the names of two tribes (Segloes and Daunoni), two rivers (Taba and Panovius) and an island (Manavi), and it was this very diversity which led to their dismissal as simply a collection of odd places (Rivet and Smith 1979: 212). More recently, however, the validity of the list has been reasserted because of the particular use of the term *loca*, and it has been argued that the names represent either the outpost forts beyond Hadrian's Wall or, more probably, tribal meeting-places or markets where people were allowed to meet only under Roman supervision (Mann 1992).

Diplomatic relationships are often shadowy and difficult to identify archaeologically, but further hints may be provided by the discovery beyond the northern frontier from the late second century onwards of a number of large coin hoards which are likely to represent the payment of subsidies to Scottish tribes (figure 9.3). From Rumbling Bridge, Kinross-shire, comes a hoard of over a hundred coins ending in AD 184. A very large hoard of over 1900 silver coins found at Falkirk had been assembled primarily under the Severi (AD 193–217) and augmented before its final deposition

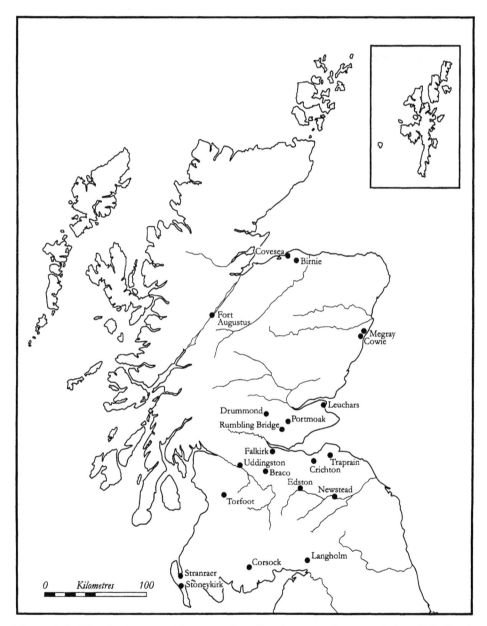

Figure 9.3   Distribution map of late second- to fourth-century Roman coin hoards in North Britain (after Robertson 1978, 187, 193 and 195 with additions).

some fifteen to twenty years later with coins of the next two emperors, while a hoard of 290 silver coins ending in about AD 222, discovered close by the hill-fort at Edston in Peeblesshire, has a very similar content (Holmes and Hunter 1997). More dramatic have been the results of excavations at Birnie, Moray. Here for the first time two hoards, one of third-century denarii and the other still to be identified, have been found in context, buried in native pots a few metres apart outside a large round house (*Discovery and Excavation in Scotland*, 2000: 58–9 and information from Fraser Hunter). Large hoards of late third- or fourth-century date are known, mainly from antiquarian accounts, from several locations well beyond the frontier, for example, at Fort Augustus, dating to the reign of Diocletian (AD 284–305) and at Stoneykirk, dating from the reigns of Constantine I to Decentius (AD 306–353) (Robertson 1978: 209–11).

The Local Population: Trade

It has long been assumed that long-distance trading contacts beyond what became the established Roman frontier in northern England were a regular feature of Roman and native interaction. Certainly the presence of Roman artefacts on native sites is frequently attested (see pp. 151–5 below and figure 9.6). However, it had been noted that such material was most accessible to native communities in the periods of actual occupation (Macinnes 1989: 112), and a recent re-examination of the samian ware from Traprain Law stresses the absence of any indication of an influx of pottery either before or immediately after the periods of Roman occupation of Lowland Scotland in the first and second centuries (Erdrich et al. 2000: 451–2). Thus, for much of the period the Roman frontier seems to have acted as a barrier to economic exchange. A similar pattern has been argued by Fulford (1989) in relation to parts of Germany.

During the occupation the Roman army seems to have played a major role in whatever system of exchange was involved (Macinnes 1989: 112–14). The strong congruence in the forms of samian vessels found on Traprain Law and on various military sites demonstrates a close relationship between the two, at least for the early Antonine period (Erdrich et al. 2000: 452–3). The simplest explanation is that the indigenous population obtained Roman material goods from the military supply system, presumably either by commercial exchange or by barter from the *vicus* of the nearest fort. It is clear, however, that such access to Roman goods was not universal, being largely confined to the élite or wealthier elements of native society. Nor were all native groups equally attracted by Roman material goods.

Traprain Law is one of the few sites in Scotland that has produced evidence of continued contacts with Rome in the third and fourth centuries. The coin list from the site, excluding those associated with the late Roman hoard of silver plate discussed above, runs through to about AD 400, though with a gap from about AD 160 to 250. The late third- and fourth-century coins constitute two-thirds of the total from the site. However, they are of low denomination base metal with little or no intrinsic value, and the overall pattern of their loss is not representative of the currency circulating at the time (Sekulla 1982: 288–9). This implies that they are unlikely to represent booty and do not reflect regular economic interaction with sites that were fully integrated into the contemporary provincial economy. The coins have been seen as indicative of a different function of the site as a ceremonial centre (Hill 1987), though this interpretation is neither convincing, nor does it explain how the material arrived at the site. Since the quantities involved are relatively small and the time-span lengthy, the most likely explanation would seem to be that this later Roman material does reflect irregular, intermittent trade contacts beyond the frontier, though such trade may have had diplomatic rather than purely economic overtones.

Leaving aside debates about the extent to which economic factors may have motivated Roman territorial expansion, there is no doubt that the exploitation of resources was a high priority for Rome once the conquest of an area was complete. This normally took three forms: the extraction of natural resources, most commonly metals; the utilization of human resources through enslavement or recruitment into the Roman army; and taxation. There is no direct evidence of either the first or last in Scotland, but Britons were certainly recruited into the Roman army. Because the presence of several irregular units of Brittones is first attested epigraphically in Germany in the mid-second century, it was once believed that these troops represented men recruited, or even transported *en masse*, from the Scottish Lowlands. Archaeological evidence that the forts involved had first been occupied by the same units in the later first century served to disprove this postulated connection, and clearance of population as a result of the Roman advance into Scotland is not sustained by the settlement evidence. The Brittones might still have been recruited in North Britain, however, for such irregular troops were generally drawn from the least civilized parts of the frontier provinces, and recently the presence of T. Haterius Nepos as *censitor Brittones Anavion[enses]* in Annandale at the very beginning of the second century has been linked with the conscription of the local male inhabitants (Birley 2001). The only epigraphic record of a native from Scotland comes from Colchester in the early third century, where a man called Lossio Veda describes himself on a religious dedication as a Caledonian (*RIB* 191). He was presumably a person of some substance, since he paid for the inscription himself, though whether he was a soldier, a merchant or a noble hostage is unknown.

The Impact on the Indigenous Population: Environment and Landscape

It has been asserted recently, on the basis of the analysis of a pollen core from Fozy Moss, that the Roman army played a major part in the clearance of the natural forest cover in the area of Hadrian's Wall (e.g. Dumayne 1994). Though it is inevitable that the demands of the military for building timber will have had some impact, if only locally, significant Roman involvement in forest clearance cannot be substantiated (Hanson 1996). Most published pollen analyses suggest that extensive woodland clearance began in the second half of the first millennium BC and was linked to the long-term expansion of settlement and agriculture (e.g. Dumayne-Peaty 1998). Where they are available, site-based pollen analyses in Lowland Scotland and northern Northumberland consistently indicate a largely cleared landscape at the time of the Roman arrival (e.g. Jobey 1978: 23–4; Boyd 1984). There is also increasing archaeological evidence that arable agriculture was established even in the more remote uplands by the Pre-Roman Iron Age. Indeed, recent aerial survey work has indicated the presence of Iron Age and Roman period settlement sites and associated extensive agricultural exploitation in the immediate vicinity of Fozy Moss itself (Gates

1999). However, there are occasional hints in the archaeological record of a short-age of suitable building timber in certain areas. By the mid-second century AD, for example, the massive squared timbers which had been used in the first century for the construction of Roman military gateways and towers seem to have been less readily available, and greater use was made of roundwood in fort-building generally.

While on campaign the Roman army lived off the land. Moreover, it was not an uncommon tactic to destroy crops and kill livestock in order to threaten the economic basis of the enemy and bring them to battle. Both actions may have had quite a dramatic impact on the agricultural landscape, but the effects are likely to have been localized and short-lived. However, a marked decline in levels of cultivation and a regeneration of woodland has been noted in a number of pollen diagrams from eastern and north-eastern Scotland, dating in broad terms to the early first millennium AD (Whittington and Edwards 1993). The suggested explanation for these phenomena is that they are a direct result of the ravaging action of the Roman army while on campaign through hostile territory, though there are difficulties with the precision of the associated carbon-14 dates. This is an interesting hypothesis concerning an area within which Roman activity was primarily antagonistic, though the suggested impact seems out of proportion to the size and scope of the military actions which are thought to have stimulated it, not least because the effects seem to have lasted for up to a millennium. Nor can the concomitant suggestion of depopulation and decline be supported in the archaeological record of settlement patterns in the north and east. By contrast, in central Scotland recent analysis of pollen samples from the ditch towards the western end of the Antonine Wall suggest that arable cultivation was taking place nearby and did not decline until the end of the Roman occupation (information from A. Dunwell), though there were hints of a decline in grazing pressure during the Roman period in the analyses from the fort at Bar Hill (Boyd 1984).

The Impact on the Indigenous Population: Settlement and Land Use (figure 9.4)

It has long been argued that the Roman conquest and occupation brought about major changes in native settlement patterns. In particular, the move from defensive to non-defensive, usually enclosed, settlement has been seen as a direct consequence of the imposition of the *pax Romana*. But the pattern of settlement development was more complex. While field survey established that numerous hill-forts in the uplands between the Tyne–Solway and the Forth–Clyde were overlain by enclosed settlements (Jobey 1974a: 22; RCAHMS 1997: 158–61), excavation suggested that this move to non-defensive settlement was already underway before the Roman arrival. At Broxmouth, East Lothian, complete excavation of a small Iron Age hill-fort revealed a complex development probably stretching over several hundred years, culminating in a phase of unenclosed stone-built houses (Hill 1982a). Roman artefacts do not appear to have been current on the site until after these houses had fallen into disuse. Similarly, a number of the free-standing non-defensive enclosures in Northumberland can be shown to have had timber precursors, in two cases dated by carbon-14 to the Iron Age (Jobey 1978: 24–7). However, none of the stone-built sites can yet be

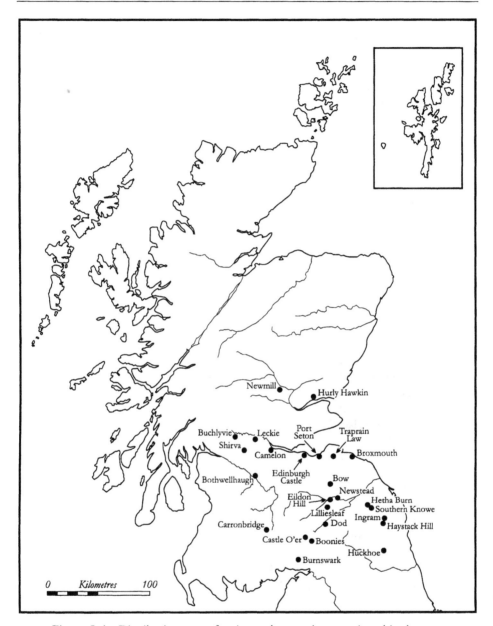

Figure 9.4 Distribution map of native settlement sites mentioned in the text.

demonstrated to have been founded earlier than the first century AD, and a number cannot be earlier than the Roman period (e.g. Jobey 1974b).

A number of naturally or potentially defended sites also remained in use, though whether their defences continued to be maintained is unclear. The classic example is Traprain Law, East Lothian, sited on a natural eminence that dominates the fertile coastal plain. Almost continuous occupation throughout the Roman Iron Age can be demonstrated from the rich artefactual record (Burley 1956), but increasing credence has been given by some to a suggestion (Hill 1987: 88) that during the Roman Iron Age the site was primarily a ceremonial centre. However, recent analysis of the finds distribution points to a number of patterns which are more distinctive of domestic than ritual activity (Erdrich et al. 2000: 444–9 and 452). Hearths and domestic artefacts, including spindle whorls, loom-weights, quernstones and whetstones, show a fairly consistent spread across most of the area examined. The distribution of samian pottery concentrates to the south of the site, particularly in the lower levels, possibly indicating the location of midden deposits, while in the upper levels the focus of depositional activity shifts to the north-west with some signs of industrial activity in the form of crucibles and melted glass. Thus, while domestic activity is attested across the entire site, there is some suggestion of shifting foci and variable function over time. The precise nature of the occupation during the Roman period of the similar volcanic plug on which Edinburgh Castle now stands is not clear, but recent excavations recovered enough Roman material to indicate that it too was a high-status site (Driscoll and Yeoman 1997: 130–7). Small-scale work at Eildon Hill North, Roxburghshire, which rivals Traprain Law in size, suggested that the defences were quite insubstantial, serving more as a territorial marker than a barrier (Owen 1992: 68–9). Moreover, the site, previously thought to have been cleared to allow the construction of a Roman watch-tower at its centre, seems to have continued in use in the second century AD. There is also occasional evidence from other, smaller defensive sites of occupation during the Roman period. At Castle O'er in Dumfries-shire carbon-14 dates indicate maintenance and development of the defences into the Roman period (RCAHMS 1997: 78–82 and 153).

Evidence of a more immediate impact of the Roman presence, whereby native settlements were displaced in order to build Roman forts or other installations, is surprisingly slight. A timber round house at Bothwellhaugh, Lanarkshire, seems to have been burnt down prior to construction of the bath-house outside the Antonine fort there (Keppie 1981: 49), but the small Iron Age enclosure at Camelon, Falkirk, appears to have been only temporarily displaced by the occupation of the annexe of the adjacent Antonine fort, for a second phase of round-house construction overlies the Roman features (Proudfoot 1978). Similarly at Carronbridge, Dumfriesshire, construction of a Roman temporary camp nearby does not seem to have disturbed the occupation of the settlement enclosure (Johnston 1994). Unfortunately, the relationship of the enclosure to the adjacent Roman road was not established, though it clearly must have impinged on the area within the outer of the two ditches (figure 9.5).[2] The nature of the settlement pattern in the later Roman period is potentially problematic. Most of the settlement sites investigated fail to produce material later in date than the second century AD and as a result it has been suggested that they were abandoned shortly thereafter (Hill 1982b: 9–10). Some have even gone so far as to suggest that Severus and Caracalla solved the frontier problem in North Britain by massacring the local population or transporting them away *en masse* (see p. 143 above for a similar hypothesis in the second century). There are, however,

2   The excavator suggests that the two concentric enclosure ditches at Carronbridge were not in contemporary use. But there is no stratigraphic evidence to support this assertion, and the almost complete absence of features outside the inner ditch makes the separate existence of the outer one less than convincing.

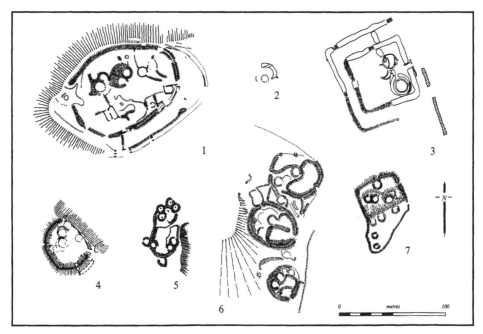

Figure 9.5 Plans of selected Romano-British settlements referred to in the text: 1. Huckhoe; 2. Newmill; 3. Carronbridge; 4. Boonies; 5. Southern Knowe; 6. Haystack Hill; 7. Hetha Burn (after Jobey 1959, 221; 1964, 49 and 60; 1974b, 123; Burgess 1984, 168; Johnston 1994, 238; Watkins 1980, 187).

various objections to the hypothesis of abandonment, and even more to the suggestion of a drastic cause. First, given that Roman artefacts seem to have been differentially available according to social, political or economic factors, no chronological implications can be drawn from their absence from sites of potential Roman date. In particular, the almost total lack of Roman material in the later third and fourth centuries, when the army was not physically present in the area, may reasonably be taken to reflect nothing more sinister than lack of access to such material. The structural history of such sites was not static and many demonstrate expansion over time. Indeed, at Burnswark a scooped settlement overlies the south-western rampart of the Roman south camp, and platforms for round-houses are visible in its northern corner overlying the second-century AD Roman fortlet, suggesting reoccupation of the site after the Romans had departed (RCAHMS 1997: 180–3).

Some sites both continued to be occupied and had access to later Roman material. Traprain Law is one, demonstrating its continuing domination of contacts with Rome, and recent finds from excavations at Edinburgh Castle suggest occupation there extending into the fourth century (Driscoll and Yeoman 1997: 130–7). But not all examples are obviously of high status. The stone-built enclosure at Huckhoe in Northumberland is only about 1 acre in internal area (figure 9.5) but provides structural and artefactual evidence of occupation from the earlier Iron Age to the post-Roman period (Jobey 1959). The site appears to have had access to both a range and quantity of material in the Roman period not readily paralleled on similar, though generally smaller, stone-built settlements. Recent field-walking and excavation at Lilliesleaf, Roxburghshire, a single-ditched rectilinear enclosure, has produced coins of late third- and fourth-century date (Bateson and Holmes 1997: 531), though assessment of other Roman material from the site is still awaited. In the two latter cases, proximity to the road network may have continued to facilitate easier access to Roman material.

A recent reassessment has attempted to link the demise of souterrains, underground passageways now widely regarded as food stores (Watkins 1980), with the departure of the Roman military and the cessation of the market for surplus grain (Armit 1999: 593–4). Mainly located in the eastern Lowlands north of the Forth, with outliers in Lothian and the Borders, their use cannot be demonstrated to extend much beyond the Roman period. But their continued construction after the Roman withdrawal in the mid-second century is indicated by the reuse of much Roman masonry from nearby forts in the examples at Shirva, Dunbartonshire, and Newstead, Roxburghshire. At the other extreme, Newmill in Perthshire has produced a carbon-14 date attesting its origins in the later Iron Age (Watkins 1980: 169 and 178). Thus, linking their floruit to Roman activity cannot readily be sustained. The more likely explanation for their demise remains a change in the social structure that underpinned the use of local communal storage facilities, perhaps related to increased political centralization.

Traditionally the appearance and decline of the Lowland brochs, the distinctive dry-stone towers best known in the Highlands, have been considered almost solely in the context of Roman military activity. They have been variously explained as the homes of northern invaders, filling the power vacuum after the Roman departure, or as the bases for mercenaries invited south to assist in the defence of territory either for or against Rome. But there is no evidence that the occupation of the broch at Leckie, near Stirling, was ended by Roman attack. Nor is there anything to indicate the involvement of the Romans in the demolition of the brochs at Bow, Midlothian, Buchlyvie, Stirlingshire, or Hurly Hawkin, Angus (Macinnes 1984: 237–8). Rather, the range and quantity of Roman artefacts from these sites indicate that their inhabitants were on friendly terms with Rome. Similarly, the absence of artefacts indicative of cultural links with the far north and west of Scotland makes it difficult to accept that they were the homes of northern immigrants. Moreover, the brochs show no departure in their internal arrangements from traditional local house forms, and in some cases, as at Buchlyvie and Hurly Hawkin, continuity of occupation can also be demonstrated. Thus, the brochs should be seen as an integral part of local architectural developments, their more elaborate form offering an alternative mode of material symbolism or display for the wealthier elements of indigenous society (Macinnes 1984).

One possible beneficial effect of the *pax Romana* is an increase in population. A survey of non-defensive, enclosed settlements in the eastern Lowlands between Tyne and Forth, generally regarded as of Romano-British date, provides clear indications of expansion, some 30% showing an increase in the number of houses over time (Jobey 1974a). In some cases additional houses were inserted overlying or immediately outside the enclosure walls or within the yards, as at Southern Knowe, Northumberland (figure 9.5). In others the enclosure itself was expanded to incorporate further houses, as for example at Haystack Hill or Hetha Burn in Northumberland (figure 9.5). It is more difficult to demonstrate the spawning of entirely new settlements, but in some areas their density is considerable, with, for example, some 150 houses recorded in 21 enclosures within a two- to three-mile stretch of the Breamish valley in Northumberland. Unfortunately, as noted above, the phenomenon is not closely dated. A similar pattern is apparent from excavations at some of the timber-built sites, such as at Boonies in Dumfriesshire, where the number of timber houses within the enclosure increased from one to five (Jobey 1974b) (figure 9.5).

Some settlement forms were introduced by Rome. Though no towns ever developed north of Hadrian's Wall, civilian settlements outside forts (*vici*) are attested at several sites, particularly those associated with the Antonine Wall. Rarely, however, have any of these settlements been subject to large-scale investigation, so that our knowledge of them is little more than rudimentary. Indeed, there is still debate about the relationship between such settlements and the fort annexes (e.g. Bailey 1994: 305–11). Associated field systems indicate that the inhabitants were directly involved in farming, as confirmed by excavation at Croy Hill and indicated on aerial photographs at Carriden and at Castledykes in Lanarkshire, where the ditches of a temporary camp are reused. A settlement at Carriden of sufficient significance to have its own administrative organization is implied by a communal dedication to Jupiter made by the inhabitants of the *vicus*. The most extensive civilian settlement in Scotland in the Antonine period is that to the east of the fort at Inveresk, East Lothian, its importance confirmed by two inscriptions recording the presence there of the imperial procurator. Again, aerial photography has confirmed the presence of extensive field systems. Excavations have confirmed their date and revealed various structures extending for approximately a kilometre from the fort (Bishop 2002).

The primary role of the *vici* would have been to serve the economic and social needs of the local garrison, providing goods and services, and accommodation for unofficial 'wives' and children. The presence of such non-combatants is occasionally attested on altars and tombstones. Examples are recorded from Auchendavy on the Antonine Wall, from Birrens, Dumfriesshire, Netherby, Cumbria, and from Risingham in Northumberland (*RIB* 2182–3; 2115; 967, 984; 1246, 1248, 1250–2, 1254, and 1258). It may not be insignificant that, as outpost forts to Hadrian's Wall, the last three were occupied over a longer time-scale than other forts in the area, the latter two into the third century, when the marriages of military personnel ceased to be proscribed. The civil settlements would have been imposed on the indigenous pattern along with the forts with which they were associated. They need not have accommodated any members of the local population, though the Celtic ethnicity of individuals occasionally recorded on tombstones may hint at such involvement. One of the tombstones from Risingham records the unnamed infant daughter of Blescius Diovicus, whose Roman name is clearly derived from its Celtic roots, but other name forms suggest non-local origins. Even if mainly populated by individuals from other provinces, however, the market role of the *vici* is likely to have been one of the primary mechanisms by which the indigenous population obtained Roman artefacts, and consequently these settlements were also a potential vehicle of Romanization.

The Impact on the Indigenous Population: Subsistence and Food Supply

One major potential Roman impact on the local economic system was the requirement to support the food needs of the military garrison. During the Antonine occupation this would probably have numbered some 22,000–25,000 men. Calculations based on the most recent estimate of the military grain ration suggest that they would have consumed between 8000 and 10,000 tons of wheat per annum, with a further 8350–8900 tons of barley for the cavalry horses (Hanson 1997).[3] A recent reassessment of the daily meat ration would give an annual total for the putative maximum garrison of only 537 tons. Allowing for the preference for beef and pork amongst the military, this would translate into 2800 cattle, 4800 pigs and between 4800 and 14,400 sheep, based on the estimated dressed weight of carcasses.

It is now generally accepted that the Iron Age subsistence economy in North Britain was one based on mixed farming. There are sufficient sites where bone evidence survives to suggest that the main domestic species exploited were cattle, sheep, pigs and goats, but not enough to allow more detailed study. Although the role of arable agriculture is generally under-represented in the pollen record, archaeological evidence of later prehistoric arable cultivation continues to grow. Rotary quernstones are common finds on Iron Age and Romano-British settlement sites (e.g. Jobey 1959: 269–76; 1974b, 133–4; Hill 1982a: 181) and plough-marks are regularly discovered preserved beneath the ramparts of Roman forts, for example, at Cramond. Remains of narrow or cord-rig cultivation have been widely recorded, particularly in the Borders, even in what are now environmentally unsuitable locations. Though attaching precise dates to these field remains is still a problem (Topping 1989), they do seem in the main to be associated with later prehistoric settlement sites, and in some cases, such as at Wallsend and Newcastle, can be shown to have been still extant when Roman forts were built over them.

Dated regional pollen diagrams indicate that mixed farming involving barley cultivation seems to have been the norm in the pre-Roman Iron Age (e.g. Whittington and Edwards 1993). Barley is better suited to the damper climate and shorter growing season that predominates in Scotland. A similar pattern of local land use is recorded in pollen analyses from Roman fort sites in central Scotland (e.g. Butler 1989: 273). The record of macrofossil plant remains also indicates an emphasis on barley cultivation (Boyd 1988: 104–5). In the Breamish valley in northern Northumberland, for example, a mid-second-century AD date has been obtained from quantities of barley deposited in a ditch fill of a native enclosure at Ingram South, located only two miles from the Devil's Causeway Roman road (Frodsham 2000: 27). However, wheat is attested as a relatively minor part of the plant assemblage from some sites in Dumfriesshire and northern Northumberland (e.g. van der Veen 1992: 34–9; Johnston 1994), while recent excavations on the Iron Age settlement enclosures at Port Seton in Lothian indicate the presence of wheat in quite large quantities,

---

3 The calculations were made in respect of the estimated strength of the garrison in the first century, but the additional demands of manning a linear barrier meant that the garrison was unlikely to have been much less in the primary Antonine period despite the reduction in the area occupied.

mainly emmer but with higher proportions of spelt in later contexts (Huntley 2000: 161 and 169–70).

Thus the military meat requirement should have been available in the areas where the troops were stationed, as should the barley and a reasonable proportion of the wheat. Estimating the impact of these demands on the local economy requires that they be translated into a percentage of local production figures. Basing an estimate on the experimental yield figures from the Butser Ancient Farm, the area necessary to produce the entire military wheat and barley requirement would be between 12,000 and 26,000 acres (about 4850–10,500 hectares), depending on whether or not the fields were manured. Similarly, extrapolating from advice on potential output offered to small farmers at the beginning of the twentieth century, the animal requirements represent the product of approximately 9000 acres of grazing land. In relation to the size of the area under Roman control, the annual requisition or purchase of the product of between 21,000 and 35,000 acres (about 8500–14,160 hectares) is large, but not excessive, and would have been further reduced by the necessity to import most of the wheat. Moreover, these demands would have been garnered as a percentage of the product from a much wider area so as to ensure that the supply would be sustainable in the longer term.

Expressed differently, assuming the occupation of some fifty Roman military installations in the second century AD, the requirements even at the upper end of the estimate represent the product of about 3 per cent of the land within a three-kilometre radius of each Roman fort or fortlet. Allowing for land not under cultivation, this figure seems even less excessive. In the more fertile parts of eastern Scotland, Roman demands may have served to stimulate the local economy to produce a surplus (Breeze 1989: 229), assuming they were not already doing so. Alternatively, in areas with more marginal environmental conditions or the absence of a socio-economic structure which could readily be adapted to the potential of a market economy, the Roman presence may have had a depressing effect on the subsistence economy, as has been argued was the case in northern England (Higham 1989). On present evidence, the first of these scenarios seems more likely for Lowland Scotland. Pollen evidence for forest clearance seems to indicate that agricultural expansion continued through the Roman period, though recent work in the western Lowlands suggests the possibility of some localized woodland regeneration (Dumayne-Peaty 1998: 209). Similarly, examination of native settlements in the more marginal areas of northern Northumberland and the Scottish borders suggests an increase rather than a decrease in population during the Roman period, and attention has been drawn to the possible correlation between settlements showing signs of expansion and those associated with probable arable field systems (Gates 1982: 38).

The Impact on the Indigenous Population: Material Culture

Roman impact on indigenous material culture has traditionally been seen as considerable, so that many of the artefacts from the area which characterize the period are attributed to diffusion from the south rather than being seen as local developments. This includes the distinctive glass bangles and blue or green glass melon-beads that are relatively common site finds (Stevenson 1976). Similarly, the three large ironwork hoards from Carlingwark Loch, Blackburn Mill and Eckford in Lowland Scotland are thought to have been deposited by Roman auxiliary troops of Celtic origin (Manning 1981).

The diffusionist paradigm which underlies these interpretations is no longer as widely followed, and indigenous production is to be preferred unless there is direct evidence to the contrary. The distribution pattern of the glass bangles, heavily concentrated in southern Scotland, makes them difficult to see as other than local products. Crucibles, some containing coloured glass, and moulds for dress-fasteners are recorded from Traprain Law, confirming the local manufacture of at least some glass and bronze artefacts (Burley 1956: 181 and 220). Moreover, the probable local origin of many of the iron tools is indicated by recent comparative metallographic and radiographic analysis of iron knives from the hoards at Carlingwark Loch and Black-burn Mill, and from the large hill-fort at Traprain Law, with material from the Roman fort of Newstead (Hutcheson 1997). The iron used in the Roman fort had been more efficiently smelted, since it contained less slag, and the blades examined had been produced by a more sophisticated smithing procedure involving composite construction.

However, there does appear to be an increase in both the volume and range of material available to native communities in the Roman Iron Age compared to what went before, though more precise chronological patterning remains elusive in the absence of independent dating for the material other than its association with Roman imports. To some extent this increase may be explained by changes in the process of deposition during the Roman Iron Age, but it seems likely that it also reflects a real increase in the availability of the appropriate raw materials. Thus, analyses indicate the reuse of bronze (more correctly brass) of Roman origin in the manufacture of native artefacts (Tate et al. 1985; Dungworth 1997: 48–9). By contrast, on present evidence there seems to have been little reuse of Roman iron or transfer of either smelting or smithing technology from Roman to native (Hutcheson 1997: 71–2).

The presence of Roman finds on native sites has long been the subject of record. The actual quantity of material appears to be quite small, though recent assessment has prompted the suggestion that the distribution pattern, based on excavation and chance discoveries, may considerably underestimate the volume of Roman metalwork in circulation (Hunter 1996, 2001: 290–1) (figure 9.6). The artefacts are sometimes of surprising quality, and a scarcity of the more mundane items, such as coarse pottery, is apparent. By the Antonine period both the quantity and geographical distribution of material increases, with finds extending into the north and west of the country (Macinnes 1984: 241–2). A variety of settlement types are represented, though distribution is biased towards the more elaborate and presumably higher-status settlement forms such as brochs, duns, crannogs and souterrains, the considerable storage capacity of the latter indicating the ability of the occupants to produce a substantial surplus.[4] Traprain Law is pre-eminent in terms of the range, quality and

---

4   Given the tendency for archaeological work to focus on higher-status sites, the possibility that the distribution of Roman finds on native sites reflects a bias in data collection must be considered. However, relatively extensive modern excavations at a number of enclosed settlements, such as at the Dod, Selkirkshire, and of unenclosed houses and a souterrain at Newmill, Perthshire, all of which on other evidence can be shown to have been occupied during the Roman period, produced no Roman artefacts.

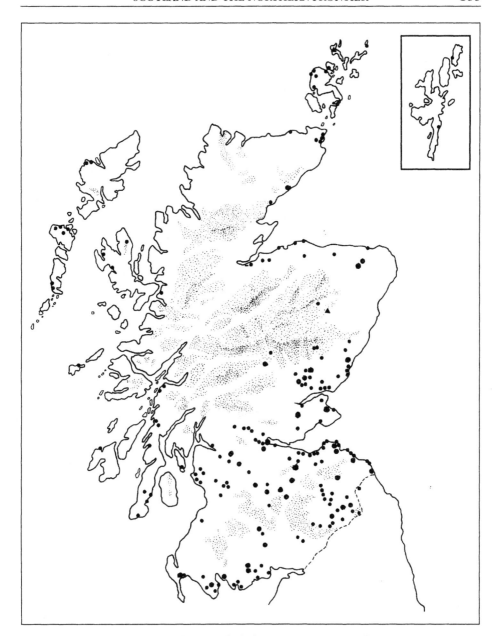

Figure 9.6   Distribution map of Roman finds from native contexts (after Hunter 2001, 290).

quantity of material received, including highly Romanized items such as door-keys, toilet instruments and even an iron stylus. These provide some indication of the level of contact with the Romans and its potential impact on the social and cultural life of the inhabitants of the hill-fort. Traprain also dominates Roman/native exchange thereafter, as noted above, being one of the few sites which continued to receive Roman material in the later third and the fourth centuries (Macinnes 1989: 112–13).

The distribution of Roman finds from native sites suggests that contact with the occupying forces was limited, and largely confined to the upper elements within the local social hierarchy. Such a distribution is not entirely commensurate with the supposed stimulating effect of the imposition of monetary taxation and a market economy (Breeze 1989: 228–9), but it seems to have taken several generations before the native population within the province of Germania Inferior accepted and integrated Roman pottery or other Roman commodities into their own sphere (cf. Willems 1981–4). Since the native peoples of Scotland were not integrated into the more developed socio-economic system which characterized many Iron Age peoples on the fringes of the Roman Empire, and thus were not accustomed to a market economy or coin use, then it becomes more difficult to believe that the short presence of Roman military forces would have led to far-reaching changes in their socio-economic organization. The distribution of coinage gives no indication that native society adopted a monetary economy, though there is a paucity of small-denomination coinage in the province as a whole until the later third century.

Access to Roman goods is frequently regarded as contributing towards maintenance of a prestige goods economy in southern Scotland (Macinnes 1984: 241–2). However, it has recently been suggested that the material may also have been adopted in the same way as other 'exotic' artefacts and deposited in hoards to symbolize the community's alliances and contacts with the wider world (Hunter 1997: 121). By contrast, the absence of such material from hoards in the north-east of the country is taken to indicate an emphasis on local identity in the face of Roman threat, for it can be demonstrated that Roman artefacts were in circulation in the area since they are found occasionally in burials, and Roman bronze was reused in the local production of massive bronze armlets (Tate et al. 1985). This also serves to highlight regional variations in the response to the Roman presence.

Roman goods did not reach native hands by chance or simply trickle down to them as cast-offs. Though there is a broad congruence between what was in use in Roman forts and their associated *vici* and what is found on native sites, the indigenous population were clearly expressing preferences and exercising choice in their selection of material. This is immediately apparent from the percentage of high-quality artefacts and the relative scarcity of more mundane items. More detailed analysis provides further support for this assertion. A recent comparative study of the distribution of different brooch types indicates a preference for those with clear echoes of native decorative traditions (Hunter 1996: 121–3). The wearing of brooches seems to have been somewhat alien to pre-Roman Iron Age society, which showed a marked preference for pins. Thus, the popularity of Roman brooches, perhaps serving as status symbols, was tempered by an element of conservatism. It is interesting to note, however, that Traprain Law shows a slightly different pattern with a greater proportion of military-style brooches, perhaps reflecting a greater degree of cultural assimilation.

The potential two-way nature of exchange mechanisms and, accordingly, the presence of native artefacts on Roman sites have never been systematically assessed (but see Allason-Jones 1991 for a brief survey). This is made problematic by the difficulty involved in identifying the ethnic origins of substantial elements of material culture in the area. Glass bangles and bronze 'dress-fasteners' are commonly found on Roman forts as well as native sites (Wild 1970; Stevenson 1976). Wild interprets the fasteners as harness mounts, suggesting that they were items of military equipment, and Stevenson sees most of the bangles as the products of incomers from the south, though accepting that some were probably made at Traprain Law. But if both are simply accepted as indigenous products, their presence on Roman sites implies that trade contacts between Roman and native were not entirely one-sided. This may also explain the presence on military as well as native sites of particular types of bronze penannular brooches, which have a clear native British ancestry (Fowler 1960: 169–71 and 174–5), ring-headed pins and bone 'weaving' combs (Allason-Jones 1991: 3–4).

The Impact on the Indigenous Population: Socio-political Structure

One change that may have come about in response to the Roman presence is a form of political unification. It is from classical literary sources that we obtain the names of the indigenous political groupings in Scotland which are conveniently referred to as tribes. The name Caledonians came to be used generally in that literature for the inhabitants of northern Scotland, but in Dio's account of the campaigns of Septimius Severus they are referred to as a confederation of the tribes north of the Forth, and contrasted with the Maeatae representing a similar merging of the more southerly tribes (76.12). During the later third and fourth centuries AD we see the appearance of what became the kingdom of the Picts, which again seems to have grown out of the previous tribal-based social structure. An anonymous panegyric delivered in AD 310 to the emperor Constantine, who campaigned in Scotland, refers to the Caledonians and other Picts, while in AD 367 the Picts are described as divided into two parts, the Dicaledonae and Verturiones (*Pan. Lat. Vet.* vi(vii) 7.2; Ammianus Marcellinus 27.8.4). This process of political fusion seems to be mirrored beyond the Rhine and Danube frontiers with the appearance of the Alamanni in the third century, but linking it directly with the Roman presence remains a speculative, albeit attractive, hypothesis (Mann 1974: 41).

The Impact on the Indigenous Population: Religious Life

Roman vessels seem to have played a significant role in indigenous ritual practices in Scotland, being found quite frequently in association with water (Hunter 1997: 117 and 127). But this indicates a continuity of ritual practice, merely utilizing exotic material as an alternative form of conspicuous consumption. Three large, primarily ironwork, hoards have been singled out for detailed examination in the past: Carlingwark Loch in Kirkcudbrightshire, Blackburn Mill in Roxburghshire and Eckford in Berwickshire. They are generally accepted as votive deposits, because of their discovery in lakes. Though they appear to contain artefacts of both Roman and native manufacture, the origins and significance of the deposits have been the subject of much dispute. On the one hand, they have been seen as products of the Roman presence, their contents entirely derived from Roman military contexts and likely to represent deposition by auxiliary troops of Celtic origin from southern Britain or the continent (Manning 1981). On the other, they have been thought to represent the actions of native refugees from the south, transhipped to the frontier zone as an act of Roman policy (Piggott 1953). In neither case could they be regarded as indicative of local religious activity. However, a recent review, drawing attention to the probable local origin of many of the iron tools indicated by metallographic and radiographic analysis (Hutcheson 1997), emphasizes their significance as indicators of change in local ritual practice, perhaps reflecting a greater emphasis on acts of communal rather than personal deposition (Hunter 1997: 116–17). This would not be an unprecedented reaction to the social stress likely to have been caused by the presence of a force of occupation.

Whether the same social forces also stimulated renewed interest in traditional sites of religious significance is speculative, but we do see the ritual deposition of quantities of Roman material in cave sites, particularly in north-east Scotland. The best-known example is Sculptor's Cave, Covesea, on the Moray Firth. Originally a burial site of later Bronze Age date, the cave has produced counterfeit Roman coins, bronze pins and toilet articles. From Constantine's Cave and Kinkell Cave in Fife, both of which displayed a considerable depth of cultural deposits, have come a range of Roman pottery, including olive-oil amphorae, a glass bottle and the handle of a bronze jug (Hunter 1996: 119). These assemblages of Roman material may be interpreted as representing the inclusion of exotic and powerful material within local ritual offerings. It is not uncommon for Roman troops to adopt the local gods of the area in which they were stationed, as is readily attested by the numerous Latin dedications to local gods, often combined with Roman ones, found along Hadrian's Wall and its outpost forts. Particularly notable are the dedications to Cocidius, whose cult centre seems to have been somewhere in the vicinity of the Roman fort at Bewcastle. No equivalent dedications are known from Roman military sites in Scotland, with the exception of the statuette dedicated to Brigantia from Birrens (*RIB* 2091). Reference to Medio Nemeton (middle grove or sanctuary) in the list of names in the Ravenna Cosmography, which is thought to refer to sites on the Antonine Wall, suggests that the Romans may have adopted at least one native cult centre. Dedications to Silvanus and Britannia may represent attempts to propitiate local generic spirits, but the paucity of such dedications implies that the level of Roman interaction with local religious life in the area was minimal. This may well reflect the relatively short duration of the occupation of most of Scotland, and in particular the limited level of recruitment from the indigenous population into military units serving locally.

There is little evidence of Roman influence on burial practices in North Britain, other than in the origin of some of the grave goods. The most frequently attested Iron Age burial rite in Lowland Scotland involves inhumation in a stone cist. Several such burials with Roman grave goods are known, largely as a result of antiquarian discoveries (Hunter 1997: 123 and figure 12.3). Multiple inhumations have been recorded adjacent to the Roman forts at Camelon and Inveresk, and in both cases assumed to be military, or closely related (Breeze et al. 1976; Gallacher and Clarke 1993). But the burial ritual involved has more in common with local traditions, since cremation was the norm at Roman sites in Britain until the later second century AD, and at Camelon the individuals were buried with their weaponry, a most unusual occurrence for a Roman burial. One example of a cremation in the Roman fashion within a cairn from High Tors, Luce Sands, Wigtownshire, was originally interpreted as a military burial, but reassessment of the identification and range of associated Roman artefacts, including an iron ring with onyx intaglio and a crucible, has broadened the possibilities to include a trader or smith (Breeze and Ritchie 1980). The date of the finds would indicate operations after the period of Roman occupation.

Conclusion

For many years it has been almost axiomatic in studies of the period that the Roman Conquest must have had some major medium- or long-term impact on Scotland. On present evidence this cannot be substantiated either in terms of environment, settlement, economy or, indeed, society. The Roman impact appears to have been surprisingly limited. The general picture remains one of broad continuity and gradual development, rather than one of disruption and major change. In this context the short time-span and intermittent nature of the occupation should not be forgotten. Though some sections of society, particularly the élite, may have been affected to a greater extent by virtue of their greater contact, the mass of the population seems to have remained largely untouched. Even where Roman artefacts are attested on settlement sites, they tend to represent only one phase in a lengthy period of occupation generally characterized by continuity of the indigenous lifestyle. Where changes did take place, they tend to be longer-term developments which it is difficult to attribute with any certainty to the Roman presence.

In the main, the peoples of northern Britain had little in common with Rome and, prior to the Roman Conquest, had a less developed socio-economic system, which lacked a complex political hierarchy, proto-urban centres (*oppida*), or independent coin use, all traits which typified the south-east of England and contributed to its rapid Romanization. However, these differences should not be taken as a value judgment to indicate that the north was economically peripheral or some sort of cultural backwater. The peoples of the area were merely exhibiting a different trajectory of development within which Roman cultural norms and values were seen as less relevant to the majority of the population.

ACKNOWLEDGEMENT

I am grateful to Lorraine McEwan for preparing the line drawings.

FURTHER READING

Reconstructing Iron Age Societies, edited by A. Gwilt and C. Haselgrove (1997) is a useful collection of papers on the Iron Age, which provides an up-to-date overview of some of the issues important to an understanding of indigenous society. Particularly important for the area under consideration here are the papers by Dungworth and Hunter. *Later Prehistoric Settlement in South-east Scotland*, edited by D. W. Harding (1982) is a useful, if now slightly dated, collection of papers on various aspects of the nothern Iron Age. Reports on otherwise unpublished sites, and more general papers by Hill and Macinnes, are particularly important. *Between and Beyond the Walls: Essays on the Prehistory and History of North Britain in Honour of George Jobey*, edited by R. Miket and C. Burgess (1984) is a very useful collection of papers on aspects of the northern Iron Age. Of particular importance are the overviews provided by Burgess, Macinnes and Welfare.

Breeze and Dobson's *Hadrian's Wall* (third edition, 2000) is a regularly updated standard text that puts the long-lived frontier into its wider historical context. *Rome's North-west Frontier: The Antonine Wall*, by W. S. Hanson and G. S. Maxwell (second edition, 1986) is the standard text on its subject and puts Rome's most northerly frontier into its wider social and historical context.

F. Hunter's paper, 'Roman and native in Scotland: new approaches', *Journal of Roman Archaeology*, 14 (2001), 289–309, is an important and up-to-date survey of the distribution and significance of Roman material from native contexts in Scotland. L. Macinnes' 'Brochs and the Roman occupation of Lowland Scotland', *Proceedings of the Society of Antiquaries of Scotland*, 114 (1984), 234–49, is a now classic paper which demonstrates the important relationship between Rome and the indigenous élites.

REFERENCES

Allason-Jones, L. 1991. Roman and native interaction in Northumberland. In V. A. Maxfield and M. J. Dobson (eds) 1991. *Roman Frontier Studies 1989*. Exeter, 1–5.

Armit, I. 1999. The abandonment of souterrains: evolution, catastrophe or dislocation? *Proceedings of the Society of Antiquaries of Scotland*, 129, 577–96.

Bailey, G. B. 1994. The provision of fort annexes on the Antonine Wall. *Proceedings of the Society of Antiquaries of Scotland*, 124, 299–314.

Bateson, J. D. and Holmes, N. M. McQ. 1997. Roman and medieval coins found in Scotland, 1988–95. *Proceedings of the Society of Antiquaries of Scotland*, 127, 527–61.

Birley, A. R. 2001. The Anavionenses. In N. J. Higham (ed.), *Archaeology of the Roman Empire: A Tribute to the Life and Works of Professor Barri Jones*. BAR (International Series) 940. Oxford, 15–24.

Bishop, M. (ed.) 2002. *Roman Inveresk: Past, Present and Future*. Duns.

Boyd, W. E. 1984. Environmental change and Iron Age land management in the area of the Antonine Wall. *Glasgow Archaeological Journal*, 11, 75–81.

—— 1988. Cereals in Scottish antiquity. *Circaea*, 5.2, 101–10.

Breeze, D. J. 1989 The impact of the Roman army on North Britain. In J. C. Barrett, A. P. Fitzpatrick and L. Macinnes (eds), *Barbarians and Romans in North-west Europe from the Later Republic to Late Antiquity*. BAR (International Series) 471. Oxford, 227–34.

Breeze, D. J., Close-Brooks, J. and Ritchie, J. N. G. 1976. Soldiers' burials at Camelon, Stirlingshire. *Britannia*, 7, 73–95.

Breeze, D. J. and Dobson, B. 2000. *Hadrian's Wall*, 3rd edn. London.

Breeze, D. J. and Ritchie, J. N. G. 1980. A Roman burial at High Torrs, Luce Sands, Wigtownshire. *Transactions of the Dumfriesshire and Galloway Natural History and Archaeological Society*, 55, 77–85.

Burley, E. 1956. A catalogue and survey of the metal-work from Traprain Law. *Proceedings of the Society of Antiquaries of Scotland*, 89, 118–226.

Butler, S. 1989. Pollen analysis from the west rampart. In S. S. Frere and J. J. Wilkes, *Strageath: Excavations within the Roman Fort*. London, 272–4.

Collingwood, R. G. and Wright, R. (eds) 1965. *Roman Inscriptions in Britain I: Inscriptions on Stone*. Oxford.

Driscoll, S. T. and Yeoman, P. A. 1997. *Excavation within Edinburgh Castle in 1988–91*. Society of Antiquaries Monograph 12. Edinburgh.

Dumayne, L. 1994. The effect of the Roman occupation on the environment of Hadrian's Wall: a pollen diagram from Fozy Moss, Northumbria. *Britannia*, 25, 217–24.

Dumayne-Peaty, L. 1998. Human impact on the environment during the Iron Age and Romano-British times: palynological evidence from three sites near the Antonine Wall, Great Britain. *Journal of Archaeological Science*, 25, 203–14.

Dungworth, D. 1997. Copper metallurgy in Iron Age Britain: some recent research. In A. Gwilt and C. C. Haselgrove (eds), *Reconstructing Iron Age Societies: New Approaches to the British Iron Age*. Oxford, 46–50.

Endrich, M., Giannotta, K. M. and Hanson, W. S. 2000. Traprain Law: native and Roman on the northern frontier. *Proceedings of the Society of Antiquaries of Scotland*, 130, 441–56.

Fowler, E. 1960. The origins and development of the penannular brooch in Europe. *Proceedings of the Prehistoric Society*, 26, 149–77.

Frodsham, P. 2000. Worlds without ends: towards a new prehistory for central Britain. In J. Harding and R. Johnston (eds), *Northern Pasts: Interpretations of the Later Prehistory of Northern England and Southern Scotland*. BAR (British Series) 862. Oxford, 15–31.

Fulford, M. G. 1989. Roman and barbarian: the economy of Roman frontier systems. In J. C. Barrett, A. P. Fitzpatrick and L. Macinnes (eds), *Barbarians and Romans in North-west Europe from the Later Republic to Late Antiquity*. BAR (International Series) 471. Oxford, 81–95.

Gallacher, D. B. and Clarke, A. 1993. Burials of possible Romano-British date from Inveresk, East Lothian. *Proceedings of the Society of Antiquaries of Scotland*, 123, 315–18.

Gates, T. 1982. Farming on the frontier: Romano-British fields in Northumberland. In P. Clack and S. Haselgrove (eds), *Rural Settlement in the Roman North*. Durham, 21–42.

—— 1999. *The Hadrian's Wall Landscape from Chesters to Greenhead: An Air Photographic Survey*. Hexham.

Gillam, J. P. 1974. The frontier after Hadrian: a history of the problem. *Archaeologia Aeliana*, 5th ser. 2, 1–12.

Hanson, W. S. 1996. Forest clearance and the Roman army. *Britannia*, 27, 354–8.

—— 1997. The Roman presence: brief interludes. In K. J. Edwards and I. B. M. Ralston (eds), *Scotland: Environment and Archaeology, 8000 BC–1000 AD*. London, 195–216.

Hanson, W. S. and Maxwell, G. S. 1986. *Rome's North-west Frontier: The Antonine Wall*, 2nd edn. Edinburgh.

Harding, D. W. (ed.) 1982. *Later Prehistoric Settlement in South-east Scotland*, Edinburgh.

Higham, N. J. 1989. Roman and native in England north of the Tees: acculturation and its limitations. In J. C. Barrett, A. P. Fitzpatrick and L. Macinnes (eds), *Barbarians and Romans in North-west Europe from the Later Republic to Late Antiquity*. BAR (International Series) 471. Oxford, 153–74.

Hill, P. 1982a. Broxmouth hillfort excavations 1977–78. In D. W. Harding (ed.), *Later Prehistoric Settlement in South-east Scotland*. Edinburgh, 141–88.

—— 1982b. Settlement and chronology. In D. W. Harding, (ed.), *Later Prehistoric Settlement in South-east Scotland*. Edinburgh, 4–43.

—— 1987. Traprain Law: the Votadini and the Romans. *Scottish Archaeological Review*, 4.2, 85–91.

Hingley, R. 1997. Resistance and domination: social change in Roman Britain. In D. J. Mattingly (ed.), *Dialogues in Roman Imperialism: Power, Discourse, and Discrepant Experience in the Roman Empire*. Journal of Roman Archaeology, Supplementary Series no. 23. Portsmouth, RI, 81–100.

Hodgson, N. 1995. Were there two Antonine occupations of Scotland? *Britannia*, 26, 29–49.

Holmes, N. M. McQ. and Hunter, F. 1997. Edston, Peeblesshire. In R. Bland and J. Ornstein (eds), *Coin Hoards from Roman Britain*. Volume 10. London, 149–68.

Hunter, F. 1996. Recent Roman iron age metalwork finds from Fife and Tayside. *Tayside and Fife Archaeological Journal*, 2, 113–25.

—— 1997. Iron age hoarding in Scotland and northern England. In A. Gwilt and C. C. Haselgrove (eds), *Reconstructing Iron Age Societies: New Approaches to the British Iron Age*. Oxford, 108–33.

—— 2001. Roman and native in Scotland: new approaches. *Journal of Roman Archaeology*, 14, 289–309.

Huntley, J. P. 2000. The charred and waterlogged plant remains. In C. Haselgrove and R. McCullagh *An Iron Age Coastal Community in East Lothian: The Excavation of Two Later Prehistoric Enclosure Complexes at Fishers Road, Port Seton, 1994–5*. Edinburgh, 157–70.

Hutcheson, A. R. J. 1997. Ironwork hoards in northern Britain. In K. Meadows, C. Lemke and J. Heron (eds.), *TRAC 96: Proceedings of the Sixth Annual Theoretical Roman Archaeology Conference, Sheffield 1996*. Oxford, 65–72.

Jobey, G. 1959. Excavations at the native settlement at Huckhoe, Northumberland, 1955–7. *Archaeologia Aeliana*, 4th ser. 37, 217–78.

—— 1974a. Notes on some population problems in the area between the two Roman Walls. *Archaeologia Aeliana*, 5th ser. 2, 17–26.

—— 1974b. Excavations at Boonies, Westerkirk, and the nature of Romano-British settlement in eastern Dumfriesshire. *Proceedings of the Society of Antiquaries of Scotland*, 105, 119–40.

—— 1978. Iron age and Romano-British settlements on Kennel Hall Knowe, North Tynedale, Northumberland (1976). *Archaeologia Aeliana*, 5th ser. 6, 1–28.

Johnston, D. A. 1994. Carronbridge, Dumfries and Galloway: the excavation of Bronze Age cremations, Iron Age settlements and a Roman camp. *Proceedings of the Society of Antiquaries of Scotland*, 124, 233–91.

Keppie, L. J. F. 1981. Excavation of a Roman bathhouse at Bothwellhaugh, 1975–76. *Glasgow Archaeological Journal*, 8, 46–94.

Macinnes, L. 1984. Brochs and the Roman occupation of Lowland Scotland. *Proceedings of the Society of Antiquaries of Scotland*, 114, 234–49.

—— 1989. Baubles, bangles and beads: trade and exchange in Roman Scotland. In J. C. Barrett, A. P. Fitzpatrick and L. Macinnes (eds), *Barbarians and Romans in North-west Europe from the Later Republic to Late Antiquity*. BAR (International Series) 471. Oxford, 108–16.

Mann, J. C. 1974. The northern frontier after AD 369. *Glasgow Archaeological Journal*, 3, 34–42.

—— 1992. Loca. *Archaeologia Aeliana*, 5th ser. 20, 53–5.

Manning, W. H. 1981. Native and Roman metalwork in northern Britain: a question of origins and influences. *Scottish Archaeological Forum*, 11, 52–61.

Miket, R. and Burgess, C. (eds) 1984. *Between and Beyond the Walls: Essays on the Prehistory and History of North Britain in Honour of George Jobey*. Edinburgh.

Owen, O. A. 1992. Eildon Hill North. In J. S. Rideout, O. A. Owen and E. Halpin (eds), *Hillforts of Southern Scotland*. Edinburgh, 21–71.

Piggott, S. 1953. Three metalwork hoards of the Roman period from southern Scotland. *Proceedings of the Society of Antiquaries of Scotland*, 87, 1–50.

Proudfoot, E. V. W. 1978. Camelon native site. *Proceedings of the Society of Antiquaries of Scotland*, 109, 112–28.

Rivet, A. L. F. and Smith, C. 1979. *The Place-names of Roman Britain*. London.

Robertson, A. S. 1978. The circulation of Roman coins in North Britain: the evidence of hoards and site finds from Scotland. In R. A. G. Carson and C. Kraay (eds), *Scripta Nummaria Romana*. London, 186–216.

Royal Commission on Ancient and Historical Monuments in Scotland. 1997. *Eastern Dumfriesshire: An Archaeological Landscape*. Edinburgh.

Sekulla, M. F. 1982. The Roman coins from Traprain Law. *Proceedings of the Society of Antiquaries of Scotland*, 112, 285–94.

Stevenson, R. B. K. 1976. Romano-British glass bangles. *Glasgow Archaeological Journal*, 4, 45–54.

Tate, J., Barnes, I. and MacSween, A. 1985. Analysis of massive bronze armlets. In T. Bryce and J. Tate (eds), *The Laboratories of the National Museum of Antiquities of Scotland*. Volume 2. Edinburgh, 89–94.

Topping, P. 1989. Early cultivation in Northumberland and the Borders. *Proceedings of the Prehistoric Society*, 55, 161–79.

van der Veen, M. 1992. *Crop Husbandry Regimes: An Archaeobotanical Study of Farming in Northern England 1000 BC–AD 500*. Sheffield.

Watkins, T. 1980. Excavation of a settlement and souterrain at Newmill, near Bankfoot, Perthshire. *Proceedings of the Society of Antiquaries of Scotland*, 110, 165–208.

Whittington, G. and Edwards, K. J. 1993. *Ubi solitudinem faciunt pacem appellant*: the Romans in Scotland, a palaeoenvironmental contribution. *Britannia*, 24, 13–25.

Wild, J. P. 1970. Button and loop fasteners in the Roman provinces. *Britannia*, 1, 137–55.

Willems, W. 1981 and 1984. Romans and Batavians: a regional study in the Dutch eastern river area. *Berichten Rijksdienst Oudheidkundig Bodemonderzoek*, 31, 5–201, and 32, 42–491.

Chapter Ten

Cities and Urban Life

Michael J. Jones

Urbanization in Roman Britain

The larger urban settlements of Roman Britain, those which might be distinguished with the title of 'cities', constitute one of the clearest indications of the Roman impact on Britain. Civic life was one of the defining elements of Classical society (Drinkwater 1987). The characteristic elements of the principal urban centres – substantial public buildings, strong fortifications and a grid pattern of streets – were imported forms introduced from the Empire. It was convenient for the Roman authorities to have a single base for the administration of each tribe, a system already established in much of Gaul (Woolf 1998).

The subject of urbanism in Roman Britain is still a matter of much debate, and conceptual approaches have been undergoing upheaval in recent years. In particular, the extent of the contribution made by the native aristocracy to the development of the tribal (*civitas*) capitals is now seen as more fundamental to the process of urbanization than any part played by the army, except perhaps in the first phases of the military *coloniae* (Millett 1990). Although it is unlikely that there was much coercion on the part of the Roman authorities, the much-quoted section from Tacitus' *Agricola* (21), that the Britons 'were encouraged to build temples, fora and houses', suggests that they were being persuaded of the political value of adopting Roman civic forms. The Roman occupation provided the élite with a Roman-style urban setting as a context for their rivalries, initially through supporting the development of public amenities, and later through the medium of their private residences (both urban and rural).

The cities thereby created also served not only as administrative bases but in addition as markets and centres of specialist crafts. Although some settlements linked to military sites in the north and west grew to considerable size, the largest urban growth occurred mainly in the south-east of Britain (figure 10.1); this is a reflection of the extent of centralization of the tribes (Cunliffe 1991). Even then, the nature of British society at this time meant that only about twenty-five cities were established – about 5 per cent of the numbers found in the Mediterranean areas of Italy or North

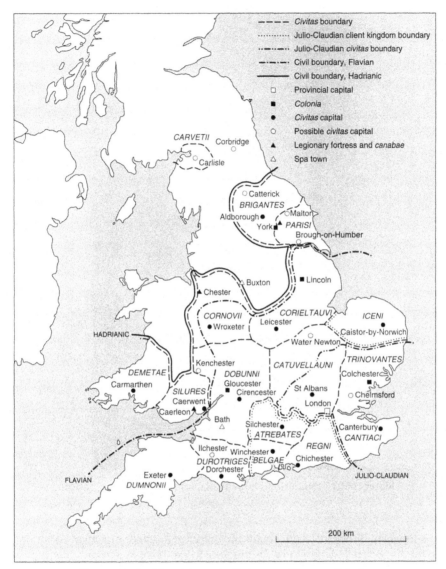

Figure 10.1 The cities and tribal areas of Roman Britain.

Africa, where an urban tradition in the Graeco-Roman mould already existed. Considering these factors, the pace of urbanization is impressive, with much of the effort coming from the start of the Flavian period (AD 69) through to the mid-second century. After this date, no major new towns were established.

There were setbacks – notably when fires took hold of the mainly timber structures of the early towns, and some were deliberate: Boudicca's destruction of London, Colchester and Verulamium (St Albans) in about AD 60/1 has preserved some details of these earliest phases of urban development. There may also have been particular stimuli: it has been suggested that the visit of Hadrian to Britain may

Figure 10.2 Inscription set up by the Civitas Silurum at Caerwent.

have been such, either from the emperor's presence or encouragement, or in preparation for his presence. Unfortunately, but for a few notable exceptions, it is impossible to date urban developments precisely enough to link them to historical events.

Characteristics and Status

The characteristics of a Romano-British city have been defined in one recent study (Burnham et al. 2001), which suggested the following criteria: planned, organized settlements of a minimum size of about 15 hectares (although some less significant sites were larger than this: the key difference was functional) containing a concentration of population and a variety of building types. These buildings housed corporate activity as well as specialization and industrial production (some of it zoned). The settlements in question are those distinguished by a certain level of wealth and status, and a range of cultural activities, a political and administrative function and also a

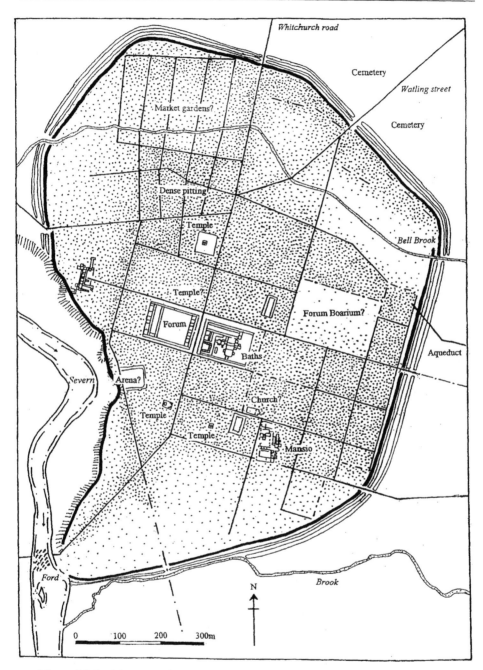

Figure 10.3 The City of Viroconium Cornoviorum (Wroxeter) *c.* AD 125–400.

linked religious role, and with fortifications by the late third century at the latest. The emphasis of much current research is on how towns functioned in society, rather than on form or status.

The legal status of the cities varied, and is understood largely from evidence found in other provinces. The highest status was that of colony (*colonia*). In Britain, three former legionary fortresses were designated as such: Colchester (AD 49), Lincoln (*c.* AD 90), and Gloucester (*c.* AD 96–8?) (Hurst (ed.) 1999). York, while still an occupied fortress, became the capital of the north (*Britannia Inferior*) in the early third century, and the civil settlement was probably promoted to *colonia* status at this time. It is possible that London, which may have begun as a *conventus civium romanorum* – an exception to the usual categories – was promoted from the time it became capital: it was later referred to as *Augusta*. The core inhabitants of the *coloniae* had full Roman citizenship, which the legionaries already possessed, and which was given to all provincials in any case in AD 212 by the Emperor Caracalla. The next rank, probably with Latin citizenship, was that of *municipium*; Verulamium is the only documented example, but London and York may have held the same rank for a while. The vast majority of the tribal capitals were probably classed as *civitates peregrinae* (i.e. of 'provincial' or 'foreign' peoples), thereby retaining a sense of their British identity (figure 10.2). In some ways, and in due course, the distinctions between the various types were insignificant: for instance, the patterns of fortification from the late second century, and of coin loss, are similar for all major towns, and contrast with those of the minor settlements (Reece 1991).

All the cities had constitutions derived ultimately from that of Rome, containing strict rules for the governance of the town. There were annual magistracies involving various duties, including that of organizing religious cults, for those who could afford to take part. The town council (*ordo*) is considered to have been nominally 100 strong, made up of councillors (*decuriones*). In the fourth century, the four cities which held capital status benefited from security and investment.

The Evidence, and the Impact of New Data and Approaches

Some sites are now largely deserted and can be at least partly understood from aerial photographs (figure 10.3), but most are still towns, and since few remains survive above ground, the study of these sites normally involves excavation. The physical evidence has survived only partially and fortuitously, and each city may have something to add to the provincial picture, the general pattern of which is now fairly clear in many respects (Wacher 1995).

Britain may have produced more new evidence for the use of Latin than other areas in recent years, thanks to recent discoveries at Vindolanda and Bath, but there has been little in the way of new epigraphic material to change radically our view of urbanization. Rather, the great growth in knowledge has come in the form of stratified sequences and their contents. Following a period of post-Second World War reconstruction affecting certain sites, redevelopment accelerated during the 1960s, provoking a response in terms of rescue excavation – but the subsequent support to enable full analysis came only after some delay, so that the results of previous work are still emerging. Sufficient material was at hand by the mid-1970s for a first major synthesis in 1975, and the scale of field activity meant that it subsequently took much effort to update this volume twenty years later (Wacher 1995). There is now generally less in the way of large-scale investigations, but it is true that we are still digesting the results of the previous decades. Meanwhile field programmes are continuing at sites where the evidence is more easily accessible, notably at Silchester and Wroxeter.

The resulting, more balanced picture has reinforced the impression of diversity. Re-excavation of some previous investigations has corrected sequences, and particularly added to our understanding of the earliest and latest phases of the town. Other notable characteristics of recent research include a shift away from concentration on monumental buildings and large residences to the suburbs, waterfronts and cemeteries, aspects which are still poorly understood at the vast majority of sites. With investigation of the waterlogged deposits came opportunities for recovering organic materials, not only artefacts of wood, leather or textiles which made up a good proportion of material culture, but also samples of biological material for evidence on the environment. The study of environmental samples is also providing information on such aspects as diet and living conditions, and on the landscape and its exploitation (Dobney et al. 1999). Other recent advances include quantitative analysis to indicate changing population densities (Faulkner 2000), and study of data from cemeteries: both aspects warrant much greater attention. High-quality information in such large amounts, and databases compiled as part of a current national programme, provide opportunities for studying social and economic patterns such as intra-site zonation and the limits of settlement.

Some of the emphasis in recent years has shifted from the cities to the so-called 'small towns' or market centres, which mainly saw their flowering in the third and fourth centuries. Only the most significant of these are mentioned here. Quite a few of them were centres of mass production (e.g. *Durobrivae* (Water Newton) for the pottery industry), or associated with large-scale mineral extraction. It is still uncertain whether their growth was at the expense of the cities, that is, as a result of decentralization of certain activities, or merely represents economic and population growth.

Varying approaches

Until the 1970s the study of Roman Britain was undertaken principally from a Roman perspective, and largely within a historical framework. Understanding of the concept of 'Romanization' was based on an imposition of Imperial ways on the natives, even though Francis Haverfield, who had introduced the term a century ago, saw it as representing interaction between the two cultures. Not surprisingly, the British who did lead the study of Roman Britain tended to identify themselves with the standpoint of the Imperial rulers (Hingley 2000). The recent concern of archaeology with 'culture change', and the withdrawal from Empire which has encouraged a 'post-colonial perspective' among younger generations, have affected our view of Roman Britain (Millett 1990; R. F. J. Jones (ed.) 1991; Webster and Cooper 1996). For instance, the artistic achievements of Romano-British society should not be judged purely on the criteria applied to Graeco-Roman models. With the realization of the part played by the native aristocracy in urban development comes an understanding too of the way in which the new settlement forms reinforced the existing status quo.

The theoretical developments in archaeology contemporary with shifts in perspective have involved an increasing dependence on archaeological evidence, and led to greater interest in social and economic life and the ideological thread which ran through it. This change partly follows movements in urban geography and sociology applied to modern society, in which civic society experiences a greater concentration of activities and processes, all leading to a faster pace of life (Pounds 1994: 341–78; Millett 2001). There were taverns and traders, professional offices and noxious industries. Some current views of urban society argue that there was a two-way relationship between the material culture of the time and the human actions which produced it. While this is true of modern conurbations and perhaps of some of the *metropoleis* of the Roman Empire, it might be considered to be less applicable to the relatively small cities of Roman Britain, which were only as large as modern villages or at the most market towns. Yet the use of space and architectural design may well have affected human experiences and in turn social attitudes – and certainly from the time of Augustus there *was* deliberate use of monumental architecture and engineering achievements to impress and overawe the local population. Although the nature of Roman cities was similar across much of the Empire, it is no longer assumed that the Roman army played the key role in building the early cities, but it was a significant presence in Britain, and opinions still vary on the extent to which official Roman help, advice or expertise was made available, or whether there was a deliberate policy of urbanization or Romanization (see, for instance, Mattingly 1997). Decisions as to the provision and exact form of the various amenities, however, represented the choices made by the élite of each city, perhaps stimulated by suggestions from professional advisers, including representatives of the provincial government, or by impressions made by visits to sites in Britain or beyond.

An enhanced appreciation of the length of the Roman occupation also makes us aware of the changes during that period, notably in the change in Imperial attitudes to Britain, resulting partly from crises elsewhere, and those of the native aristocracy. From initial enchantment with the Roman city as an instrument for maintaining social position by sponsoring public works, later there was resentment at the burdens of office and a move to using private reception areas for establishing credentials.

The chronological and thematic analyses which follow should be seen in the context of these social and environmental perspectives.

Origins and Development

A form of urbanization, marked by increasing nucleation, was taking place in the tribal centres of south-east Britain before the Roman Conquest. That process stemmed partly from contacts with and influences from the Roman world, especially after Julius Caesar's visits in 55–4 BC (Haselgrove 1989; Cunliffe 1991). Their coinages indicate centralized political authority, and their social structure was becoming more complex and stratified. Access to imported luxury items was limited to those of a certain rank, and their ownership reflected a greater sense of private property and the visible expression, through such goods, of rank and status. The subsequent adoption of Romanized forms of wealth display, such as sponsoring public monuments, did not therefore represent a major cultural change.

The larger *oppida* of the first centuries BC and AD were not urban centres in the Roman sense, but some clearly demonstrate Roman influence. At Silchester, for instance, evidence of a street system dating to about 20 BC has been discerned within the existing fortified settlement (Fulford and Timby 2000). It might therefore be argued that the beginnings of urbanization can be detected at these *oppida* a century or so before the Claudian conquest. The native aristocracy's leanings towards the acceptance of the security and material benefits of an imperial power meant that they played a major role in the transition to Roman-style urbanism.

There was another significant presence in this formative period: the Roman army, which traditionally has been seen as a major contributor to both the siting and the building of towns. The establishment of a network of forts attracted natives and encouraged trading communities to set up stalls adjacent to the fort-gates. That these *vicus* sites often remained centres of population after the garrison moved on was accordingly ascribed purely to the long-term influence of a military presence; but it is now clear that many forts were established close to (and sometimes even within) existing concentrations of native population, and that the subsequent transition to an urban settlement when the army had moved on was not an inevitable step. A settlement away from the later routes with no market or other function in the developed economy would not necessarily survive. On the second point, the extent of the army's role in providing technical expertise and in actually helping to build structures, again it would be wrong to assume that the native community was not capable of organizing or undertaking this process itself; but perhaps ex-military engineers were at times involved. Whereas the extent of input from the military remains uncertain, however, the influence of existing layouts on those settlements converted from army bases – notably at the *coloniae* – is clear. The siting of Roman cities in Britain owes something, then, to the existing political geography, but this pattern was partly overlaid by other strategic factors, including the need for accessible communications – many routes were already built and used by the army.

In terms of social, religious and political needs – three intertwined elements – most of the Roman centres merely adapted the native sites to the new Imperial context. The imported elements, requiring huge investment, consisted of various public amenities and (initially basic) accommodation for the population, including traders. The cities were centres of culture, spectacle, craft specialisms, exchange and distribution, and they consumed much in the way of food and materials produced in the immediate hinterland, as well as importing luxury items

The earliest towns to develop were those in the existing tribal centres of what is now south-east England: settlements of the Trinovantes, Catuvellauni, Cantiaci, Regni, Atrebates and Belgae. Their foundations were generally successful. Further major settlements were established subsequently in the regions to the north and west, with some not thriving until well into the second century. Three of these early cities – Colchester, Lincoln and Gloucester – were military colonies, former legionary fortresses converted to receive retired legionaries in groups as they were discharged. The transition from military to civil site is of interest here – as it is at the fortresses of Exeter and Wroxeter, which became *civitas* capitals.

The speed of development of each town would have been largely constrained by the level of resources available to the community and the motivation of certain individuals or groups – including the municipal authority itself – to provide particular elements. The evidence for the awarding of chartered status is too scarce for us to be able to associate particular physical developments to this act, but there may have been some link. Major complexes took several years, perhaps decades, to complete, and the construction of a circuit of walls and gates must have absorbed a large percentage of

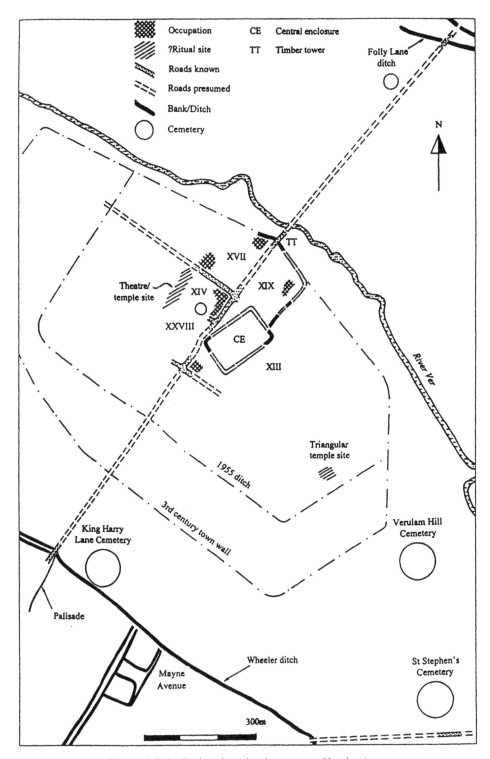

Figure 10.4 Early urban development at Verulamium.

the public budget. Buildings were frequently altered, or even totally rebuilt to another plan, to meet the needs of the new users. Moreover, only so much could be achieved at a time in logistical terms, apart from considerations of finance and expertise. It is likely that architects and sculptors from Gaul and the Rhineland were working at several different sites (Blagg 1989).

The earliest towns

The first quarter-century after the Roman invasion of AD 43 witnessed considerable Roman urban development in Britain. Several of the existing tribal centres adopted Roman forms. They included some client kingdoms which had already established friendly relations with the Roman authorities. London was an exception in being favoured by its strategic location as an entrepôt for the whole province. It soon succeeded Colchester as the provincial capital, although Colchester may have remained the principal focus of the Imperial cult for some time.

The large-scale excavations at Verulamium of the 1930s and 1950s yielded a useful sample for early urban development in Britain, which has served as a (changing) model for several decades. The latest analysis (Niblett 2001) confirms that the settlement was beginning to nucleate around the route leading down the hill from the Folly Lane burial, but focused south of the river, and around the pre-Roman 'Central Enclosure' (figure 10.4). Its best-known structures are a row of workshops in *insula* XIV, providing high-quality goods for the local élite. This settlement may have covered only about 12 hectares, and at the time lacked a street grid. The burnt horizon created by the Boudiccan destruction allows us to analyse what was happening in terms of urban development at the other two sites affected – Colchester and London. This evidence is supported by that from excavations at the Atrebatic centres of Chichester, Winchester and Silchester. All were on or adjacent to Iron Age centres, and were showing signs of urban development before AD 60. The exceptional early developer is Bath, but as a cult centre rather than a town.

Unity and diversity

The most recent excavations in London (*Londinium*), which are yielding evidence of the highest quality, have shown that it was being developed during the Claudian period as a trading centre with many immigrant merchants and artisans. The years of recovery from 61 saw considerable growth, partly organic – including that at Southwark across the Thames – but not entirely random: some sort of planning control was in place, especially on the eastern hill. The huge forum, the amphitheatre adjacent to the fort, and the palace for Carausius or Allectus (290s) are among the most notable public structures (figure 10.5). Major harbour installations and the organic artefacts and samples from the related deposits have been discoveries of great significance (Perring 1991; Milne 1995).

Colchester (*Colonia Claudia Victricensis*?), founded as a colony in AD 49, can lay claim to being the first Roman city in Britain, partly reusing the site and layout of the legionary fortress (figure 10.6), and to exhibiting some of the earliest fully Romanized elements (Crummy 1997). Notable was the Temple to the Deified Claudius, erected after his death in AD 54. Large-scale investigation of the military/civilian

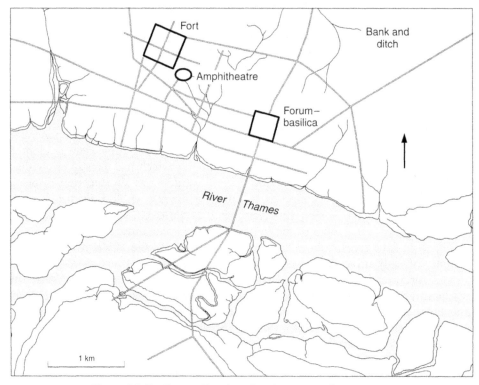

Figure 10.5   Roman London showing principal structures.

transitional phases has demonstrated how the legionary barracks, only a few years old before becoming obsolete, were adapted for civilian occupation.

Colchester probably accommodated all the veteran legionaries who retired before 60. Two other colonies were founded at Lincoln and Gloucester before the end of the century (Fulford 1999). Their foundations, and the land around taken into official hands, provided an expedient mechanism for settling former legionaries in the disused legionary bases. It is likely that several hundred men and their families were accommodated. Although there were some natives and immigrants among them, it is possible that their original colonists, substantially of Mediterranean origin (perhaps 50 per cent were Italians at Colchester, falling to 20–25 per cent at Lincoln and Gloucester), considered themselves to be a special, exclusive group.

The towns which they developed from the rigorous fortress street layouts may have influenced the forms of urban development in the *civitas* capitals, but it is now clear that the *coloniae* were not identical to each other. Like the tribal centres, each community chose from a menu of styles, according to their preferences and resources, the architectural statements they wished and could afford to make about their city. There was a significant early religious centre at all three – it is at the *coloniae* where we might expect the centres of the imperial cult to have been located. In other ways, it is apparent from the evidence of the range of structures, coins and artefacts that, certainly by the third century, they differed little from the native cities. A study of

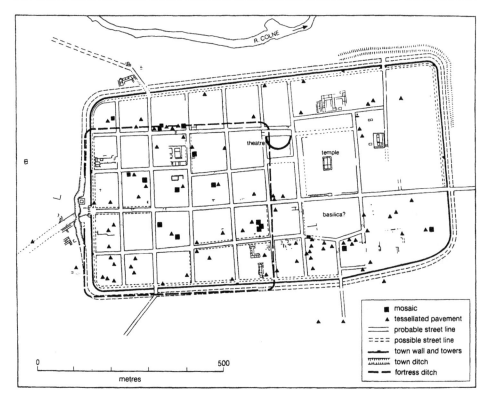

Figure 10.6 Camulodunum, showing the relationship of the early fortress to the later *colonia*.

environmental data might show a difference in diet, with a preference for more Mediterranean taste, for a couple of generations. At both Lincoln and Gloucester, the legionary defences were initially retained and refaced in stone and an early temple precinct built (M. J. Jones 1999a, 1999b; Hurst 1999). At Lincoln, the hillside to the south was also walled later, and extensive suburbs developed; the extent of occupation at Gloucester was not so great but has been underestimated. The promotion of the civil settlement at York (*Eboracum*) to the rank of *colonia* dates from the early third century, perhaps from its selection to be capital of *Britannia Inferior*, or following Septimius Severus' residence during the campaigns in Scotland. The principal focus lay across the river from the fortress.

The civitas capitals

Verulamium (St Albans), whose earliest phases have been described above, really came of age with the establishment of a street-grid and the construction of the large forum-basilica complex completed about AD 80. The study of Silchester *(Calleva Atrebatum)* has benefited both from aerial photography, which has revealed much of its (latest) form, and from recent investigation of its civic basilica, amphitheatre and fortifications, and currently a sample of the residential area. At Winchester (*Venta*

Belgarum), the later cemeteries are notable for a group which contained late Roman military equipment. Togidubnus' third site, at Chichester *(Noviomagus Regnorum)*, was likely to have been his favoured town, and its cemeteries have also been investigated. Canterbury (*Durovernum Cantiacorum*) had been an Iron Age centre but has not yet produced evidence to counter the impression that it developed substantially only from the Flavian period (AD 69–96).

In contrast to the other tribal centres discussed above, Caistor-by-Norwich *(Venta Icenorum)* did not lie on the site of the political centre of the tribe, which probably continued as an independent client kingdom until Prasutagus' death and the subsequent revolt led by his widow Boudicca. The Corieltauvi, the tribe occupying the present East Midlands to the north-west of the Iceni, consolidated their base at Leicester *(Ratae Corieltauvorum)* as its capital rather than that at Old Sleaford, possibly since this lay only 20 miles south of the *colonia* at Lincoln. Cirencester *(Corinium Dobunnorum)* was a new foundation, following military occupation based in the southern part of what became the town. The important native centre at nearby Bagendon was gradually given up in favour of the new site (Holbrook 1998). Dorchester *(Durnovaria)*, was the centre for a tribe – the Durotriges – that had offered considerable resistance to the Roman army.

Further west, Exeter *(Isca Dumnoniorum)* began life as a legionary fortress, and some elements of the military occupation appear to have survived in use for a time after the army left. Wroxeter (*Viroconium Cornoviorum*), like Exeter, developed on the site of a legionary fortress (whose street plan was partially incorporated). Like Caerwent (*Venta Silurum*) further south, its principal phase of development was in the Hadrianic–Antonine periods. The same is true for the most westerly tribal capital, that at Carmarthen (*Moridunum Demetarum*), whose exact site was only formally identified in the late 1960s to the east of a two-phase fort.

Brough-on-Humber (*Petuaria Parisiorum*) remains a problematic identification. The fortifications suggest a military function – perhaps associated with the British fleet – rather than an urban site. Against this is the inscription dating to 144 recording the dedication of the *proscaenium* (stage) of a theatre by an official of the *civitas*. Aldborough (*Isurium Brigantium*) is the least known of the definite *civitas* capitals. It lay on the main route north (Dere Street), to the north-west of York, and probably succeeded a fort.

Other extensive walled settlements

Three other sites to the north of Aldborough all deserve mention, although essentially they remained in the military zone, because of the extensive nature of their civilian settlement: Carlisle, Corbridge and Catterick. None of these took the form of the *civitas* capitals of the 'civilian' areas of the province, but it is possible that both Carlisle and Corbridge functioned as administrative centres for their districts. At Catterick *(Cataractonium)*, a civilian settlement developed along the line of Dere Street both north and south of the River Swale. The later Roman period witnessed its greatest growth, the rudiments of a street-grid and the building of a wall and ditch (Wilson 2002).

These three sites provide useful examples of the larger type of urban settlements which developed in the military zone of Roman Britain. They all exhibit particular growth in the third and fourth centuries rather than earlier, and in that sense are more akin to the so-called 'small towns' – a better term for them might be 'secondary agglomerations', as widely used in France. For present purposes, it is sufficient to note here that some of the 'minor' towns in the civilian area of the province also grew to the same scale, were in due course enclosed by fortifications and exhibit at least a modicum of internal planning, but were not in the same category as the cities.

Analysis

In this section, various themes are reviewed: first the topographical and structural aspects, then cultural, environmental and socio-economic matters, and finally the later chronological periods.

From the point of view of town planning, it is easier to detect political expediency rather than the textbook ideals of Vitruvius in the choice of site, influenced by both native and Roman military predecessors. The second of these are most apparent at the sites of former legionary fortresses, which were rigidly laid out. Whether standard units were employed, as suggested for Colchester from the legionary period, and for other towns (Crummy 1985), is something to be borne in mind and tested, but it cannot easily be confirmed. Not all town-grids were entirely regular: there is considerable diversity, and some show evidence of later modifications – the original phases of urban development are still emerging at several sites. The principal public buildings often clustered on the two main streets and at the heart of the town, expressing the new political realities in Romanized form. That there was deliberate zonation, particularly for commercial and cemetery areas, and even open spaces, seems clear, but we still have much to learn about how land-use could vary through time. Study of the urban fringes, their functions and their mobility has been neglected.

Vast amounts of resources were expended on public works, not only on buildings but also on streets and associated drainage systems and fortifications (figure 10.7). These were largely the responsibility of the municipal authorities to provide and to maintain, but private benefactions were obtained where possible, and could be used to seek popularity and status. Not surprisingly, some schemes were never completed or simply did not function properly. Public programmes provided a great amount of work for those producing the raw materials as well as those involved in actual construction, and it is clear that some imported expertise was available, particularly from Rhineland-based specialists. This Continental influence is, as we might expect, discernible at the *coloniae* and in the south-east, but that is not to downplay the quality of some of the imported classical elements even visible at towns on the edge of the frontier zone. The creation of monumental buildings represented a necessary step to the expression of their new Roman identity by native élites. Construction work might take decades, and timber or proto-versions may have preceded the full development of stone versions; even then, they were subject to later modification.

This was particularly so in the case of the forum–basilica complex, the administrative, judicial and market centre, and in some towns also incorporating or adjacent to the principal religious focus. Major temples, as centres for the imperial cult, might be expected at the *coloniae* (figure 10.8), where they could be on a massive scale, and at London as the provincial capital, but not elsewhere (see Todd 1985 for the wider

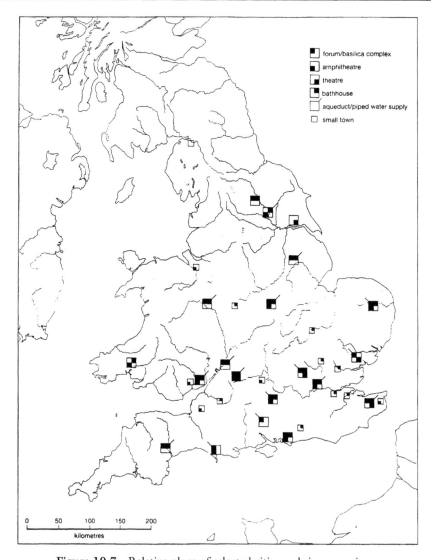

Figure 10.7 Relative plans of selected cities and size groupings.

context). Whereas classical temples were on the whole rare, those of the various Romano-Celtic types characteristic of the north-west provinces were common, and not only in the cities. Buildings associated with the oriental cults, including Mithraism, occur more sporadically, and very few Christian churches are known – partly because they emerged as a distinctive type only from the late fourth century. Nor is there an obvious reason why certain cities also provided an extra market (*macellum*), unless many more await discovery.

There was considerable variation among the fora – not only in terms of the provision of temples, but also regarding other arrangements, such as the location, plan and scale of the *curia* (council chamber). The reasons for the variations are not always clear but

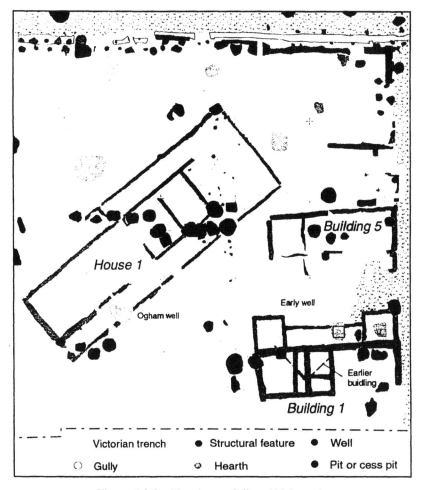

Figure 10.8   Housing at Calleva (Silchester).

were presumably connected with the priorities of the sponsors as well as architects' preferences (Blagg 1991; M. J. Jones 1999b). An examination of the ways in which these structures were used will be aided by the level of detailed information which has been produced by recent work at Caerwent (Brewer and Guest 2001; figure 10.9). The ideological element in this is also a matter of interest (Revell 1999).

The same variety can be seen in the plans of the other essential, the public baths, and at some cities more than one suite was provided (Delaine and Johnston 1999). They were the first structure to appear after the forum, and they provided a context for another form of social activity, with ritual and political implications, new to the British. They also represented an impressive use of a wide range of Roman engineering expertise. Theatres, if provided, were often adjacent to another public structure, but are comparatively rare in Britain, whereas amphitheatres, arenas for public spectacle, seem to have been more common, although normally extramural and often derived from a military predecessor. Rarely do we find both, a fact which has led to the speculation that they could serve both functions, but more examples surely await

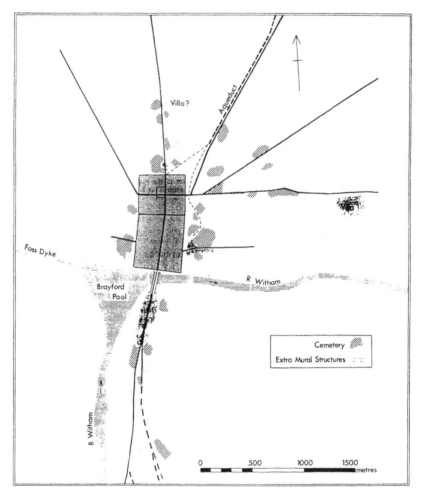

Figure 10.9   Plan of Lindum Colonia (Lincoln), showing suburbs and cemeteries.

discovery. Aqueducts supplying water from springs outside the town are fairly common, but mainly of a simple design, as at Dorchester. Examples of more ambitious types, like the pressurized system at Lincoln, which is still imperfectly understood and which may even never have worked, and of water-towers (*castella*) for distribution, are rarer (Stephens 1985; Burgers 2001). Although wooden supply pipes are also common, systems are rarely studied as elements of a holistic water-management system: these features were usually planned as parts of a larger whole, sometimes involving fountains and complex drainage systems, controlled by the municipal authorities.

Finally, among public works mention should be made of fortifications, a subject which has generated much dispute, arising partly from the difficulty of dating them precisely. As a result, the question as to whether the main context for their provision was a short-term reaction to political events or a longer-term manifestation of civic aspiration by individual communities is unresolved. It is known that imperial permission was required, and this explains why in the first century defended towns were those built at tribal centres under the control of client kings – notably those associated with Togidubnus in the south, and, of a different order, the three military *coloniae*. Colchester's negligence in not defending the original colony, so laying it open to Boudicca's destruction, was not repeated at Lincoln or Gloucester: here the legionary defences were strengthened with new stone structures soon after their foundation. An early fortification is now being revealed at London, and it is possible that there are more temporary defences to be found dating from the immediately post-Boudiccan period (Crummy 1999). Otherwise, the cities did not require to be defended: the towns of Gaul, with a few notable exceptions including the *coloniae*, were similarly unfortified. The devotion of public and private resources to the development of public amenities was in any case the priority for most sites till the late second century. The fact that the project of erecting defences would have had to vie with other schemes favours the longer chronology, rather than a military threat, but the problem cannot be settled without much more precise dating, such as that available from dendrochronological analysis for the riverside wall at London.

It is notable that, apart from the first-century examples, the sequence at many towns was similar, with an earlier bank and ditch system succeeded in the third century by a stone wall inserted into the bank, necessitating a new ditch. Some later examples, as at Canterbury, were stone-fronted from the start, and some others only built after the late third century had no rampart-bank. The sequence at the *coloniae* appears to have been consistent with that of the *civitas* capitals from the late second century on, and they also shared in the general fourth-century strengthening, in which projecting semicircular towers were a common feature. Whether the towns could be effectively defended is another question: it seems unlikely that a local militia could cover the whole circuit, and probable that the primary motivations were status and deterrence. The variations in design are best explained as reflecting the preferences of each community, and the resources in terms of expertise and funding available: this also suggests that the works were not carried out to strict military instructions. Detailed study of particular cities, including Cirencester (Holbrook 1998) and Lincoln (M. J. Jones 1980; (ed.) 1999), has shown that repairs were common and there was not necessarily uniformity around the circuit. It has been possible to argue from this fact that the walls were constantly being repaired according to need, and that it might therefore be misleading to postulate a provincial pattern (Wacher 1998). It does seem likely that there was competition between cities to provide fortifications, including impressive gates, as a sign of status. Although no examples are known from Britain of highly decorated walls (as at Cologne), the presence of flush-pointing and artificial incising does indicate that attempts were made to impress viewers and visitors.

As we have noted previously, it was in the area of housing that aristocratic competition was most evident in the later Roman period, both in towns and in the rural context. In contrast, the earliest urban residences were comparatively simple affairs, established quickly in order to enable trading. Some may have taken the form of simple rooms (*tabernae*) in blocks let out to immigrant traders, as at London and Verulamium, or to the first colonists at Colchester. Most urban residences – whether in the cities or in the 'minor towns' – were of the simple 'strip' type, and most of these consisted of shops and workshops set along street-frontages both inside the walled area and on main routes outside (figure 10.10). Although initially in timber (not that their interiors need have been primitive), stone became gradually more fundamental

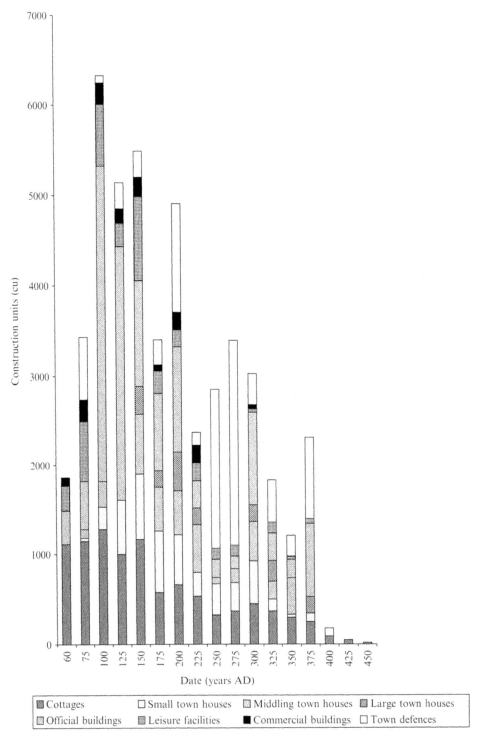

Figure 10.10 Changing levels of investment in public and private buildings in Romano-British cities.

in their construction. Prosperous traders appear to have extended their buildings to the rear or might even absorb the neighbouring property. Although we know from other evidence some of the range of commercial and industrial trades practised, it is very rarely that evidence survives for individual establishments, whether metalworking, other manufacturing, or providing foodstuffs. Investigation of the dumps in their backyards might provide clues.

It would be wrong to assume that the houses of the wealthier classes included no commercial elements, for as well as letting out street-frontages for shops, reception rooms were used for entertaining clients. This would have been a more effective practice when large residences, of the courtyard type, became more common after c.150. Associated with this change was an increased incidence of tessellated pavements and of painted walls and ceilings. Many of these houses continued to stand, sometimes being extended, well into the fourth century, and were joined by others. But it would be fair to say that Britain saw few fully developed peristyle houses in Mediterranean style – although it is known that some were owned by foreign proprietors. Whether this stemmed from a lack of funds, will or expertise is uncertain, but alternatively it may reflect the different nature of the élite social group, that is, perhaps the houses in Britain were designed for only a single family unit rather than an extended family (who might of course be resident in the same owner's rural villa). Complete examples of the larger residences, as revealed at sites such as Caerwent, lend themselves to some further social analysis, including theories of circulation and exclusion and their use for competitive display. A careful study of the artefactual assemblages found in houses can reveal the way the household operated (Allison 1997). Other large residences in towns include inns and mansions, provided at many towns for official purposes, and, as at Cirencester, what appear to be late Roman farms on the western edge of the town centre.

Town housing is still a relatively neglected area of study, particularly in terms of modern investigation, partly through a tendency to concentrate on monumental centres. It would be true to say that our knowledge of extramural suburbs has fared even worse, largely for the same reason. That is not to say that there have not been notable advances in recent years, notably at Lincoln and London. Development mainly commercial in nature expanded across and well to the south of the respective rivers at both sites. This growth is also notable in that it involved major landfill operations over damp ground. Some amphitheatres and temples were also commonly found outside the walls. Outside the western defences at Colchester (and beyond a temple), area excavation also indicated extensive cultivation beds 2 metres wide; the types of vegetable grown are difficult to identify without good preservation. The main point to be made is that extramural settlement was often very extensive, and to exclude it from considerations of physical or population size is misleading. While the economic viability of premises not adjacent to gates or main routes could be affected by the construction of defences, the suburbs could also reflect a city's changing fortunes as expressed through the spread of occupation. The appearance of commercial suburbs was linked, according to some views, to the growth in size of intramural residences rather than to economic growth: but this was the period when similar expansion was taking place in the minor towns. At some growing cities, the suburbs might extend over an earlier cemetery, as at Lincoln, and at others, including Canterbury, the cemeteries extended back towards the city over former suburban development. The urban settlement had an official boundary, but on the urban fringes there were often industrial zones, including those connected with extraction for the building industry, sources of timber for fuelling kilns and furnaces (including those of the baths) and market-gardening (recently suggested for a large area in the northern part of Wroxeter).

Cemeteries were a major component of the suburban area, and a key indicator of the population and its health. Cities were the sites where burial was most clearly organized, in areas zoned for use as cemeteries and sometimes marked by boundaries, even within individual cemeteries. Cremation, the universal rite in the earlier period, might leave only slight traces. Modern investigation has noted the existence of grave-markers, sometimes tombstones, and often associated goods including personal possessions, or offerings, including poultry bones and glass phials. When inhumation became more common as the second and third centuries progressed, burial became more archaeologically visible and, as well as wooden coffins or shroud burials, certain favoured groups were provided with tombs or *mausolea*, some in metropolitan Roman style. The range of types offers an opportunity to study social stratification, aspirations and identity (R. F. J. Jones 1991b).

Unfortunately, very few large-scale cemeteries have been examined and analysed under modern conditions, and on the whole these have tended to be of fourth-century date, when burial practice was most ordered and most burials occur: did they include some rural settlers? Those studied, including London (Barber and Bowsher 2000), Chichester, Winchester, Colchester and Dorchester (Poundbury), show a bias in favour of males, and occasional hints of groups identifying themselves by special artefacts (foreign militia (?) at Winchester) or tomb decoration and burial style (suggested as Christians at Poundbury). We need more large samples if we are to begin to understand the general level of health, pathology, size and longevity of the population of Roman Britain: even diet-type can now be established by scientific analysis. Interestingly, the community at Poundbury showed little evidence of class differentiation on the evidence of the skeletal remains (Farwell et al. 1993), while more recent analysis has suggested that one element had a diet rich in oil, possibly representing incomers from the Mediterranean (see below, pp. 248–9).

Cultural, Social, Economic and Environmental Aspects

The artistic achievements of Roman Britain were considerable, but should not be judged simply in terms of a classical perspective of artistic quality. Imported expertise, especially in architecture and relating building skills and design, did, however, make far more permanent structures, which have survived well in the archaeological record for Britain. Their use again reflects a radical shift in the patronage by the élite from 'Celtic' styles and trappings of warfare to Romanized forms. The availability of natural resources could help create centres of expertise, but the output of their workshops need not be confined to the locality: limestone sculpture was understandably prominent in the cities on the oolitic limestone belt, from Lincoln down to Cirencester and Bath, but work in it was also found in London and elsewhere (Henig 1995: 109–18).

Architecture was a particularly potent instrument for impressing the native population, and encouraging the view that imported Roman technology and expertise was something to be admired and emulated. We have noted already how public buildings, exemplified by the forum, provided an impressive space in which rituals were set that reinforced the power of the establishment. Public buildings in Britain may not on the whole have been of the scale and sheer sumptuousness of some of the most extravagant found in the Mediterranean provinces or later provincial capitals, but they do exhibit many constituent elements of the repertoire available in the Empire (Blagg 1989).

One distinctive aspect, the colonnade, conveyed the new order. Some examples partly or completely enclosed civic centres, and they were commonly used also in public baths and classical temples, perhaps as much as 10 metres high. Engaged columns are also found as monumental arches or as pilasters. In some cases, for smaller colonnades, half- or quarter-tile segments could be rendered in mortar, and perhaps fluted if appropriate stone was not available. Among sculptural decoration, the Corinthian order of capital columns was common, but Doric and Ionic types are also known. When examined in the context of other sculpture, the evidence from Britain tends to suggest closest links with northern Gaul and the Rhineland.

Constructional details of walls are emerging in greater numbers, with finds from rural sites such as the windowed fragment of fallen wall from the Meonstoke villa and evidence for two-storey buildings at Carlisle giving an idea of superstructures. The use of different types of stone and tile for patterning here is particularly instructive. Remains of paint or 'whitewash' have been identified on several structures, while devices to suggest stone joints, stucco, rustication and marbling – clearly Mediterranean in inspiration – are also in evidence (Johnson and Haynes 1996). The forum at Gloucester employed materials of different colours for different elements. Horizontal courses, often of tiles, are found in some high-status masonry walls, having also a bonding function. Timber superstructures are less well understood, even to the extent of the relative frequency of exposed or plastered beams. Some roof finials and antefixes occur, but were presumably fairly rare, and red tiles were generally more common than stone or slate roofs.

With regard to internal decoration, fresco wall-painting (Ling 1985, 1993) was widespread in buildings of any pretension, and this might include those of traders as well as public buildings and aristocratic residences. Wall decoration was essentially a Roman import, in terms of both technique and style, and has no native elements. There are a few examples of some excellent-quality walls and ceilings – those at Verulamium and Leicester come to mind – but the British evidence on the whole survives poorly and is not closely dated. They were designed to be seen as part of an ensemble together with floor mosaics, within their architectural context.

We might presume that cities had major workshops for decoration, as it is suggested that there were also *officinae* (workshops) for craftsmen producing floor mosaics (Johnson 1993; Ling 1997; Neal and Cosh forthcoming). Several hundred examples have been found, but few pavements dating before the mid-second century. With the investment in better residences, mosaic-laying became more generally established, especially in the cities, although simple geometric patterns or plain floors were most common. There may have been separate traditions in the south-east (possibly based at Verulamium and/or Colchester), and in the midlands and west (from Leicester to Cirencester). It is not clear why there was stagnation in the third century – few new impressive mosaics date to that century – before a definite revival and flowering in the fourth century in towns and villas. Four possible schools were identified some time ago, although these are probably better interpreted as regional traditions, their bases possibly linked to tribal capitals. Those of the best quality appear at Cirencester and Dorchester and their regions. The significance of the iconography and the use of symbolism are matters still being explored.

These various specialists involved in the building trades formed part of a considerable range of crafts making up the economic life of the towns. Several generations took part in an urban building boom from the late first century, initially in public works, but later primarily in houses and fortifications. It is even possible to talk of a 'consumer revolution' from the great increase in the availability of physical items in the home, whether utilitarian, ornamental or ritual. But, although the model of the 'consumer city' is now regarded as inadequate (Parkins 1997), the town was dependent on local agricultural production, and also on extractive industries and manufacturing often based at the urban fringe. It provided goods and markets where urban and rural products could be bought and sold. Among these were many objects of various metals, pottery, glass, and other materials, including textiles, as well as food. It is presumed that by the later Roman period at least a cash economy prevailed, but it is difficult to know how much trade was actually controlled by the tribal or military authorities.

There is plenty of evidence for long-distance trade, bringing not only samian and other pottery from Gaul and the Rhineland, but also more exotic foodstuffs and materials from various parts of the Mediterranean. For instance, the ornamental building-stone types found in London include sources from various Mediterranean marble quarries, and the same is true for other cities. London, by virtue of its location, was the principal port of the province, but it is clear that much was moved by sea around Britain and that river transport was also significant: it would have been essential for the movement of stone for building. Lincolnshire limestone was used in the monumental arch at London, Pennine sandstone in the forum columns at Lincoln, and Charnwood granites at Leicester. Substantial harbour installations of different periods have been found in London, where warehouses are also found, and there are hints of wharves and docks at other cities, if only for river traffic. Once established, routes and vessels could be employed to take other materials.

Investigation of these waterfront sites is a relatively recent development in archaeology, but in addition to information on river conditions has yielded much valuable information from waterlogged deposits. These include dumps of material in deposits laid down to advance or consolidate riverbanks, and can include large samples of environmental material.

The various species of plants, insects and mammals consequently identified are providing valuable information on aspects of the economy and environment which have been neglected until recently but which are helping to provide a more balanced perspective of urban life. Progress has been made especially in London, York and Lincoln: at the last, fourth-century riverfront dumps produced huge quantities of cured shoulders of beef, suggesting civic organization of the food supply (Dobney et al. 1996, 1999). Such evidence also adds to the data on animal husbandry. A model for London compatible with the evidence suggests that slaughter and tanning were undertaken outside the city, and butchery and of course consumption within. Remains of plants and small mammals are adding to our knowledge of urban living conditions (the black rat was a Roman import and other pests are known), of local landscape, both wild and cultivated, and the range of vegetables and fruit available. The Roman period in Britain continued and accelerated the increasing choice which began to be available in the south-east in the previous century. Imported delicacies at several sites included *garum* (fish sauce), and some fish species.

The biological evidence noted above for the local landscape raises the question of the urban hinterland, that is, that part of the surrounding countryside, including market centres, which had a close economic relationship with the major towns and contained the land required to feed the urban population (Roskams 1999). Cattle, sheep and pigs, in that order, dominate the mammalian record in terms of meat produce, although cattle often served as traction animals before slaughter. Understanding these relationships begs a number of questions, not least the nature of the economy and to what extent it was embedded, politically controlled, and how taxes and rents were paid. Neither the systems nor the use or extent of the hinterland was necessarily static and unchanging, and also bearing on this issue is the relationship of the city to its official territory, in the case of the *coloniae*, or to the *civitas* as a whole. The absence of definite evidence of centuriation – regular land allotment – around the *coloniae* means that we cannot as yet define the size or location of the *territoria* assigned to them. Possible archaeological indicators for a city's influence on its region include distribution patterns of artefacts such as pottery and stamped tiles. Valuable minerals, whether stone, metal or salt, may have been under official control.

Cereals made up a significant element of the Roman diet, along with pulses. Research in and around York has shown that the Ninth Legion at first imported its own grain, and that it took a generation or so before the land around was being reorganized to serve the needs of the garrison and its associated civil settlement. A similar delay may have been usual at all such sites, but it is clear that Roman influence and contacts considerably extended the range of foodstuffs available. The analysis of environmental samples has produced much evidence for 'exotic' imports: figs, coriander, grapes, walnuts, olives, wine, and dates among them, although it is true that later in the period those that could be were also grown in Britain (M. K. Jones 1991). Oysters are a common find in rubbish deposits, possibly sourced at the British coast and also exported. There were obviously divergences according to both resources and cultural preferences. In general, the still limited but significant evidence to date suggests that the urban meat supply was officially organized, and that the diet in general was much in line with that found in the other north-west provinces. It may be that the model set by the incoming army, dominated by beef and cereals, influenced native preferences at first; beef became a more important element of the native diet after the Conquest (King 1991). The *coloniae* do not appear to differ significantly from the tribal centres, except perhaps in the first one or two generations, but it is true that few sites have yet been adequately sampled.

All this growing archaeological evidence for social and economic activity helps bring us nearer to the people who actually inhabited the towns, and there is an increasing interest in modern scholarship to explore a more holistic view of the experience of town life, and a realization that there was a ritual element attached to many activities. Obviously the physical environment, made up of the design and layout of buildings (the 'organization of space'), their general condition and state of repair, lighting, sounds and smells, and the concentration of people, casually encountered or participating in some official ritual or economic activity, all affected this experience and produced the urban 'mentality'. Some echoes of our own day can be discerned: a society which comforted itself with material goods, and clothing which expressed a cultural preference rather than indicating ethnic origins. Thus the cities served to spread Roman ideas and practices. Among those present, at times, would have been country-dwellers, peasants as well as aristocrats, immigrant traders, professionals such as doctors and educators, and occasionally visiting officials, in addition to the more static groups.

Some individuals are known from inscriptions, but these tend to be more prominent members of society and (particularly at the early *coloniae*) ex-military personnel, and are not a representative sample of the whole population (Birley 1979). They include city councillors, Gauls and Greeks (most assumed to be traders or merchants), ex-legionaries of Italian or Mediterranean origin at the early colonies and their descendants, people identifying themselves as sculptors, Christians, priests, potters and craftsmen working in several different trades, including metalworking. Slaves and freedmen are also documented.

Although it presumably absorbed a regular influx of country-dwellers, the urban population mix was clearly different from that of the countryside, especially in terms of those skilled in certain professions and trades. Some were descendants of the inhabitants of the native settlements, whose inter-relationships may have been altered as a result of incorporation into the Roman province. The nature of urban housing in the early decades suggests that either the population density was high or that only small groups lived together. The evidence from both Caerwent and Silchester suggests that in the later period about 15 per cent of the walled town contained domestic, roofed space: were their population densities and social mixes therefore similar? It would also be possible to draw inferences from comparative assemblages of artefacts from different types of housing and from different cities – e.g. did the earliest generation of colonists have a different material culture from the inhabitants of the contemporary tribal centres, since we assume that at this stage they were drawn largely from different groups? Quantitative analysis of domestic artefacts can, if 'read' carefully, provide an insight into social life – for instance, in changes in emphasis in the use of pottery, metal and glass vessels in preparing food, and receiving visitors in élite residences. In contrast, the poorer classes, including those involved in the craft industries and their families, lived in the simpler homes and have left fewer clues.

The examination of burials is clearly of potential value in studying populations. All but the infants were of course buried outside the city walls, and even infant burials are found in cemeteries in the later period, perhaps as part of changing values inspired by religions such as Christianity. Previously, remains of neonatal, stillborn or unwanted healthy infants might be disposed of adjacent to houses. Inscriptions provide us with a small but possibly misleading sample of the age of death. Even aristocrats often died young, and most analyses of longevity suggest that less than 20 per cent lasted beyond the age of 50. Very few lived past 70, but there were exceptions: one woman from Lincoln was apparently a nonagenarian. Their heights were not so different from those of most of the twentieth century; according to one estimate, at an average of 1.63 metres for women and 1.69 metres for men (5ft 4in and 5ft 7in respectively). But analysis of bones indicates that osteo-arthritis and dental decay were widespread among those of middle age; pain was a regular feature of life. From other evidence it appears that eye ointments were frequently dispensed, possibly for tra-choma, and unhygienic conditions probably led to other conditions also arising from an insanitary environment.

The question of population size is a difficult one. Some estimates have suggested that the twenty or so cities of Roman Britain contained a population of roughly a quarter to half a million, i.e. approximately 10 per cent of the total for the province as a whole. This is an interesting figure in itself, for it brings out the fact that, even though the Roman period may have represented the most urbanized in Britain until the eighteenth and nineteenth centuries, still up to 90 per cent lived and mostly worked on the land. Most average cities are judged to have contained of the order of 5000 residents, with larger towns 10,000 or above, and only London at its height – c. AD 100 – perhaps double this figure (some suggest that at its apogee it may have had 50,000+ inhabitants). Faulkner's attempts to assess population density (e.g. 1996, 2000) provide an opportunity to study this problem 'bottom-up'. The evidence so far from burials and comparison with other provinces would, however, be consistent with the order of magnitude already proposed.

Change through Time: the Third and Fourth Centuries

It is clear from what has been said already that there was a shift in the emphasis of investment as time went on. The late first and second centuries witnessed the great era of public amenities, some cities perhaps overreaching themselves and trying to achieve a level that was unsustainable. There were few new public buildings in the third century, although modifications and repairs were common, but already heavy spending was being devoted to fortifications and private residences. Some towns were still expanding, others apparently diminishing in scale and population, but perhaps they were becoming another type of town. By the third century at the latest it is difficult to note any significant differences between cities of varying legal status, whether in terms of physical fabric or artefactual/ecofactual assemblages. There was a generally similar culture, with variations discernible at the regional or local level – for instance, in the quality of mosaic pavements or that of sculpture, according to the local availability of materials and expertise. This period also saw a move of many pottery industries out of urban fringe sites to rural locations, for reasons as yet not entirely understood; it cannot be seen in purely market terms, but implies some influence on demand by the tribal authorities, and may be part of a wider movement that saw much economic activity move to minor towns.

The radical changes in the administrative system introduced by Diocletian at the end of the third century, and continued by Constantine I, had significant effects for the ruling classes in Britain. The new élite which emerged and which shows signs of considerable wealth was linked to the military bureaucracy: their residences and portable wealth show up strongly in the archaeological record but in themselves hardly indicate that Britain as a whole was increasingly wealthy. More and more, what happened in Britain was influenced by political events in the Empire. Not that there were major setbacks at first: considerable resources were still being expended on urban and rural residences, and there is some evidence of maintenance of public amenities: but civic architecture was no longer an expression of the community's prosperity. Certain public buildings were now put to other uses appropriate to the changing conditions: the basilicas at Silchester and Caerwent were commandeered for metalworking, with the administrative accommodation possibly now confined to the offices to the rear. The cities were also centres for the collection of taxes and for storing supplies: the appearance of security was in due course enhanced by a programme of modernizing and strengthening the fortifications, in effect making them more like the strongholds of later centuries. On the evidence of the pattern of coin loss, Richard Reece (1991) detects an earlier fall-off in the eastern part of Britain than in the west.

Those which fared best were probably the four capitals: London, Cirencester (or Gloucester?), Lincoln and York. These cities were also made bishoprics shortly after Constantine declared tolerance of Christian practice, and were invited to send representatives to the first Christian council in the west, held at Arles in 314. It is not yet apparent if the coming of the new provincial officials had an immediate physical impact on the capitals: no definite governors' offices or palaces, nor any definite bishops' cathedrals have been identified – although even episcopal churches did not generally emerge as distinctive buildings until the last decades of the fourth century. In time, the bishoprics spread to other cities. Of the possible candidates for urban churches proposed in Roman Britain, doubt has been cast on just about all of them: that at Silchester adjacent to the forum, and that in the Butt Road cemetery at Colchester, on grounds that they may not be Christian, while a possible candidate at London is known only fragmentarily, but a new impressive discovery at Wroxeter (still to be excavated) is more convincing. The timber example in the forum at Lincoln cannot be closely dated, and may be of sub-Roman or Anglo-Saxon date. Paganism remained more common, yet it is clear from finds such as lead baptismal tanks that these bishops were ministering to practising Christians, even in rural communities. We might expect that it was the urban centres where Christianity flourished most visibly: those wishing to keep in favour with the new imperial rulers might be persuaded to adopt it, even if only nominally.

The End of Urban Life in Roman Britain

A quantitative analysis of the intensity of occupation of several of the cities by Faulkner (2000) has suggested that many were in decline by the mid-fourth century, in terms of the population size, building quality and the use of public amenities. At the same time, it is clear that there was some urban and civic activity into the fifth century at certain sites. A different sort of town, in both physical and economic terms, with slight timber structures and a more self-sufficient economy, was emerging in the last generation or so of the official Roman period in Britain. This is the most reasonable interpretation of the ubiquitous 'dark earth' layers found to overlie the latest Roman stone structures at several towns (Watson 1998). But it could also represent landscaping, horticulture or agriculture, or abandonment.

The general evidence for Roman Britain's demise is described in more detail in other contributions to this volume. The question here is what became of the larger urban centres. It is clear that they ceased to be the major centres of population, with impressive classical stone architecture, well-maintained public amenities and a range of craft specialisms that had formerly characterized them. Their subsequent fate owed much to regional conditions. Several towns continued to be occupied in some form during the fifth century: this is clear, for instance, from wear patterns on stone surfaces at Bath, from the laying of a new water supply at Verulamium. Some were subsequently used to provide convenient 'Roman' identities in order to legitimate new rulers. Wroxeter is perhaps the most remarkable example of this post-Roman 'classicization'. The fora at Lincoln and at Exeter, and the amphitheatre at London, accommodated Christian cemeteries and possibly associated churches. Their walled circuits and building remains, and oral traditions looking back to the Roman days, might influence their subsequent function. But towns, in the Roman sense, were a thing of the past by AD 450.

FURTHER READING

The many standard works on Roman Britain include sections on urban settlements. John Wacher's *The Towns of Roman Britain* (second edition, 1995) remains the only full-scale synthesis of the subject, and has both analytical sections and detailed accounts of each city. Guy de la Bedoyere (1992) contains many useful building reconstructions by the author. Both adopt a largely historical, Romano-centric approach to the material, and should therefore be read in conjunction with Millett (1990) which eloquently sets out the case for the native contribution to the development of a 'Romanized' culture. This 'social' interpretation is finding its way into the more general literature on Roman Britain. The same author's *Roman Britain* (1995) takes the same standpoint, but is more approachable for non-specialists. For comparisons with Gaul and Germany, see A. King (1990), and now G. Woolf (1998), and M. Carroll (2001).

Three volumes of conference proceedings also contain sections on individual cities and other synthetic papers; F. Grew and B. Hobley (1993) also examines the imperial context of urban construction; S. Greep (1993) covers much of southern England; H. Hurst (1999) contains not only accounts of existing knowledge of the four British colonies, but important discussions (and divergent opinions) on several related matters, including biological evidence, hinterlands and civic space. R. F. J. Jones (1991) contains another set of useful essays summarizing the state of knowledge and pointing ways forward. The 'small towns' are dealt with in some detail in B. Burnham and J. Wacher (1990). Apart from volumes of excavation reports on most cities, there are now excellent general syntheses on some. Notable among these are P. Crummy's excellently illustrated *City of Victory* (1997), Rosalind Niblett's *Verulamium* (2001), and Philip Barker and Roger White's *Wroxeter* (1998), Patrick Ottaway's *Roman York* (1993), and two books on *Roman London*, by Dominic Perring (1991) and Gustav Milne (1995). More are in preparation, and London has since benefited from some conference volumes (see bibliography). A collection of excavation reports on Cirencester (edited by N. Holbrook, 1998) is a most useful up-to-date account of various aspects.

For the difficult period of the fourth and fifth centuries, Esmonde Cleary (1989) remains fundamental. Faulkner (2000) is the best of several new works on this subject to have appeared in the past few years.

For theoretical approaches, the proceedings of the annual Theoretical Roman Archaeology conferences contain several papers on urban aspects of Roman Britain, some of them of ephemeral interest.

REFERENCES

Allison, P. M. 1997. Roman households: an archaeological perspective. In H. M. Parkins (ed.), *Roman Urbanism*. London, 112–46.

Barber, B. and Bowsher, D. 2000. *The Eastern Cemetery of Roman London: Excavations 1983–90*. London.

Barker, P. and White, R. 1998. *Wroxeter: The Life and Death of a City*. Stroud.

Bird, J., Hassall, M. W. C. and Sheldon, H. (eds) 1996. *Interpreting Roman London: Papers in Memory of Hugh Chapman*. Oxford.

Birley, A. R. 1979. *The People of Roman Britain*. London.

Blagg, T. F. C. 1989. Art and Architecture. In M. Todd (ed.), *Research on Roman Britain 1960–89*. Britannia Monograph Series 11. London, 203–18.

—— 1991. Buildings. In R. F. J. Jones (ed.), *The Defences of the Lower City*. Archaeology of Lincoln 7.2. Lincoln, 3–14.

Brewer, R. J. and Guest, P. 2001. Caerwent: *Venta Silurum. Current Archaeology*, 174, 232–40.

Burgers, A. 2001. *The Water Supplies and Related Structures of Roman Britain*. BAR (British Series) 324. Oxford.

Burnham, B. and Wacher, J. S. 1990. *The Small Towns of Roman Britain*. London.

Burnham, B., Collis, J., Dobinson, C., Haselgrove, C. and Jones, M. J. 2001. Themes for Urban Research, *c.* 100 BC to AD 200. In S. James and M. Millett (eds), *Britons and Romans*. CBA Research Report 125. London, 67–76.

Carroll, M. 2001. *Romans, Celts and Germans: The German Provinces of Rome*. Stroud.

Crummy, P. 1985. Colchester: the mechanics of laying out a town. In F. Grew and B. Hobley (eds), *Roman Urban Topography in Britain and the Western Empire*. CBA Research Report 59. London, 78–85.

—— 1997. *City of Victory: The Story of Colchester – Britain's First Roman Town*. Colchester.

—— 1999. Colchester: making towns out of fortresses and the first urban fortifications in Britain. In H. R. Hurst (ed.), *The* Coloniae *of Roman Britain*. Journal of Roman Archaeology, Supplementary Series 36. Portsmouth, RI, 88–100.

Cunliffe, B. W. 1991. *Iron Age Communities in Britain*, 3rd edn. London.

de la Bedoyère, G. 1992. *Roman Towns in Britain*. London.

Delaine, J. and Johnston, D. E. (eds) 1999. *Roman Baths and Bathing*. Journal of Roman Archaeology, Supplementary Series 37. Portsmouth, RI.

Dobney, K., Hall, A. and Kenward, H. 1999. It's all garbage . . . A review of bioarchaeology in the four English *colonia* towns. In H. R. Hurst (ed.), *The* Coloniae *of Roman Britain*. Journal of Roman Archaeology, Supplementary Series 36. Portsmouth, RI, 15–35.

Dobney, K., Jaques, D. and Irving, B. 1996. *Of Butchers and Breeds: Report on Vertebrate Remains from Various Sites in the City of Lincoln*. Lincoln Archaeological Studies 5. Lincoln.

Drinkwater, J. F. 1987. Urbanisation in Italy and the Western Empire. In J. S. Wacher (ed.), *The Roman World*. London, 345–87.

Esmonde Cleary, A. S. 1989. *The Ending of Roman Britain*. London.

Farwell, D., Molleson, T. and Ellison, A. 1993. *Excavations at Poundbury*. Volume II. *The Cemeteries*. Dorchester.

Faulkner, N. 1996. Verulamium: interpreting decline, *Archaeological Journal*, 153, 79–103.

—— 2000. *The Decline and Fall of Roman Britain*. Stroud.

Fulford, M. G. 1999. Veteran settlement in 1st-century Britain and the foundations of Gloucester and Lincoln. In H. R. Hurst (ed.), *The* Coloniae *of Roman Britain*. Journal of Roman Archaeology, Supplementary Series 36. Portsmouth, RI, 177–80.

Fulford, M. G. and Timby, J. 2000. *Late Iron Age and Roman Silchester: Excavations on the Site of the Forum-Basilica 1977, 1980–86*. Britannia Monograph Series 15. London.

Greep, S. J. (ed.) 1993. *Roman Towns: The Wheeler Inheritance: A Review of 50 years' Research.* CBA Research Report 93. London.

Grew, F. and Hobley, B. (eds) 1985. *Roman Urban Topography in Britain and the Western Empire.* CBA Research Report 59. London.

Haselgrove, C. 1989. The later Iron Age in Southern Britain and beyond. In M. Todd (ed.), *Research on Roman Britain 1960–89.* Britannia Monograph Series 11. London, 1–18.

Henig, M. 1995. *The Art of Roman Britain.* London.

Hingley, R. 2000. *Roman Officers and English Gentlemen. The Imperial Origins of Roman Archaeology.* London and New York.

Holbrook, N. (ed.) 1998. *Cirencester: The Roman Town-defences, Public Buildings and Shops (Cirencester Excavations V).* Cirencester.

Hurst, H. R. 1999. Topography and identity in *Glevum colonia,* in H. R. Hurst (ed.), *The* Coloniae *of Roman Britain.* Portsmouth, RI, 113–35.

Hurst, H. R. (ed.) 1999. *The* Coloniae *of Roman Britain: New Studies and a Review.* Journal of Roman Archaeology, Supplementary Series 36. Portsmouth, RI.

James, S. and Millett, M. (eds) 2001. *Britons and Romans: Advancing an Archaeological Agenda.* CBA Research Report 125. London.

Johnson, P. 1993. Town mosaics and urban *officinae.* In S. J. Greep (ed.), *Roman Towns.* CBA Research Report 93. London, 147–65.

Johnson, P. and Haynes, I. (eds) 1996. *Architecture in Roman Britain.* CBA Research Report 94. London.

Jones, M. J. 1980. *The Defences of the Upper Roman Enclosure.* Archaeology of Lincoln, 7.1. Lincoln.

——1999a. Roman Lincoln: changing perspectives. In H. R. Hurst (ed.), *The* Coloniae *of Roman Britain.* Portsmouth, RI, 101–12.

——1999b. Lincoln and the British fora in context. In H. R. Hurst (ed.), *The* Coloniae *of Roman Britain.* Portsmouth, RI, 167–74.

Jones, M. J. (ed.) 1999. *The Defences of the Lower City.* Archaeology of Lincoln, 7.2. Lincoln.

Jones, M. K. 1991. Food production and consumption – plants. In R. F. J. Jones (ed.), *Britain in the Roman Period,* 29–34.

Jones, R. F. J. 1991a. The Urbanisation of Roman Britain. In R. F. J. Jones (ed.), *Britain in the Roman Period.* Sheffield, 53–66.

——1991b. Cultural change in Roman Britain. In R. F. J. Jones (ed.), *Britain in the Roman Period.* Sheffield, 115–20.

Jones, R. F. J. (ed.) 1991. *Britain in the Roman Period: Recent Trends.* Sheffield.

King, A. C. 1990. *Roman Gaul and Germany.* London.

——1991. Food production and consumption – meat. In R. F. J. Jones (ed.), *Britain in the Roman Period.* Sheffield, 21–8.

Ling, R. J. 1985. *Romano-British Wall-Painting.* Shire Archaeology 42. Princes Risborough.

——1993. Wall painting since Wheeler. In S. J. Greep (ed.), *Roman Towns.* CBA Research Report 93. London, 166–70.

——1997. Mosaics in Roman Britain: discoveries and research since 1945. *Britannia,* 28, 259–95.

Mattingly, D. J. (ed.), 1997. *Dialogues in Roman Imperialism.* Journal of Roman Archaeology, Supplementary Series 23. Portsmouth, RI.

Millett, M. 1990. *The Romanization of Britain: An Essay in Archaeological Interpretation.* Cambridge.

——1995. *Roman Britain.* London.

——2001. Approaches to urban societies. In S. James and M. Millett (eds), *Britons and Romans.* CBA Research Report 125. London, 60–6.

Milne, G. 1995. *Roman London.* London.

Neal, D. S. and Cosh, S. R. (forthcoming). *Roman Mosaics of Britain.* 4 vols.

Niblett, R. 2001. *Verulamium: The Roman City of St Albans.* Stroud.

Ottaway, P. 1993. *Roman York.* London.

Parkins, H. M. (ed.) 1997. *Roman Urbanism: Beyond the Consumer City.* London and New York.

Perring, D. 1991. *Roman London.* London.

Pounds, N. J. G. 1994. *The Culture of the English People: Iron Age to the Industrial Revolution.* Cambridge.

Reece, R. M. 1991. *Roman Coins from 140 Sites in Britain.* Oxford.

—— 1999. *Colonia* in context: *Glevum* and the *civitas Dobunnorum.* In H. R. Hurst (ed.), *The* Coloniae *of Roman Britain.* Portsmouth, RI, 73–85.

Revell, L. 1999. Constructing *Romanitas*: Roman public architecture and the archaeology of practice. In P. Baker, C. Forcey, S. Jundi and R. Witcher (eds), *Theoretical Roman Archaeology Conference Proceedings 1998.* Oxford, 52–8.

Roskams, S. 1999. The hinterlands of Roman York: present patterns and future strategies. In H. R. Hurst (ed.), *The* Coloniae *of Roman Britain.* Portsmouth, RI, 45–72.

Stephens, G. R. 1985. Civic aqueducts in Britain. *Britannia,* 16, 197–208.

Todd, M. 1985. Forum and Capitolium in the early Empire. In F. Grew and B. Hobley (eds), *Roman Urban Topography in Britain and the Western Empire.* CBA Research Report 59. London, 56–66.

Todd, M. (ed.) 1989. *Research on Roman Britain 1960–89.* Britannia Monograph Series 11. London.

Wacher, J. S. 1995. *The Towns of Roman Britain,* rev. edn. London. [First published in 1975.]

—— 1998. The dating of town walls in Roman Britain. In J. Bird (ed.), *Studies in Rome's Material Past in Honour of B. R. Hartley.* Oxford, 41–50.

Watson, B. (ed.) 1998. *Roman London: Recent Archaeological Work.* Journal of Roman Archaeology, Supplementary Series 24. Portsmouth, RI.

Webster, J. and Cooper, N. (eds) 1996. *Roman Imperialism: Post-colonial Perspectives.* Leicester Archaeology Monographs 3. Leicester.

Wilson, P. R. 2002. *Roman Catterick and its Hinterland.* CBA Research Reports 128–9. London.

Woolf, G. 1998. *Becoming Roman: The Origins of Provincial Civilization in Gaul.* Cambridge.

Chapter Eleven

Gallo-British Deities and their Shrines

MIRANDA ALDHOUSE-GREEN

This is an exciting time to review the evidence for Romano-British cult practices and cosmologies, since a considerable amount of recent research has focused on such important Roman provincial issues as colonialism and resistance, acceptance and coercion, all of which would have had an impact on religion. The old models of Romanization have rightly been subjected to critical scrutiny and, at last, elements of socio-anthropological theory – long utilized in approaches to prehistoric archaeology – are being applied to Roman Britain in general and to Romano-British religion and ritual in particular. The application of these new cognitive models allows us to think in innovative ways about the material culture of cult and belief, about ways of seeing earth world and the supernatural world, and about the functional interpretation of religious expression, whether in the form of iconography, epigraphy or the use of sacred space.

This essay seeks to present some of the evidence for cults, deities and sanctuaries that apparently had their genesis in the cosmological systems and paradigms of western Europe outside the Mediterranean littoral. Despite such a remit, it is not easy to draw sharp distinctions between beliefs and ritual practices of British origins and those of the Graeco-Roman world, partly because *romanitas* arguably pervaded parts of Britain for at least a hundred years prior to the official conquest in AD 43 (Henig 1998; Creighton 2000) and therefore probably influenced British religion during this 'pre-Roman' period. In addition, there were undoubtedly persistent linkages between Britain and temperate Gaul for centuries before the Claudian invasion, and parts of Gaul itself would have been heavily infiltrated by the ideologies and material culture of Mediterranean Europe. So, in a sense, it is somewhat specious to try and ring-fence Britishness or even Gallo-Britishness in any approach to Romano-British rituals, beliefs and divinities. Nonetheless, it is possible to identify certain religious themes, supernatural beings and methods of veneration situated within a cosmovisual network that provided an alternative or partnered framework when set against the grammar of *romanitas*. Certain cults appear to have crossed the English Channel from Gaul, either with Continental pilgrims, traders, artists or units of the Roman army (Green 1998a); others seem to have been born British. What is more, it is becoming increasingly possible to identify elements of ritual practice that had an ancestral locus within the later Iron Age.

Britannitas and Romanitas

Martin Henig (1998) would have us believe that Britain welcomed the Romans in AD 43 and, indeed, that some prominent first-century Britons, like Togidubnus, embraced *romanitas* as a 'liberation', arguing that our distorted view of aggressive Roman imperialism stems from too much acceptance of the implicitly distorted military models peddled by such writers as Tacitus. In broadly similar vein, John Creighton (2000) speaks of Britain as being 'riddled with Romans' in the hundred or so years between Caesar's visits to Britain and the official Claudian invasion. Other scholars, such as Jane Webster (1995) and John Drinkwater (2000) speak in terms of the 'profound social dislocation' caused by colonial occupation, and the need to recognize the severity of the coercive impact that the Roman cosmological package had on the British population.

Each of these opposed canons has its adherents in current academic discourse and each can draw upon evidence to support the oppression and liberation theories. The pendulum of debate is likely to continue swinging between these two poles but, as is true for most extremes, the most convincing interpretations may lie somewhere in between. In any case, it is unlikely that identical attitudes towards Rome prevailed in all parts of Britain or percolated through all strata of society. What may have been good for Togidubnus was, if we can place any credence on the textual evidence, clearly not so good for Boudicca. The Mediterranean 'power-drinking' paraphernalia, with its strong resonance with Classical *symposia*, which is present in certain high-status late Iron Age tombs in south-east England (Arnold 2001) is not found among the Silures of Wales, and there is plenty of evidence to suggest that in parts of Britain remote from Continental Europe *romanitas* may have had little effect on old ways of life (Green and Howell 1997). What is undoubtedly true is that, for the first time during the second half of the first century AD, Britain became an identifiable entity; what had been a series of more or less fragmented polities metamorphosed into Britannia, what we call Roman Britain. In terms of religion, ways of expressing the supernatural world became solidified, codified into a grammar of behaviour, attitude and currency of expression many of whose elements shared a generic commonality with Gaul, the Rhineland, Iberia and, indeed, with Italy itself. Such currencies included formalized sacred architecture, the naming of deities and worshippers in inscriptions, and the use of formulaic, repetitious iconography, serving as a visual language of religious identification. All of these features came ultimately from Rome. However, in seeking to comprehend the material culture of religious expression in the western Roman provinces (including Britain), it is necessary to appreciate one overarching and fundamental factor, namely that religion was not simply a matter of belief in and honour of the gods but was a highly complex affair involving negotiative power-relationships between groups and individuals and between Britain and Rome (Woolf 1998).

Conquest and Crisis

For some people living in Britain in the mid-first century AD, both the prospect and the actuality of an official Roman military presence must have represented a hugely destabilizing threat to the established religious order. If we believe Julius Caesar (*Gallic War*, VI.13), the influential caste of the Druids had its origins in Britain, spreading from there into Gaul. The basis of the Druids' authority (Green 1997) lay in religious matters and, thus, any potential external challenge to indigenous cult practices would have caused them considerable unease. But we also learn from Caesar (*Gallic War*, I.16) and from Cicero (*De Divinatione*, I.90) that the offices of political leader and Druid could be combined, notably in the case of the Aeduan chief Diviciacus in the mid-first century BC. It would appear to follow, therefore, that the introduction of Roman values and ideologies into Britain, whenever that began to occur, initiated a serious fracturing of religious identity, incurring cosmological anxiety, diminution of self-confidence and severe disruption among the conservative elements within the higher ranks of British society, despite claims (above) that the ruling 'dynasts' of south-east Britain enthusiastically embraced *romanitas*.

Is it possible to glimpse the products of this anxiety in the material culture of Conquest Britain? Are the results of such tensions visibly expressed in the archaeo-logical record? So far, there have been few attempts to identify signs of ritual responses to this kind of crisis but, if we look for them, perhaps they begin to emerge for the period between the fifties BC and the sixties and seventies AD. One of the ways in which such a response might manifest itself is in human sacrifice, a ritual act for which there is secure evidence in European antiquity (Green 2001b), though it was probably always triggered by particular stresses within communities and was never commonplace. Interestingly, there is an increasing body of evidence suggesting that ritual murder was being sporadically enacted during the hundred years between Caesar's visits to and Claudius' invasion of Britain and even beyond. This is of particular note since Classical writers place great emphasis on the barbarity of human sacrifice, using the theme as a stock *topos* to describe the behaviour of uncivil-ized, 'other' peoples outside the Graeco-Roman world. If these authors are correct in identifying recurrent human sacrificial practice at the time they were chronicling events in Gaul and Britain in the first centuries BC and AD (when the majority of the texts were compiled), then we might fairly read such activity in terms of responses to threats of socio-religious dislocation engendered by the advance of *romanitas*.

The discovery of 'Lindow Man' in a Cheshire peat-bog, during the summer of 1984, received considerable publicity at the time, and he has continued to enjoy a high profile in both the media and in popular and academic books on the archaeology of ancient Britain. This young man – his skull fractured, his throat cut and subjected to death by strangulation – was cast naked into a remote marsh, having consumed a 'ritual' meal, in the form of a griddled loaf made from seeds, cereal grains and including pollen from mistletoe, a plant mentioned in Pliny the Elder's *Natural History* (XVI.95) in the first century AD as being especially associated with Druidic ritual. While the radiocarbon dates on the body and the surrounding peat have caused problems, the general consensus is this individual met his death in the mid-first century AD, at about the time when the Roman governor Suetonius Paulinus led

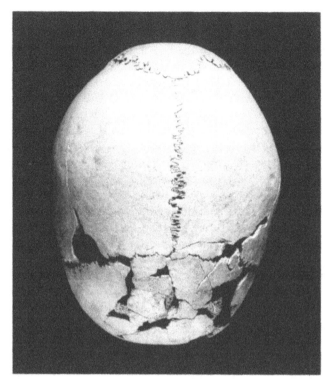

Figure 11.1   Defleshed human skull from Folly Lane, Verulamium. © English Heritage.

his army north-west to annihilate the Druidic holy place on Anglesey, on a route which would have passed close to Lindow (Stead 1986).

   At about the same time that Lindow Man was despatched, far away at Folly Lane, Verulamium, in Hertfordshire, a person of high status was given an elaborate funeral, perhaps lying in state for a time before his remains were consumed on a great pyre within a specially constructed enclosure. John Creighton (2000: 184) has suggested that he was perhaps the ruler of a client kingdom, friendly to Rome and thus both conversant with and susceptible to Roman ways, but at the entrance to his ceremonial enclosure, and deposited at the time it was constructed, were the inhumed bodies of three women, of different ages but the bones of all showing signs of hip deformities that would have severely affected their mobility (Niblett 1999: 20). The inference is that these women were killed as 'attendant sacrifices' to accompany the leader to the other world or, perhaps, to neutralize the pollution and ill-luck his death may have been perceived to bring (Green 2001b). It is significant that more than a century later, in the vicinity of the enclosure, the skull of a teenage boy was defleshed before being deposited deep in a pit outside a temple, having first been displayed on a pole for a time (Niblett 1999: 83–8). Discovered more recently, in 2000, a group of human bones from a 'swallet hole' at Alveston, near Bristol, exhibit treatment suggesting that their owners did not die naturally but may have been the victims of ceremonial killing: part of a skull, belonging to a young woman of about 18, showed that she died as a result of a heavy blow to her head; more sinister still were signs that

0   100mm

Figure 11.2 Copper-alloy plaque decorated with bird-head triskele, from Llyn Cerrig Bach, Anglesey. © National Museum of Wales.

a human leg-bone had been split by someone intent on extracting the marrow, in other words, cannibalism. The latest Accelerator Mass Spectrometry dates on the bone assemblage from Alveston come out firmly at around the time of the Roman Conquest. It is worth noting, too, that one of the people whose partial remains were interred at Alveston had suffered from Paget's disease, a geriatric condition causing the sufferer to adopt a 'simian' stance; the ritual treatment of such an individual resonates strongly with what happened at Folly Lane at about the same time. Elsewhere in Britain, also, there is evidence of ritual practice involving human beings at the time of Roman military interest: the votive aquatic deposits at Llyn Cerrig Bach on Anglesey contained not only the well-documented metalwork, the latest of which dates from the Conquest period, but also the remains of animals and people (Macdonald 1996: 32). The Roman fort at Newstead contained a number of peculiar pit-deposits, including the heads of cattle and horses, and in one was the body of a human dwarf (Curle 1911). This is interesting, for it may belong to a recurrent act of ritual behaviour involving human sacrificial victims spanning the whole Iron Age and ranging over a wide region, including Britain, Gaul and northern Europe, namely the selection of deformed or disabled victims (Green 2001b); we have seen this already at Folly Lane (above). Simon Clarke reminds us that tensions must have existed between the Roman worldview and that of the indigenous population on whom the military installation of Newstead was imposed, and who lived in the extramural zone in close proximity to the fort (Clarke 1999: 36–45). Acts of deposition like this, taking place in defiance of the strict Roman rules regarding disposal of the dead outside settlements, must have made positive, visible and highly vocal statements concerning *habitus* and identity, *britannitas* and *romanitas*. Taken individually, none of the discoveries points unequivocally to human sacrifice, but cumulatively the evidence is suggestive, and it may be significant that we appear to be able to identify a flurry of this kind of activity during the Conquest period in Britain.

Tensions and Negotiations

Memories of the ancestors

About 50 BC a wooden shrine was constructed on Hayling Island, Hampshire. First, an irregular quadrangular enclosure was constructed around a small inner rectangular building just outside which was a pit or timber upright; shortly afterwards, the sanctuary was modified: the outer enclosure was made squarer and the central structure was replaced by a round-house. Its identification as a sacred building is due partly to its plan but more especially on account of the large 'votive' assemblage of coins, martial gear and brooches, many of the items ritually broken before their deposition. It is likely that the construction of this sanctuary, in the very late pre-Roman period, was associated with a ruling local dynasty, that of Commius the Atrebatian, a staunch ally of Caesar in Gaul before becoming bitterly opposed to him and moving out to southern Britain. The establishment of such a dynastic cult-centre here is supported by the circulation of coin issues in southern England bearing legends and imagery suggestive of ancestral veneration: inscriptions on the coinage of Commius' successors, Tincomarus and Verica, allude to their identity as sons of Caesar's erstwhile friend, though Verica, at any rate, must have been using the term *filius* as a formulaic dynastic title rather than as a claim for Commius' paternity.

For students of cult practice in early Roman Britain, developments at the Hayling Island shrine in the years immediately following the Claudian invasion are highly

Hayling Island Temple

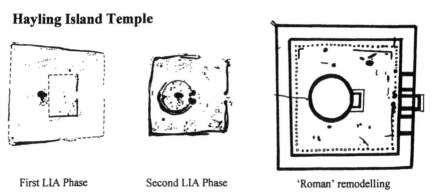

First LIA Phase   Second LIA Phase   'Roman' remodelling

Figure 11.3 The late Iron Age and Romano-British shrines at Hayling Island, Hampshire (after J. Creighton, *Coins and Power in Late Iron Age Britain*. Cambridge University Press, 2000, fig. 7.5).

significant, for now the building was replaced by a more massive edifice built of stone, although still maintaining the overall plan of inner circle and rectilinear outer court-yard, whose boundary walls were modified to form a galleried portico (Downey et al. 1980). Indeed, the plan of the sanctuary is that of the traditional 'Romano-Celtic' temple, with its inner *cella* and surrounding ambulatory. But, as in the earlier phases, no specific evidence points to the identity of the deity worshipped and Creighton's suggestion (2000) that Hayling might have been founded by the Commian dynasty and persisted in the early Roman period as a focus of ancestral veneration is persuasive. Other early ritual centres might be similarly identified: the great rectilinear enclosure built in the mid-first century AD at Thetford, Norfolk (Gregory 1991), is almost certainly a ritual structure, and it is significant – in this respect – that, more than 300 years later, the rich gold and silver treasure dedicated to the obscure Italian

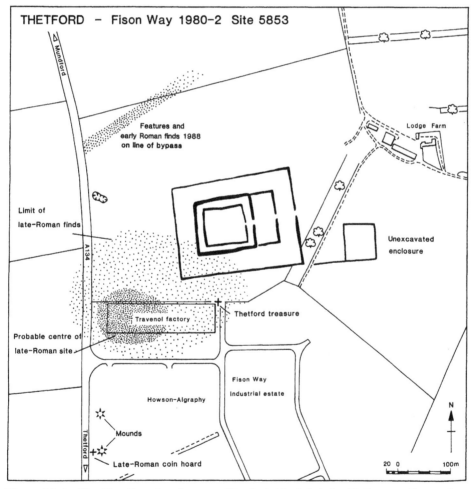

Figure 11.4 The 'Boudiccan' enclosure at Thetford, Norfolk (after T. Gregory, *Excavations in Thetford, 1980–1982. Fisons Way. Vol. 1.* East Anglian Archaeology Monograph 53, 1992, xiv, fig. 1).

god Faunus, in association with a range of native British deities (see below, p. 216) was deposited here (Johns and Potter 1983). The treasure was dedicated in about AD 390, but its site of interment may have been carefully chosen in reflection of a much earlier ancestral cult, perhaps connected to the Icenian royal house, maybe even to Prasutagus and Boudicca. It may be, therefore, that in identifying cult-centres in early Roman Britain, we should not expect that all were dedicated to gods and goddesses, in the conventional sense, but acknowledge that, to Britons in crisis, the cults of the ancestral ruling dynasts were perhaps considered more powerful.

The phenomenon of Sulis

Close to the river Avon and set against the dramatic backdrop of the Cotswold escarpment, on the site of the spa town of Bath, three natural springs pump out hot water at an average rate of a quarter-million gallons a day. Ferruginous minerals give the water a fiery red glow and the steam rising from the springs hangs swirling round them as if shrouding a hidden presence. It is small wonder that, in antiquity, this mysterious and numinous place was venerated as a *locus consecratus* (Cunliffe 1995). Although the evidence is sparse, it is almost certain that there was a shrine here in pre-Roman times: after all, the springs would always have been highly visible in the landscape, and their heat must have seemed explicable only in terms of supernatural agency. When Barry Cunliffe began to investigate the site in the late 1970s, he found a causeway of gravel and rubble, predating the Roman-period reservoir built to contain the fast-flowing hot water, apparently constructed so that pilgrims could walk out over the marshy ground to approach and pay homage to the sacred spring. Very few offerings of this pre-Roman phase have been identified except for a group of eighteen Iron Age coins; even these, however, could represent archaic survivals and may have belonged to the early Roman horizon of offering activity.

At the time when the Claudian invasion forces penetrated the West Country, Bath provided a crucial crossing-point over the Avon, and a Roman fort would have been established quickly to control the crossing and its traffic. Very early on in the Roman period, the natural hot springs became the focus of a monumentalized sanctuary that included the sacred spring itself contained in a reservoir, an imposing temple with an external altar and an elaborate bath-suite; surrounding the temple, altar and spring was a large courtyard bounded by a colonnaded portico. The original phase of building belongs to the later first century AD, but what is perhaps surprising is that the presiding deity, for whom the great edifice was constructed, was a local British goddess, Sulis, her identity being securely established by the numerous inscriptions from the shrine which mention her name. As the layout of the sanctuary was initially designed, the spring in its reservoir, the holy of holies, could be seen wherever visitors were within the sacred precinct but, towards the end of the second century AD, something happened to change the way the shrine worked, in so far as the living waters were enclosed in a great vaulted chamber, thus making it at the same time less visible, gloomier and more mysterious, as if religious officials had decided to exercise more control over access to the goddess herself (see below, pp. 228–9).

Sulis was probably a healing divinity whose power was founded on the ability of her sacred hot springs to alleviate suffering and cure maladies (whether of physical or spiritual origin). She may well have been venerated for centuries before the Romans

Figure 11.5   Altar to Sulis Minerva, Bath. © Miranda Aldhouse-Green.

arrived and turned her shrine into a centre for formal pilgrimage and tourism but, when the stonemasons erected the great permanent buildings in the first century AD, Sulis' identity was also changed: she was hybridized and conflated with a goddess familiar to the Romans, Minerva, one of the three state deities of the Roman pantheon. Indeed, the gilt-bronze head from the cult-statue of the goddess, hacked from its body sometime in antiquity, shows us an image that is entirely Classical. Only the inscriptions inform us that the divine spirit of the spring-water was British: some mention Sulis alone, others twin her with Minerva, but – significantly – almost all dedications mentioning both names put that of Sulis first, as if the British divine persona was the primary focus of worship. The practice of conflating Roman with indigenous god-names was endemic within the Roman Empire, and should, perhaps, be read as a mechanism for the negotiation of socio-religious identities which may have been presented in terms of equal (or near equal) partnership between *romanitas* and local tradition. This model begs questions as to whether codified and formalized sacred identities existed before Roman influence or whether – as Webster (1995) has suggested – the naming of deities, whatever the ethno-genesis of those names, represented Roman word-power in action. My view (Green 2001a) is that names like Sulis might indeed be the product of the Roman presence but, like the new iconographic repertoire of the period, may have resulted from a perceived desire for native societies to establish a new, alternative religious grammar of expression to act as counterpoint or resistance to wholesale *romanitas*.

Figure 11.6   Schist plaque depicting three women, Bath. © Miranda Aldhouse-Green.

This is not the platform upon which to examine the temple-site of Bath and its finds in great detail; the temple, its baths, inscriptions, iconography and offerings are described in many well-presented publications (Cunliffe 1995). But I should take the opportunity here to point to a few features that appear to demonstrate independence from Roman traditional religious values and systems. Some of the iconography is particularly interesting in this respect since it can sometimes betray tensions associated with identities: for instance, the Classical style of the Minerva cult-statue is balanced by a highly schematic local depiction of three women, perhaps the *Suleviae* mentioned in the epigraphy of the site. The 'Gorgon' pediment is also redolent of conflicting traditions: a fierce and vibrant male carved face glared down upon visitors as they entered the temple, a version of the Medusa of Classical myth, but transgendered and incorporating the solar and aquatic symbolism of the shrine with the *gorgoneion* of Minerva's breastplate. What is more (and to my knowledge, no one has pointed this out before) the lobate motif on the forehead may be a potent manifestation of pre-Roman imagery, for it is highly reminiscent of emblems present on the faces of monumental anthropomorphic figures of pre-Roman Iron Age Continental iconography, such as those from Pfalzfeld, Heidelberg and Glauberg in Germany, all of which depict beings in human form but adorned with 'leaf-crowns', identified as mistletoe leaves (Green 2000). The forehead motif visible on all these images has been suggested as representative of the buds and berries of this plant, and an identical design can be seen on the Bath 'Gorgon', as if deliberately seeking to identify with the past. It may be that the craftsman who carved this pediment was of Gaulish origin, as has been suggested for much of the stone-masonry on the site (one sculptor named Priscus belonged to the Carnutes, in the environs of

Chartres). It is certainly the case that people from eastern Gaul visited the sanctuary: we know from dedications that pilgrims came from the tribal territories of the Mediomatrici and the Treveri, both in the vicinity of the Rhineland (Cunliffe 1995: 102).

What do we know of the people who were present at Sulis' sanctuary, either as religious practitioners or pilgrims? We know from an inscribed tombstone that the goddess had her own resident clergy: Gaius Calpurnius Receptus died at the ripe old age of 75 and was commemorated for ever by his widow, the freedwoman Calpurnia Trifosa; although he officiated at Sulis' shrine, it is tempting to believe that he owed his longevity, at least in part, to his proximity to her healing waters. Another priest, Lucius Marcius Memor, a *haruspex* (a Roman official who divined the will of the gods by inspecting the innards of sacrificed animals) set up a statue to Sulis. He is usually regarded as evidence for the enactment of highly Romanized cult practices at this British shrine, but the fact that he recorded his gift to the goddess may mean that he

Figure 11.7   Lead curse-tablet from Bath. © Roman Baths Museum.

Figure 11.8 Altar dedicated by the Treveran Peregrinus to Loucetius Mars and Nemetona.
© Miranda Aldhouse-Green

was present here as a suppliant visitor rather than a professional *sacerdos*. Other pilgrims immortalized by their funerary inscriptions included retired soldiers or those either on leave as tourists or, perhaps, sent to Bath to recuperate from injury or disease; many – whom the goddess could not help – died young but one old man, a city-magistrate from *Glevum*, died at 80 years old. The majority of the altars and tombstones record visits from worshippers of some status; otherwise they, or their relatives, would not have been able to afford such expensive expressions of veneration or respect, but a discrete form of communication with the goddess, the large group of lead or pewter curse-tablets, written with messages in cursive script by wronged suppliants, rolled up and cast into the reservoir as pleas to Sulis for vengeance, represent a social spectrum that included slaves and record several persons with Gallo-British names (Cunliffe 1995: 102–8). These tablets, which belong to a well-known Graeco-Roman religious tradition, form one of the most numerous types of portable offering at Sulis' spring. Others include items of personal adornment, such

0   500mm

Figure 11.9   Stone relief depicting Mercury and his Gaulish consort Rosmerta, Gloucester.
© Gloucester City Museum.

as brooches, bracelets, earrings and finger-rings; many pilgrims brought monetary
gifts, often of low value but, in a few instances, representing as much as two months'
salary for the devotee. It is clear from some of the *defixiones* that Sulis was perceived
as the personification of the spring, and it was thus entirely fitting that offerings to the
presiding deity were placed in the very water itself, just as had occurred in parts of
Europe, including Britain, during the Bronze and Iron Ages in sacred watery or
marshy places. The presence of pewter vessels in the holy reservoir at Bath, some
inscribed with dedications to Sulis, reflects the significance of physical contact with
the numinous spring-water; they were probably used as receptacles for lustration,
their purpose being to scoop up the sacred liquid and pour the essence of Sulis'
healing spirit over her supplicants.

Divinities other than Sulis herself were venerated at Bath. Peregrinus the Treveran
brought with him to Britain the deities of his distant homeland, Loucetius Mars and
his consort Nemetona (her name deriving from a Gaulish term for a sacred
place). The *Suleviae*, probably a form of triple mother-goddess, have already been
mentioned; dedications to these deities are known not only from Aquae Sulis but
were venerated also at Cirencester and Colchester as well as in Gaul (Duval 1976:

56). A small carved plaque depicts the Roman god Mercury, with his *petasos* and *caduceus*, accompanied by a female, probably the Gaulish goddess Rosmerta, but her representation belongs to a small, idiosyncratic group of images from Britain, including Gloucester and Corbridge, distinctive in their possession of a wooden bucket, highly reminiscent of vessels found in certain high-status Late Iron Age tombs from south-east England and northern Gaul. If this attribute has been correctly identified, then we should perhaps read its presence on Romano-British images as an exemplar of archaizing 'retro-symbolism', wherein pre-Roman artistic traditions were preserved within the new religious order in a manner similar to that suggested as being present on the forehead of the Bath Gorgon. The stone depicting Mercury and Rosmerta from Bath is also home to a triad of tiny figures dressed in hooded cloaks, known as *Genii cucullati*, who were worshipped in Roman Britain and Gaul, and who were represented, perhaps deliberately, in the heavy outdoor winter *sagum* of north-west Europe rather than in the flowing garments of Mediterranean lands.

Coventina: a northern British water-goddess

Unlike the presiding goddess of *Aquae Sulis*, certain deities venerated in Roman Britain were never 'twinned' with Roman equivalents but were identified epigraphically as wholly British: such is the case with the cult of a female water-spirit, Coventina at Carrawburgh on Hadrian's Wall. The several streams flowing in antiquity along the the valley overlooked by the Roman fort at Carrawburgh made the valley-bottom marshy. The site of Coventina's Well was focused on a spring, the waters pumped from which were still prized by local people in Victorian times, though lead-mining activities have since caused the water to dry up. In the early second century AD, the spring was contained within a functioning cistern, presumably by soldiers stationed here, but by about AD 130, the well began to take on an apparently new significance as a religious centre.

The coin evidence suggests that the cult of Coventina blossomed to its apogee in the late second and early third centuries AD and was tailing off in the fourth century; the great pulse of activity appears to have been towards the end of the second century when the majority of the coins were deposited in the water, sometimes in large sums; such a surge of religious fervour may have occurred because, for whatever reason, 'the worshippers felt the need to reaffirm their belief' (Allason-Jones and McKay 1985). One deposit of coins had been placed in part of a human cranium before being offered to Coventina; the cranium was that of a woman, whose skull was perhaps given a ritual burial a long while after her death. Apart from money, the goddess's followers donated a number of intimate possessions, including personal ornaments, probably because, as for Sulis' devotees, the offerings of objects worn on the body were perceived to carry with them elements of the devotees themselves. One of the worshippers lost or dedicated a silver finger-ring inscribed to the *Matres* (Allason-Jones and McKay 1985).

Pilgrims worshipping at the Carrawburgh spring set up inscribed altars to Coventina (albeit with several varieties of spelling of her name), whom they represented iconographically, appropriately enough, as a water-nymph. The sanctuary appears to

Figure 11.10 Stone relief depicting triple Coventina, Carrawburgh. © Newcastle University Museum of Antiquities.

have consisted of a square cistern containing the spring, left open to the sky, surrounded by a concentric enclosure bounded by stone walls, with an entrance in the middle of the west side. According to epigraphic evidence, Coventina drew her worshippers from the north-west provinces of the Empire, principally from the Lower Rhine and Scheldt regions of what is today the Netherlands. Her cult seems occasionally to have been exported: two dedications were set up in the Lugo region of north-west Spain and another has been found at Narbonne in southern Gaul. But the large number of inscribed stones from the Carrawburgh shrine makes certain Coventina's north British origin. One of the curious features of the shrine was the deposition of so many stone dedications in the well itself. They were placed there in two groups, arguably for different reasons: some may have been cast into the spring-water as offerings, in the same way as the coins and ornaments; others may have been put into the well for protection, to conceal them, probably after the cult's importance had waned, maybe in a final act of faith.

Coventina's cult, like that of Sulis, was focused on a holy spring; this is what drew pilgrims to her sanctuary in the far north of Britain. The cistern of water was at the centre of her shrine, arguably taking the place of the normal *cella*, and it is thus inconceivable that the goddess's identity was not inextricably linked with aquatic symbolism. In any case, the iconography clearly indicates that Coventina was a water-goddess. But we have little, if any, specific evidence for her role as a divine healer; there is no sign of the anatomical votive offerings or *tamata* that characterize cognate sites in Gaul, such as Chamalières (Romeuf 2000) or *Fontes Sequanae* (Green 1999). But the same is true of Bath (with the exception of two pairs of model breasts) and it may be that the habit of casting replicas of body-parts into water, in rogatory or thanksgiving rituals, was less embedded within British contexts. Like Sulis, Coventina was undoubtedly a powerful local divinity, the personification of the spring-water. But Lindsay Allason-Jones (1985, 11) is probably right in referring to her as an ' "all-rounder" goddess'.

Nodens and Lydney

The great cult establishment at Lydney in Gloucestershire (Wheeler and Wheeler 1932) was carefully sited so as to overlook the vast River Severn near its estuary; on a clear day, it would also have been possible for pilgrims to see other sanctuaries, such as the temple of Mercury at Uley, from the hilltop. It is evident that many shrines in the West Country were deliberately positioned so as to allow for inter-visibility between them, perhaps as part of a recognized pilgrim route. There is no evidence that the temple at Lydney was founded before the third century AD, and it may have been built even later. It seems to have fitted in with a pattern of cult activity in the south-west, dating to the later third and fourth centuries AD, wherein a number of new temples were constructed and old foundations refurbished: a new sanctuary was built inside the old hill-fort at Maiden Castle, Dorset, and the Lydney temple was similarly positioned within the ramparts of an Iron Age stronghold. Indeed, the practice of placing Romano-British shrines inside earlier hill-forts is well known throughout southern Britain, and may have been prompted by perceptions associated with ancestral memory and the symbolic linkage between place and past.

Lydney was founded close to Iron Age and Roman iron-mines and, indeed, the ferruginous water of its springs may well have been recognized as a potent source of healing power. The sacred precinct consisted of a rectangular temple, a suite of baths and – probably – accommodation for pilgrims to sleep overnight. It is highly likely that, as at *Aquae Sulis*, not far away, professional clergy presided over the temple rituals and controlled the activities of pilgrims. Indeed, one of them is known from the inscription on a mosaic from the site: he was Titus Flavius Senilis, who styled himself an 'interpreter of dreams'; and he must have been one of the priests who acted as a mediator between the shrine's suppliants and the divine presence. He may even have been the owner of a diadem depicting a solar deity riding in a chariot, or of the chain headdress found on the site.

Inscriptions from the Lydney temple provide information that the presiding deity was called Nodens, a British god who is known in only one other location, in Lancashire. Like Sulis, Nodens was sometimes twinned with deities of Roman origin: he was known simply either as Nodens (Nodons) or Mars Nodons or he was paired with Silvanus. Curiously, though, no anthropomorphic images of Nodens have ever been discovered; instead, nearly a dozen figures of dogs are recorded, presumably deposited in the sanctuary as offerings by grateful or hopeful pilgrims, in recognition of the well-known healing symbolism attributed to this beast in antiquity. Live dogs were kept at the great Classical curative shrine to the Greek healer-god Asklepios at Epidaurus in the Peloponnese and, in this context, it is of particular interest that some unpublished finds from Lydney include parts of what may be dog-collars, similar in form to that worn by the most famous of the dog figurines, the bronze statuette of a young deerhound. It may even be that Nodens himself could have been perceived as taking on the form of an animal; one of the canine images from Lydney has a human face. Nodens was not the only British deity for whom dog symbolism was important: another southern British healing shrine, at Nettleton Shrub in Wiltshire (Wedlake

Figure 11.11 Facsimile of copper-alloy figurine of a young deerhound, from the Lydney temple. © Bristol City Museum.

1982), consisting of an elaborate octagonal structure, was dedicated to Apollo Cunomaglus (Hound-Lord). The small settlement surrounding the temple may well have grown up there in order to service the cult precinct. The shrine at Nettleton was established by the later first century AD, but its popularity was at its peak in the mid-third century, when a major cult centre was developed, with hostel, shops and a priest's house built to support the shrine and cater for the comfort of its pilgrims.

The function of Nodens as a healer is suggested not only by his association with dogs but from some of the other finds, including a bronze model arm, whose hand displays the spoon-shaped fingernails characteristic of someone suffering from iron deficiency: the iron-rich minerals of the spring-water may well have brought this sick pilgrim to seek help at Lydney. Other diagnostic finds include so-called oculists' stamps, tiny inscribed stones or pieces of pottery used to mark sticks of eye ointment. Many of these *collyrium* (salve) stamps are recorded at Gallo-Roman healing shrines, such as Grand, Vichy and Bolards (Green 1999). The aquatic symbolism so central to therapeutic sanctuaries in Gaul and Britain is not absent from Lydney. Its position high above the great River Severn, with its clear view of the episodic tidal surge known as the Severn Bore, must have had considerable influence in terms of the powers attributed to the god: the mosaic given to the temple by the priest Senilis is full of marine imagery, as is the 'solar' diadem he may have worn. But the presence of iron and earlier mining may also have been significant for the way the god was perceived: that same diadem bears the image of a half-human, half sea-beast, brandishing a pick in each hand. One of the unpublished finds from the temple precinct recently brought to light is a beautifully made miniature iron pick, perhaps a votive offering from a pilgrim who was aware of the mineral-rich land on which Nodens' sanctuary was built and who acknowledged the contribution of iron to the spiritual essence of the place. Finally, the solar imagery on the diadem should also be noted:

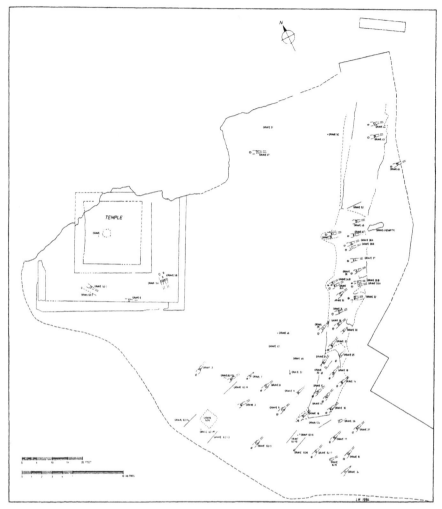

Figure 11.12   Plan of the cemetery associated with the Henley Wood temple (after L. Watts & P. Leach, *Henley Wood, Temples and Cemetery Excavations 1962–69*. York: CBA Research Report 99, 1996, 45, fig. 30).

the link between the sun and healing was well established in western provincial curative shrines (Green 1991: 119–21). This is seen at its most overt in sanctuaries dedicated to the Gaulish Apollo, particularly Apollo Belenus at Sainte-Sabine and Apollo Vindonnus at Essarois, whose temple pediment bore the image of the radiate sun-god. The bronze deerhound from Lydney bears curious rayed motifs at each shoulder and haunch that should perhaps be interpreted as solar motifs.

Cults of the ancestors: burial in hallowed ground

A recurrent phenomenon in the material culture of Roman Britain, particularly in the later phases, is the association between cemeteries and rural sanctuaries. A number of shrines were clearly in regular use as repositories for the dead. The temple at Henley Wood in north Somerset was the location for a small cemetery of eighty or so people, of whom most seem to have been buried in the fifth or sixth century AD, after the shrine building had gone out of use, but the earliest grave was certainly dug while the structure was still intact (Smith 2001: 93). The first round sanctuary building at Nettleton Shrub in Wiltshire dates to the later second century AD and the octagonal temple was constructed in the mid-third century. On the edges of the precinct were three spatially and chronologically discrete cemeteries, between them covering the period from the first to fourth centuries (Wedlake 1982: 77). Several other temples were the repositories for single or multiple burials and this should not surprise us, in so far as – like Christian churchyards – sanctuaries would provide relevant sacred contexts for the disposal of the dead. But the presence of burial grounds associated with rural religious precincts may have other meanings too: perhaps the community's ancestors were thus incorporated into the local pantheon of spirits, their presence serving to reinforce the identity of the living, to protect them from malign forces and contribute to their prosperity.

Gaulish gods in Roman Britain

In discussing the identity of pilgrims at Bath (above, p. 200), allusion was made to the import of foreign divinities from Continental Europe, such as Loucetius and Nemetona from the territory of the Treveri; and the two-way direction of such traffic in deities has been exemplified by the distribution of dedications to Coventina outside her British homeland. Even Sulis was apparently exported to the Rhineland (E. Birley 1986: 54). Britannia owed much of her rich religious diversity to Continental traditions; that much is clearly demonstrated by both epigraphy and iconography. Many cults were imported via army personnel, but there were other travellers – merchants, entrepreneurs, craftspeople – who sojourned in Britain for a time or became permanent settlers, while retaining allegiance to their indigenous divine patrons. People of the Tuihanti, a tribe occupying the eponymous region of Twenthe in the Netherlands, dedicated a shrine at Housesteads on Hadrian's Wall to an obscure group of deities with Germanic names: Mars Thincsus and two female spirits, called Beda and Fimmilena and known collectively as the Alaisiagae (E. Birley 1986: 77). The converse was also true: Marcus Aurelius Lunaris held the influential appointment of *Sevir Augustalis* (priest of the Imperial Cult) at York and Lincoln in AD 237; he was a trader between Britain and Gaul, and he dedicated an altar at Bordeaux to a goddess named 'Boudig', in gratitude for her protection (Frere 1987: 162). This deity's name means 'victorious one' and is cognate with that much earlier British heroine of the Iceni, Boudicca; Boudig was almost certainly an indigenous goddess. Similarly British-born was the northern British deity Maponus, worshipped at, for instance, Vindolanda; he was a hunter-god, sometimes twinned with Apollo. A dedication to him, found at the healing spring shrine of Chamalières in the Auvergne, may reflect the cult of a Briton abroad.

    A range of important and popular Gallic divinities found their way to Britain; some caught on and became very popular, others seem to have been followed by only a few. The cult of the Mother Goddesses, known epigraphically as *Deae Matres* or *Matronae* (the latter title especially prevalent among Rhenish worshippers) gained a

Figure 11.13 Stone group of three mother-goddesses with children, from Cirencester. © Corinium Museum.

Figure 11.14 Stone group of three *Genii Cucullati* and a goddess, from Cirencester. © Corinium Museum.

considerable body of followers in Britain, there being clusters of epigraphic dedications and iconographical representations in the Cotswolds, along Hadrian's Wall, in Lincolnshire and London. They were frequently represented as a triad of goddesses, sometimes with a discernible age variation between the three. A recent find, from Aldworth in West Berkshire (Henig and Cannon 2000), suggests that there may have been a shrine associated with the *Matres* in the vicinity: this consists of a spear-shaped sceptre terminal, similar to those found at sacred sites such as Felmingham Hall in Norfolk and Brigstock (Northamptonshire) (Green 1976: pl. IX and pl. XXV 6), but decorated with the busts of three females. The Aldworth find may originally have come from the sanctuary at Lowbury Hill (Oxfordshire) nearby; three such ceremonial 'spears' were found there. At least one temple to the Mother Goddesses was established in the Ashcroft area of Cirencester; the town has produced a number of triplistic female images nursing babies, in company with older children or with baskets of fruit or loaves of bread. The triadic theme was strong here: in addition to the three Mothers, iconography includes a representation of one woman but with three apples in her lap, and several groups consisting of three hooded, apparently male, figures with a single seated female companion. Mention has already been made of these triadic figures wearing the hooded Gallic *sagum* or British *birrus*, since they appear on the Mercury and Rosmerta plaque at Bath. These *Genii cucullati* were commonly venerated on the Cotswolds and, like the *Deae Matres*, were also popular in the region of Hadrian's Wall. Their affinity with the goddesses, together with the egg emblems they sometimes carry, suggests that the *cucullati* had a role cognate with that of the Mothers.

One of the most venerated Gaulish deities in western Europe was the horse-goddess Epona; evidence of her worship, in the form of epigraphic dedications or images, is found all over Gaul and the Rhineland: she even had her own festival day (18 December) in the Roman calendar of holy days (Green 1995: 184–7). But she did not travel well across the Channel: there is only a handful of evidence to suggest that she had a following in Britain, including dedications from Auchendavy on the Antonine Wall and from one or two sites on Hadrian's Wall, mirroring Epona's popularity among the military on the Rhine frontier. There are a few scattered references to her cult further south, include a graffito to her on a jar from Alcester (Warwickshire), an image of the goddess on the cheek-piece of a helmet from South Collingham in the Midlands, two fragmentary statuettes from Colchester and Caerwent and an interesting – but, alas, unprovenanced – bronze group of Epona with two ponies from Wiltshire (Johns 1971).

The pairing of Gallo-British and Roman god-names, exemplified by Sulis Minerva at Bath, was repeated all over Britain, frequently involving divinities of Gaulish origin, who were twinned with mainstream Classical deities such as Apollo and Mars. Thus, Apollo Grannus, whose main cult centres were at Grand in the Vosges and Aquae Granni at Aix-La-Chapelle (Green 1986: 161), found his way to Inveresk in the far north of Britain; and Apollo Anextiomarus, worshipped at South Shields, belonged principally to the tribal territory of the Aulerci Cenomanni (E. Birley 1986: 44). The great Treveran god Lenus Mars was venerated at Caerwent, the *civitas* capital of the Silures and by someone of low – perhaps servile – status at the Chedworth Roman villa (*RIB* 309, 310). The name of the Gaulish hammer-god Sucellus was inscribed on a silver finger-ring belonging to someone at York (Green 1986: fig. 4b). Teutates and Taranis were two Gallic deities mentioned by the Roman poet Lucan, in his epic civil war poem *The Pharsalia* (I.444–6), written in the first century AD: both are attested archaeologically in Gaul and both were worshipped in Britain:

Figure 11.15 Copper-alloy figurine of Epona with two ponies, unprovenanced, Wiltshire.
© The British Museum.

Toutates was twinned with Mars at Barkway (Hertfordshire) (Green 1976: 209) and
was venerated also at Kelvedon in Essex and Great Walsingham, Norfolk (Bagnall
Smith 1999: 32). An army officer, originally from Spain, dedicated an altar to Taranis
(more accurately Tanarus), the thunder-god, pairing him with Jupiter (*RIB* 452).
This may be the same Gaulish version of the Roman sky-god who was frequently
represented by the symbol of a spoked wheel, representing the sun (Green 1991:
86–106): a depiction of the 'wheel-god' comes from Corbridge, and several altars
bearing wheel motifs and dedicated to Jupiter come from forts on Hadrian's Wall.
The same Gaulish deity may be represented by the elaborate column-capital
from Cirencester which, together with an inscribed stone alluding to the restoration
of a column to Jupiter, almost certainly came from a Jupiter-Giant column (Green
1984), similar to those from eastern Gaul and the Rhineland (Bauchhenss and Nölke
1981).

Figure 11.16 Silver plaques depicting a warrior and inscribed to Cocidius, Bewcastle. © Carlisle Museum.

A skein of spirits and a god for all seasons

All over Roman Britain, people worshipped their personal choice of divine entity, whether of local or foreign origin, and whether confined to one shrine or venerated more widely. Two male deities, apparently confined to Hadrian's Wall and with specific distribution patterns within this region, were Cocidius and Belatucadrus: the latter was worshipped along the western section, with the densest concentration of dedications at Brougham; he may have attracted followers from the lower socio-economic groups, since his altars are small and ill-inscribed. Eric Birley (1986: 60–2) has suggested that the group of uninscribed anthropomorphic male images with horns from the area might represent Belatucadrus. Cocidius attracted a largely military clientele, and – moreover – one that enjoyed relatively high rank, including a legionary centurion and equestrian officers. The Ravenna Cosmography has identi-fied Bewcastle, north of the Wall, as *Fanum Cocidi*; the largest number of inscriptions mentioning the god comes from this fort, including two silver plaques each depicting a schematized warrior figure, armed with spear and shield (Green 1986: fig. 54). Concentrated in the eastern sector of the Wall was a set of poorly inscribed dedica-tions to the Veteri or Hveteri, with a great deal of spelling variation on their altars (E. Birley 1986: 62–4); sometimes they are referred to in the singular, at others as multiple spirits. A goddess called Setlocenia (*RIB 841*) seems only to have been invoked at Maryport in Cumbria: she is recorded on a single dedication, made by a German. Such isolated cults occur quite frequently: Abandinus at Godmanchester (Cambridgeshire) and Antenociticus at Benwell on Hadrian's Wall (E. Birley 1986: 64) appear similarly to have represented highly localized cults.

That *britannitas* survived – apparently happily married to *romanitas*, while maintaining its own religious identity – well into late Roman Britain is suggested by the extraordinary find of gold and silver treasure from Thetford in Norfolk (on the site of the old Boudiccan enclosure). The Thetford Treasure consisted of eighty-one items, including gold jewellery and a set of thirty-three silver spoons, belonging to a religious *collegium* or guild, who deposited the hoard in the late fourth or early fifth century AD (Johns and Potter 1983). The spoons perhaps represented a particular level of offering or even reflected the gift of a measure of wine, oil or other substance (Painter 1997: 93–110). Many of the spoons are inscribed with dedications to an obscure Latian pastoral god called Faunus, but his name is sometimes paired with local spirits with Gallo-British names, the most evocative being 'Medugenus' ('mead-begotten'), whose name appears on four of the spoons. It is tempting to see Medugenus as the British equivalent of the bibulous Graeco-Roman god Bacchus, whose cult involved his initiates in the ecstatic consumption of liquor in the expectation of transcendental, out-of-body experience: it is surely no coincidence that silver liquor-strainers were included in the Thetford hoard. What is, perhaps, the most enlightening element in this cache of sacred material is the presence of British god-names in a context that is otherwise apparently so very Italian: the jewellery, the liturgical equipment and Faunus himself seemingly belong entirely to the Roman end of the Romano-British spectrum, although Kenneth Painter (1997: 102) has suggested that he was perceived as more of a local deity than his name would have us believe; but Medugenus and his siblings serve as a reminder that Britain retained a religious identity of its own until Britannia itself ceased to be.

FURTHER READING

One of the most accessible texts on the subject of Romano-British sanctuaries is Anne Woodward's *Shrines and Sacrifice* (1992). The most up-to-date research on the subject is contained within Alexander Smith's *The Differential Use of Sacred Space in Southern Britain, from the Late Iron Age to the 4th Century* AD (2001). For specific sanctuaries, Barry Cunliffe's *Roman Bath* (1995) is the most concise text on the subject of Sulis' sanctuary, but for greater depth, see his two research volumes *The Temple of Sulis Minerva at Bath: The Site* and *The Finds* (1985–8). Wedlake's *Nettleton Shrub* (1983) and Wheeler's *Lydney* (1932) reports remain the best starting-points for study of these two sites, as does Allason-Jones's *Coventina's Well* (1985) for this shrine. For an account of the Maiden Castle temple, see Niall Sharples, *Maiden Castle* (1991).

For thought-provoking discussion of the Iron Age Roman transition, see John Creighton's *Coins and Power in Late Iron Age Britain* (2000), Miranda Green's *Exploring the World of the Druids* (1997) and Jane Webster's 'At the end of the world: druidic and other revitalization movements in post-conquest Britain and Gaul', *Britannia*, 30 (1999), 1–20, and for the significance of sepulchral evidence, the reader is directed to *Burial, Society and Context in the Roman World*, edited by John Pearce et al. (2000). The reader will find an up-to-date discussion of the evidence for human sacrifice in Late Iron Age and Roman Britain in Miranda

Green's *Dying for the Gods* (2001). For useful discussions of Gallo-Roman religious issues, see Ton Derks's *Gods, Temples and Ritual Practices* (1998) and Greg Woolf's *Becoming Roman. The Origins of Provincial Civilization in Gaul* (1998)

For good syntheses of religion in Roman Britain, see Martin Henig's *Religion in Roman Britain* (1984) and Miranda Green's *The Gods of the Celts* (1986). For studies of iconographical issues, Miranda Green, 'God in Man's image', *Britannia*, 29 (1998), 17–30, raises concerns about ethnogenesis and independence. For illustrated catalogues of Romano-British cult imagery, the reader is referred to the *Corpus Signorum Imperii Romani* volumes for Britain, particularly Martin Henig, *Roman Sculpture from the Cotswold Region* (*CSIR* 1, fasc. 7, 1993). For epigraphic studies, see Eric Birley's survey (1986) and, for a newer discussion, Marilynne Raybould, *A Study of Inscribed Material from Roman Britain*, particularly chapter 3 (1999), and Miranda Aldhouse-Green and Marilynne Raybould, 'Deities with Gallo-British names recorded in inscriptions from Roman Britain', *Studia Celtica*, 33 (1999), 91–135.

REFERENCES

Aldhouse-Green, M. J. 2000. *Seeing the Wood for the Trees: The Symbolism of Trees and Wood in Ancient Gaul and Britain*. Centre for Advanced Welsh & Celtic Studies Research Paper 17. Aberystwyth.

——2001a. Alternative iconographies: metaphors of resistance in Romano-British cult-imagery. In *VII Internationales Colloquium über Probleme des Provinzialrömischen Kunstschaffens*. Cologne.

——2001b. *Dying for the Gods: Human Sacrifice in Ancient Europe*. Stroud.

Aldhouse-Green, M. J. and Raybould, M. 1999. Deities with Gallo-British names recorded in inscriptions from Roman Britain. *Studia Celtica*, 33, 91–135.

Allason-Jones, L. and McKay, B. 1985. *Coventina's Well*. Chester.

Arnold, B. 2001. Power drinking in Iron Age Europe. *British Archaeology*, 57 (February), 14–19.

Bagnall Smith, J. 1999. Votive objects and objects of votive significance from Great Walsingham, Norfolk. *Britannia*, 30, 21–56.

Bauchhenss, G. and Nölke, P. 1981. *Die Iupitersaülen in den germanischen Provinzen*. Cologne and Bonn.

Birley, E. 1986. The deities of Roman Britain. In W. Haase (ed.), *Principat*. Volume 18. *Religion. Aufstieg und Niedergang der Römischen Welt*. Berlin, 3–112.

Clarke, S. 1999. Contact, architectural symbolism and the negotiation of cultural identity in the military zone. In P. Barker, C. Forcey, S. Jundi and R. Witcher (eds), *TRAC 98*. Oxford, 36–45.

Creighton, J. 2000. *Coins and Power in Late Iron Age Britain*. Cambridge.

Cunliffe, B. 1985–8. *The Temple of Sulis Minerva at Bath*. 2 vols. Oxford.

——1995. *Roman Bath*. London.

Curle, J. 1911. *A Roman Frontier Post and its People: The Fort of Newstead in the Parish of Melrose*. Glasgow.

de la Bedoyère, G. 1999. *The Golden Age of Roman Britain*. Stroud.

Derks, Ton. 1998. *Gods, Temples and Ritual Practices*. Amsterdam.

Downey, R., King, A. and Soffe, G. 1980. The Hayling Island temple and religious connections across the Channel. In W. Rodwell (ed.), *Temples, Churches and Religion in Roman Britain*. BAR (British Series) 77. Oxford, 289–304.

Drinkwater, J. 2000. Review of Ton Derks, *Gods, Temples and Ritual Practices. The Transformation of Religious Ideas and Values in Roman Gaul*, 1998. *Britannia*, 31, 458–9.

Duval, P.-M. 1976. *Les Dieux de la Gaule*. Paris.

Fitzpatrick, A. P. 2000. Ritual, sequence and structure in Late Iron Age mortuary practices in north-west Europe. In J. Pearce, M. Millett and M. Struck (eds), *Burial, Society and Context in the Roman World*. Oxford, 15–29.

Frere, S. S. 1987. *Britannia*, 3rd edn. London.

Green, M. J. 1976. *A Corpus of Religious Material from the Civilian Areas of Roman Britain*. BAR 24. Oxford.

—— 1984. *The Wheel as a Cult-Symbol in the Romano-Celtic World*. Brussels.

—— 1986. *The Gods of the Celts*. Gloucester.

—— 1991. *Sun Gods and Symbols of Ancient Europe*. London.

—— 1995. *Celtic Goddesses: Warriors, Virgins & Mothers*. London.

—— 1997. *Exploring the World of the Druids*. London.

—— 1998a. God in Man's image: thoughts on the genesis and affiliations of some Romano-British cult-imagery. *Britannia*, 29, 17–30.

—— 1998b. Humans as ritual victims in the later prehistory of Western Europe. *Oxford Journal of Archaeology*, 17, 169–89.

—— 1999. *Pilgrims in Stone: Stone Images from the Gallo-Roman Sanctuary of Fontes Sequanae*. BAR (International Series) 754. Oxford.

Green, M. J. and Howell, R. 1997. *Celtic Wales*. Cardiff.

Gregory, T. 1991. *Excavations in Thetford, 1980–1982, Fisons Way*. Volume 1. East Anglian Archaeology 53. Norwich.

Haselgrove, C. 1999. The Iron Age. In J. Hunter and I. Ralston (eds), *The Archaeology of Britain*. London, 113–34.

Hassall, M. W. C. and Tomlin, R. S. O. 1979. Roman Britain in 1978: II Inscriptions. *Britannia*, 10, 339–56.

Henig, M. 1984. *Religion in Roman Britain*. London.

—— 1993. *Roman Sculpture from the Cotswold Region*. CSIR I.7. Oxford.

—— 1998. Togidubnus and the Roman liberation. *British Archaeology*, 37 (September) 8–9.

Henig, M. and Cannon, P. 2000. A sceptre-head for the matres cult and other objects from West Berkshire. *Britannia*, 31, 358–61.

Johns, C. M. 1971. A Roman bronze statuette of Epona. *British Museum Quarterly*, 36, 37–41.

Johns, C. M. and Potter, T. 1983. *The Thetford Treasure*. London.

King, A. and Soffe, G. 1991. Hayling Island. In R. F. Jones (ed.), *Roman Britain: Recent Trends*. Sheffield, 111–13.

—— 1999. L'Organisation interne et l'enfuissement des objets au temple de l'âge du fer à Hayling Island (Hampshire). In J. Collis (ed.), *Society and Settlement in Iron Age Europe; l'habitat et l'occupation du Sol en Europe. Actes du XVIIe Colloque de l'AFEAF, Winchester – Avril 1994*. Sheffield, 113–26.

Macdonald, P. 1996. Llyn Cerrig Bach: an Iron Age votive assemblage. In S. Aldhouse-Green (ed.), *Art, Ritual and Death in Prehistory*. Cardiff, 32–3.

Niblett, R. 1999. *The Excavation of a Ceremonial Site at Folly Lane, Verulamium*. Britannia Monograph Series 14. London.

Painter, K. 1997. Silver hoards from Britain in their Late-Roman context. *Antiquité Tardive*, 5, 93–110.

Parker Pearson, M. 2000. Great sites: Llyn Cerrig Bach. *British Archaeology*, 53 (June), 8–11.

Pearce, J., Millett, M. and Struck, M. (eds) 2000. *Burial, Society and Context in the Provincial Roman World*. Oxford.

Potter, T. W. 1997. *Roman Britain*. London.

Raybould, M. 1999. *A Study of Inscribed Material from Roman Britain*. BAR 281. Oxford.

Romeuf, A.-M. 2000. *Les ex-voto gallo-romains de Chamalières (Puy de Dôme)*. Paris.

Royal Commission on Historical Monuments. 1962. *Eboracum: Roman York*. London.

Sharples, N. 1991. *Maiden Castle*. London.

Smith, A. 2001. *The Differential Use of Constructed Sacred Space in Southern Britain, from the Late Iron Age to the 4th Century AD*. BAR (British Series) 318. Oxford.

Stead, I. M., Bourke, J. B. and Brothwell, D. 1986. *Lindow Man: The Body in the Bog*. London.

Watts, L. and Leach, P. 1996. *Henley Wood, Temples and Cemetery Excavations 1962–69*. CBA Research Report 99. York.

Webster, J. 1995. Roman word-power and the Celtic gods. *Britannia*, 26, 153–61.

—— 1997. Necessary comparisons: a post-colonial approach to religious syncretism in the Roman provinces. *World Archaeology*, 28, 324–38.

—— 1998. Freedom fighters under a mystic cloak. *British Archaeology*, 39 (November), 18.

—— 1999. At the end of the world: druidic and other revitalization movements in post-conquest Gaul and Britain. *Britannia*, 30, 1–20.

Wedlake, W. J. 1982. *The Excavation of the Shrine of Apollo at Nettleton, Wiltshire 1956–1971*. London.

Wheeler, R. E. M. and Wheeler, T. V. 1932. *Report on the Excavation of the Prehistoric, Roman and Post-Roman Site in Lydney Park, Gloucestershire*. Oxford.

Woodward, A. 1992. *Shrines and Sacrifice*. London.

Woolf, G. 1998. *Becoming Roman: The Origins of Provincial Civilization in Gaul*. Cambridge.

CHAPTER TWELVE

Roman Religion and Roman Culture in Britain

MARTIN HENIG

The Romans defined themselves as a people of special religiosity (*pietas*) and strict adherence to the *mos maiorum* (which meant, to them, something more than mere 'custom'). Although accommodating to the religious practices of others (except when they included objectionable rites like human sacrifice), and very ready to conflate their own gods with those of the nations which they incorporated into their Empire, even eventually welcoming some foreign deities such as Cybele and Isis into their own State pantheon, there was always a recognizable, sometimes even a predominant, element which can be called Roman, even in an outlying province like Britain.

Roman Gods and Imperial Cult

Actual transplanted Roman cult was the exception. First, it is likely that the *coloniae* of Colchester, Gloucester and Lincoln each had a *capitolium* where Jupiter Optimus Maximus together with Juno and Minerva received veneration, and other chartered towns no doubt had similar cults. Three temple-like buildings were attached to the forum of the *municipium* of Verulamium, though it is not certain whether any of them was a temple of Jupiter. This forum was built in Flavian times and dedicated in the governorship of Agricola (Frere 1983: 55–72). One of the best indications of an early cult of the god in a town is the base of a column dedicated to Jupiter Optimus Maximus in honour of the Divine House (the Imperial Family) at Chichester (*RIB* 89; Figure 12.1), though this almost certainly belongs to King Togidubnus' client kingdom and might have been regarded as the conflation of the Roman Jupiter with a native, Celtic conception of the god. Also, we cannot be sure whether or not there was actually a temple of Jupiter here, although a temple (almost certainly of classical form) was dedicated to Neptune and Minerva, likewise in honour of the *Domus Divina*, and was authorized by the king, as attested by a Purbeck marble inscription found in North Street, near the centre of the city (*RIB* 91; Bogaers 1979; figure 12.2). The northern part of the Atrebatic realm centred on Silchester, and a bronze eagle from the basilica, probably dating to the second century (Henig

Figure 12.1 Part of a monument to Jupiter, Chichester, West Sussex: water nymphs (Photo by courtesy Grahame Soffe).

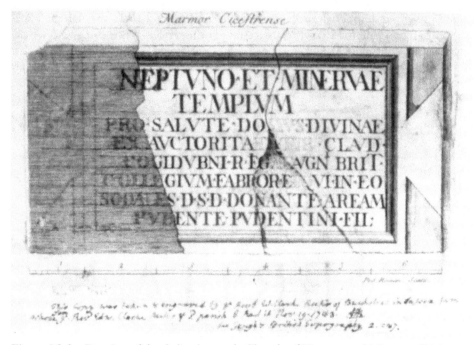

Figure 12.2 Drawing of the dedication to the Temple of Neptune and Minerva, Chichester, *c.*1783 (Institute of Archaeology, Oxford).

1995: 98, illustration 64), may have belonged to a full-size Jupiter statue of Capitoline type.

The veneration of deified emperors has left rather more evidence in Britain. The cult was officially centred on the Temple of Divus Claudius at Camulodunum, authorized by the Roman Senate after the death of that emperor in AD 54 (Tacitus, *Annals*, XIV.31; Fishwick 1972). Previous to that there may have been an altar dedicated to Rome and Augustus, as at Lyons in Gaul and Cologne in Germany. Here, leading men of the British tribes could serve as priests and pledge their loyalty to the Roman State as members of the Provincial Council. The altar, especially the temple, was so much a foreign implant that it became a symbol of loathing among the opponents of Roman rule, the *arx aeternae dominationis* in Tacitus' pithy phrase (*Annals*, XIV. 30), for Queen Boudicca of the Iceni and her rebellious followers seven years later. Part of the reason is said to have originated in the considerable amounts of money expended on the buildings, as well as on feasts and sacrifices, by men who could not afford such expenditure. However, it is probable that part of that problem would have lain in the custom of excessive gift-giving in a society where ostentatious expenditure had always been a rule of life. In any case, not all tribes rebelled against Rome and her gods; the Catuvellauni of Verulamium remained loyal and were, in consequence, early victims of Trinovantian and Icenian reprisal; the Atrebates under Togidubnus likewise took the Roman side.

The temple of Claudius was later rebuilt but may have lost its importance as London came to assume the role of capital of the province; on the evidence of a well-cut monumental inscription to the Numen Caesaris Augusti by the Province of Britain (*RIB* 5; figure 12.3) the centre of the cult may shortly have moved, a hypothesis given additional probability by the finding of a tomb monument (*RIB* 21) on Ludgate Hill, for a *provincialis* (a slave in the service of this cult), who would have served at the altar. The bronze head of Hadrian found in the Thames at London Bridge cannot be used as direct evidence because Imperial statuary would have been

Figure 12.3   Slab found in Nicholas Lane, London, which can be restored 'To the Numen of the Emperor, the Province of Britain set this up', after RIB 5.

Figure 12.4 Pediment of the Temple of Sulis Minerva, Bath (Photo: Institute of Archaeology, Oxford).

set up in a wide range of locations, and dedications to the *numina* (the divine spirit) of living emperors are found in many contexts, from cities, rural sanctuaries and army stations.

The best iconographic evidence for the Imperial cult is to be found at Bath. Here, the difficulty for us of trying to detach what is officially Roman from Romano-British cult is to be seen at its most acute. The iconography of the pediment at once suggests a highly sophisticated programme (Henig 1999, 2002; figure 12.4). The mask in the centre evidently conflates the Medusa mask worn on Minerva's breastplate with a head of Neptune. As at Chichester, here are the same two deities paired as representing water and land, and it is possible that the patron of the temple was Togidubnus who, if he was indeed the paramount king (*Rex Magnus Britanniae*) over the Belgae as well as other areas, would very probably have controlled Bath at the time the temple was built. The mask is on a shield encircled by two oak-wreaths ... The allusions here are to the Roman shield of virtue (*clipeus virtutis*) and the wreath (*corona civica*). With regard to a mask in a shield, we may recall the use of this motif in the Forum of Augustus in Rome. The wreath was awarded to Augustus and other Roman emperors, such as Vespasian, for supposedly saving the lives of citizens and is featured on the coinage. Victories on globes are self-explanatory, but probably point to victories in Minerva's realm, the land; tritons are members of Neptune's marine *thiasos* and symbolize victory at sea, notably the Augustan triumph at the Battle of Actium in 31 BC, which effectively established the Principate, and the sea crossing and successful invasion of Britain in AD 43. A star in the pediment and another on the architrave recall the *sidus Iulium* and the star in which both Claudius and Vespasian were subsequently deified. In part, at least, the temple was surely associated with the Imperial cult.

Of course, the building was primarily a temple to Sulis Minerva, whose first name is surely British (and the native elements in her cult are rightly considered elsewhere in this volume: see pp. 200–2), but for the Roman army officers involved in her worship, such as Marcus Aufidius Maximus of Legio VI or Gaius Curatius Saturninus of Legio II, who both visited Bath in the second century (*RIB* 143, 144, 146), she was evidently, for all practical purposes, a manifestation of the Italian Minerva Medica, who was venerated in Rome. The temple of Sulis was a variant on the classic type of Roman temple in the Corinthian order, with capitals which can be precisely dated to the Flavian period. It contained a cult statue of the goddess of which the gilt-bronze head alone remains; this is a very fine and accomplished example of bronze-casting, again probably early Imperial. What we know of religious rites here certainly includes the Etrusco-Roman practice of consulting entrails of sacrificial victims, for a *haruspex*, a specialist in 'gut-gazing', by the name of Lucius Marcius Memor, set up a dedication to the goddess (Cunliffe and Davenport 1985: 65 and 130 no. 9A. 1), and the sanctuary was supplied with professional *sacerdotes* as we have the tombstone of one, the 75-year-old Gaius Calpurnius Receptus, whose *tria nomina* show him to have been a Roman citizen (*RIB* 155). The presence of dream interpreters is also perhaps implied by a well-cut dedication set up *ex visu*, 'as the result of a vision or dream' (*RIB* 153). The many lead tablets from the sacred spring (*fons Sulis*), carrying imprecations against malefactors, are couched in Roman legal Latin, expressing the formal contractual nature of the bargains made with the gods (Tomlin 1988). As for offerings themselves, it has been suggested (Sauer 1999) that the dedication of coins in springs as opposed to weapons, etc. is to a large degree an Italian practice brought north by the Imperial armies.

Apart from the temple and cult statue, the sanctuary contained an altar on which it seems coal was burnt (Solinus, *Collectanea Rerum Memorabilium*, 22.10), probably a building used in incubation (sacred sleep) entered through a sculpted screen donated by a local guild, the spring of the goddess after which the sanctuary was named, a great suite of baths, a *tholos* of Greek design and probable Hadrianic date, perhaps containing a special, Imperial dedication by Hadrian himself, and almost certainly a theatre. The sanctuary was, in fact, fully as sophisticated as the great sanctuaries of the Mediterranean world, such as Olympia, Delphi or Eleusis, albeit on a smaller scale.

Other sacred sites in Britain were smaller and, in certain respects, less Roman and more native in their architecture and furnishings. But a visitor to, say, the temple of Mercury at Uley or of Mars Nodens at Lydney, both in Gloucestershire, would not have felt lost. At Uley the beautiful over life-size image of the god was carved from Cotswold limestone. It was based on a master-work by Praxiteles and, although the artistic style of the sculpture was British, it shows great confidence in the handling of classical forms. As well as the iconography, votive altars and lead tablets similar to those from Bath, but addressed to Mercury rather than Sulis, show that the contractual basis of cult was no different. Mars Nodens' shrine with its guest-house, baths and probable *abaton* is also Roman in its organization. The inscription on a fourth-century mosaic shows that its priest (who still sported the Roman *tria nomina*) was called Praepositus Religionum and that there was also a dream interpreter on site (*RIB* 2448.3). As Sir Mortimer Wheeler observed, in some ways the cult here recalled the healing cults of the Mediterranean, more especially Epidauros, with its *abaton* and sacred temple hounds, evidenced at Lydney by figurines. At Epidauros they licked the wounds of the afflicted and supposedly brought healing.

In studying cult it is important to establish whether the votaries were Roman or strongly Romanized or not, thereby having some basis on which to suggest their understanding of religion. Thus an arch dedicated to Mars Rigonemetos near Lincoln would seem from the name of the god alone, as with Sulis Minerva, to lead straight to native cult, to a local Mars of a *nemet* or sacred grove. However, Q. Neratius Proxsimus was a Roman citizen, who came from the Samnite country south of Rome, and was assuredly also a leading citizen of the *colonia* at Lincoln (Petch 1962). He, no doubt, envisaged this Mars as being the same protective deity he knew from his homeland, and who, as Cato proclaims, protected the woods and fields. Added to his veneration for Mars was that of the *numina* of the emperors. The worship of the emperor's *numen* was widespread in Britain and, even where one can be fairly sure that the dedicators were of Celtic origin and that their ways of thinking were far less Romanized, this aspect of cult linked foreign religious sentiment to Rome. Thus a Purbeck marble plaque from Colchester contains the dedication of a freedman called Imilico (who might, in fact, have been an African) to the Imperial *numina* and Mercury Andescociuoucus (*RIB* 193); similarly the well-known bronze statuette of Mars from the Foss Dike, Lincolnshire, which was paid for by Bruccius and Caratius, adds the Imperial *numina* (*RIB* 274). Here we can see Romanized religion, but not necessarily Roman religion.

One reservoir of traditional practice, the Roman army, remains to be mentioned. It was naturally conservative in its religious practices, as is shown by a roster of religious observances, carried out by an auxiliary unit at Dura Europos in Syria, preserved on papyrus and concerned entirely with the festivals of traditional Roman deities and commemorations of deceased emperors and empresses. The evidence from this document (which scholars have called the *Feriale Duranum*) can be supplemented by what can be learned from inscriptions found on military sites in Britain, such as Corbridge (Richmond 1943). Clearly, every Roman fort was regarded as an image of Rome in microcosm, and the same customs were observed, as though preserved in aspic, from one end of the Empire to the other. A great deal of fascinating evidence for official or Italian-style religion thus comes from such army sites.

Jupiter Optimus Maximus, as the chief god of the Roman State, was venerated frequently, most importantly at the beginning of each year on 3 January and on the anniversary of the reigning emperor's accession. A large number of such altars were excavated at Maryport on the Cumbria coast and were, until recently, thought to have been dedications from the edge of the parade-ground, set up annually by the prefect in office and buried in the following year. It has now been realized that they were not from the parade-ground but from a temple of the god outside the fort (Breeze 1997). Other deities closely connected with the Roman administration and venerated on altars from military stations include Mars, Minerva, Apollo, Diana, Hercules (here regarded as a god rather than a hero) and Sol (generally regarded as a different deity from Apollo). Some of the 'official' gods and goddesses were ones we would regard as personifications: Victory (often of the emperor), Fortune, the Genius of the Place or

I ᐱ O ᐱ M
ETNMINB ᐱAVG
M ᐱVA R ᐱSEVƎRVS
ᐱ B ᐱ CoS ᐱ
ARAM ᐱ CVM
CANCELLIS
ᐱD ᐱ S ᐱ P ᐱ

Figure 12.5   Altar to Iuppiter Optimus Maximus from Dorchester, Oxfordshire. After RIB 235.

Unit, Concord, Salus (health). The Nymphs and Fountains protected the aqueduct of the fortress of Legio XX at Chester (*RIB* 460). Hadrian may have introduced the cult of Discip(u)lina, in accord with his policy of smartening up the army (Henig 1984; 77–8). Then there were territorial goddesses, Rome of course, but also Britannia. An interesting case was Brigantia, on the surface a purely native deity but perhaps a Severan creation to establish a sense of identity for northern Britain (Britannia Inferior). The only certain representation of Brigantia comes from Birrens (*RIB* 2091) and was set up by a military engineer called Amandus. Although some recent commentators have dated the stone back in the second century, the style of the relief looks later and an *architectus* is just the expert who would have been sent to a mothballed fort to see if it could be brought back into commission. Brigantia not only has a mural crown, but the spear, shield, helmet and Medusa breastplate of Minerva, and the wings of Victory. An oriental feature is the omphaloid stone beside her, perhaps equating her with Dea Syria, with whom the empress Julia Domna was equated, as on the dedication set up by Marcus Caecilius Donatianus at Carvoran (*RIB* 1791).

The emperor, in the guise of the Numen of the living ruler (see above), is often mentioned on altars set up by soldiers. For instance, Marcus Varius Severus, a *beneficiarius consularis*, a legionary detached for policing duty, set up at the posting station at Dorchester in Oxfordshire an altar surrounded by screens (*RIB* 235: figure 12.5) dedicated to Jupiter Optimus Maximus *and* the Numinibus Augustorum.

In addition, dead emperors venerated as Divi play a significant part in the cult outlined in the *Feriale Duranum*. One aspect of Roman religion that is found from time to time, especially in army centres but also in the towns, concerns *damnatio memoriae*, the deliberate erasure of the emperor's name or even occasionally of the god he especially venerated. Thus at Corbridge, on a temple dedication of AD 162–8 to Sol Invictus (*RIB* 1137), an attempt was made to remove the name of the deity, probably because he was associated with Commodus or perhaps, if the stone survived that long, Elagabalus. The official removal of the name of Domitian, for instance, on the forum dedication at Verulamium (Frere 1983: 69–72) and of Geta on dedications to Severus and his sons (e.g. *RIB* 740 from Bowes) or the Gallic emperor Postumus on a dedication slab from Lancaster (*RIB* 605) were essentially religious acts, analogous to more recent attempts at erasure of memory, in the toppling of statues of Stalin in Eastern Europe.

The extent to which personal, Italianate cult was practised (that is, without specific reference to local Celtic practice) should not be underestimated. Gaius Tetius Veturius Micianus, prefect of the Sebosian Cavalry, concluded a hunting expedition on the moors near Stanhope in Country Durham by setting up a fine altar to Silvanus Invictus 'on fulfilment of his vow... for bagging a wild boar of remarkable fineness which many of his predecessors [as prefect] had been unable to take' (*RIB* 1041). Interestingly, he had used a secondhand altar to the Numina of the Augusti. There is an altar from York dedicated by a prefect called Publius Aelius Marcianus to both Jupiter and the Penates, traditional Roman gods of the home, for having protected him and his household (*RIB* 649). A husband and wife at Caerleon, Cornelius Castus and Julia Belismicus, venerate Fortune and Bonus Eventus (*RIB* 318). In the early fourth century, visitors to the great villa at Woodchester were admonished by an inscription on a mosaic floor to 'Worship Bonus Eventus duly' (*RIB* 2448.2).

With regard to the last, special mention should be made of the particular gods of person and place, the Genius, the Lares, Fortune and Bonus Eventus. Especially evident are the many sculptures of Genii, sometimes, as on a relief at Tockenham, Wiltshire, wearing the Roman toga. Fortuna too is a Roman conception and has her familiar attributes of rudder, wheel and horn of plenty, for example, on a relief at Marlborough, Wiltshire. Both deities appear with another, possibly a Lar, on a relief from the villa at Stonesfield, Oxfordshire (Henig and Booth 2000: 131, illustration 5, 17b). The nymphs were also vital in connection with water supply, as is shown by the Chester altar to the Nymphs and Fountains (*RIB* 460) set up by Legio XX or the painting of the nymphs in the basement shrine of the villa at Lullingstone, Kent (Henig 1984: 173).

The personal aspect of Roman religion is demonstrated by the varied devices on the engraved gemstones (signets) which men and women wore on their fingers and which provide a wonderful conspectus of the gods and goddesses they venerated (Henig 1978). With some minor exceptions, a few eastern deities and one or two possible Celtic ones, all the gods shown belong to the Graeco-Roman pantheon. Most of the important Roman deities are strongly represented. A number of gems depict Jupiter, including a so far unique intaglio from Colchester, which shows Jupiter with the Cretan goat who nurtured him on Mount Ida. Other gods include Mars, Mercury, Apollo, Diana, Minerva and Venus. The presence of Fortuna, the Genius, Ceres, Bonus Eventus, Silvanus and a wide range of cupids and satyrs show the essentially personal role (protection of hearth and home) of such devices. A few gems, including examples from Corbridge, Northumberland, and North Cerney, Gloucestershire, show a worshipper making an offering at a country shrine (perhaps of Priapus). The gods will bring prosperity and health to the wearers.

Religious Practices

The way the gods were approached is best shown by the so-called curse tablets. These were scratched on sheets of lead, and have been found at Bath, Uley, Lydney, Pagans Hill and other sites (Henig 1984: 142–5). Although, at first glance, they look like an aspect of Celtic cult, in fact the concept of making a contract with a deity, in which one asks the god to do something and promises payment if the act desired is done, comes from the realm of Roman law. The language is very precise and legal and matched by contracts in the secular world. First, the address has to be right. On visiting a temple one needed to know exactly how to address the power who reigned there. At Delphi, Apollo would have been called Phoebus, for example; a specific Diana (Diana Nemorensis) presided at Aricia on Lake Nemi; the Minerva at Carbo in north Italy was different from Minerva elsewhere. Therefore, whether one was a Roman army officer or a local peasant, the Minerva at Bath was always Sulis or Sulis Minerva, never simply Minerva. Thus, a typical invocation begins 'Docilianus, son of Brucetus, to the most holy goddess Sulis' (Tomlin 1988: 122 no. 10). Then follows the complaint, 'I curse him who has stolen my hooded cloak.' But here legal niceties come in: if the implication is that the thief is a man and the crime was perpetrated by a woman, the goddess will be unable to help. Similarly, if the thief was a slave of either sex, it had to be remembered that technically a slave was a chattel, and the curse was without power. Thus Docilianus adds 'whether man or woman, whether slave or free'. Another plaintiff at Bath was worried about whether the goddess's power was limited only to believers. What about Christians? Better add 'Whether Pagan or Christian' (Tomlin 1988: 232 no. 98). Only after this opening can Docilianus make his request, the *nuncupatio* proper: 'inflict death . . . don't allow him sleep . . . or children now and in the future.' However, it is not a simple curse but a call for restitution 'unless (or until) he has brought my hooded cloak to the temple of my divinity'. Sometimes a reward is offered to the deity, a tenth part perhaps, or a specified item.

The central rite of classical Roman religion, whether civilian or military, was blood sacrifice upon an altar; the gods required propitiation or gifts with something living. Additionally, libations of wine and offerings of seeds and fruit were acceptable. One of the clearest representations of a sacrifice is on the right-hand side of the Bridgeness distance slab from the Antonine Wall (*RIB* 2139; figure 12.6). There we see the commander of Legio II Augusta, identified by the *vexillum* flag behind his head, pouring a libation from a *patera*. Despite numerous variations, such a scene would have been familiar to almost everyone in Britain. As mentioned above, the Genius from Tockenham, Wiltshire, is shown wearing his toga, as he too pours a libation upon an altar (figure 12.7). On the Bridgeness slab, the legate is about to perform a *suovetaurilia*, one of the most expensive of sacrifices as it meant killing a prime boar (*sus*), a first-quality ram (*ovis*) and a bull (*taurus*), all potential breeding stock. The officiant (legionary legate) is wearing a toga and will shortly pull its folds up over his

Figure 12.6 Right side of the Antonine Wall distance slab from Bridgeness, West Lothian, showing the Legate of II Augusta performing the *suovetaurilia* (Photo: M. Henig).

head. The *popa*, probably the figure shown on the left side of the scene, will then fell the beasts, whose entrails might then be examined by a *haruspex* (though only one practitioner of this ancient, originally Etruscan, craft has yet been identified in Britain). There may also have been other sorts of diviner involved in the rites. The practice of augury is suggested by a sard intaglio from Silchester which shows, in addition to a jug used for pouring libations, a curved staff or *lituus* used by augurs in studying the heavens, as well as in asperging victims prior to sacrifice (Henig 1978: no. 410; figure). Little votive axes, found on sites of all sorts, represent the Roman rite of sacrifice at an altar, and may have been given as a sort of substitute by the poor, for whom a ram, let alone an ox, would have been beyond their means.

Altars of the form shown on the Bridgeness relief were, of course, universal, through Britain as elsewhere in the Empire, but larger sanctuaries had altars

Figure 12.7 Relief of a genius set into the south exterior wall of the church at Tockenham, Wiltshire (Photo: M. Henig).

constructed of stone blocks which were elaborately decorated with reliefs, as in the case of altars at Rome. The site for such an altar is known in front of the Temple of Claudius at Colchester; it is very likely that the so-called screen of gods reconstructed from stone blocks recovered from the Riverside wall at London was another. It bore images along its sides of major Roman deities. Similarly figured, the blocks which seem to be cornerstones of the altar of Sulis Minerva at Bath comprise a third.

Archaeological evidence for sacrifice is likely to be scarce, apart from the presence of large quantities of animal bones on some temple sites. It may be noted from the *Feriale Duranum* that it was customary to sacrifice male animals to gods and female ones to goddesses, and hence the fact that many of the bones from the sanctuary at Bath were those of cows is, perhaps, significant.

Commitment and Enthusiasm

More ecstatic involvement is often thought to have belonged to mystery religions, but action might be impelled by dreams and visions. A monument to Sulis was put up at Bath 'ex visu' (*RIB* 153). Another inscription on an altar set up as a result of a vision may have been set up by someone who was, literally, in mortal fear, as it is an altar to Nemesis from the Nemeseum of the amphitheatre at Chester (Henig 1984: 156, illustration 77). There were dream-books which could be consulted and dream-interpreters to visit, the name of one of whom is given as Victorinus on a late Roman mosaic from the cella of the temple of Nodens at Lydney Park, Gloucestershire (Henig 1984: 136, illustration 58).

But the best example is the verse inscription from Carvoran, mentioned above (*RIB* 1791), addressed by the tribune Marcus Caecilius Donatianus to the empress Julia Domna, whom he equates with Juno, Peace, Dea Syria and the Magna Mater. The language seems genuine and heartfelt. Even though there is an element of State cult here, there is far more of the inclusiveness and questing of the religious syncretism of the Middle Empire. The verse brings to mind the appearance of Isis to Lucius in the final book of Apuleius' *Golden Ass*. Indeed, this desire to gain a personal revelation from a deity is a feature which can be especially associated with the gods introduced from the east. Thus dedications to the version of Jupiter imported from Doliché in Asia Minor (Jupiter Dolichenus) are likewise often set up *ex visu* or *admonitus*; the god took care of his worshippers.

This is even clearer from the much better evidence for the Mithras cult which although, in fact, largely a Roman creation purported to have come from Persia (Henig 1984: 97–109; Clauss 2000). As with Dolichenus, merchants and, above all, soldiers were the main worshippers. The temples (*mithraea*) were small basilical buildings constructed to resemble caves, and within them cult ceremonies took place (figure 12.8). On the end wall was the primal act of Creation. The young sky-god Mithras, in Persian dress, sacrifices a bull from which all life comes. On either side of him stand his supporters, likewise in Persian dress, one with torch raised, Cautes representing day and life; the other with torch lowered, Cautopates, night and death. Only fragments of major taurocthonies remain from the Mithraea of London and Housesteads, for example, but there are small votive versions from York and London, the latter dedicated by Ulpius Silvanus, an emeritus of Legio II Augusta (figure 12.9).

Figure 12.8 The Mithraeum outside the fort at Carrawburgh, Northumberland (Photo: M. Henig).

Astrology was central to the cult and many of the figures shown, the scorpion, snake and hound who take the bull's vital juices (semen and blood), have an astral signifi-cance. Silvanus' taurocthony is set within the circle of the zodiac. An extraordinary carving half in relief and half in the round from Housesteads shows Mithras bursting forth from the cosmic egg, an idea garnered from Orphic beliefs, set within an ovate border again containing the signs of the zodiac. Here is Mithras Saecularis, 'Lord of Ages' (Henig 1984: 99, illustration 38).

The central ceremonies of Mithras involved feasts in which the votaries reclined on couches in the aisles. Progress through various grades of initiation involved dressing up, as recorded by observers, but also ordeals including mock burial, as suggested by a rectangular pit excavated at Carrawburgh. The ultimate aim of the votary was doubtless salvation, unity with the sun and with Mithras, who were associated with each other and often conflated.

Another salvation cult whose origins are more certain is that of Isis. Like Mithras, she evidently had an important temple in London where she is attested by an altar dedicated to her by a third-century governor or acting governor, Marcus Martianus Pulcher (Henig 1984: 113–14). Isis had been venerated in Rome from the time of the Republic, but from the Flavian period she had achieved very considerable official acceptance. A jug inscribed *Londini ad Fanum Isidis* of Flavian date, found in Southwark, shows she had a temple here at that time and, as the jug is almost complete, there is a good chance it was deliberately buried (after it was deemed ritually unusable) on site. Miniature representations of Harpocrates, son of Isis, from the Thames confirm Pliny the Elder's remarks on the growing acceptability of the

Figure 12.9   Marble taurocthony from Walbrook Mithraeum, London (RIB 3) (Photo: Musuem of London).

Egyptian gods. From Wroxeter there are intaglios showing both Isis and her consort, Serapis. A portrait of Serapis is among the marbles from the Walbrook Mithraeum, but here he may have stood in for Ahura Mazda and did not have a cult. Another head in British stone from Silchester may point to his veneration here, and from York there is the building record of a temple of Serapis erected by a legate of Legio VI, Claudius Hieronymianus (*RIB* 658; figure 12.10). This stone displays sacred cult standards associated with this deity on its sides.

A third eastern cult, widespread in the Empire, was that of Cybele and Attis. Cybele, a powerful nature deity originating from Pessinus in Asia Minor, was equated with Julia Domna by Donatianus, as we have seen, but she was not a beneficent mother-goddess like Isis but had far darker characteristics. In her myth the shepherd Attis, forsaking her for love of the nymph Sangaritis, had been driven mad by the jealous and vengeful goddess and had castrated himself (Vermaseren 1977). In like manner, some of her votaries made themselves eunuchs for her sake. One of the most controversial objects from Roman London is a clamp used for castration, decorated with busts of Attis and Cybele, as well as the days of the week, horse protomes and bull protomes. Of course, it might have been used in gelding animals, like other plain examples which have been found, but this example could equally have been used in removing the human *vires*, preventing the flow of blood which would have followed

Figure 12.10 Dedication of Temple to Serapis, York. In the Yorkshire Museum (RIB 658) (Photo: courtesy of the late Ralph Merrifield).

the actual cut with a sharpened flint or potsherd and which proved fatal to Attis himself. This rite (which the emperor Julian called a 'sacred harvest') generally took place on 24 March, the *dies sanguinis*. There is no direct evidence for *galli*, the eunuch priests of Attis, from Britain, though a bronze figurine of Attis, with his trousers open to reveal his immature genitals, was also recovered from here. There must have been a temple of Attis at Gloucester too, as a representation of an immature Attis is figured on an altar from that *colonia*, as is a half-length figure of the youth whose fleshy features suggest immaturity or perhaps emasculation. From a cemetery outside the walls a plaque also depicts a head of Attis, but another plaque shows an Attis-like figure as a huntsman.

The death and resurrection rituals of Attis made his cult the centre of a burial guild; the tree-bearers (*dendrophori*) were non-eunuch supporters of Attis, who seem to be attested by a graffito on a pot from a cemetery at Dunstable, dedicated by the *dendrophori* of Ver(ulamium), where they may have had their headquarters at the Triangular Temple on the east side of the city (Henig 1984: 158, illustration 78, 159). It is of some interest that items connected with cult and burial, recovered immediately south of London Bridge on the site of Southwark Cathedral, contain a statue of a huntsman wearing a Phrygian cap, and this may have been the site of a similar temple. The Gloucester evidence suggests a third.

However, in the case of London–Southwark and Gloucester, the huntsman with the Phrygian cap is evidence for a connection with the wider field of Roman–Celtic cult, for it seems Attis was here conflated with a local deity, who is attested in London and especially the Cotswold region and may have been called Apollo Cunomaglus, 'Apollo the hound prince'. Later this syncretic god was possibly merged into a highly distinctive local version of Orpheus, who is shown, accompanied by his hound, on mosaics like those of Woodchester and Barton Farm in Gloucestershire and Littlecote in Wiltshire (Henig 1995: 153–4).

Late Paganism

The distinctiveness of the British Orpheus pavements, which place Orpheus in the middle of a circle with beasts circulating in registers around, has long been recognized. The concept of the unchanging centre and the ever moving world outside it may owe something to neo-Platonic and Orphic speculation. This is especially evident at Littlecote (figure 12.11), where, although some scholars have interpreted the mosaic-floored tri-conch chamber as merely a summer dining-room, the imagery which serves to conflate Orpheus with Apollo and Bacchus in an esoteric fashion suggests use of the room as a centre of private cult, the centre for exotic rites (Walters 1984). The visitor enters the room over a threshold displaying a cantharus flanked by sea panthers and then, after crossing a geometric patterned pavement, another cantharus with a pair of panthers. The next section may represent the pool of memory from which the votary of Orpheus must drink after death to secure a blissful immortality. Orpheus himself is figured in the centre of a room with three alcoves. He is surrounded by four beasts representing the transformations of Bacchus when he fled from the Titans, and four deities representing the Seasons, ruled over by Apollo. The three apses have sun-like motifs (for Apollo), but panther heads (for Bacchus) at the centre of the chord on each. The only objects from the site which might confirm the nature of the rites are two bronze appliqué busts of Bacchus, one exceedingly fine, and rather earlier (Henig 1995: 71, illustration 39), a Hadrianic conflation of Bacchus with Hadrian's lover Antinous, but perhaps pressed into service to ornament a couch in this room.

Ritualized eating, drinking and ecstatic dancing are shown on a mosaic from Trier. Such rites go back a long way and are most famously represented in the cult room of the Villa of the Mysteries outside Pompeii. In Britain there is considerable evidence for the veneration of Bacchus in Late Roman times (Henig 2002). Some of it is circumstantial, for example, the villa mosaics at Stonesfield, Oxfordshire, and Thruxton, Hampshire, both showing Bacchus and his panther, although the latter was possibly laid 'ex voto'. A marble statuette of Bacchus was buried with the owner of a villa at Spoonley Wood, Gloucestershire, presumably to succour him in the next world as the god had protected him in this one. The Great Dish and other dishes in the Mildenhall Treasure show Bacchic dancing, and it is quite likely that this was much more than mere decoration. Most exciting of all is the realization that the old Temple of Mithras beside the Walbrook in London had been rededicated to Bacchus. A marble statuette figures the god with his panther, together with a satyr and maenad, Pan and Silenus on his donkey. The inscription reads 'hominibus bagis bitam', 'You give life to wandering men' (*RIB* 1; figure 12.12). In addition to this and two marble torsos of Bacchus, a silver bowl and a lidded casket embellished with scenes of conflict but, as an elephant and panthers are prominent, very possibly recalling the Indian Triumph of Bacchus. The casket is in fact a *cista mystica*, here containing an infuser used to hold narcotic substances to lace the wine drunk in celebration of the god's saving power. Pottery cups were also found here.

Figure 12.11 Mosaic at Littlecote, Wiltshire, engraved by George Vertue in the eighteenth century.

Figure 12.12 Marble group of Bacchus and his followers from the former Walbrook Mithraeum, inscribed '*hominibus bagis bitam*' (RIB 1) (Photo: Museum of London).

No doubt the votaries were a closed group of worshippers, as were those who are represented on the inscriptions from the Thetford Treasure. As the inscriptions upon the spoons attest, here the god worshipped was Faunus, among the most ancient of the deities of Latium, but here given various Celtic epithets. Among the gold jewellery is a ring showing an overflowing wine bowl (the wine represented by an amethyst) flanked by woodpeckers standing for Faunus' father Picus (which means woodpecker). Another ring figures the goat-like features of Pan with whom Faunus was sometimes equated. However, the gold buckle has a plate figuring a satyr, though perhaps again to be regarded as Faunus. Spoons and little strainers suggest eating and drinking. The men and women attested on the inscriptions may not have stopped at dining, but dancing and even erotic congress between them may have been central to what was surely a salvation cult. This marks the other side of Roman religion, not the rather boring, formal cult activity which has so often been seen as its hallmark, but a vital union with deity highlighting mankind's deepest needs. The Thetford Treasure demonstrates that Roman cult, far from being the antithesis of native religion, was complementary to it (Johns and Potter 1983).

Christianity in a Pagan World

Christianity in Roman Britain is an enormous theme and this is not the place to discuss the subject in general (for which see Thomas 1981; Mawer 1995). Had Christianity not become the State religion of the Empire in the fourth century, or had it declined and disappeared, as a result, perhaps, of Julian succeeding in his aim of restoring paganism, the archaeological remains of Christianity from the Province would intrigue us as much as do those of Mithraism. Christianity can be differentiated from other mystery cults because it originated in an exclusive monotheistic religion, Judaism, and because, like its parent, it was monotheistic and exclusive. Nevertheless, it did have some features found in other cults. The presentation of votives, plaques and silver vessels, at Water Newton, Cambridgeshire (Painter 1999) is an obvious link with the behaviour of contemporary pagans. Indeed, the same ritual formulae for gift-giving are sometimes used. Purification by water, best attested in fonts such as that recognized in a corner of the Roman fort at Richborough, Kent, and the Christianization of the spring, perhaps dedicated to the nymphs at Chedworth, Gloucestershire, provide another example. In Dorset, the Hinton St Mary mosaic, with its central head of Christ and other Christian symbols, juxtaposed with a pagan scene, Bellerophon slaying the Chimaera, and even more the intrusion of a chi-rho, the symbol of Christ, on the chord of the apse on the largest of the mythological floors at Frampton, show some desire to integrate old and new. The Bath curse tablet which supposes that someone hanging around Sulis Minerva's baths and temple might have been a Christian argues as much. It is easy to regard a gold ring found at Suffolk showing a chi-rho, a tree of life and a dove as marking a real break with the past, but it can be seen as answering the same human needs as a signet-ring depicting a deity; or as the British equivalent of one of those 'silver shrines for Diana' made by Demetrius and his colleagues in the guild of silversmiths at Ephesus. This is a miniature, portable, lead shrine of Minerva from Dorchester, Dorset (figure 12.13). Gods, whoever they were or are, protect those who seek their help.

FURTHER READING

The study of the Roman aspects of religion in Britain has to begin with the religion of the Empire as a whole. A good starting-point is R. M. Ogilvie, *The Romans and their Gods* (1969). Exhaustive treatment of religion in Rome can be found in Mary Beard, John North and Simon Price, *Religions of Rome* (1998).

My own book, *Religion in Roman Britain* (1984), attempts to cover the range of cults apart from Christianity from a Roman (rather than a Celtic) perspective; it may be supplemented with *The Art of Roman Britain* (1995) as I believe art is central to our understanding of how the Romans saw the gods. I am coming to believe that the native people of Britain took a far more decisive role in developing a sophisticated religious life in Roman Britain, and the evidence for this is given in *The Heirs of King Verica* (2002). For an excellent study of a highly Romanized sanctuary see Barry Cunliffe, *Roman Bath Discovered* (2000). Georgia Irby-Massie, *Military Religion in Roman Britain* (1999) is a solidly inclusive work. For the eastern cults, John Shepherd's *The Temple of Mithras, London. Excavations by W. F. Grimes and A. Williams at the Walbrook* (1998) discusses the most lavish of British Mithraea and the shrine of Bacchus which succeeded it. Manfred Clauss, *The Roman Cult of Mithras* (2000) is the best modern

Figure 12.13 Lead shrine to Minerva from Dorchester, Dorset (Photo: Institute of Archaeology, Oxford).

treatment. R. E. Witt, *Isis in the Graeco-Roman World* (1971) is brilliantly readable, as is M. J. Vermaseren, *Cybele and Attis. The Myth and the Cult* (1977), though the latter contrives to miss almost all the British evidence. A volume of papers ranging from a study of the Genius to the cults of Bacchus and Faunus and late Roman syncretism, many of them concerned with Britain, are included in M. Henig and A. King, *Pagan Gods and Shrines of the Roman Empire* (1986).

Finally, anyone wishing to make a contribution to understanding Romano-British religion will have to consult the *Roman Inscriptions of Britain,* of which two volumes (one on inscriptions on stone and another on inscriptions on other objects) have so far been published, and the great sculpture corpus, the *Corpus Signorum Imperii Romani,* likewise in progress.

REFERENCES

Bogaers, J. E. 1979. King Cogidubnus in Chichester: another reading of RIB 91. *Britannia,* 10, 243–54.

Breeze, D. J. 1997. The regiments stationed at Maryport and their commanders. In R. J. A. Wilson (ed.), *Roman Maryport and its Setting: Essays in Memory of Michael G. Jarrett.* Maryport, 67–9.

Clauss, M. 2000. *The Roman Cult of Mithras: The God and his Mysteries.* Edinburgh.

Collingwood, R. G. and Wright, R. P. 1965. *The Roman Inscriptions of Britain* I. *Inscriptions on Stone.* Oxford.

Cunliffe, B. 2000. *Roman Bath Discovered.* Stroud.

Cunliffe, B. and Davenport, P. 1985. *The Temple of Sulis Minerva at Bath. I. The Site.* Oxford University Committee for Archaeology 7. Oxford.

Fishwick, D. 1972. Templum Divo Claudio Constitutum. *Britannia,* 3, 164–81.

Frere, S. S. 1983. *Verulamium Excavations II.* London.

Henig, M. 1978. *A Corpus of Roman Engraved Gemstones from British Sites.* BAR (British Series) 8. Oxford. [First published in 1974.]

—— 1984. *Religion in Roman Britain.* London.

—— 1995. *The Art of Roman Britain.* London.

—— 1999. A new star shining over Bath. *Oxford Journal of Archaeology,* 18, 419–25.

—— 2002. *The Heirs of King Verica.* Stroud.

Henig, M. and Booth, P. 2000. *Roman Oxfordshire.* Stroud.

Henig, M. and King, A. 1986. *Pagan Gods and Shrines of the Roman Empire.* Oxford University Committee for Archaeology 8. Oxford.

Irby-Massie, G. 1999. *Military Religion in Roman Britain.* Leiden.

Johns, C. and Potter, T. 1983. *The Thetford Treasure.* London.

Mawer, C. F. 1995. *Evidence for Christianity in Roman Britain: The Small Finds.* BAR (British Series) 243. Oxford.

North, J. and Price, S. 1998. *Religions of Rome.* Cambridge.

Ogilvie, R. M. 1969. *The Romans and their Gods.* London.

Painter, K. 1999. The Water Newton Silver: votive or liturgical? *Journal of the British Archaeological Association,* 152, 1–23.

Petch, D. F. 1962. A Roman inscription, Nettleham. *Lincolnshire Architectural and Archaeological Society,* NS 9, 94–7.

Richmond, I. A. 1943. Roman legionaries at Corbridge, their supply-base, temples and religious cults. *Archaeologia Aeliana,* 4th ser. 21, 127–224.

Sauer, E. 1999. The Augustan army spa at Bourbonne-les-Bains. In A. Goldsworthy and I. Haynes (eds), *The Roman Army as a Community.* Journal of Roman Archaeology Supplementary Series 34. Portsmouth, RI, 52–79.

Shepherd, J. 1998. *The Temple of Mithras, London: Excavations by W. F. Grimes and A. Williams at the Walbrook*. London.

Thomas, C. 1981. *Christianity in Roman Britain to AD 500*. London.

Tomlin, R. S. O. 1988. The curse tablets. In B. Cunliffe, *The Temple of Sulis Minerva at Bath. 2. The Finds from the Sacred Spring*. Oxford University Committee for Archaeology 16. Oxford, 59–277 [abbreviated as *Tab. Sulis*].

Vermaseren, M. J. 1977. *Cybele and Attis: The Myth and the Cult*. London.

Walters, B. 1984. The 'Orpheus' mosaic in Littlecote Park, England. In R. Farioli Campanati (ed.), *III colloquio internazionale sul mosaico antico*. Ravenna, 433–42.

Witt, R. E. 1971. *Isis in the Graeco-Roman World*. London.

CHAPTER THIRTEEN

The Human Population: Health and Disease

CHARLOTTE ROBERTS AND MARGARET COX

Today, as always, our physical and mental health is probably the factor that concerns us most and affects how we conduct our lives. Even when we are well, we can never anticipate illness and know that our illness can be treated quickly and effectively. It is thus a truism that health is a prerequisite for the success of any society. One only has to look to modern developing societies to appreciate the problems they face (McElroy and Townsend 1996) in acquiring the basic necessities of life such as a clean water supply; without this, health suffers and early mortality may ensue. We do not have to go far back in time to realize that it is only during the past century or so that we in Britain have seen the improvements in living conditions, diet, access to health care and the development of medical applications such as antibiotics that we take for granted today. If we consider our ancestors further back in time, we must question how much ill-health they encountered, their attempts to introduce measures to prevent disease and to treat it, and comparisons with today. If encounters with ill-health were influential in determining the success or otherwise of past societies, then we should be considering the people who shaped those societies and their health. In pursuing this line of thinking, we must inevitably turn to the archaeological evidence for people, as the primary evidence for the health of human beings comes from the remains of the people themselves. This chapter considers the nature of this evidence, the associated problems of analysis and interpretation, the evidence for health and disease in Roman Britain, and offers some thoughts on how healthy the Romano-Britons were, and the impact of their health on the functioning of their society.

The History of Study

The study of palaeopathology has had a long history in Britain and has enjoyed significant advances over the past twenty years. While practitioners analysing human remains from archaeological sites have, until recently, remained in the background of enquiry, there has been an increased recognition of the value of studying skeletal remains. This has probably arisen because there are now many more specialists in this field and specific training is now available to guide analysis. The establishment of one-year master's courses in archaeology departments at various universities in Britain has provided that training. Many of these graduates originally come from archaeology and anthropology undergraduate courses, and are now working much more closely with field archaeologists when they are excavating cemetery sites. In addition, when analysing skeletons, they are collaborating much more with other 'specialists' in order to produce an integrated report that considers the human remains within their cultural and environmental context. This is of significant benefit to archaeology as a whole, and even relegating human bone reports to appendices in archaeological publications is no longer inevitable. While initial and early work in palaeopathology concentrated on individual skeletons with interesting diseases (case studies), we now see a much more holistic and population-based approach to examining people's health in the past.

Studying palaeopathology using skeletal remains

While human remains are the primary evidence for people in the past, the study of the remains of our ancestors is the primary evidence for disease. It is, of course, possible to consider written and illustrative evidence for disease, and this may be the only evidence available for some diseases, such as those that affect only the soft tissues, but these types of data can be misleading and need care with interpretation. There are, however, also problems with the study of human remains. It is therefore important, before discussing the evidence for health and disease in Roman Britain, to understand the processes inherent in the study of palaeopathology and the potential limitations.

There are two ways in which a disease may be reflected in the skeleton: these are bone formation (hypertrophy) and bone destruction (including atrophy) or both. The bone formed may be of two types, woven or lamellar; woven or immature bone is the initial response to a disease and can indicate active disease at the time of death, and lamellar bone is mature bone that replaces it. Lamellar bone indicates a chronic and long-standing disease. Destruction of bone may show signs of healing, such as rounding of the edges of a lesion, but the disease causing it may also have been active at death and no healing may be evident. An individual's immune system status (strong or weak) is instrumental as to whether a disease is seen on the skeleton and how severely the bone may be affected. In effect, exposure to many foreign organisms (pathogens) during the growing years is essential to establish a strong immune system. The lesions that result occur in specific distribution patterns that may allow a particular disease to be diagnosed. For example, in the infectious disease tuberculosis, the skeleton is usually affected in the spine and/or hip or knee, and the lesions are mainly destructive. We are aware of lesion distribution patterns from the consideration of data from clinical sources, and we have to assume that the bone changes of different diseases have not altered through time; of course, this may not be the case. The teeth can also suffer destruction, for example, through caries (too much sugar in the diet and poor care of teeth), but they may also accrue additional material such as calculus (hardened plaque) which may contain evidence for diet.

When a person is collecting data on disease from the skeleton the process of collection starts with a detailed description of the abnormal lesions, followed by a consideration of the nature of the lesions (forming/destroying) and their distribution pattern. This is the most common method of analysis, although radiography plays a significant part of the analytical procedure for many; this allows the interior structure of bones and teeth to be viewed and health problems to be identified before they are seen externally. People could have died before the disease became obvious or they may have suffered a disease that would never be visualized without radiography. Where adequate funding is available, histopathology can also add to our understanding (Bell and Piper 2000). Another recently developed method of investigation has increased in use for diagnosis of disease, and that is biomolecular analysis. Over the last ten years some researchers have managed to extract and amplify (by the polymerase chain reaction or PCR) DNA and other biomolecules of organisms causing disease to prove that certain individuals had a specific disease. This methodological development has allowed diagnosis of disease before it was evident in the skeleton (Mays et al. 2001), confirmation of diagnoses of disease made on the basis of bones (Taylor et al. 2000), and also the identification of disease that never affects the skeleton, such as the plague (Raoult et al. 2000) and malaria (Taylor et al. 1997). While there may be problems with this method of analysis, such as survival of ancient DNA and contamination with foreign DNA, there are likewise problems with other methods of analysis for disease in the skeleton.

Wood and others (1992) and Waldron (1994) have succinctly outlined the problems palaeopathologists face when trying to identify and interpret health in past populations, and the reader is referred to those publications for more details. However, a few points can be made here. We must first be aware that bones in particular can react in only two ways to disease (formation or destruction of bone) and therefore a series of diseases could lead to the same or similar bone changes. It is therefore important to produce 'differential diagnoses', that is, the potential disease processes that could have caused the lesions, and then processes of elimination conclude which one was involved. Unfortunately, many skeletons that are excavated in Britain are poorly preserved and incomplete, and therefore diagnosing disease can prove difficult. When considering the evidence of disease in a skeleton, it is necessary to be aware that what is observed is the accumulation of indicators of health over the lifetime of the individual. One is viewing this evidence at a static point in the person's life, their death, and it is often impossible to know at what point in their life a disease afflicted them. If woven bone (see above) is seen, then we can infer the disease causing it was active at the time, but lamellar bone formation suggests that the person had had the disease for a long period of time, that is, it was chronic. In fact, those skeletons we see in a population with chronic healed lesions are really the healthy members of society because their immune systems combated the acute stages of the disease. They may have progressed to the chronic stage (healed lesions) or they may not. Clearly, the presence of a skeleton with no evidence of disease could suggest a number of scenarios. The person may have died in the acute stages of a disease before bone changes occurred; the person may have had a disease but died before the bone damage became obvious; or the person may have died from a disease that did not affect the skeleton (e.g. cholera). Of course, all these scenarios need to be suggested, but it is rarely possible to focus on one. It is also almost impossible to say what the cause of death was when considering only a skeleton. Even a weapon embedded in a bone associated with a wound showing no evidence of healing cannot be assumed to be the cause of death of the person (unless we can be sure that it will have damaged a vital organ or blood vessel). It may be that it only contributed to the cause of death, producing damage to vital structures that led to death by excessive loss of blood. In effect, the haemorrhage ultimately caused the death of the person. Similarly, the presence of woven bone indicates a specific health problem at the time of death, but it does not prove the disease caused death. One final consideration is that some damage to the skeleton could be post-mortem, so it is important to be able to differentiate between ante-mortem and post-mortem change to avoid misinterpretation.

Health and Disease in Roman Britain

The evidence

This chapter focuses on the evidence for diseases as seen from skeletal remains, while Jackson (1988) particularly considers the written, iconographic and to a lesser extent archaeological data for medical practice at this time. As mentioned above, it is only recently that people working in palaeopathology have really focused on populations of people via their skeletons, although the representative nature of these populations has to be questioned. Do these people represent the living population they were derived from? They are certainly dead, but do their health patterns represent what was seen in the general population? Was the entire group buried in the cemetery or were some (the children, for example) buried elsewhere? If the whole cemetery was not excavated, is the sample biased in any way? In effect, whatever cemetery site is considered, it is extremely unlikely to recover the entire social group at a particular point in time.

With respect to skeletal samples from sites of Roman date, there are many published and unpublished reports on the bookshelves, but it is often the larger sites that have received the most attention once the report has been published, for example, those from Cirencester, Gloucestershire (Wells 1982) where 362 burials were analysed, Colchester, Essex (Pinter-Bellows 1993) where 575 individual skeletons were considered, and Poundbury, Dorset (Farwell and Molleson 1993) where 1131 graves revealed skeletons. The recent report by Conheeney (2000), on London's 'Eastern' cemetery will encourage more work on this sample of over 500. However, the reasons for re-examining samples for research purposes are usually determined by sample size and awareness of the existence and location of the curated material. Many skeletons from Roman sites are curated in smaller museums in locations away from centres such as London. Unless researchers have a particular objective in mind, e.g. the study of Roman skeletons from Warwickshire, most skeletal collections curated in museums will remain relatively unstudied. The authors believe that this situation will be rectified as research questions about the health of Roman Britain become more focused and developed. However, the need for a centralized database, which documents skeletal collections available for study, and their location, is paramount to these developments. A key consideration in the representative nature of skeletal remains from Roman Britain is the dearth of information on health that can be derived from remains that were cremated (McKinley 2000) as was the case for most of the first and second centuries AD. Consequently, our analysis provides a picture of disease only in the third and fourth centuries AD. This is perhaps unfortunate as what we do not see are the ramifications on health of the transition from a more rural and tribal-based economy to one that is increasingly urbanized, with more centralized centres of industrialized specialization. While we might see the impact of the end of Roman Britain on health, we do not see the impact of Roman rule and the beginnings of Roman influence.

Roberts and Cox (forthcoming) considered published and unpublished data on health and disease from a total of 51 Roman dated cemetery sites, thus representing 5716 individual skeletons; 47 of the sites derive from England. This was a large increase in sites and skeletons from the Iron Age and reflects changed burial practice and an increase in population. It must be remembered, however, that this sample of the dead population of this period represents only a small proportion of the estimated population for that time. Millett (1995: 21) suggests that 3.6 million people lived in rural areas, that the urban population may have been 250,000 and that an additional 125,000 came from the army. Most of the skeletons from cemeteries considered derive from urban contexts. It is impossible to be certain of population numbers during the period of Roman influence in Britain, and the skeletons considered as representing health status at that time are only a minute subset of the original population. As discussed above, we must therefore be aware of the biases and limitations of the material available for study. While cremation and inhumation burial was practised at various times throughout the period, and there exist some large cremation cemeteries, the former are not considered. The main reason for this omission was that the information that may be derived from cremation burials on health and disease is normally substantially reduced because of the nature of the burial rite (McKinley 2000).

The context

It is generally accepted that the interpretation of the evidence for health and disease from human skeletal remains cannot be undertaken without considering the context from which the remains derive. Key aspects of the social, economic and cultural setting in which these past populations lived can only enhance our understanding of why specific health problems arose. However, while the health record for the past, based on skeletal remains, can be very patchy and problematic, there may also be gaps in our knowledge about, for example, the structure of houses, the constituents of diet, or the industries present. The archaeological record is fragmentary, but we should aim to use what is available in order to interpret and understand why health was compromised at certain points in our history. The archaeological record, in the form of artefacts, ecofacts and structures, potentially provides the information necessary. However, it is usually the case that a cemetery site will not have an associated excavated settlement, or that there will be any real understanding of living conditions and diet. This makes direct correlation between health status and context impossible. Furthermore, there appears to be a concentration of work in urban centres rather than rural settlements. While for urban sites this is very useful, for rural sites the data is lacking. In general, we do have an understanding of life in Roman Britain, and we must use this to the best of our ability to interpret the evidence for disease.

The landscape

The general landscape of Roman Britain was less forested than in the Iron Age but still contained areas of woodland, while later in the period (from AD 250) extensive land clearance was apparent (Jones 1996; Dark 2000). Clearance of land for farming also contributed to provision of fuel for everyday activities such as cooking, keeping warm and heating bathhouses, but it was also required for kilns and furnaces for pottery and tile manufacture, and smelting of metal ores. Clearance of land provided much-needed building materials too, and the open spaces made provision for grazing animals.

This period saw an opening up of Britain through the construction of roads. This allowed some people to travel around more easily, extend trade networks and establish better communication, but it will also have allowed disease to spread more easily. In the south and east of England there was close contact with Gaul, as seen by imports to Britain from around the first century BC (Darvill 1987). What impact this contact had on health in the south of England, compared to communities further afield, has not been examined, but it is hypothesized that one would expect to see a difference. If we consider how widely and frequently people travel around the world, and the health problems they encounter (and introduce to the population) at their destinations, we must seriously consider the impact of the development of an extensive network of roads in Roman Britain and the expansion of international trade.

Housing in town and country

Housing varied in construction between rural and urban areas, geographically and also for those of differing socio-economic status. House construction and organization (walls, roof, ventilation, arrangement inside) today contribute considerably to poor health. For example, better insulation and heating (and less ventilation) has contributed to an increase in respiratory disease, and a number of factors have been identified within the home as leading to an unhealthy population (Harrison 2000). One could argue that prior to the Roman period, when housing mainly consisted of thatched-roofed structures, ventilation might have been better. One could also argue (although one could not prove) that a change to some of the house construction, especially in urban and rural villas where stone- or brick-built structures and tiled roofs were the norm, may have decreased ventilation. Being relatively better insulated, they may have predisposed people to increased health problems.

Rural: In many rural areas, especially in the early Roman period, round or oval-shaped houses are most prominent (Hingley 1989), while the Roman-style rectangular building (single- or multi-roomed) predominates in southern Britain; central hearths are a prominent feature in all. The rectangular structures vary in the number of rooms, and aisled (central room) and corridor (series of rooms linked by a passageway) types are also seen. Building materials provided for wattle and daub walls and thatched roofs, but stone-walled structures are also seen. Small communities dominated rural southern and eastern England; for example, farmsteads with primarily rectangular buildings are seen enclosed by a bank and ditch. In the north and west of England, circular and sub-rectangular groups of buildings dominated. Finally, hill-forts and other defended sites also remained in use from the Iron Age, thus illustrating that there was a variety of types of rural housing to suit geography and geology, and period, within the Roman era. Social status also affected the type of building people had access to. Ellis (2000) suggests that the poorer members of society at that time lived in wattle and daub walled structures, with earthen floors and thatched roofs. The richer members of Roman society built villas in the country, but these varied in organization and magnificence, and probably reflected relative prosperity; they were certainly a way of illustrating wealth, but they also contributed to the economy. Perhaps there may have been differences in health in the people who lived in these different houses, and levels of sanitation and hygiene would have varied.

Urban: The Roman period facilitated an expansion of urbanization begun in the Iron Age. Larger towns were well organized around a grid system of roads, and they also encompassed a series of public buildings that provided services and administration for the urban community. Larger populations would have been supported in these urban communities and, thus, diseases depending on population density may be expected, such as respiratory disease. Initially houses had two levels and were of wattle and daub construction; this was later replaced by stone (Wacher 2000). Thatch, tile or slate roofs completed the structure, and there was a central hearth. Houses usually incorporated a workshop and shop, thus combining functions. There were also very large town houses for the rich, with mosaic floors and wall paintings. Smaller towns, which appeared in the later Roman period, were not as well organized as those described above. Many were characterized by a concentration of multi-functional structures (workshops and houses) and a lack of public buildings (Esmonde Cleary 1999). Larger and more richly built houses for the higher social classes were also seen. These smaller towns were very prominent centres in the later Roman period, when the larger towns declined and public buildings were neglected (Millett 1995).

Diet and economy

Agriculture was well established in the form of domesticated plants and animals by AD 43. Romanization saw agricultural intensification. Wheat, barley, oats, flax, beans and peas, root crops, fruit trees and a range of vegetables were grown and provided a varied diet. Meat was also consumed, and cattle, sheep, pigs, horses, wild boar, domestic fowl and deer contributed the main sources of meat. Sheep increased in use through the period (Millett 1995), and cattle and pig became more popular as a meat source in the late Roman period. The Romans introduced new breeds of cattle into Britain, which may have brought with them diseases such as tuberculosis, a potential health hazard to humans. Rural sites additionally provide evidence for a greater variety of food sources, such as wild animals. The waste products of animals were useful for a number of industrial developments in the Roman period, such as tanning and horn-working. It is suggested that most of the population at this time had a basic balanced diet (Jackson 1988) with bread, meat, fish, fruit and vegetables. Of course, with the presence of the Roman army in the country, there would have been additional demands on food and fuel, and it is possible that some parts of the population may have been malnourished as a consequence, though there is no skeletal evidence for this. The climate, and hence the weather, is suggested for this period by Lamb (1981 in Dark 2000) to have been similar to today, although later in the period colder conditions prevailed, which may have affected normal crop production. This too could have caused dietary hardship.

Industrial activity

It has been argued that industrial activity may be reflected in the skeleton in the form of osteoarthritis of joints. This is considered as joint degeneration, but increased robustness of bones (and asymmetry), remodelled muscle, tendon and ligament attachments, and specific work-related fractures such as that of 'clay shovelling' (Crawford Adams 1983) may also be considered. However, Jurmain (1999) has argued that the relationship is not as simple as it may seem. Such enterprises as the construction of Hadrian's and the Antonine Wall in the second century AD may have contributed to physical wear and tear on those involved with quarrying, mining and building, as would the massive urban constructions involved in the landscape of Roman towns. A large range of small- and large-scale industries was operating, and these generated a variety of goods. Working with animals or their products, masonry, carpentry, quarrying (stone, flint, chalk, gravel, clay and sand) and mining (coal, gold, iron, copper, lead and tin), building, pottery and tile manufacture, and metalworking comprise just a small proportion of the different types of occupations in which people at this time may have been engaged. Each would have had their occupational hazards. For example, caring for animals, butchering them and dealing with their products, may have exposed people to zoonoses, or those diseases of animals that can be transmitted to humans (e.g. anthrax, tuberculosis). Working in pottery and tile manufacture may have exposed people to dust inhalation and burns, and even lead poisoning, and smelting of metals could have caused poisoning (see the study by Oakberg et al. 2000).

Hygiene

In the Roman period we see the first evidence of attention to hygiene and sanitation, with attempts to control waste of all kinds. This need not imply that no such efforts were made previously, simply that we have little evidence for them. This is seen most obviously in urban contexts in the form of water distribution via aqueducts, pipes and fountains, disposal of water through sewer systems, and the provision of toilets and baths. Military sites also had similar provisions (e.g. Housesteads Fort on Hadrian's Wall in northern England; Wacher 1979), while smaller towns and villages did not (there was possibly less need for formal organization of such facilities). Thus, in theory, the better off living in urban contexts may have had access to a clean water supply, although we must be careful to remember that, even with a water supply, it may have become contaminated at times and posed a threat to the health of vulnerable people.

The practice of dentistry, medicine and surgery at this time is also evident (see Jackson 1988), although mainly through documentary data. For example, toothpastes and toothpicks are described for keeping the teeth clean, and the practice of medicine and surgery followed Hippocratic thinking. It is debatable whether these were familiar to much of the population at this time and, if they were, whether access was equal for the rich and the poor.

Health and Disease: the Roman Evidence

The consideration of context is essential to our understanding of why particular health problems appeared in the Roman period. The previous section provided a brief overview of the conditions under which people of this period were living, all of which can be reflected in the evidence of disease in their remains. If we consider first that most conditions we have noted were chronic in nature, and thus had been survived, mortality rates in the Roman period indicate that these people died because of some trauma or disease, probably involving the soft tissues. In addition, infant mortality in a population reflects the fragile time period of infancy, when this part of the population is vulnerable to acute illness, and possibly some to infanticide (Mays 1993). The correlation of age at death and disease, however, when most of the evidence of disease that is seen is chronic, is somewhat meaningless (even if adult age estimation was accurate – see Cox 2000 for an overview of the problems). For example, a healed fracture may have occurred in the person's lifetime ten years before death, and thus their age at death need not correlate with the timing of the fracture. Nevertheless, we must remember that the older a person was, the more potential they had for contracting disease. We do not specifically consider disease in the context of age in this chapter as we are focusing on evidence of (mostly) healed chronic conditions. The evidence is considered within the discussion of lifestyle and environment as indicated above.

Diet and nutrition

'We are what we eat' describes how important food and water are for life, and how the quality and quantity of diet may affect our well-being. While the quality and quantity of food and water consumed in the Roman period were vital to health, the processes that food and water underwent before consumption were probably even more important. For example, if one considers the use of lead for glazing pottery, and for making water pipes and vessels, plus the use of lead tableware, there was potential for lead poisoning to develop. However, this would only be the case when food and drink were acidic, and lead pipes would not be a hazard if they were in hard-water areas. While there have been some studies of lead levels in skeletal remains from this period (e.g. Waldron 1982), it is by no means clear whether most of our population at this time, particularly those living in towns, had lead poisoning (see Waldron 1983 for the problems of analysis). However, the presence of iron deficiency anaemia, or the joint disease gout, both of which may be related to high lead levels, indirectly suggests that some people may have been exposed to high levels of lead. Perhaps these were the wealthier members of society and/or those who worked in the lead-mining industry and the manufacture of goods made of lead. Equally though, these conditions can occur without any exposure to lead. Certainly this area of research needs revisiting.

Dietary indicators in skeletal samples may reflect not only the diet being eaten but the workload associated with the economic system being practised; that is, the method of production of food may affect the skeleton. Specific evidence for diet is

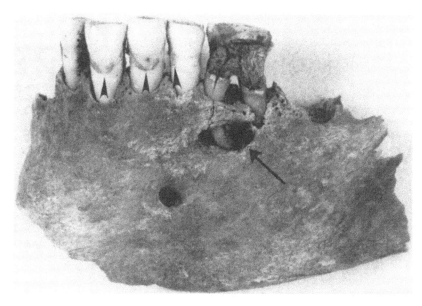

Figure 13.1 Dental abscess cavity in the bone of the lower jaw with evidence of caries of the associated tooth, and dental calculus on the canine and premolar teeth (Gambier-Parry Lodge, Gloucester 532).

seen in the form of dental disease, and lack of particular nutrients in the diet may be reflected in the bones and/or teeth (e.g. vitamin deficiencies). Destructive lesions of the teeth (caries) were seen in 7.5% (2187) of the total teeth observed (29,247) of the 5716 individuals considered (51 cemetery sites). If one compares these data with other published data for this period we see varying rates ranging from Cooke and Rowbotham (1958) of 4.6% of 4963 teeth affected, Emery (1963) with 11.4% of 870 teeth, and Freeth (1999) who reports 12.4% of female teeth and 9.1% male teeth. This is generally an increase from the previous Iron Age of 2.9% (Roberts and Cox, forthcoming) and probably reflects the increased consumption of fermentable carbo-hydrates (sugars) in cereal crops. However, there is evidence for the consumption of honey, sap, fruits, and imports of figs and dates, which may all have contributed to this frequency. The development of caries requires fermentable carbohydrates, a lack of oral hygiene, a low level of fluoride in the water supply and plaque on the teeth. Fluoride levels and their correlation (or not) with caries at this time is an area that requires research.

A complication of caries may be the development of a dental abscess at the base of the root of the tooth (figure 13.1), although an abscess may be the result of severe dental wear exposing the central pulp cavity of the tooth and infection (figure 13.2). Again at this time we can see that some parts of the population suffered abscessing, a painful condition. Frequency rates for abscesses are probably underestimated (be-cause radiography is not routinely employed in analysis), and only those abscesses that have perforated the bone of the jaw are identified, but we do have some evidence. From a total of 25,095 'tooth positions', 970 (3.9%) had evidence of an abscess (384 individuals of 3620 adults or 10.6%). However, many teeth had been lost

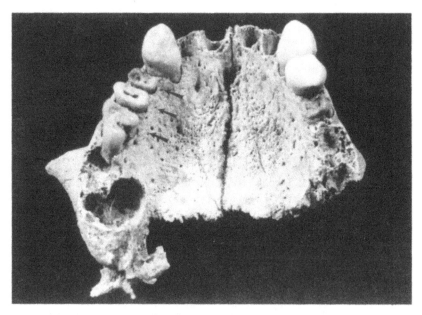

Figure 13.2 Extreme upper jaw dental wear on the right premolar and 1st molar teeth with exposure of the pulp cavity. Probable dental abscess cavity at the site of the 2nd molar (Barratt Cemetery, Baldock, Hertfordshire Burial 2).

ante-mortem (recognized as 'filling in' of the tooth socket with bone), and one of the causes of tooth loss could have been a dental abscess (in addition to caries). The frequency rate for abscesses is an increase from the Iron Age (3.1%). Ante-mortem tooth loss (5042 of 35,762 'tooth positions' or 14.1%, from 29 cemetery sites; Roberts and Cox, forthcoming) is similar to that reported by Freeth (1999) of 13.5% for females and 14.1% for males, but less than that reported by Brothwell and Blake (1966) of 23.9%.

If people do not clean their teeth then plaque accumulates, which allows caries to develop (figure 13.1). The action of fermentation of carbohydrates by plaque bacteria results in an acidic oral environment and the tooth structure can then be destroyed. Plaque (a saliva protein which contains microorganisms) becomes calculus as crystals are incorporated into the structure; this is a much harder deposit and survives archaeologically. The data we have suggest that calculus was a considerable problem. Of 3620 adult skeletons, 405 (11.2%) revealed calculus, and for five sites we have an absolute prevalence rate of 39.5% of 4034 teeth. Freeth (1999) records an even higher frequency of 47.6% of the total teeth observed for both sexes. While this indicates that plaque is not being efficiently removed (if at all), it may also reflect consumption of a high-protein diet.

Deficiencies in diet, or under- or malnutrition, may be identified in a number of ways. For example, dental enamel defects, representing a deficiency in enamel formation during its development, may result from dietary deficiency. It has been used extensively in palaeopathology as indicating stress in small children, mostly interpreted as malnutrition, and in agricultural populations (e.g. Larsen 1995). However, we do know that these defects can be caused by other factors (see Hillson 1986), including infectious disease and psychological stress. Nevertheless, their presence does indicate stress of some kind. From a total of 3620 adults, 239 had defects on their teeth (6.6%). However, absolute rates from six sites indicate a 6.8% rate from the 328 of 4796 teeth affected, which is little different to the individual rate.

More specific indicators of dietary deficiency may be seen in the evidence for anaemia, which would have been iron deficiency at this time. Of course, there are many causes for iron-deficiency anaemia other than dietary deficiency. These include exposure to infectious disease, excessive haemorrhage from a gut infection or gut parasites, or even exposure to high lead levels; all these possible causes could have been operating in this period (Stuart Macadam and Kent 1992). Although absolute frequency rates cannot be determined, on an individual basis 306 of 3620 adults had evidence of cribra orbitalia (anaemia) in the orbits of their skulls (figure 13.3) or 8.5%. However, a more detailed study of the skeletons from Poundbury, Dorset (Stuart Macadam 1991), suggests that of those skeletons with preserved orbits, 26% of the adults and 36% of the non-adults were affected. It appears from the archaeozoological record that during this period people had access to adequate amounts of iron in their diet, and therefore infectious disease load may be responsible for the evidence here (see pp. 264–6 for evidence of infection).

A further indicator of stress that has not really been considered extensively for any period of time in British prehistory and history is that of Harris Lines of arrested growth, or horizontal radio-dense lines, visible on radiographs, that indicate stress

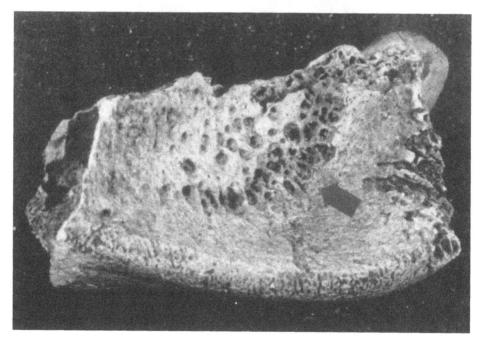

Figure 13.3 Cribra orbitalia (holes) in the orbit of Burial 510 (Gambier-Parry Lodge, Gloucester).

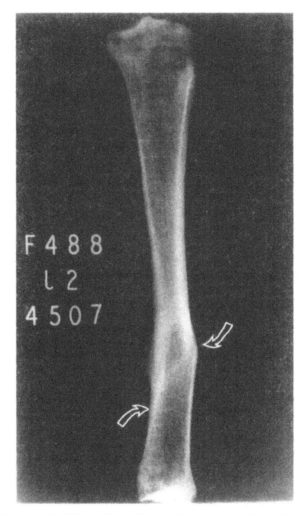

Figure 13.4 Radiograph of Harris lines of arrested growth (and healed fracture) in the tibia (Baldock, Hertfordshire F488 L2 4507).

during growth (see figure 13.4). As the bone grows, periods of arrest of growth may be initiated by a dietary deficiency or childhood disease (e.g. see Hughes et al. 1996). The reasons for the lack of attention paid to this abnormality in skeletal remains could be many, including the ability of the body to make these lines invisible by remodelling of the bone during life, and the lack of resources for radiography. Stature, however, which can also be an indicator of health during growth, is commonly recorded and appeared to range for males between 159 and 178 centimetres with a mean of 169 centimetres (5 feet 6 inches), which was an increase from the Iron Age (of 1296 individuals). In the female population the stature range was 150–168 centimetres (5 feet 2 inches) with a mean of 159 centimetres (of 1042 individuals); this was a slight decline on Iron Age female stature (Roberts and Cox, forthcoming).

Other conditions indicating problems of metabolism, which may be related to diet, include osteoporosis, scurvy and rickets, although few individuals from the sites are recorded with these conditions, and they will not be discussed further. Osteoporosis, a common condition today, especially in older females after the menopause (Stini 1990) and related to lack of exercise, calcium and protein when the skeleton is growing, is reflected in lower bone mass for age. It is most often seen in the spine, hip and knee, and may be reflected in the form of fractures at those sites. Its relative lack of appearance in the Roman period may suggest problems with diagnosis, the confounding effects of post-mortem damage to the skeleton leading to bone loss, or simply that the condition was less common than it is today.

Vitamin C deficiency (scurvy) is experienced by people with a diet lacking in enough of the vitamin to maintain healthy, strong, blood vessels. It is seen in the skeleton as new bone formation as a response by the body to haemorrhage from fragile blood vessels in a characteristic pattern (Ortner and Ericksen 1997). Vitamin D is necessary for the absorption of calcium and phosphorus into the body for the manufacture of strong well-mineralized bones. Some Vitamin D comes via the diet (oily fish) but most comes from the action of sunlight on the skin; thus higher frequencies may be expected in urban situations where people may be inside more as part of their daily lives; this occurs much later in Britain, during the industrial revolution in Europe (Howe 1997). Bending and distortion of long bones of the skeleton, expansion of their ends and changes in the skull may be indicators (Ortner and Mays 1998). We see little evidence of either condition in this period (although see figure 13.5), which suggests that people were ingesting adequate levels of vitamin C and being exposed to good levels of ultraviolet light. While urbanism had developed at this time, it seems not to have impacted on health in this way.

Lifestyle

The effects of the living environment on health may be explored by considering the evidence for respiratory disease, and congenital and neoplastic disease. All of these types of condition are seen in skeletal material from this period. Many respiratory diseases have been identified in living populations as being associated with polluted indoor and outdoor environments (e.g. Ezzati and Kammen 2001). Likewise, congenital disease (i.e. conditions where a person is born with a defect in normal development) and neoplastic disorders ('new growths', tumours or cancer) may also be caused by problems in the living environment (Aufderheide and Rodríguez Martin 1998). While in living populations the factors causing these conditions may be identified, for past populations this is much more difficult. Skeletal analysis for this period revealed a surprisingly diverse array of different types of tumours compared to earlier times (44 of 3620 adults). For example, at the cemetery of 'Derby Racecourse' an individual with an osteochondroma of the humerus (figure 13.6) was noted (Roberts 1985), and at Alington Avenue, Dorchester, Waldron (1989) records a meningioma. However, the most common type of tumour is the benign ivory osteoma, usually of the skull (32 individuals), which is common and asymptomatic.

Conditions of a congenital or developmental nature mainly included disorders of the spine. These can include spina bifida occulta, or lack of fusion of the posterior aspects of the sacrum and/or lower spine, which is usually asymptomatic. Sacralization

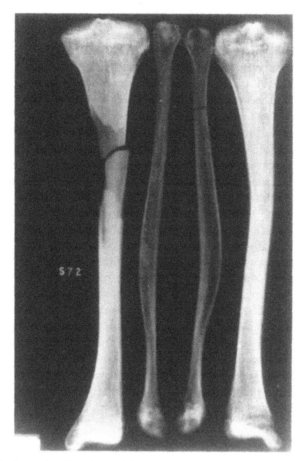

Figure 13.5 Radiograph of bending of the tibiae and fibulae suggesting rickets in childhood (Gambier-Parry Lodge, Gloucester 572).

and lumbarization are also common and may have produced low back pain. In these conditions, the fifth lumbar vertebra fuses to the sacrum or the first sacral vertebra detaches from the main body. Interestingly, recent observations of young males who died in the First World War are revealing a very high prevalence of these conditions. This may indicate that a low socio-economic and nutritional status are significant determinants (Cox, unpublished reports 2001). There were also rarer conditions, such as a type of dwarfism called mesomelia from Alington Avenue (Rogers 1986), an individual with a club foot from Kingsholm, Gloucester (Roberts 1989), and congenital dislocation of the hip, the latter two probably affecting mobility. A total of 174 individuals of 5716 were affected by congenital defects. None of the conditions observed is life-threatening and many would not have been evident to the person concerned. It is probable that infants born with life-threatening conditions did not survive and infant remains are usually fragmentary. However, one must consider the possible effects of conditions such as clubfoot and dwarfism on the individual and the society in which they lived. While stigma can be associated with some medical

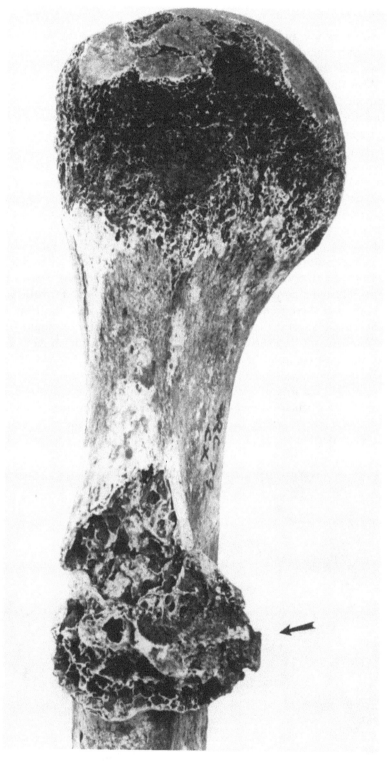

Figure 13.6 Humerus with changes in the shaft suggesting osteochondroma (Derby Racecourse CX).

conditions, we cannot assume that people were stigmatized in the past or that they were disabled by their condition (Roberts 2000). The evidence from the data considered suggests the presence of those factors causing congenital and neoplastic disease. What those factors specifically were is difficult to judge, but they may have included pollutants in the broadest sense in the environment.

Evidence for respiratory disease in the form of maxillary sinusitis and lung infection (rib involvement) is also noted for this period (figure 13.7), although it is very doubtful that the frequencies seen are the real frequencies. Ribs are often not considered a major and regular area to record for disease, and sinuses may be complete and therefore inaccessible for observation. Neither is commonly reported or (we suggest) recorded for many cemetery sites. However, both may arise from indoor or outdoor pollution, as well as other factors. Industry in Roman towns, particularly, may well have produced the conditions for respiratory disease. However, it should not be forgotten that bone formation on the ribs may also result from pulmonary tuberculosis or pneumonia, and sinusitis could result from the complications of dental abscesses (see Roberts et al. 1998). Thirty-two of 3620 adults had evidence of inflammation of their sinuses and 36 had new bone formation on their ribs. In both cases these frequencies are higher than those from the Iron Age, and one might wish to suggest that differences in levels of ventilation might have been a factor. However, the data quality does not allow us to make definitive statements.

Two of the most common health problems identified in skeletons from archaeological sites are joint disease and trauma, and for this period we see increases in the number of individuals affected by both these conditions when compared to the Iron Age. There is a particular problem with considering the frequency of joint disease because osteologists recording the changes do not record them consistently. In addition, joints degenerate at different rates in people, and the changes may purely

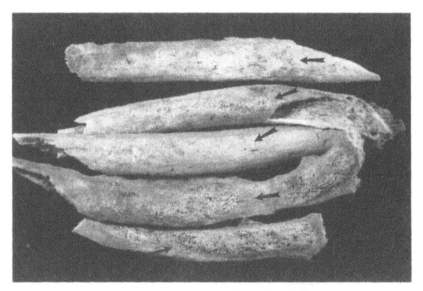

Figure 13.7 New bone formation on the internal surface of ribs from Cirencester, Gloucestershire.

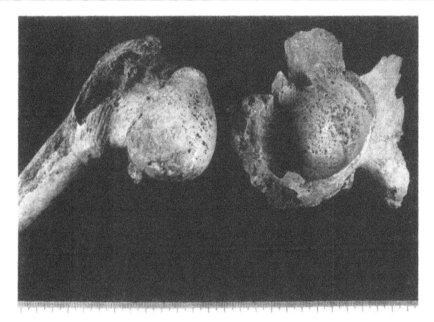

Figure 13.8 Changes in the hip bones of an individual from Odiham, Hampshire, suffering from osteoarthritis (osteophytes, porosity and eburnation).

represent ageing (for example, the presence only of bone formation on and around the joint margins, or osteophytes). Osteoarthritis, however, is usually diagnosed if two or more features are present in a joint (Rogers and Waldron 1995). These changes include osteophytes, porosity on the joint, eburnation or polishing, or fusion of the joint (figure 13.8). Erosive lesions on the joints can also occur, which usually represent erosive joint disease such as psoriatic or rheumatoid arthritis. It is extremely important also to record the distribution pattern of the changes in order to diagnose a specific disease. Despite these diagnostic recommendations and problems, the data we have suggest that 822 individuals displayed some evidence for joint disease; 311 of 3620 adults (8.6%) had spinal changes (figure 13.9) and 463 (12.8%) had changes in other joints.

One particular abnormality seen in the spine (Schmorl's node) represents a degeneration of the intervertebral disc and the protrusion of its contents into the vertebral body. This was seen in 179 sexed adult skeletons (4.6%), but some absolute prevalence data from four sites reveal that 495 of 2793 vertebrae had this condition (17.7%). This is believed to represent weight-bearing stress on the spine during the teens and would suggest that this percentage of the population was engaged in arduous physical activity from an early age. Increasing age may cause degeneration of joints, as we have already seen, but it can also be associated with obesity, the female sex and occupation (Rogers and Waldron 1995). It would be useful to be able to suggest a specific association with a particular cause for this period, but the data do not allow this. All we can say is that people's joints appeared to experience degenerative change and disease during this period, as at all others. Other joint diseases are recorded, but in such small numbers that discussion is not warranted. However, 23 individuals from nine sites revealed evidence for diffuse idiopathic skeletal hyperostosis (figure 13.10). This condition appears more frequently in later periods and in monastic populations (Rogers and Waldron 1995, 2001), but is seen as fusion of the spine and bone formation at sites of soft tissue attachments to bones. The first evidence in Britain may be from the Neolithic period (Rogers 1990). It is suggested that this condition is associated with increasing age in obese diabetic males. Another joint disease, gout, particularly affects the great toe bones and is seen today in older males and in those consuming a rich diet and excessive amounts of alcohol (Rogers and Waldron 1995); it also has a genetic predisposition. High levels of uric acid (normally excreted in the urine) build up and are deposited as crystals in the joints, which leads to erosion. Whether high levels of lead contributed to the frequencies also needs considering (Rogers and Waldron 1995). It is in the Roman period that we see the first evidence for gout at Cirencester and Poundbury; perhaps this indicates people of higher status eating a rich diet.

Trauma is seen in 505 sexed adults (14% of 3620) for this period and dislocations in seven individuals (three from Poundbury and Cirencester respectively). Trauma is usually seen in the form of healed fractures in skeletons from archaeological sites, and this period is no exception (e.g. see figure 13.11). Unfortunately, there is very little absolute prevalence data which would provide us with an indication of the real rates for fractures. Dislocations, where the two bones of a joint are traumatically displaced out of alignment, are rarely seen because of the tendency for dislocations to reduce themselves, that is, they may pop back into place (or they may be deliberately reduced). If either of these scenarios is present then the change we use to identify dislocation, the presence of a new joint surface, will not be present. Detachment of

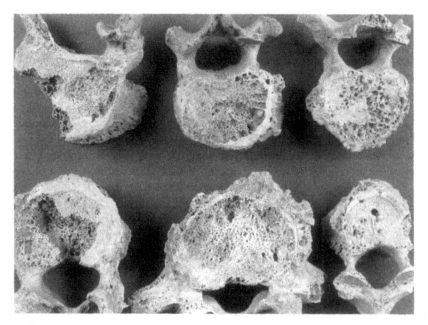

Figure 13.9 Changes on the spine due to degeneration (Gambier-Parry Lodge, Gloucester 579).

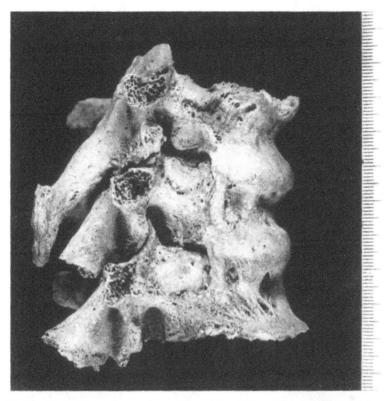

Figure 13.10 Three thoracic vertebrae affected by diffuse idiopathic skeletal hyperostosis (fusion) from a skeleton from Odiham, Hampshire.

the neural arch, or the back of the (usually) last lumbar vertebra, was seen in 49 individuals from 14 sites and is associated with an inborn (congenital) weakness at this site with associated trauma (bending and lifting, weight-lifting, etc. – Merbs 1989). Seen in different frequencies around our world's population, its presence in this period may be indicating some aspect of lifestyle.

It is, unfortunately, not possible to make considered deductions about the significance of fractures or trauma in this period because of the flaws inherent in the data and our inability to discern accurately the causes of most types of trauma. However, all parts of the body were affected (figures 13.12, 13.13 and 13.14). Weapon injuries are evident, although not in high numbers. These latter injuries may represent interpersonal violence, and periods of incursion and unrest, but they could equally be the result of accidents. An interesting fracture to the spinous processes (the back of the vertebra) of the last cervical (C7) and/or first thoracic (T1) vertebrae is, in living populations, associated with shovelling heavy soils (Knusel et al. 1996). Three individuals are identified with this condition at Kempston, Bedfordshire (Boylston and Roberts 2000) and at Baldock (Roberts 1984). It is surprising that more individuals from this period have not been identified with this condition, as presumably people at this time were undertaking this particular activity; there is evidence for shovels and spades, and a great deal of building and agricultural work took place.

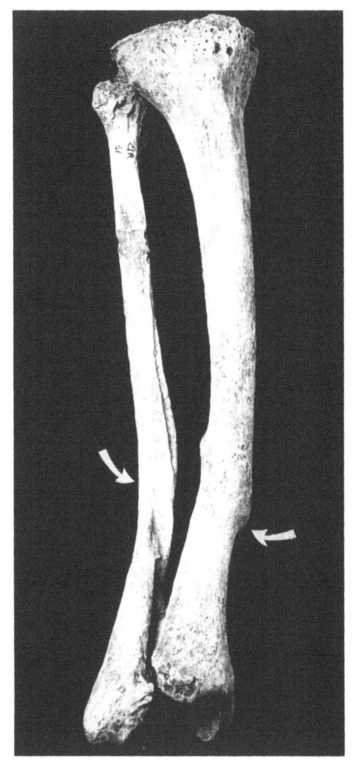

Figure 13.11 Healed fracture to the tibia and fibula with angulation on healing (Cirencester, Gloucestershire 61).

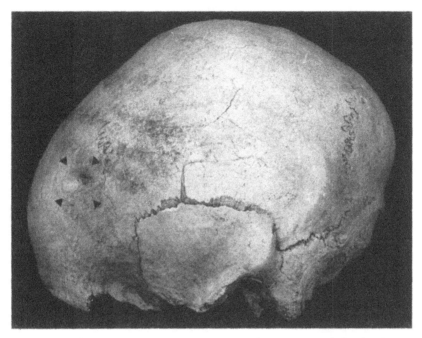

Figure 13.12 Skull showing small healed depressed fracture to the left side of the frontal bone (Cirencester, Gloucestershire 39).

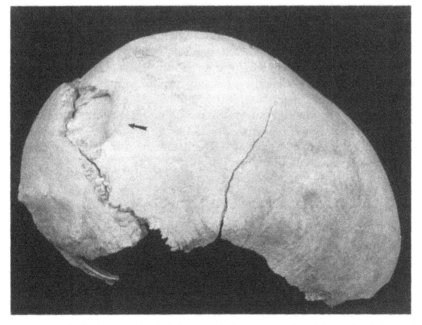

Figure 13.13 Skull showing healed depressed fracture to the right parietal bone (Hyde Street, Winchester 17).

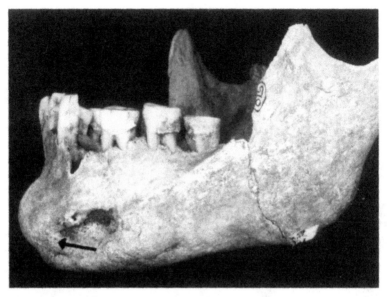

13.14 Healed mandible fracture on the left side (Gambier-Parry Lodge, Gloucester 510).

While we have a wealth of evidence for medicine and surgery in the written literature for this period (see Jackson 1988), there is very little evidence for this in the skeletons themselves. It is likely that most treatments left no mark on the skeleton, but drilling holes in the head (trepanation) and amputation are identified at this time. Five trepanations are noted from Baldock, Newarke Street (Leicester), Cirencester, Trentholme Drive, York, and Whitchurch (Shropshire); the details of these individuals are summarized in Roberts and McKinley, forthcoming). Three had associated head injuries, which perhaps suggests the reasons behind the trepanation, but only two were healed. There may be many reasons for performing trepanations, which include headaches, migraine, epilepsy or purely to let the spirits out, and when there is no evidence for a head injury we can only guess the reason. Other evidence for surgery was noted at Alington Avenue, Dorchester, by Waldron (1989) in the form of an amputated limb, and at Poundbury, Dorchester, by Molleson and Cox (1988) who describe a possible embryotomy.

Hygiene and sanitation

Levels of hygiene and sanitation may be reflected (but not always) in levels of infectious disease. The most common manifestation of infectious disease is a non-specific infection, that is, the specific causative pathogen is not known. This is usually seen in the form of pitting and/or new bone formation on bone surfaces, and the most common place for this to be observed is on the long bones, more specifically on the lower leg. The changes seen on the ribs and sinuses are the same (described above) and may be specifically associated with a particular cause, as we have seen. However, most of the evidence can only be interpreted as 'presence of non-specific infection'. This may indicate a number of factors, for example, poverty, poor standards of hygiene, sanitation and living conditions, and trauma to the lower legs (Aufderheide and Rodríguez Martin 1998). Additionally, the changes in the lower legs may be also seen in the specific infections of leprosy and treponemal disease (Aufderheide and Rodríguez Martin, 1998). The skeletons considered for this period revealed that 381 of 3620 sexed adults (10.5%) had non-specific infection, but the majority had the condition visible on their lower leg bones in the form of periostitis (involvement of the periosteum or membrane covering the bones in life). Fewer people had more severe involvement of other layers of the bone, such as osteitis (involving the next layer down, or cortex) or osteomyelitis (the medullary cavity or central area of the bone). The number of people with non-specific infection at this time is an increase from the Iron Age, but rates are not as high as the (later) post-Roman period. Due to the multifactorial causative nature of non-specific infection of the skeleton, it is not possible to say exactly what was causing the condition here.

Other infections that may be termed specific in nature are those where the causative organism is known. We first see evidence for leprosy in Britain in the Roman period. It has been recorded at Cirencester, Gloucester (Manchester and Roberts 1986) and Poundbury, Dorset (Reader 1974). Leprosy, caused by *Mycobacterium leprae*, is transmitted via droplet infection (coughing and sneezing, and even breathing) in higher population densities and in people living in poverty. The bones of the face, hands and feet are particularly damaged, mainly because of the damage the bacteria cause to the sensory, motor and autonomic nerves. The frequency of leprosy does not increase until the later medieval period in Britain. Its appearance in the Roman period is suggested to represent its importation with invading Roman armies (Manchester 1991). The fact that these early examples are in the south of England would seem to make sense, since the invasion was in the south-east of England, but both these cemeteries are of later Roman date, that is, fourth century AD. Perhaps these people were incomers involved with trade and having contact with the Continent. However, we cannot know whether leprosy was around earlier in the period because of the rite of cremation, making the evidence almost impossible to discern. The related disease of tuberculosis (TB) is also seen for the first time, although we should be expecting to see it very soon after the domestication of animals in the Neolithic period in Britain, assuming they were infected. Perhaps the Romans introduced new breeds of cattle and these were infected with TB. Tuberculosis is caused by *Mycobacterium tuberculosis* if transmitted human to human by droplet infection, or by *Mycobacterium bovis* if contracted by humans from ingesting infected meat and milk. It is therefore linked with animal domestication and/or people living in close contact with each other. We have both these situations occurring in the Roman period, although only twelve individuals with tuberculosis have been identified from this period (see Roberts and Buikstra, forthcoming, for details). Nine of the cases are from the south of England (Dorset, Hampshire, Gloucestershire) with three from the site of Ancaster, Lincolnshire; this may simply reflect the higher number of Roman cemetery sites excavated in the south compared to the north, and better survival of bone in these areas.

Other infections manifest in the skeletal evidence from this period are various. They include possible meningitis (inflammation of the membranes covering the brain and spinal cord), poliomyelitis caused by a virus that can lead to paralysis of parts of the body, and Paget's Disease which, it is believed, may be caused by a viral infection. Meningitis has been suggested by Schultz (1999, 2001) to lead to new bone formation on the inside (endocranial) of the skull, although this is still being disputed. Five individuals from this period were recorded with this change. One young adult female from the site of Gambier-Parry Lodge, Gloucester (Roberts, 1987) had extensive bone formation on her skull, and she was also very short in stature (4 feet 3½ inches or 130.8 centimetres) but proportionately so. This type of dwarfism probably reflects damage to the pituitary gland that sits in the pituitary fossa of the skull; this can affect normal growth because of the symbiotic relationship between the pituitary and thyroid glands, the latter of which produces growth hormone when stimulated by the former. Damage to the pituitary gland can occur as a result of tuberculous meningitis, which may be the explanation for this young female's condition. Poliomyelitis was recognized in four people from Cirencester by Wells (1982) and in one person at Baldock, Hertfordshire, by McKinley (1993). Atrophy or wasting of limb bones, perhaps representing paralysis, was identified. However, we must be careful not to attribute a specific diagnosis to these changes, because several other conditions inducing paralysis could be responsible.

In considering the evidence for health and disease in Roman Britain, it is clear that the data need much more work, and future data collected would benefit from a more systematic and scientific approach. It would be interesting to consider the data from cemetery sites of this period in terms of differences between males and females, different age groups and funerary context (e.g. urban and rural, villa and town houses, poor and rich, north and south, Highland and Lowland). However, because of the nature of the data published (and unpublished) it has not been possible to do this.

The nature of the evidence and its effect on interpretations

We have much archaeological evidence from Roman Britain to indicate the conditions in which these people lived. However, our information on health and disease from human skeletal remains which we would usefully correlate (or not) with these data, is not sufficiently robust to make other than general comments. Most of the data considered are in the form of either the presence or absence of specific diseases, or presented as individuals affected in any one population. The authors suspect that much of the root cause of the poor quality of osteological data lies with the way archaeology operates as a field discipline. There are rarely sufficient resources to record, analyse, interpret and present skeletal data in a manner that is useful for future research. Curators and those responsible for allocating resources for osteological analysis have failed to set standards in osteological analysis and recording and, further to this, United Kingdom osteologists must also take some responsibility for not organizing themselves in terms of standards for recording. The latter at least is being remedied by the British Association of Biological Anthropology and Osteoarchaeology. While it would be preferable to collect all the primary data oneself when considering specific research questions and ideas, or testing particular hypotheses, this is not practically possible. Thus, reliance on other workers in the field is inevitable. While time and money are key restricting variables on the quality of data, there are also at times problems with a lack of expertise among practitioners in the identification, recording and presentation of data. These factors, set amid a framework that has been devoid of standards, have ultimately affected the data presented here and its potential for meaningful interpretation.

Health and disease in Roman Britain and its meaning

Despite the problems and limitations inherent in our discipline, if we consider the problems of the data but do not allow them to prevent us interpreting such data as we have, there are a number of observations about health and disease in later Roman Britain that can be made. We have plenty of evidence for the type of foods people had access to. There were enough fermentable carbohydrates in the diet to cause carious teeth, and the amount of calculus on the teeth suggests poor oral hygiene and a high level of protein in the diet. This is supported by the amount of meat produced for consumption at this time, as seen from animal bones from archaeological sites. Levels of iron, therefore, for most were adequate, although some individuals had changes in their skeletons induced by iron deficiency. There is very little osteological data to suggest that major elements were lacking in the diet, again suggesting that it was well balanced for most people, and stature increased from the Iron Age for males, while female height decreased a little, but not significantly. Did this vary between town and country, rich and poor, and in males and females? Without good-quality data it is impossible to say, or to undertake statistical analysis of the data for significance of trends.

Levels of hygiene and sanitation appear to have been generally good for many at this time, as witnessed by evidence for the establishment of a system for providing clean water and disposing of sewage, with latrines and bathhouses featuring in towns particularly. Although non-specific infections are recognized, their specific aetiology is unknown and severe cases (i.e. involving all layers of bone) are rarely reported. Oral hygiene, however, appears not to have been practised widely as the majority of dentitions had plaque (calculus) deposits. Evidence for the indoor and outdoor living environment (air quality) suggests that there may have been instances where people were exposed to pollution, but the problem was not severe or widespread. Outdoor pollution will only have been a problem for those people working or living near (or in) industrial areas in towns. Many questions remain to be addressed: were more men than women affected by infection? Did men have better diets than women and more access to facilities for 'keeping clean'? Was the level of sanitation different for the poor and the rich, and in the town or the country? Was pollution more of a problem for women due to their assumed domestic work over open fires, or were males more affected because of their involvement in industry? These can be addressed when standards of recording and reporting reflect adequate basic standards within the discipline.

Joint disease and trauma appear to be fairly common but, as we have seen, their presence may be initiated by many factors. The data may be suggesting that workload was responsible for some of the evidence, although domestic accidents and ageing could equally be responsible. There is certainly evidence for interpersonal violence in the form of blade injuries to the skull, but how violent was it to live in Roman Britain and when? Was trauma more common in males rather than females, and did this reflect the nature of their lifestyles and occupations? Does its occurrence reflect periods of unrest? Was trauma more common in the town or country and did patterns of fractures differ? Did the rich or the poor have higher levels of joint disease? If the former, perhaps this reflected increased longevity for the rich, and if the latter this may indicate that those from lower socio-economic groups carried most of the workload, as is always so. These are questions that we are not yet in a position to answer. Neither are we in a position, on the basis of the skeletal evidence, to comment on how widely medicine and surgery were practised at this time. A few trepanations, one amputation and an embryotomy are the only direct data for surgical intervention, even though there is much contemporary written data for therapeutics.

Future research

The consideration of health and disease in the Roman period in Britain is a fruitful area of study, considering the possibility of linking the data to relevant archaeological evidence for what life was like. However, before this can be done with any degree of accuracy, there is an urgent need to ensure that any future data recorded from our ancestors at this time follow strict and accepted methods of recording. An example is that of Buikstra and Ubelaker (1994), developed primarily for North American purposes, but recording recommendations are currently being developed for British skeletal material by the British Association of Biological Anthropologists and Osteoarchaeologists; Roberts (1996) also describes what a typical skeletal report may contain. The data should also be presented in a way that will be meaningful, that is, primarily as absolute prevalence rates (e.g. see table 1) but also as the number of individuals affected.

In addition, any diagnosis of disease should include detailed descriptions of the changes with their distribution patterns (or at least references to diagnostic criteria used), and very problematic or rare diagnoses must also be illustrated. The data should also be considered in their cultural context, or the data will have no meaning. One cannot consider indicators of dietary stress without dealing with the evidence from archaeological sites for diet and economy, and neither can evidence for infection be considered without reference to housing, the general environment and levels of sanitation and hygiene. Taking a multidisciplinary and holistic view of health in the Roman period will not only help the advance of palaeopathology in Britain by understanding how the occurrence and frequency of health problems changed through time. It will also contribute to archaeology as a whole. Without the people of the past there would be no other archaeological evidence for this period and the health status of the population would surely have influenced social, political and economic development in Roman Britain.

Table 1. Absolute frequency rates for trauma in long bones in a hypothetical skeletal population.

Bone	Numbers observed	Numbers affected	Percentage affected
Humerus	100	23	23.0
Radius	200	46	23.0
Ulna	100	19	19.0
Femur	400	37	9.3
Tibia	200	50	25.0
Fibula	100	38	38.0
Total	1100	213	19.4

REFERENCES

Aufderheide, A. and Rodríguez Martin, C. 1998. *Cambridge Encyclopedia of Human Paleo-pathology.* Cambridge.

Bell, L. and Piper, L. 2000. An introduction to palaeohistology. In M. Cox and S. Mays (eds), *Human Osteology in Archaeology and Forensic Science.* London, 255–74.

Bennion, E. 1986. *Antique Dental Instruments.* London.

Boylston, A. and Roberts, C. A. 2000. The Roman inhumations. In M. Dawson, *Archaeology in the Bedford Region.* Bedfordshire Archaeological Monograph 4. Bedford, 309–36.

Brothwell, D. R. and Blake, M. L. 1966. The human remains from the Fussell's Lodge long barrow: their morphology, discontinuous traits and pathology. In P. Ashbee, Fussell's Lodge long barrow excavations 1957. *Archaeologia,* 100, 48–63.

Buikstra, J. E. and Ubelaker, D. (eds) 1994. *Standards for Data Recording from Human Skeletal Remains.* Archeological Survey Research Seminar Series 44. Fayetteville, AR.

Conheeney, J. 2000. The inhumation burials. In B. E. Barber and D. Bowsher, *The Eastern Roman Cemetery of Roman London: Excavations 1983–1990.* Museum of London Archaeological Services Monograph 4. London, 277–96.

Cooke, C. and Rowbotham, T. C. 1958. A craniometric and dental investigation of 301 Romano-British skulls and jaws circa AD 150. *Journal of Dental Research,* 37, 753.

Cox, M. 2000. Ageing adults from the skeleton. In M. Cox and S. Mays (eds), *Human Osteology in Archaeology and Forensic Science.* London, 61–81.

Crawford Adams, J. 1983. *Outline of Fractures.* Edinburgh.

Dark, P. 2000. *The Environment of Britain in the First Millennium AD.* London.

Darvill, T. 1987. *Prehistoric Britain.* London.

Ellis, S. 2000. *Roman Housing.* London.

Emery, G. T. 1963. Dental pathology and archaeology. *Antiquity,* 37, 274–81.

Esmonde Cleary, S. 1999. Roman Britain: civilian and rural society. In J. R. Hunter and I. Ralston (eds), *Archaeology of Britain: An Introduction from the Upper Palaeolithic to the Industrial Revolution.* London, 157–75.

Ezzati, M. and Kammen, D. 2001. Indoor air pollution from biomass combustion and acute respiratory disease in Kenya: an exposure-response study. *Lancet,* 358 (9282), 619–20.

Farwell, D. E. and Molleson, T. 1993. *Poundbury.* Volume 2. *The Cemeteries.* Dorset Natural History and Archaeological Society, Monograph Series 11. Dorchester.

Freeth, C. M. 1999. *Dental Health in Cultural Biocultural Perspective. The Prevalence, Pattern and Distribution of the Dental Diseases in British Archaeological Populations from Geographic, Demographic and Temporal Viewpoints.* Unpublished PhD thesis, University of Bradford.

Harrison, P. 2000. Where can you breathe easy? *Times Higher Educational Supplement* (24 November), 26.

Hillson, S. 1986. *Teeth.* Cambridge.

Hingley, R. 1989. *Rural Settlement in Roman Britain.* London.

Howe, G. M. 1997. *People, Environment, Disease and Death.* Cardiff.

Hughes, C., Heylings, D. J. A. and Power, C. 1996. Transverse (Harris) lines in Irish archaeological remains. *American Journal of Physical Anthropology,* 101, 115–31.

Jackson, R. 1988. *Doctors and Diseases in the Roman Empire.* London.

Jones, M. E. 1996. *The End of Roman Britain.* Ithaca, NY.

Jurmain, R. D. 1999. *Stories from the Skeleton: Behavioral Reconstruction in Human Osteology.* Amsterdam.

Knusel, C., Roberts, C. A. and Boylston, A. 1996. When Adam delved . . . An activity-related lesion in three human skeletal populations. *American Journal of Physical Anthropology,* 100, 427–34.

Lamb, H. H. 1981 Climate from 1000 BC to 1000 AD. In M. Jones and G. Dimbleby (eds), *The Environment of Man: The Iron Age to the Anglo-Saxon Period.* BAR (British Series) 87. Oxford, 53–65.

Larsen, C. S. 1995. Biological changes in human populations with agriculture. *Annual Review of Anthropology,* 24, 185–213.

McElroy, A. and Townsend, P. K. 1996. *Medical Anthropology in Ecological Perspective.* Boulder, CO.

McKinley, J. 1993. *Human Skeletal Report from Baldock.* Unpublished.

——2000. The analysis of cremated bone. In M. Cox and S. Mays (eds), *Human Osteology in Archaeology and Forensic Science.* London, 403–21.

Manchester, K. 1991. Tuberculosis and leprosy: evidence for interaction of disease. In D. Ortner and A. C. Aufderheide (eds), *Human Paleopathology: Current Syntheses and Future Actions.* Washington, DC, 23–35.

Manchester, K. and Roberts, C. A. 1986. *Palaeopathological Evidence of Leprosy and Tuberculosis in Britain.* Unpublished SERC Report (Grant 337.367), University of Bradford.

Mays, S. 1993. Infanticide in Roman Britain. *Antiquity,* 67, 883–8.

Mays, S., Taylor, G. M., Legge, A. J., Young, D. B. and Turner-Walker, G. 2001. Paleopathological and biomolecular study of tuberculosis in a Medieval skeletal collection from England. *American Journal of Physical Anthropology,* 114, 298–311.

Merbs, C. F. 1989. Trauma. In M. Y. Iscan and K. A. R. Kennedy (eds), *Reconstruction of Life from the Skeleton.* New York, 161–89.

Millett, M. 1995. *Roman Britain.* London.

Molleson, T. I. and Cox, M. 1988. A neonate with cut bones from Poundbury Camp, 4th century AD, England. *Bulletin de la Société Royale d'Anthropologie et de Préhistoire,* 99, 53–9.

Oakberg, K., Levy, T. and Smith, P. 2000. A method for skeletal arsenic analysis applied to the Chalcolithic copper smelting site of Shiqmina, Israel. *Journal of Archaeological Science,* 27, 895–901.

Ortner, D. J. and Ericksen, M. 1997. Bone changes in infancy in the human skull probably resulting from scurvy in infancy and childhood. *International Journal of Osteoarchaeology,* 7, 212–20.

Ortner, D. J. and Mays, S. 1998. Dry bone manifestations of rickets in infancy and childhood. *International Journal of Osteoarchaeology,* 8, 45–55.

Pinter-Bellows, S. 1993. The human skeletons. In N. Crummy, P. Crummy and C. Crossan, *Excavations of Roman and Later Cemeteries, Churches and Monastic Sites in Colchester, 1971–1988.* Archaeological Report 9, Colchester Archaeological Trust. Colchester, 62–92.

Raoult, D., Aboudharam, G., Crubézy, E., Larrouy, G., Ludes, B. and Drancourt, M. 2000. Molecular identification by 'suicide PCR' of *Yersinia pestis* as the agent of medieval black death. *Proceedings of the National Academy of Sciences,* 97, 12800–3.

Reader, R. 1974. New evidence for the antiquity of leprosy in early Britain, *Journal of Archaeological Science,* 1, 205–7.

Roberts, C. A. 1984. *The Human Skeletal Report from Baldock, Hertfordshire.* Bradford: Calvin Wells Laboratory, University of Bradford [Unpublished.]

——1985. An osteochondroma from Derby Racecourse Roman cemetery. *Paleopathology Association Newsletter,* 50, 7–8.

——1987. A possible case of pituitary dwarfism from the Roman period. *British Medical Journal,* 295, 1659–60.

——1989. *The Human Remains from 76 Kingsholm, Gloucester.* Calvin Wells Laboratory, University of Bradford. [Unpublished.]

—— 1996. The biological evidence or what the people say. In E. O'Brien and C. A. Roberts, Archaeological study of church cemeteries: past, present and future. In J. Blair and C. Pyrah (eds), *Church Archaeology: Research Directions for the Future*. CBA Research Report 104. York, 159–181.

—— 2000. Did they take sugar? The use of skeletal evidence in the study of disability in past populations. In J. Hubert (ed.), *Madness, Disability and Social Exclusion: The Archaeology and Anthropology of Difference*. London, 46–59.

Roberts, C. A. and Buikstra, J. E. (forthcoming). *Tuberculosis: Old Disease with New Awakenings*. Gainesville, FL.

Roberts, C. A. and Cox, M. (forthcoming). *Health and Disease in Britain: Prehistory to the Present Day*. Gloucester.

Roberts, C. A., Lewis, M. E. and Boocock, P. 1998. Infectious disease, sex and gender: the complexity of it all. In A. Grauer and P. Stuart Macadam (eds), *Sex and Gender in Paleopathological Perspective*. Cambridge, 93–113.

Roberts, C. A. and McKinley, J. (forthcoming). A review of British trepanations in antiquity, focusing on funerary context to explain their occurrence. In R. Arnott and S. Finger (eds), *Proceedings of the International Symposium on Trepanation in Antiquity, Birmingham*. Amsterdam.

Rogers, J. 1986. Mesomelic dwarfism in a Romano-British skeleton. *Paleopathology Association Newsletter*, 55, 6–10.

—— 1990. The human skeletal material. In A. Saville, *Hazleton North, Gloucestershire, 1979–1982. The Excavation of a Neolithic Long Cairn of the Cotswold-Severn Group*. English Heritage Archaeological Report 13. London, 182–98.

Rogers, J. and Waldron, T. 1995. *A Field Guide to Joint Disease in Archaeology*. Chichester.

—— 2001. DISH and the monastic way of life. *International Journal of Osteoarchaeology*, 11, 357–65.

Schultz, M. 1999. The role of tuberculosis in infancy and childhood in prehistoric and historic populations. In G. Pálfi, O. Dutour, J. Deák and I. Hutás (eds), *Tuberculosis, Past and Present*. Szeged and Budapest, 503–7.

—— 2001. Paleohistopathology of bone: a new approach to the study of ancient disease. *Yearbook of Physical Anthropology*, 44, 106–47.

Stini, W. A. 1990. Osteoporosis: etiologies, prevention and treatment. *Yearbook of Physical Anthropology*, 33, 151–94.

Stuart Macadam, P. 1991. Anaemia in Roman Britain. In H. Bush and M. Zvelebil (eds), *Health in Past Societies*. BAR (British Series) 567. Oxford, 101–13.

Stuart Macadam, P. and Kent, S. (eds) 1992. *Diet, Demography and Disease: Changing Perspectives on Anaemia*. New York.

Taylor, G. M., Rutland, P. and Molleson, T. 1997. A sensitive polymerase chain reaction method for the detection of *Plasmodium* species DNA in ancient human remains. *Ancient Biomolecules*, 1, 193–203.

Taylor, G. M., Widdison, S., Brown, I. N. and Young, D. 2000. A mediaeval case of lepromatous leprosy in 13th–14th century Orkney. *Journal of Archaeological Science*, 27, 1133–8.

Wacher, J. 1979. *Roman Britain*. London.

—— 2000. *A Portrait of Roman Britain*. London.

Waldron, T. 1982. Human bone lead concentrations. In A. McWhirr, L. Viner and C. Wells, *Romano-British Cemeteries at Cirencester*. Cirencester, 203–20.

—— 1983. On the post-mortem accumulation of lead by skeletal tissues. *Journal of Archaeological Science*, 10, 35–40.

—— 1989. *The Human Remains from Alington Avenue*. [Unpublished.]

—— 1994. *Counting the Dead: The Epidemiology of Skeletal Populations*. Chichester.

Wells, C. 1982. The human burials. In A. McWhirr, L. Viner and C. Wells, *Romano-British Cemeteries at Cirencester*. Cirencester, 135–202.

Wells, C. and Woodhouse, N. 1975. Paget's disease in an Anglo-Saxon. *Medical History* 19, 396–400.

Wood, J. E., Milner, G. R., Harpending, H. C. and Weiss, K. M. 1992. The osteological paradox: problems of inferring health from the skeletal samples. *Current Anthropology*, 33, 343–70.

CHAPTER FOURTEEN

The Family in Roman Britain

LINDSAY ALLASON-JONES

Our evidence for family life in Britain before the Roman invasion relies almost solely on what can be extrapolated from excavation evidence and artefacts research. During the Roman period we are fortunate in having access to more detailed information – the written evidence on tombstones and religious dedications, such as altars, as well as curse tablets and writing tablets. From these we can deduce that the family was an important element in the cosmopolitan community which made up Roman Britain. It is, however, precisely because Britain was so cosmopolitan, with immigrants from all the provinces of the Empire living in the country, that no single definition of the typical Romano-British family can be offered.

It has often been presumed that the Roman way of life was the norm throughout the Roman Empire and that the Roman ideal of the family would have been followed in all the provinces. According to this ideal, each family would have had a father at its head – the *pater familias* – who had legal rights over his wife, his children, the children of his sons, and his slaves. On the death of the *pater familias* his adult sons would be promoted to *pater familias* of their own households while the widow and younger children became *sui iuris*, which meant that they were independent of a *pater's* control. However, widows and adult female orphans were still expected to have a guardian appointed from the immediate family circle to sanction their actions. Under Roman law a woman could not act as the head of a family or exercise *potestas* (control) and without *potestas* she could not own property, adopt a child or exercise legal control over her children. It is not clear how much this pattern was followed to the letter outside Rome or, indeed, if it was strictly adhered to outside patrician circles in the city itself. In provinces such as Britannia, where there was a tradition in some tribes of women being considered equal to men (Tacitus, *Annals*, XIV), it is unlikely to have found universal favour.

Most of the population of Britain before the Roman invasion appears to have lived in extended family groups, and many rural families may have continued in this tradition at least until the second century AD and possibly, in some of the more remote areas, throughout the Roman period. The typical Iron Age and early Romano-British rural dwelling was a large building which would have been occupied by two or three inter-related families, with similar extended families living in the same enclosed compound (Ehrenberg 1989: pp.160–1). These settlements would have been self-sufficient, relying on what the inhabitants could grow, hunt or gather, with limited contact or exchange with other communities.

The Roman invasion resulted in a considerable change to this way of life. Sometimes this change was rapid, as in the case of settlements destroyed by enemy action or demolished to make way for forts or military zones; elsewhere the change was slower as towns began to develop and families started to move into the larger conurbations. This drift towards urban dwelling will have had a particular impact on the extended family, as town life and urban architecture favoured the nuclear family; even if the development of towns had not encouraged the economic migration of young men and women, the army's need for recruits would have taken sons from their homes and undermined the traditional extended family groups.

Extended families were not peculiar to the Britons. Among the incomers there is also evidence that extended families were common, with many military and civilian immigrants bringing with them grandmothers and aunts: for example, Campania Dubitata from southern Russia found herself in Ribchester, in Lancashire, with her daughter, grandson and son-in-law (a *singularis consularis* in the cavalry regiment of Sarmatians: *RIB* 594), while the German woman Ursa lived with her brother, sister-in-law and nephew at the fort at Chesters on Hadrian's Wall (*RIB* 1483). Even though it refers to a German family, this latter inscription may reflect the legal tradition that the eldest son was usually appointed as guardian to the unmarried women in his family on the death of his father. The Roman government tried on a number of occasions to exempt serving soldiers from this duty but to no avail, and as a result the *vici* and *canabae* of forts and fortresses in Britain may have housed a number of widowed mothers as well as the sisters and nieces of soldiers. Tadius Exuperatus at Caerleon in Wales, for example, appears to have taken charge of his mother Tadia Vallaunius and his sister Tadia Exuperata on the death of his father (*RIB* 369) while Lifana seems to have been taken into the household of her uncle, Lucius Senofilus, at Carvoran (*RIB* 1830).

As more and more military personnel, as well as merchants and traders, arrived in Britain from all over the Empire, they came into contact with each other and the local population. Several mixed marriages are known in Roman Britain, of which the most famous are those of Regina, the Catuvellaunian girl married to Barates, a Palmyrene (*RIB* 1065), and Vibia Pacata, thought to have been an African woman, married to the Pannonian centurion Flavius Verecundus at Westerwood on the Antonine Wall (Wright 1964: 178, no. 7; *CSIR* I.4, no. 86), but these are not the only examples. Centurions, in particular, were often married to women from different provinces to themselves. Centurions and decurions appear to have always been permitted to marry, and although there was a rule that officers should not marry women from the province in which they were stationed, this rule may have been only loosely observed or even ignored in the case of centurions (Allason-Jones 1999: 42–3); Salviena Lepidina, for example, is likely to have met her husband while he was stationed in Britain (*CIL* VIII. 2907), but many centurions and decurions would have been already married when they arrived in Britain and would have brought with them wives from other provinces.

Figure 14.1 The tombstone of Regina at South Shields.

That mixed marriages were not confined to centurions, or to foreigners already married when they arrived, can be deduced from a reference to the Boudiccan revolt which indicates that much of the hostility of the Boudiccan troops was directed to those local women who had already married Roman veterans (Cassius Dio, *Roman History,* LXII.2.7). Once the province had settled down, however, marriage between British girls and army veterans seems to have been more readily accepted and eventually generally approved of. By the second century AD, marrying a veteran may have been considered a sensible match for a girl if her suitor had not wasted his salary of twenty-five years on drink and gambling and, as an additional benefit, any children born of such a marriage would have had Roman citizenship. Many veterans settled in the *vici* or towns, where they had a respected position in society and maintained their lifestyle by setting themselves up in business as traders or craftsmen;

Figure 14.2   The tombstone of Flavia Augustina, Aeresius Saenus and their children at York (Photo: Otto Fein).

this led to numerous families in the military zones with young children whose fathers were in their late forties or fifties but whose mothers were only in their twenties or thirties; Flavia Augustina and Gaius Aeresius Saenus and their two children at York are a good example of this 'typical' military zone family (*RIB* 685).

   The children of these mixed marriages must often have been confused as to their identity. Unless one of their parents was from Italy, Latin may not have been the language spoken at home, and it is probable that many children were able to speak several languages: Latin for official or public occasions, their mother's native language and/or their father's native language, plus the local dialect of the area they were living in at the time. That young children are able to learn several languages at once and switch effortlessly from one to the other is well known, but it is also recognized that the impact of several cultural traditions at the same time within the home often results in stress for both the parents and the children, leading to family breakdown or behavioural problems. This will have been evident in those families where the parents came from different ethnic backgrounds, but may also have been found in immigrant families from other provinces, such as Sacer, the son of a citizen of the Senones, who lived in Lincoln with his wife and son (*RIB* 262), or the Greek Flavius Helius, who also lived in Lincoln with his family (*RIB* 251).

Language difficulties may not have been the only problems experienced by those in mixed marriages; differences in religious beliefs would also have created stress. Men from Italy would have expected their wives to tend the domestic shrine in the home but rely on the *pater familias* to carry out the official religious duties and dedications on behalf of the family outside the home – a German soldier called Maduhus, for example, dedicated to the goddess Coventina 'for himself and his family' (*RIB* 1526), following Roman tradition (see also *RIB* 1837, 2039, 2045, 2124, 2176), but there are other dedications which suggest that women in Britain occasionally took this responsibility on themselves, such as Tranquila at Carrawburgh, who fulfilled a vow 'for herself and her family' (*RIB* 1539). However, if the wife came from a Celtic tribe of one of the north-west provinces, while her husband came from Syria, then it would only be in carrying out the official rites expected of all the people in the Roman Empire, such as attending the ceremonies of the cults of the Deified Emperor, Jupiter or Roma, that they would act as a family in a religious context. Several religions precluded family participation, such as the exclusively male cult of Mithras, although even in Mithraea there were occasional dedications which included a member's family (e.g. *RIB* 1599 and 1600). It may have been their efforts to follow their native religions which revealed to an individual just how far they were from home if they had married outside their tribe, or moved to a different tribal area or province.

For Romans from mainland Italy, as well as for the native Britons and peoples from the tribes from the north-western provinces, monogamy was the norm. However, while none of the epigraphic evidence provides a named polygynous or polyandrous family in Britain, it is clear that in some of the provinces polygamy was common, and immigrants from those provinces continued to live in polygmous family units while in Britain. The wording of army retirement diplomas, for example, recognizes the marriage of retiring auxiliaries, 'with those who are their wives at the date of this grant, or in the case of the unmarried, any wives they may subsequently marry, provided they only have one each' (Hassall and Tomlin, 1983; 347–8, no. 40; Roxan 1985: no. 97). This official statement was designed to ensure that only the children of one wife were registered as legitimate – and thus entitled to citizenship or recognition as the heirs of their fathers – but it also indicates that the military authorities were aware that many auxiliaries came from cultures where polygamy was the norm.

The incoming Romans seem to have been fascinated by the marital habits of some of the British tribes. Julius Caesar recorded that 'groups of ten or twelve men have wives in common, and particularly brothers along with brothers, and fathers with sons, but the children born of the union are reckoned to belong to the particular house to which the maiden was first conducted' (*De Bello Gallico*, V.14). This view of

British family life appears still to have been believed several generations later, when the Empress Julia Domna asked the wife of the Caledonian chieftain Argentocoxus 'about the free intercourse of her sex with men in Britain' (Cassius Dio, *Roman History*, LXXVII.16.5). Each British tribe would have had its own traditions and it is not inconceivable that some either had or still practised polyandry, but it is also possible that Roman writers – always on the alert for unorthodox behaviour among provincials and barbarians – had misunderstood a legal system whereby a widow became technically the wife of her new guardian on her husband's death. It is also possible that a system was practised which was similar to that of the Levirate in Nubia, in which widows capable of child-bearing are taken into the household of their husband's brother in order to keep any subsequent children within the tribal subgroup and to keep the family from dying out. This system has been practised throughout history whenever warfare has made inroads into the young male population, leaving large numbers of fertile widows.

While it is likely that throughout the Empire men who practised the eastern habit of polygamy had large families, the evidence from Roman Britain suggests that the average family had only two children. Forensic examination of female skeletons in the 1950s and 1960s led to the suggestion that some women in the province were producing up to five children, but the methodology which led to this conclusion – the theory that the number of children delivered leaves identifiable, measurable traces on the pelvis called scars of parturition – has now been discredited. From tombstone evidence it is known that Carinus, a citizen of Rome who died at Dorchester, had three children: Rufinus, Carina and Avita (*RIB* 188), as did Caesoria Corocca and her husband Rentius at Caerleon (*RIB* 371), while Sempronius Sempronianus at London (*RIB* 15) had two brothers, and Vindicianus mourned a brother and a sister at Old Penrith (*RIB* 934), but these appear to be the exception rather than the rule.

While several natural reasons for the preponderance of small families have been offered, such as lead contamination in the drinking water or poor nutrition, these reasons were equally plausible in medieval and post-medieval Britain, when large families were commonplace. The evidence from Roman Britain indicates that social status and consequent living conditions did not affect the size of the families, and two children appears to have been the preferred option. This suggests that family planning was widely practised in Roman Britain.

The medical writers of the time provided much advice on the subject of contraception, including a number of methods which would have been effective if followed conscientiously (Allason-Jones 1989: 38–42); for example, alum, vinegar, olive oil and brine, contraceptives recommended by the second-century Greek writer Soranus, were still being recommended in the 1930s by Marie Stopes. However, the medical writers could only offer nostrums based on observation rather than sound physiological knowledge, and amulets and potions were just as strongly recommended.

If their contraceptive method failed, women might resort to abortion. Although this was forbidden in the Hippocratic Oath, most of the ancient medical writers who discussed female health described abortion methods. The *Digest* suggests that there was no prohibition on abortion as such (Gardner 1986: 158) and the Severan law which forbade a wife to abort without her husband's consent appears to have been more concerned with her deceit than the act of abortion (*Digest*, 47.11.14, 48.8.8, 48.19.39). In Roman law the foetus was not considered to have a soul or any individuality; its destruction, therefore, was not regarded as murder. The only legal hindrance was a ban on the sale of abortifacients (along with aphrodisiacs), which was included in a law on poisons, but this was because of the lethal contents of some of the prescriptions rather than because of any perceived moral issues (*Digest*, 48.8.3.2, 48.19.38.5).

A third method of controlling the size of families – and one which is invariably linked with Roman family planning – was infanticide. In his section on childbirth, Soranus gives advice on recognizing babies who were not worth rearing because they were sickly or malformed (*Gynecology*, II.12), but his reasoning appears to have been based on purely medical grounds; other literary evidence makes it clear that babies could be exposed if financial constraints made their birth unwelcome. The many references to infanticide in the works of Plautus (e.g. *Casina*, prol. 41, 79; *Cistellaria*, i.3, 17, 31) suggest that the exposure of infants was a common occurrence and while this source may be regarded with some wariness – babies being left on hillsides being a useful dramatic device – it appears to have been the extent of the practice which led to the many alimentary schemes for poor families which developed in Rome. There is, however, little evidence that infanticide was practised to this extent in any of the north-western provinces. Tacitus's comment in *Germania* 19, that 'to restrict the number of children, or to kill any of those born after the heir, is considered wicked,' suggests that infanticide was not considered acceptable in some northern tribes.

In his article on infanticide through the ages, Mays (1995: 8) suggests that infanticide was practised extensively in Roman Britain, but the evidence may be the result of a statistical irregularity or indicate practice for one tribal area and not be proof of activity in the province as a whole. Early evidence of infanticide on a grand scale at Hambledon villa is now interpreted as the discovery of an official infant cemetery in a rural community, where burial in family groups was not the tradition (Allason-Jones 1989: 42–4). The 'marked peak in deaths at around full term' which Mays noted during his research may have had a natural cause – newborn infants are often at risk from viruses – while the ceremonies which accompanied the birth of a child in some tribes, such as those described by Soranus (*Gynecology*, II.12), must often have had tragic and unlooked-for consequences.

Regarding the argument that it was only the female babies which were disposed of, it is not considered possible to differentiate between male and female perinatal babies from the skeletal evidence alone with any degree of accuracy, while the preponderance of adult male skeletons in the cemeteries at Ancaster, Cirencester, Colchester, Winchester and York, for example, may simply reflect the impact of a male-dominated, military population or even separate burial areas for men and women, rather than an indication that unwanted female infants were being disposed of at birth. At Poundbury, Molleson (1989: 27–38) has noted a tendency for a high proportion of burials of females aged about 12 years of age. Her suggestion is that adolescent girls were not considered to be of much worth and were, as a consequence, not as well fed, but there is little corroborating evidence that girls were regarded as second-class citizens in Roman Britain. Indeed, a society which could trace its roots back to such redoubtable female leaders as Cartimandua and Boudicca, and in which a woman could describe herself as the head of a household, as Veloriga does on a curse tablet from Bath (*Tab.Sul.* 53), is unlikely to have accepted without argument the Roman view, voiced by Cicero, that 'all women, because of their weakness of intellect, should be under the power of guardians' (*Pro Murena*, 27). That said, it must be remembered that there were families in Britain from provinces where women were regarded as of lesser importance, and in those families female infanticide may have been practised. Equally, there are always parents in every society who, despite the normal social mores of their culture, kill their children through neglect or because of mental illness; it is interesting in this context to note that Soranus was fully aware of the dangers of baby-battering, although his warning was aimed at parents choosing a wet nurse rather than identifying post-natal depression in the mother (*Gynecology*, II.19).

The evidence of epitaphs suggests that some children were deeply mourned by their grieving parents and that it was not considered unusual to express this grief through the medium of a publicly visible tombstone. Some inscriptions simply give the names of the deceased, e.g. 'Ahteha, daughter of Nobilis' who died aged 5 at Corbridge (*RIB* 1180), and others may imply the use of a stock phrase, e.g. the 'most sweet daughter' of Fabius Honoratus and Aurelia Eglectiane at Chesters (*RIB* 1482; cf. the 'very sweet son' of Bassaeus Julius at York, *RIB* 672), but there are others where individually composed epitaphs speak of unbearable grief. An unnamed parent at Lincoln, for example, mourned a 9-year-old daughter: 'she lived a sweetest [child, torn away no less suddenly] than the partner of Dis; . . . after she was carried away suddenly . . . I have mourned thy fate' (*RIB* 265), while the similarly literary Quintus Corellius Fortis appears to have been distraught at the loss of his 13-year-old daughter, Corellia Optata: 'Ye mysterious spirits who dwell in Pluto's Acherusian realms, and whom the meagre ashes and the shade, empty semblance of the body, seek, following the brief light of life; sire of an innocent daughter, I, a pitiable victim of unfair hope, bewail her final end' (*RIB* 684). At the other end of the emotional scale, however, is Vitellia Procula at York with the rather cool reference to herself as 'mother . . . and heir in part' of her anonymous 13-year-old daughter (*RIB* 696).

Affection of children for parents and parents for children can also be noted through the use of family nicknames, such as 'Ertola, properly called Vellibia' who was mourned by Sudrenus at Corbridge (*RIB* 1181). At Maryport, a Gallatian 'when dying craved [to be buried] in the tomb of his father' (*RIB* 864). Affection between married couples may also be identified through the use of such epithets as 'beloved wife' (*RIB* 621), 'very beloved wife' (*RIB* 959), 'peerless husband' (*RIB* 11), 'devoted husband' (*RIB* 375) and 'most devoted wife' (*RIB* 17), although terms such as 'well deserving wife' (*RIB* 250) and 'very pure wife who lived 33 years without blemish' (*RIB* 1828) seem more public than personal in their expression of affection. Evidence of long marriages can be found in the tombstone of Placida, whose husband recorded that they had been married for thirty years when she died at Wroxeter at the age of 55 (*RIB* 295), while the tombstone of the veteran of the Second Legion Augusta, Julius Valens, who died at the age of 100, could have been married to his wife Julia Secundina for over fifty years, even if he had waited until his retirement in his forties before marrying (*RIB* 363); Julia Secundina herself died at the age of 75 (*RIB* 373).

In Rome and the Mediterranean provinces an early age of marriage for girls, particularly in the wealthier families, was the norm, but in Britain girls appear to have married later. Tacitus, in his discussion of the German tribes, declared that 'the girls, too, are not hurried into marriage' (*Germania*, 20), while Julius Caesar observed that for a German 'to have intercourse with a woman below the age of twenty

Figure 14.3 The tombstone of Julia at Wroxeter.

is considered perfectly scandalous' (*De Bello Gallico*, VI.21). That this Celtic view of a suitable age for marriage was shared by the British tribes may be implied by the fact that the youngest bride recorded through inscriptions in the province was 19, although in this case Claudia Martina was married to a civil servant and her family may have followed the Roman custom of an early marriage (*RIB* 21). The skeletal evidence from Poundbury has indicated that only 7.5 per cent of the female population of that area had had their first child by the time they were 17, while 54 per cent had given birth by the time they reached 21 and 62 per cent by the age of 28 (Cox, personal communication).

Although under Roman law childlessness was regarded as grounds for divorce – and considered to be the fault of the wife unless there was obvious evidence to the contrary – there were mechanisms for adopting or fostering children. A number of foster-children are recorded in Roman Britain, for example, Mercatilla the foster-daughter of Magnius at Bath (*RIB* 162), Hyllus a 'beloved foster-child' at York (*RIB* 681), Ylas the 13-year-old 'dearest foster-child' of the legionary tribune Claudius Severus at Old Penrith (*RIB* 937) and Hermagoras, the foster-child of Honoratus the

Tribune at High Rochester (*RIB* 1291). Several of these children are described as 'freed', suggesting that these were not nieces and nephews being taken into a relative's home on the death of their parents but slave children being given their freedom as part of the adoption process. According to Roman law, only men could adopt children legally and only male children could be adopted by *adrogatio*, that is by a legislative act through which the child would be given the rights of a legitimate child (Gardner 1986: 8–9). If a child was taken into a household without any legal documentation, then he or she retained their status at birth.

A Romano-British family included not only relations by birth and marriage but also the slaves and freedmen or freedwomen of the household. A freed person was tied to their previous owner by the new relationship of patron and client, but need not necessarily leave the patron's house on manumission; many appear to have continued to fulfil their old duties, and on the death of their patron even transferred to the household of the heir. Inscriptional evidence suggests that there was often an affectionate relationship between the freed servants and the families they served: Eutychus, for example, set up an altar to Silvanus Pantheus on behalf of his master Rufinus, the tribune at High Rochester, Rufinus' wife (the aristocratic Julia Lucilla), as well as himself and 'his dependants', suggesting that he was concerned as to their spiritual well-being (*RIB* 1271). The altar also, by referring to 'his dependants', indicates that Eutychus had brought his own family with him from Rome to Northumberland in the household of Rufinus.

The head of a household acted as *pater familias* to his servants as well as his family members, and while some will have regarded this as merely a legal duty, there is evidence that others considered both freed and slave members of the household as being entitled to respect and affection. At Chester, for example, Pompeius Optatus set up a tombstone to three slave children in his household: Atlianus, Antatilianus and Protus (*RIB* 560), while his neighbour, Gaius Asurius Fortis, erected a memorial to Etacontius 'his deserving freedman' (*RIB* 559). It is not clear what the relationship was between Julia Velva and her heir, Aurelius Mercurialis, at York – she may have been his mother-in-law although the reference in her epitaph to her having 'lived most dutifully for 50 years' may suggest that she was a well-loved freedwoman – but she was included in the tomb which Aurelius Mercurialis had 'in his lifetime made . . . for himself and his family' (*RIB* 688). Other men were mourned by their freedmen, such as Verecundus and Novicius, who paid for the tombstone of the centurion Marcus Favonius Facilis, presumably in the absence of anyone with closer family ties (*RIB* 200). At York, Caecilius Musicus arranged the burial of Aelia Severa, the widow of his late master Caecilius Rufus; in this case it is noticeable that the slave had taken the name of his master on manumission as was the Roman custom (*RIB* 683).

Under Roman law slaves could not contract marriages, but in many households stable relationships were formed. The couple concerned may have regarded these as true marriages; for example, Cunitius and Senovara, the slaves of Cunomolius and Minervina at Bath, were recorded as man and wife on a curse tablet (*Tab.Sul.* 9). These marriages, however, were no bar to either partner being sold by his or her owner and separated from his or her spouse. Slave parents also had no control over the fate of their children, who could be sold at any stage.

Serving soldiers under the rank of centurion were also not allowed to make a legal marriage contract until the Severan Edict of 197. That this ban had been enacted before the Roman invasion of Britain is shown by Cassius Dio's comment that: 'he, Claudius, gave the rights of married men to the soldiers, since in accordance with the law they were not permitted to marry' (60.24.3). Herodian's explanation of this ban was that 'all these things [that is, wives and children] are normally considered alien to military discipline and an efficient readiness for war' (3.8.4). If this law was adhered to then, theoretically, there should be no wives and children of serving soldiers in Britannia until the end of the second century AD. There was, of course, no legal constraint on soldiers making more informal arrangements: Robin Birley, for example, has taken the term *contubernia* in Vindolanda Letter 181 to mean 'concubine' rather than its alternative meaning of 'messmate', interpreting the text to refer to the concubine or de facto wife of Tagamatis, the flag-bearer (Birley 1990: 30). However, a number of inscriptions have been found which suggest that the ban on formal marriage was not observed among the auxiliary units in Britannia. Dagvalda, for example, was 'a soldier in the First Cohort of Pannonians' whose death on Hadrian's Wall was mourned by a woman who claimed to be his wife Pusinna (*RIB* 1667). Aurelius Marcus, a soldier in the century of Obsequens, set up a tombstone at Carvoran to a woman he described as 'his very pure wife', Aurelia Aia; in this case the wife is recorded as having come from Salona in modern-day Croatia, and it may be postulated that she had followed her husband to Britannia rather than met and married him here (*RIB* 1828). Even legionaries flouted the law: Gaius Valerius Justus, a record clerk in Legio XX, was willing to admit having been married when he mourned the loss of 'his most chaste and pure wife' Cocceia Irene on a tombstone in the fortress cemetery at Chester, where a *beneficiarius* called Titinius Felix was also commemorated by his widow, Julia Similina (*RIB* 505). Some of the many memorials to soldiers' wives or erected by soldiers' widows may date to after AD 197, when Septimius Severus 'gave [soldiers] permission to wear gold rings and to live in wedlock with their wives' (Herodian, 3.8.5), but it is doubtful that all of them do. It is, indeed, improbable that large numbers of Celts (considered by the Romans to be particularly moral in their outlook on life) would have agreed to their daughters cohabiting with foreign soldiers and moving around the Empire with the army unless some form of recognizable and acceptable ceremony had been followed to give the relationships respectability and the girls some expectation of a stable home life.

Britannia was not unusual in having married soldiers in the ranks. Margaret Roxan's survey of 904 tombstones in the frontier regions of the Empire has revealed 102 military widows and 55 widowers who were still serving (Roxan 1989: 462–7). Roxan has also noted that the number of soldiers' families named in the *diplomata* changed through time (Roxan 1981: 265–86) with a noticeable rise in the number of named families after AD 120. She suggests that the period of imperial expansion before AD 120 made it difficult for serving soldiers to form long-term relationships, while the more settled situation after AD 120 resulted in troops being garrisoned at one fort for long periods, giving them time to meet and marry.

In practice, a high proportion of retirement diplomas acknowledge that the retiring soldiers were already in long-standing formal relationships, indicating that the army had accepted that soldiers would marry. In denying soldiers the right to marry legally, the State was simply avoiding any responsibility for dependants, and it would be interesting to know how the military authorities viewed the presence of the soldiers' mothers and sisters in this context. There is certainly evidence for families following soldiers both on tours of duty and on active campaigns; Cassius Dio, for example, describes 'not a few women and children and a large retinue of servants' following the army of Varus (53.20.2–5) and Julius Caesar referred to carts filled with female luggage at the back of one of his convoys (*De Bello Africa*, 75). While accepting the existence of these families, the army's legal position makes it unlikely that any official provision of transport was on offer, either across the English Channel or up and down the province. Families would have had to make their own arrangements should the father find himself transferred to another fort or another province.

The legal status of children born to serving soldiers before the Severan Edict would have been uncertain. Children born during their father's military service were classed as illegitimate and could thus have no claim on their father's estate if he did not leave a will. Even if he had made written provision for these children, they might still have had problems in proving their identity in a court of law, as a soldier could not register the birth of a child; such cases are known to have kept the legal profession busy in other provinces (see Gardner 1986: 34; also *Papyrus Michigan*, VII.442, and Ricco-bono et al., *Fontes*, 3.5, 3.19).

Women who allied themselves to serving soldiers under native law would also have found it difficult to reclaim their dowries on their husband's death if their marriage had not been recognized by the authorities; nor could their families prosecute for adultery on their behalf (*Digest*, 23.2.12–1). Even if a woman had married legally, her marriage would be declared dissolved and any subsequent children illegitimate if her husband enlisted after marriage. This, theoretically, could have affected the 5500 Sarmatians who were conscripted between AD 169 and 180 and sent to Ribchester as well as the *numerus Hnaudifridi* at Housesteads and the Tigris bargemen at South Shields, yet all these units appear to have had families with them. Whether the military authorities acknowledged a woman's relationship with a soldier or not, if she wanted his financial support for herself and her children then her best chance was to follow him wherever he went.

An auxiliary's salary was not generous and it is probable that any dependants a soldier might have would have had to find some paid work in order to contribute to the family's income. In areas where the military presence was well established and the garrisons were rarely changed, mothers, sisters and wives might set themselves up in business, but in less settled times, when a soldier might be transferred often, there would be fewer opportunities. Carol van Driel Murray's discussion of the lives of soldiers' families in the Dutch East Indies in the nineteenth century may offer a comparable picture of how these women survived (van Driel Murray 1995: 3–21).

Women from military families were not the only ones whose lives were inextricably bound up with the careers of their fathers, husbands or brothers. In towns the right to serve on the *ordo*, the council which governed the *coloniae* and *municipia*, was reserved for men over the age of 30 who satisfied the relevant property qualifications, but the honour was shared by the whole family, as is shown by Aelia Severa, wife of a decurion at York, calling herself *honesta femina*, a title reserved for women of the curial class (*RIB* 683). However, the honour could be a mixed blessing as the *ordo* was responsible for collecting taxes, and if any money was outstanding the *ordo* had to make up the shortfall from their own pockets – a curial family could easily be bankrupted by their duty.

In shops and businesses in the towns and on farms in the country families worked together as units. Very few of these individuals are known by name but occasionally there is a glimpse of extended and nuclear families acting together, such as the case of Decentius, his wife Alogosia, his brother Uricalus and sister-in-law Docilosa, and his nephew and niece Docilis and Docilina, who swore an oath against perjury at Bath (*Tab.Sul.* 94). In Scotland, a man called Salmanes set up a tombstone to his son of the same name; it has been suggested that this was a Jewish trading family which travelled from fort to fort (A. Birley 1988: 128; *RIB* 2182). Higher up the social scale were the merchant Marcus Verecundius Diogenes, '*sevir* of the colony of York, and *quinquennalis*, also tribesman of the Bituriges Cubi' (*RIB* 678) and his wife, Julia Fortunata from Sardinia (*RIB* 687).

Family life is not always without its problems and Romano-British family life was no exception. Several curses recorded on lead tablets hint at adultery, such as 'he who carried off Vilbia from me' at Bath (*RIB* 154) and the love triangle at Old Harlow between Etterna, Timotneus and a third party (Wright and Hassall 1973: 325, no. 3), while a curse tablet from London, which curses 'Tretia Maria and her life and mind and memory and lungs mixed up together, and her words, thoughts and memory; thus may she be unable to speak what things are concealed', suggests a family row (*RIB* 7) as does 'Tacita, hereby accursed is labelled old like putrid gore' (*RIB* 221). In the case of a wife's adultery, divorce was obligatory under Roman law, otherwise her husband was considered to condone the act. Insanity was not grounds for divorce; on the contrary, if a woman was declared insane she could not divorce her husband, nor could her family obtain a divorce on her behalf.

Divorce under Roman law was not a complex procedure. A marriage was formed by the man and woman consenting to the match before witnesses and could be just as easily dissolved by either party renouncing their commitment. The only exception was a freedwoman married to her previous owner, who was not allowed to divorce him unless he consented. Problems might occur if there was any argument about the return of the dowry to the woman's family but no specific references to such cases have survived in Britain. Legitimate children were the financial responsibility of their father, including any children born after their parents' divorce, but a mother could claim custody and in these cases her ex-husband was expected to pay maintenance for his children (Gardner 1986: 146–7). The wife herself could not claim any maintenance. How complex divorce was under Celtic law is not so clear, but the story of Cartimandua and her divorce from Venutius indicates that it was possible; nowhere in the literary evidence does it suggest that divorce was only available to the upper classes (Tacitus, *Histories*, III).

A tombstone from Maryport, which reads 'To the spirits of the departed (and) of Morirex (who lived) 70 years. Appointed in place of his sons, his heirs set this up' (*RIB* 861), may be interpreted as that of a man whose sons had predeceased him. Alternatively, it could suggest a family which had broken up. Another tombstone from Risingham, on the other hand, reveals a different type of family problem when it refers to 'he [the son who] had been prevented by illness' and so had been 'substituted [as heir] instead of the son, following the natural succession' (*RIB* 1256). Many families will have lost children to disease or accident and the constant movement of families around the province and between the provinces will have made such losses particularly hard to bear as small graves had to be left behind in a distant land; Fabius

Honoratus and his wife Aurelia Eglectiane would not have been the only military family to have been in this unfortunate position (*RIB* 1482).

The importance of having family ties may be indicated by the tradition of including the phrase 'son of' or 'daughter of' on a tombstone, particularly when the epitaph was erected by someone outside the immediate family. Indeed, the need to have someone responsible for ensuring that you had a decent burial and some kind of suitable memorial after your death led to those without families creating substitute groupings: Julius Vitalis, armourer of the Twentieth Legion Valeria Victrix, for example was buried at Bath 'at the cost of the Guild of Armourers' (*RIB* 156). Others joined burial clubs, such as Pervinca, daughter of Quartio, whose tombstone was set up at Housesteads by a group of unrelated people who appear to have been part of a tontine (*RIB* 1620). Burial clubs were particularly popular with slaves such as Hardalio, whose tombstone was set up at Halton Chesters by 'the guild of his fellow slaves' (*RIB* 1436). Despite having money withheld from their salaries to pay for their funeral, military men appear to have preferred to appoint a colleague to act in place of their family and ensure that their last requests were carried out: examples include Dannicus, trooper of the Cavalry Regiment Indiana at Cirencester (*RIB* 108), Aventius, *curator* of the Second Cavalry Regiment of Asturians at Chesters (*RIB* 1480) and Caecilius Avitus, Gaius Cestius Teurenicus and Florianus, all buried at Chester (*RIB* 492, 494, 496).

The family in Roman Britain was a complicated unit. It could consist of a simple nuclear unit of a man, his wife and their two children, all of whom shared the same ethnic background. Or it might involve several generations, including slaves and freedmen, with every individual coming from a different province, speaking different languages, worshipping different gods and having different expectations about what being a family member entailed. What is clear, however, is that being part of a family – whether a genetic family or a group of unrelated people who acknowledged that they had familial responsibilities to each other – was considered of prime importance. In the changing world of Roman Britain, the family might be the only stable element in a person's life, and the large numbers of religious dedications by individuals on behalf of themselves and their families or on behalf of themselves and their households reflects how keen people were to maintain that stability.

FURTHER READING

For the background to Roman family law, see *Women in Roman Law and Society* by Jane F. Gardner (1986) and *The Roman Mother*, by Suzanne Dixon (1988). Both volumes, however, should be read with the understanding that the legal system of the Roman Empire was often subject to provincial variations, and the legal constraints on family life recognized in Rome may not have been acknowledged in Britain.

For a study of the names, careers and probable origins of individuals in Roman Britain, see *The People of Roman Britain* by A. Birley (1979, paperback 1988). For a general study of the female population aimed at the general reader, see *Women of Roman Britain* by Lindsay Allason-Jones (1989). For those women and children attached to the army, see 'Women and the Roman Army in Britain' by Lindsay Allason-Jones in *The Roman Army as a Community* (ed. A. Goldsworthy and I. Haynes (1999) and 'Women of the frontiers' by M. M. Roxan in

Roman Frontier Studies 1984. Proceedings of the XVth International Congress of Roman Frontier Studies (ed. V. A. Maxfield and M. J. Dobson, 1989).

Soranus' *Gynecology* is available in a translation by O. Temkin (1956).

REFERENCES

Allason-Jones, L. 1989. *Women of Roman Britain*. London.

—— 1999. Women and the Roman army in Britain. In A. Galsworthy and I. Haynes (eds), *The Roman Army as a Community*. London, 41–51.

Birley, A. 1988. *The People of Roman Britain*. London. [First published in 1979.]

Birley, R. 1990. *The Roman Documents from Vindolanda*. Newcastle upon Tyne.

Dixon, S. 1988. *The Roman Mother*. London.

Ehrenberg, M. 1989. *Women in Prehistory*. London.

Gardner, J. F. 1986. *Women in Roman Law and Society*. London.

Hassall, M. W. C. and Tomlin, R. S. O. 1983. Inscriptions. *Britannia*, 14, 336–41.

Mays, S. 1995. Killing the unwanted child. *British Archaeology*, 2 (March), 8–9.

Molleson, T. I. 1989. Social implications of mortality patterns of juveniles from Poundbury Camp Romano-British Cemetery. *Anthropologische Anzeiger* 47, 27–38.

Riccobono, S., Baviera, J., Ferrini, C., Furlani, J. and Arangio-Ruiz, V. (eds) 1940–3. *Fontes iuris Romani anteiustiniani*. 3 vols. Florence.

Roxan, M. M. 1981. The distribution of Roman military diplomas. *Epigraphic Studies*, 12, 265–86.

—— 1985. *Roman Military Diplomas, 1978–1984*. Institute of Archaeology Occasional Paper 9. London.

—— 1989. Women on the frontiers. In V. A. Maxfield and M. J. Dobson (eds), *Roman Frontier Studies 1989: Proceedings of the XV International Congress on Roman Frontier Studies*. Exeter, 462–7.

Soranus. 1956. *Gynecology*, trans. O. Temkin. Baltimore, MD.

Van Driel Murray, C. 1995. Gender in question. In P. Rash (ed.), *Theoretical Roman Archaeology: Second Conference Proceedings*. Aldershot, 3–21.

Wright, R. P. 1964. Inscriptions. *Journal of Roman Studies*, 54, 177–85.

Wright, R. P. and Hassall, M. W. C. 1973. Inscriptions. *Britannia*, 4, 324–37.

CHAPTER FIFTEEN

Personal Ornament

ALEXANDRA CROOM

Roman jewellery was made out of everything from gold and silver and copper alloy, to semi-precious stones, coral, glass, jet and even iron and bone, while gilding, tinning and silvering gave copper alloy the appearance of richer materials. Jewellery was worn by all levels in society, but material alone is not enough to identify who would have purchased it; as nowadays, small items of gold and silver such as ear-rings and finger-rings would have been affordable by a larger section of the population than could buy items such as necklaces or bracelets, which used a greater quantity of metal. However, while some forms of jewellery were made only in precious metals, such as chains with a wheel motif made only in gold or silver, or coins set in gold jewellery, very often the same designs were carried out in a range of materials to suit all purses.

Gemstones and glass were only rarely facet-cut and there seemed to be a greater interest in colour than glitter, while the most precious, and most expensive, jewel was considered to be the pearl.

There were clear changes in fashion over the centuries, with an increasing elaboration in jewellery, and a clear interest in texture and the play of light developing in the third century. The use of open-work and granulation in particular reflects these new fashions, while black seems to have become fashionable at the same time, with increasing quantities of jet jewellery and the use of black glass beads.

In the ancient world jewellery was frequently considered to be a female form of ornament, while men wore 'functional' items such as brooches, amulets, and finger-rings that doubled as signet rings. However, in the provinces local native traditions allowed men to wear some items of jewellery, and this may also be found in Roman Britain. In a rare consideration of male jewellery during this period, R. Philpott identified 31 burials considered to be male with items of personal ornament. They included twelve with brooches, six with rings and one with an amulet. There were a further four or five with bracelets, including examples made out of beads, most of early post-Conquest date (Philpott 1991: 144). Another burial, so far unique, had an expanding 'bracelet' around the thigh (Philpott 1991: table A30, Albert Road, Dorchester).

Grave Goods

Philpott's study of Romano-British burial practice has looked at personal ornaments not from the perspective of individual items, but as sets considered suitable for burial with their owner. Philpott has found examples of jewellery as grave furniture from the first century onwards although most of the largest collections come from the fourth century, when there was a fashion for sets of jewellery to be buried with girls or young women. The jewellery was either worn or collected in a group at the head or foot of the grave, sometimes originally in a box or bag. There is a clear difference between the quantity of jewellery worn and those deposited in a group. A grave from South Shields (Croom 1994: 54), for example, had a collection of unworn jewellery consisting of nine bracelets, six finger-rings and a bead necklace or bracelet, while at Dunstable two pins, two necklaces and seven bracelets were found in a bag within the grave (Philpott 1991: table A30). The evidence from graves where women were buried wearing jewellery, on the other hand, shows that surprisingly little was worn at any one time.

The most common arrangement is for only one category of jewellery to be worn, such as a single bracelet or a bracelet on each arm, one finger-ring or four on one hand, or one anklet or pair of ear-rings. It is quite unusual for a set of jewellery to be worn, such as in a burial in Colchester where a woman wore four bracelets, three finger-rings and a bead necklace (Philpott 1991: table A30), although there may be some regional bias in the practice. Philpott (1991: table 31) has calculated that where jewellery was worn, 84 per cent wore solely one category of ornament and only 16 per cent wore more than one type. When combinations occur, the most common choice was a bead necklace and bracelets.

A major drawback to the study of this grave material is the variable nature of the surviving evidence. Many of the graves were excavated many years ago, when the level of site recording was poor, and there is now little or no information about the location of the jewellery in the grave or the order of individual beads. For example, a grave from Walmgate, York, excavated in 1892, contained over 600 small coral beads, nearly 300 blue glass beads, 92 jet beads, approximately 80 freshwater pearls, 16 amber beads and 8 of green glass. There was also a jet pendant with its associated jet necklace, 14 jet bracelet beads and 4 jet hairpins (Allason-Jones 1996: figure 15). As currently displayed, the loose beads have been separated out by colour to make three necklaces of very different lengths, a bracelet of pearls and amber beads and a ring or loop of green beads. Due to the lack of information from the original excavation, it is impossible to say whether this is correct or not. This rethreading in neat, symmetrical order appeals very much to modern tastes, but may not have appealed so much to the Roman, as much more random threading seems to have been common. The grave at South Shields (Croom 1994: figure 7) produced a short necklace or bracelet of 100 beads, out of which the correct positioning of 71 of the beads could be recovered. These were threaded in no apparent order (3 blue, 3 yellow, 19 blue, 1 yellow, 11 blue, 1 yellow, 7 blue, 1 large green, 8 blue, 1 yellow, 16 blue), and two necklaces from a grave at Winchester show a similar random mix of bead shape, size and colour (Guido 1979: plate Ia). Even the beads on a wire necklace from Poundbury have a random mixture of four bead types, although a more symmetrical arrangement would easily have been possible (Guido and Mills 1993: figure 72, no. 5).

The information from more recent excavations can sometimes be no better than those of a hundred years ago, with the publication reports of necklaces in graves frequently concentrating on the colour and shape of individual beads without considering the necklace as a whole. Too often the exact location of the necklace in the grave, the order of the beads or even the length of the complete necklace are not recorded.

The most recent comprehensive study of Romano-British jewellery has been that of C. Johns (1996a). As well as considering materials, manufacture and symbolism, she has looked at each of the different categories in turn and considered how fashions changed over time. Although she considers the surviving gold and silver jewellery from this country, she also studies the more humble and everyday items made from cheaper materials. Looking at the jewellery only from this province has thrown up some interesting contrasts with jewellery elsewhere; there are some types, found in other north-western provinces which do not appear in this country, including necklaces with semi-precious stones set in box fittings. This may simply be because by chance no example has yet been turned up, or it may be because these are types rare or absent from the province. She has also noted a number of items of jewellery that are uniquely Romano-British. One of these is the dragonesque brooch, which is an S-shaped brooch with an animal head on either terminal with cast or enamel decoration on the body (figure 15.1a). It is often seen as being very Celtic in feel, although there are no known pre-Roman examples, and is in fact an interesting example of local fashion being absorbed into the mainstream.

Another form of jewellery not found on the Continent is the glass bangle, studied most recently by J. Price (figure 15.1h). Although common in pre-Roman Europe, they were not made in Britain until the Roman period, and the concept seems to have been brought over by the Roman military and adopted with enthusiasm. The bracelets were made from the early first century into the second, but some time during the second century they fell out of fashion. They were seamless bangles which were either plain or had decorative cords, trails and spots in contrasting colours on their outer surfaces. The most common colours were blue-green and opaque white, but examples are known in yellow-brown, dark blue and dark green. The cords were made of twisted glass, such as blue and white, yellow-brown and white, and sometimes even three colours such as blue, red and yellow (Price 1988: 341).

Jet

A third distinctive Romano-British item of jewellery is the carved jet pendant (figure 15.1b). These are flat-backed ovals carved in relief on the front with a Medusa head, family portraits, clasped hands or, in the case of an example from Vindolanda, a kissing couple, and it has been suggested from some of this subject-matter that they were betrothal gifts. From examples found in graves, it appears they were usually worn hanging from jet bead necklaces of incredible workmanship. They consist of small discs cut with deep notches on both faces so that they fit exactly with their neighbours to create an apparently solid and yet highly flexible rope of jet (Allason-Jones 1996: figure 15). Jet became more popular in the late Roman period, and a

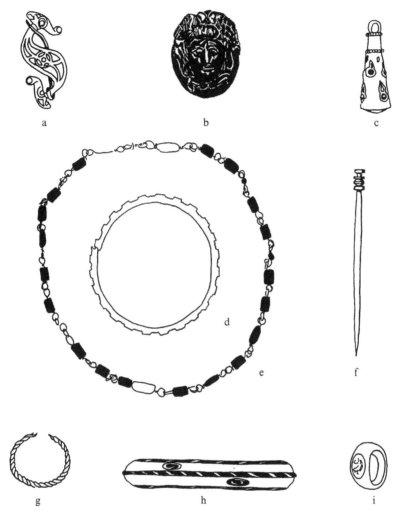

Figure 15.1   **a** Dragonesque brooch; **b** jet pendant; **c** Hercules' club pendant; **d** bracelet; **e** bead and wire necklace; **f** hairpin; **g** wire ear-ring; **h** glass bangle; **i** finger-ring with intaglio.

large number of other, simpler designs were used for necklace beads, often cut with facets or grooves to let light play on their shiny black surfaces. Bracelets were also made out of jet, either as separate beads or solid bangles. Simple rigid shale bracelets had been worn in pre-Roman times, but by the time jet examples became popular in the late third century they were made in a much wider range of decorated forms, including dot and ring motifs or carved into a mock cable pattern. Jet beads used in bracelets tend to have two holes so that the beads cannot turn easily and are therefore often flat on the back and decorated only on the front. Some are a simple long and narrow shape, but others are D-shaped with edge-cut decoration, found in a wide range of sizes, suggesting that they were worn graduating in size so that the bracelet was less bulky against the inner wrist.

Jet was used for necklaces, bracelets, hairpins, and finger-rings (often following the designs common in metal), although not, to current knowledge, for ear-rings. Jet seems in many ways to be considered a 'female' material, used also for weaving equipment such as distaffs and spindle-whorls (Allason-Jones 1996: 17). It would be of interest to consider the evidence for men wearing rings made out of such a 'female' material, although this is not as easy as it might seem; the size of finger-rings is not a reliable guide as there were fashions for both rings on upper joints of the fingers and on thumbs.

Beads

Jet beads were often used in necklaces by themselves, but are occasionally found mixed with glass beads. M. Guido's first study of glass beads (1978) has now been supplemented by a study of those of the later period (1999), which often discusses the development of the bead type during the Roman period. She has shown that some bead types continued on from the Iron Age, others were introduced by the Romans and, in the late period, unusual types were brought in from nations outside the Roman Empire. Blue and green were by far the most common colours, but beads of most other colours are also known in smaller numbers. Work on complete bead necklaces or bracelets relies, however, on the study of those found in graves, and there is still much to be learnt about the length of necklaces and whether this changes over time.

Beads could also be used threaded onto fine wire and then linked together to form decorated chains, a form found throughout the Roman Empire (figure 15.1e). The best were made of gold wire strung with emeralds left in their natural hexagonal shape. For those who could not afford emeralds, there were cheaper versions made with copper alloy wire and green glass beads. Few people could probably tell the difference between the emeralds and the beads, and there is at least one necklace which has a green glass bead among its emeralds.

Ear-rings

L. Allason-Jones (1989) has made a detailed study of ear-rings in Roman Britain, and although she has noted that they are simpler and generally smaller than Continental examples, she has identified eighteen probable types and shown that they are more common in Roman Britain than previously thought. There are two main styles of ear-ring, divided between those based on hoops and those based on hooks. The most common type is a penannular loop tapering to each terminal. These show a range of decoration very similar to that of bracelets, being made either out of twisted wire (with up to four separate wires, perhaps originally in varying colours), or of hoops with crenellation or edge-cut decoration (figure 15.1d, g). Another type of hoop was made of thin wire with the ends overlapped and twisted, forming an annular loop that would make a permanent or semi-permanent ear-ring. Both types of hoop could be hung with beads or pendants, such as the Hercules' club (a stylized conical wooden club with the knots represented by raised or enamelled ovals, also found as pendants for chain necklaces: figure 15.1c).

The other form of ear-ring has a hook attachment, keeping the decorative element closer to the ear-lobe. Simple wire examples had the visible end twisted into a spiral or attached to a coloured bead, while more complex ones had one or two hollow bosses, or embossed rosettes. The great majority of ear-rings were made out of copper alloy, but there is one third-century type that seems to have been made only out of gold. It consists of a box setting for a glass or semi-precious stone surrounded by a decorative flange, and sometimes with hanging pendants.

Hairpins

A more functional item of personal adornment was the hairpin (figure 15.1f). In the Mediterranean region Roman women always wore their long hair pinned up, and the resulting hairstyles were an important element of display for them. After the invasion of Britain, women throughout the country quickly adopted the fashion, and the thick, straight pins used to hold the hair in place are one of the most common site finds in Britain. A simple, twisted bun can be held up with a single pin, but it is likely that more were commonly used for added security; a bun of preserved hair from York still has two matching pins in place and a skull with hair from Egypt has four mismatched pins (Allason-Jones 1996: figure 17).

The number of pins required probably changed over time, according to the nature of the hairstyles currently in fashion. A recent study (Cool 2000b: 48) has shown that there is a noticeable drop in the number of pins found on late fourth-century sites, which could reflect a fashion for much simpler hairstyles in this period, perhaps because Christian women were supposed to cover their hair and there was no longer an opportunity to show off fashionable hairstyles.

Hairpins were made from a variety of materials, the most commonly surviving type being bone or antler. They could also be made from copper alloy and, less commonly, iron, jet and even glass. Until the late second century, the most common forms of bone pins had heads no wider than the shank. By the mid-third century, however, the predominant forms had larger heads in a wide range of designs, including spherical, flame-shaped, flat-topped, bead-and-collar and faceted cubes (Greep 1995: 1113). Outside this range of very common designs, there was a wide range of much rarer and less typical designs, some of which could be very elaborate. Copper alloy pins have a different range of designs and are often longer than the bone pins, perhaps relating in some way to a different purpose or use. Other pins were composite, such as bone pins with jet heads, iron pins with glass bead heads and copper alloy pins with glass insets in the head.

Brooches

The brooch is one of the most studied of Roman personal ornament, mainly because there are quite distinct forms with regional and chronological variations that can be identified and classified. With the establishment of this basic framework, more work is now perhaps needed in identifying the function of brooches. In the ancient world the brooch was used to hold clothes together (it was therefore not the purely decorative item that the modern brooch is) and as such would be worn by both men and women. Among the wide range of designs which came into and drifted out of fashion it is almost certain that there were types which were worn exclusively by either men or women. Even in modern times men's and women's jewellery tends to have different styles, and in a society where the sexes were more strictly separated this is even more likely to have been the case. As has been seen above, in the first and second centuries, female costume required a brooch on each shoulder to hold it together. Sometimes chains or strings of beads were hung between the brooches and a number of brooches (not always matched pairs) still connected by chains to loops on their bases have been found. These linked brooches clearly belong to women, and it is likely that most brooches with a loop on the base were also worn in this way and are therefore also female. This style of fashion, and therefore also this kind of brooch, died out in the late second century.

In the first and second century it is possible that women used a third brooch to fasten their mantles, either on their shoulder or centrally on their chest, but when women adopted the new form of dress, the tunic did not need brooches and the mantle is always depicted as being unfastened. Therefore, by the third century the majority of brooches recovered from sites are likely to belong to men (particularly soldiers), who had always used a brooch to fasten their cloaks. The brooch was almost exclusively worn on the right shoulder to leave the right arm unencumbered by folds of cloth. In the fourth century elaborate crossbow brooches seem to have become a symbol of rank for men, therefore brooches do not seem to have been as common as in previous centuries (with the implication that most men were presumably wearing items such as capes that did not need brooches).

On the whole, brooches in Britain were quite delicate, with an overall length rarely over 7 centimetres (and often much smaller) until the late period and the development of the ostentatious crossbow brooches. Some of the smallest brooches surviving, some with pin lengths of only 1 centimetre, are the type now called plate brooches. These are one category of brooch that may have had a purely decorative purpose, since some are so small they would seem to be awkward to use holding two layers of cloth together, although an alternative interpretation is that they had been especially designed to fasten delicate or very fine cloth. These brooches, often highly decorated, frequently took the shape of animals and objects, with images such as a man on horseback, a cockerel, a hare, a shoe and an axe (Hattatt 2000: figures 217–22). These may have had some religious significance, or they may have merely appealed to the whimsical nature of the wearer, but for whatever reason, the fashion for them died out during the third century.

Brooches should always be considered as part of the costume they were integral to, but items of less functional personal ornament may also say something about the clothing worn. For example, occasionally anklets have been found, including examples worn in graves. They were never as popular as bracelets, and the length of women's gowns meant that they would not often be very visible. Future study could perhaps indicate whether they were fashionable at one particular time when gowns were worn short, or by women from cultures with a different style of costume, or if they were popular with women such as female entertainers, who revealed more of their body than usual. Armlets worn on the upper arm (when most costume seem to have at least elbow-length sleeves), toe-rings and the leg-ring worn by a man in Dorchester also all need to be considered in greater detail.

Finger-rings

Rings were another item of jewellery that could be worn by both men and women. Rings were made of every material available, from gold to iron, and ranged in design from the very simple to florid over-elaboration, with the implication that they were available to all levels of society. Some were cast plain hoops, while others were made of wire twisted into a spiral or knot at the front. Others were set with single stones, while the most ornate had multiple settings, gold coins, filigree or open-work designs. The most characteristic Romano-British ring has a hoop that is narrow at the back, wide at the front and with an intaglio or other stone set flush within the width of the hoop (figure 15.1i). Oval intaglios are almost always set with their long axis along the length of the ring rather than at right angles, and it is more usually circular, plain stones or pastes that are set on narrow hoops so that they extend on either side as in the modern fashion. From the third century, the design of rings altered so that the front of the ring grew flatter and there was a more distinct shoulder between front and hoop, creating a new area on the ring to be exploited for the elaboration fashionable in this period.

Intaglios are usually made from a semi-precious stone, cut into an oval and engraved with a small image, although cheaper versions could be made of glass. It has been recognized that, although they were originally intended to be used as personal seals for sealing letters or goods for protection or verification, they came to have both amuletic and decorative purposes as well. In the first and second centuries the stones used were often translucent ones such as carnelian and amethyst, which sometimes meant the image was difficult or impossible to see until impressed in wax. In the third century the fashion was for opaque stone, such as red jasper, where the image was clearly visible on the ring (Henig 1978: 31).

The range of images used was very large, including religious figures such as Mars, Venus, Bacchus, Bonus Eventus, Fortuna and guardian spirits, images of (often rural) life such as hunters and herdsmen and their animals, monsters and mythical creatures such as griffins and sea-centaurs, individual animals such as lions, horses, birds, and even shrimps, an ant and a roast fowl. The reasoning behind the choice of image may reflect the owner's wish to have a gem with amuletic properties, so that soldiers in particular seemed to like Mars, Fortuna and Victory, or one that reflects their interests, such as hunting scenes or theatre masks, or has some other significance to their own lives that is now unknown to us. Some, of course, may have been chosen for no other reason than that the buyer liked the image. It is not even clear how much choice a buyer actually had, but it is likely that the rich or those who were willing to pay more could commission a design, while the majority of people had to make a choice from what was made available to them. For those without much money to waste, the cheapest versions of intaglios were made out of moulded glass in light blue-green or blue, and usually had an extremely simple stick figure for an image that is sometimes little more than an abstract shape.

The find of a jeweller's hoard from Snettisham has thrown some interesting light on jewellers' workshops. The hoard was stored in a pottery jar and consisted of coins, intaglios, silver jewellery, an unfinished gold ring, silver ingots, scraps of silver and gold, a burnisher and a seal box. It is of great interest in that some items were brand new, some were unfinished, some showed wear and some were in need of repair.

There were 110 loose intaglios and 17 set in silver rings, and while there was a range of designs, the majority were of the same four: 25 per cent depicted Bonus Eventus, 20 per cent Ceres, 13 per cent Fortuna and 12 per cent a parrot. There has been a suggestion that the untypical range of intaglio devices may have some significance. H. Cool (2000a: 37) has recently studied snake-headed jewellery in hoards and has raised the possibility that the high number of this otherwise rare ring type, and the unusual choice of intaglio designs, might suggest that the jeweller had some connection with a religious cult and was making items to suit the tastes of his chosen market.

Religious Offerings

Cool's work on snake jewellery is part of a recent interest in looking at hoards of jewellery and the use of jewellery in religious contexts. Johns' (1996b) work on treasure hoards has shown that jewellery can be found in safe-keeping or storage hoards, or as temple wealth. Elsewhere in the Empire it is known that items of jewellery were often included in dowry agreements, where they were intended to act as a financial reserve in the marriage while remaining the property of the woman, and were often described purely in terms of their weight in metal. It has been suggested that women may have held much of their personal wealth in the form of jewellery and that where treasure hoards contain coin, plate and jewellery, it is likely that they represent the wealth of the whole family (Johns 1996b: 3). Jewellery was also considered to be a high-value gift, suitable for offerings, and may therefore also be found in temple deposits (Johns 1996b: 14).

Cheaper items of jewellery such as brooches, rings and bracelets also seem to have been used as gifts for temples or shrines, as a number of such sites have large numbers of jewellery items. In most cases these are copper alloy items such as brooches, finger-rings and bracelets. At Uley, brooches were more common in the earlier period (when brooches were in fashion) while bracelets were more common in the fourth century. Discussions of the reasons for the offering of jewellery at sites where weapons and tools were also seen as suitable offerings have suggested a number of cults in parallel; and it has been suggested that the jewellery offerings reflect a cult of fecundity and healing (Woodward and Leach 1993: 334).

Amulets

As their world seemed a dangerous and unpredictable place, Romans sometimes resorted to magic in the shape of amulets; these could be used to improve performance, cure illnesses or give protection in an uncertain world. Made as copper alloy or bone pendants, one of the most common designs was the phallic symbol, probably intended to bring good luck to the wearer. Another was the fig hand, where the tip of the thumb is visible between clenched fingers, which was a protective gesture against the evil eye; amulets combining both elements are known. Cow and dog teeth, still with the complete root and drilled through for suspension, were also used as charms. Although literary evidence gives some uses for a dog-tooth amulet, there is no surviving evidence for the purpose of the cows' teeth. There are other items that were probably also charms, such as bells on bracelets and pierced coins, whose function is also now lost, and there were probably many other, fully organic, charms that have also not survived.

Cosmetics

Something else that has not survived in archaeological terms are cosmetics. At least some women in Roman Britain would have worn make-up, but only objects identified as cosmetics grinders and implements for mixing and applying cosmetics survive to hint at the practice and it is unclear how widespread it was. Hair oil was also used by both men and women elsewhere in the Empire, but again it is difficult to recover the evidence of it archaeologically in this country. However, rare examples of preserved hair in graves at Poundbury were covered in oil (Farwell and Molleson 1993: 205), showing that the fashion was known in this province, but again there is not enough evidence to say how widespread it was. Its use may have been restricted to a short period of time when it was ultra-fashionable, or to certain types of community such as urban sites, or even to a small section of the population, such as those with a Mediterranean background; or it may have been absolutely universal. As with so much about personal ornaments, there is still much to learn.

FURTHER READING

The Jewellery of Roman Britain, by C. Johns (1996), is the most recent and comprehensive study of this topic, with an excellent bibliography for more detailed research. For individual categories of jewellery there are a number of different works; *Roman Jet in the Yorkshire Museum*, by L. Allason-Jones (1996) gives a good overview of jet in Roman Britain and includes some fine photographs of mixed grave goods from York, while *The Glass Beads of the Prehistoric and Roman periods in Britain and Ireland* and *The Glass Beads of Anglo-Saxon England c. AD 400–700*, by M. Guido (1978, 1999) provide information on all the glass bead types known, although they do not discuss necklace assemblages. *A Corpus of Roman Engraved Gemstones from British Sites*, by M. Henig (1978) explains the use, designs and symbolism of intaglios and provides a catalogue of all known examples at the time of writing. *A Visual Catalogue of Richard Hattatt's Ancient Brooches* (2000) includes the illustrations from all his books on ancient brooches. *Treasures and Trinkets*, by T. Murdoch (1991) has a good range of Roman jewellery from Roman London, while *Burial Practices in Roman Britain: A Survey of Grave Treatment and Furnishing AD 43–410*, by R. Philpott (1991) includes a large section on jewellery as grave goods.

REFERENCES

Allason-Jones, L. 1989. *Ear-rings in Roman Britain*. BAR (British Series) 144. Oxford.
—— 1996. *Roman Jet in the Yorkshire Museum*. York.
Cool, H. E. M. 2000a. The significance of snake jewellery hoards. *Britannia*, 31, 29–40.
—— 2000b. The parts left over: material culture into the fifth century. In T. Wilmott and P. Wilson (eds), *The Late Roman Transition in the North*. BAR (British Series). Oxford, 47–66.
Croom, A. T. 1994. Small finds. In M. E. Snape, An excavation in the Roman cemetery at South Shields. *Archaeologia Aeliana*, 5th ser. 22, 43–66.

Farwell, D. E. and Molleson, T. I. 1993. *Poundbury*. Volume 2. *The Cemeteries*. Dorchester.

Greep, S. 1995. The worked bone, antler and ivory. In K. Blockley, M. Blockley, P. Blockley, S. S. Frere and S. Stow, *Excavations in the Marlowe Car-park and Surrounding Areas*. Part II. *The Finds*, 1112–70.

Guido, M. 1978. *The Glass Beads of the Prehistoric and Roman Periods in Britain and Ireland*. London.

—— 1979. Glass beads and catalogue. In G. Clarke, *Pre-Roman and Roman Winchester*. Part II: *The Roman Cemetery at Lankhills*. Oxford, 292–300.

—— 1999. *The Glass Beads of Anglo-Saxon England c. AD 400–700*. Woodbridge.

Guido, M. and Mills, J. M. 1993. Beads (jet, glass, crystal and coral). In D. E. Farwell and T. I. Molleson, *Poundbury*. Volume 2. *The Cemeteries*. Dorchester, 100–2.

Hattatt, R. 2000. *A Visual Catalogue of Richard Hattatt's Ancient Brooches*. Oxford.

Henig. M. 1978. *A Corpus of Roman Engraved Gemstones from British Sites*. BAR (British Series) 8. Oxford.

Johns, C. 1996a. *The Jewellery of Roman Britain*. London.

—— 1996b. The classification and interpretation of Romano-British treasures. *Britannia*, 27, 1–16.

Murdoch, T. 1991. *Treasures and Trinkets*. London.

Philpott, R. 1991. *Burial Practices in Roman Britain: A Survey of Grave Treatment and Furnishing AD 43–410*. BAR (British Series) 219. Oxford.

Price, J. 1988. Romano-British glass bangles from eastern Yorkshire. In J. Price and P. R. Wilson (eds), *Recent Research in Roman Yorkshire*. BAR (British Series) 193. Oxford, 339–66.

Woodward, A. and Leach, P. 1993. *The Uley Shrines: Excavation of a Ritual Complex on West Hill, Uley, Gloucestershire: 1977–9*. London.

Chapter Sixteen

Textiles and Dress

John Peter Wild

The clothing and textiles of Roman Britain, not surprisingly, reflect the province's climate and physical environment. The clothing needs of the individual, however, could be adequately met by exploitation of the fibre resources, animal and plant, which were immediately to hand. Sheep's wool was the principal fibre of Britain, followed by flax and, to a lesser extent, hemp and animal hair (Wild 1970: 4–21, 2002). The processes of conversion – fibre preparation, spinning and weaving – had reached a high level of sophistication long before the Roman invasion. There is no space to discuss them here, but it is important to emphasize one point: the concept of a bolt of cloth cut and tailored into garments was alien to the western world in antiquity. The weaver (and often the spinner) set to work with a specific garment in mind and it came from the loom in a recognizable form (Granger-Taylor 1982). In principle therefore, the study of clothing or furnishing textiles and the methodology of their production should be a single field of enquiry: in practice, however, the disparate nature of the scattered sources of evidence makes this a difficult exercise.

Knowledge of the clothing of Roman Britain rests on three sources: funerary art, written documents and preserved textiles (Wild 1968, 1985). Each has its limitations, but the most serious obstacle is the difficulty of combining them into a rounded picture. A garment depicted on a tombstone can rarely be assigned a name drawn from the documents, and neither can yet be recognized in the corpus of fragmentary textiles from archaeological sites. Some progress is being made, however, and the following account can be offered, with all due caution.

Male Costume

The everyday garb of the civilian in Britain consisted of a wide-fitting tunic (the 'Gallic coat'), topped by a voluminous, sleeveless, hooded cape (Wild 1968: 168–80, 1985: 369–76). According to season he wore a scarf, and perhaps a second tunic, usually invisible beneath the coat. This attire – or significant elements of it – is depicted on at least five tombstones from northern Britain (figure 16.1) and countless funerary monuments in Gaul and the German provinces (Roche-Bernard 1992).

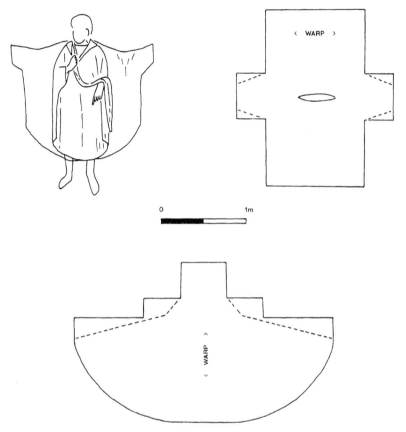

Figure 16.1   The 'Gallic coat': above left, the coat as worn; above right, the Reepsholt coat in the form in which it was woven; below, outline of a late Roman cape from Egypt.

The Gallic coat was a wide, loose-fitting tunic, worn without a belt and falling in deep folds from the arms and elbows (figure 16.1). It had wide sleeves (but sometimes none) and reached to just below the knee. A surviving example, the wool coat from Reepsholt in north Germany (figure 16.1), demonstrates its proportions: length at front and back 97 centimetres, body width 1.15 metres and overall width including sleeves 1.82 metres (Wild 1968: 169, 1985: 370). The Reepsholt coat was woven in 2 by 2 twill to a cruciform plan on a warp-weighted loom, the weaver beginning at the cuff of one sleeve and ending at the cuff of the other. The sleeves and sides of the body could be secured by sewing or, as a relief at Neumagen in Germany suggests, by lacing at intervals.

None of the representations in Gaul or Britain indicates any form of decoration, apart from fringes occasionally at the lower hem or ends of sleeves. In that respect the coat differed from the tunic of metropolitan Italy with its two vertical tapestry-woven *clavi* (stripes) down front and back.

The Gallic evidence shows that the coat was worn by men at all levels in provincial society from at least the Claudian period until the late fourth century (Roche-Bernard 1992; Böhme-Schönberger 1997). Social distinctions were probably marked by subtle differences in fabric quality and garment finish, which are not conveyed by the relief sculpture. Its Latin name is unknown and so it cannot be recognized in Roman written sources. It may share a common ancestor with the Italian tunic, but its prehistory is obscure; classical writers repeatedly describe the tight-fitting shirt and trousers of the Gallic warrior class, but not the attire of the peasant, which arguably became the attire of the Romano-Briton.

In inclement weather a cape was worn over the coat. In shape it was a semicircle, at least two metres in diameter, with an integral hood projecting from the centre. As worn, the two halves of the straight edge were stitched or laced together, sometimes leaving a slit open at the bottom. (On Philus' tombstone at Cirencester the end of a belt appears to project through the slit (Wild 1968: 178 figure 9).) A jet figurine, also from Cirencester, shows that the hood, which normally lay flat on the back between the shoulders, was laced across the top (Wild 1968: 177, 1985: 374). On the tombstone of the York legionary veteran C. Aeresius Saenus and his family both Saenus and his young son Saenius Augustinus wear capes pulled aside to reveal their coats beneath.

The Gallic cape was probably referred to as a *caracalla*, a garment that was regularly the target of clothing thieves in the baths at Bath. A similar cape, the *birrus*, was an important British export from at least the third century (Wild 2002: 1). Its particular form may be reflected in a complete surviving semicircular cape with integral hood from an unknown site in Egypt (Granger-Taylor 1982).

The material of the coat and cape was almost certainly wool. Given the popularity of 2/2 diamond twill in Britain, this was probably the standard weave for both garments, although the twill textiles from Vindolanda reveal a wide spectrum of fabric weights and qualities (Wild 2002: 14–18). What role – if any – linen played in everyday clothing is uncertain. A few Gallic reliefs still bear traces of yellow paint

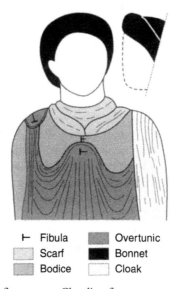

⊢ Fibula   ▨ Overtunic
▢ Scarf   ■ Bonnet
▨ Bodice   ▢ Cloak

Figure 16.2 Drawing of a figure on a Claudian funerary monument from Ingelheim in the Rhineland showing the costume with fibulae worn by women in early Roman Britain.

on coats and capes, possibly representing the colour of undyed wool; but, given the polychromy of earlier Gaulish costume, clothing dyed in bright colours, certainly red and blue, was probably common.

Practical clothing for the working environment is also attested in Roman Britain, such as the characteristic folded loincloth of the gladiator (Wild 1968: 185–7, 1985: 379–83). The ploughman in a well-known bronze figurine from Piercebridge is shown in a weather-proof, shoulder-length, hooded cape (*cucullus*) (which a near-parallel from Trier, Germany, suggests was of leather (Wild 1985: plate V, 15)), a short sleeveless coat and leggings. From an urban context the list of clothing stolen in Bath includes mittens (*manicilia*), a head-band (*capitularis*), two shirts of uncertain shape ((*vestes*) *paxsae*), two bath-robes (*balneares*) and a cloak (*sagum*; Wild 2002: 26).

Traditional Roman dress made little headway in Britain (Wild 1968: 188–92, 1985: 383–5). The toga, the most celebrated garment, was essentially a sub-rectangle of white wool cloth (Wilson 1924; Goette 1989; Sebaste and Bonfante 1994: 13–45; Croom 2000). Over the centuries its shape was adapted to the modes of draping which changing fashion dictated. Tacitus comments (*Agricola*, 21) with pardonable exaggeration that the *toga* became *frequens* in Britain under the Flavians; but the indications from Gaul and Italy are that it was regarded more as a status symbol of Roman citizenship than practical clothing. It was probably donned on official occasions by urban magistrates and resident imperial administrators: sculptors were sometimes unsure how to represent it on the tombstones of Roman citizens who may in fact never have worn it.

A more successful introduction, military uniform, was confined to the forces of occupation (Fuentes 1987; Sumner 2002). The legionary, as seen for instance on the stele of Favonius Facilis at Colchester, wore a wide-fitting sleeveless tunic reaching to the knee and contained at the waist with a belt. It is not clear whether the tunic had *clavi*, and its colour is in dispute. On campaign a rectangular cloak, the *sagum*, was worn over it, secured on the right shoulder with a fibula. (The fibula's pin pointed upwards, its head downwards, *not* as it is conventionally drawn in excavation reports.) The *sagum* might also serve as a blanket. Undress uniform included a hooded cape, the *paenula*, which differed in some respects from the local styles of cape. How often the legionary wore short trousers (*braca*) of leather or cloth is uncertain. He might wear a scarf.

The clothing of auxiliary troops, like their weapons and armour, was as diverse as their origins, and it is difficult to generalize (Sumner 2002). The evidence suggests that many preferred to wear a long-sleeved shirt with a closer fit, which in the western provinces was probably derived from the shirt of the Gaulish and Germanic warriors. It was of wool, but probably not woven as a one-piece garment. Such a shirt is shown regularly on the funerary stelae of the second and third centuries, by which time legionaries appear to have adopted it too.

Two classes of find from the pre-Hadrianic levels at the Stanegate fort of Vindolanda have cast an entirely new light on soldiers' clothing in Britain: textile fragments and written documents on leaf-tablets (Wild 2002: 14–18, 25–6). The original function of only a few of the textiles, however, can be established. They include remains of a light-weight rectangular cloak with a 'purple' tapestry-woven gamma motif in each corner (belonging to the commandant's household and later recycled), lengths of wool band for leg-bindings, a sock cobbled together from twill cloth, and a curious cap plaited from hair-moss with a projecting fringe. The documents record *inter alia* lists of clothing supplied to the garrison. In addition to the predictable *tunicae, saga* and *paenulae* there are items such as a *stica* (long-sleeved shirt), *udones* (leggings), a *sudarium* (neckerchief), a *capitulare* (head-band) and two sorts of loincloth (*subligar, lumbare*). Officers provided themselves with an impressive array of formal dress for dining that would not have shamed a dinner-party in Rome.

Compared to the rapidly changing fashions in hairstyles, shoe patterns (van Driel-Murray 2001) and fibula morphology, clothing fashion moved slowly. At the beginning of the third century, however, new trends can be discerned that reflect rising metropolitan interest in the sensible clothing of the Celtic-speaking West (*birrus, caracalla*) and the flamboyant costume of Syria and Iran (Wild 1968: 234, 1985: 413). Both site finds and contemporary art show that the élite, even in Britain, had access to exotic fabrics such as silk damask (woven in Syria from imported Chinese silk yarn) and were not embarrassed to wear garments decorated with bright, figured, tapestry-woven roundels and *clavi*.

The trend is exemplified in two expensive garments, a *dalmatica* and a *chlamys*, each made at a leading textile centre, which were presented in AD 220 to a retiring member of staff by Claudius Paulinus, governor of Lower Britain (Wild 1968: 222, 225–6). The dalmatic was not unlike the Gallic coat, wide-bodied and wide-sleeved, but with prominent *clavi* and, in later years, other forms of decoration. How often it was to be seen in Britain is a moot point. The *chlamys* was a large and heavy half-moon cloak, pinned on the right shoulder with a crossbow brooch. Once the preserve of high-ranking officers, it was often worn (to the emperor's displeasure) by upper-class Romans to underline their fashionable military pretensions. It is figured on jet medallions from York.

In later Roman art the *chlamys* is associated with elaborate forms of the long-sleeved shirt, sporting various types of *clavus*, shoulder panels, knee-level panels and wrist bands. At first glance this is what the *orantes* in the wall-painting of the Christian chapel at Lullingstone appear to be wearing; but in fact their shirts have a single wide pearl-edged band set centrally in the Partho-Persian manner (Wild 1968: 193, 1985: 387). They are more likely to be figures from the Bible than Lullingstone residents.

The heavy-duty so-called 'chip-carved' copper-alloy belt fittings widely distributed across lowland Britain in the fourth century were once attributed to Germanic elements in the Roman army. That they were primarily military may be broadly correct; but in the light of their distribution they may also be seen as another manifestation of the aristocratic vogue for military attire, worn with a long-sleeved shirt and *chlamys* (Swift 2000). Most Romano-Britons, however, probably continued to wear the coat and cape.

Female Costume

A tombstone from Murrell Hill, Carlisle (figure 16.3) depicts most of the elements of everyday female costume in Roman Britain (Wild 1968: 194–9, 1985: 388–92). The deceased (with fan) is shown in a full-fitting, loose-sleeved, Gallic coat, a cloak draped about her shoulders and with an undergarment visible only at her ankles.

Figure 16.3 The tombstone of a lady with a fan and her son from the Roman cemetery at Murrell Hill, Carlisle (Photo: Otto Fein).

There are at least ten representations of the coat on adult females in Britain, all from the military zone. Taken with the evidence from Gaul, it is apparent that the coat worn by women differed only in length (it reached the ankles) from that of men. The point is neatly illustrated by another exceptional find, a well-preserved coat from a second-century female grave at Les Martres-de-Veyre near Clermont-Ferrand in central Gaul (Roche-Bernard 1992: 11–13, 153). From neck to lower hem the coat measures 1.25 metres, but 1.70 metres from cuff to cuff. It would probably reach the ankles (there is a tuck around the waist), but it is *very* loose-fitting. The sleeves were attached separately to the garment body, but all three components were of the same wool half-basket weave with reinforced selvedges and corded starting/finishing border.

In Britain the relevant tombstones all date to the second and third centuries AD; but no representation of a woman in a coat belonging to the first century can be cited from any of the north-west provinces. The reason may be the conservative outlook of at least the first two or three generations of provincial women, who retained their traditional Iron-Age dress with multiple fibulae (see below; Böhme 1985; Garbsch 1985; Wild 1985: 393–9). Indeed, the origin of the coat worn by women is debatable: it may simply have been borrowed, with modification, from the male clothes-chest, supposing that the contemporary conventions of gender differentiation permitted that. The dalmatic certainly had both a male and a female version.

There is no evidence that women wore a hooded cape like the *caracalla* mentioned above. Rather, they preferred a large rectangular cloak, a simple textile that would have been made in a variety of styles appropriate to the season and social standing of the owner. It was not pinned with a fibula, but draped around the shoulders in various modes. The commonest (see figures 16.2 and 16.3) is for the corners of the cloak to be either flung over the shoulders from the front or concealed under folds that swathed the upper part of the chest and throat.

The undergarment worn by the Murrell Hill figure (figure 16.3) has already been mentioned (Phillips 1976). Another largely unseen item may have been stockings: the grave at Les Martres-de-Veyre contained a pair of knee-length wool stockings made from pieces of cloth sewn together. Some Gallic women wore a close-fitting bonnet, but there is no sign of it in Britain: an old-fashioned accessory, it impeded display of the latest hairstyle.

What may be a variant of the coat appears occasionally in the art of Gaul and Britain (Wild 1985: 399–401). It has long sleeves – longer than those of the standard coat – but a less full body, which is girt. Servant girls in scenes of funerary banqueting in Gaul are dressed in it; but it also features on the stelae of independent ladies. Julia Brica at York conceals most of her tunic under a cloak, but both the girdle and a flounce or tuck can be seen: most of the tunic on the infant Vacia at Carlisle is visible, and it is identical. How this type of tunic relates to the coat is not obvious.

A merchant travelling up the Danube and down the Rhine to Britain shortly after the Claudian conquest would have noticed throughout his journey how tenaciously local womenfolk clung to bygone modes of dress. A standard ensemble (long-sleeved bodice, *peplos*-like over-tunic and cloak) was common to all; but they expressed visually their precise ethnic and tribal affiliations through specific regional types of fibula and styles of headdress (Garbsch 1965, 1985). The disadvantage of the later Gallic ensemble was that it obscured such distinctions.

The sources on which knowledge of this essentially Iron Age costume rests, early Roman funerary monuments and contemporary grave finds of metal dress accessories, are very thin on the ground in Britain, and it is consequently difficult to estimate the degree of dress conservatism in the province (Wild 1968: 199–208). The Claudian tombstones of the Rhineland, however, enable us to characterize the costume itself (figure 16.2).

Next to the skin the British woman wore a tight-fitting bodice (of wool?) with long narrow sleeves that ended in cuffs which were folded back (Wild 1985: 393–9, plate XI).

The sculptors showed quite explicitly a vertical slit down the front of the garment, closed by fibulae: presumably the division made it easier to put the bodice on and off.

Over the bodice came a loose tubular over-tunic, supported and secured by a pair of matching fibulae, one on each shoulder. Additionally, the tunic's upper edge was often pinned to the underlying bodice by a third fibula, set horizontally. The outfit was topped by a rectangular cloak which might be fastened on the right shoulder with yet another fibula.

The inventories of first-century graves in north Gaul and the Rhineland indicate how prevalent this costume was: three brooches – two matching, one non-matching – characterize the furnishing of female cremation burials, and wealthier graves contained more. Intact grave groups are comparatively rare in Britain; but fibulae with head-loops, such as the Backworth type, were designed to be worn in pairs, head down, one on each shoulder and linked by a chain or string of beads. Brooch finds suggest that this long-lived costume did not finally die out until the later second century.

Comparatively few residents of the north-west provinces dressed to the height of Italian fashion (Croom 2000). The wives of government officials and high-ranking military officers on short tours of duty in Britain probably did so (Wild 1985: 406). Having noted already the modish dinner suits owned by Flavius Cerealis, commandant at Vindolanda, it is hard to believe that his wife Sulpicia Lepidina did not bring an extensive wardrobe with her for her own social gatherings. At its most basic the matron's costume consisted of a sleeveless (or short-sleeved) tunic (*stola*) and a large rectangular cloak. The tunic was ankle-length and worn with a girdle. The cloak was draped, not pinned on the shoulder. The written sources demonstrate that far more was actually available, but as usual it is difficult to match the iconographic to the documentary evidence. Colour and fabric character, moreover, were important social markers which modern research is only just beginning to explore.

In later Roman Britain there was greater awareness of how the rest of the Empire dressed. Scraps of gold thread from purple and gold tapestry-woven panels and *clavi*, traces of cloth dyed with mollusc (Tyrian) purple and fragments of silk damask in fourth-century graves are reflections of the expensive garb which ladies of the urban upper class and their peers in the countryside were now able to afford (Wild 2002).

Children's Clothing

During the first few months of life a baby was constrained within 'swaddling bands', for supposed therapeutic reasons. Once it was on its feet, the artist depicted the child as a miniature adult (Wild 1968: 218–19). Saenius Augustinus at York wears coat and cape like his father (figure 16.3); the son of the lady with the fan at Murrell Hill (figure 16.2) is also in coat and cape; Sempronia Martina (aged 6) at York is the image of her mother Julia Brica in girded tunic and draped cloak. What sculpture does *not* show (but finds from Roman Egypt do) is that children often wore recycled garments which had already served older siblings well and were in any case made from reclaimed adult clothing, especially cloaks.

Textiles apart from Clothing

Textiles serving as household furnishings (cushions, blankets) and general utilities (sacks, sails) tend to be overlooked. There is a surprising amount of documentary evidence for them in Roman Britain, but few attributable textile remains or iconographic information (Wild 2002: 22–7). The inhabitants of the *praetorium* at Vindolanda are on record as receiving two *lodices* (blankets or coverlets), a *bedox* (a coverlet or curtain of a local type), four *tosseae* (rugs) and five coloured *vela* (curtains or hangings). The *tossea* appears again in a military context at Carlisle and may be identical with the *tapete*, a British wool rug that was an important export in the fourth century. Thieves at Bath took a *caballaris* ('horse' blanket) and a *stragulum* (bed-sheet). A Londoner is recorded as possessing a *mappa* (napkin) and *sabanum* (towel), just the kind of household linen that was regularly used to shroud the dead in the gypsum burials at York and Dorchester.

Roman furniture was not upholstered, so mattresses, bolsters, cushions and coverlets were necessary loose furnishings, as the banqueting scenes on tombstones reveal. Wall-hangings were probably not unknown: the Lullingstone *orantes* in their arcades have close parallels on preserved decorative wall-hangings from Roman Egypt – wall-painting was the cheaper medium.

The Roman Impact

Some old fashions died hard in Britain. The multifibulate female costume of Iron Age Europe was not superseded here until the second century. The man's coat and cape, which may have had a similar origin, were less obviously alien, closer to basic Roman costume, and so there was less incentive to adapt. By the third century Italy was succumbing to new, less restrained fashions in dress, and those in Britain who could afford it followed suit. The vogue for Roman-style household furnishings developed early: as a facet of interior decoration, it was in tune with the new villa culture.

FURTHER READING

The civilian clothing of Roman Britain is discussed in its European context by Wild, 'Clothing in the north-west provinces' (1968) and Wild, 'The clothing of Britannia' (1985), where the relevant evidence is examined in depth. Costume in Gaul and the Rhine and Danube provinces is reviewed by Böhme, 'Tracht und Bestattungssitten' (1985), Garbsch, 'Die norisch-pannonische Tracht' (1985) and Roche-Bernard, *Costumes et Textiles* (1992). Military costume across the Empire is covered by Sumner, *Roman Military Clothing* (2002). Croom, *Roman Clothing* (2000) and the classic works of L. M. Wilson, *The Roman Toga* (1924) and *The Clothing of the Ancient Romans* (1938), survey Italian fashions. For textile-manufacturing processes consult Wild, *Textile Manufacture* (1970), and 'The textile industries' (2002).

REFERENCES

Böhme, Astrid. 1985. Tracht und Bestattungssitten in den germanischen Provinzen und der Belgica. In H. Temporini and W. Haase (eds), *Aufstieg und Niedergang der Römischen Welt*, vol. II, 12, 3. Berlin and New York, 423–55.

Böhme-Schönberger, Astrid. 1997. *Kleidung und Schmuck in Rom und den Provinzen*. Aalen.

Croom, A. T. 2000. *Roman Clothing and Fashion*. Stroud.

Fuentes, Nicholas. 1987. The Roman military tunic. In M. Dawson (ed.), *Roman Military Equipment: Proceedings of the 3rd Roman Military Equipment Research Seminar*. BAR S336. Oxford, 41–75.

Garbsch, J. G. 1965. *Die norisch-pannonische Frauentracht im 1. und 2. Jahrhundert*. Münchner Beiträge zur Vor- und Frühgeschichte 11. Munich.

——1985. Die norisch-pannonische Tracht. In H. Temporini and W. Haase (eds), *Aufstieg und Niedergang der Römischen Welt*, vol. II, 12, 3. Berlin and New York, 546–77.

Goette, H. R. 1989. *Studien zu römischen Togadarstellungen*. Mainz.

Granger-Taylor, Hero. 1982. Weaving clothes to shape in the ancient world: the tunic and toga of the Arringatore. *Textile History*, 13, 3–25.

Hald, Margrethe. 1980. *Ancient Danish Textiles from Bogs and Burials*. Copenhagen.

Jørgensen, Lise Bender. 1992. *North European Textiles until AD 1000*. Aarhus.

Munksgaard, Elisabeth. 1974. *Oldtidsdragter*. Copenhagen.

Phillips, E. J. 1976. A workshop of Roman sculptors at Carlisle. *Britannia*, 7, 101–8.

Roche-Bernard, Geneviève. 1992. *Costumes et textiles en Gaule romaine*. Paris.

Scholz, B. I. 1992. *Untersuchungen zur Tracht der römischen Matrona*. Cologne.

Sebaste, J. L. and Bonfante, L. (eds) 1994. *The World of Roman Costume*. Madison, WI.

Sumner, Graham. 2002. *Roman Military Clothing I: 100 BC–AD 200*. Oxford.

Swift, Ellen. 2000. *Regionality in Dress Accessories in the Late Roman West*. Montagnac.

van Driel-Murray, Carol. 2001. Vindolanda and the dating of Roman footwear. *Britannia*, 32, 185–97.

Wild, J. P. 1968. Clothing in the north-west provinces of the Roman Empire. *Bonner Jahrbücher*, 168, 166–240.

——1970. *Textile Manufacture in the Northern Roman Provinces*. Cambridge.

——1985. The clothing of Britannia, Gallia Belgica and Germania Inferior. In H. Temporini and W. Haase (eds), *Aufstieg und Niedergang der Römischen Welt*, vol. II,12,3. Berlin and New York, 362–422.

——2002. The textile industries of Roman Britain. *Britannia*, 33, 1–42.

Wilson, L. M. 1924. *The Roman Toga*. Baltimore, MD.

——1938. *The Clothing of the Ancient Romans*. Baltimore, MD.

CHAPTER SEVENTEEN

Economic Structures

MICHAEL FULFORD

Any attempt to understand the economic life of Roman Britain must acknowledge at the outset the severe constraints imposed by the lack of relevant source material. While we can be reasonably certain from the range and detail of the information recorded on documents such as the Vindolanda tablets (Bowman and Thomas 1989) that there was considerable documentation of property and financial transactions, including records of taxes paid, such as those on provincial imports or exports, or of the contributions of individual *civitates*, precious little survives. A rare surviving observation, that of Appian writing in the second century (*Praefatio* [to *Roman History*] 5), implying that Britain was not yet paying its way, suggests the existence of records upon which such generalizations could be made. In reality there is a handful of surviving written sources distributed through the four centuries or so of the Roman administration, none exceeding a few lines in length; the *Agricola*, of forty-six short 'chapters', is the exception. Complementing these is a range of archaeological evidence derived from both material and biological sources. Each of these has to be considered in terms of its context and particular limitations before its potential significance can be established.

To give an example: Strabo, writing towards the end of the first century BC observes that Britain had a reputation for the export of 'corn, cattle, gold, silver, iron, hides, slaves and hounds' (*Geography*, IV.v. 2–3). The author is silent on a number of important questions: he does not tell us in what quantities these commodities were exported, nor from what regions of Britain, nor to what destinations across the Channel, nor whether this traffic had been a regular feature of relations between British societies and their Continental neighbours. From an archaeological perspective, it is difficult to take these remarks further in the current state of knowledge because almost none of these commodities can be easily traced in the archaeological record. While metals certainly survive, characterization studies have not yet advanced sufficiently for us to report reliably either British gold or British iron across the Channel. In the case of the perishables, the majority survive only in particular environmental conditions and, while future analysis of trace elements and isotope ratios in samples of grain, leather and bone might lead us towards isolating groups of material from either side of the Channel with shared characteristics, at present we cannot test Strabo's remarks further. However, as we shall see, there is reasonable certainty of a substantial cross-Channel traffic from the evidence of materials clearly imported into Britain before AD 43.

Taken from the perspective of the archaeological record, we also have problems in establishing its significance from the surviving remains. To take the example of basic but key perishable commodities, such as cereals, meat, textiles and timber, we have little hope of reconstructing past populations and their movement either within Britain or beyond. Correspondingly, with artefacts, even in such categories as pottery or stone where we can determine provenance quite precisely and adopt a quantitative approach to the study of their distribution, we do not yet have sophisticated techniques for extrapolating original populations from the sample of surviving examples.

In the light of these cautionary remarks, the study of the economic life of Roman Britain may seem a hopeless pursuit, but in reality, despite the unpromising nature of the source material, there is much that can be established and used to contribute to a number of key debates. Foremost among these is the question of the population, upon which all economic activity in the province was founded, followed by the exploitation of natural resources and the development of manufacturing activity and craft specialization. In the case of population we have no census information or any other form of numerical data, apart from the estimates associated with determining the changing size of the army in Britain. Even here, where some degree of certitude might be expected, there are critical limitations, such as our imperfect understanding of the numbers of auxiliary regiments present in any one year, and our uncertainty as to the level of strength of any unit at any time. In the case of the native population, we have no evidence to determine whether underlying conditions favoured either growth or decline. If anything, our sources would argue that conditions favoured a downward trend. Strabo alerts us to an export trade in slaves in the years between Caesar and Claudius, and it would be reasonable to assume that during the years of conquest, when taking slaves was an expected prize of war, the volume of human trafficking increased. Even if a proportion of those taken remained in Britain to assist the incomers, such as the office of the procurator in its exploitation of the mineral resources of the province, or was sold to help landowners develop their estates in the peaceful south, others would probably have left the island.

Britain was, presumably, also not entirely immune from the plagues which affected other parts of the Empire, though its insularity would have afforded it some protection. In the troubled years of the mid and late third century that degree of isolation may have made the island an attractive refuge for estate owners in Gaul and Germany. Investment on the part of incomers has been suggested as one explanation for the rise of villa estates in the west of Britain in the late third century (Branigan 1976; cf. Smith 1978). Even though written sources record organizations such as the Church and private landowners with multiple estates held in various parts of the Empire, establishing convincing archaeological evidence for a migrating or mobile aristocracy is hard to determine. It is even harder to ascertain whether such developments were accompanied by larger movements of people, such as the estate workers. The difficulty of identifying secure evidence for popular migration becomes more acute in the fourth century, with controversy surrounding the possible movement into the diocese of people from outside the empire (cf. Swift 2000). This could be in two forms:

unlawful movement across the North or Irish Sea, or the organized settlement of barbarian groups as *laeti* or *foederati*. Of the latter we have no evidence before the end of the fourth century, but of the former we can cite, for example, the listing in the late fourth- or early fifth-century document, the *Notitia Dignitatum*, of certain coastal garrisons and forts in east and south-east Britain as under the command of a *comes litoris Saxonici*. This has been taken by some to indicate settlement by Saxons of the regions thus defended (for a review of the debate, see Pearson 2002: 125–38).

In trying to establish both absolute numbers of population and relative change through time, reliance has come to be placed on the interpretation of settlement evidence, particularly that derived from a combination of excavated data and surface survey (Millett 1990: 181–6). The latter is dependent on the presence of datable material such as pottery, a constraint which limits its effectiveness to those regions, mostly in 'lowland Britain', where pottery was widely circulated and consumed. Without systematic sampling by excavation to recover evidence for independent scientific dating, the situation in the south-west, the north of Britain, and in much of Wales – regions where there was little circulation of Roman material culture – remains very difficult to determine. Thus the archaeological basis for estimating numbers and changes in the rural population is probably limited to about half of the area of the early Roman province or the late Roman diocese. In this context we might hope to obtain figures for the number and extent of settlements occupied at any one period, but, because so much pottery and other finds have long chronologies, the date of a period is likely to range between half a century and a century and a half. In turning to the individual settlement, estimating the numbers of inhabitants – and change through time – is fraught with problems. This is obviously also an issue for urban and other nucleated settlements where parallels from the medieval period have been sought (Frere 1987: 256–7). In the case of walled towns, it would seem that, if the enclosed area is a secure indicator of population numbers, after rapid growth in the first and second centuries, at the end of which most were defended, numbers might have been fairly static between the second and the fourth century. This is based on the observation that, almost without exception, the course of late third-century town walls tends to follow that of the earlier earthen defences of the late second century. Where good evidence survives for the expansion or shrinkage of the extramural suburbs or *vici*, it is possible to elaborate the hypothesis based on defended area.

The same broad generalization probably applies to the countryside as well, with the greatest density of settlement – in 'lowland' Britain at least – reached between the early second century and the mid-fourth century AD. Even in areas where there has been an intensive survey, such as the East Anglian Fenland, there is a reluctance to differentiate trends of settlement behaviour within the Roman period, and only one Roman period distribution is presented (Hall and Coles 1994). On the other hand, from central southern Britain a more variable picture may be discerned between the first and the mid-second century AD, with some evidence of abandonment of settlements (Fulford 1992).

In trying to wrest some general observations or trends from this difficult array of evidence, where the presence or absence of archaeological visibility counts for so much, we can claim with some confidence that there is not yet evidence of significant decline in the number and extent of settlements before the second half of the fourth century when the circulation of material culture begins to decline. Even in this context we need to be cautious and consider first the difficult relationship between declining material culture and population. However, and more positively, we might also hazard that the population in the second century, bearing in mind the growth of urban centres and the military establishment, was considerably greater than at the beginning of the first century AD. At the regional level and with more detailed and systematic work, distinctive evidence of settlement behaviour of the kind that has already been reported for the Fenland is likely to emerge. Limited though these conclusions are, further inferences will be drawn from them below.

It is important now to consider the extent to which agriculture had developed from that of the pre-Roman Iron Age. A crucial question is whether there were surpluses sufficient to support urban and other dependent communities, particularly the army garrisoned in Britain, and whether or not there were, from time to time, further surpluses available for export across the Channel to feed markets and Imperial needs outside Britain. By the same token it is important for us to consider the extent to which agricultural resources were at any time inadequate and whether external sources were looked to for supplying Britain (Fulford 1984). In exploring these issues we need to be sensitive to theoretical considerations which point out that, in terms of the overall demand on the land of Britannia, the addition of military and urban populations need not have posed a particular stress on agricultural production (Millett 1990: 56–7). Equally, in the debate about how much forts on the northern frontier or in the uplands of Wales were dependent on external supplies, we need to recognize the potential for the production of surplus at the local level (Manning 1975). In both examples the empirical evidence challenges the theoretical position, and it is important to seek to understand an apparently irrational situation.

Aspects of the market changed through time. Urban centres were established and continued to develop, particularly in the first and second centuries, and there were changes in the military disposition. After the governorship of Agricola, the absolute number of troops garrisoned in Britain declined from its early peak of four legions and associated auxiliary regiments by about a quarter in the second century. Further reduction followed, and a strong case has been made for a relatively small establishment, perhaps only a quarter of its maximum strength, by the fourth century (James 1984). Overall, given the length of the Roman administration of Britain, it is appropriate to try and establish how the situation in respect of food supplies changed through time. The basis for doing this is not straightforward. On the one hand there is the biological evidence of faunal and plant remains; on the other there is the evidence of more or less archaeologically durable containers, such as those made of pottery or wood. There is also the question of the extent to which the pattern of movement of any durable material can be used as proxy evidence for the traffic in perishable goods. Significant changes in the balance of imported durable goods as opposed to locally produced material might signify a trend which relates to all kinds of goods and commodities. Thus, in order to pursue the issue of the movement of subsistence goods, it is necessary for both the artefactual and the biological evidence to be evaluated.

Quite certainly the production of food remained the mainstay of economic life in Britain throughout. The production of cereals, notably varieties of wheat and barley, coupled with the raising of lifestock – cattle, sheep and pigs – was at the heart of the agricultural economy. The centrality of this activity is not only implicit in the density and variety of rural settlement across Britain, but also in the regularity with which the archaeological record delivers substantial assemblages of animal bone which are dominated by the three domesticates, while the less robust record of plant remains, often selectively and sparingly represented in carbonized form, consistently produces evidence for cereal production and processing. Turning this evidence into figures of the quantities of grain and meat produced is well nigh impossible; so too is the tracking of the movement of these perishable commodities within Britain and abroad. Profiles of the age of death of animals may be revealing; the incidence of a significant proportion of young cattle, reared for their meat, for example, may suggest the presence of animals brought into a town or fort from the countryside. Similarly, the association of the seeds of weeds characteristic of particular habitats different from that of the settlement under investigation may indicate the presence of grain imported from elsewhere. While these kinds of evidence do not lead to hard numbers, the incidence in assemblages of presences and absences and change through time can allow us to make judgments about the changing relative importance of the locally to the regionally or provincially produced or to the imported commodities.

But for Strabo, we would have no evidence that Britain exported corn, cattle and hides at the end of the first century BC. Nor is there significant corroborative evidence in the form of quantities of artefacts of British origin on Continental sites to serve as a proxy of the archaeologically invisible traffic. On the other hand, and helpfully, there is material evidence, mostly surviving in the form of imported metalwork, including coins, and ceramic evidence dating from the last quarter of the first century BC, from the south-east of Britain, which points to significant relations with Gaul and the Mediterranean (summarized in Cunliffe 1991: 434–43; Tyers 1996: 48–52). Although Strabo does not characterize the nature of the reverse traffic to Britain from Continental Europe, the presence of these imported goods provides a basis for estimating its scale and extent, notably the concentration of finds in nucleated settlements such as Baldock and Braughing, Camulodunum, Verulamium and Calleva, in the context of a broader geographical distribution largely confined to the south-eastern counties of Britain. Among the imports there is evidence for the importation of wine, olive oil, fish sauce and other foodstuffs packaged in amphorae to set against the archaeologically invisible export of corn and cattle. It is probably right to consider these imports as luxuries and of a comparatively small volume, but it is also appropriate to speculate about whether other foodstuffs were being imported alongside the archaeologically durable material. The presence of the weed seed *Agrostemma githago* (corn-cockle), normally associated with southern European environments, alongside carbonized cereals in Late Iron Age contexts at Calleva can be interpreted as proxy evidence for the importation of grain (Jones 2000; Fulford and Timby 2000: 505).

While there is much more to be understood about the nature and social impact of the traffic between British tribes and their Roman neighbours before AD 43, the fact that surpluses, albeit of an unknown scale, of food and other materials were available for export provides a context for understanding how support of the Roman army, at least in terms of food and raw materials, could conceivably have been assimilated by the new province. It remains to be determined what happened to the trade in these commodities after AD 43. Were all subsistence resources put at the disposal of the governor and the procurator, or did the existing arrangements continue with military supplies from across the Channel compensating for the outgoing native foodstuffs? Certainly there was no cessation in the inflow of the range of material goods present before AD 43, but those involved in their purchase and consumption might have been different. The Roman army itself was evidently a major consumer of just these goods. It is clear that, in the absence of securely quantified information, the extent to which the Roman army and the province might have looked beyond the shores of Britain for its subsistence requirements is debatable. Agricola's reform (chapter 19) of corn supply within Britain in the early eighties is strong evidence for the existence of local networks. Neverthless, the fact that native food supplies were not sufficient to meet the needs of the new province is indicated directly by the presence of imported grain in the Claudian fortress at Alchester (E. Sauer, personal communication), pre-Boudiccan London (Straker 1987) and elsewhere, as well as indirectly by the introduction and spread of pests associated with the storage of grain (Fulford 1984). In the case of 'non-essential' foodstuffs such as wine, olive oil, fish sauce, dried fruit, etc., there can be little argument. The survival of the robust ceramic amphorae which transported these goods from Gaul, Italy, Spain and elsewhere, and their abundant representation in pottery assemblages in pre-Flavian fortresses, forts and urban centres, is sure testimony of the presence of those imported commodities. The occasional discovery of the remains of wooden wine barrels, reused as well linings and thus preserved in waterlogged conditions, also hints at the possible scale of the import trade in wine from Gaul and Germany (e.g. Frere and Tomlin 1992: 1–10). The importance of trade and supply links back to Continental Europe is underlined by the foundation and development of London from the late forties.

London's pivotal role in the development of the province is implied by the construction of the main roads which radiate out from the town. On the back of the traffic exploiting the new routes we can see in the sixties and seventies the emergence of a successful pottery industry situated along Watling Street at Brockley Hill and elsewhere between Verulamium and London. Its products are found widely dispersed across the province, reflecting perhaps the impact of that radial route network (Tyers 1996: 132–4, 199–201). It is not an unreasonable hypothesis that perishable foodstuffs passed outwards along the same road network. Certainly, with the notable exception of the Fosse Way linking Exeter with Lincoln, there are few routes which cut across the strongly London-centred network established in the third quarter of the first century AD. However, there is no evidence yet, as represented by the distributions of artefacts, for the Fosse Way acting as a major trading route in the early Roman period. While the main reason for the development of London is its role as a port to handle trade with the rest of the Empire, this does not preclude it also functioning as a centre to redistribute to the north and north-west foodstuffs coming in by road from the south and south-east.

In the absence of much specific surviving evidence for subsistence foods, such as cereals, or a means of establishing whether they were imported or not, some attempt has been made to exploit the potential of the proxy evidence of other materials, particularly pottery, in trying to determine the patterns of flow of perishable goods. In broad terms it has been suggested that the general reduction in the scale of imports in the second and early third century can be seen also to reflect a declining reliance on imported foodstuffs (Fulford 1984). Certainly the latest deposit of grain with a non-local origin from the northern frontier is from the fort at South Shields and is of late third- or early fourth-century date. It is not clear whether the grain is of southern British or Gaulish origin (Van der Veen 1994). As far as foodstuffs carried in amphorae are concerned, the range of vessels in the second century is very largely restricted to olive-oil carriers from the Guadalquivir in Baetica and Gaulish wine and oil carriers from Narbonensis (Tyers 1996: 85–104). The former carry stamps of which the latest are of Severan date; thereafter these vessels cease to be exported to Britain. There is little doubt that by the end of the first quarter of the third century, the importation of any foodstuffs, whether carried in durable amphorae or evidenced by actual food remains, had virtually ceased. While a devil's advocate might press the case for a transition from durable to more perishable packaging, there is no evidence for the latter. Wine barrels, for example, of third- or fourth-century date have not so far been identified. The cessation in the importation of Spanish amphorae also coincides with that of tableware represented by Central and a significant proportion of Eastern Gaulish plain and decorated sigillata (Tyers 1996: 105–16). That convergent relationship of consumer durables and packaged foodstuffs may help us to understand an earlier development, which may be linked to the trade or supply in foodstuffs.

In the early second century the principal source of sigillata supplied to Britain shifts from factories in the south of Gaul, situated at La Graufesenque near Toulouse to kilns located in the centre of Gaul in the proximity of Clermont-Ferrand, first at Les Martres de Veyre, then at Lezoux. Such a move does not have a clear rational explanation, not least because the distance to the markets or destinations principally supplied remained much the same. At the same time, in Britain itself there is a shift in the location and associated distribution patterns of major suppliers of cooking ware. On the one hand, workshops located around Poole harbour in south Dorset become the principal source of cooking ware in the west of Britain as far north, in the first instance, as Hadrian's new frontier, while in the Thames estuary potteries principally located on the north Kent coast became a major source of a similar range of pottery supplied up the east coast, also as far as the northern frontier (Allen and Fulford 1996; Tyers 1996: 182–8). Other workshops in the Midlands also become major suppliers of the northern frontier (e.g. Tyers 1996: 122–4, 190–1). This move within Britain can be seen as representative of a change in emphasis which draws on the wider resources of the province, where London appears to cease to have the same importance as a pivotal point in the redistribution of imported and locally supplied goods. While the west of Britain seems to link into its own regional network, London perhaps retains its pre-eminence in respect of eastern Britain, reflected in the coastal emphasis of certain distributions (e.g. Tyers 1996: 119–20). Strictly speaking, these changes might be explained as pottery-specific, but the correspondence in time with the reorganization of the main sources of supply of imported sigillata suggests that wider reorganizational forces were at work. Where the supply of subsistence food-stuffs is concerned, we might extrapolate from the pottery evidence to argue that greater reliance was being placed on British rather than overseas supplies from the reigns of Trajan and Hadrian onwards. With the virtual demise of evidence for cross-channel traffic from the early third century, it is reasonable to suppose that all basic foodstuffs were supplied from within Britain. Moreover, it is from this period that certain strands of evidence emerge which might argue for Britain playing an enhanced role in the supply of foodstuffs to Germany and Gaul.

From London there is the paradoxical situation of a major investment in the waterfront along the north bank of the Thames in the second quarter of the third century at a time when, as we have seen, there is little empirical evidence for any trade or traffic in foodstuffs (Brigham 1990). Along the east coast of Britain, initially at Brancaster on the north Norfolk coast and at Reculver on the north Kent coast, there is investment in new auxiliary forts, perhaps from as early as the late second or early third century. These were followed before the mid to late third century by further constructions at Caistor-by-Yarmouth, Bradwell and perhaps Walton in Suffolk (Pearson 2002). While it is possible that security against the possible threat of raiders from across the North Sea was the over-riding explanation for these constructions, it is also important to note that, where excavation has taken place, the archaeological assemblages have produced considerable evidence for coastal trade as well as traffic across the North Sea (Darling and Gurney 1993; Allen and Fulford 1999). At Walton, for example, there is some evidence for the use of Eifel lava in the building of the fort. With the settlement of the northern frontier by Caracalla, we might envisage that resources which had previously been despatched to the north and collected at bases like South Shields were now available for deployment elsewhere, perhaps to supply Caracalla's expeditions in Germany. The east coast forts were well placed to assist in such activity.

Assessing the extent to which foodstuffs were either imported or exported from Britain in the third and fourth centuries is difficult, thanks to the rarity of both botanical evidence and the traditional ceramic or wooden containers which might identify such trade. The use of amphorae remained largely confined to the Mediterranean region, and late Roman amphorae from North Africa and elsewhere are found in only small quantities in Britain. From this we might infer that connections with the Mediterranean world were trivial in comparison with those of the first and second centuries. However it is interesting to note that, from two late Roman contexts at Silchester (*insula IX*), there is evidence for lentils and figs, neither of which is easily cultivated in Britain (M. Robinson, personal communication). The fig occurred in a very late fourth- or early fifth-century well. The two finds raise again the question of the extent to which foodstuffs may have been transported in perishable containers of textile or leather, as well as wooden barrels. That connections with Gallia Belgica and the German provinces were of greater importance is signalled by the number of overlapping distributions in Britain and Gallia Belgica of late Roman artefacts, such as coins from mints in London and Trier, Rhenish glass, pottery from a variety of sources in Britain, Gaul and Germany, and metalwork (Fulford 1989: 197, fig. 6). This inter-relationship is given greater weight by important written sources which mention a major supply of grain organized to relieve famine among the cities of the Rhineland in the reign of Julian in 359. One reading of one source is that the particular measures laid on in this instance supplemented an already existing arrangement (Frere 1987: 343–4). Apart from the proxy items of trade mentioned above, which, like the Mediterranean amphorae, in volume represent a fraction of the early imperial supply of goods from Gaul and Germany to Britain, there is no other direct source of evidence to substantiate the scale and frequency of this food supply to the Rhineland. We are left, then, in some uncertainty of the scale and frequency of the movement of foodstuffs in and out of Britain in the late Roman period (cf. Fulford 1978), but we have to be reminded that our understanding has to be set into a context where late Roman Britain in both town and country shows greater evidence of material prosperity than at any other time. We shall return to this observation below.

References to the exploitation and trade in metals from Britain occur among the major written sources of the early imperial period. If Tacitus was being rhetorical in his reference to gold and silver being the reward of victory (*Agricola*, 12), Strabo's reference in a different context to the export of gold, silver and iron perhaps offers a more reliable starting-point. Indeed, we can find evidence for the mining of gold and lead (from which silver could be extracted) from the first century AD. In addition, even if we lack certainty about the date of exploitation in a specifically Roman context, we can probably add copper and tin to the list from the same period. Indeed, it is likely that all these minerals were being regularly exploited in Britain from the Iron Age and earlier. Much of our specific chronological evidence for the Roman period rests on the existence of stamped ingots, particularly for copper and lead, but it is the latter, almost certainly because of imperial interest in the silver component, where the epigraphy is the most revealing. Otherwise we are dependent on the evidence of settlement activity in the close proximity of known mineral sources and the assumption of a link between the two.

From as early as AD 49 stamped ingots indicate exploitation of the lead of the Mendips, and by the Flavian period there is comparable evidence for the additional production of lead from North Wales and the Pennines. The difficulty here is determining the relationship between lead production and silver production and, given the separate demands for both metals, we can have no confidence that the evidence of one confirms the extraction of silver. Independent of the imperial demand for silver, at a local level the establishment of military forts, with their associated bath-houses, and then the growth of towns with similar requirements would have provided a ready market for lead from the forties onwards. The addition of the letters EX ARG on some stamped ingots, notably from two groups, one which can reasonably be attributed to the Mendips in the reign of Vespasian and the second associated with Derbyshire production centred at Lutudarum, is interpreted as *ex argentariis*, 'from the lead-silver works' (Frere et al. 1990: 38–66). Whether or not silver had already been extracted from these or any other of the stamped ingots is unclear, as analysis indicates both high and low levels of silver (as parts per million) (Tylecote 1976). The only period with datable stamped silver ingots which have been found in the British Isles is the fourth century, but there is no certainty that the silver is of British origin. Indeed one ingot from Canterbury is from the workshop of Leo at Trier (Frere et al. 1990: 29–33). While numbers of stamped lead ingots from various ore-fields have been found in Britain, presumably lost in transit, only four of what might arguably be inferred as ingots of British origin have been reported from across the Channel. One of these was reported from a location close to the Channel at St Valéry-sur-Somme, while a second was found at Lillebonne, close to the mouth of the Seine. The other two were found close to Châlon-sur-Saône, the latter river being one of the great supply routes of Gaul.

Unless there are factors relating to the survival of lead ingots which favour Britain, rather than Gaul or Germany, the clear inference to be drawn from the numbers and distribution of these pigs found in Britain is that most of the lead production at least was destined for consumption within the province. The destination of the silver, however, was presumably direct to the Imperial treasury (cf. Todd 2002). Given the lack of natural resources in Gallia Belgica and Germania, it is reasonable to assume that a proportion of the lead, perhaps reworked in a context where the epigraphy was removed, was exported to Gaul, Germany and beyond. For whatever reason, no ingot found in Britain has been found stamped with an Imperial designation later than the joint reign of Marcus Aurelius and Lucius Verus, AD 164–9. However, the pigs referred to above, from Lillebonne and Châlons-sur-Saône and which might be of British origin, carry stamps of Septimius Severus. What this signifies, whether a loss of interest on the part of the procurator and the emperor who ultimately controlled the exploitation and related export of the lead, with an essential continuity of production and export by civilian entrepreneurs and *societates*, for some of whom we have epigraphic evidence, is far from clear. Alternatively, the diminution of stamping may have marked a significant threshold in the history of the industry, representing the closure of mines and workings. On the other hand, there is considerable evidence for continued production in the late Roman period, not only represented by the presence of unstamped ingots from fourth-century contexts in settlements associated with lead-mining, but also by stamped ingots of pewter, an alloy of lead and tin, in London (Frere et al. 1990: 68–70), and the presence of significant quantities of late Roman artefacts of lead in Britain, notably baptismal tanks and sarcophagi. As for the continued export of lead, the late Roman Ploumanac'h wreck off the north coast of Brittany yielded a cargo of 271 ingots, weighing some 22 tonnes, among which were 14 incised inscriptions naming the *civitates* of the *Brigantes* and the *Iceni* (L'Hour 1987). We are probably right to conclude that from the late second or early third century the procurator ceased to be interested in tracking the movement of the lead or silver-lead from the mines and, by inference, in having an interest in the metal once it had left the mines. Those leasing mines were presumably liable for rent to the emperor, but the assumption is that this would have been paid in ways which are archaeologically invisible, but perhaps through the silver extracted at source. While the difficulties in determining trends in the volume of lead (and silver) production cannot be overestimated, the fact that stamping of all kinds all but ceased by the early third century probably does indicate a reduction in production.

Other metals have not produced ingots stamped in the same way, and assessment of the duration, distribution and scale of production is fraught with difficulties. Gold is, perhaps, to be linked with the duration of occupation of associated supervisory forts, such as at Dolaucothi, but, as with lead, there are arguments for continued civilian production after the loss of Imperial interest (Burnham 1997; Arnold and Davies 2000: 99–100). Stamped ingots of copper from Anglesey and north Wales are not independently dated, but one signifies an organization based in Rome (*RIB* II, 2403.3). Only one among some 19 ingots of tin of probable Roman date is stamped (*RIB* II, 2405.1). It is probably of fourth-century date and was recovered from Cornwall. The lack of specific evidence for early Roman working in the south-west has been linked to an assumed ease of availability of Spanish tin and has been taken to imply a lack of interest in its production in the early Roman period. While there can be no certainty about the lack of activity based on the absence of stamped ingots, the evidence for pewter manufacture, particularly in the third and fourth centuries, is certainly a testament to late Roman production. Indeed, tin may reasonably be seen as one of the reasons for continued interest in Britain on the part of Byzantium in the late fifth and sixth century.

The ubiquitous demand for iron for a variety of civil and military purposes has ensured abundant evidence from a variety of sources for its exploitation throughout the Roman period. The major production areas were the Weald and the Forest of Dean, but numerous other sources were also exploited, such as in Northamptonshire, north Norfolk, south-east Wales, Devon, etc. Estimating the scale of production and change through time is extremely difficult. In the case of the Weald, Cleere and Crossley (1986) have drawn attention to the evidence for the spread westwards of ironworking sites and for the apparent decline of production from about the mid-third century. That this coincides with the period when the stamping of lead ingots virtually ceased may provide reinforcement for the view that the latter did indeed represent a decline in the production of that metal.

The Forest of Dean, on the other hand, shows plentiful evidence for the production and the export of ores for smelting at relatively remote sites down-river along the Severn estuary through the third and fourth centuries and hints at the scale of demand (Fulford and Allen 1992). Around the Forest several large settlements, such as *Ariconium*, *Blestium* and Worcester, can be associated with this activity. It is a reasonable assumption that Britain was self-sufficient in iron throughout the Roman period, but the extent to which material was exported after Strabo's time is uncertain. The involvement of the *Classis Britannica* in production, as evidenced by the finds of its stamped tiles in the south-east of the Weald at settlements associated with iron production, strongly implies that iron was being supplied by that organization to the military on the northern frontier (where inscriptions attest the presence of the fleet) and elsewhere (Frere and Tomlin 1993: 1–25). Equally, similar evidence from stamped tiles for the fleet across the Channel at Boulogne would support the inference that British iron continued to be exported during the Roman period. For such a central activity in the economic life of Britain, it is frustrating that it is so difficult to estimate either the changing scale in the production of the raw blooms or the extent to which both larger and smaller centres specialized in the smelting of the ore, as opposed to the forging of iron artefacts.

Other raw materials which were exploited during the Roman period were stone and timber. Except for the south-east of Britain, where suitable sources of stone for carving for architectural or artistic purposes were limited, military and civilian settlements tended to exploit local resources. Limestone from the Jurassic system, stretching north-eastwards from Somerset to Lincolnshire, was the principal source of freestone for the towns of the south-east so that, for example, stone attributed to quarries in and around Bath is noted at Silchester, while material from Lincolnshire and Northampton has been identified in London (Fulford 1989: 188–9). Imported freestone from Boulogne and the Paris Basin is reported from, respectively, Richborough and Fishbourne (Hayward, personal communication). Predictably, stone used as rubble or as *petit appareil* did not travel great distances except where local materials were in really short supply. Such examples, where stone used in this way travelled more than about fifty miles, include Kentish Ragstone, probably quarried from sources close to the upper reaches of the Medway River, and used in quantity in a variety of buildings in London from the Flavian period onwards. Access by water, both to the quarries and to the point of consumption, as evidenced by the Kentish ragstone cargo of the Blackfriars wreck, was a key factor in this supply (Marsden 1994). Relatively remote sources of stone, such as Lincolnshire limestone at Bradwell, were similarly employed in the building of forts and other installations around the eastern shores of Britain from the Wash to Kent in the third century (Allen and Fulford 1999).

Decorative marbles for use as veneers in walling and flooring were also imported from more distant sources in the Pyrenees and the Mediterranean, but are comparatively rare outside London and towns in the south-east (Pritchard 1986). In terms of estimated volume, the cladding of the great monument at Richborough, Kent, in white Carrara marble represented an exceptional use of this material. Within Britain itself, the shelly, grey Purbeck marble from south Dorset was a popular material for decorative purposes and, in the first and second centuries, was widely used in the south-east and, to a more limited extent, in the west, reaching as far north as the legionary fortress at Chester.

Timber was extensively exploited both for constructional purposes and for fuel, but we have little evidence for gauging the extent to which sources other than local ones were used. Evidence that some timber used in London in the first century AD was stamped might suggest that both distant and varied sources were used, the stamp helping to distinguish different suppliers. Oak was the favoured material for building in both military and civilian contexts. The quantities required for certain projects, such as the building of a legionary fortress, would in themselves suggest that material would have to have been acquired from distant sources (Shirley 2001). Much civilian and military building was in timber at first, with gradual replacement in stone thereafter. It is a moot point whether increasing difficulty in finding timber supplies, rather than cultural circumstances, was a factor in determining the change to building in masonry. Nevertheless, even where the principal material for a structure changed to stone, the requirements for roofing and joinery would still have necessitated significant supplies of timber. One insight into the value of wood is provided by a wooden writing tablet found in London, which records in AD 117 the sale of about 5 acres (15 *arpennia*) of woodland in Kent for the seemingly modest sum of 40 *denarii*, the equivalent of about one-seventh of a legionary's annual pay (Tomlin 1996). There is a scarcity of evidence for the management of woodland, but a recent review of the pollen evidence from Roman Britain indicates only limited further clearance of woodland in relation to what was achieved in the prehistoric period (Dark 1999). Although exhaustion of suitable fuel has been suggested as one possible explanation for the decline of the Wealden iron industry, the only pollen sequence taken from close to an area with a consistent fuel demand, that of the Oxfordshire pottery industry, indicates little impact of that activity on the local environment (Dark 1999: 265).

Consideration of fuel takes us to the role of manufacturing and trade in the economic life of Roman Britain (Fulford 1991). We have already seen, in the context of trying to understand the extent to which foodstuffs moved in or out of Britain, that a range of imported goods dominated Roman material culture in Britain in the first and second centuries. Although the economics of production and distribution would have suggested that there was scope for the more local manufacture of many of the goods imported into Britain, this was slow to happen. Pottery, with its ubiquity and its durability, may serve as a good model for the development of indigenous industries of all kinds. Specialized production of a range of Roman forms including flagons and mortaria, in distinctive white clays, developed in the mid to late first century AD in the south-east in workshops close to London, as at Brockley Hill between London and Verulamium, and in the Alice Holt Forest to the south-west on the Hampshire–Surrey border (Tyers 1996). By the mid-second century several pottery industries, consisting of groups of workshops, had emerged in the Midlands, as in the Nene Valley and at Mancetter in Warwickshire, and the south, as in Colchester, Oxfordshire and south-east Dorset. By this time the repertoire had developed further to include slipped drinking vessels and other specialized wares. Although there were attempts to produce sigillata, most notably at Colchester, imports continued to dominate until the demise of Gaulish and Rhenish production by the mid-third century (Tyers 1996).

While, for the most part, pottery intended for cooking and storage did not travel more than about twenty-five to fifty miles from source, some of the more specialized production, such as mortaria, was traded widely. One significant exception, which survived until the late fourth century, was the production and distribution of cooking and related kitchen wares from south-east Dorset. This Poole harbour production was widely traded across the province up to both the Hadrianic and the Antonine frontier, with a particular emphasis in western Britain. Otherwise we may cite, for example, Brockley Hill mortaria, produced between the later first and mid-second century, distributed widely across the province, while in the second century we have evidence of a similarly extensive distribution of Colchester mortaria, but with a marked south-east and east coast bias (Tyers 1996: 119–20, 132–4). These are reported right up to the Antonine frontier, a north-seeking emphasis which is also evident in the distribution of fine ware from the Nene Valley and mortaria from Mancetter, in the second century (Tyers 1996: 123–4, 127–8). All of these, and other cooking-ware producers based some distance south of the frontier, such as those of Dales ware (Humberside) and Derbyshire ware, reveal the influence of the northern military market and its associated civilian dependants. The additional costs reflected in the further distance the products had to travel were somehow absorbed, so that, for the most part, more localized workshops did not develop.

Significant new production emerged in the mid to late third century in the New Forest and among the well-established workshops in Oxfordshire. For the first time there was a repertoire of imitation sigillata available in southern Britain to compensate for the absence of imported material. Thereafter, until the first signs of declining output in the second half of the fourth century, the distribution and number of major producers stabilized. Only in the north in Yorkshire does there appear some new production of decorated wares in the fourth century at workshops located near Malton at Crambeck (Tyers 1996: 188–9).

The model presented by the ceramic evidence for the establishment of insular workshops from the late first century onwards, and for a lessening dependence on imported goods, can probably be applied more widely to other categories of material. In the case of hand querns, essential for the production of flour, for example, there is considerable evidence for the importation of lava querns from the Eifel Mountains in Germany until the late first or early second century, alongside continuing native production. By the second century appropriate further production in Britain had become established, with major sources located in the west in the Forest of Dean and in the Pennines. In the south we can observe how, even at a considerable distance from source, Forest of Dean querns replace apparently similar but more localized production. As with examples of pottery production, such as the south-east Dorset black-burnished ware, distance does not seem to be a barrier to the distribution of certain types of quern. While perceptions of quality and durability may be factors in the apparent success of certain industries at the expense of others, the distance the goods travelled does not always seem to have influenced their price. Thus in Britain we see evidence locally and on a smaller sale of apparently economically irrational distributions comparable with those associated with major Continental producers of tableware or amphora-contained commodities.

Pottery and stone represent examples where both products and the source of production can be relatively easily identified. In a whole host of other manufacturing activities, such as textile production, manufacture of metal goods, of which iron was probably the most important and abundant, tanning, brewing, bone-working, wood-working, glass-making, etc., etc., this fingerprinting is much more difficult. Distinguishing without the benefit of epigraphic evidence between workshops which might have had a province-wide clientele from those with a local significance is correspondingly equally testing. Nevertheless, the range of material culture and the specialist skills required to produce what is, albeit for reasons of relative preservation, only partly preserved in the archaeological record, constitute very distinctive elements of economic life in Roman Britain, creating the distinctiveness in material culture terms of the Roman as opposed to the preceding Iron Age and succeeding Anglo-Saxon periods.

The circulation of coinage, alongside abundant finds of artefacts and ecofacts in town and country of 'Romanized' or 'lowland' Britain from the second century, and most especially from the late third century onwards, represents a proxy for the myriad of transactions relating to the highly specialized activities indicated by the archaeological record. The Vindolanda tablets offer further insight into the complexities of this activity (Bowman 1994: 65–81). How far the changing volume of low-value coinage from one emperor or phase of minting can be linked to changing levels of economic activity is debatable not least because there is some connection between increased volume and inflation. Nevertheless, cash was not the only driver of economic activity. However, there is clearly a link between the eventual cessation in the importation of coinage into Britain in the first decade of the fifth century and the end of much of the specialized production that otherwise characterized Roman Britain. Although there are clear difficulties in establishing with certainty when the production of a particular artefact type ended, it is generally accepted that there is little evidence of new forms of material culture outside the Anglo-Saxon sphere after the beginning of the fifth century. It is tempting here to make a connection between coin and production in general in the third century, when there is a substantial period after the Severan settlement of the north when almost no new money appears to have entered Britain and only early Imperial small change continued to circulate until the 260s and 270s. This period also coincides with stagnation in material culture, where it is difficult to identify forms which could be considered as new and typical of the third century, that is, before the 'renaissance' of the Gallic and British empires of the last quarter or third of the century. Artefacts tend to be classified either as of the late second/early third century, or of the late third/fourth century, but not of the third century. Equally the period coincides with the ending of major streams of archaeologically recognizable imported goods, such as sigillata and amphora-contained commodities such as Spanish olive oil. The parallel between the situation at the beginning of the fifth century and that from the 220s merits further exploration in trying to understand some of the underlying motors of economic life in Britain.

In pursuing this line of enquiry it is important, despite the extraordinary and selective nature of the evidence available to us, to reflect further on some of the paradoxes and contradictions of the economic evidence. In the early Roman period, between the Conquest and the Severan settlement, there is evidence for almost continuous development and growth. Up to the Flavians, there was only a brief interlude in the process of military conquest and territorial expansion in the second half of the reign of Nero. Accompanying this expansion was urban development, investment in the building of roads and investment in mineral extraction. Given that some manpower probably left the province as booty, it is hard not to accept that the Conquest brought with it civilian immigration as well as the army itself, whether in the shape of the craftsmen who set up small industries, or the merchants who were attracted to supplying the rich military market. The presence and identity of these immigrants is reflected, for example, in early Roman burial rites which do not relate to indigenous traditions (Philpott 1991). Veterans stayed behind to profit out of conquest (Fulford 1999). It is difficult not to accept that, although there might have been a theoretical capacity for Britain to be able to sustain such growth with its own resources, the reality was, as we have seen, that there was considerable reliance on overseas food and materials. In these circumstances, it seems paradoxical that a significant proportion of the evidence for this import traffic is consumer goods such as tableware and glass. How were such goods paid for when the Conquest and the establishment of the provincial infrastructure were demanding so much of the province itself? Since distance from the consumer does not seem to have influenced the location of the workshops, we may assume that the cost of transport was subsidized. If this was the case, perhaps the entire supply was subsidized or owned by the State. Such an explanation might account for the supply of Baetican olive oil which, given the possibility of closer sources of supply from the south of Gaul, was evidently economically irrational. All of these goods were consumed by the army; but they also reached civilian consumers in large quantities, either at a subsidized price (which did not build in the transport costs) or as a direct payment in kind for services and supplies. Similar arrangements probably prevailed in relation to the eccentric distribution of Dorset black-burnished ware to explain its extensive and west-oriented distribution from the second century onwards.

Withdrawal of the systems of patronage underpinning these supply arrangements led to dramatic changes: the demise of the south Gaulish sigillata industry at the end of the first century AD and the switch to central Gaulish suppliers; the demise of the supply of Spanish olive oil and central Gaulish sigillata at the beginning of the third century AD. The latter seems to have coincided with the loss of interest in further military adventure in Britain after the Severan campaigns. While expenditure of central resources on Britain after the Caracallan settlement appears to have been at an all-time low, there are hints, as we have seen, that British supplies could be helpful to Rome across the Channel and the North Sea. Although the recapture of Britain by Constantius Chlorus in 296 might have been driven in part by historic reasons, the shades of Caesar and Claudius, the event does underline the importance which Rome attached to the British provinces.

The late third and fourth century provides a complete contrast to the earlier period. The evidence for cross-Channel trade is nugatory, although at the same time there is further evidence for British food supplies to the Continent, certainly as late as the 360s. On the other hand, it is precisely in the first half of the fourth century that the British countryside exhibits the greatest opulence; towns too appear to flourish. The greatest focus of that prosperity lies in the west, in the area around Bath, central and north Somerset, south-east Wales and the Cotswolds. Such wealth appears to manifest itself at a time when both the military establishment was much reduced and the size of the civil population appears not to be significantly greater than it was in the second century. The wealth and distribution of villas seem to bear no close relationship with urban centres in Britain. Given that internal demands to support the army and develop an infrastructure were less than in the early Roman period, the possibility arises that the rural wealth of late Roman Britain owes much to systems of patronage of Imperial inspiration exploiting the relatively peaceful conditions of the island to feed its Continental forces and civil service. Such patronage could go some way to explaining the apparently irrational western bias in the distribution of rich villas; otherwise one might have expected an easterly or more even distribution, reflecting greater proximity to the Continent. Dependency on a market outside Britain could help to explain the urgency with which forces were raised from within Britain to try and wrest control of the Empire from certain usurpers. The expeditions of Magnus Maximus in the 380s and then of Constantine III in 407 can be seen as desperate attempts to retake control of the Continent in order to ensure the continuity of arrangements with British suppliers. By the same token, the arrival earlier of Theodosius in 367 to restore order in the wake of the *barbarica conspiratio* once again reflects that larger concern for the security of Britain on the part of the emperor.

Once the demand for grain and other supplies dried up, and the State ceased payment for these and for whatever armed forces survived in Britain, it was inevitable that the fabric of Roman Britain would collapse. So much in Britain owed its origins to patronage that once the key influences ceased there was no structure to hold together even the minor components of that system; hence the very rapid demise of the Roman province. If Britain had remained a backwater in the fourth century, economically independent of the Continent, a greater continuity might have been expected. What made the difference was the cessation of payments, previously represented by the losses of silver *siliquae* in southern Britain, for foodstuffs, wool, etc. in the deteriorating circumstances of the later fourth century. The decision to close the prefecture in Trier in the 390s and move the centre of power to Arles was surely a very considerable blow for British landowners.

FURTHER READING

Most recent surveys of Roman Britain include a section on aspects of trade and industry, but for a focused treatment of the 'Economy of Roman Britain' see Fulford (1989). The chapter on 'The Economy' in B. Jones and D. Mattingly, *An Atlas of Roman Britain* (1990), provides many distribution maps and other illustrations.

Studies of Britain can be seen in a wider context in Part 2 of P. Garnsey and R. Saller's *The Roman Empire* (1987) and in Part 1 of M. McCormick's *Origins of the European Economy*

(2001) or K. Greene's survey of archaeological evidence in *The Archaeology of the Roman Economy* (1986). J. du Plat Taylor and H. Cleere, in *Roman Shipping and Trade: Britain and the Rhine Provinces* (1978), examine Britain's trade relations with the Rhine provinces.

A range of reading will help to understand the implications of supplying the needs of the state, including the Roman army. Drawing on detailed documents preserved at the Roman fort of Vindolanda, A. Bowman's *Life and Letters on the Roman Frontier* (1994) is a marvellous introduction to the complexities of the subject and the richness of these sources. For a more general survey of a legion's role, see the essays in R. Brewer (ed.), *The Second Augustan Legion and the Roman Military Machine* (2002), and for issues relating to supply see Allen and Fulford (1996 and 1999).

There are many important contributions on individual subjects, but the following ones may be a helpful start. For the role of coinage and currency in understanding economic life, see R. Reece, *The Coinage of Roman Britain* (2002); for a masterly overview of pottery, see P. Tyers, *Roman Pottery in Britain* (1996); for the role of London as a port, see G. Milne, *The Port of Roman London* (1985) and P. Marsden, *Ships of the Port of London* (1994). For a study of a single industry, see H. Cleere and D. Crossley, *The Iron Industry of the Weald* (1986), while D. Peacock's *Pottery in the Roman World: An Ethnoarchaeological Approach* (1982) is an excellent introduction to the production of pottery, bricks and tiles.

At the level of the individual site there is always much economic information to be gleaned. Two examples illustrate this theme: from the port perspective, see T. Dyson (ed.), *The Roman Quay at St Magnus House, London* (1986); from that of an urban settlement, see M. Fulford and J. Timby, *Late Iron Age and Roman Silchester* (2000), particularly the Synthesis (Part 7).

REFERENCES

Allen, J. R. L. and Fulford, M. G. 1996. The distribution of south-east Dorset black-burnished Category 1 pottery in south-west Britain. *Britannia*, 27, 223–81.

—— 1999. Fort building and military supply along Britain's Eastern Channel and North Sea coasts: the later second and third centuries. *Britannia*, 30, 163–84.

Arnold, C. and Davies, J. L. 2000. *Roman and Early Medieval Wales*. Stroud.

Bowman, A. K. 1994. *Life and Letters on the Roman Frontier*. London.

Bowman, A. and Thomas, J. D. 1983. *Vindolanda: The Latin Writing Tablets*. Britannia Monograph 4. London.

—— 1994. *The Vindolanda Writing-Tablets (Tabulae Vindolandenses II)*. London.

Branigan, K. 1976. Villa settlement in the West Country. In K. Branigan and P. Fowler (eds), *The Roman West Country: Classical Culture and Celtic Society*. London, 120–41.

Brigham, T. 1990. The late Roman waterfront in London. *Britannia*, 21, 99–183.

Burnham, B. C. 1997. Roman mining at Dolaucothi: the implications of the 1991–3 excavations near the Carreg Pumsaint. *Britannia*, 28, 325–36.

Cleere, H. and Crossley, D. 1986. *The Iron Industry of the Weald*. Leicester.

Cunliffe, B. 1991. *Iron Age Communities in Britain*. London and New York.

Dark, P. 1999. Pollen evidence for the environment of Roman Britain. *Britannia*, 30, 247–72.

Darling, M. J. with Gurney, D. 1993. *Caister-on-Sea: Excavations by Charles Green 1951–1955*. East Anglian Archaeology 60. Dereham.

Frere, S. S. 1987. *Britannia: A History of Roman Britain*, 3rd edn. London.

Frere, S. S., Roxan, M. and Tomlin, R. S. O. (eds) 1990. *The Roman Inscriptions of Britain* II.1. Gloucester.

Frere, S. S. and Tomlin, R. S. O. (eds) 1992. *The Roman Inscriptions of Britain* II.4. Stroud.

—— 1993. *The Roman Inscriptions of Britain* II.5. Stroud.

Fulford, M. 1978. The interpretation of Britain's late Roman trade: the scope of medieval historical and archaeological analogy. In H. Cleere and J. du Plat Taylor (eds), *Roman Shipping and Trade: Britain and the Rhine Provinces*. London, 59–69.

—— 1984. Demonstrating Britannia's economic independence in the first and second centuries. In T. F. C. Blagg and A. C. King (eds), *Military and Civilian in Roman Britain*. BAR (British Series) 136. Oxford, 129–42.

—— 1989. The economy of Roman Britain. In M. Todd (ed.), *Research on Roman Britain 1960–89*. Britannia Monograph 11. London, 175–201.

—— 1991. Britain and the Roman Empire: the evidence for regional and long-distance trade. In R. F. J. Jones (ed.), *Roman Britain: Recent Trends*. Sheffield, 35–47.

—— 1992. Iron Age to Roman: a period of radical change on the gravels. In M. Fulford and E. Nichols (eds), *Developing Landscapes of Lowland Britain. The Archaeology of the British Gravels: A Review*. London, 23–38.

—— 1999. Veteran settlement in late 1st-century Britain and the foundations of Gloucester and Lincoln. In H. Hurst (ed.), *The Coloniae of Roman Britain: New Studies and a Review*. Journal of Roman Archaeology, Supplementary Series 36. Portsmouth, RI, 177–80.

Fulford, M. and Allen, J. R. L. 1992. Iron-making at the Chesters Villa, Woolaston, Gloucestershire: survey and excavation 1987–91. *Britannia*, 23, 159–216.

Fulford, M. and Timby, J. 2000. *Late Iron and Roman Silchester. Excavations on the site of the Forum-Basilica 1977, 1980–86*. Britannia Monograph 15. London.

Hall, D. and Coles, J. 1994. *Fenland Survey: An Essay in Landscape and Persistence*. London.

James, S. T. 1984. Britain and the Late Roman Army. In T. F. C. Blagg and A. C. King (eds), *Military and Civilian in Roman Britain*. BAR (British Series) 136. Oxford, 161–86.

Jones, M. 2000. The plant remains. In M. Fulford and J. Timby, *Late Iron and Roman Silchester*. Britannia Monograph 15. London, 505–12.

L'Hour, M. 1987. Un site sous-marin sur le côte de l'Armorique: l'épave de Ploumanac'h. *Revue Archéologique de l'Ouest*, 4, 113–31.

Manning, W. H. 1975. Economic influences on land use in the military areas of the highland zone during the Roman period. In J. G. Evans, S. Limbrey and H. Cleere (eds), *The Effect of Man on the Landscape: The Highland Zone*. London, 112–16.

Marsden, P. 1994. *Ships of the Port of London*. London.

Millett, M. 1990. *The Romanization of Britain*. Cambridge.

Pearson, A. 2002. *The Roman Shore Forts: Coastal Defences of Southern Britain*. Stroud.

Philpott, R. 1991. *Burial Practices in Roman Britain: A Survey of Grave Treatment and Furnishing AD 43–410*. BAR (British Series) 219. Oxford.

Pritchard, F. A. 1986. Ornamental stonework from Roman London. *Britannia* 17, 169–89.

Shirley, E. 2001. *Building a Roman Legionary Fortress*. Stroud.

Smith, J. T. 1978. Halls or yards? A problem of villa interpretation. *Britannia*, 9, 351–8.

Straker, V. 1987. Carbonised cereal grain from first-century London: a summary of the evidence for importation and crop-processing. In P. Marsden (ed.), *The Roman Forum Site in London: Discoveries before 1985*. London, 151–5.

Swift, E. 2000. *Regionality in Dress Accessories in the Late Roman West*. Montagnac.

Todd, M. 2002. Mining, bullion and the balance of payments in the Roman West. *Laverna*, 13, 81–90.

Tomlin, R. S. O. 1996. A five-acre wood in Roman Kent. In J. Bird, M. Hassall and H. Sheldon (eds), *Interpreting Roman London*. Oxford, 209–15.

Tyers, P. 1996. *Roman Pottery in Britain*. London.

Tylecote, R. F. 1976. *A History of Metallurgy*. London.

Van der Veen, M. 1994. Reports on the biological remains. In P. Bidwell and S. Speak, *Excavations at South Shields Roman Fort I*. Newcastle, 243–69.

CHAPTER EIGHTEEN

Rural Settlement in Northern Britain

RICHARD HINGLEY

Background

Most of the south of this area forms part of the so-called 'military zone' (Haverfield 1905). This region is often contrasted to the 'civil zone' of the south, although there are some problems with the way that the zones have been characterized (James and Millett 2001). The northern part of the study area extends well outside the province to the north, into areas that remained free of Roman occupation in what is today Scotland.

The archaeological evidence for the Roman period has often been compartmentalized into various categories. These include military archaeology, urbanism, native settlement, etc. This compartmentalization has created a problem. Villas and towns have long been a source of fascination (Hanson and Macinnes 1991; Hingley 2000: 151; Evans 2001) and this has encouraged a long tradition of archaeological work on these sites. They are felt to relate to the successful Romanization of the native population. Roman military monuments have provided an equally powerful attraction to archaeologists. By contrast, with the exception of the seminal work of George Jobey, there has been a scarcity of studies of the extensive landscapes of native settlement that characterize much of the north (Haselgrove 1996; Nevell 1999; Frodsham 2000). Native settlements are considered to represent the continuation of a tradition that evolved from Iron Age origins. As these settlements do not constitute the homes of 'Roman' populations they have often not been seen as the subject-matter of Roman archaeology. To the north the monumental brochs and duns of Scotland have been a subject of extensive research by Iron Age archaeologists (Haselgrove 1999a). By contrast, the native settlement landscapes of central Britain are often seen in a negative light, the backdrop to what is considered the important evidence left by Roman military activity (Willis 1999; Frodsham 2000).

Several works by Roman specialists stress the need to examine the native background to military issues in northern Britain (for example, Keppie 1989; Hanson and Breeze 1991; Breeze 1996; Hanson 1997). This increase in interest has developed alongside projects that have explored Roman and native interaction in the Netherlands and, more recently, in Germany (Bloemers 1989; the 'thematic session II on Romans and natives' in Maxfield and Dobson 1991; Haffner and von Schnurbein 1996; Creighton and Wilson 1999; and Wigg 1999). Our understanding of Roman military and native interaction in northern Britain, however, remains poor and native sites are often defined in negative terms. It is argued that they often produce few Roman artefacts, if any at all (Keppie 1989: 67–8; Breeze 1996: 114). Higham has suggested that artefact-discard rates at Roman forts or *vici* on the one hand and adjacent settlements on the other are as different as those of a modern western city compared to a Third World community (Higham 1986: 224). Keppie (1989: 72) has argued that 'It is a reasonable conclusion that the Roman impact on non-Roman Britain was slight and short-lived.'

A contrasting approach has developed recently and this is based upon the idea that the Roman impact on native communities was dramatic and significant (Hanson and Macinnes 1991). A number of innovative recent articles promise new understandings of the evidence (for example, Willis 1999 and Hunter 2001a). The evidence indicates that, although individual sites often produce few finds, Roman objects must have been fairly common in the north, while regional variations in the character of assemblages enables ideas about differing types of contact to be developed (Hunter 2001a: 291). It appears to be true that many sites produce only limited numbers of Roman finds, but these objects have not always been reported in full in excavation reports in the past (Willis 1999: 100). This has helped to create the idea that Roman finds were actually scarcer than now appears to be true. In addition, the scarcity or absence of Roman goods on many sites should not be taken as a sign of failure (Taylor 2001: 56). Other methods for representing status – such as feasting, the ownership of cattle, or architectural elaboration – are also likely to have existed within native society. To suppose that all sectors of society desired Roman objects and had access to them gives a biased view that focuses upon the influence of Rome (in other words, it is Romano-centric). We also need to think about the presence of this Roman material in more positive terms, as even occasional finds indicate contact. A number of native sites, however, yield considerable quantities of Roman objects, and it is probable that over much of the study area certain sections of the population had the ability and desire to obtain these goods.

The archaeological data for native settlement is highly variable (Willis 1999: 83), as is the evidence for the occurrence of Roman finds in native contexts (Hunter 2001a). This variety may represent a range of different lifestyles in the north and also differing relationships between native communities and the Roman administration (Hunter 2001a: 289). It will be argued that, as in the southern areas of the province, the Roman administration manipulated local society in various ways. We do not need to assume, however, that the influence of Rome on these communities was entirely one-sided. The local population are likely to have exploited the opportunities offered by Roman contact, and it will be suggested that the character of native society influenced the disposition of Roman military forces and the ways that the Roman administration exercised power.

Concepts: 'rural' and 'settlement'

This paper addresses rural settlement – that is, those settlements that did not have an urban or military character or a specialized industrial function (see Taylor 2001: 46), but a primarily agricultural base. The concepts 'rural', 'urban', 'military' and 'industrial' have significance only within the Roman province. Within *Britannia*, sites that archaeologists title 'towns' (colonies, *civitas* capitals and small towns), 'military' sites (fortresses, forts, camps, etc.) and specialized 'industrial' complexes occur. These terms do not, however, have a significant meaning within the areas of the north that remained free of Roman rule. In these parts Roman military sites, if they occur at all, were occupied for short periods, and all settlement was effectively rural.

A settlement, for the purposes of this paper, is an area of domestic occupation that was substantial enough to leave surviving physical traces. The archaeological evidence suggests that the later prehistoric and Roman period witnessed a significantly increased structural elaboration of particular localized places in the landscape, which archaeologists choose to term 'settlements' (for the limitations of this term see Brück and Goodman 1999: 5). Individual settlements were often defined by the creation of boundary earthworks and/or the construction of elaborate houses (Hingley 1989; Haselgrove forthcoming). As we shall see, however, not all settlements were enclosed, and human occupation and activity also extended more broadly across the landscape (Haselgrove and McCullagh 2000).

Information for these broader landscapes of settlement includes evidence of the distribution of settlement, land boundaries, field systems, route-ways, roads and resource areas (Taylor 2001: 52). Few detailed studies have been made of the complex landscapes that characterize the archaeological record across Roman-period Britain. Promising new directions in landscape archaeology are, however, beginning to develop (for a case study in north-eastern England see Taylor 2001: 53).

The character of the study area

The nature of the landscape across this area is highly variable and this will have influenced agricultural regimes. The geology and topography contributed towards the landscapes that people inhabited. Much of the area is highland, varying from the moors of northern England, southern and western Scotland to the mountainous terrain of north-western England, northern and western Scotland (see Ballantyne and Dawson 1997; Dark and Dark 1997; Higham 1986; Whittington and Edwards 1997). Soils vary across the study area, from the fertile lowland areas of the coastal plains of the east and of the river valleys to the thin and infertile soils of much of the uplands (Davidson and Carter 1997). The climate also varies, with a shorter growing season in highland areas, and this will have influenced agricultural regimes, which must have varied across the area.

Communities had occupied and exploited much of the north for millennia before the arrival of the Romans (Dark and Dark 1997; Dark 1999; Hingley and Miles 2001). Environmental evidence across the centre and north of Britain suggests that much of the landscape had been cleared of trees by the time of the Roman invasion; across this area woodlands must have survived as managed resources that were exploited by the native populations. The information presented by pollen diagrams suggests that further clearance occurred during the period of Roman control. Evidence for cereal cultivation occurs in many of the pollen sequences from the area of the province and from the land to the north (Tipping 1994; Edwards and Whittington 1997; Dark 1999).

Estimates of population for the Roman province suggest that it may have been between 2.5 and 3.6 million (Hingley and Miles 2001). The dense networks of settlement that exist in some parts of the study area could suggest a total population of as much as 1,000,000. The habitations of these people would have been dispersed across the landscape but concentrated in the more fertile parts, river valleys and coastal plains. Current evidence suggests that some areas, particularly parts of the north-west of England, may have been fairly marginal (Nevell and Walker 1999). This apparent marginality may be the result of problems in the recovery of archaeological evidence, and presents a challenge for future fieldwork.

The impact of Rome on native communities

The Roman army carried out a series of campaigns across the north (see Hanson and Macinnes 1991; Breeze 1996; Hanson 1997). It is important to keep in mind the potentially destructive character of Roman contact with some of the societies of Britain throughout the period of contact and control (Hanson and Macinnes 1991: 85–6; Hingley and Miles 2001). Archaeological evidence for this impact is hard to locate, although some information from the north could indicate that native communities were disrupted by contact with Rome. It has been argued that the violence of the Roman campaigns in the north-east of Scotland may have led to a partial regeneration of the forest cover (Whittington and Edwards 1993). That other areas appear to witness increased forest clearance suggests varying relationships between the Roman forces and native communities in different parts of northern Britain, although the evidence for regeneration in the north-east is, perhaps, not fully convincing (Hanson 1997: 214).

Armit (1999) has discussed a 'souterrain abandonment horizon' in the late second and early third centuries in Fife and Perthshire, which he suggests may correlate with the campaigns of the Roman emperor Severus against the Maeatae. The settlements with souterrains may have been abandoned as a result of Roman military activity, although the dating evidence for the construction and filling in of souterrains requires a fuller assessment. It is also notable that the two enclosed settlements at Port Seaton (East Lothian) appear from the radiocarbon evidence to end around AD 80–120 and may have been abandoned because of their vulnerability to the Roman fleet (Haselgrove and McCullagh 2000). Future research might focus upon the issue of the impact of Rome upon the communities across the north and the province as a whole.

The Character of the Settlement Evidence

The evidence that we have is very uneven across the area (see Haselgrove forthcoming, for northern England). Relatively few excavations have occurred and much of the information is derived from archaeological surveys. In some parts detailed aerial photography has been carried out. An extensive knowledge exists of cropmark landscapes in south-east Perthshire (figure 18.2; RCAHMS 1994), the central part of the Hadrian's Wall corridor (Gates 1999), the Yorkshire Wolds (Stoertz 1997) and East Lothian (Haselgrove and McCullagh 2000). In other areas aerial reconnaissance has produced some evidence (Bewley 1994; Still et al. 1997: 4), while elsewhere know-

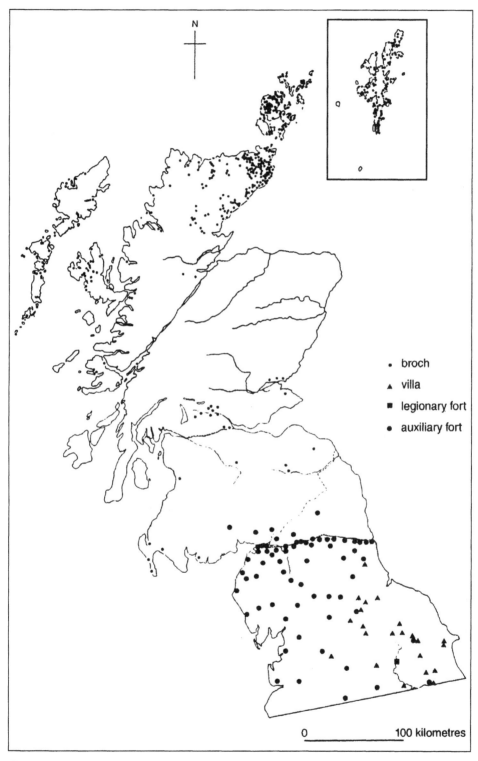

Figure 18.1 The distribution of Roman forts, villas and brochs across northern Britain (after Rivet (ed.) 1966, Millett 1990a, figure 48, and Millett 1995, figure 7. The forts are those occupied towards the end of the reign of Hadrian and mark the culmination of the retrenchment after the withdrawal from Scotland; Millett 1995, 19).

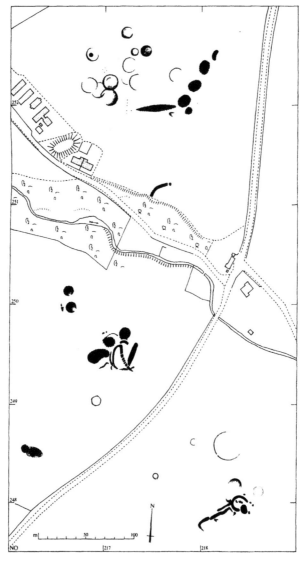

Figure 18.2 A crop-mark landscape at Pitordie, south-east Perthshire, including evidence for roundhouses, souterrains and other structures (after RCAHMS 1994, page 66, Crown © RCAHMS).

ledge is very incomplete (Collens 1999) or non-existent. Field survey projects have revealed extensive archaeological landscapes, for instance, in north-east Perthshire (RCAHMS 1990), eastern Dumfriesshire (RCAHMS 1997) and northern England (for instance, Bowden 1996). In some areas field-walking of arable fields has produced scatters of artefacts (Rahtz et al. 1986: Haselgrove et al. 1988; 40; Caruana 1989; Tolan-Smith 1997; Knight et al. 1998; Halkon and Millett 1999: 45–66, figure 24), while finds are very rare in other places in which the technique has been applied (for instance, the Clyde Valley; Bill Hanson, personal communication).

The results derived from archaeological survey and from excavation can be combined to build an understanding of patterns of settlement. Attempts to construct coherent pictures of Roman-period landscapes show how patchy our knowledge remains (RCAHMS 1994; Hingley et al. 1997; Stoertz 1997; Armit 1999; Nevell 1999). The evidence may suggest that each region had its own particular pattern of settlement. In some areas patterns appear quite distinct, as in the Yorkshire Wolds with their complex enclosed landscapes (Stoertz 1997), or the areas to the south and to the north of Firth of Forth respectively (Macinnes 1982). Recent work in the first of these two areas is beginning to develop a subtle understanding of landscape organization which is derived from the aerial photographic and excavated evidence (Taylor 2001: 53 and figure 15). Studies of this nature are very rare in Britain (Taylor 2001: 52) but future projects of this type should help us to comprehend the variety of ways in which human communities occupied and exploited landscapes. In future, additional evidence and analysis may allow these complex patterns to be unravelled in various parts of the study area.

I shall consider a general model that has been developed for three distinct regions that cover very large areas. The evidence that exists, however, indicates how very complex the situation is likely to have been at a more local level. The subject deserves a far more comprehensive study than is possible in this paper and provides a challenge for future study.

Three regions

A model developed by Higham attempts to explain general patterns of settlement. This author observed that the villa zone of Roman Britain effectively stopped just north-west of a line drawn between Aldborough and Wroxeter. Both Breeze and Higham suggested that in southern Scotland the brochs and duns represented alternative types of high-status settlement. Between the two lies a zone in which, excluding the Roman army and administration, little trace of such a hierarchy has been identified. The approximate geographical boundaries of this central zone lie in the east on the Tees and the Tweed, in the west on the Mersey and in south-west Scotland on the Central Uplands and the River Nith (Higham 1989: 168). It encompasses the region that was heavily garrisoned in the hinterland of Hadrian's Wall and those areas beyond it in which the Roman army took a particular interest in the Hadrianic and post-Hadrianic period (the latter form an effectively blank area on figure 18.1). It also includes the land to the south, including north-western England, where Roman military sites survived throughout much of the period of Roman control. I shall examine these three zones individually.

North-east England: Villas, referred to in the classical literature, were the rural homes of the wealthy town-based élite. Villas, in archaeological terms, are fairly substantial stone-built houses of rectangular form that were built in rural contexts. They sometimes incorporated luxurious fittings; hypocausts, tessellated floors, painted walls and bathhouses (Hingley 1989). The civil districts of the lowlands of the province have been defined as the 'villa landscape' (see Dark and Dark 1997: 43), although the term has rather limited value as villas are not distributed evenly. Parts of the south of the study area, in east Yorkshire around York and as far north as Durham, included landscapes that supported villas; the north-east of England formed the northernmost extent of this so-called villa landscape. Villas appear rare, but new discoveries (figure 18.3; for example, Brown 1999; Durham University Archaeological Services 2000) indicate that they were once more common.

There has been a lengthy debate about whether these villas comprised the homes of native landowners or retired army veterans (Branigan 1989). Work on the German frontier suggests that some villas were built by retiring auxiliary soldiers who were native to the area. This is indicated by the gradual development of villa-type buildings within native settlements of traditional timber long-houses (Carroll 2001: 71–2). Sites such as Holme House, Piercebridge, on the Tees, and Beadlam, at the eastern edge of the Vale of Pickering, may represent a similar development within northern England. At Beadlam (Neal 1996) the villa was built on top of a pre-existing enclosure site, while at Holme House (Harding 1984) the building was fitted into an enclosure in which a round building (possibly a house) remained the central building. At Dalton Parlours (north-east Yorkshire) a villa developed within a pre-existing enclosure system (Wrathmell and Nicholson 1990). Other villas in east Yorkshire follow a similar trend to those of eastern England in general in developing within or on top of pre-existing native enclosures (see Ramm 1978: 73–80, who describes these enclosures as a Roman innovation, although it is now clear that they form a native tradition).

On the Wolds of east Yorkshire villas are probably fairly common; they may derive from the distinctive Iron Age societies of this area with their characteristic burial and settlement traditions (Ramm 1978; Millett 1990b). There may have been a shift in the nature of élite display from a burial to a settlement context in the late Iron Age. Another area in which villas appear fairly common is close to the late Iron Age centre of Stanwick (north Yorkshire). Recent work here suggests that Roman material culture, including pottery and other objects, became common on some sites during the early to mid first century AD (Abramson 1995; Fitts et al. 1999; Willis 1999: 101; Haselgrove forthcoming). The villas may have developed on high-status native settlements within a zone in which Roman pottery imports had become fairly common prior to and during the early Roman period. Thorpe Thewles (Cleveland) perhaps shows this type of development early in the Roman period but then stops abruptly, apparently in the second century (Heslop 1987).

It is often argued that villas in southern Britain developed as part of the system of local self-government within the *civitates* and that villas were the homes of the native élite households that administered these units (Millett 1990a; Halkon and Millett 1999: 226). The north-eastern examples may have fulfilled a comparable role, as towns occur within the area. Towns at Aldborough and Brough-on-Humber operated as *civitas* capitals (Burnham and Wacher 1990: figure 1), while York, Catterick and Malton developed in association with military sites. Recent work has located roadside settlements in east Yorkshire (see the evidence for Shiptonthorpe discussed by Halkon and Millett 1999: 226) and these may have been comparable to the 'small towns' of southern Britain. Further fieldwork may indicate that these settlements once existed rather more widely across the north-east.

The distribution of the villas may have varied from those of other regions. A survey (Halkon and Millett 1999: 226 and illustration 8.3) has suggested that villas and

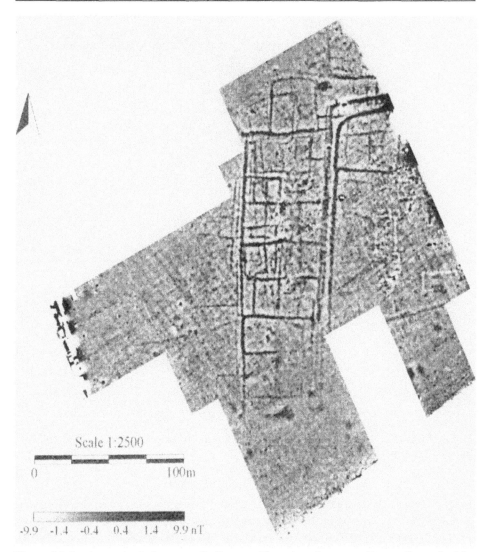

Figure 18.3 A geophysical survey of a Roman villa and settlement at Quarry Farm, Ingleby Barwick, Stockton-on-Tees. The villa lies to the east (right) of the enclosures (after Durham University Archaeological Services 2000, figure 10).

other sites with Romanized finds assemblages to the south of the Wolds clustered close to the Roman road network. Across the north-east in general the few villas occur close to Roman roads and in 'haloes' close to the towns (Branigan 1989: figure 18.3 shows the proximity of villas to Roman roads around Brough, Aldborough, Catterick and Stanwick). Away from the roads more traditional types of rural settlement may have continued (for an example see Inman et al. 1985; Halkon and Millett 1999: 226), although very little work has been undertaken to assess this suggestion and further research is required on this topic across the north-east. This evidence

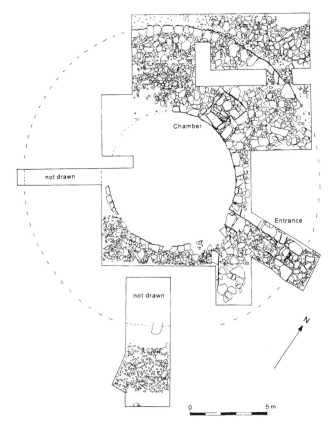

Figure 18.4 The broch at Fairy Knowe, Buchlyvie, Stirling (after Main 1998, illus. 9. Reproduced by permission of the Society of Antiquaries of Scotland and the authors).

suggests that the Romanized pattern of settlement that is common in the south may only have spread to parts of the north-east. The villa distribution also does not overlap substantially with that of forts (Breeze and Dobson 1985).

The north and west: This part of the study area is characterized by a variety of 'substantial roundhouses' (Hingley 1992: 12). Examples include brochs (figure 18.4) and duns, which formed very substantial stone-built houses with complex wall construction. Brochs have been argued to have a fairly distinctive and complex form (Parker Pearson and Sharples 1999: 363–4; although see also Dunwell 1999: 347). Duns are rather more variable in character and do not form an entirely coherent group (Hingley 1992: 13; Hingley et al. 1997: 447). Other forms of substantial roundhouse also occur, including crannogs (timber houses often built on islands in lochs) and timber houses (Hingley 1992; Armit 1997a). The tradition of the building of substantial roundhouses commenced in the later prehistoric period but continued into the Roman Iron Age (Armit 1997a; 102–16). Brochs and duns were more common in certain areas of the Scottish Highlands and islands (often called the 'Atlantic' areas) than in the Lowlands, and other forms of settlement characterize the southern and eastern areas, although substantial roundhouses do occur in some parts.

The substantial stone-built houses of Scotland are usually interpreted as the homes of powerful households (there has been some recent disagreement over this; Armit 1997b; Sharples and Parker Pearson 1997). The distance of Scotland from the influences of urban life in the south of the province may explain the reason for the use of the native model of the broch, dun or crannog on high-status settlements. These individual structures represented complex architectural forms that were based upon native templates. The substantial roundhouse will not have performed exactly the same role within native society as the villa, as the architectural form of these types of houses differed dramatically. This indicates that the use of space provided by the two types of house will also have varied.

Two excavated brochs produced quantities of Roman objects. At Fairy Knowe (Stirlingshire) the Roman finds included pottery (coarse wares, samian, amphorae and mortaria), glass and coins (Main 1998: 400), while Leckie (Stirlingshire) produced a broadly similar range (Mackie 1982). It has been argued that Lowland brochs were built by native chieftains who had a co-operative relationship with Rome (Macinnes 1994). Two additional brochs, Hurly Hawkins (Tayside) and Torwoodlee (Borders), have also produced significant concentrations of Roman material (Fraser Hunter, personal communication). Another site that produced quantities of Roman material is the hill-fort of Traprain Law (East Lothian; Hunter 2001a); perhaps this was a significant centre with an important relationship to Rome. Special relationships perhaps enabled people on these sites to obtain Roman goods, either through trade and/or as gifts. Hunter (2001b: 295) has speculated that in the south-east of Scotland the Roman finds indicate a strong hierarchy in the access of people to Roman goods, which forms a contrast to other areas of the north. Many of the Roman objects on these sites related to dining, and people may have been using these containers for eating and drinking. The variety of the pottery types that are represented possibly indicates that these objects were being introduced into the context of native feasting habits (Fraser Hunter, personal communication). They may have been used in a way that created a social distinction between dominant members of the household and others within their immediate communities (Meadows 1999). Personal ornaments are also a common find, and these may have been used in a comparable manner (Hunter 2001a).

It is likely that some of the people who lived in substantial roundhouses did not have such a close association with Rome (or, alternatively, such a strong desire to change their eating habits) for they do not all produce significant quantities of Roman material. For instance, a substantial roundhouse at Aldclune (Perthshire) produced just one fragment of samian (Hingley et al. 1997), while the broch at Edin's Hall (near Berwick-on-Tweed) produced no Roman artefacts despite fairly extensive excavations (Dunwell 1999: 348), although it is not certain that it was occupied at this time. Substantial roundhouses such as these may represent the homes of powerful households, but perhaps these people had a different attitude to Rome and did not require Roman goods. Alternatively, if the Roman objects were obtained from traders who supplied the army, perhaps people at substantial houses in some parts of Lowland Scotland did not have such direct access to the suppliers of these goods.

Some peoples with access to Roman objects did not build substantial roundhouses and this suggest that there is no exact correlation between high status and the building of substantial houses across the whole of Scotland. A rectilinear enclosure at Lilliesleaf North (Borders), close to the major Roman military complex at Newstead (*Trimontium*), produced large quantities of finds, including Roman pottery and glass (Clarke and Wise 1998; Simon Clarke, personal communication). A variety of Roman artefacts was found during recent examination of an unenclosed settlement at Birnie (Moray), including two coin hoards, three brooches and significant native objects (Hunter 2001b and Fraser Hunter, personal communication). These two sites suggest that Roman material occurred on a variety of types of native settlement across the north.

Souterrains were built on many pre-Roman and Roman period sites in Scotland (Hingley 1992: 29; Armit 1997a, 1999) and some of these sites have also produced Roman objects. Souterrains may often have served a storage function and they are very common in particular in the open settlement landscapes of Fife and Perthshire (RCAHMS 1994: 63–8; Armit 1999). Armit has proposed that they were built using a native design, effectively to supply the Roman army with grain. The frequency of the occurrence of souterrains in Fife, Perthshire and Angus (Armit 1999), where they probably occurred on many of the settlements, may indicate settlements that produced and sold an agricultural surplus to the Roman army. Souterrains are rare on sites with substantial roundhouses.

The evidence, therefore, does not support the idea that a consistent network of households with access to large quantities of Roman goods existed in substantial houses. The highly variable nature of the settlement evidence and artefact discard indicates that the situation was actually far more complex. Some of the households that lived in substantial houses either did not have a close relationship with Rome or did not obtain Roman objects. The souterrains in Fife and Perthshire and the sites at Lilliesleaf and Birnie suggest that different patterns of life and perhaps varying relationships with Rome existed in different parts of the north, while the substantial roundhouses of the Atlantic area rarely produce Roman objects.

The central area: Dark and Dark (1997: 11) have defined the north of England as a 'native landscape'. The native character of this landscape contrasts with the south and east, where it is usually argued that a process of 'Romanization' led to the development of a civil society (Millett 1990a; Dark and Dark 1997). This native landscape effectively characterizes the whole of the north, including areas to the north and west considered above. It is, however, important to stress that this supposed 'native landscape' was not homogeneous. We have seen that substantial roundhouses occurred in many areas of the north and west, while other native settlements varied widely in character across the area.

Higham and Breeze argued that the population of the area between the northern extent of the villa landscape and the southern extent of the distribution of substantial houses and souterrains did not possess a hierarchical pattern of settlement. In addition, the towns that occur in this area (Corbridge and Carlisle), and also the *vici*, appear to have been fully dependent on the Roman army. This absence of hierarchy may have been a result of the role of the Roman army within this area (Higham 1989:

168; see also Breeze 2001). There was a permanent military presence across much of northern England, focused upon the Hadrian's Wall corridor but also spreading some way to the north and south. The military may have taxed the local population in order to obtain some of the raw materials and supplies that they required, including animals, grain and other foodstuffs.

We have seen that to the south of this area the native élite were possibly used by the Roman administration to run local government. Their role in running the *civitas* may have allowed them to build up the surplus that was then used to create a Roman-type lifestyle. Some powerful households in Lowland Scotland acquired imported Roman objects as a result of contacts built up with visitors from the province, and these people may have had some form of economic relationship with Rome. The direct taxation of the local population by the army across the areas of central Britain may effectively have prevented the development of this local élite.

When the archaeological evidence for this study area is examined, however, a number of problems emerge with this idea. First, if substantial roundhouses in Scotland are taken to represent a hierarchical pattern of settlement, then it has to be accepted that this pattern predates the Roman influence, for all these types of houses have a pre-Roman origin (Hingley 1992). Indications of a hierarchical settlement pattern may also exist in a pre-Roman context in the Yorkshire Wolds and around Stanwick (see above). Therefore, if hierarchical patterns of settlements occur to the north and south in the pre-Roman period, why are they absent from this central area? Perhaps the character and extent of the military area was actually itself a consequence of the absence of a pre-Roman élite – the presence of the army may have been required to control the native population.

It has been proposed that a more egalitarian social structure may have characterized this central area (Willis 1999: 102) and perhaps it was more difficult for Rome to impose order in the absence of an existing native élite. We have to be careful, however, as it is not certain that a settlement hierarchy was entirely absent. Failure in the past to locate high-status sites may be partly due to the scarcity of modern archaeological excavations on native sites across this area. Some sites produce more Roman material than would be expected. For instance, field-walking on a crop-mark enclosure at Sandybrow (Cumbria) produced an unusually large quantity of Roman pottery (Caruana 1989: 66). In addition, other ways of demonstrating status might well have existed; it is not necessarily true that all dominant households will have wished and been able to acquire Roman objects. Can the character of so-called 'native settlements' inform us further? For instance, the creation of a substantial and elaborate settlement enclosure boundary might represent one means of defining high status. Perhaps relations of inequality were created and symbolized through the mobilization of dependent labour from subservient households that helped to create enclosure earthworks around certain high-ranking settlements (Hingley 1992: 32).

Enclosed and unenclosed settlements

Enclosed settlement appears to have formed the dominant type across much of Iron Age Britain (Haselgrove 1999b: 117) and Roman-period native settlements

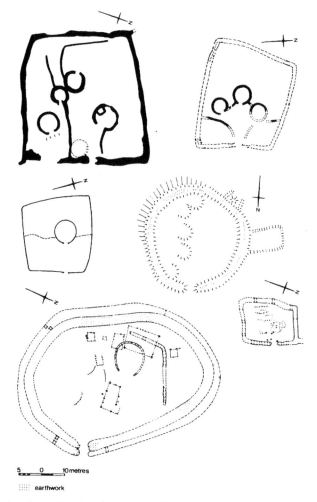

Figure 18.5 A variety of enclosed 'native settlements' in central Britain (after Hingley 1989, figure 26).

across northern Britain included a variety of types of enclosed sites. Indeed, some enclosed settlements of later prehistoric date continued in occupation in Roman times.

Enclosed settlements were typified by an enclosed space formed by an earth bank or stone wall, often associated with an external ditch (Hingley 1989: 60; Dark and Dark 1997: 80). These settlements varied in size from small enclosed examples to the extensive hilltop fortifications called hill-forts; most of the latter had probably gone out of use by the Roman period, although occupation may have continued on some sites. Enclosed sites appear to represent the most common form of native settlement across southern Scotland, much of northern and north-eastern England (Higham 1986: 186–97; Willis 1999; Haselgrove forthcoming). They are of a variety of types in terms of the shape that they adopt and the type of boundary (figure 18.5). In

Cleveland, the Tyne valley and perhaps in the north-east of England in general, sub-rectangular and rectangular enclosures predominate (Still et al. 1997, Haselgrove forthcoming). Enclosed settlements are also common in south-eastern Scotland (Armit 1997a: 104; Haselgrove and McCullagh 2000: 187) and elsewhere in central and eastern Scotland (Hingley 1992). These are often of curvilinear form, but with the occasional rectangular enclosure (RCAHMS 1997; Wise 2000; Haselgrove and McCullagh 2000: 187). The character of settlement patterns in the north-west of England and south-western Scotland is far less clear-cut. On the Salway Plain enclosed settlements appear fairly common (Higham and Jones 1985: 77–9, 95–6; Bewley 1994). In Cheshire, Merseyside and Lancashire evidence is emerging for enclosed sites, although these are few and far between (Haselgrove 1996; Collens 1999; Nevell 1999), while evidence for south-west Scotland is equally scarce (Alexander 2000).

The frequency of enclosed settlements, however, masks far more extensive landscapes of complex evidence. Enclosures form a type that is commonly recognized throughout northern England and southern Scotland because of their high visibility (Haselgrove and McCullagh 2000: 186–7), while unenclosed (or open) settlements can be more difficult to locate. The pattern of settlement in Fife and Angus, to the north of the Firth of Forth, is often termed 'open' or 'unenclosed' (Macinnes 1982) and comparable settlements occur further north, for instance, in Perthshire (figure 18.2) and Moray (Hunter 2001b). Recent analysis of the evidence has shown the highly variable nature of many unenclosed settlement landscapes (RCAHMS 1994, 1997).

Open settlements are probably far more common across much of the study area than the current evidence would suggest. For instance, at Melsonby, Stanwick (north Yorkshire), geophysical survey and excavation revealed an open settlement of mid to later Iron Age date (Fitts et al. 1999: period 1). Elsewhere it is appears likely that open and enclosed settlements do not form entirely distinct types. For some enclosed settlements evidence indicates that the enclosure actually formed part of much more extensive and varied settlement (Haselgrove and McCullagh 2000: 187). At Gardener's House Farm, Dinnington (Northumberland) geophysical survey produced evidence for an extensive settlement including a number of enclosures (figure 18.6; Biggins et al. 1997). At Thorpe Thewles (Cleveland) the enclosed settlement formed an early phase in the development of what became an extensive open settlement (Heslop 1987). On other sites open settlements developed on top of enclosure sites during the late Iron Age and Roman period (Jobey 1974; Dunwell 1999: 348).

It would be convenient to suppose that enclosed settlements might have been of higher status than the open settlements, but the evidence does not necessarily support this. The information for open settlements that were the setting for the deposition of valuable objects at Birnie and Melsonby suggests that the situation was probably more complex; both types of settlement may sometimes have been the homes of households that had access to valuable items. Further work on the native settlements is required to assess the frequency and distribution of Roman objects and the regional character of settlement evidence, but we should not necessarily assume that high-status households were entirely absent from any part of the study area until more intensive study has been undertaken.

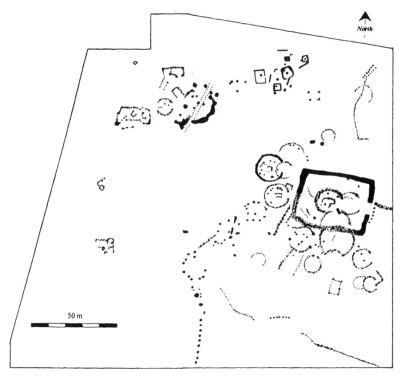

Figure 18.6   Gardener's House Farm, Dinnington (Northumberland) magnetometer survey showing an enclosed site surrounded on at least two sides by an extensive settlement (after Biggins et al. 1997, figure 6, used by permission of the author).

Research Agendas for Native Settlement in the Roman North

Rather than seeing native society in northern Britain as irrelevant to Roman archaeology, or as simple and backward, we are actually left with a rather complex picture (Hanson and Macinnes 1991: 85; Willis 1999). Regional variations suggest that people were living and interacting with Rome in different ways throughout the area, as indeed they were across the whole of the empire (Mattingly 1997). The relationship of native communities to Rome requires to be highlighted more fully than it has been. After all, Rome had a considerable ability to influence local settlement development, but it is also true that the nature of local organization must also have impacted upon the actions of the Romans.

I have reviewed an idea that we can define three broad zones of organization. First, in the north-east of England some members of the native élite were able to construct villas. Roman towns also existed within the area, and the wealth of the élite was probably based on the production of surplus agricultural goods and possibly also upon their position with regard to local government. A complementary way of achieving high rank may have been to join the Roman auxiliary forces (Roymans 1990). This villa economy was focused largely upon the Roman towns and lines of communication. Villas did not spread evenly across the entire area and to describe this as a 'villa landscape' (Dark and Dark 1997: 43) is a huge simplification. In fact the majority of the population probably continued to live in settlements that resembled pre-Roman types, although we have very little understanding of their ways of life because of traditions of archaeological research that have led to the neglect of these sites.

In a second zone to the north there was a fairly dense distribution of Roman forts, sometimes with associated *vici*, and the native settlements that occurred in large numbers did not usually include elaborate houses. In this area the Roman military may have taxed the population directly in kind and this could have prevented the development of surplus wealth by any local élite. As a result, native settlements characterize this area to the exclusion of villas, and the Roman towns and *vici* that occur were fully dependent on the Roman army. Nevertheless native settlements across this area do not fit into a standardized pattern. Some settlements may have been the homes of households that demonstrated their power through the creation of elaborate settlements, or through some other means. In addition, so little excavation work has occurred on native settlements in this area that it may emerge in due course that some people had access to quantities of Roman objects.

In the third zone, further north in Lowland Scotland, Roman pottery, glass vessels and metalwork occur, but significant quantities of finds are restricted to a relatively small number of settlements. On some of these settlements, substantial structures in a native form existed, including brochs, duns, hill-forts and souterrains. These may suggest the presence of households that had significant contact with the Roman administrators and with traders. The pre-Roman ancestry of the substantial round-house traditions suggests that the Roman administration may have exploited an inherited situation in the Lowland areas of this northern zone. Other types of sites, however, also had access to Roman objects, and the evidence does not suggest a consistent form of organization across the area. In addition, in the Atlantic areas of Scotland Roman finds are few and far between, although substantial roundhouses are common (Hunter 2001a); the distance of these areas from the Roman-controlled areas may be relevant here.

Turning to the nature of native society across all three regions, the contrasts in the character of native society that relate to the character of the social hierarchy may have influenced the policy of Rome for a substantial period in the second to fourth centuries. If the central area had a genuine absence of high-status settlement, the extent of military domination may have related to an unstable area in which Rome could not use a pre-existing native élite to create order (see Groenmann-van Waater-inge 1980 for this idea). By contrast, in the areas to the north and to the south control may have been created through alternative measures.

Further research will be necessary if the patterns that have been explored in this paper are to be interpreted in greater detail. In particular, excavation projects that promise new understanding of the deposition of both Roman and high-status native finds should be encouraged (see Clarke and Wise 1998; Hunter 2001b) but we also require a fuller understanding of native settlement in general. Can we detect and study in greater detail alternative methods for symbolizing status? Much more work is also required to map and comprehend patterns of settlement, as has been undertaken in some areas for the pre-Roman Iron Age (for instance, the Tees Lowlands and parts of Northumberland). Projects that pursue these approaches should aim to examine landscape history at the level of the locality, as this approach promises useful results. Regionally based studies should aim to synthesize the information in a more detailed fashion than has been possible in this paper, and to relate the broad variations in rural settlement patterns to the character of the physical landscape, the climate, the political and the settlement history. At the same time we need to develop our understanding by creating more flexible interpretations of the wide variety of evidence that helps us to target our attention on important themes.

ACKNOWLEDGEMENTS

I am very grateful to David Breeze, Steve Dickinson, Paul Frodsham, Bill Hanson, Colin Haselgrove, Fraser Hunter, Christina Unwin and Steve Willis for the helpful comments that they made on earlier versions of this paper and to Simon Clarke and Fraser Hunter for providing information on Lilliesleaf and Birnie prior to full publication.

REFERENCES

Abramson, P. 1995. A late Iron Age settlement at Scotch Corner, North Yorkshire. *Durham Archaeological Journal*, 11, 7–18.

Alexander, D. 2000. Later prehistoric settlement in west central Scotland. In J. Harding (ed.) *Northern Parts*. BAR (British Series) 302. Oxford, 157–65.

Armit, I. 1997a. *Celtic Scotland*. London.

—— 1997b. Cultural landscapes and identities: a case study in the Scottish Iron Age. In A. Gwilt and C. C. Haselgrove (eds), *Reconstructing Iron Age Societies*. Oxford, 248–53.

—— 1999. The abandonment of souterrains. *Proceedings of the Society of Antiquaries of Scotland*, 129, 577–96.

Ballantyne, C. and Dawson, A. 1997. Geomorphology and landscape change. In K. Edwards and I. Ralston (eds), *Scotland: Environment and Archaeology, 8000 BC–AD 1000*. Chichester, 23–44.

Barrett, J., Fitzpatrick, A. and Macinnes, L. (eds) 1989. *Barbarians and Romans in North-West Europe*. BAR (International Series) 471. Oxford.

Bevan, B. (ed.) 1999. *Northern Exposure: Interpretative Devolution and the Iron Ages of Britain*. Leicester Archaeology Monograph 4. Leicester.

Bewley, B. 1994. *Prehistoric and Romano-British Settlement on the Solway Plain*. Oxbow Monograph 17. Oxford.

Biggins, J. A., Biggins, J. et al. 1997. Survey of the prehistoric settlement at Gardener's House Farm, Dinnington. *Durham Archaeological Journal*, 13, 43–53.

Bloemers, T. 1989. Acculturation in the Rhine/Meuse Basin in the Roman period. In J. Barrett, A. Fitzpatrick and L. Macinnes (eds), *Barbarians and Romans in North-West Europe*. BAR (International Series) 471. Oxford, 175–97.

Bowden, M. 1996. Recent archaeological fieldwork in the Howgill Fells. *Transactions of the Cumberland and Westmorland Antiquarian and Archaeological Society*, 86, 1–11.

Branigan, K. 1989. Villas in the North. In K. Branigan (ed.), *Rome and the Brigantes: The Impact of Rome on Northern England*. Sheffield, 18–27.

Breeze, D. 1990. The impact of the Roman army on the native peoples of northern Britain. In H. Vetters and M. Kandler (eds), *Der Römische Limes in Österreich*. Akten des 14 Internationalen Limeskongresses 1986 in Carnuntum 1986. Vienna, 85–97.

—— 1996. *Roman Scotland*. London.

—— 2001. The edge of the world: the imperial frontier and beyond. In P. Salway (ed.), *The Short Oxford History of the British Isles: The Roman Era*. Oxford, 173–202.

Breeze, D. and Dobson, B. 1985. Roman military deployment in Northern England. *Britannia*, 16, 1–20.

Brown, J. 1999. *Romano-British Villa Complex: Chapel House Farm, Dalton on Tees, North Yorkshire*. York.

Brück, J. and Goodman, M. 1999. Introduction: themes for a critical archaeology of prehistoric settlement. In J. Brück and M. Goodman (eds), *Making Places in the Prehistoric World: Themes in Settlement Archaeology*. London, 1–19.

Burnham, B. and Wacher, J. 1990. *The 'Small Towns' of Roman Britain*. London.

Carroll, M. 2001. *Romans, Celts and Germans*. Stroud.

Caruana, I. 1989. Fieldwalking in the Solway Plain, 1983–84. *Transactions of the Cumberland and Westmorland Antiquarian and Archaeological Society*, 89, 51–68.

Clarke, S. and Wise, A. 1998. *Lilliesleaf North 1998. Interim report*. [Privately published.]

Collens, J. 1999. Flying on the edge: aerial photography and settlement patterns in Cheshire and Merseyside. In M. Nevell (ed.), *Living on the Edge of Empire*. Manchester, 36–40.

Creighton, J. and Wilson, R. J. A. 1999. Introduction: recent research on Roman Germany. In J. Creighton and R. J. A. Wilson (eds), *Roman Germany*. Portsmouth, RI, 9–34.

—— (eds) 1999. *Roman Germany: Studies in Cultural Interaction*. Journal of Roman Archaeology. Supplementary Series 32. Portsmouth, RI.

Dark, K. and Dark, P. 1997. *The Landscape of Roman Britain*. Stroud.

Dark, P. 1999. Pollen evidence for the environment of Roman Britain. *Britannia*, 30, 247–72.

Davidson, D. and Carter, S. 1997. Soils and their evolution. In K. Edwards and I. Ralston (eds), *Scotland: Environment and Archaeology, 8000 BC–AD 1000*. Chichester, 45–62.

Dunwell, A. 1999. Edin's Hall fort, broch and settlement, Berwickshire (Scottish Borders). *Proceedings of the Society of Antiquaries of Scotland*, 129, 303–58.

Durham University Archaeological Services. 2000. *Quarry Farm, Ingleby Barwick, Stockton-on-Tees*. Durham.

Edwards, K. J. and Ralston, I. (eds) 1997. *Scotland: Environment and Archaeology, 8000 BC–AD 1000*. Chichester.

Edwards, K. and Whittington, G. 1997. Vegetational changes. In K. Edwards and I. Ralston (eds), *Scotland: Environment and Archaeology, 8000 BC–AD 1000*. Chichester, 63–82.

Evans, J. 2001. Material approaches to the identification of different Romano-British site types. In S. James and M. Millett (eds), *Britons and Romans*. CBA Research Report 125. London, 26–35.

Fitts, R., Haselgrove, C. et al. 1999. Melsonby revisited: survey and excavation 1992–95. *Durham Archaeological Journal*, 14–15, 1–52.

Frodsham, P. 2000. Worlds without ends: towards a new prehistory for Central Britain. In J. Harding (ed.), *Northern Parts*. BAR (British Series) 302. Oxford, 15–31.

Gates, T. 1999. *The Hadrian's Wall Landscape from Chesters to Greenhead: An Air Photographic Survey*. Hexham.

Groenmann-van Waateringe, W. 1980. Urbanisation and the north-west frontier of the Roman Empire. In W. Hanson and L. Keppie (eds), *Roman Frontier Studies 1979*. BAR 71. Oxford, 1037–44.

Gwilt, A. and Haselgrove, C. C. (eds) 1997. *Reconstructing Iron Age Societies*. Oxbow Monograph 71. Oxford.

Haffner, A. and Schnurbein, S. von. 1996. Kelten, Germanen, Römer im Mittelgebirgsraum zwischen Luxemburg und Thüringen. *Archäologisches Nachrichtenblatt*, 1, 70–7.

Halkon, P. and Millett, M. 1999. *Rural Settlement and Industry: Studies in the Iron Age and Roman Archaeology of Lowland East Yorkshire*. Otley.

Hanson, W. 1997. The Roman presence: brief interludes. In K. Edwards and I. Ralston (eds), *Scotland: Environment and Archaeology, 8000 BC–AD 1000*. Chichester, 195–216.

Hanson, W. and Breeze, D. 1991. The future of Roman Scotland. In W. Hanson and L. Slater (eds), *Scottish Archaeology: New Perceptions*. Aberdeen.

Hanson, W. and Macinnes, L. 1991. Soldiers and settlement in Wales and Scotland. In R. F. J. Jones (ed.), *Roman Britain: Recent Trends*. Sheffield, 85–92.

Harding, D. 1984. *Holme House, Piercebridge*. Edinburgh.

Harding, J. (ed.) 2000. *Northern Pasts: Interpretations of the Later Prehistory of Northern England and Southern Scotland*. BAR (British Series) 302. Oxford.

Haselgrove, C. C. 1996. The Iron Age. In R. Newman (ed.), *The Archaeology of Lancashire: Present State and Future Priorities*. Lancaster, 61–73.

—— 1999a. Iron Age societies in central Britain: retrospect and prospect. In B. Bevan (ed.), *Northern Exposure*. Leicester, 253–78.

—— 1999b. The Iron Age. In J. Hunter and I. Ralston (eds), *The Archaeology of Britain*. London, 114–34.

—— (forthcoming). The later Bronze Age and the Iron Age in the Lowlands. In R. Daniels and A. Harding (eds), *Archaeology in the North*.

Haselgrove, C. C., Ferrell, G., Healey, E. and Turnbull, P. 1988. *The Durham Archaeological Survey 1983–87*. Durham.

Haselgrove, C. C. and McCullagh, R. 2000. *An Iron Age Coastal Community in East Lothian: The Excavation of Two Later Prehistoric Enclosure Complexes at Fisher Road, Port Seaton, 1994–5*. Edinburgh.

Haverfield, F. 1905. The Romanization of Roman Britain. *Proceedings of the British Academy*, 2, 185–217.

Heslop, D. H. 1987. *The Excavation of an Iron Age Settlement at Thorpe Thewles*. London.

Higham, N. 1986. *The Northern Counties to AD 1000*. London.

—— 1989. Roman and native in England north of the Tees: acculturation and its limitations. In J. Barrett, A. Fitzpatrick and L. Macinnes (eds), *Barbarians and Romans in North-West Europe*. BAR (International Series) 471. Oxford, 153–74.

Higham, N. and Jones, B. 1985. *The Carvetii*. Gloucester.

Hingley, R. 1989. *Rural Settlement in Roman Britain*. London.

—— 1992. Society in Scotland from 700 BC to AD 200. *Proceedings of the Society of Antiquaries of Scotland*, 122, 7–53.

—— 2000. *Roman Officers and English Gentlemen: The Imperial Origins of Roman Archaeology*. London.

Hingley, R. and Miles, D. 2001. The human impact on the landscape. In P. Salway (ed.), *The Short Oxford History of the British Isles: The Roman Era*. Oxford, 141–72.

Hingley, R., Moore, H., Triscott, J. E. and Wilson, G. 1997. The excavation of two later Iron Age fortified homesteads at Aldclune, Blair Atholl, Perth & Kinross. *Proceedings of the Society of Antiquaries of Scotland*, 127, 407–66.

Hunter, F. 2001a. Roman and native in Scotland: new approaches. *Journal of Roman Archaeology*, 14, 289–309.

—— 2001b. *Excavations at Birnie, Moray 2000*. Edinburgh.

Inman, R., Brown, D., Goddard, R. E. and Spratt, D.A. 1985. Roxby Iron Age settlement and the Iron Age in north-east Yorkshire. *Proceedings of the Prehistoric Society*, 51, 181–214.

James, S. and Millett, M. (eds) 2001. *Britons and Romans: Advancing an Archaeological Agenda*. CBA Research Report 125. York.

Jobey, G. 1974. Notes on some population problems in the area between the two Roman walls I. *Archaeologia Aeliana*, 5th ser. 2, 17–26.

Keppie, L. 1989. Beyond the Northern Frontier: Romans and Natives in Scotland. In M. Todd (ed.), *Research on Roman Britain 1960–89*. Britannia Monograph 11. London, 61–74.

Knight, D., Garton, D. and Leary, R. 1998. The Elmton fieldwalking survey: prehistoric and Romano-British artefact scatters. *Derbyshire Archaeological Journal*, 118, 69–85.

Macinnes, L. 1982. Pattern and purpose: the settlement evidence. In D. Harding (ed.), *Later Prehistoric Settlement in South-east Scotland*. Occasional Publication 8. Edinburgh, 57–74.

—— 1994. Brochs and the Roman occupation of Lowland Scotland. *Proceedings of the Society of Antiquaries of Scotland*, 114, 235–49.

Mackie, E. 1982. The Leckie broch, Stirlingshire: an interim report. *Glasgow Archaeological Journal*, 9, 60–72.

Main, L. 1998. Excavations of a timber round-house and broch at the Fairy Knowe, Buchlyvie, Stirlingshire, 1975–8. *Proceedings of the Society of Antiquaries of Scotland*, 128, 293–418.

Mattingly, D. 1997. Dialogues of power and experience in the Roman empire. In D. Mattingly (ed.), *Dialogues in Roman Imperialism: Power, Discourse and Discrepant Experiences in the Roman Empire*. Journal of Roman Archaeology, Supplementary Series 23. Portsmouth, RI, 7–24.

Maxfield, V. and Dobson, M. (eds) 1991. *Roman Frontier Studies 1989*. Exeter.

Meadows, K. 1999. The appetites of households in early Roman Britain. In P. Allison (ed.), *The Archaeology of Household Activities*. London, 101–20.

Millett, M. 1990a. *The Romanization of Britain*. Cambridge.

—— 1990b. Iron Age and Romano-British settlement in the southern Vale of York and beyond. In S. Ellis and D. Crowther (eds), *Humber Perspectives: A Region through the Ages*. Hull, 347–56.

—— 1995. *Roman Britain*. London.

Neal, D. 1996. *Excavations on the Roman Villa at Beadlam, Yorkshire*. Leeds.

Nevell, M. 1999. Iron Age and Romano-British rural settlement in north-west England: marginality, theory and settlement. In M. Nevell (ed.), *Living on the Edge of Empire*. Manchester, 9–12.

Nevell, M. (ed.) 1999. *Living on the Edge of Empire: Models, Methodology and Marginality*. Manchester.

Nevell, M. and Walker, J. 1999. Introduction: models, methodology and marginality in Roman archaeology. In M. Nevell (ed.), *Living on the Edge of Empire*. Manchester, 9–12.

Parker Pearson, M. and Sharples, N. 1999. *Between Land and Sea: Excavations at Dun Vulan, South Uist*. Sheffield.

Philpott, R. and Adams, M. 1999. Excavation of an Iron Age and Romano-British settlement at Irby, Wirral, 1987–96. In M. Nevell (ed.), *Living on the Edge of Empire*. Manchester, 64–73.

Rahtz, P., Hayfield, C. and Bateman, J. 1986. *Two Roman Villas at Wharram Le Street*. York.

Ramm, H. 1978. *The Parisi*. London.

Rivet, A. L. F. (ed.) 1966. *The Iron Age in Northern Britain*. Edinburgh.

Royal Commission on Ancient and Historic Monuments in Scotland. 1990. *North-east Perth: An Archaeological Landscape*. London.

—— 1994. *South-east Perth: An Archaeological Landscape*. London.

—— 1997. *Eastern Dumfriesshire: An Archaeological Landscape*. London.

Roymans, N. 1990. *Tribal Societies in Northern Gaul*. Amsterdam.

Salway, P. (ed.) 2001. *The Short Oxford History of the British Isles: The Roman Era*. Oxford.

Sharples, N. and Parker Pearson, M. 1997. Why were brochs built? In A. Gwilt and C. C. Haselgrove (eds), *Reconstructing Iron Age Societies*. Oxford, 254–65.

Still, B., Vyner, B. and Benley, R. 1997. A decade of air survey in Cleveland and the Tees Valley hinterland and a strategy for air survey in County Durham. *Durham Archaeological Journal*, 5, 1–10.

Stoertz, C. 1997. *Ancient Landscape of the Yorkshire Wolds: Aerial Photographic Transcription and Analysis.* Swindon.

Taylor, J. 2001. Rural society in Roman Britain. In S. James and M. Millett (eds), *Britons and Romans*. York, 46–59.

Tipping, R. 1994. The form and fate of Scotland's woodlands. *Proceedings of the Society of Antiquaries of Scotland*, 124, 1–54.

Tolan-Smith, M. 1997. The Romano-British and later prehistoric landscape. In C. Tolan-Smith (ed.), *Landscape Archaeology in Tynedale*. Tyne-Solway Ancient and Historic Landscapes Research programme, Monograph 1. Newcastle-upon-Tyne, 69–78.

Whittington, G. and Edwards, K. J. 1993. *Ubi solitudinem faciunt pacem appelant*: the Romans in Scotland, a palaeo-environmental contribution. *Britannia*, 24, 13–26.

—— 1997. Climate change. In K. Edwards and I. Ralston (eds), *Scotland: Environment and Archaeology*. Chichester, 11–22.

Wigg, A. 1999. Confrontation and interaction: Celts, Germans and Romans in the Central German Highlands. In J. Creighton and R. J. A. Wilson (eds), *Roman Germany*. Journal of Roman Archaeology, Supplementary Series 32. Portsmouth, RI, 35–53.

Willis, S. 1999. Without and within: aspects of culture and community in the Iron Age of north-east England. In B. Bevan (ed.), *Northern Exposure*. Leicester, 81–110.

Wise, A. 2000. Later prehistoric settlement and society: recent research in the Central Tweed Valley. In J. Harding (ed.), *Northern Pasts*. BAR (British Series) 302. Oxford, 93–9.

Wrathmell, S. and Nicholson, A. 1990. *Dalton Parlours: Iron Age Settlement and Roman Villa*. Yorkshire Archaeology 3. Bradford.

Chapter Nineteen

Rural Settlement in Southern Britain: A Regional Survey

Anthony King

Settlement Types

The leitmotif of this chapter is regional diversity. A secondary theme is derived from that much used term 'Romanization'. Classification of settlement types (often in order to describe regional diversity) poses problems of definition that are closely linked to ideas of what is Roman in relation to the countryside of Roman Britain. Principally, these revolve around the definition of the term 'villa', but also extend to definition of what is meant by village, farm and the all-embracing descriptor 'rural settlement' in the Romano-British context.

A tripartite division of terms has been adopted here – farms, villages and villas – which could be regarded as simplistic, but has the merit of being easy to apply in most cases. The great majority of villas are easy to define as such: they have material characteristics such as mortared rectilinear masonry, ceramic or stone roof-tiles, and planning features such as clusters of rooms, porticoes, bath buildings, etc. Villa plans can be complex, and have given rise to a variety of interpretations among specialists (cf. J. T. Smith 1978, 1997: 3–20; Cosh 2001: 219ff.). Embellishments to villas include decorative wall-plaster, mosaics, underfloor heating and architectural ornamentation in classical style (Blagg 2001). The exact definition of a villa has been much debated (cf. Hingley 1989: 21, 1991: 75–6; Scott 1993: 1–8; J. T. Smith 1997: 10–11), but need not detain us here, except for those more problematic cases that lie on the boundary between villas and farms. Simple masonry rooms of rectangular plan overlying earlier round-houses (e.g. Whitton, Glamorgan; Jarrett and Wrathmell 1981) have been defined as villas on the basis of the rectilinearity of plan and the masonry technique. Buildings that have villa characteristics because of their plans, but are built of timber, not stone (e.g. Boxmoor period 1, Hertfordshire; Neal 1978: figure 12), are also defined as villas. This has the implication that field-survey surface scatters of ceramic or stone roof-tiles, but lacking obvious masonry building debris, should also be accepted as potential villa sites, on the assumption that the tiles are being used for timber rectangular structures of villa type (cf. Whitwell 1970: 89).

Villas, of course, were farms in terms of their function in the vast majority of cases, but the term 'farm' in this chapter is applied to those buildings that were essentially the inheritors of the regional vernacular traditions of the Iron Age (Hingley 1989: 23–4, 31–5). They are much more variable in their nature than villas. Earth-fast timber, clay and daub and dry-stone walling techniques are used, usually for circular or ovoid structures, but simple rectangular buildings are also known. In plan, buildings are usually single-roomed, only rarely being multiple. However, round-houses on farms often occur in groups of two or more, raising the issue of variable function. The majority of farms are also enclosed, usually in single-ditched compounds or courtyards, but there is wide variation (Hingley 1989: 55 ff.), and the nature of data acquisition, principally through air photography and geophysical survey, almost certainly means that unenclosed farms are numerically under-represented.

Villages are the most difficult to define, since they can grade into villas and farms on the one hand, but are also large enough to be regarded as 'small towns' in some respects (Hanley 1987; Hingley 1989: 76–80). Probably the most usable definition of a village is a grouping of buildings, usually six or more, of roughly equal size and apparent status. This separates villages from large villas, which could easily have attained village size in terms of population, but which have a greater internal differentiation of status and generally a greater unity of planning than the former. Villages that straddle Roman roads usually take the alternative definition of roadside settlement or small town (Burnham and Wacher 1990) and are not considered further here.

Regional Variation

The southern *civitates* (i.e. East Anglia, the Midlands, South Wales, south-west and south-east England) cover a large part of the province of Britannia, and there are considerable variations in the density and nature of rural settlement within that area. Although topographical considerations play a part in the differences between regions, the human geography is equally, if not more, important as an influence. There are several distinctive zones of settlement, which can be loosely characterized as follows.

Devon and Cornwall

Small nucleated settlements of varying type dominate this region, including groups of courtyard houses, 'rounds' and other types of farmstead. Many sites show continuity from the Iron Age, and many appear to retain their defences (Thomas 1966a; Johnson and Rose 1982; Quinnell 1986; Todd 1987: 216–31).

Cornish rounds, as the name implies, are circular or oval in form with an embanked enclosure, but some of them are rectilinear (Johnson and Rose 1982: figure 3). They are very common, numbering over 1500 examples, mainly in west Cornwall (Todd 1987: 224). Virtually all the well-attested examples are Roman in date, such as Trethurgy, which commenced in the late second century and eventually comprised five oval drystone buildings around the periphery of the enclosure (Quinnell 1986: 123–7). The site lasted until the fifth century. Another recently excavated example, at Reawla, Gwinear, dates to the second to fourth centuries, and saw an enlargement during its existence (Appleton-Fox 1992). Finds from this type of site tend to be few in number, and the level of material culture is generally low. The Devon equivalent of the round is generally more square in form (Griffith 1988, 57–60, 1994: 93–5) and is a single or double-ditched enclosure. The banks of the enclosures are not massive, and are probably for demarcation and stock control. A typical example is the square enclosure at Hayes Farm, Clyst Honiton (Simpson et al. 1989). Another at Pomeroy Wood, Devon, is interesting in having a group of round-houses in a rectilinear enclosure built over an abandoned first-century Roman military base (Fitzpatrick et al. 1999).

A highly specialized and geographically restricted settlement type is the village or smaller group of courtyard houses, usually in an open settlement. The houses are often clustered together physically, or with small passageways between them. Occasionally they are singletons within a settlement of other building types. Chysauster and Carn Euny, West Penwith, Cornwall, are the best-known examples, and the type is essentially confined to the tip of the peninsula and the Isles of Scilly (Todd 1987: 168–72). Courtyard houses are not found elsewhere in the Roman province, but have some similarities with complex stone-built sites in Ireland, such as the *clochan* groups of the Dingle peninsula (Cuppage et al. 1986: 384; Ashbee 1996: 136). The most recently published excavation of a courtyard house is Halangy Down, Isles of Scilly (Ashbee 1996), where the house apparently grew cumulatively between the second and fourth centuries. The open oval courtyard in the centre formed a focus for chambers with round-house characteristics leading off from it. The walls are very thick earth and rubble banks with stone facings. Material culture at Halangy Down and other excavated courtyard houses indicates a relatively high status, with imported pottery, beads, etc., from Roman Europe. The excavations at Carn Euny also demonstrate a similar status, and have Roman finds running from the second to the fourth centuries. Iron Age origins for courtyard houses are clearly seen at Carn Euny, and in form the houses tend to have elongated side chambers (Christie 1978: 313, 333, 385–8).

Iron Age defended sites in Devon and Cornwall, such as promontory forts and hill-forts, tend to have very limited evidence of Roman-period domestic settlement (Grant 1995; Johnson and Rose 1982: 156), which may be indicative of a move into the unenclosed or weakly defended sites described above. Quinnell (1986: 124–6) suggests that this embodies an expansion of settlement (and population) in Cornwall during the Roman period. At the Iron Age hill-slope fort of Milber Down, Devon, occupation apparently ceases in the fort itself, but is found in a small rectilinear first-century farmstead just outside the perimeter (Griffith 1988: 41; Grant 1995: 103). This appears to be a similar sequence to Castell Henllys in South Wales (see below). Another settlement location that seems to display very little evidence for occupation in the Roman period is Dartmoor (Quinnell 1994: 82) and the other high moorlands of the south-west. These regions were in decline at this time, and indeed had been experiencing a reducing level of population from much earlier in the Iron Age.

Villas are almost non-existent in this zone, except to the south-east of Exeter, where villas, e.g. Honeyditches, Seaton (Silvester 1981), and other Roman settlement gravitate towards estuary and valley-side locations (Griffith 1988: 52–3; Brown and Holbrook 1989: 39).

South Wales

A dispersed settlement pattern predominated in this region, and was essentially a continuation of that of the Iron Age (Hogg 1966; Arnold and Davies 2000, 65–89; Manning 2001: 73–90). During the Roman period settlement density increased, mainly in areas that were already a focus of settlement activity. However, hills, marshes and estuaries were a deterrent to intensive settlement, as were poor soils in many areas. There are some villas in the south-eastern part of this zone, but in the main it is dominated by enclosed or unenclosed farms that frequently display continuity from the Iron Age. A possible explanation for the lack of villas is resistance to Roman culture, but Arnold and Davies (2000: 65–6) prefer poor agricultural productivity due largely to social constraints as an explanation, rather than active resistance.

In south-west Wales (James and Williams 1982; Williams and Mytum 1998), there is strong continuity, usually in small defended sites, e.g. promontory forts, or undefended enclosures. At Castell Henllys, Pembrokeshire, the defended site is abandoned and a farmstead constructed immediately outside (Williams and Mytum 1998: 132), and at other defended sites, e.g. Walesland Rath, Pembrokeshire, the Roman buildings are positioned over some of the defensive elements (Wainwright 1971). The latter site is a type of ring-fort, similar to contemporary and early medieval Irish examples, where they are much more numerous (Stout 1997). They appear to be high-status settlements (Williams and Mytum 1998), and in a couple of cases, e.g. Trelissey, Pembrokeshire, rudimentary villas are constructed within them (Thomas and Walker 1959; Arnold and Davies 2000: 74, figure 7.4). Some of the sites display abandonment in the early Roman period, but later reoccupation at a lower socio-economic level, e.g. Walesland Rath. In the early Roman period, round-houses continue to be constructed, but tend to change to rectilinear buildings by the later period (Arnold and Davies 2000: 76).

In south-east Wales (Robinson 1988: vii–xxiv; Walters 1992: 84–90), the main area of settlement is on better-quality lands in the Vale of Glamorgan. Here some villas are interspersed among farms of various types, in a settlement pattern reminiscent of the lowland *civitates* but with a much lower density of villas. One of the settlement types in this area was the embanked and ditched farmstead, originating in the Late Iron Age and in some cases developing simple villas within them by the late Roman period, e.g. Whitton, Glamorgan (Jarrett and Wrathmell 1981), Llandough, Glamorgan (Owen-John 1988). Villa development is slow and late – even at the best-known, Llantwit Major, Glamorgan (Nash-Williams 1953; Arnold and Davies 2000: 85–6), where a simple row-type villa is constructed in the mid to late second century, in all probability, over earlier timber buildings. Not until the early fourth century does the enlarged villa with double courtyard and mosaics emerge, only to be abandoned by about AD 350, as were virtually all Welsh villas by the mid-fourth century (Arnold and Davies 2000: 87).

A simpler type of rural settlement is also known in the region: small-scale but complex enclosures, with round-houses in the early period and rectilinear buildings, sometimes in stone, by late Roman times, e.g. Biglis, Glamorgan (Parkhouse 1988), Caldicot, Gwent (Vyner and Allen 1988). Evidence for Roman occupation of the hill-forts in south Wales is slight compared with the north of the principality (Manning 2001: 78).

North-western Midlands

In this region there is a sparse scatter of villas, and easier soils dominated by enclosed farms (Webster 1975: 79–93; Whimster 1989: 35–65; Booth 1996). Some rural settlements develop simple stone-built rectilinear buildings in the late Roman period, especially in the southern part of this region.

The low number of villas, even around the *civitas* capital of Wroxeter (Webster 1975: figure 37), seems to indicate a lack of resources and inclination to develop Romanized rural sites. Those that are known, e.g. Whitley Grange near Shrewsbury (White 1997), are relatively well appointed with mosaics, but none is large.

In the Marches, well-defined single- or double-ditched rectilinear enclosures are common, nearly all probably originating in the Iron Age and continuing into the early Roman period. They seem to be of relatively high status, are usually positioned as individual sites rather than conjoined or in clusters, and may have been the preferred type of rural site in the region, rather than villas. Two good examples, one single- and one double-ditched, were excavated at Sharpstones Hill, near Shrewsbury (Barker et al. 1991): both had round-houses within, and continued up to the second century, but not beyond. Others at Eardington (Hunn 2000) and Bromfield (Stanford 1995) display similar characteristics, but the sequence at the latter was interrupted by the positioning of a Roman marching camp immediately adjacent.

The single-ditched enclosures tend to be more ovoid or circular in shape in the western part of the region, and more rectilinear in the eastern, more low-lying areas (Whimster 1989: 36–40, 64). Whimster implies that this is due to Roman influence, because the rectilinear settlements were in regions where Roman military sites were common, but the excavation evidence (above) would suggest that many of the rectilinear enclosures were already in existence by the time of the Roman conquest.

The settlement evidence is strongest in the river valleys, e.g the Severn in Shropshire (White 1997), the Tame in Staffordshire (C. Smith 1979) or the Arrow in Warwickshire (Palmer 1999: 219–20). In the Tame valley, the typical settlement is a farmstead with round-houses in a loose grouping of interlinked rectilinear enclosures. Many originate in the Iron Age, but only 20 per cent go on after the third century. Those that do are often under or near later medieval settlements, and Smith suggests (1979: 10–11) that a more nucleated settlement pattern was starting to emerge in the late Roman period, which foreshadows medieval developments. Settlement density in the Tame valley in the early Roman period was one site per 2.275 square kilometres, giving each site about 225 hectares of land. This is comparable to other regions, but some parts of the East Midlands, such as Northamptonshire, appear to have been more densely occupied (C. Smith 1979: 10–11).

Wetlands

These zones of low-lying poor drainage show evidence of being deliberately settled and drained during the Roman period. The two main areas are the Fens (Phillips 1970; Gregory 1982; Potter 1989; Hall and Coles 1994: 105–21) and the Severn estuary including the Somerset Levels (Allen and Fulford 1987; Rippon 1996, 1997: 65–118), but smaller wetland areas such as Romney Marsh also display signs of Roman intervention (Cunliffe 1988). Each of the two main areas has its own characteristics, notably a greater sense of centralized organization in the Fens, focused on the apparently official quasi-urban centre set up at Stonea, Cambridgeshire (Jackson and Potter 1996). The main impetus for Roman settlement in the Fens occurred in the early second century, involving drainage and communication works, rectilinear droveways and fields. Interestingly, the organization of the settlement pattern was not very regimented, despite the apparently official nature of the whole operation. This contrasts with earlier Roman exercises in landscape reorganization elsewhere in the Empire, with their carefully surveyed centuriations. The settlements themselves were unenclosed and extensive, on the whole, with many 'Romanized' characteristics such as rectilinear layout. However, the buildings were made of ephemeral materials and do not survive well. Excavated examples demonstrate rect-angular constructions in wattle and daub, sometimes in groups of rooms together not unlike a villa (e.g. Welney Washes; Phillips 1970: 231–3, figure 16). The later Roman period sees evidence of flooding, for instance, in the southern Fenland in the mid-third century (Potter 1981: 132). In general, settlement densities were declining in the late Roman period.

The other main wetland area, the Severn estuary, is more variable in its nature. The Welsh side, the Gwent Levels (Rippon 1996: 25–35), saw its initial development in the late first and second centuries, because of the nearby military sites and the town at Caerwent. Land reclamation took place perhaps as a result of military initiatives, and the ensuing settlement was variable but poor, on the whole. On the English side, land reclamation also occurred as a result of communal action, which was probably locally organized rather than a result of official intervention. It was also later in date, and the ensuing settlement, of a somewhat sporadic nature, reaches its greatest extent in the late Roman period (Rippon 1997: 110–12). Rippon points out (1997: 116–17) that the reclamation of this region was different to other wetland areas, such as the Fens, in the lack of evidence for exploitation of seawater for salt production. The implica-tion is that the area was drained for conversion to agricultural land, rather than for exploitation of the existing natural resources.

In both main areas, there are some villas, particularly on the better ground on the periphery of the drained areas, e.g. the eastern Fen edge (Gregory 1982; Gurney 1986), but none is very wealthy.

The Villa Zone

The main zone of villa settlement was in central southern and south-eastern England, East Anglia, Lincolnshire and the East Midlands, where they were probably the dominant rural settlement type. Numerically, however, other types of farmstead and village may still have been more strongly represented and more populous. There are various sub-groups.

The Cotswolds and Somerset

This area is notable for having many large and wealthy villas, usually with a main phase of development in the late third or early fourth century, following a beginning in the mid-second century, and a continuation well into the fourth century (Branigan 1976a: 34–6, 1976b; RCHM 1976; McWhirr 1981: 81–104; Henig and Booth

2000: 79–113). Many of the villas are significant sites by any standard, and bear favourable comparison with fourth-century architecture elsewhere in the Empire (Hurst 1987: 29–32; Walters 1996).

Great Witcombe, Gloucestershire (Leach 1998) can be taken as a good example of this. The site displays little evidence before the mid-second century, but from the early third century there was major development of two large wings linked by a central corridor and ornamental *triclinium*. Significant embellishments to the *triclinium* and elsewhere followed in the late third or early fourth century. There was a change in use about AD 380, resulting in a poorer standard of living, followed by desertion in the post-Roman period. Other villa sites in the region also have complex sets of rooms of late Roman date, usually either dining or bathing facilities, which betray a sophisticated sense of architectural form and space (Walters 1996).

In some cases, e.g. Frocester (Price 2000), Barnsley Park (Webster et al. 1981–5; J. T. Smith 1985), villa development is of late Roman date over an early Roman farm of rectilinear timber buildings. It is unusual to see villa development in the first century, the best-known exception being the Ditches villa, North Cerney, Gloucestershire (Trow and James 1988), where an apparently high-status defended enclosure of the Late Iron Age has a stone-built villa of fairly simple type constructed within it only a few decades after the conquest. The site is reminiscent of villas in the eastern parts of Britain, and provides a strong contrast with others in the Cotswolds. This is heightened by the lack of development at the Ditches, and its abandonment by the end of the third century. The early impetus at the Ditches, perhaps also seen at Ditchley and Shakenoak in Oxfordshire (Henig and Booth 2000: 38), may be linked with the adjacent Late Iron Age *oppidum* and its concomitant élite associations.

There is evidence of intensification of rural settlement in the Roman period compared with the Iron Age (Fowler 1976: 177–9). One manifestation of this is the growth of villages, the most notable example being Gatcombe, Avon (Branigan 1977; Leech and Leach 1982: 67), where a group of simple rectangular masonry buildings, some aisled, seem to form a conglomeration of at least three farms of third- or fourth-century date, collectively being enclosed by a defensive wall. The excavator interpreted the site as a villa estate centre, with the main villa itself probably having been destroyed by post-medieval development (Branigan 1977: 188–9), but the case can equally be made for the farms as a village, as at the second- to fourth-century roadside settlement at Catsgore, Somerset (Leech 1982b). Similarly at Kingscote, Gloucestershire (Timby 1998: 287–93), a villa estate has been proposed for a site of about 30 hectares and up to 75 buildings. This seems more like a small town, but the question of definition remains open.

An unusual feature of the region is the use of caves in the Mendips, evidence for relatively wealthy domestic occupation coming from Wookey Hole and elsewhere (Branigan and Dearne 1992: 49–50).

Wessex

Villas in this region generally run from the second to the mid-fourth century, few being much earlier or later. A typical example is Halstock, Dorset (Lucas 1993), part of a significant cluster of villas around the town of Ilchester on the Somerset/Dorset border (Putnam 1984: 55 ff.; Leech 1982a: 210). It was built over a Late Iron Age settlement that had been abandoned in the mid-first century. Villa buildings of simple type were constructed from the mid-second century onwards, and there were large-scale changes in the third century, culminating in the development of a courtyard villa with mosaics and a two-storey monumental entrance, that had its *floruit* in the fourth century.

The overall density of villas is variable and dependent on both the pattern of urban settlements, which acted as foci in many cases because of the road and river systems (cf. Hodder and Millett 1980; Walters 2001: 140–1) and also topography (cf. Johnston 1978: 72–4; Tomalin 1987: 11–12), with a marked lack of villas in un-favourable areas for agriculture, such as the Weald, the New Forest, higher parts of Salisbury Plain and Cranborne Chase. The upland parts of the Berkshire Downs display little evidence for villas, in contrast to base-of-scarp villas in the Vale of the White Horse (Gaffney and Tingle 1989: 89 ff., 239 ff.). Most of the population on the Berkshire Downs lived in open settlements or ditched enclosures with origins in the Iron Age. Villas in this environment tend to be simple, such as Maddle Farm, and datable to the third and fourth centuries (Gaffney and Tingle 1989).

In much of Wiltshire, Hampshire and Dorset, it is possible to gain a fairly full picture of the relationship between villa and non-villa settlement, due to the work of the Royal Commission on Historical Monuments and individuals such as M. Corney (2000: 35–6). Iron Age rural sites in Wessex have long been studied and are relatively well understood (Bowen and Fowler 1966: 43 ff.; Cunliffe 1993: 179 ff.). From excavations at enclosed settlements, such as Gussage All Saints (Wainwright 1979), Winnall Down (Fasham 1985) and Ructstalls Hill (Oliver and Applin 1979), it is possible to see that settlements do not, on the whole, continue from the Iron Age into the Roman period in unchanged form. Circular ditched farmstead enclosures, often of Middle Iron Age origin, are usually abandoned in favour of smaller, some-times multiple, rectilinear enclosures. There is some evidence that the end of the Middle Iron Age or the beginning of the Late Iron Age marks a period of disruption to rural settlement in this region (Cunliffe 1984: 32 ff.), and this is probably a stimulus to reorganization of settlement forms in the early Roman period (cf. Fulford 1992: 29). Many sites occupy the same position throughout this transition, but some, such as Worthy Down, Hampshire (Dunning et al. 1929; King 1985) and Park Brow, Sussex (Rudling 1998, 47), have a pattern of shifting settlement foci within a zone of about 1 square kilometre. Another hiatus for these settlements occurs in the later Roman period, when many are abandoned, with lesser traces thereafter, including linear fence lines and ephemeral structures.

Some of the farms are large enough to be classified as villages, especially on Salisbury Plain, where sites such as Coombe Down (Entwhistle et al. 1993) and Chisenbury Warren (Bowen and Fowler 1966: 50–2; Cunliffe 1993: 251–2) seem to indicate continuation and expansion of large Iron Age settlements. They lack obvious Roman characteristics, perhaps because of their comparative remoteness from urban centres, and in this respect they resemble villages in northern Britain that were distant from civilian development.

The development of Iron Age settlements into Roman villas can be seen at the so-called 'banjo' enclosures that often have Roman-period surface scatters, and occa-sionally evidence for stone buildings, such as Bramdean (Perry 1966). The Danebury Environs Project has specifically focused on this question, and has demonstrated several sites in the Test valley where Late Iron Age settlements become villas, usually aisled buildings and other fairly simple villa buildings in a courtyard arrangement (Cunliffe 1993: 221, 1994). Aisled buildings are a feature of the villas of central southern Britain, often attaining a prominent position in the villa layout, such as Sparsholt (Johnston 1978: 80), Brading (Tomalin 1987: 22) or Thruxton (Henig and Soffe 1993) and an imposing elaboration of architectural form, as at Meonstoke (King 1996). Their purpose appears to be multi-functional, having both agricultural storage and domestic occupation evidence (the latter especially in the later Roman period). It is possible that they represent a stone-built rectangular 'Roman interpretation' of pre-Roman round-houses (cf. Hadman 1978).

South-eastern England

West Sussex is one of the few regions of Roman Britain to show precocious early development of villas, possibly as a result of the client kingdom there (Rudling 1998: 43–6, 1982, 275–7). The most famous of them is Fishbourne (Cunliffe 1971), and it reflects a Mediterranean/Gallic architectural form that was imported in all its basic essentials, including probably the skilled labour force, within a few decades of the invasion. Some fifteen others are known, all of lesser pretensions than Fishbourne, but nevertheless well appointed and luxurious for their date. They are widely distributed within the territory of Chichester, and may represent the residences of the *civitas* élite, each with its own block of land (Cunliffe 1973: 79). Interestingly, the early flowering of villas was not sustained, so that by the second century, villas analogous to those in other regions were being constructed, and by the mid or late third century many of those on the coastal plain were being abandoned, probably a result of insecurity along the 'Saxon Shore' (Drewett et al. 1988: 218).

Canterbury provides a contrast with Chichester in having a distinct lack of villas focused on its territory (Blagg 1982), and in this respect it is similar to both Silchester and London, though perhaps for different reasons. The land around the town has good potential for villas and other rural settlements, unlike London and to a lesser extent Silchester, so it is possibly for cultural reasons that wealthy citizens of the *civitas Cantiacorum* decided to prefer the town to the country. Generally speaking, it is the river valleys of west Kent that saw the wealthiest and densest concentrations of villas in the south-eastern corner of Britain. In the Darent valley, for instance, there is a villa every couple of kilometres (Detsicas 1983: 107 ff.; Andrews 2001), the best-known being Lullingstone, with its exceptional evidence for late Roman transformation into a Christian country residence (Meates 1979). River valleys are preferred locations for more Romanized forms of rural settlement elsewhere too, and may be associated with the working of more difficult soils by improved tools during the Roman period (cf. Bird 1987: 178 for Surrey).

An aspect of the transition to more 'Roman' forms of building can be seen at Park Brow, Sussex (Black 1987: 96–7; Rudling 1998: 47), where five poorly dated rectangular single-roomed houses of timber and daub were found, with evidence for red-painted plaster, window-glass and roof-tiles. They may represent individual cottages (Cunliffe 1973: 98) or two discrete groups equivalent to the rooms of a villa (Black 1987: 96–7). Elsewhere, rectangular structures (rather than round-houses) have been noted under early Roman villas, for instance, at Park Street, Hertfordshire (Rook

1997). Similar simple rectangular buildings of wood or stone have been excavated at the unenclosed village site at Chalton, Hampshire (Cunliffe 1977), and probably represent a widespread but poorly understood building tradition over much of south-eastern Britain.

The Thames valley

In the lower Thames valley, there is little evidence for rural settlement, mainly because of the modern London metropolitan area (Sheldon and Schaaf 1978). The settlement pattern is apparently dispersed with few clusters, except for riverside settlements up-stream of London (Cotton et al. 1986: 63–7). Few villas are known (only thirty-seven in the Greater London area), and they tend to be distant from the river and the city (fifteen kilometres or more) on higher ground (Perring and Brigham 2000: 155–7).

In the territory of Silchester, remarkably little rural settlement has been found, except in the Kennet valley to the north of the town, where settlements and a few villas, e.g. Aldermaston Wharf, Berkshire, overlook the valley (Lobb and Rose 1996: 86–92). This lack of settlement around the town may be due to a predominantly pastoral landscape in this region (Fulford 1982: 406). The Kennet valley itself sees an expansion of settlement onto more marginal land in the Roman period, possibly indicating a population increase. In the Middle Thames area, settlement evidence is poorly understood, but is similar in nature. Farms appear to have Middle Iron Age origins in several cases, and continue into the early Roman period, but are abandoned by the end of the second century. The settlements are rectilinear enclosures linked to field boundaries and 'droveways', as in Oxfordshire and the upper Thames valley (Miles 1982a), and contain either round-houses, e.g. Binfield, Berkshire (Roberts 1995) or tiled-roofed simple rectangular buildings, e.g Thames Valley Park, Reading (Barnes et al. 1997). At the former site, meagre material culture, but numbers of loomweights, led the excavator to suggest a low-status site specializing in weaving and associated pastoralism.

Further upstream, in the vicinity of Dorchester-on-Thames, Oxford and the Upper Thames, evidence for settlement is much more plentiful, the quantity of crop-marks on the river terrace gravels suggesting settlement densities as high as any in Britain (Henig and Booth 2000: figure 4.1). Large multi-period sites have complex se-quences of predominantly rectilinear enclosures, as at Lechlade and Appleford (Miles 1982a; Henig and Booth 2000: 99–100), within which stand individual farms and, on occasion, sites that develop into villas, such as Roughground Farm (Allen et al. 1993) or Barton Court Farm (Miles 1986). At the latter, a bipartite enclosure of the early Roman period overlay a Late Iron Age rectilinear enclosure on a different alignment. Within the Roman site, a simple rectangular timber build-ing with plastered walls and two post-built granaries represent incipient Roman building ideas. By the late Roman period, after a probable occupation break, another realignment and enlargement of the enclosures had taken place, within which was built a masonry villa of fairly simple type. At other farms with little or no evidence of Roman-style buildings, round-houses may have been succeeded by wooden sill-beam constructions, as probably occurred at Northmoor (Allen 1990: 79–83). This site also shows a possible break in occupation at the end of the Iron Age, a phenomenon observable elsewhere in the region and beyond (Fulford 1992: 28–36), which may

account for the renewed occupation being organized differently, with more rectilinearity in both enclosures and buildings.

Carefully organized rectilinear enclosures are evident at several villa sites in the
Upper Thames region, most notably at Ditchley, where the villa enclosure was later
walled to form a courtyard with agricultural outbuildings (Henig and Booth 2000:
86–7). In general, the villas in this region are positioned away from the river itself,
and are much more common on the higher ground to the north, where they take on
the characteristics of Cotswold villas, many being large and long-lived (Miles 1988:
65–6; Henig and Booth 2000: 90–2). The most significant of these is North Leigh,
with its three ranges around a large courtyard, and evidence for extensive subsidiary
buildings by the fourth century (J. T. Smith 1997: figure 42c). It was large enough to
house a substantial population, and indeed, multiple occupancy has been suggested
on the basis of the repetition of bath units and other features within the main ranges
(J. T. Smith 1978: 177, 1997: 299). North Leigh cannot be regarded as a village,
despite being large enough, but should be seen as the centre of a large estate.
Elsewhere in the Upper Thames area, evidence for villages is slight, with the exception of a few farms that gain significantly in size by the late Roman period to take on
village characteristics (Henig and Booth 2000: 72, 92).

The Chilterns, South Midlands, Essex

There are many villas in this region, often of early date and rapid development, but
few last beyond the mid-fourth century. Other forms of settlement include extensive
unenclosed villages, some large enough to be classified as towns, also many farms with
Iron Age antecedents.

South-east Essex has few villas, but many settlements of other forms. They are
thickly spread on the gravels of the Thames terraces, the two most notable being
Mucking (Going 1993: 19–21, 1996: 99–100) and Orsett (Carter 1998). At the
former site a rectangular, strongly ditched enclosure was created in the Late Iron Age,
close to more informal enclosures of Middle Iron Age origin. These had round-
houses within them, but interestingly, the large-scale excavations revealed that the
majority of houses were positioned outside the enclosures – this may well be the case
elsewhere, but has never been properly tested by excavation. After the Conquest, the
landscape was organized in a series of large linear ditched allotments, focusing on a
rectilinear double-ditched enclosure of the late first century, containing an aisled
building, a Roman-style granary and other wooden buildings. Occupation had
declined by the late Roman period, and had possibly ceased to be a domestic
settlement after the second century. By the later fourth century, it is suggested that
Mucking was effectively *agri deserti* (Going 1993: 21). Orsett, a few kilometres away,
is remarkable in being a Conquest-period heavily defended enclosure, about 50 × 60
metres, containing a high-status round-house. This is interpreted as native resistance
to the Roman Conquest, albeit displaying some evidence of Roman influence in its
planning (Carter 1998: 168–9). After this phase, the inner defences were partially
backfilled and simple wooden post-built structures were erected around the original
house, which continued until the end of the first century. Thereafter, the site becomes
a fairly typical farm, and like Mucking, declined by the late fourth century.

Further north, a villa cluster around the lower Colne valley has been linked with the *colonia* of Colchester (Dunnett 1975: 94–7, 113), and is likely to have been within its *territorium*. Generally, however, villa settlement is mainly found to the west of Colchester at some distance inland, on higher ground and more easily worked soils, with some evidence of clustering around the small towns (Dunnett 1975: figure 25, 1–2, 101). Notable among these is the villa at Rivenhall (Rodwell and Rodwell 1986, 1993), where excavations have revealed a sequence in which a large villa and court-yard were erected in the early second century, over a regularly laid-out Late Iron Age enclosure. The villa has parallels in northern Gaul, and is a good example of architec-tural ideas derived from other provinces.

In Hertfordshire, a significant cluster of villas in the Chilterns has Verulamium as its focus (Neal 1978; Branigan 1985: 100–40; Hunn 1995). Villas are built from the late first century on the whole, with notable early exceptions like Gorhambury (Neal et al. 1990). Some of the villas have Late Iron Age antecedent settlements, often with poorly understood rectangular buildings (Rook 1997). After development through the second century, there are clear signs of decline in the third century (cf. Faulkner 2000: 71–2), a brief revival in the early fourth, but from the mid-fourth century onwards, many decline to a lower standard of living (Niblett 1995: 77–87). A few, however, continue to the end of the fourth century, and it has been argued in the case of Latimer (Branigan 1971) that occupation well into the fifth century is a strong possibility. Non-villa settlement is not well understood in this area, but excavations at Chells revealed a weakly enclosed farm of the first century that expanded substantially in the following century, eventually going out of use in the third quarter of the fourth century (Going and Hunn 1999).

Further north in Bedfordshire and Buckinghamshire, there is a significant increase in settlement numbers in the middle and upper Ouse valley during the Roman period compared with the Iron Age (Simco 1984: 29; Zeepvat 1987: 8–10; Dawson 2000a: 113, 125, figure 10.4;). Villas are set up in low-lying positions in the river valley, often on south- or east-facing slopes, close to water sources and on good soils – a good example being Bancroft, Buckinghamshire (Williams and Zeepvat 1994: 12). Most are second-century, over or near Iron Age predecessor settlements, e.g. Odell (Simco 1984: 24–5), but some are not founded until the third century. Even so, the latter are often over sites with evidence of round-houses. Farms with round-houses and complex arrangements of extensive sub-rectangular enclosures, e.g. Wavendon Gate, Buckinghamshire (Williams et al. 1996), are typical of the non-villa settlement in the region. Open settlements of village type are not very common, but could be extensive. Kempston, Bedfordshire, covers 10 hectares, and has evidence of a rectilin-ear organized layout (Dawson 2000a: 125–6). This is similar to sites in the Fens to the north, such as Grandford, Cambridgeshire (Potter and Potter 1982). On more difficult soils such as the clays west of Bedford, settlement is more sparse, usually in individual enclosed sites of Iron Age origin (Dawson 2000b: 133–4). Similarly in Essex, sites on clay appear to be less densely scattered than on lighter soils, but nevertheless amount to one site every one and a half to two kilometres during the Roman period, leading Drury and Rodwell (1980: 69–70) to suggest that the distribution of settlement was not much different in density from that recorded in the Domesday survey.

East Anglia, East Midlands, Lincolnshire

In this region, there is a general scatter of villas, usually second to mid-fourth century, showing some evidence of clustering around the minor urban centres (Moore 1988: 56) or on favoured geology (Whitwell 1970: 80; Todd 1973: 78–80). Substantial villas are not common, and examples with ranges and courtyards, such as Winterton, Lincolnshire (Goodburn 1978) or Orton Hall Farm, Peterborough (Mackreth 1978), place an emphasis on agricultural production and storage rather than elaboration of the main buildings (Smith 1997: 166–8). The latter site is in the Nene valley, not far from the small town of Water Newton, around which a significant concentration of villas results in a density of one every two kilometres or less along the river valley (Browne 1977: 21).

The best evidence for rural settlement is often from river valleys and lighter soils, e.g. Nene (Wild 1978), Welland (Simpson 1966) and Trent valleys (Whimster 1989: 20–5, 66 ff.), where settlement densities are among the greatest in the whole of Roman Britain. Settlement of all types increases by comparison with the Iron Age, and zones such as the Suffolk boulder clays have evidence for farms where previously very few existed (Moore 1988: 56). In the Trent valley, complex groups of crop-marks have been interpreted as extensive enclosures of Iron Age and Roman date, the most interesting being at Cromwell, Nottinghamshire, where the crop-mark response is particularly good (Whimster 1989: 20–4). A simple villa and aisled building sit within a formally laid-out double-ditched enclosure, 250 × 200 metres, apparently succeeding a series of smaller conjoined enclosures along a trackway, although the exact sequence has yet to be tested by excavation (Whimster 1989: 78–9). This, however, is the only villa in this part of the valley, and a considerable number of farms existed in the immediate environs (Todd 1973: 78; Whimster 1989). It has been suggested that some or all of them may have been dependencies of the villa (Bourn et al. 2000: 99), but an alternative would be semi-independent farmsteads, one of which underwent villa development for reasons of cultural choice.

Non-villa settlement is similar to Essex and the South Midlands in having unenclosed or weakly enclosed villages and farms. Many of these sites are visible as extensive crop-marks showing ditched fields and loosely organized areas of settlement, e.g. Lynch Farm, Peterborough (Jones 1975), which unusually is of the late Roman period. A more organized settlement with sub-rectangular enclosures originating in the Iron Age is Wakerley, Northamptonshire (Jackson and Ambrose 1978: 171–3), where round-houses of the Late Iron Age are succeeded by a simple aisled building and other rectilinear buildings in the early Roman period.

Round-houses in fact continue into the early Roman period on many farmsteads and villages, but of some note is their existence on villa sites as well. These take the form of stone-built circular foundations, apparently a masonry and mortar version of the traditional round-house form. Several are known from the Midlands (Keevil 1996: 46; Keevil and Booth 1997; Taylor 2001: figure 13), most notably at the village or villa-estate at Stanwick, Northamptonshire (Neal 1989), and from southern Britain (Rudling 1997), and both domestic and sacred interpretations have been made concerning this curious phenomenon.

Conclusion

Fieldwork in the last thirty years has resulted in an enormous increase in our knowledge of Roman rural sites. This has been mainly due to systematic air photography and extensive open-area excavations, which together have particularly enhanced understanding of farms and other non-villa sites. Landscape investigations, such as those at Mucking, Essex, have been invaluable in this respect, and it is greatly to be hoped that similar projects can be funded and undertaken in future.

The late twentieth-century upsurge in fieldwork has not changed some traditional views of Romano-British rural sites, for instance, that villas are usually in favoured positions, on good soils and with ready access to resources and markets. Instead, we have a much better grasp of such issues as the nature of wetland drainage and settlement, and of the density of farms along river valleys in the lowlands, particularly on river terrace gravels. There are biases in this new evidence, of course, such as the greater sensitivity of gravels to crop-mark formation, but current and future research programmes are working to counter this.

This chapter has attempted to bring out the nature of rural sites of all types, region by region, in the southern *civitates*. In some respects, this approach underplays the traditional emphasis put on villa studies in Romano-British research, but no apology is necessary for omitting recent work on such matters as room usage in villas (Cosh 2001), since this level of detail would unbalance the general overview.

A largely morphological paradigm has been adopted for this chapter, with distinctions being drawn on the basis of shape, rectilinearity, etc. From this perspective, the regions present markedly different characteristics, as outlined above, and over southern Britain as a whole it can be seen that villas dominate, albeit patchily, the southern and eastern sectors, together with strongly rectilinear and indeed often formally organized enclosures, even for farms. Moving west into the West Midlands and Devon, villas are much less common, but farms in sub-rectangular enclosures dominate instead. Further west still, in Cornwall and South Wales, circular or sub-circular enclosures become more common. What does this pattern signify?

As an answer, it is tempting to make the simple equation, round = native Iron Age tradition; rectangular = imported Roman tradition, and it may well be the case that this has merit as an explanation. However, it avoids the question of motivation for these differences – whether villas, for instance, are primarily profit-making economic structures, their owners taking on Roman ideas for reasons of personal economic advancement, or alternatively that they are social status symbols, expressing a willingness to embrace what owners considered to be an advantageous version of Roman lifestyle (cf. Gregson 1988; Hingley 1989; Scott 1993; J. T. Smith 1997; Taylor 2001 for further discussion). The nuances of personal choice versus social expectation are almost certainly reflected in the mix of rural sites in each region. For instance, social constraints probably led to conservatism in rural settlement in some regions, notably in the west.

When considering the chronology of rural sites in southern Britain, continuity from the Iron Age is apparent on many sites, but there is also a significant increase in the number of new sites in the Roman period, implying a concomitant increase in the population (cf. Millett 1990: 181–6). There is also evidence for disruption in the Late Iron Age and the abandonment of some rural sites in the early Roman period, in central southern Britain and the Upper Thames valley. Is this a regional phenomenon due to warfare or a similar cause of discontinuity? This needs to be pursued further, since warfare undoubtedly took place in the Late Iron Age, and its effects on rural settlement are not well understood. Conversely, was it simply a result of *pax romana* that rural settlement apparently increased in the Roman period, or are we too dependent on the biased evidence of a better-surviving Roman material culture when evaluating site numbers through different periods?

The question of evidence survival also applies to the late Roman period, since it is increasingly apparent that rural sites of all types, not just villas, decline or disappear in most regions in the second half of the fourth century. There is considerable new building or reconstruction up to the early or mid-fourth century, and thereafter it tails away, dramatically so after AD 375 (Faulkner 2000: 71–2, 144–6). Villa numbers decline more steeply than farms, and from slightly earlier in the century, but even so, farm enclosures, as a rule, are no longer being made in the late Roman period, nor is there any longer evidence for round-house construction, which appears to have gone out of fashion in nearly all areas by the third century (Hingley 1989: 30; Fitzpatrick et al. 1999: 402). The replacement house type on farms was probably using rectangular sill-beam construction, for which there is remarkably little evidence. The latest settlements also probably tended to be unenclosed, or within fences rather than ditched enclosures. On the face of it, the decline in site numbers implies a decline in population, but the more plausible alternative is that the archaeological evidence is simply more difficult to recover (Esmonde Cleary 2001: 93–6). It is clear that significant changes were occurring on rural sites well before the normally accepted end of Roman Britain. We are, in effect, seeing in the late fourth century the beginnings of settlement structures and patterns that would characterize the post-Roman period, and it should be a priority of Romano-British research to investigate the nature of this change.

FURTHER READING

The literature on rural settlement in its many aspects is very extensive, but general works are relatively limited. Among the most important are: R. Hingley, *Rural Settlement in Roman Britain* (1989); K. and P. Dark, *The Landscape of Roman Britain* (1997); C. Thomas (ed.), *Rural Settlement in Roman Britain* (1966). Useful surveys on a regional basis are included in B. Cunliffe, *The Regni* (1973); R. Dunnett, *The Trinovantes* (1975); M. Todd, *The Coritani* (second edition, 1991); R. Whimster, *The Emerging Past* (1989). On the rural economy: R. Hanley, *Villages in Roman Britain* (1987); M. Todd (ed.), *Studies in the Romano-British Villa* (1978); K. Branigan and D. Miles (eds), *The Economies of Romano-British Villas* (1988). Most aspects of villas are covered in A. L. F. Rivet (ed.), *The Roman Villa in Britain* (1969); J. T. Smith, *Roman Villas: A Study in Social Structure* (1997); G. de la Bedoyère, *Roman Villas and the Countryside* (1993); E. W. Black, *The Roman Villas of South-East England* (1987); K. Branigan, *The Roman Villa in South-West England* (1976); and E. Scott, *A Gazetteer of Roman Villas in Britain* (1993).

REFERENCES

Allen, J. R. L. and Fulford, M. G. 1987. Romano-British settlement and industry on the wetlands of the Severn Estuary. *Antiquaries' Journal*, 62, 237–89.

Allen, T. G. 1990. *An Iron Age and Romano-British Enclosed Settlement at Watkins Farm, Northmoor, Oxon*. Oxford.

Allen, T. G., Darvill, T., Greek, S. and Jones, M. 1993. *Excavations at Roughground Farm, Lechlade, Gloucestershire: A Prehistoric and Roman Landscape*. Oxford.

Andrews, C. 2001. Romanisation: a Kentish perspective. *Archaeologia Cantiana*, 121, 25–42.

Appleton-Fox, N. 1992. Excavations at a Romano-British round; Reawla, Gwinear, Cornwall. *Cornish Archaeology*, 31, 69–123.

Arnold, C. J and Davies, J. L. 2000. *Roman and Early Medieval Wales*, Stroud.

Ashbee, P. 1996. Halangy Down, St Mary's, Isles of Scilly, excavations 1964–1977. *Cornish Archaeology*, 35, *passim*.

Barker, P. A., Haldon, R. and Jenks, W. 1991. Excavations on Sharpstones Hill near Shrewsbury, 1965–71. *Transactions of the Shropshire Archaeological and Historical Society*, 67, 15–57.

Barnes, I., Butterworth, C. A., Hawkes, J. W. and Smith, L. 1997. *Excavations at Thames Valley Park, Reading, 1986–88*. Wessex Archaeology Monograph 14. Salisbury.

Bird, D. G. 1987. The Romano-British period in Surrey. In J. Bird and D. G. Bird (eds), *The Archaeology of Surrey to 1540*. Guildford, 165–96.

Black, E. W. 1987. *The Roman Villas of South-East England*. BAR (British Series) 171. Oxford.

Blagg, T. F. C. 1982. Roman Kent. In P. Leach (ed.), *Archaeology in Kent to AD 1500*. CBA Research Report 48. London, 51–60.

—— 2001. *Roman Architectural Ornament in Britain*. BAR (British Series) 329. Oxford.

Booth, P. 1996. Warwickshire in the Roman period: a review of recent work. *Transactions of the Birmingham and Warwickshire Archaeological Society*, 100, 25–58.

Bourn, R., Hunn, J. R. and Symonds, J. 2000. Besthorpe Quarry, Collingham, Nottinghamshire: a multi-period occupation site. In R. Zeepvat (ed.), *Three Iron Age and Romano-British Settlements on English Gravels*. BAR (British Series) 312. Oxford, 71–117.

Bowen, H. C. and Fowler, P. J. 1966. Romano-British rural settlements in Dorset and Wiltshire. In C. Thomas (ed.), *Rural Settlement in Roman Britain*. London, 43–67.

Branigan, K. 1971. *Latimer: Belgic, Roman, Dark Age and Early Modern Farm*. Bristol.

—— 1976a. *The Roman Villa in South-West England*. Bradford-on-Avon.

—— 1976b. Villa settlement in the West Country. In K. Branigan and P. Fowler (eds), *The Roman West Country*. Newton Abbot, 120–41.

—— 1977. *Gatcombe Roman Villa*. BAR (British Series) 44. Oxford.

—— 1985. *The Catuvellauni*. Gloucester.

Branigan, K. and Dearne, M. 1992. *Romano-British Cavemen*. Oxbow Monograph 19. Oxford.

Branigan, K. and Fowler, P. (eds) 1976. *The Roman West Country*. Newton Abbot.

Branigan, K. and Miles, D. (eds) 1988. *The Economies of Romano-British Villas*. Sheffield.

Brown, S. and Holbrook, N. 1989. A Roman site at Otterton Point. *Proceedings of the Devon Archaeological Society*, 47, 29–42.

Browne, D. M. 1977. *Roman Cambridgeshire*. Cambridge.

Burnham, B. and Wacher, J. 1990. *The 'Small Towns' of Roman Britain*. London.

Carter, G. A. 1998. Excavations at the Orsett 'Cock' enclosure, Essex, 1976. *East Anglian Archaeology*, 86.

Christie, P. M. 1978. The excavation of an Iron Age souterrain and settlement at Carn Euny, Sancreed, Cornwall. *Proceedings of the Prehistoric Society*, 44, 309–433.

Corney, M. 2000. Characterising the landscape of Roman Britain: a review of the study of Roman Britain 1975–2000. In D. Hooke (ed.), *Landscape, The Richest Historical Record.* Amesbury.

Cosh, S. R. 2001. Seasonal dining-rooms in Romano-British houses. *Britannia*, 32, 219–42.

Cotton, J., Mills, J. and Clegg, G. 1986. *Archaeology in West Middlesex.* Uxbridge.

Cunliffe, B. 1973. *The Regni.* London.

—— 1977. The Romano-British village at Chalton, Hants. *Proceedings of the Hampshire Field Club and Archaeological Society*, 33, 45–67.

—— 1984. Iron Age Wessex: continuity and change. In B. Cunliffe and D. Miles (eds), *Aspects of the Iron Age in Central Southern Britain.* Oxford University Committee for Archaeology Monograph 2. Oxford, 12–45.

—— 1988. Romney Marsh in the Roman period. In J. Eddison and C. Green (eds), *Romney Marsh: Evolution, Occupation, Reclamation.* Oxford University Committee for Archaeology Monograph 24. Oxford, 83–7.

—— 1993. *Wessex to AD 1000.* Harlow.

—— 1994. *The Danebury Environs Project, 6. Houghton Down: Excavation 1994, Interim Report.* Oxford.

Cunliffe, B. W. (ed.) 1971. *Excavations at Fishbourne, 1961–9.* Society of Antiquaries Research Report 26. Leeds.

Cuppage, J. et al. 1986. *Archaeological Survey of the Dingle Peninsula.* Ballyferiter.

Dark, K. and Dark, P. 1997. *The Landscape of Roman Britain.* Stroud.

Dawson, M. 2000a. The Ouse Valley in the Iron Age and Roman periods: a landscape in transition. In M. Dawson (ed.), *Prehistoric, Roman and Post-Roman Landscapes of the Great Ouse Valley.* CBA Research Report 119. York, 107–30.

—— 2000b. *Iron Age and Roman Settlement on the Stagsden Bypass.* Bedfordshire Archaeological Monograph 3. Bedford.

Detsicas, A. 1983. *The Cantiaci.* Gloucester.

Drewett, P., Rudling, D. and Gardiner, M. 1988. *The South East to AD 1000.* Harlow.

Drury, P. J. and Rodwell, W. 1980. Settlement in the Later Iron Age and Roman periods. In D. G. Buckley (ed.), *Archaeology in Essex to AD 1500.* CBA Research Report 34. London.

Dunnett, R. 1975. *The Trinovantes.* London.

Dunning, G., Hooley, W. and Tildesley, M. 1929. Excavation of an Early Iron Age village on Worthy Down, Winchester. *Proceedings of the Hampshire Field Club and Archaeological Society*, 10, 178–92.

Entwistle, R., Fulford, M. and Raymond, F. 1993. *Salisbury Plain Project 1992–93 Interim Report.* Reading.

Esmonde Cleary, S. 2001. The Roman to medieval transition. In S. James and M. Millett (eds), *Britons and Romans.* CBA Research Report 125. London, 90–7.

Fasham, P. 1985. *The Prehistoric Settlement at Winnall Down, Winchester.* Stroud.

Faulkner, N. 2000. *The Decline and Fall of Roman Britain.* Stroud.

Fitzpatrick, A., Butterworth, C. and Grove, J. 1999. *Prehistoric and Roman Sites in East Devon: The A30 Honiton to Exeter Improvement DBFO, 1996–9.* Volume 2. *Romano-British Sites.* Wessex Archaeology Monograph 16. Salisbury.

Fowler, P. 1976. Farms and fields in the Roman West Country. In K. Branigan and P. Fowler (eds), *The Roman West Country.* Newton Abbot, 162–82.

Friendship-Taylor, R. and Friendship-Taylor, D. (eds), 1997. *From Round House to Villa.* Hackleton.

Fulford, M. 1982. Town and country in Roman Britain – a parasitical relationship? In D. Miles (ed.) *The Romano-British Countryside.* BAR (British Series) 103. Oxford, 403–19.

Fulford, M. 1992. Iron Age to Roman: a period of radical change on the gravels. In M. Fulford and E. Nichols (eds), *Developing Landscapes of Lowland Britain: The Archaeology of the British Gravels: A Review*. Society of Antiquaries Occasional Paper 14. London, 23–38.

Gaffney, V. and Tingle, M. 1989. *The Maddle Farm Project*. BAR (British Series) 200. Oxford.

Gregson, M. 1988. The villa as private property. In K. Branigan and D. Miles (eds), *The Economics of Romano-British Villas*. Sheffield, 21–33.

Going, C. 1993. The Iron Age and the Roman period. In A. Clark *Excavations at Mucking*. Volume 1. *The Site Atlas*. English Heritage Archaeological Report 20. London, 19–21.

—— 1996. The Roman countryside. In O. Bedwin (ed.), *The Archaeology of Essex. Proceedings of the 1993 Writtle Conference*. Chelmsford, 95–107.

Going, C. and Hunn, J. R. 1999. *Excavations at Boxfield Farm, Chells, Stevenage, Hertfordshire*. Hertfordshire Archaeology Trust Report 2. Hertford.

Goodburn, R. 1978. Winterton: some villa problems. In M. Todd (ed.), *Studies in the Romano-British Villa*. Leicester, 93–101.

Grant, N. 1995. The use of hillforts in Devon during the late Roman and post-Roman periods. *Proceedings of the Devon Archaeological Society*, 53, 97–108.

Gregory, T. 1982. Romano-British settlement in West Norfolk and on the Norfolk Fen edge. In D. Miles (ed.), *The Romano-British Countryside*. BAR (British Series) 103. Oxford, 351–76.

Griffith, F. M. 1988. *Devon's Past: An Aerial View*. Exeter.

—— 1994. Changing perceptions of the context of prehistoric Dartmoor. *Proceedings of the Devon Archaeological Society*, 52, 85–99.

Gurney, D. (ed.) 1986. *Settlement, Religion and Industry on the Fen Edge: Three Romano-British Settlements in Norfolk*. East Anglian Archaeology 31. Norwich.

Hadman, J. 1978. Aisled buildings in Roman Britain. In M. Todd (ed.), *Studies in the Romano-British Villa*. Leicester, 187–95.

Hall, D. and Coles, J. 1994. *Fenland Survey: An Essay in Landscape and Persistence*. London.

Hanley, R. 1987. *Villages in Roman Britain*. Princes Risborough.

Henig, M. and Booth, P. 2000. *Roman Oxfordshire*. Stroud.

Henig, M. and Soffe, G. 1993. The Thruxton Roman villa and its mosaic pavement. *Journal of the British Archaeological Association*, 146, 1–28.

Hingley, R. 1989. *Rural Settlement in Roman Britain*. London.

—— 1991. The Romano-British countryside: the significance of rural settlement forms. In R. F. J. Jones (ed.), *Roman Britain: Recent Trends*. Sheffield, 75–80.

Hodder, I. and Millett, M. 1980. Romano-British villas and towns: a systematic analysis. *World Archaeology*, 12, 69–76.

Hogg, A. H. A. 1966. Native settlement in Wales. In C. Thomas (ed.), *Rural Settlement in Roman Britain*. London, 28–38.

Hunn, J. R. 1995. The Romano-British landscape of the Chiltern dipslope: a study of settlement around Verulamium. In R. Holgate (ed.), *Chiltern Archaeology: Recent Work*. Dunstable, 76–91.

—— 2000. Hay Farm, Eardington, Shropshire: an Iron Age and Romano-British enclosure. In R. Zeepvat (ed.), *Three Iron Age and Romano-British Rural Settlement on English Gravels*. BAR (British Series) 312. Oxford, 119–44.

Hurst, H. R. 1987. Excavations at Box Roman villa, 1967–8. *Wiltshire Archaeological and Natural History Magazine*, 81, 19–51.

Jackson, D. A. and Ambrose, T. 1978. Excavations at Wakerley, Northants, 1972–75. *Britannia*, 9, 115–242.

Jackson, R. P. and Potter, T. W. 1996. *Excavations at Stonea, Cambridgeshire, 1980–85*. London.

James, H. and Williams, G. 1982. Rural settlement in Dyfed. In D. Miles (ed.) *The Romano-British Countryside*. BAR (British Series) 103. Oxford, 289–312.

James, S. and Millett, M. (eds) 2001 *Britons and Romans: Advancing an Archaeological Agenda*. CBA Research Report 125. York.

Jarrett, M. and Wrathmell, S. 1981. *Whitton: An Iron Age and Roman Farmstead in South Glamorgan*. Cardiff.

Johnson, N. and Rose, P. 1982. Defended settlement in Cornwall – an illustrated discussion. In D. Miles (ed.), *The Romano-British Countryside*. BAR (British Series) 103. Oxford, 151–207.

Johnson, P. (ed.) 1996 *Architecture in Roman Britain*. CBA Research Report 94. York.

Johnston, D. 1978. Villas of Hampshire and the Isle of Wight. In M. Todd (ed.), *Studies in the Romano-British Villa*. Leicester, 71–92.

Jones, R. F. J. 1975. The Romano-British farmstead and its cemetery at Lynch Farm, near Peterborough. *Northamptonshire Archaeology*, 10, 94–137.

Keevil, G. 1996. The reconstruction of the Romano-British villa at Redlands Farm, Northamptonshire. In P. Johnson (ed.), *Architecture in Romano Britain*. York, 44–55.

Keevil, G. and Booth, P. 1997. Settlement, sequence and structure: Romano-British stone-built roundhouses at Redlands Farm, Stanwick (Northants), and Alchester (Oxon). In R. and D. Friendship-Taylor (eds), *From Round House to Villa*. Hackleton, 19–45.

King, A. C. 1985. Excavations at Worthy Down, South Wonston, 1985. *Hampshire Field Club and Archaeological Society Newsletter*, NS 5, 16–17.

—— 1996. The south-east façade of Meonstoke aisled building. In P. Johnson (ed.), *Architecture in Roman Britain*. York, 56–69.

Leach, P. 1998 *Great Witcombe Roman Villa, Gloucestershire*. BAR (British Series) 266. Oxford.

Leech, R. H. 1976. Larger agricultural settlements in the West Country. In K. Branigan and D. Fowler, *The Roman West Country*. Newton Abbot, 142–61.

—— 1982a. The Roman interlude in the south-west: the dynamics of economic and social change in Romano-British South Somerset and North Dorset. In D. Miles (ed.), *The Romano-British Countryside*. BAR (British Series) 103. Oxford, 209–67.

—— 1982b. *Excavations at Catsgore 1970–1973*. Bristol.

Leech, R. H. and Leach, P. 1982. Roman town and countryside 43–450 AD. In M. Aston and I. Burrow (eds), *The Archaeology of Somerset: A Review to 1500 AD*. Bridgewater, 63–81.

Lobb, S. and Rose, P. 1996. *Archaeological Survey of the Lower Kennet Valley, Berkshire*. Wessex Archaeology Monograph 9. Salisbury.

Lucas, R. N. 1993. *The Romano-British Villa at Halstock, Dorset. Excavations 1967–1985*. Dorset Natural History and Archaeological Society Monograph 13. Dorchester.

Mackreth, D. F. 1978. Orton Hall Farm, Peterborough: a Roman and Saxon settlement. In M. Todd (ed.), *Studies in the Romano-British Villa*. Leicester 209–28.

McWhirr, A. 1981. *Roman Gloucestershire*. Gloucester.

Manning, W. 2001. *Roman Wales*. Cardiff.

Meates, G. W. 1979. *The Lullingstone Roman Villa, I*. Maidstone.

Miles, D. 1982a. Confusion in the countryside: some comments on the Upper Thames region. In D. Miles (ed.), *The Romano-British Countryside*. Oxford, 53–79.

—— 1988. Villas and variety: aspects of economy and society in the Upper Thames landscape. In Branigan and Miles (eds), *The Economies of Romano-British Villas*. Sheffield, 60–72.

Miles, D. (ed.) 1982b. *The Romano-British Countryside: Studies in Rural Settlement and Economy*. BAR (British Series) 103. Oxford.

—— 1986. *Archaeology at Barton Court Farm, Abingdon, Oxon*. CBA Research Report 50. York.

Millett, M. 1990. *The Romanization of Britain: An Essay in Archaeological Interpretation*. Cambridge.

Moore, I. E. 1988. *The Archaeology of Roman Suffolk*. Ipswich.

Nash-Williams, V. 1953. The Roman villa at Llantwit Major in Glamorgan. *Archaeologia Cambrensis*, 102, 89–163.

Neal, D. S. 1978. The growth and decline of villas in the Verulamium area. In M. Todd (ed.), *Studies in the Romano-British Villa*. Leicester, 33–58.

—— 1989. The Stanwick villa, Northants: an interim report on the excavations of 1984–88. *Britannia*, 20, 149–68.

Neal, D. S., Wardle, A. and Hunn, J. 1990. *Excavation of the Iron Age, Roman and Medieval Settlement at Gorhambury, St Albans*. English Heritage Archaeological Report 14. London.

Niblett, R. 1995. *Roman Hertfordshire*, Wimborne.

Oliver, M. and Applin, B. 1979. Excavation of an Iron Age and Romano-British settlement at Ructstalls Hill, Basingstoke, Hampshire, 1972–5. *Proceedings of the Hampshire Field Club and Archaeological Society*, 35, 41–92.

Owen-John, H. 1988. Llandough: the rescue excavation of a multi-period site near Cardiff, South Glamorgan. In D. M. Robinson (ed.), *Biglis, Caldicot and Llandough*. BAR (British Series) 188. Oxford, 123–77.

Palmer, S. C. 1999. Archaeological excavations in the Arrow Valley, Warwickshire. *Transactions of the Birmingham and Warwickshire Archaeological Society*, 103, 1–230.

Parkhouse, J. 1988. Excavations at Biglis, South Glamorgan. In D. M. Robinson (ed.), *Biglis, Caldicot and Llandough*. BAR (British Series) 188. Oxford, 1–64.

Perring, D. and Brigham, T. 2000. Londinium and its hinterland: the Roman period. In Museum of London Archaeological Service, *The Archaeology of Greater London: An Assessment of Archaeological Evidence for Human Presence in the the Area now covered by Greater London*. London, 119–70.

Perry, B. 1966. Some recent discoveries in Hampshire. In C. Thomas (ed.), *Rural Settlement in Roman Britain*. London, 39–42.

Phillips, C. W. (ed.) 1970. *The Fenland in Roman Times*. London.

Potter, T. W. 1981. The Roman occupation of the central Fenland. *Britannia*, 12, 79–133.

—— 1989. Recent work on the Roman Fens of eastern England and the question of imperial estates. *Journal of Roman Archaeology*, 2, 267–74.

Potter, T. W. and Potter C. F. 1982. *A Romano-British Village at Grandford, March, Cambridgeshire*. British Museum Occasional Paper 35. London.

Price, E. 2000. *Frocester: A Romano-British Settlement, its Antecedents and Successors*. Stonehouse.

Putnam, B. 1984. *Roman Dorset*. Wimborne.

Quinnell, H. 1986. Cornwall in the Iron Age and the Roman period. *Cornish Archaeology*, 25, 111–34.

—— 1994. Becoming marginal? Dartmoor in later prehistory. *Proceedings of the Devon Archaeological Society*, 52, 75–83.

Rippon, S. 1996. *The Gwent Levels: The Evolution of a Wetland Landscape*. CBA Research Report 105. York.

—— 1997. *The Severn Estuary. Landscape Evolution and Wetland Reclamation*. London.

Roberts, M. R. 1995. Excavations at Park Farm, Binfield, 1990: an Iron Age and Romano-British settlement and two Mesolithic flint scatters. In I. Barnes, C. A. Butterworth, J. W. Hawkes and L. Smith *Early Settlement in Berkshire*. Wessex Archaeology Monograph 6. Salisbury, 93–132.

Robinson, D. M. (ed.) 1988. *Biglis, Caldicot and Llandough. Three Late Iron Age and Romano-British Sites in South-east Wales, Excavations 1977–79*. BAR (British Series) 188. Oxford.

Rodwell, W. J. and Rodwell K. A. 1986 and 1993. *Rivenhall: Investigations of a Villa, Church and Village 1950–1977*. CBA Research Reports 55 and 80. York.

Rook, T. 1997. The view from Hertfordshire. In D. and R. Friendship-Taylor (eds), *From Round House to Villa*. Hackleton, 53–7.

Royal Commission on Historical Monuments (England). 1976. *An Inventory of Iron Age and Romano-British Monuments in the Gloucestershire Cotswolds*. London.

Rudling, D. R. 1982. Rural settlement in Late Iron Age and Roman Sussex. In D. Miles (ed.), *The Romano-British Countryside*. BAR (British Series) 103. Oxford, 269–88.

—— 1997. Round 'house' to villa: the Beddingham and Watergate villas. In D. and R. Friendship-Taylor (eds), *From Round House to Villa*. Hackleton, 1–8.

—— 1998. The development of Roman villas in Sussex. *Sussex Archaeological Collections*, 136, 41–65.

Scott, E. 1993. *A Gazetteer of Roman Villas in Britain*. Leicester.

Sheldon, H. and Schaaf, L. 1978. A survey of Roman sites in Greater London. In J. Bird, H. Chapman and J. Clark (eds), *Collectanea Londiniensia: Studies presented to Ralph Merrifield*. London, 59–88.

Silvester, R. 1981. Excavations at Honeyditches Roman villa, Seaton, in 1978. *Proceedings of the Devon Archaeological Society*, 39, 37–88.

Simco, A. 1984. *Survey of Bedfordshire: The Roman Period*. Bedford.

Simpson, S., Griffith, F. and Holbrook, N. 1989. The prehistoric, Roman and early post-Roman site at Hayes Farm, Clyst Honiton. *Proceedings of the Devon Archaeological Society*, 47, 1–28.

Simpson, W. G. 1966. Romano-British settlement on the Welland gravels. In C. Thomas (ed.), *Rural Settlement in Roman Britain*. London, 15–25.

Smith, C. 1979. The historical development of the landscape in the parishes of Alrewas, Fisherwick and Whittington: a retrogressive analysis. *Transactions of the South Staffordshire Archaeological and Historical Society*, 20, 1–14.

Smith, J. T. 1978. Villas as a key to social structure. In M. Todd (ed.), *Studies in the Romano-British Villa*. Leicester, 149–85.

—— 1985. Barnsley Park villa: its interpretation and implications. *Oxford Journal of Archaeology*, 4, 341–51. [See also the reply by Webster, 6, 1987, 69–89.]

—— 1997. *Roman Villas: A Study in Social Structure*. London.

Stanford, S. C. 1995. A Cornovian farm and Saxon cemetery at Bromfield, Shropshire. *Transactions of the Shropshire Archaeological and Historical Society*, 70, 95–141.

Stout, M. 1997. *The Irish Ringfort*. Dublin.

Taylor, J. 2001. Rural society in Roman Britain. In S. James and M. Millett (eds), *Britain and Romans*. CBA Research Report 125. London, 46–59.

Thomas, C. 1966a. The character and origins of Roman Dumnonia. In C. Thomas (ed.), *Rural Settlement in Roman Britain*. London, 74–98.

Thomas, C. (ed.) 1966b. *Rural Settlement in Roman Britain*. London.

Thomas, W. G. and Walker, R. F. 1959. Excavations at Trelissey, Pembrokeshire, 1950–1. *Bulletin of the Board of Celtic Studies*, 18, 295–303.

Timby, J. 1998. *Excavations at Kingscote and Wycomb, Gloucestershire*. Cirencester.

Todd, M. 1973. *The Coritani*. London.

—— 1987. *The South-West to AD 1000*. Harlow.

Todd, M. (ed.) 1978. *Studies in the Romano-British Villa*. Leicester.

Tomalin, D. 1987. *Roman Wight: A Guide Catalogue*. Newport.

Trow, S. and James, S. 1988. Ditches villa, North Cerney. An example of locational conservatism in the early Roman Cotswolds. In K. Branigan and D. Miles (eds), *The Economies of Romano-British Villas*. Sheffield, 83–7.

Vyner, B. and Allen, D. W. 1988. A Romano-British settlement at Caldicot, Gwent. In D. M. Robinson (ed.), *Biglis, Caldicot and Llandough*. BAR (British Series) 188. Oxford, 65–122.

Wainwright, G. 1971. The excavation of a fortified settlement at Walesland Rath, Pembroke-shire. *Britannia*, 2, 48–108.

—— 1979. *Gussage All Saints: An Iron Age Settlement in Dorset*. Archaeological Report 10. London.

Walters, B. (Bryn) 1992. *The Archaeology and History of Ancient Dean and the Wye Valley*. Cheltenham.

—— 1996. 'Exotic' structures in 4th-century Britain. In P. Johnson (ed.), *Architecture in Roman Britain*, CBA Research Report 94. York, 152–62.

—— 2001. A perspective on the social order of Roman villas in Wiltshire. In P. Ellis (ed.), *Roman Wiltshire and After. Papers in Honour of Ken Annable*. Devizes, 127–46.

Webster, G. 1975. *The Cornovii*. London.

Webster, G., Fowler, P., Noddle, B. and Smith, L. 1981–5. The excavation of a Romano-British rural establishment at Barnsley Park, Gloucestershire, 1961–79. *Transactions of the Bristol and Gloucestershire Archaeological Society*, 99, 21–77; 100, 65–189; 103, 73–100.

Whimster, R. 1989. *The Emerging Past: Air Photography and the Buried Landscape*. London.

White, R. 1997. Summary of fieldwork carried out by the Wroxeter Hinterland Project 1994–7. *Transactions of the Shropshire Archaeological and Historical Society*, 72, 1–8.

Whitwell, J. B. 1970. *Roman Lincolnshire*. Lincoln.

Wild, J. P. 1978. Villas in the Lower Nene valley. In M. Todd (ed.), *Studies in the Romano-British Villa*. Leicester, 59–69.

Williams, G. and Mytum, H. 1998. *Llawhaden, Dyfed: Excavations on a group of small defended enclosures, 1980–4*. BAR (British Series) 275. Oxford.

Williams, R. J., Hart, P. and Williams, A. 1996. *Wavendon Gate: A Late Iron Age and Roman Settlement in Milton Keynes*. Buckinghamshire Archaeological Society Monograph. 10. Aylesbury.

Williams, R. J. and Zeepvat, R. 1994. *Bancroft: A Late Bronze Age/Iron Age Settlement, Roman Villa and Temple/Mausoleum*, Buckinghamshire Archaeological Society Monograph 7. Aylesbury.

Zeepvat, R. 1987. Romano-British settlement in the Upper Ouse and Ouzel valleys. In D. Maynard (ed.), *Roman Milton Keynes. Excavations and Fieldwork, 1971–82*. Buckinghamshire Archaeological Society Monograph 1. Aylesbury.

Zeepvat, R. (ed.) 2000. *Three Iron Age and Romano-British Rural Settlements on English Gravels*. BAR (British Series) 312. Oxford.

Chapter Twenty

Domestic Animals and Their Uses

ANNIE GRANT

The daily lives of Romano-British farmers were inevitably intimately linked to the husbandry of their crops and livestock, but animals also impacted directly or indirectly on many aspects of the lives of every man, woman or child living in Roman Britain. The need for buildings to house and manage animals dictated the layout of farms and villas, crop cultivation had to take account of animal grazing and fodder requirements, the location of towns, villages and military settlements was influenced by the distances it was possible to travel by horse, or move goods in animal-drawn carts. Many craftsmen and shopkeepers were dependent on animal products, priests and priestesses needed animals in order to perform essential rites and rituals, the clothing of most of the population would have included woollen or leather items, much, although perhaps not the majority, of the food consumed would have included ingredients that were animal in origin, animal fat provided illumination, some animals spread disease, others were pets and so the list goes on.

The sources of evidence that can illuminate the history of the complexity and scope of human–animal interactions is very broad, encompassing documents, images, structures, artefacts and ecofacts. It would be foolish here to attempt a broad-based summary; this chapter concentrates primarily on the information provided by excavated animal remains and builds on earlier work by this author (Grant 1989) and that of others, particularly Tony King and Mark Maltby (see bibliography). It is necessarily selective in the topics chosen for discussion and also has a geographical bias as the majority of large, well-dated and comprehensively studied faunal assemblages are from the Midlands and the south.

There has been much recent theoretical debate about the meaning of 'Roman' as applied to Britain, and what any process of Romanization might imply in terms of both everyday activities and human identity. Recent post-colonial debates about identity place Roman against Celt, colonist against resister, and such debates are important in helping us to challenge simplistic assumptions about the Romanization of Britain (for example, Webster and Cooper 1996). There are also other interpretational frameworks. Woolf (1998: 206) argues that the Roman and Gallic identities were clearly in opposition only in the earliest stages of Roman conquest, and that other contrasts in

Romano-Gallic, and perhaps also in Romano-British society, included rich and poor, military and civilian, and urban and rural. This chapter uses archaeozoological data to explore some aspects of the role of animals in Roman Britain and some of the tensions and contrasts that characterized the Romano-British way of life.

The Beginning: Military, Civilian and Native

When the first Roman soldiers set foot on British shores, they encountered a native Iron Age society that in many parts of the country was continuing a way of life rooted in traditions dating back for centuries, but in other parts was undergoing rapid change and development. This latter is nowhere more apparent than in a group of settlements in southern Britain that are set apart from their neighbours and antecedents by the presence of luxury items and imported goods, including Mediterranean foodstuffs such as olive oil and *garum*, transported in amphorae. Substantial quantities of shellfish, particularly oysters, provide evidence of other trading networks that, even if they were more local, were over distances and at scales previously unparalleled in Britain. There are other characteristics of food procurement and consumption at some of these Late Iron Age *oppida* that also set them apart from most contemporary Iron Age settlements. Pork and chicken provide a higher proportion of the meat consumed and, where there is information of sufficient detail, the restricted range in the mortality patterns of cattle in particular, but also of pigs, suggests that many of the animals whose meat was consumed had not been raised by the settlements' inhabitants (figures 20.1 and 20.3; Grant 2000).

Military settlements

The earliest Roman settlements were established very rapidly following the Claudian invasion in AD 43, and the first task of any invading force must have been to ensure their shelter and safety, and adequate food supplies. The animal bone remains from some very early fortresses suggest that local animals provided the meat eaten. Sheep are small and slender, typical of native Iron Age animals, and cattle are generally smaller than on the Continent (King 1999a: 144; Grant 2001).

The establishment of a new, demanding and powerful group of consumers within farming communities, which may have had only a limited capacity to produce a surplus (Grant 1991: 483), had the potential to bring about a considerable disruption; the army may have taken as much from the native farmers as it required, with little or no regard for the consequences. However, if the army intended to remain for any length of time, they would need to ensure that local animal husbandry and agriculture were not fatally undermined. Faunal assemblages from many early forts include higher proportions of cattle than are common at contemporary native settlements, but the beef consumed was mainly from old or even elderly animals. The cattle mortality profile dated to the Flavio-Trajanic occupation of the auxiliary fort of Leucarum at Loughor in west Wales is typical (figure 20.1; Sadler 1997). Studies of the military diet (Davies 1989: 187–206; Webster 1998: 262–4) have shown that cereal and vegetable products provided the basis of the army diet, but cereal cultivation required cattle for ploughing and other agricultural tasks; young animals may have been spared to be trained for the plough and to replace the breeding stock, thus

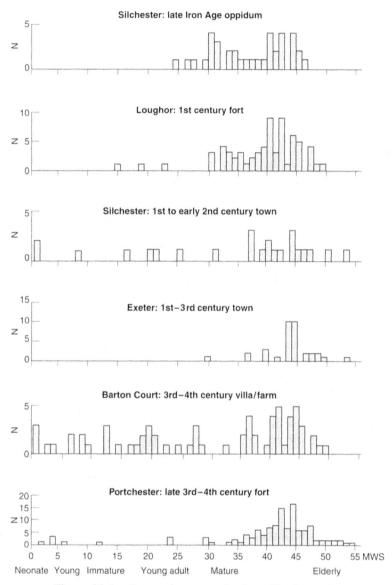

Figure 20.1 Contrasting age at death profiles for cattle.

ensuring the continuing viability or even growth of herds. Fully grown cattle may also have been preferentially chosen for slaughter to provide hides for leather, which the military required in significant quantities. This pattern of cattle culling, also noted at some Late Iron Age *oppida* such as Silchester (Grant 2000), was to continue as a feature of many military and also urban settlements through the Roman period (figure 20.1; Grant 2000: figure 213).

Pork also played a significant role in the military diet. Pigs can produce large litters up to twice a year and are thus a source of rapidly replaceable food. Pork can be preserved well, a feature that may have made pork or pork products very valuable for an army on the move. In Britain, a higher than average percentage of pig bones is a defining feature of settlements whose inhabitants have access to privileged resources (Grant 1989: 142), or who are primarily consumers rather than producers; both of these are characteristics of the invading Roman army. At the early 'fortlet' at Charterhouse in northern Somerset, built to protect mineral resources, the bones of pigs outnumber those of sheep (Gee 2001). All parts of the skeleton were present, suggesting that animals were requisitioned locally and butchered on site.

King's work on species proportions from sites in the Roman world in general (King, 1978, 1999a) and military sites in particular (1984, 1999b) equates cattle and pigs with 'Roman' and sheep with 'native', in respect of their relative importance in the diet, and many of the early forts conform to the 'Roman' pattern. However, there are some early military settlements where sheep bones dominate the faunal assemblages, perhaps reflecting pre-existing husbandry traditions that determined the availability of animals.

If local animals provided most of the meat consumed by the invading army, many horses must have been brought from the Continent with the first invading troops; it takes time to train horses for military use, particularly the chargers required by the cavalry. One of the earliest finds of donkey remains was in an early military deposit (Hamshaw-Thomas and Bermingham 1993) and may have been from an animal brought with the army from the Continent as a pack animal. There is evidence for an increasing involvement in horse-breeding in the last century BC (Grant 1984a: 521) and no doubt many locally bred horses were also requisitioned by the army. The growing military and economic importance of horses is reflected in a significant increase in the average size of horses in the Roman period (Audoin-Rouzeau 1994).

Some of the food eaten in the early military settlements was from wild animals (Davies 1971). The native game mammals, red and roe deer, boar and hare, may have been hunted for sport or to provide additional stronger-tasting meat, but they were not extensively exploited, and although their bones are found at many or even most forts, they occur in small numbers. In contrast, the remains of other wild resources, oysters, cockles, whelks and other marine or estuarine creatures, are found on most early military sites, regardless of location. The transport of seafood to selected inland settlements in the south had been established by the end of the first century BC but the Roman army extended this distribution across the occupied territory.

Civilian and native settlement

The origins of the earliest civilian settlements inevitably had a significant influence on their early development. Some early towns, settlements or villa estates developed from military establishments or on 'green-field' sites; others had their origins in Late Iron Age or earlier settlements, with or without an intervening military presence. At Fishbourne, in Sussex, pig remains (50 per cent) dominated the bone assemblage from the earliest occupation, which included a Roman military phase. The construction in AD 75/80 of a villa of a scale and luxury that scarcely finds a parallel in Europe, let alone in Britain, appears to have had surprisingly little impact on the relative importance of the remains of the three principal domesticates in food refuse. Pig bones remain dominant in second- and third-century deposits, although their contribution to the bone assemblages declines slightly. Change is more evident in the age at death of both the pigs and the sheep: on average, the pigs were killed at a younger age and the sheep at an older one in the villa than in the pre-villa phases. These developments may be related to changing tastes or in the focus of the villa or surrounding rural husbandry, with sheep reflecting an increased importance placed on wool production. Many of the cattle in both villa and pre-villa phases were killed before they reached maturity (Grant 1971).

In contrast, at nearby Chichester the bone remains from early military levels were dominated by cattle; pig bones accounted for only 10 per cent of those from the principal domesticates. The proportions of the three main domesticates remain remarkably stable through the development of the town to the fifth century (Levitan 1989). In the early Roman period the majority of cattle remains were from mature animals, while the sheep bones were from a slightly wider range of ages, patterns that were to continue through the first and second centuries.

An early military settlement was followed by a civilian occupation at many settlements of a more modest nature. In the military phase of the roadside settlement at Wilcote in Oxfordshire, the site may have operated as a staging post and the soldiers would have been well placed to receive supplies from outside the local area. Nonetheless, sheep bones dominate the assemblage (68 per cent). By the end of the first century, a flourishing 'fully Roman' settlement had been established; sheep-bone proportions remain very high into the second century, although there is some increase in cattle and a decline in pig remains. Most of the sheep were killed before they were skeletally and probably also reproductively mature, and many of the cattle remains were also from immature animals (Hamshaw-Thomas and Bermingham 1993). Despite its Roman military origins, the faunal assemblage from this settlement has many Iron Age characteristics, and this may provide an indication of the settlement's population.

In those early Romano-British rural settlements that had their origins in the Late Iron Age, any change might be expected to be gradual, its speed perhaps dependent on proximity to the new roads and the developing towns. At Dragonby in Lincolnshire, species proportions in Iron Age deposits typify those of very many contemporary sites (approximately two-thirds from sheep, a quarter from cattle and under a tenth from pigs); these proportions remain fairly stable throughout the first century. However, by the second century cattle bones became almost as common as those of sheep while pig-bone proportions remained constant throughout the main phases of occupation (Harman 1996). Just over half the cattle in the both the Iron Age and the first to third century AD had been slaughtered when they were mature, with the rest killed at a range of ages, including some when they were very young, a profile very similar to that from the early Roman period at Silchester (figure 20.1).

At the rural settlement at Waveden there was already a dominance of cattle bones in Late Iron Age deposits, and this was maintained into the early Roman period and later (Dobney and Jaques 1996). The majority of the Iron Age cattle were kept until they were mature, but in the early Roman period there is a slight increase in the proportion of younger animals. Species proportions in early urban deposits at Silchester are similar to those in Late Iron Age deposits, but here too there was an increase in the proportion of juvenile cattle in the early Roman period (figure 20.1; Grant 2000).

The demand for meat from those who were not themselves involved in the production of food, particularly from the military and many of those living in the towns, must have placed significant demands on the rural population. A shift from, say, sheep to cattle husbandry, an increase in the size of herds and flocks, or a change in the balance of products required might take many years to achieve, with implications for land use, crop cultivation, and farm architecture and organization. The heavier soils of the lower-lying areas had begun to be cultivated in the Late Iron Age, and lowland settlements frequently have higher percentages of cattle than those sited on higher ground (Grant 1989: 136). However, it is unlikely that the scale of cattle husbandry prior to the Roman invasion would have been able to meet immediately a significantly increased demand for beef in all areas. Larger herds of animals also require access to larger areas of land for pasture, but at the same time more land was required for the cultivation of the all-important cereals. Satisfying the competing needs of land for cattle-rearing and crop cultivation will inevitably have required a co-ordinated approach to the development of the agricultural and pastoral landscapes of Britain.

An increase in pork production can be achieved more easily and quickly than an increase in beef production; this may be one reason why pig bones are frequently more common in early Roman settlements than in many Iron Age settlements. Interestingly, wild mammals, including the larger species such as deer, rarely play a major role in the Romano-British civilian diet (Grant 1981).

There is no typical early 'Romano-British' settlement in the sense of either the type of meat consumed or the nature of the local animal husbandry that supplied that meat. On the contrary, there is considerable variety in species proportions and, significantly, in the age at slaughter of the main domestic animals, which does not seem to be neatly related to the size, origins or status of a settlement. Among the small number of sites discussed above as examples, there are some where, once the early pattern of animal exploitation and meat consumption was established, either before or just after the Roman invasion, it was maintained into the second century or even later. There are others where there was significant change in the early Roman period. Further research is required to establish whether the factors that had the most significant influence on the early development of Romano-British animal husbandry and meat consumption were the local environment, pre-existing traditions, the development of a market for animal products and distribution networks, social and economic status, food preferences, population migration, or new ideas and ideologies; all may have played a part.

The Development of Towns: Consumption and Production

Urban consumption

The increasing complexity that is characteristic of urban centres makes the interpretation of bone assemblages very challenging. Excavations usually open only very small 'windows', and different views of the same settlement may provide contrasting perpectives. For example, bone remains from the early Roman defensive ditches at Silchester suggested cattle as the dominant species (cattle 66%, sheep 26% and pigs 8 %; Maltby 1984a). Contemporary deposits from the centre of the town gave a rather different picture (cattle 48%, sheep 27% and pigs 26%; Grant 2000). Nonetheless, there can be no doubt that cattle were the most important species in respect of their contribution to the Romano-British urban diet: a fully grown cow or ox might have provided around 200 kilograms of edible food compared to 15 kilograms from a sheep, 60 kilograms from a pig and much less for immature animals (Vigne 1992). The contributions of cattle, sheep and pigs to the food eaten in the forum-basilica area at Silchester have been calculated as, respectively, 68, 4 and 28 per cent (Grant 2000: 428).

Deposits of cattle remains dominated by skulls and limb extremities in many Romano-British towns including Chichester, Winchester, Silchester, Leicester and Lincoln point to the development of centralized processing and distribution of beef (Levitan 1989; Maltby 1989, 1994; Dobney et al. 1997; Gidney, 1999). Networks established by the military as a means of provisioning their early settlements were doubtless exploited to supply the growing populations of towns. Further evidence of the organization of the urban meat supply can be seen in the narrow range of ages in cattle mortality profiles in many urban deposits, which provide evidence of a continuation of the culling practices used by the military. The speed with which an organized urban meat supply, based on selective culling, was established seems to have varied. At Exeter and Lincoln, sub-adult cattle are rare from the first century onwards. At Silchester and Leicester, the cattle bones found in early Roman deposits were from animals slaughtered at a wider range of ages; in the later Roman period almost all the remains were those of mature cattle (figure 20.1; Gidney 1999; Grant 2000).

It is perhaps inevitable that cattle were chosen to provide the major component of the urban meat supply, as an increased investment in raising these animals was vital to the expansion of cereal cultivation. Rearing cattle for food production also becomes an increasingly viable strategy when concentrations of people are living together, and the meat and offal provided by each of these large animals can be shared. An efficient system for carcass processing and meat distribution and preservation is also essential if cattle are to be exploited on a large scale. There is evidence for the development of new butchery practices relating to an intensive processing of cattle carcasses, including the possible preservation of shoulders of beef by smoking or salting (Maltby 1989; Dobney 2001: 61).

In contrast to cattle, sheep mortality profiles from urban deposits typically include animals from a wide range of ages, with some animals that may have been bred specifically for consumption and others slaughtered later after they had made significant contributions of wool and milk; the differences in urban and rural settlements are less marked for sheep than for cattle (figure 20.2).

Pigs also played an important role in feeding the growing urban populations and were doubtless bred specifically to perform this function. Fish and shellfish remains found in urban settlements inland demonstrate the continuation and further development of longer-distance trade in foodstuffs. At Silchester the ratio of shell to animal-bone fragments increased from 1:21 in the mid-first century to 1:1.5 in the mid-second century (Grant 2000). Chickens first appear in the archaeological record in Britain in the Late Iron Age, but they increase in importance in the Roman period; their remains, together with those of geese and ducks, are common in Romano-British towns. Most urban contexts also include very small numbers of wild bird remains that may have provided protein when other sources were in scarce supply

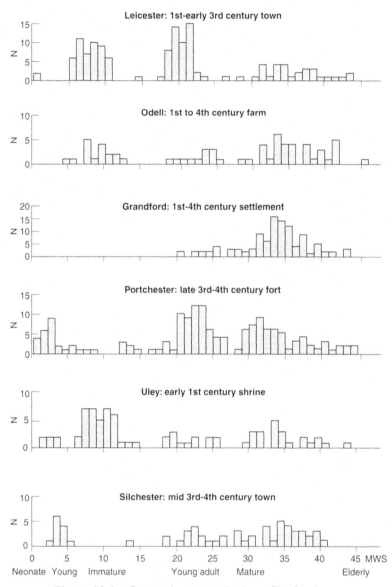

Figure 20.2 Contrasting age at death profiles for sheep.

(Parker 1988). Dietary diversity was perhaps most easily provided through the consumption of animals, birds and fish that were not closely tied into the agricultural cycle or required to produce a range of secondary products.

Urban production

A proportion of the food consumed in towns may have been provided by the townspeople themselves, particularly in the smaller urban centres. The land around

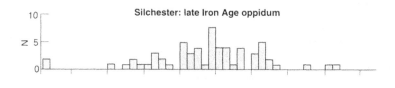

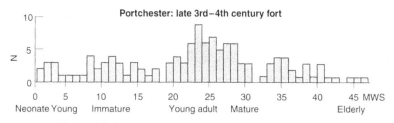

Figure 20.3 Contrasting age at death profiles for pigs.

towns was often farmed, and animals may also have been raised within town walls. Of the three principal domesticates, pigs are most easily reared in urban environments, and it has sometimes been suggested that pork consumed in towns was from pigs raised by the town-dwellers. However, where there is a high proportion of male animals, or a fairly restricted age profile, as in the fourth-century assemblage from Lincoln and indeed in the pre-Roman material from Silchester (Dobney et al. 1997: 73, figure 70; Grant 2000: figure 198), it is more likely that the animals consumed had been raised elsewhere.

Remains of animals from a wide range of ages, including both neonatal and elderly individuals, may be indicative of an involvement in animal breeding: it seems unlikely that neonatal animals would have been transported very far from their birth-place. Neonatal cattle bones are sometimes found, for example, at Kingscote and in the early Roman period at Silchester (Maltby 1998; Grant 2000), but they are rare in most urban assemblages. Neonatal sheep remains have been found at a number of urban settlements, particularly in the smaller towns, including Kingscote and Haybridge (Maltby 1998; Johnson and Albarella 2002). They were found in first- and early second-century contexts at Silchester (Grant 2000), but they are absent from Lincoln (Dobney et al. 1997) and second- to third-century deposits at Exeter (Maltby, 1979). Such differences may be useful in helping to identify social and economic hierarchies in urban development.

Towns also functioned as producers of a range of animal products, and indeed they were well placed to do this. It was only with the advent of refrigeration that fresh meat could be moved any distance except on a live animal, so a wide range of crafts and manufacturing activities grew up in urban centres to exploit the inedible waste from animal slaughter. The large dumps of cattle-bones may include waste from butchery but also from leather-processing, the extraction of fat and glue from animal bones and horn-working – horn cores are conspicuously absent from some deposits, suggesting their removal for processing as a specialist craft (Maltby 1989). Large deposits of burnt cattle mandibles in fourth-century deposits at Lincoln have been interpreted as the waste from specialist production of lamp oil, or oil for use as soap, medicines or in cosmetics (Dobney et al. 1997: 25). Some towns may have been manufacturing sauce from locally caught fish (see below).

Rural Development: Small Farms and Villa Estates

Animal-bone remains provide direct evidence for consumption, but only indirect evidence for animal husbandry. Faunal assemblages from rural settlements that were contributing to an urban or military food supply will be lacking those animals that had once been part of the local flocks and herds but were sent to market and slaughtered elsewhere. This movement of animals will inevitably have distorted our view of rural animal husbandry and the activities and behaviours of the rural population.

Rural bone assemblages typically include the remains of animals killed at a range of ages, suggesting husbandry strategies that focused on a diversity of primary and secondary products (figures 20.1–3). Herd maintenance must also have been a major preoccupation for rural farmers locked into a mode of production that was based on supplying a demand generated elsewhere and providing their own food. The wealthy, including villa owners, inevitably had the most flexibility to raise animals to meet their own demands, and perhaps to produce goods to trade for further food-stuffs; a relatively high percentage of pig-bones is typical of the wealthier villas, with both production and significant consumption indicated (Grant 1989; King 1978, 1999a). Falkner (2000: 150–1) has postulated the existence of two economic systems – the estate owners producing for a market, and the native farmers with a more self-sufficient husbandry. Although native farmers may have been self-sufficient in respect of meat and cereals, the production of a surplus of animals and animal and agricultural products must have been crucial in providing the means to access the non-local products that are found even in some modest settlements.

The contribution of sheep to the urban food supply was small when compared to that of cattle, but still significant. Sheep played another crucial role in the rural economy: wool production was well established in Britain long before the Roman Conquest, but it became increasingly important in the following centuries. In bone assemblages in the third or fourth centuries at a wide range of towns and smaller settlements, there is an increase in the remains of mature sheep, animals that would have proved several clips of wool before being sold off for meat (for example, O'Connor 1986; Levitan 1989; Dobney and Jaques 1996; Dobney et al. 1997; Grant 2000). In some parts of the country, notably in the east of England, there seems to have been a particular emphasis on wool from an early period. Over half the animal remains found in all phases of occupation (first to fourth centuries) at Grand-ford, a Fenland settlement in Cambridgeshire, were those of sheep, most of which had not been killed for consumption until they were mature and would have provided several clips of wool (figure 20.2; Stallibrass 1982).

Pigs may have been bred at some settlements mainly for home consumption, but other settlements must have been producing pigs for the urban and military market too, providing a valuable 'cash crop'. Pig remains from rural farming settlements such as Barton Court Farm are typically from animals that died at a wide range of ages, but with a tendency to include a higher proportion of immature animals in comparison to some urban sites (figure 20.3; Wilson 1984) We can only rarely gain any impression of the scale of rural production: estimates of minimum numbers of animals in faunal assemblages provide very low figures, deflated to an unknowable extent by excavation strategies, survival factors and rubbish-disposal practices. However, the exceptional remains from the Uley shrines have provided some indication of local agricultural wealth and its capacity to produce a surplus. Levitan (1993) has conservatively estimated that in a fifty-year period in the fourth century approximately 1100 apparently healthy goats and sheep were sacrificed.

Animal improvements

The importance of cattle in the Romano-British economy, and the consequent attention to their husbandry, is visible in a significant increase in the average height of cattle at a number of locations in the south of England at an early date. Improved breeding, including cross-breeding with imported animals, and improved feeding, can all bring about size increase and it is possible that all played a role. There was also some improvement in the sheep livestock, although this may have happened slightly later than the increase in cattle size in many areas. The impetus for sheep improvement may have been a developing requirement for wool, which may have come slightly later than the need for a improvements in animals that provide traction, meat and leather. Our knowledge of the development of pig breeding is limited by the scarcity of remains of mature animals; as they produce no secondary products and are most frequently killed before they reach their full size, there may have been less attention paid to this species (see also Grant 1989: 142–3).

The jawbone of a mule (a cross between a mare and an ass) found in a mid-second-century context in London (Armitage 1979) may offer evidence for the development of Romano-British understanding of animal breeding, although it is possible that this animal was brought to Britain by boat. Deliberate animal breeding is unambiguously evidenced in the very considerable variation in size and shape of Romano-British dogs: dog remains from single locations include animals that range from the size of a fox terrier to that of a boxer (for example, Chapman and Smith 1988; Harman 1996).

The Later Roman Period: Prosperity and Decline

Although the general trend is to an increase in cattle, there is a continuation of significant diversity in faunal remains into the third and fourth centuries. At many towns and smaller settlements, at least half of the bone remains are those of cattle, but this is not universally the case. At Silchester, for example, the proportion of cattle-bones in deposits inside the town fell from nearly 50 per cent in the mid-first century to under 30 per cent in the mid-third to fourth centuries (Grant 2000).

At the villa at Fishbourne, the proportion of cattle-bones increased and that of pig remains declined over time, but even in the deposits associated with a possibly casual occupation of part of the villa following a major fire at the end of the third century, cattle-bones still made up less than half the assemblage, and nearly a third of the bone remains were from pigs (Grant 1971). In the fourth century, the villa at Piddington in Northamptonshire was divided up and occupied by a number of separate family units. The former wealth and luxury were no longer apparent and buildings had begun to fall into disrepair but, unexpectedly, the consumption of pork increased (Ayres 1995). Even if the last inhabitants were no longer living in luxurious surroundings, they may have still been producing goods or services to trade for meat. High proportions of pig bones have been noted by King (1999a: 190) at a number of industrial sites that may have traded their goods for meat: the Piddington pigs are mainly young adult and mature animals and may not necessarily have been reared on site, although a small proportion were from very young animals (figure 20.3). At some villas, deer-bone proportions increase in late phases associated with evidence of decline; declining villa productivity may have provided the impetus to seek alternative sources of meat (Grant 1981).

Other sites indicate the continuation of effective distribution networks through to the late fourth century. Lincoln was a thriving town at this time, and most of the meat consumed in the city was beef: almost 80 per cent of the bone remains were those of cattle, the majority of which were adult animals (Dobney et al. 1997). The army continued to exploit local and perhaps regional resources, with cattle providing most of the meat consumed at military settlements. The efficient organization of the beef supply to the late fort of Portchester in Hampshire is indicated by a consistent butchery technique, a restricted age range, and a considerable diversity in the size of the animals, suggesting that they had been drawn from a number of herds (figure 20.1; Grant 1975). In contrast, sheep and pig remains are from animals killed at a very wide range of ages; these animals may have been raised locally and may have been killed on demand to meet immediate needs (figures 20.2 and 20.3). Although many of the sheep were mature at death, a significant proportion seem to have been raised specifically for their meat; at Portchester, meat may have been in relatively plentiful supply.

Behaviour and Identity

The significance and context of meat consumption

The size and ubiquity (except in very acidic environments) of animal bones may tempt us to overemphasize the role of meat in past diets. If the much rarer and smaller (sometimes microscopic) remains of waste from the consumption of vegetable foods are supplemented by indirect evidence (field systems, granaries, storage pits, quern stones and grinders, etc.) and information derived from documentary and ethnographic sources, we must assume that the majority of food consumed was vegetable and probably more specifically cereal in origin, as has already been noted in respect of the military diet.

Food that is eaten infrequently may acquire a particular status or symbolic value. It is thus useful to turn the focus of investigation from animal husbandry and food supply to the context, significance and even timing of meat consumption. Corbier (1989: 223) has drawn attention to the duality of the role of meat in ancient Rome: 'Consumption appeared as though organised around two poles: one was exceptional or occasional, linked in general to a religious ceremony; the other was if not everyday at least common, and . . . one might call it secular.'

It is possible or even likely that a similar duality existed in the role of meat consumption in Britain in both the pre- and post-Conquest periods. The widespread practice of whole-animal burial and the deposition of 'special' deposits of parts of animals with their flesh apparently intact in Iron Age contexts has made it relatively easy to recognize some aspects of exceptional or religious animal slaughter, if not of consumption (Grant 1984b). Ritual feasting has been suggested to explain the remains of butchered animals that have been found together with unbutchered remains at some exceptional sites, such as sanctuaries (Green 1992: 97). Ongoing work on bone assemblages from Iron Age habitation sites is suggesting that meat consumption may have been largely seasonal, and perhaps therefore almost always exceptional (Grant 2002).

In Roman religion, sacrificial slaughter was usually followed by consumption of the victim. The distinction between religious and secular slaughter and consumption may therefore be difficult to draw, except when consumption took place in a context that was clearly religious. At the Late Iron Age and Romano-British temple at Uley in Gloucestershire, the animal remains were classified as either 'votive' or 'non-votive', the former primarily goats, sheep and domestic fowl, and the latter cattle, pigs, wild animals and fish (Levitan 1993). There were no burials of complete articulated animals at Uley, but although the incidence of butchery marks is low, it is still likely that the meat of both votive and non-votive animals was consumed. Sheep were the preferred sacrificial victims at a number of other Romano-British temples, including Harlow in Essex and Great Chesterford in Cambridgeshire (Legge et al. 1992). There is less direct evidence for the religious slaughter of cattle, but despite Ovid's assertion that religion spared the ox as man's companion in labour, many oxen were sacrificed in the Roman world (Corbier 1989: 225–6) and cattle and pigs also play a significant role in Celtic religion (Green 1992).

The Uley data suggest and the Roman documentary evidence asserts that the same species may be exceptional or religious, or common or secular at different times and in different contexts. In some parts of the Roman Empire, meat from sacrificial animals was sold in shops and markets for consumption in private homes (Frayn 1995), thus crossing the religious/secular divide, and further complicating interpretation of bone remains. There may have been other religious/secular distinctions, including the differences between fresh meat available immediately after slaughter and the preserved meat and fat that was available long afterwards.

How then might we begin to distinguish between exceptional and ordinary in a Romano-British context? One approach is to look at the evidence for the consumption of foodstuffs that have a less ambiguous status. Wild mammals, wild birds, fish and shellfish seem from both documentary and archaeological evidence largely to fall outside the religious sphere of consumption in this period, although the antlers of deer may have had a particular votive significance (see below). In trying to distinguish between deposits that accumulated as a result of religious or secular consumption, it might be profitable to investigate associations between the remains of different species. Perhaps because they are so common on Romano-British urban and military sites, shellfish have largely been ignored by both excavators and specialists, but their presence or absence may help us to understand better the depositional processes and the derivation of particular deposits of faunal remains. Other dualities, including rich/poor, may also be exposed through such investigations.

Another approach is to investigate the development of butchery. Distinctive butchery techniques, including evidence for the preparation of joints for smoking or salting, and large deposits of cattle remains from animals that appear to have been slaughtered outside town walls (see above) suggest the growth of a secular consumption of beef that perhaps developed in tandem with the exploitation of the carcasses of cattle for leather and other materials. Although specialist butchers may have been employed to slaughter animals for sacrifice, if Roman practices were adopted this slaughter would have taken place within the town and not extramurally. With more careful analysis of butchery techniques, we may ultimately begin to recognize significant differences.

Ovicaprid remains from a number of temples, including Uley, Harlow, Great Chesterford and Chelmsford (Legge et al. 1992; Luff 1992; Levitan 1993) include a particularly high proportion from young animals, perhaps preferentially selected for sacrifice (figure 20.2). There also seems to have been a seasonal rhythm to the sacrifice of ovicaprids and thus of religious consumption. Whether this was autumn, as has been suggested by Levitan and Legge, or winter/early spring depends on the interpretation of tooth eruption data, but it is clear that many of the sacrifices had been made within a limited period of the year. Remains from urban or other settlement contexts that indicate seasonal slaughter and concentrations of young animals may also signal sacrificial consumption. Third/fourth-century deposits associated with the forum-basilica at Silchester included a particularly high proportion of fowl, most of which were male, and a number of very young sheep (figure 20.2) and may at least in part have been derived from sacrifices (Grant 2000).

Remains of food species are also associated with human burials, both inhumations and cremations. Fowl are particularly common in the Eastern Cemetery in London and also occur in cremation burials at rural sites: at Wavedon bones from at least three chickens were found with a group of burnt human remains and a cremation vessel (Reilly 1996; Barber and Bowsher 2000). Some of the remains appear to be food offerings buried with the deceased, but others may be the refuse from feasting that took place during the burial rites, another form of exceptional consumption.

Beef, and perhaps also pork, are meats that appear to have become increasingly commonly consumed in the secular sphere, whether that was at household or community level, while mutton or lamb and perhaps chicken were meats that played a particular, although not exclusive, role in the religious sphere. Deposits that include collections of very young animals of any species might also have some religious significance. Further work will be required to test these hypotheses.

Diet and the development of taste

Discussion of dietary change has tended to focus on the relative proportions of cattle-, sheep- and pig-bone remains as indicative of the place of beef, mutton/lamb and pork in the diet (for example, King 1984, 1999a). Although this approach is very useful in offering a broad-brush impression of dietary change, the production of meat is frequently a secondary rather than a primary aim of cattle and sheep husbandry (see above) and its availability is dependent on the competing demands of agriculture and the production of secondary products. Beef, mutton/lamb and pork have been the main components of the British meat diet from the Neolithic period to the present day, so it cannot be these ingredients that provide the defining characteristics of any culturally differentiated cuisine but other ingredients and flavourings, the cooking methods, the frequency of consumption and the ways in which the food is served. The Vindolanda tablets list a wide range of foodstuffs, both vegetable and meat, and also provide an indication of the different ways in which the resources provided by a single animal might be consumed: young pig, pig's trotter, pork cutlet, ham, pork crackling and pork fat are all listed (Bowman 1994: 69–70). Unfortunately, such differences are not easy to detect from archaeological remains, but other elements of a developing Romano-British cuisine might be deduced from animal remains.

In comparison to the Iron Age, there was a much greater diversity of animal products eaten. Deer bones are about as rare in the Roman period as in the Iron Age, but remains of birds, both domestic and wild, fish and shellfish are very much more common finds on Romano-British sites than in the earlier period. A taste for these foods began to develop before the Conquest: amphorae that once contained fish sauces (*garum*, *liquamen* or *allec*) and perhaps salted fish were imported into Britain before the Roman Conquest. Although fish and shellfish are unlikely to have made more than a very small contribution in terms of calories consumed, their strong flavour and those of fish sauces would have transformed the taste of any meat or other ingredients cooked with them. By the later Roman period, fish sauce may have been manufactured in some of the larger towns, perhaps making it more widely available (Bateman and Locker 1982; Jones 1988; Dobney et al. 1997). In the pre-Roman period horses and dogs were eaten, but in the Romano-British period the increasing rarity of butchery marks on their bones suggests that tastes had changed, or that new food avoidances had been developed or learned.

The butchery of animal carcasses is limited by anatomy but guided by the cooking methods to be employed, and there is a clear change in techniques that can be directly related to a Roman influence. Cut marks on animal bones from the very early fort at Alchester demonstrate the use of heavy chopping tools and an intense fragmentation that contrasts with the careful use of knives that characterizes the Iron Age tradition (Grant 2001). The techniques used here were somewhat haphazard, contrasting with much more standardized techniques observed at later forts (Grant 1975; Stokes 2000). Perhaps the earliest garrison at Alchester did not include a specialist butcher, leaving the soldiers to prepare animals that they had commandeered from local farmers, but they may nonetheless have been preparing and cooking their food in a Continental manner. In the Late Pre-Roman Iron Age at Silchester, butchery cuts indicate an Iron Age method of meat preparation, despite evidence for the consumption of imported ingredients from the Roman Empire; techniques do not begin to change until the early Roman period (Grant 2000). Some smaller settlements with continuous occupation from the Iron Age through the Roman period show a rather later adoption of 'Roman' butchery techniques (Grant 1989: 141). Research that integrates a wider range of information about food, including animal and plant remains, butchery marks, imported goods and pottery types, will offer a more sophisticated understanding of the development of food consumption and cuisine (Hawkes 1999).

Ritual deposition and burial

Animals played a significant role in Celtic myth and religion, and among the many manifestations of the centrality of animals in the life of pre-Roman Iron Age societies was the practice of depositing whole animals or parts of animals, together with food remains, in pits or ditches of habitation sites. The continuation of elements of this practice into the Roman period is indicated at a number of early sites, even where pottery and building styles show the rapid adoption of at least some elements of a Romanized lifestyle (for example, Hamshaw-Thomas and Bermingham 1993). Ritual depositions of parts of animals became increasingly common in villas in the third and fourth centuries (Scott 1991). Scott suggests that there was a revival of Celtic religion in the third and fourth centuries, but there are differences in both the type and the context of the animal deposits, and in the inclusion of human infants; this latter is a distinctly Roman practice.

Many wells within towns and settlements fell into disuse during the life of the settlement and were filled in. Much of the fill material appears to be food and other refuse, but in some there are complete animal skeletons of domestic species, including dogs and horses, and of deer, and also whole skulls and antlers. Some also contain human remains, particularly those of newborn babies (for example, Grant 1975; Chaplin and Barnetson 1980; Chaplin and McCormick 1986; Chapman and Smith 1988). A disused well is a convenient place to dispose of food species that died of disease, or of animals that were not normally eaten, and it has also been suggested that some of the animals had fallen into wells accidentally. However, this would not explain finds of deer antler, as this was a valuable raw material and not likely to have been carelessly discarded. Deliberate or ritual deposition seems possible, as has been suggested to explain the nearly complete red deer antler and the remains of at least sixteen dogs found in the fill of a late second- to early third-century Roman well at Staines (Chapman and Smith 1988). A careful burial of a horse, a dog and a juvenile red deer in a 'spiral arrangement' was found in the London's Eastern Cemetery (Barber and Bowsher 2000: 320, figure 111). In some respects, this cemetery deposit is reminiscent of an Iron Age 'special deposit', but this particular grouping of species is not usual in the earlier period. The juxtaposition of these three species here and in well deposits may have a particularly Romano-British significance; the primary role of each of them is other than for food: horses for riding, dogs for herding, guarding or as pets and deer for antler.

Horse bones are unexpectedly common at a number of cemeteries. Barber suggests that general refuse from the town may have been incorporated in secondary contexts and grave backfills at the Eastern Cemetery in London, but he also notes the association of horses and dogs with human remains in other cemeteries in Britain and in France (Barber and Bowsher 2000: 320). At Broughton some of the horse bones were cremated and are less convincingly explained as rubbish (Worley, unpublished). The recent find of a complete dog skeleton buried upright against the side of a second- or third-century pit within the town walls of Silchester (Clarke and Fulford 2002) is further indication that this species may have had a particular significance in Romano-British ideology, perhaps one that had developed from Celtic origins.

The ideological, religious and cultural role of animals in Roman Britain has been rather little explored, but there is considerable potential to pursue this further, particularly through detailed and fine-grained analysis of individual deposits (see Grant 2002); such work is likely to be very valuable in helping us to understand the development of Romano-British identities and ideologies.

Conclusions

The Romano-British period marks the beginning in Britain of perhaps one of the most crucial and important developments in the history of human and animal inter-relationships. It is the first time since the Neolithic period when there is widespread evidence for the consumption on a regular basis of food that was not produced by the consumers. This heralds the beginnings of a separation of producer from consumer and has an importance that is not just economic, but affects the ways in which animals are perceived, including their role in ideology and religious practices.

A number of broad general trends in animal husbandry and meat consumption have previously been established for the Romano-British period, of which the increasing role of cattle over time, and a differentiation between highly 'Romanized' sites relying mainly on the products of cattle and pigs, and native sites relying more on sheep are the main features (King 1978, 1999a). This approach has raised awareness of some of the potential of animal remains, but the broad picture masks a very considerable diversity in animal husbandry and meat consumption in the Romano-British period that cannot be fully accommodated in this model. Other models, particularly functionalist and determinist models for the interpretation of faunal remains, have inhibited our understanding of the complexities of the role of animals in religion and ritual, and of the ideology of meat consumption, eating habits and taste.

This chapter has used archaeozoological data to explore some of the many dualities and contrasts inherent in Romano-British society and in doing so has highlighted what we do not yet know as much as what we do. In particular, it has attempted to raise our expectations of the potential of faunal remains. With current excavation policies we cannot be optimistic about the chances of studies of very large assemblages of animal bones appearing in the pages of site monographs in the next decade, but there are many new lines of enquiry possible that may provide some compensation by both broadening and deepening our knowledge and understanding of the Romano-British period. It will, however, be crucial to develop approaches that take more account of detailed contextual information and integrate the full range of archaeological data.

FURTHER READING

Overviews of animal remains in Roman Britain include those by Grant (1989), King (1978, 1999a) and Maltby (1984b). O'Connor and van der Veen (1999) look more specifically at agricultural production, addressing both animal and crop husbandry. Those wishing to gain a greater understanding of the nature of the archaeozoological evidence, its strengths and limitations, are recommended to consult both recent 'textbooks' (for example, Davis, 1987; Reitz and Wing, 1999; O'Connor, 2000) and detailed studies of large Roman faunal assemblages including Maltby (1979), Wilson (1986), Dobney et al. (1997) and Grant (2001).

Alcock (2000) provides a readable overview of food in Roman Britain, including the food eaten, cooking, dining, shops and markets, but to explore further aspects of food, culture, ideology, status and ritual see, for example, Goody (1982), Corbier (1989), papers in Garwood et al. (1991), Green (1992), recent volumes of the Theoretical Roman Archaeology Conference proceedings, for example, Meadows (1995) and Roskams and Saunders (2001).

Classic texts on animals in the Roman world include Toynbee (1973) and White (1970). Toynbee offers a general overview of the wide variety of roles played by animals in life in the Roman Empire, covers frogs and toads to elephants, and ranges from transport, war, food supply and veterinary medicine to attitudes to animals; her sources are largely documentary and iconographic. White takes a broad view of the economic and practical aspects of Roman (largely Italian) farming and covers crops and soils, animal husbandry and estate management. Papers in Whittaker (1988) and Wilkins et al. (1995) cover a wider range of topics, including husbandry and pastoralism, the social and religious contexts of food and eating and food medicine, while Hyland (1990) provides an authoritative account of the role and significance of a single species, the horse.

REFERENCES

Alcock, J. P. 2001. *Food in Roman Britain*. Stroud.

Armitage, P. 1979. Roman mules. *London Archaeologist*, 3, 339–46.

Audoin-Rouzeau, F. 1994. *La Taille du cheval en Europe de l'Antiquité aux Temps Modernes*. Juan-les-Pins.

Ayres, K. 1995. *Analysis of animal bones from Piddington Roman villa, Northamptonshire.* Unpublished thesis, School of Archaeological Studies, University of Leicester.

Barber, B. and Bowsher, D. 2000. *The Eastern Cemetery of Roman London. Excavations 1983–1990.* Museum of London Archaeological Service, Monograph 4. London.

Bateman, N. and Locker, A. 1982. The sauce of the Thames. *London Archaeologist,* 4, 204–7.

Bowman, A. K. 1994. *Life and Letters on the Roman Frontier: Vindolanda and its People.* London.

Chaplin, R. and McCormick, F. 1998. The animal bones. In I. M. Stead and V. Rigby (eds), *Baldock: The Excavation of a Roman and Pre-Roman Settlement 1968–72.* London, 396–415.

Chaplin, R. E. and Barnetson, L. P. 1980. Animal bones. In I. M. Stead (ed.), *Rudston Roman Villa.* 149–55.

Chapman, J. and Smith, S. 1988. Finds from a Roman well in Staines. *London Archaeologist,* 16, 3–6.

Clarke, A. and Fulford, M. 2002. Silchester, a crowded late Roman city. *Current Archaeology,* 177, 364–9.

Corbier, M. 1989. The ambiguous status of meat in ancient Rome. *Food and Foodways,* 3, 223–64.

Davies, R. W. 1971. The Roman military diet. *Britannia,* 2, 122–42.

—— 1989. *Service in the Roman Army.* Edinburgh.

Davis, S. 1987. *The Archaeology of Animals.* London.

Dobney, K. 2001. A place at the table; the role of vertebrate zooarchaeology within a Roman research agenda. In S. James and M. Millett (eds), *Britons and Romans: Advancing an Archaeological Agenda.* York, 36–45.

Dobney, K. M. and S. D. Jaques 1996. The mammal bone. In R. J. Williams, P. J. Hart and A. T. L. Williams (eds), *Wavedon Gate: A Late Iron Age and Roman Rural Settlement in Milton Keynes.* Buckinghamshire Archaeological Society Monograph Series 10. Aylesbury, 203–33.

Dobney, K. M., Jaques, S. D. and Irving, B. G. 1997. *Of Butchers and Breeds.* Lincoln.

Faulkner, N. 2000. *The Decline and Fall of Roman Britain.* Stroud.

Frayn, J. 1995. The Roman meat trade. In J. Wilkins, D. Harvey and M. Dobson (eds), *Food in Antiquity.* Exeter, 107–14.

Garwood, P., Jennings, D., Skeates, R. and Toms, J. (eds) 1991. *Sacred and Profane.* Oxford.

Gee, R. 2001. *The Faunal Assemblage from Charterhouse on Mendip.* Unpublished thesis, Department of Archaeology, University of Durham.

Gidney, L. 1999. The animal bones. In A. Connor and R. Buckley (eds), *Roman and Medieval Occupation in Causeway Lane, Leicester.* Leicester, 310–29.

Goody, J. 1982. *Cooking, Cuisine and Class.* Cambridge.

Grant, A. 1971. The animal bones. In B. W. Cunliffe (ed.), *Excavations at Fishbourne.* Volume II. *The Finds.* London, 377–88.

—— 1975. The animal bones. In B. W. Cunliffe (ed.), *Excavations at Portchester Castle.* Volume I. *Roman.* London, 378–408.

—— 1981. The significance of deer remains at occupation sites of the Iron Age to the Anglo-Saxon period. In M. Jones and G. Dimbleby (eds), *The Environment of Man, the Iron Age to the Anglo-Saxon Period.* BAR 87. Oxford, 205–13.

—— 1982. The use of toothwear as a guide to the age of domestic ungulates. In B. Wilson, C. Grigson and S. Payne (eds), *Ageing and Sexing Animal Bones from Archaeological Sites.* BAR (British Series) 109. Oxford, 91–108.

Grant, A. 1984a. The animal husbandry. In B. W. Cunliffe (ed.), *Danebury: An Iron Age Hillfort in Hampshire*. Volume 2. *The Excavations 1969–1978: The Finds*. London, 496–548.

—— 1984b. Survival or sacrifice: a critical appraisal of animal burials in Britain in the Iron Age. In J. Clutton-Brock and C. Grigson (eds), *Animals and Archaeology. 4. Husbandry in Europe*. BAR (International Series) 227. Oxford, 221–7.

—— 1989. Animals in Roman Britian. In M. Todd (ed.), *Research on Roman Britain 1960–89*. London, 135–46.

—— 1991. The animal husbandry. In B. Cunliffe and C. Poole (eds), *Danebury: An Iron Age Hillfort in Hampshire*. Volume 5. *The Excavations 1979–1988: The Finds*. London, 447–87.

—— 2000. Diet, economy and ritual: evidence from the faunal remains. In M. Fulford (ed.), *Iron Age and Roman Silchester: Excavations on the Site of the Forum-Basilica at Silchester 1977, 1980–86*. London, 423–80.

—— 2001. Preliminary note on the animal bone remains from Alchester. In E. Sauer, Alchester, a Claudian 'vexillation fortress' near the western boundary of the Catuvellauni: new light on the Roman invasion of Britain. *Archaeological Journal*, 157, 63.

—— 2002. Scales of reference: approaches to the study of behaviours and change. In K. Dobney and T. P. O'Connor (eds), *Bones and the Man: Studies in Honour of Don Brothwell*. Proceedings of York Bioarchaeology Research Forum. York.

Green, M. 1992. *Animals in Celtic Life and Myth*. London.

Hamshaw-Thomas, J. F. and Bermingham, N. 1993. Analysis of faunal remains. In A. R. Hands (ed.), *The Romano-British Roadside Settlement at Wilcote, Oxfordshire I, Excavations 1990–92*. BAR (British Series) 232. Oxford.

Harman, M. 1996. Mammalian bones. In J. May (ed.), *Dragonby: Report on Excavations at an Iron Age and Romano-British Settlement in North Lincolnshire*. Oxford, 141–61.

Hawkes, G. 1999. Beyond Romanisation: the creolisation of food. A framework for the study of faunal remains from Roman sites. *Papers from the Institute of Archaeology*, 10, 89–96.

Hyland, A. 1990. *Equus. The Horse in the Roman World*. London.

Johnson, C. and Albarella, U. 2002. *The Iron Age and Romano-British Mammal and Bird Assemblage from Elms Farm, Heybridge, Essex*. (Site Code, HYEF93–95.) Portsmouth.

Jones, A. J. K. 1988. Fish bones from excavations in the cemetery of St Mary Bishophill Junior. In T. P. O'Connor, *Bones from the General Accident Site, Tanner Row*. The Archaeology of York, 15.2. York, 126–31.

King, A. 1978. A comparative survey of bone assemblages from Roman sites in Britain. *Bulletin of the Institute of Archaeology*, 15, 207–32.

—— 1984. Animal bones and the dietary identity of military and civilian groups in Roman Britain, Germany and Gaul. In T. Blagg and A. King (eds), *Military and Civilian in Roman Britain*. BAR (British Series) 137. Oxford, 187–217.

—— 1999a. Diet in the Roman world: a regional inter-site comparison of the mammal bones. *Journal of Roman Archaeology*, 12, 168–202.

—— 1999b. Animals and the Roman army: the evidence of animal bones. In A. Goldsworthy and I. Haynes (eds), *The Roman Army as a Community*. Journal of Roman Archaeology Supplementary Series 34. Portsmouth, RI, 139–49.

Legge, A., Williams, J. and Williams, P. 1992. The determination of season of death from the mandibles and bones of the domestic sheep (*Ovis aries*). In R. Maggie, R. Nisbet and G. Barker (eds), *Archeologia della Pastorizia nell' Europa Meridionale 2. Rivista di Studi Liguri*, A.57 (1991), 49–65.

Levitan, B. 1989. The vertebrate remains from Chichester Cattlemarket. In A. Down (ed.), *Chichester Excavations VI*. Chichester, 242–67.

—— 1993. Vertebrate remains. In A. D. Woodward and P. J. Leach (eds), *The Uley Shrines*. London, 257–345.

Luff, R. M. 1992. The faunal remains. In N. P. Wickenden (ed.), *The Temple and Other Sites in the North-eastern Sector of Caesaromagus.* York, 116–24.

Maltby, M. 1979. *The Animal Bones from Exeter, 1971–1975.* Sheffield.

——1984a. The animal bones. In M. Fulford (ed.), *Silchester Defences: Excavations on the Defences 1974–80.* London, 199–215.

——1984b. Animal bones and the Romano-British economy. In C. Grigson and J. Clutton-Brock (eds), *Animals and Archaeology 4: Husbandry in Europe.* BAR (International Series) 227. Oxford, 125–38.

——1989. Urban-rural variations in the butchering of cattle in Romano-British Hampshire. In D. T. W. Serjeantson (ed.), *Diet and Crafts in Towns: The Evidence of Animal Remains from the Roman to the Post-Medieval Period.* BAR (British Series) 199. Oxford, 75–106.

——1994. The meat supply in Roman Dorchester and Winchester. In A. R. Hall and H. K. Kenward (eds), *Urban-Rural Connections: Perspectives from Environmental Archaeology.* Oxford, 85–102.

——1998. The animal bones from Roman 'small towns' in the Cotswolds. In J. Timby (ed.), *Excavations at Kingscote and Wycomb, Gloucestershire.* Cirencester.

Meadows, K. I. 1995. You are what you eat: diet, identity and Romanisation. In S. Cottam, C. D. Dungworth, S. Scott and J. Taylor (eds), *TRAC 1994: Proceedings of the Fourth Theoretical Roman Archaeology Conference, Durham.* Oxford, 133–40.

O'Connor, T. P. 1986. The animal bones. In P. Zienkiewicz (ed.), *The Legionary Fortress Baths at Caerleon. II. The Finds.* Cardiff, 224–48.

——2000. *The Archaeology of Animal Bones.* Stroud.

O'Connor, T. P. and van der Veen, M. 1998. The expansion of agricultural production in late Iron Age and Roman Britain. In J. Bayley (ed.), *Science in Archaeology: An Agenda for the Future.* London, 127–43.

Parker, A. J. 1988. The birds of Roman Britain. *Oxford Journal of Archaeology,* 7, 197–226.

Reilly, K. 1996. The bird bones. In R. J. Williams, P. J. Hart and A. T. L. Williams (eds), *Wavedon Gate: A Late Iron Age and Roman Rural Settlement in Milton Keynes.* Buckinghamshire Archaeological Society Monograph Series 10. Aylesbury, 230–3.

Reitz, E. J. and Wing, E. S. 1999. *Zooarchaeology.* Oxford.

Roskams, S. and Saunders, T. 2001. The poverty of empiricism and the tyranny of theory. In U. Albarella (ed.), *Environmental Archaeology: Meaning and Purpose.* Dordrecht, 61–74.

Sadler, P. 1997. Faunal remains. In A. G. Marvell and H. S. Owen-John (eds), *Leucarum: Excavations at the Roman Auxiliary Fort at Loughor, West Glamorgan 1982–4 and 1987–8.* London.

Scott, E. 1991. Animal and infant burials in Romano-British villas: a revitalization movement. In P. Garwood, D. Jennings, R. Skeates and J. Toms (eds), *Sacred and Profane.* Oxford University Committee for Archaeology 32. Oxford, 115–21.

Stallibrass, S. 1982. The faunal remains. In T. W. Potter and C. F. Potter (eds), *A Roman-British Village at Grandford, March, Cambridgeshire.* London, 98–127.

Stokes, P. 2000. A cut above the rest? Officers and men at South Shields Roman fort. In P. Rowley-Conwy (ed.), *Animal Bones, Human Societies.* Oxford, 145–51.

Toynbee, J. M. C. 1973. *Animals in Roman Life and Art.* London.

Vigne, J.-D. 1992. The meat and offal (MOW) method and the relative proportions of ovicaprines in some ancient meat diets of the north-western Mediterranean. *Rivista di Studi Liguri,* A.57 (1991), 21–47.

Webster, G. 1998. *The Roman Imperial Army.* Norman, OK.

Webster, J. and Cooper, N. (eds) 1996. *Roman Imperialism: Post-colonial Perspectives.* Leicester.

White, K. D. 1970. *Roman Farming.* London.

Whittaker, C. R. (ed.) 1988. *Pastoral Economies in Classical Antiquity.* Cambridge.

Wilkins, J., Harvey, D. and Dobson, M. (eds) 1995. *Food in Antiquity.* Exeter.

Wilson, B. 1986. Faunal remains: animal bones and shells. In D. Miles (ed.), *Archaeology at Barton Court Farm, Abingdon, Oxfordshire.* Oxford Archaeological Unit and the Council for British Archaeology, Fiche 8, A1–G14. Oxford.

Woolf, G. 1998. *Becoming Roman: The Origins of Provincial Civilization in Gaul.* Cambridge.

Worley, F. 2001. *Roman Cremated Animal Remains from Brougham, Cumbria.* Conference (Beyond Bones) Presentation at the Groningen Institute of Archaeology, February 16. [Unpublished.]

CHAPTER TWENTY-ONE

The Army in Late Roman Britain

PAT SOUTHERN

The history of the Roman army in Britain from the late third to the late fourth century is one of marked transformation. From the early fourth century, far-reaching administrative and military reforms were instituted by Diocletian and continued by Constantine. Diocletian divided the existing provinces into smaller units and grouped them in dioceses under the control of *vicarii*, who were commanded by the praetorian prefects. The two provinces of Britannia were divided, the four new units being governed by the *vicarius* of the diocese of Britain (*Codex Theodosianus*, 11.7.2).[1] Britannia Secunda and Flavia Caesariensis were created from the former Britannia Inferior, Britannia Prima and Maxima Caesariensis from Britannia Superior. An elusive fifth province called Valentia was recreated or newly established by Theodosius after 367, but there is no agreement on its location.

By the end of Constantine's reign, the Roman army over the entire Empire had been reorganized. The old distinctions between legions and auxiliary troops no longer applied; military forces were divided into two main groups: the rapid response mobile field armies (*comitatenses*) and the frontier armies (*ripenses*, *alares* and *cohortales*). The *comitatenses* were the highest grade troops; and a law of Constantine, dated June 325, makes it clear that the *ripenses* were of a higher grade than the *alares* and *cohortales* (*Codex Theodosianus*, 7.20.4; Southern and Dixon 1996: 9–38). The cavalry formations of the *comitatenses* were commanded by the *magister equitum*, the infantry by the *magister peditum*, newly created officers who may have ranked as highly as the praetorian prefects. The frontier armies were collectively labelled *limitanei*, a term which embraced all the troops of the *limes*, whether they were old-style legions, *alae* or *cohortes*, or the new units variously called *numeri*, *equites* and *cunei*. In the fourth century the *limitanei* were always regular troops, entitled to donatives and rations like the rest of the army, but by the sixth century the term denoted a peasant militia tied to the land and responsible for its defence. Anachronistic usage of the term by later Greek and Roman authors has led to confusion.

---

1   The four new provinces are recorded in the Verona List of 312–14; the first *vicarius* is attested in 319.

The Army and the British Frontiers

By the end of the fourth century, the outposts of the northern frontier, with the possible exception of Netherby, had been vacated (Hodgson 1991: 90 *contra* Breeze and Dobson 1987: 273–5). Hadrian's Wall was still garrisoned by old-style alae and cohorts, but the Pennine forts were manned by new style *numeri* and *equites*, units which were originally part of the mobile field army. Some territory had been given up. Much of Wales and the West were possibly abandoned; though some fort-sites may have remained in occupation, this was not necessarily military. The fortress at Chester was well maintained long after 350, but its legion, *XX Valeria Victrix*, is not attested after the end of the third century (Mason 2000: 210). Military command of the whole island was divided between the forces of the *Dux Britanniarum* in the north and the *Comes Litoris Saxonici per Britannias* in the south, with an additional small field army, probably brought in by Stilicho about 395 under the *Comes Britanniarum* (see below, p. 410)

This late fourth-century scenario is largely derived from the *Notitia Dignitatum*, an administrative handbook listing government officials and the headquarters of army units with their commanders (Mann 1976: 1–10, 1989: 6–7). Its overall purpose and its many attendant problems have been much debated (Hassall 1976: 103–17). In the *Notitia* Hadrian's Wall appears to be garrisoned by the same units that are attested there in the third century, implying that this section of the document is hopelessly out of date. But the list of Wall garrisons includes units such as the *ala Herculiana* and the *equites Crispiani*, named respectively for Maximian, a colleague of Diocletian, and for Crispus, a son of Constantine, and thus cannot be dismissed as entirely anachronistic. It is widely, though not universally, agreed that the British sections were compiled about 395 (Mann 1976: 1–10; cf. Jones 1964), but that the *Notitia* was amended up to about 428, implying that the occupation of Britain must have extended beyond 410, as earlier scholars believed. Hodgson (1991: 84–5) summarizes and reviews the various theories on this subject. Another fundamental problem is that the place-names of the *Notitia* cannot all be equated with known sites, and the northern forts where fourth-century occupation is archaeologically attested significantly outnumber those listed in the *Notitia* under the command of the *Dux*. One explanation for this could be that only the headquarters forts are listed in the document (Frere 1987: 217–24).

The Defence of Britain in the Late Third Century

The Empire of the third century was plagued by secession and frequent usurpation. At the beginning of Gallienus' sole reign in 260, the Gallic Empire under Postumus split from the central government, taking over most of the west from Raetia to Britain. A few years earlier, Gallienus had withdrawn vexillations from two legions in Britain, II Augusta (at Mainz in 255, *CIL* XIII.6780) and XX Valeria Victrix (in Pannonia by 260, *ILS* 546). There is no evidence that these troops ever returned, and it is not known if these two legions were ever brought up to full strength. Probably about 276, II Augusta moved from Caerleon to Richborough, where there was space for only about 1000 men. There is no evidence that a part of the legion was outposted so that it is possible that its numbers were never made up

(*RIB* 334 of 255–60 or 258–60 is the latest dated record of the unit at Caerleon; Hodgson 1991: 87).

In Britain, recruitment of soldiers and officers, and the careers of administrative and military personnel, would have been adversely affected during the Gallic Empire from 260 to 274. The normal tour of duty for provincial governors and unit commanders was roughly three years, followed by another more prestigious posting in a different province, but after 260 this avenue of promotion would be limited to the provinces controlled by Postumus and his successors. Units in Britain probably looked to their own men for renewed officer material, even up to the rank of commander, since equestrian officers from a wider background will have been harder to find. For instance, in the early fourth century the acting commander (*praepositus*) at Birdoswald was a centurion (*RIB* 1912).

The northern frontier was not the centre of military attention in the last decades of the third century. The forts on Hadrian's Wall seem to have been in decline and, while none was entirely abandoned, in some of them buildings went out of use and had collapsed. It would appear that by the end of the third century the units on Hadrian's Wall were much reduced in strength and that the northern frontier was not under threat (Breeze and Dobson 1987: 212).

In other parts of Britain there was a tremendous upsurge in construction and reconstruction from the 270s onward (Salway 1981: 277), probably an Imperial policy decision to be dated shortly after the reunification of the Empire by Aurelian in 274. He won back the provinces that had broken away from the centre and thus for the first time in fifteen years he had access to the full resources of the Empire. He understood the need for increased exertion in defence, employing a vigorous army backed up by massive defensive fortifications. His policies were continued by Probus (Frere 1987: 329). Under these two emperors there was at last an opportunity to put into operation a co-ordinated plan for defence in an era when threats had begun to intensify over much of the Empire (Johnson 1989: 41–2).

The hinterland of Hadrian's Wall saw significant reorganization from the later third century. The fort at South Shields was restructured from about 274 and it is suggested that was linked to the departure of *cohors V Gallorum* and the installation of the *numerus barcariorum Tigrisiensium*, listed there in the *Notitia* (Hodgson 1991: 87). The new fort at Piercebridge, which is similar in architectural style to South Shields, the fort at Newton Kyme and the fort at Lancaster, built in the style of the so-called Saxon Shore forts, may also belong to this period of restructuring (for Wales, see above, pp. 106–8). There seems to have been a redistribution of troops in the north; it has been suggested that some of the Pennine forts may have been abandoned, specifically the fourteen forts in which the *Notitia* lists the new-style units of *numeri* (Breeze and Dobson 1978: 19–21; Hodgson 1991: 87). If troops were moved out of some of the Pennine forts, the new forts at Piercebridge, Newton Kyme and Lancaster could have taken up the surplus.

Another possibility is that some of the northern units were relocated to a new frontier in the south, now indelibly labelled the Saxon Shore (Johnson 1976; Johnston 1977; Maxfield 1989). The postulated dates for the coastal forts range from about 220 to the late fourth century, suggesting an ongoing problem on the coasts, dealt with by increased fortification. In the *Notitia* the Saxon Shore forts are listed under a unified command, but it is not certain that this was the case from

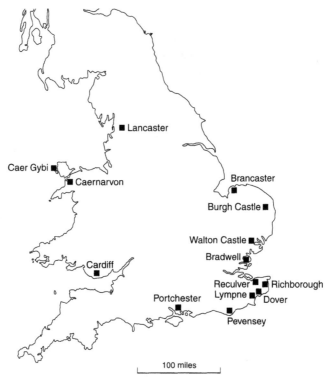

Figure 21.1   Forts of the Saxon Shore.

the outset, wherever this is taken to be. Debate has centred on the date when it may have been unified and whether both sides of the Channel were included in a central command (Johnson 1976: 81–102). It is widely agreed that the coastal defence system was not always called the 'Saxon Shore'. Eutropius, whose work dates to about 370, provides the first certain notice in literature of the *Saxones* (9.21). The Saxon Shore was thus known as such only towards the end of its life.

It has been suggested that two of the coastal forts, Reculver and Brancaster, were built about 220. Architecturally, these forts have everything in common with forts of the early Empire, with their playing-card shape, internal towers and earthen ramparts, and very little in common with the classic shore forts, characterized by massive free-standing walls and large projecting towers. An inscription from Reculver, supported by pottery evidence, seems to provide an early third-century date for that fort (Richmond 1961: 224–8, opting for A. Triarius Rufinus, *cos* 210; more convincingly, Frere 1987: 170 suggests Q. Aradius Rufinus, *cos* after 225, fitting better with the spacing on the stone). The similarities in size, shape and style of the fort at Brancaster lead to the conclusion that it was broadly contemporary with Reculver. The garrisons were old-style units. *Cohors I Baetasiorum* was moved from Maryport to Reculver and tile-stamps indicate that *cohors I Aquitanorum equitata* moved to Brancaster. Other coastal bases come into the reckoning. A small fort was established around the remains of the first-century triumphal monument at Richborough, probably in the mid-third century. A fort existed at Dover from the later second century and another may be presumed at Lympne (*RIB* 66). The two units which are known to have moved south may have been intended to assist the *Classis Britannica*, which is attested until about 250 and then disappears from the record (*CIL* XII.686 from Arles is the last known mention; Cleere 1989: 22). The early third-century dating for Reculver and Brancaster has been challenged (Mann 1989: 4). Their conservative style may have been influenced by the forts they left behind. Mann has also attempted to revise the date of the Reculver inscription, so that it may not be tied to the early third century (Mann 1977b: 15). Casey has taken the argument still further, allowing the possibility that these forts could belong to the 260s (Casey 1994: 118).

Serious raids of the Germanic tribes across the Rhine from the late 250s may have been the catalyst for the establishment of the Gallic Empire. The raids may not have been solely land-based and it is possible that it was Postumus who made the first defensive measures to defend the coasts of Britain and Gaul in the 260s, and Aurelian who continued the process in the early 270s. It may be noted that Aurelian was responsible for the design of the defences of Rome at this very time. The difference in architectural style between Reculver and Brancaster and the 'classic' shore forts need not represent any considerable lapse of time; it could simply represent the difference between earlier traditions of fort construction and the defensive concepts of Aurelian, Probus and their successors. The forts at Burgh Castle, Bradwell, possibly Walton Castle, Richborough, Dover and Lympne are dated to the period 270–90 (Johnson 1989: 41–2, pointing out the lack of hard evidence for dating). Portchester may have been added by Carausius, while Pevensey, on grounds of its ovoid shape, has been considered to be later; but Casey (1994: 120–1) amends the dating of this fort, arguing that it does not differ from the others and could be contemporary with them.

It is suggested that a line of watch-towers existed on the approaches to London on the Thames estuary, acting in concert with the shore fort garrisons, though the only tower so far known is that at Shadwell, situated on the river but at some distance from the coast (Casey 1994: 125). If the intruders were seaborne, mobile and bent on hit-and-run raids on inland sites, it made perfect sense to guard estuaries and navigable rivers. In the west, forts similar to the southern coastal installations were established at dates which were probably various. They were sited to guard estuaries, presumably to deal with attacks from Irish tribes, the Hiberni and Scotti. The forts include Cardiff and Lancaster (see pp. 106-7) and smaller installations at Caernarfon and Caer Gybi at Holyhead, the last-named resembling the late third- and fourth-century naval bases on the Rhine and Danube. The dating of the fort at Cardiff is not yet certain, though it was built after 268 (Casey 1994: 124–5).

It is not clear how the coastal forts operated. The internal buildings are not laid out on traditional lines and it has been suggested that civilians lived inside the forts (Esmonde Cleary 1989: 61). The original garrisons are unknown apart from the two northern cohorts that were installed at Reculver and Brancaster, and II Augusta at Richborough.

In any event, if they were to be effective, the forts required naval support. Prior to the building of the forts, it is clear that the fleet used at least some of the sites as bases, since *Classis Britannica* tiles have been found at Portchester and Lympne, and the prefect of the fleet set up an altar at Lympne between 135 and 145 (see *RIB* 66). Work on the *Notitia* has drawn attention to the evident pairing of harbours and landing-places (Mann 1989: 10–11), implying that the forts operated as marine bases, with facilities for beaching ships or repairing them in sheltered waters. A squadron of ships attached to each fort would be able to patrol offshore to give early warning of attack, perhaps even defeating or dispersing the enemy at sea. The army and the fleet could have worked together; an inscription attesting the presence of a *gubernator*, a river pilot, of VI Victrix at York indicates that the army could take charge of aquatic operations (*RIB* 653; Mann 1989: 6–7). The naval patrols described by Vegetius (*De Re Militari*, 4.37) may have been operative long before he wrote (Mann 1989: 3). He describes camouflaged scout ships with sails and rigging painted blue or green, matching the uniforms of the sailors; in British waters slate-grey might have been a better option.

The land-based units with a cavalry complement such as the part-mounted *cohors I Aquitanorum equitata* and units later attested in the *Notitia*, such as the *equites Dalmatae*, may have acted as the ancient counterparts of modern transport and communications sections, coupled with rapid-response functions if invaders eluded the patrols and landed. It is unlikely that the enemy would obligingly come up to the walls and lay siege to the forts, even though they were built strongly enough to withstand an attack. The forts played little or no part in the battles occasioned by Constantius' invasion of Britain (Casey 1994: 116, 125).

Communications between the south coast forts would have been quicker and easier by sea. The forts are not linked by road, but it is significant that Canterbury is linked by road with Richborough, Reculver, Dover and Lympne; the city was walled in the late third century, a coin of Postumus being sealed under the internal rampart. Casey suggests the city was a rest centre for troops from the forts (Casey 1994: 126). It is now known that a substantial town had grown up by the late third century around the fort and port at Richborough; this too may have had off-duty facilities for the south-east garrisons.

Carausius and Allectus

M. Aurelius Mausaeus Carausius is unheard of before he seized power in Britain in 286 or 287. He may already have served in Britain, perhaps in some unrecorded campaign which accounted for Diocletian's assumption of the title *Britannicus Maximus* – a title he soon dropped when Carausius rebelled. Previous service in Britain would explain why the troops accepted Carausius without demur. The soldiers would be influenced by cash payouts, but these alone might not have been sufficient to silence all opposition (Frere 1987: 362–7; Casey 1994: 46–8).

Carausius was initially appointed to clear the seas of raiders (Casey 1994: 50–1). Mann (1989: 5) suggests that he was prefect of the fleet, perhaps under a new title and operating under a reformed organization. The command involved ships and soldiers, its main base being Boulogne. Carausius commanded vexillations of several legions and a motley collection of native troops, non-Romans and barbarians, as the panegyrist calls them (*Panegyrici Latini* 8 (5).12; Casey 1994: 94–5). It was alleged that he was accused of colluding with the enemy so that he could share the booty after their raids. A condemned man, he fled to Britain, where he could rely upon armed force.

For a decade Carausius and his assassin and successor Allectus held Britain against the Tetrarchs. On the army in Britain there is little information. Carausian coinage attests two legions, II Augusta and XX Valeria Victrix, but VI Victrix based at York is conspicuously absent (Casey 1994: 93, pointing out that the legion did not serve in Gaul). Carausius perhaps entrusted the defence of the north to its resident garrisons while he attended to the south. Only at Carlisle is there evidence that Carausius was acknowledged in the north, but there is no evidence that he was resisted; had there been the slightest sign of such evidence the panegyrists who lauded the achievements of Maximian and Constantius and criminalized those of Carausius would have pounced on it and bleated it through the Imperial courts.

It is likely that the shore defences were planned when Carausius seized power. There is no support for D. A. White's (1961) argument that Carausius constructed them in order to defend his realm against Imperial forces. This is not to say that he did not take advantage of the forts – his coins are found in abundance in them – and he may have added the fort at Portchester (Casey 1994: 115–16). The efforts of Maximian to dislodge him failed and are passed over in a few words by the panegyrist, who blames the weather. The panegyri to Maximian of 287 (*Panegyrici Latini*, 10(2). 12.1) held out great hopes of defeating the rebels; the next one, of 291, ignores the campaign altogether (Nixon and Rodgers 1994: 107). The panegyric to Constantius of 297 refers to bad weather. Carausius seems to have controlled the entire fleet since Constantius had to build ships before launching his attack on Britain (Casey 1994: 131, 137).

The coinage of Carausius is found over much of Gaul and it is likely that his vexillations were based there rather than in Britain, since this is where he was most vulnerable. It seems that he still controlled the coasts of Gaul, but when his base at Boulogne fell to Constantius his assassination by Allectus was triggered, though the account in the sources may be garbled. Allectus enjoyed a short reign before Constantius and his praetorian prefect Asclepiodotus invaded and defeated him in 296. The panegyric of 297 is the sole source for the campaign against Allectus (Salway 1981: 308–13; Frere 1987: 330–1; Casey 1994: 137–8). It is not known whether or not Allectus stripped the northern frontier of its troops to face the invasion in the south. The frontier had already run down and some of the Pennine forts had already been abandoned for reasons quite unconnected with Allectus. The final battle seems to have been fought by Allectus' Frankish mercenaries. There is no firm evidence that northern troops were present.

The Fourth Century: Reforms, Rebellions and Retribution

The theory that the Wall garrisons were depleted by Allectus is bound up with the notion of disaster in the north in 296, now generally discounted (Breeze and Dobson 1987: 214, 242). This was put forward as an explanation for the extensive repairs to the mural frontier at the turn of the third and fourth centuries. This was presumably a policy decision on the part of the Western emperor, but it is not certain if work began in 296 or ten years later, when Constantius returned to conduct a northern campaign.

In a climate that is not kind to buildings, the dilapidation of the Wall, its forts and its outposts need not be attributed to damage by an enemy. There had been no extensive repairs since the reign of Severus. Constantius repaired the outpost forts and some of the forts and smaller installations on the Wall. He ignored forts in the

eastern sector at Halton Chesters and Rudchester, but the rebuilding at Birdoswald
was extensive, including the commander's house, the headquarters and the baths. At
Housesteads rebuilding is indicated, but exactly what and where is not clear. It is
suggested that this must mark the appearance of the new 'chalets', which have also
been found at Birdoswald, Greatchesters and Wallsend on Hadrian's Wall, and north
of the Wall at High Rochester (where they may precede the reign of Diocletian) and
at Risingham.[2]

It is not certain who inhabited the new chalets. The buildings are usually laid out in
rows like the older, more regular barracks, but the ground plans show lines of
individual buildings, with a gap, too small to be called an alleyway, between them.
It is suggested that one soldier and his family lived in each detached block, which
would mean that the overall strength of the garrison would be much reduced from its
normal early Empire complement, where eight men shared each *contubernium*.
Though some of the *vici* around the forts in the north were abandoned, the dates
when this occurred are uncertain, so the abandonment cannot be directly related to
the appearance of chalets inside the forts. Nor is it feasible that the chalets housed
the additional units of *exploratores* at Risingham and High Rochester, because these
units are attested only in the early third century, so they and the chalets cannot be
shown to be contemporary. The chalets are one of the great 'don't knows' of Roman
archaeology.

The reasons for the northern campaign of 306 are obscure. If the repairs to the
Wall forts began in 296, the northern tribes who witnessed the recommissioning of
the frontier may have became alarmed. A decade of growing agitation, finally
erupting into war, is not beyond the bounds of possibility. The presence of Rome
frequently acted as a catalyst on tribal society, creating amalgamations and unity of
purpose where there was none before. This may explain why the Picts are now first
mentioned. When a new ethnic name is recorded, it does not necessarily denote the
appearance of a new people. More probably the Caledones Maeatae and other groups
had amalgamated under a strong leader.

The little we know of Constantius' campaign has many parallels with that of
Severus a century before (*Panegyrici Latini*, 6(7). 1–2; Salway 1981: 317–19; Frere
1987: 335). The Roman forces reached the far north of the island and probably used
sea-borne forces in conjunction with land troops. The former Severan bases at
Cramond and Carpow may have been reused. This is the sum total of knowledge
about this war. Temporary camps abound in eastern Scotland, but none has yet been
attributed to Constantius. His army was probably composed of legionary vexillations,
alae and cohorts already in Britain, but he may also have brought in *numeri* and
equites to regarrison the Pennine forts in order to secure routes and communications
in the rear while he operated in the north. Constantius may have raised tribal units in
Gaul and Germany. A unit of Alamanni under their leader Crocus is attested by
Aurelius Victor (*De Caesaribus*, 29.41); they were later to play a role in the elevation
of Constantine to the purple; it is likely that other such formations were included in
the campaign force.

2   *RIB* 1912 and 1613 record rebuilding at Birdoswald and Housesteads respectively. Breeze and Dobson
1987: 214–17 document repairs to numerous elements of the frontier; Shotter 1996: 115. On chalets see
Bidwell 1991, 9–15, especially 10 on early chalets at High Rochester.

Like Severus, Constantius died at York. His son Constantine was with him and was immediately declared emperor by the troops, but the path to sole power was not straightforward. The effect on Britain is not known, except that Constantine took troops from the island to support his invasion of Italy; some were in his forces when he defeated Maxentius at the Milvian Bridge in 312. Coin evidence indicates that Constantine revisited Britain after this victory, one of the likely motives being to raise troops for the coming internal wars. It is suggested that he removed the garrisons north of Hadrian's Wall, leaving the outposts vacant (Breeze and Dobson 1987: 223; Hodgson 1991: 88).

Under Constantine, the administrative and military reforms set in motion by Diocletian came to fruition. Diocletian concentrated on strengthening the frontiers. In dividing the provinces into smaller units, Diocletian reduced the number of troops contained in each. The effect on the army in northern Britain was to divide the commands of the Chester and York legions and locate them in two different provinces, echoing the extension of the shore forts over more than one command. He increased the total number of legions but may have reduced the individual unit strengths from 5000 or 6000 to only 1000, though this may have applied only to the newly raised legions (Southern and Dixon 1996: 6–7, 23–33). The entourage of the emperor, the *comitatus*, assumed greater importance under Diocletian but it was not yet the foundation of the *comitatenses* of the later army. Whenever armies were assembled for campaigns, vexillations had to be gathered from the frontier formations and then dispersed when the campaign was over. It was Constantine who established the *limitanei*, comprising legions, *alae* and cohorts which were stationed on the frontiers, and the mobile *comitatenses*, comprising large cavalry elements. In Britain there seems to have been no field army until about 395, when Stilicho brought in (or possibly sent) a small force of about nine units under the *Comes Britanniarum*. Both Lupicinus in 360 and Theodosius in 367 had to bring units of the Continental field armies with them when they were sent to Britain.

The northern frontier and its hinterland, and the coastal forts, were manned by *limitanei*. The commanders of these two groups of *limitanei* are listed in the *Notitia* as the *Dux Britanniarum* and the *Comes Litoris Saxonici*. The title *dux* originally denoted a military leader, not a regular military rank, used when an officer was charged with a specific task. Diocletian established the *duces* as permanent commanders, divesting nearly all the governors (*praesides*) of their military functions. This process could not have taken place overnight. Only a few *duces* had been installed by the end of Diocletian's reign, but by the death of Constantine *duces* had probably been established in most frontier provinces (Mann 1977a: 12; Birley 1981: 344–52 on *duces*). There was never any standardization of ducal commands, which were tailored to the needs of particular frontiers. Some *duces* took charge of civil administration as commanders of provincial armies. It was a great advantage that *duces* were not limited to one province and could oversee long sections of frontier.

The command of the *Dux Britanniarum*, Duke of the Britains in the plural, clearly extended over more than one province. In its final form, as noted in the *Notitia*, it included Hadrian's Wall and the hinterland, but not the western parts of the hinterland, which may have been given up in the 380s. The date of the appointment of the first *dux* is a matter of speculation, since the only evidence derives from the *Notitia*, supported by Ammianus' description of the events of 367, when the *dux* Fullofaudes

Command of the *Dux Britanniarium* in the *Notitia Dignitatum* (Occidens 40.18–56)

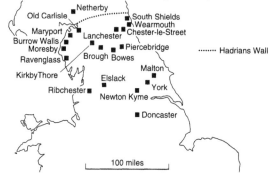

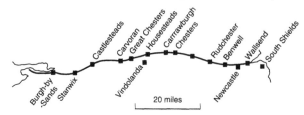

Item per lineam valli (Also along the line of the wall)Halton Chesters

Figure 21.2 Command of the Dux Britanniarum.

was ambushed and perhaps killed; at any rate, Theodosius replaced him with a trusted officer called Dulcitius (27.8.1 and 10). It is assumed that Fullofaudes was in fact the *Dux Britanniarum*, even though this is not specifically stated. This still does not clarify when the first appointment was made. At the beginning of the fourth century, rebuilding at Birdoswald was carried out under the *praeses* and not the *dux*, but this need not imply that there was no such commander at the beginning of the fourth century, since Constantius may have appointed a *dux* for the northern campaign of 306. If not, then it is assumed that the post was in existence at least by Constantine's death in 337. The headquarters of the *Dux Britanniarum* may have been at York, in Britannia Secunda (Mann 1977a: 12).

The command of the *Comes Litoris Saxonici* may have started under another *dux*, being upgraded at some time in the fourth century. Originally the term *comes* was a non-specific label for companions of the emperor, from all levels of society both civilian and military. Constantine formalized the system, using the title to denote an official of high rank, but the territorial *comites* do not appear until after his death. The *Comes Litoris Saxonici* cannot predate his reign, but once again the only evidence for the command derives from the *Notitia*, with slightly contentious backing from Ammianus (27.8.1), who describes the *comes maritimi tractus* Nectaridus, who was killed in 367. Most authors agree that the *comes maritimi tractus* is indeed the *Comes Litoris Saxonici* in literary guise, though it is possible that in 367 the appointment of *comes* had been instituted to protect the coasts, but perhaps it was known by a different title, and the appellation of the Saxon Shore had yet to be added to it.

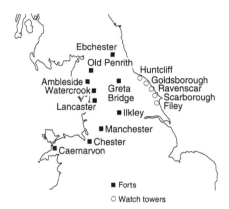

Figure 21.3 Forts occupied in the fourth century.

No ancient source clarifies whether the Saxon Shore denoted the frontier settled and defended by Saxon federate troops, or the frontier defended against Saxons. Finds of Germanic style once seemed to indicate that ethnic German soldiers must have manned the forts, but these finds are now interpreted as standard military issue and not ethnic imports. The choice of one name above all other tribal names is puzzling, since there were probably more raiders besides the Saxons, and other frontiers in the Roman world do not seem to have been named for the enemy that they faced.

The army that Constantius commanded in his expedition to Britain in 306 was probably a hybrid of the old style, pre-Diocletianic army and the new model field and frontier army that developed in the early fourth century. The army that Constans commanded during his visit in 342–3 may have been the fully fledged reorganized late Roman army. The fact that he arrived during the winter suggests urgency, but next to nothing is known of his activities. The establishment of the *areani*, usually translated as scouts, is attributed to Constans (Ammianus Marcellinus, *History*, 28.3.8). Ammianus says that they ranged far and wide, presumably gathering information, but he also says that they were based in *stationes*, implying that they reported to an assigned headquarters. It is assumed that they were native recruits, operating in the north beyond Hadrian's Wall, and that Constans was active in this frontier zone. If Constantine had taken troops from the outpost forts, there had been a thirty-year gap without resident supervision of the north, a situation for which Constans perhaps found a remedy. He may have made a treaty with the Picts, and the Scotti from Ireland; Ammianus (20.1, 20.9) says that in 360 these people broke the terms of their agreement, and since no other expedition is recorded save that of Constans, he is the most likely candidate for the establishment of such a treaty.

Constans was assassinated in 350 by Magnentius, who took troops from Britain to sustain his short-lived revolt. He had sympathizers in Britain, and retribution was harsh, under Paul Catena 'the Chain'. Perhaps only higher-ranking army officers and civil officials were affected, but the situation was so dire that the *vicarius* Martinus tried to assassinate Paul, and committed suicide when he failed. Internal discord was possibly only just over when in 360 the northern natives invaded and Julian's *magister militum* Lupicinus was sent to Britain, but no details of his expedition are recorded. In 365 there were more raids, and in 367 the serious *conspiratio barbarica* broke out, affecting all the British provinces.

The Emperor Valentinian dispatched in quick succession his *comes domesticorum* Severus, and then the *magister equitum* Jovinus. Nothing is known of what they achieved. The third general was Theodosius, whose exploits are described at length by Ammianus (27.8.1–28.3.1), not without bias, since Ammianus wrote during the reign of the Emperor Theodosius, the general's son, who accompanied his father on the British expedition. The elder Theodosius may have been *comes rei militaris*, though this is not specifically stated, and Ammianus refers to him as *dux*, in its general sense of military leader. Neither this title nor that of *comes rei militaris* indicates a rank or an official post.

Theodosius brought only four units of the Continental field army with him, the Heruli, Jovii, Batavi and Victores, amounting to perhaps 2000 men. This is not a vast number. It may indicate that the troops in Britain worked efficiently without the need for tremendous reinforcement, but the army had perhaps become demoralized. There were many deserters, to whom Theodosius issued an amnesty to encourage them to return. The enemy was probably scattered over the island in small groups, and consequently hard to bring to battle. This was not warfare of the kind where a pitched battle could decide the issue, but a prolonged search and find procedure.

Count Theodosius is the late Roman version of Gnaeus Julius Agricola, in that he is a well-documented personality, to whom all repairs and building work of vaguely the right dates tend to be attributed. Strengthening of the frontiers is to be expected after the disaster. He disbanded the *areani* because they had betrayed the Romans, and perhaps to compensate for their removal he repaired the Wall forts of Halton Chesters and Rudchester (Breeze and Dobson 1987: 224–31). The blocking of gateways in the Wall forts, once attributed to Theodosius, is now considered to have occurred at various earlier dates and need not represent extreme measures taken under duress.

The watch-towers on the east coast are usually considered to have been established by Theodosius. They are known from Filey to Huntcliff, but may have extended further in both directions, perhaps as far north as the Tyne along this eroded coast. Dating evidence can point only to a date after 367; it could thus be that they belong to measures taken by Magnus Maximus in the 380s (Ottaway 1997: 138). Whenever they were erected, they indicate the need to protect the coast from potential raiders who may have been seaborne Picts or enemies from across the North Sea, though this is discounted by some. It is not known how the towers functioned, partly because no towers linked with inland bases have been discovered, nor is there evidence that naval operations formed any part of their functions. This uncertainty is reflected in modern terminology: they are variously called signal towers, watch-towers or just towers (Wilson 1991: 142–7), and opinion is divided as to whether they belonged to the command of the *Dux Britanniarum*, because they fell within his territory, or whether they formed part of the command of the *Comes Litoris Saxonici* (Mann 1977a: 14 and Salway 1981: 383 opt for the *Dux*, Frere 1987: 345 for the *Comes*).

The Theodosian rebuilding was the last of its kind. For about forty years the arrangements he made for defence stood firm, but successive withdrawals of troops weakened the system. Some of the units removed from Britain survive in the Continental record, for instance the *Seguntienses* from Caernarfon are listed in the *Notitia* in Illyricum (Frere 1987: 356). The *milites Anderetiani* from Pevensey appear on the frontier in Germany, the *Anderetiani* in the field army in Gaul and the *classis Anderetianorum* at Paris (Mann 1989: 9).

In 383, Magnus Maximus, who may have been *Dux Britanniarum*, declared himself emperor and took British forces with him in pursuit of his claim. He perhaps abandoned Wales and the West, though there is no proof that these forts were still occupied at this date (Salway 1981: 404). Maximus was highly regarded in later Welsh tradition as Macsen Wledig; it has thus been suggested that he made arrangements with local chiefs to take over defence of their own territories. The Roman soldiers who were left in the island after 383 were probably too few in number to defend it properly, and the nine units of the field army that Stilicho sent about 395 under the *Comes Britanniarum* probably did not adequately compensate for the losses. Nothing is known of this field army, but the *comitatenses* are hard to trace archaeologically in any province, because they were usually billeted in towns and not assigned to forts. The few finds of a military nature in British towns were once regarded with suspicion, being interpreted as equipment of administrative officials. This argument has been reconsidered, but even if a military presence is indicated, it does not provide unequivocal evidence of field army units (Bishop 1991: 21–7).

During the last years of Roman Britain there was a gradual winding down of the military establishment, probably at a rate outstripping recruitment to fill the gaps. Stilicho may have taken British troops to fight against Alaric in 401, and the usurper Constantine III removed even more in 407. By the time of the final withdrawal, the Roman army in Britain had probably ceased to exist.

Conditions of Service

Unit strength of the remodelled late Roman army is much debated. The numbers of men in each fort may have been considerably reduced compared to the standards of the early Empire. The enormous numbers of men required to keep units up to full strength were probably never reached at any time, and it is likely that in the late period units were permanently under strength. Recruitment in the British provinces is undocumented, largely because soldiers lost the epigraphic habit of recording their origins and careers. The later Roman army relied increasingly on Germanic tribesmen to fill the ranks, and it is probable that this was how some units were kept up to strength in Britain, in addition to local recruitment.

There is no evidence that Germanic troops were brought to Britain as *laeti* and *foederati*, federate settlers with an obligation to provide recruits for the army. It has been suggested that the sections of the *Notitia* that might have listed *foederati* in Britain have been lost, but there is no proof for this theory (Mann 1977a: 14). There is ample literary evidence for the presence of various tribesmen, Burgundians under Probus, Frankish mercenaries under Allectus, and Alamanni with their leaders Crocus and Fraomar,[3] but otherwise they are not attested, so that either they were part of special campaign armies or they were recruited into regular army units. The rise of Germans in the regular army was widespread in the later Empire, and in Britain the *dux* Fullofaudes and the *comes* Nectaridus are presumed to be of Germanic origin.

---

3 Probus sent Burgundians and Vandals to Britain: Zosimus 1.68.1–3; Crocus and the Alamanni are attested by Aurelius Victor, *De Casesaribus*, 29.41, Fraomar by Ammianus 29.4.7.

Unit commanders in the late Empire were predominantly tribunes. The title was not standardized, in that it did not denote the same rank with the same pay scales and level of authority, but was commensurate with the grade of troops. The tribunes who commanded cohorts ranked as the lowest in the hierarchy, and the tribunes of the field army as the highest. The cohorts of Hadrian's Wall were commanded by tribunes. Commanders of *alae*, vexillations of cavalry, legions and the *numeri* were generally prefects (*praefecti*). These officers are listed in the *Notitia* as commanders of the *alae* and *numeri* under the *Dux Britanniarum*. Most of the units of the Saxon Shore forts are listed under *praepositi*, a title that had a wide application to all kinds of posts and did not denote a specific rank.

While the Empire was hard pressed during the later third and early fourth centuries, cash payments to the soldiers were commuted into payments in kind, except on those occasions when the emperor distributed cash donatives, usually on his accession and on his birthday. Supplies of food for men (*annona*) and animals (*capita*), and the production of arms, armour and clothing was centralized and State-controlled. Differentiation in pay scales was represented in multiples of the standard rations. With regard to supplies of food, Britain could boast a surplus, and shipped grain to the Continent, at least on occasion, which implies that food supplies were sufficient (Ammianus Marcellinus, 18.2.3; Zosimus 3.5.2). Each military unit may have farmed land around its base as well as requisitioning food from the local population, though this has not been proved in Britain.

The military clothing and armament of the late Empire can be reconstructed from sculptural representations and from archaeological finds. The most common finds are metal belt fittings, some of them highly decorated. In the late Empire it was the military belt rather than body armour that distinguished soldiers and state officials from civilians. Soldiers wore long-sleeved tunics, trousers and cloaks, and are often depicted in this mode of dress on sculptures and mosaics. Body armour comprised mail tunics (*lorica hamata*) or scale tunics (*lorica squamata*), helmets and shields (Southern and Dixon 1996: 89–126; Bishop and Coulston 1989, 1993).

Soldiers served for twenty years to qualify for *honesta missio*, or honourable discharge, but to qualify for full privileges as veterans (*emerita missio*) they had to serve for another four years, and then they were entitled to tax exemptions, and allotments of land or cash payments. These privileges applied to the *comitatenses* and eventually to the *ripenses*. The soldiers of the northern frontier, being the lowest ranking, may not have enjoyed the same privileges.

Though it is denied that the *limitanei* of the northern frontier formed a peasant militia, it is generally considered that they were less efficient than their predecessors, but since it is not really known precisely how the frontiers operated at any time, there is nothing to compare, and no firm evidence that the probably drastically reduced units were not performing their tasks properly. *Limitanei* were sometimes drafted into the field armies as *pseudo-comitatenses*, implying that they had not lost all their military skills. A more serious problem, which applies to all the military establishments in Britain, is that very little is known of the nature of the enemy, their origins and intentions. It is not known how the Romans perceived them or how they operated against them, and on these scores buildings and archaeological finds are mute.

REFERENCES

Bidwell, P. T. 1991. Late Roman barracks in Britain. In V. A. Maxfield and M. J. Dobson (eds), *Roman Frontier Studies 1989*. Exeter, 9–15.

Birley, A. R. 1981. *The Fasti of Roman Britain*. Oxford.

Bishop, M. C. 1991. Soldiers and military equipment in the towns of Roman Britain. In V. A. Maxfield and M. J. Dobson (eds), *Roman Frontier Studies 1989*. Exeter, 21–7.

Bishop, M. C. and Coulston, J. C. N. 1989. *Roman Military Equipment*. Princes Risborough.

—— 1993. *Roman Military Equipment*. London.

Breeze, D. and Dobson, B. 1987. *Hadrian's Wall*, 3rd edn. London.

Casey, J. 1994. *Carausius and Allectus*. London.

Cleere, H. 1989. The Classis Britannica. In V. A. Maxfield (ed.), *The Saxon Shore*. Exeter, 18–22.

Davies, J. L. 1991. Roman military deployment in Wales and the Marches from Pius to Theodosius. In V. A. Maxfield and M. J. Dobson (eds), *Roman Frontier Studies 1989*. Exeter, 52–7.

Esmonde Cleary, S. 1989. *The Ending of Roman Britain*. London.

Frere, S. 1987. *Britannia: A History of Roman Britain*, 3rd edn. London.

Goodburn, R. and Bartholomew, P. (eds) 1976. *Aspects of the Notitia Dignitatum*. Oxford.

Hassall, M. W. C. 1976. Britain in the Notitia. In R. Goodburn and P. Bartholomew (eds), *Aspects of the Notitia Dignitatum*. Oxford, 103–17.

Hodgson, N. 1991. The Notitia Dignitatum and the later Roman garrison of Britain. In V. A. Maxfield and M. J. Dobson (eds), *Roman Frontier Studies 1989*. Exeter, 84–92.

Ireland, S. 1986. *Roman Britain: A Sourcebook*. London.

James, S. T. 1984. Britain and the late Roman army. In T. F. C. Blagg and A. C. King (eds), *Military and Civilian in Roman Britain*. Oxford, 161–8.

Johnson, S. 1976. Channel commands in the Notitia. In R. Goodburn and P. Bartholomew (eds), *Aspects of the Notitia Dignitatum*. Oxford, 81–102.

—— 1989. Architecture of the Saxon Shore forts. In V. A. Maxfield (ed.), *The Saxon Shore*. Exeter, 30–44.

Johnston, D. A. (ed.) 1977. *The Saxon Shore*. London.

Jones, A. H. M. 1964. *The Later Roman Empire, 284–602*. Oxford.

Mann, J. C. 1976. What was the Notitia Dignitatum for? In R. Goodburn and P. Bartholomew (eds), *Aspects of the Notitia Dignitatum*. Oxford, 1–10.

—— 1977a. Duces and Comites in the fourth century. In D. A. Johnston (ed.), *The Saxon Shore*. London, 11–15.

—— 1977b. The Reculver inscription. In D. A. Johnston (ed.), *The Saxon Shore*. London, 15.

—— 1989. Historical development of the Saxon Shore. In V. A. Maxfield (ed.), *The Saxon Shore*. Exeter, 1–11.

Mason, D. J. P. 2000. *Roman Chester*. Stroud.

Maxfield, V. A. (ed.) 1989. *The Saxon Shore*. Exeter.

Nixon, C. E. V. and Rodgers, B. S. 1994. *In Praise of Later Emperors: the Panegyrici Latini*. Berkeley, CA.

Ottaway, P. 1997. Recent excavations of the late Roman signal station at Filey, North Yorkshire. In W. Groenmann-van Waateringe (ed.), *Roman Frontier Studies 1995*. Oxford, 135–41.

Richmond, I. A. 1961. A new building inscription from the Saxon-shore fort at Reculver, Kent. *Antiquaries Journal*, 41, 224–8.

Salway, P. 1981. *Roman Britain*. Oxford.

Shotter, D. 1996. *The Roman Frontier in Britain*. Preston.

Southern, P. and Dixon, K. 1996. *The Late Roman Army*. London.

White, D. A. 1961. *Litus Saxonicum*. Madison, WI.

Wilson, P. R. 1991. Aspects of the Yorkshire signal stations. In V. A. Maxfield and M. J. Dobson (eds), *Roman Frontier Studies 1989*. Exeter, 142–7.

CHAPTER TWENTY-TWO

Britain in the Fourth Century

SIMON ESMONDE CLEARY

The title of this chapter is one of the few in this work which is explicitly chronological rather than thematic. It thus isolates a particular period and imposes on it a unity, one which cuts across several of the themes elaborated in other chapters. This chapter will therefore respond to this agenda by examining first, the historical sources and the picture they have been used to construct; second, major classes of archaeological evidence and the ways in which they have been studied; and third, major themes in current research. This will allow conclusions to be drawn about the extent to which the fourth century may (or may not) be viewed as a distinct and distinctive period in the development of Roman Britain.

The Historical Sources

There is a variety of written sources both from within Britain and from outside which bear on the island in the fourth century. It must be admitted at the outset that all are partial and lacunose. Partly this is for reasons of their original composition: Britain was only of occasional interest; or it is the result of time and chance, which have effaced more than they have handed down (cf. Ireland 1986 for translations).

Primacy of honour has always been given to the narrative historical sources, for without them there would be no chronological structure nor overall impression of the sequence of events. But equally, Britain features only when it was the setting for events which were of interest to the historians, events principally which touched upon the Imperial succession or military triumph and disaster. Thus we read of the usurpation of the title of Augustus by Constantine I at York in 306, the midwinter visit by his son Constans in 342–3, the assassination seven years later of Constans and his replacement by Magnentius, and the consequences of Magnentius' own suppression in 353. When Julian was Caesar in Gaul in the late 350s, he seems to have used Britain as a bread-basket for resupplying the Rhine frontier, and in 360 sent his *magister armorum* (army commander) Lupicinus to Britain in midwinter with a small force to put down an invasion by the Picts and the Scots. Ammianus' summary of the state of the Empire at the accession of Valens and Valentinian I in 364 (*Res Gestae*, XXVI, 4) mentions it as one of many areas supposedly under attack. Three years later, in 367, Ammianus tells us of what has become the most famous episode in Britain's fourth-century history, the *barbarica conspiratio*, the barbarian conspiracy when Britain was subjected to simultaneous barbarian attack, in which Nectaridus, commander of the coastal defences (possibly the *Comes Litoris Saxonici*, commander of the coastal defences in the south and east) was killed, and Fullofaudes the *dux* (possibly the *Dux Britanniarum*, commander of the northern frontier) was besieged and captured. The western Augustus, Valentinian I, sent the *comes* Theodosius with an expedition-ary force to restore order on the island, where he also dealt with the consequent revolt of one Valentinus. The fact that the son of this commander, the emperor Theodosius I, wore the purple at the time of the writing of Ammianus' history may help explain the prominence given to this episode, though it does also sound to have been a significant military reverse for the Roman forces in Britain. In 383 a putsch led to the deposition and murder of the western Augustus Gratian, and his replacement with Magnus Maximus, who appears at the time to have been an army commander in Britain, where he had also served with the *comes* Theodosius. Maximus was sup-pressed in 383 by the emperor Theodosius I.

Two consistent patterns emerge from this litany of bloodshed. The first is Britain's role as a nursery of usurpers, a role which had started with Carausius in the late third century and was to continue into the early fifth with Constantine III. The imperial politics of the late Roman Empire may briefly be characterized as dynastic autocracy tempered by assassination, so it not perhaps surprising that Britain with its garrison should be implicated in some of these imbroglios. The second pattern is the chronic threat to the integrity of the Roman possessions posed by external peoples, another task for the military establishment in Britain.

A tiny handful of other references in the histories tell us such snippets as the fact that the elder Gratian, father of Valens and Valentinian I, had served in Britain, or that a German tribe, the Bucinobantes, was transferred to Britain by Valentinian I with their king Fraomar, who was put in command of a large force of Alamanni in the island. Far more useful for reconstructing the military dispositions of later fourth-century Britain is the *Notitia Dignitatum*. As well as its extensive listings of the units of the various military commands and armies, it also allows us a glimpse of the internal organization of the civil and financial administrations of the late Roman diocese of the Britains. The *vicarius* of the diocese of the Britains was probably based in London; one is known by name, Pacatianus, to whom the emperor addressed a decree (rescript) in 319. There also resided the consular governor of Maxima Caesariensis, the officials of the Finance Minister (*comes sacrarum largitionum*), including the diocesan treasury, and those of the Keeper of the Privy Purse (*comes rerum privatarum*). Late Roman London, which on occasion functioned as a mint, must have been something of a 'company town' of the late Roman State.

All the sources described above were written by people from outside Britain. Written sources actually generated within Britain in the fourth century are very few. Civil Roman Britain seems never to have had a very strong commitment to the 'epigraphic habit', inscribing on stone. In the second and earlier third century the army had erected hundreds of inscriptions, but by the fourth century this had dwindled to a trickle. So, apart from one or two military inscriptions, such as those commemorating the construction of Yorkshire signal-stations (e.g. *RIB 721* from

Ravenscar) and a few civil tombstones (e.g. *RIB* 955 from Carlisle), or a base from Cirencester (*RIB* 103) suggesting that that town lay in Britannia Prima, epigraphy is denied us as a useful source. Otherwise, some of the curse-tablets from Bath are of an orthography which suggests a later rather than an earlier date, and one (*Tabellae Sulis* 98) mentions Christians, thus by implication a group sufficiently numerous to be worthy of note. A number of graffiti are scratched on pottery and pewter vessels of fourth-century date, but are seldom more illuminating than the name of the owner. As yet we lack anything such as the Vindolanda tablets from first-century Britain or the Abinnaeus archive from fourth-century Egypt to give a more personal and day-to-day view of life as it was lived. Indeed, the overall picture of fourth-century Britain, such as it is, from these non-narrative sources is largely of dull ordinariness: a diocese and provinces administered in the usual way, with a large but not exceptional military garrison, the rudiments of Church organization and sufficient literacy to vouchsafe us some few glimpses of the concerns of the people of the island.

Developments in Modern Scholarship

When one turns to the development of thought and writing on Roman Britain through the twentieth century, the effect of the lack of a master narrative gained from the texts is clear; for the first two-thirds of the century the fourth century is not regarded as a separate period with its own problems and peculiarities. If one looks at the synthetic works of the 'great tradition' of writing on Roman Britain till after the Second World War, the approach is principally thematic. This agenda was laid down by Haverfield (1905) and followed by Collingwood (Collingwood and Myres 1936) and Richmond (1955), each of these the standard work on the subject for its generation. With such an approach, it is more possible to blur or confound chronological difference than with a more strictly narrative framework. Also, it must be remembered what a limited number of sites and a small amount of material these scholars had to work with, compared with the massive databases and range of analyses and approaches of the present day. Indeed, one campaign of excavation on one site provides Collingwood with his most noticeable break into chronological relativism; the Wheelers' excavations at Verulamium in the 1930s, with Mortimer Wheeler's powerfully written evocation of the 'bombarded city' of the third century and the 'Constantinian renaissance' of the early fourth (Wheeler and Wheeler 1936). Collingwood's treatment of the third, fourth and fifth centuries was otherwise largely a narrative derived from the various historical or other textual sources.

In the last third of the twentieth century the place of the fourth century in Romano-British studies changed out of all recognition. In part, this must be to do with the greatly expanded database both of sites and of material which the 'rescue boom' of the 1960s and 1970s, and the subsequent more orderly provision for the excavation of sites, has produced. The quantitative leap simply in the amount of evidence to hand is hard to overestimate. In parallel with this, the increasingly sophisticated study of coins (cf. Reece 2002) and pottery (Tyers 1996) as dating media have allowed sites to be dated more accurately. The combination of more sites and better dating allowed patterns of development through time to be recognized, which had simply not been available to earlier workers. But just as important, the Late

Empire started to acquire master narratives, comparable to those long deployed for the High Empire, which allowed an overall characterization of the period. This, of course, was the invention of Late Antiquity as a period in its own right, not just as a tailpiece of Gibbonian decadence and despotism. For the English-speaking world the turning-point came in 1964 with the publication of A. H. M. Jones' magisterial *The Later Roman Empire, 284–602*.

Three years later, in 1967, another of the standard works for its generation on Roman Britain was first published, Sheppard Frere's *Britannia: a History of Roman Britain*. Because of the incidence of evidence and of existing published work, as well as the author's own interests, the first two centuries and the military sequence bulk large, but Frere's own excavations at Verulamium had marked a major step in characterizing fourth-century towns. Though written too late to take advantage of Jones' framework for the Late Empire, it does mark a major change in the treatment of the third and fourth centuries. In the thematic chapters on towns, countryside, trade and industry, romanization, there is much more of a sense of development and change through time than had been the case in (or possible for) a Collingwood or a Richmond. The fourth century is recognized as qualitatively different from the second century, though in some respects it is still treated as a late flowering of traditional Roman culture.

What has been outlined above is what might be regarded as a traditional 'Romanist' view of Britain in the fourth century, a part of the Empire and a development out of the earlier Roman period. But alongside this tradition there is another, in which the fourth century is regarded essentially as the necessary precursor to the fifth. In the fifth century the historical sources tell us of the collapse of Roman power and its replacement by the incoming ancestors of the English, the Anglo-Saxons. The archaeology tells us of the collapse of the Roman way of life, forts, towns, villas, and its replacement by the settlements, cemeteries and artefacts of the Anglo-Saxons. The questions posed were over the extent to which there was a causal relationship between the end of one culture and the arrival of another, and the extent to which there was overlap and interaction between the two periods. In 1936 volume I of *The Oxford History of England* was revealingly titled *Roman Britain and the English Settlements*, where the consideration of Roman Britain by Collingwood flowed seamlessly on into an examination of the early Anglo-Saxon settlement by J. N. L. Myres. The scenario proposed by Myres, and revisited throughout a long and influential career, was that the earliest Anglo-Saxons are to be found in Britain at the time of the collapse of Roman power, and that the stories of Hengest and Horsa and Vortigern preserved in later written sources such as Gildas and Bede reflect the circumstances of their arrival as mercenaries or federates under the control of sub-Roman potentates. In subsequent work Myres tried to identify specifically 'Germanic' objects in the material culture of late Roman Britain, such as 'Romano-Saxon' pottery. This ethnic ascription of objects was also influentially proposed by Hawkes and Dunning in 1965, when they argued that certain types of belt-suite and associated metalwork from late Roman contexts and early Anglo-Saxon graves were of Roman manufacture but to Germanic taste, thus betokening the presence of Germanic warriors in Britain before the end of Roman rule. A variant on this was the invocation of late Roman Britain as a background or preface to 'Celtic' Britain, that is, western and northern Britain in the fifth and sixth centuries, beyond the areas being over-run by the Anglo-Saxons, and where a culture in part descended from that of Roman Britain might be discerned (e.g. Thomas 1986).

But in the last twenty years of the twentieth century it was the archaeology of the fourth century and into the fifth that was to experience a growth in interest and publication. In 1979 the proceedings of a conference on *The End of Roman Britain*, edited by Casey, concentrated on the archaeology rather than the history. The following year Johnson's *Later Roman Britain*, while incorporating textual material, was more concerned with the archaeology of the late Roman diocese, running on into the early Anglo-Saxon period. In 1984 Arnold published his *Roman Britain to Saxon England*, which explicitly looked at the archaeology through the prism of then current interpretative models. This preference for the archaeology over the history was also a theme of the present author's 1989 *The Ending of Roman Britain*, which also expressed itself very sceptical of the value of the textual sources for the fifth century, which had till then supplied the main narrative and exegetic frameworks. Subsequent writers such as Dark (2000) and Higham (1992) have been more charitably disposed to the written sources for the fifth century, while at the same time treating the fourth century as an important period in its own right as well as being the prelude to the fifth century. More recently, Faulkner's *The Decline and Fall of Roman Britain* (2000) has provided a useful, if provocative, reassessment of the archaeology of the fourth century.

This consideration of the development of fourth-century studies has of necessity confined itself to a handful of the synthetic works, and has passed over many crucial articles on the period as a whole or on classes of site or material. But synthetic works do have the value of encapsulating the developments represented in these shorter publications. What is evident from the discussion above is that, from being a sort of tailpiece to the study of Roman Britain, the fourth century has over the last twenty years emerged as a subject in its own right, not merely an add-on to works principally concerned with the first two centuries AD. In this chapter it is proposed to adopt a series of themes which in a way climb the Hawkesian 'ladder of inference' from topics which are allegedly simple to elucidate, such as the economic basis and social structure, to the more complex, such as religion. But these themes will also be an expression of the visibility of the different aspects of the fourth century in the archaeological record, and the way that this has strongly conditioned the incidence of work on the period. The themes are: settlements and society; economic formations; agrarian formations; religious formations; before looking at the concept of 'decline'. It is hoped that these will show that there is a coherence and logic to this period, defined as it is by arbitrary chronological limits.

Rural Economy

Studies of Roman Britain tend to open with considerations of the most archaeologically visible classes of site, which are also the most 'Roman' (forts, towns, villas). While this is entirely understandable, it runs the risk of downgrading the countryside which was first, the most fundamental industry, agriculture, on which all else depended, and second, the lives and activities of the overwhelming bulk of the population, the peasantry. The problem here is to try to identify patterns and trends which relate to the fourth century and to avoid simply a general-purpose disquisition on things rural.

One may start with the agrarian economy and landscape, meaning the demands made on agricultural production and how these are reflected in the structures and layout of the countryside. The overall development of the crops grown and animals raised in the Romano-British countryside are tolerably well understood, with some appreciation of gross regional products. The staple crop was wheat, principally spelt with some emmer and also evidence for bread-wheat, the latter often associated with military sites. Barley and oats were also important cereals, possibly for brewing and animal fodder, as well as any human food use. In this there does not appear to be any particularly fourth-century variation. What may be more characteristic of the fourth century is the evidence for extensification of cereal agriculture (there may also have been intensification, but that would be hard to show from archaeology). It is noticeable that there is evidence for the imposition of field-systems onto areas where cereal agriculture is not the optimal land use, for instance, river flood-plains, hill-slopes and some upland areas. This would seem to suggest pressure for or a premium on cereal production, perhaps to meet the demands of army supply (a similar situation may be seen in the lower Rhine basin), or for the support of townspeople, or perhaps to feed an increasing population. Accurate calculation of absolute population figures is impossible; such figures as there are are produced with smoke and mirrors. But it does seem to be agreed that there is a relative increase in population over the Roman period, so a unifying feature of the agrarian economy in the fourth century may have been increased demand for grain. The situation with livestock and their products is more difficult to read (Dobney 2001). The value of cattle and sheep for secondary products (hides, wool, milk, etc.) and the importance of industries such as cordwaining and textiles is clear, as is the contribution of meat to diet. It is difficult, though, to isolate any specifically fourth-century profile in the animal-bone record, particularly at the producing sites (villas, farmsteads, etc.). But recent work on what animal bone may tell us about the supply of livestock, and thus their products, to the consuming site of Lincoln may begin to show us how we can approach the mobilization of resources over distance through political or economic power.

There may also be evidence for the importance of the countryside in the processing of raw materials and in manufacture. Most pottery production in late Roman Britain seems to have been in rural locations, ranging from large 'industries' cumulatively covering many square kilometres, to small, localized producers (cf. Tyers 1996). Explanations for this have ranged from access to raw materials to exploitation of administratively marginal locations. But these sites are generally integrated into the landscape, and the presence of 'corn-driers' and equipment such as querns shows an overlap with the implements of agrarian production. Pottery may be as much a rural 'crop' as grain or wool. The location of some of the metalworking industries, especially iron, recalls that of pottery. How and where and by whom other major rural products, particularly timber, leather, wool, were worked is much more difficult to approach through the archaeology. Nevertheless, it is a priori likely that some (much?) of this went on in the countryside, and the evidence of butchered bone, leather offcuts or wooden waste occasionally confirms this. Some of this was undoubtedly produced for surplus, either to meet tax or rental obligations, or for trade at the towns. But much of it may have circulated much more locally, for instance, on estates or within local social networks.

Rural Settlement

As with the rural economy, so it is easy to write a general description of Romano-British rural settlement, but much less easy to isolate patterns and trends specific to the fourth century. This is particularly the case when dealing with settlements other than the villa, which is essentially the only settlement type in the north and west and is numerically dominant in the south and east (cf. Hingley 1989: chapter 9). The traditional impression of rural settlement in Roman Britain is that it consisted of isolated sites, be they villas or be they farms/farmsteads/native settlements, or whatever the preferred term. This was often taken to imply a corresponding social landscape of (semi-)autonomous family groupings.

It is becoming clear, however, that in the south and east there is growing evidence for nucleated settlement. This is clearest in the Salisbury Plain area, where recent fieldwork has shown that there is a landscape of linear arrangements of building enclosures with associated field-systems, reminiscent of the appearance of deserted medieval villages. Sites such as Chisenbury Warren have long been known, but others such as Knook show the type to be more widespread. The nucleation and degree of planning suggest a considerable degree of control; it would be interesting to know whether this was exercised from the villas which ring the Plain, or from some other source, or was an expression of group identity within agrarian society. These field-systems on the chalk of the high Plain again suggest the extension of cereal agriculture onto unsuitable land. Similar sites are known from elsewhere in central southern Britain. Other areas such as Somerset, the Thames valley and parts of the East Midlands have analogous sites consisting of clusters or linear arrangements of simple housing. Large-scale excavations at Stanwick (Northamptonshire) have also showed a rural landscape that is much more complex in terms of its constituent elements and their inter-relationships than the traditional villa:farmstead dichotomy would allow. They also resemble in overall morphology and some building types some of the so-called 'small' towns, as well as sites such as Kingscote (Gloucestershire), which we find very difficult to label. The paucity of modern English vocabulary for settlement types may be hindering understanding by offering too few categories.

The incidence of these distinctive settlement types has helped make workers more alive to the very regional nature of much of fourth-century Britain. The gross distinction between the north and west and the south and east has long been recognized. But it is clear that even within these large super-regions there are smaller regions and sub-regions which have their own peculiarities. Sometimes these are imposed by topography and resources, for instance, the wetlands of the Fens or the Somerset Levels, or the sands and clays of the Weald in the south and east, or the upland pastures of the Pennines as opposed to the arable river-valleys in the north and west. Sometimes the differences are an artefact of human cultural preference, as in the clusters or absences of villas in the south and east. The analysis of differing landscapes is surely going to be one of the growth areas in ways of looking at Roman Britain. In part this is because of the growth of the powerful technical systems lumped together under the title of Geographical Information Systems (GIS), which allow the manipulation and analysis of large quantities of data. In part this is because of the growth of interest in 'landscape archaeology' and the ways of analysing landscape features to understand the human significance of that landscape, often with time-depth incorporated. It has rightly been noted that the study of the Romano-British landscape has traditionally consisted in looking at points (sites) rather than at the landscape and its constituent elements as a whole. This has been a pronounced weakness, since our perception of Romano-British landscapes is restricted largely to habitation sites. Yet work in areas such as the Fens shows that a more complex and extensive picture can be created.

Villas

Villas have always absorbed the lion's share of work on the countryside because they are archaeologically visible and seemed to show the assimilation of the Romano-British gentry and aristocracy to a more civilized way of life. Indeed, for a long time later Roman villas in Britain were seen as the fourth-century predecessors of the country houses of the eighteenth- and nineteenth-century aristocracy and gentry. This attitude spilt over into implicit assumptions about social structures, with an adult male heading a household of women, children, servants and agricultural labourers which, it is only fair to note, corresponded with the picture to be gained from fourth-century writers. It was also noted that the first half of the fourth century saw a peak both in the overall numbers of villas and in their size and complexity (particularly at the upper end of the scale). This was viewed as evidence not just for agrarian prosperity (for some, at least) but also for a growing preference for the rural over the urban among the élite. This was read in the light of fourth-century legislation against the municipal aristocracy shirking its responsibilities in the towns and of the apparent 'decline' of the 'large' towns to produce a picture of the 'flight' of the aristocracy to their country estates. Indeed, some went so far as to postulate that some of this development marked the 'flight of capital' from Gaul after the invasions of the third century.

More recently, attention has focused on the use of the plans and decoration of villas to explore alternative models for how they were peopled and used. In 1978 J. T. Smith produced his analysis of villa plans to show repetition of units, even of whole buildings, which he interpreted as showing that these villas were inhabited not by a single patriarchal family, but by lineages or groups within an extended family or kin group (cf. J. T. Smith 1997). This would imply that, instead of a villa representing a single piece of property transmissible at will, it and its land might represent an asset held and transmitted in common, of which individuals had only the usufruct during their lives.

Other, more recent, analyses have concentrated on the evidence from villa residences for patterns of use and movement, drawing on work undertaken elsewhere in the Empire on how the late Roman aristocrat wished to portray himself and to be seen (Perring 2002). This work has emphasized the presence of large, well-appointed rooms in axial or other dominating positions. These may be interpreted as the formal reception rooms where the villa proprietor welcomed important guests or his peers, and received his tenants or other social inferiors. Many of these rooms have mosaics (all that usually survives of the decorative scheme), the layout and subject-matter of some of which suggest that these rooms could also have doubled as dining-rooms for formal entertainments. The most elaborate, such as Keynsham or Woodchester, may have had rooms with highly specific functions, such as libraries or sculpture galleries, emphasizing the wealth and connoisseurship of their owners. Such interpretations do implicitly hark back to the model of a single, aristocratic proprietor rather than multiple ownership, but at least this opens up the subject by giving models to test and alternatives to consider. It is also worth pointing out that the *praetoria* or commanding officers' houses of fourth-century forts seem to be of a comparable size and a comparable scale of appointment to many villas further south. This is well exemplified by the recent excavations at South Shields, as well as at sites such as Housesteads and Vindolanda.

The comments above have been structured by the conventional separation of rural from military and urban archaeology. But what this may be obscuring is that we would be better off transcending such categories and looking instead simply at the category of élite residence, and what it tells us about that élite. In this respect some of the more recent approaches noted above, to do with the patterns of occupation and use, may be ways forward. Recent studies of earlier Imperial houses have concentrated on the importance of the public/private axis in the ordering of domestic space, the extent to which penetration into the house was a function of status, and the ways of identifying servile and low-status areas. These could well be applied to fourth-century Roman Britain. Other approaches would make more use of structuring by gender. We are still remarkably ignorant of whether and how Roman houses of any period reflected gender relations or, for that matter, age relations. This may in part be due to the difficulty of 'reading' two-dimensional plans with none of the furniture or décor which would have given the clues to a contemporary, but this does not mean that the attempt should not be made.

What we are looking at here is in large measure the post-modern interest in 'identity', how a person's social identity was created and how this then helped structure the arenas in which that identity was displayed. In the case of fourth-century élite residences in Britain, the mosaics show a clear 'Roman' identity, not only in the choice of medium but in the contexts in which they are laid and in the choice of figured designs, which uniformly display figures and scenes from Mediterranean religion and legend. Other evidence, such as the hoards of silver plate deposited at the turn of the fourth and fifth century, suggest a desire to impress through the display of highly decorated (and unusable) precious metal. Similar motives may also lie behind the choice of some fourth-century glass. Analysis of food residues may also contribute to an understanding of what went on in these rooms ('foodways' in the unlovely jargon). But equally, if J. T. Smith's analyses of house-plans be accepted, this proclamation of 'Roman' and 'élite' identities may be taking place in contexts where other identities, such as family, gender or legal title, were more powerful in shaping the physical environment.

Traditionally, villas have been seen as outposts of Roman urban civilization, and this has undoubtedly helped shape the perception of them in the fourth century as alternative poles of aristocratic activity, increasingly favoured at the expense of towns. But towns themselves in the fourth century have been a focus of much debate in their own right.

Towns

Towns are seen as the litmus test of the impact of Roman values on Britain. To the Romans they were the most important type of human community, for political, administrative and cultural reasons: their development in Britain often stands as a metonym for the development of Roman culture in the island. This has been particularly true of the so-called 'large' towns, the administrative centres with their street-grids and Roman-style public buildings and monuments. Early campaigns at towns such as Silchester and Caerwent yielded plans of those towns, but plans that were indeed two-dimensional in that they lacked any real chronology. Wheeler's Verulamium excavations did, as noted, introduce an element of change over time, but it is really with Frere's excavations at the same town that the differences between earlier and later Romano-British towns began to be clear. To generalize, by the fourth century towns had seen a rise in the number and importance of the grander urban residences ('town-houses'), while the public buildings of the second century were abandoned or diminished, and economic functions such as manufacture and redistribution appear less significant both in comparison with the second century and in comparison with fourth-century 'small' towns. Because of the importance accorded to public buildings as an index of the impact of Roman political, cultural and architectural models, this change was sometimes seen as 'decline'. Nonetheless, economically and socially these towns could still be seen as vigorous through the fourth century, albeit changed. In the sixties and seventies of the twentieth century there was much debate over 'continuity'. Was there continuity between aspects of Roman Britain and of early Anglo-Saxon England (picking up the agenda long proposed by Myres)? The continued existence of Romano-British towns, sometimes into the fifth century as at Verulamium Insula XXVII, and the presence in some towns of 'Germanic' objects, accorded well with an intellectual climate which favoured continuity. In 1980 Reece published a designedly controversial paper arguing that the Romano-British town was 'dead' in the third century, and that the town-houses of the fourth century are a cluster of the estates of the powerful 'administrative villages'. The view of what a Roman town ought to be is deeply traditionalist and the view of the fourth-century town over-jaundiced, but the paper set out to provoke, and it did. It was important in that it broke the cosy consensus for continuity and emphasized that fourth-century towns in Britain must be studied in their own right rather than as a prefiguring of the early mediaeval towns of England. More recently, Faulkner (2000) has proposed that the high levels of occupation achieved by the third century persist, just, into the early fourth century, but that then both quantitatively and qualitatively occupation drops at an accelerating pace through the fourth century, with perhaps only 10 per cent as much habitation in towns in 400 as there had been in 300. Moreover, the fourth century saw a shift away from the large town-houses to smaller, simpler structures. He also notes the huge diversion of resources into building town walls, the diagnostic public monument of the late Roman town.

What has become clear is that the traditional emphasis on the fate of public buildings and monuments was misleading, for it imported a second-century agenda into the fourth century. While some fourth-century towns had rid themselves of their inheritance of second-century public buildings, others maintained some or all of them. But some, such as the forum, seem decreasingly to have been useful. Given the importance in fourth-century town-houses of reception rooms, what we may be seeing is the transfer of the display of power from the relatively open public building to the more controlled theatre of the private residence, thus symbolizing the rise of the power of the individual at the expense of the civic. Other public buildings, such as the baths, may also have been affected by changes in public bathing as a consequence of changing attitudes to the body and its display. Temples, theatres and amphitheatres may increasingly have been affected by imperial Christian legislation against places of pagan worship and spectacle. Thus, rather than seeing some unilinear 'decline' affecting all classes of public building, one should look at how changing attitudes to a range of activities may have impacted on different types of public building and custom.

Study of the 'small' towns has come to less certain conclusions (Burnham and Wacher 1990). Unlike the 'large' towns, which all look more like each other than they look like anything else, the 'small' towns cover a wide range of sizes, layouts, building types. Some are indistinguishable from 'rural' settlements, some seem to be large temple settlements, some are mainly industrial, and there is a large 'undistributed middle' whose buildings, features such as furnaces and ovens, and artefact distributions all suggest that they are essentially 'market towns'. For the fourth century, such discussion as there has been has tended to concentrate on comparing them with the 'large' towns. The consensus has been that at this period they have usurped much of the economic primacy of the 'large' towns, as seen both in the development of the 'small' towns and in the decline of the artisan aspects of the 'large' towns. This remains impressionistic rather than quantified, and may be an over-simple antithesis. The town-houses which mark out the 'large' towns as élite residences are almost entirely absent from the 'small' towns. The 'small' towns certainly had important economic functions, but we are perhaps in danger of losing sight of other equally important aspects such as the religious (e.g. the presence at almost all of temples), and as centres for the dissemination of information downwards and upwards, articulated by their position on the communications network and perhaps in the administrative structure. There are two other aspects worth noting. The first is that Britain retains its 'small' towns in the fourth century in a way which Gaul and Germany do not, suggesting a different trajectory of social, economic and religious development. The second is that, again unlike the Continent, a number of these towns are given stone defences in the later third and fourth century (if not before). In this way they are related to the 'large' towns, though at the 'small' ones the defences enclose only a limited area, perhaps with an emphasis on protecting installations of interest to the State.

Economic Formations

The most widely used archaeological indicator of economic activity, pottery, is abundant over most of fourth-century Britain (cf. Tyers 1996). Certain other classes of artefact such as metal objects may have a more or less certain provenance. The distribution of these objects, above all pottery, away from their place(s) of manufacture is, of course, the best-known archaeological proxy for economic activity and relations. In addition, there are large amounts of fourth-century coinage in Britain, from a variety of archaeological contexts: coins certainly have to do with economic activity, but precisely what needs to be scrutinized (cf. Reece 2002). The risk is simply to catalogue instances rather than to seek deeper patterning. Therefore it will be argued here that much of what we can see in the archaeological record is engendered by three interlocking structures of production and consumption: the State, the market, social relations.

In Marxian analysis, much of the late antique world is characterized as belonging to the 'tributary mode', where the prime mover of economic activity was the extraction of surplus in the form of tribute. This sets it apart from either the postulated 'slave mode' characteristic of some times and places in the ancient world, or the 'feudal mode' held to be characteristic of the medieval world. Surplus was extracted ultimately through coercive power, and went either to the central State apparatus in the form of taxes in coin and in kind, or to intermediate structures such as the cities and the Church, as income from land and donations by the citizen or the faithful, or as rents and dues to the élite who were a rentier class. These revenues were then expended by the State in order to safeguard its own existence and to discharge its financial obligations, by the cities and Church to discharge their civic or liturgical and charitable duties, or by the élite to finance their lifestyles of conspicuous consumption and display. By the fourth century, the textual sources are unanimous in agreeing that the exactions of the State were an ever-present and ever-increasing burden on the empire's population. These exactions fell largely on the land and people of the countryside and took the form either of payment in precious-metal coin or bullion, or in kind, or in labour (munera). They were required in large measure to feed, clothe, equip and pay the army, on whose labours the continued existence of the Empire and the life of the emperor depended.

The State therefore caused large quantities of materials, some of it of low intrinsic value, to move over long distances, thus counteracting the normal laws of economic gravity of the pre-industrial world. There is clear evidence of this in the archaeology of the late Roman world. In Britain, the principal obligation of the State was to the military garrisons. The existence of the taxation and expenditure cycle through the medium of precious-metal coinage and bullion is well attested, particularly in hoards (cf. Robertson 2000). There is also an abundance of the base-metal issues struck by the State in order to help it recapture precious metal it had paid out, by giving taxpayers a means of obtaining the gold and silver in which they were required to render certain taxes. Though struck for State purposes, this base-metal coinage went on to serve other purposes (see below). Direct archaeological evidence for the supply of taxes in kind is hard to come by, though the analyses of animal bone from late Roman Lincoln, suggesting organized supply, may hint at how a probable provincial capital was supplied. Other such analyses of grain and animal bone, particularly from forts and other 'official' sites (e.g. London) may in future fill out the picture. For the moment, our best indicator remains pottery. For instance, analysis of the distribution of Oxfordshire wares shows a greater than expected amount down-river at London, Reculver and Richborough, the diocesan capital and two Saxon Shore forts; is this pottery travelling along with supplies of grain or other commodities? In the north, pottery distribution is very closely linked with military sites. (This may in part be an artefact of a disinclination to accept Roman-style material culture on the part of the rural population of the north, as discussed below, the negative thus emphasizing the positive.) This is particularly clear in the case of the Crambeck wares from east Yorkshire, whose distribution is largely confined to military sites. It is perhaps unlikely that the pottery was specifically produced at State behest to supply the army; evidence from elsewhere in the Empire does not show the central authorities micro-managing in this way. But the presence of the military garrisons and the supply networks created for them may have engendered the industry by providing the necessary transport infrastructure to make the pottery production profitable. Some of the vessels, particularly the closed forms, may have been containers for commodities, which might in part be rendered as tax.

The presence of a market economy in later Roman Britain is usually predicated (often implicitly) on the presence of large quantities of low-value coinage, the existence of towns with evidence for manufacture, evidence of artefact distributions which suggest urban marketing. Each of these perhaps merits further dissection. That low-value coins were used in the Roman world for buying and selling cannot be doubted (cf. Reece 2002). In contrast with earlier periods, late third- and fourth-century Britain had an abundance of low-denomination copper-alloy coins, either supplied by the Imperial fiscal authorities or, if such supplies were inadequate, supplemented by local counterfeiting. Nevertheless, there are three arguments which should warn against a simple assumption of market function. First, their presence may in part relate to the process of precious-metal recovery by the State and of taxpayers purchasing gold and silver. Second, the incidence of coins at different types of site has shown that it is the large towns, the administrative and taxation centres, which have a distinct pattern of coin-loss, with the 'small' towns' coin-loss pattern resembling that at rural and religious sites. Third, many coins turn up in contexts where it is far from clear that they are performing a strictly economic function, such as coins from temples or other religious contexts, where coins were perhaps a medium of exchange between the human and divine worlds. As for towns as market centres, while the evidence for manufacture at towns 'large' and 'small' in the fourth century (with the latter becoming more prominent in relation to the former) cannot be gainsaid, it is worth remembering that there is also copious evidence for 'industry' in rural locations. In part this takes the form of the winning of raw materials, but many of the major pottery industries of late Roman Britain had a rural location, and it may well be that important elements of archaeologically less visible industries such as timber and textiles (e.g. wool) took place largely in the countryside. Finally, though town-centred artefact distributions can be identified, so also can ones where towns do not seem to play an articulating role. It may be that there were other networks and systems of distribution, which, because they are less easy for us to understand, have not yielded a neat, comprehensible explanation. These arguments are not intended to deny the existence of a market economy powered by the profit motive, but they are intended to caution against assuming that the market economy was ubiquitous. At certain times and in certain places it doubtless operated, but as one of a suite of options. It now remains to consider some of the other options.

These have to some extent been adumbrated above. Economic anthropologists studying pre-industrial societies have long noted that much exchange is 'socially embedded', that is, it takes place within a network of social obligations and arrangements. On this model, goods and services circulate in patterns which are far less easily analysed and comprehended by our models. The exchange of prestige items can sometimes be isolated through the appearance of a high-status item far from its place of origin. But at the level of agricultural resources, and the circulation of low-value goods such as pottery, this can be far more difficult. As noted above, there is evidence for a non-urban location for some important manufacturing in late Roman Britain. There are also the pottery distributions which do not produce clean-cut, town-centred patterns. For instance, as well as the 'fine wares' which have received the lion's share of attention, the major ceramic industries of fourth-century Britain also produced huge quantities of utilitarian wares, which circulated in a more restricted, local area than the fine wares. Are these distributions necessarily reflective of town-centred market exchange? It has also been postulated that there may have been major rural foci of exchange, for instance, at temples, where regular or seasonal 'markets' may have been held, thus bypassing the urban economy altogether. Or it may be that on the major estates the élite controlled the production and distribution of goods as part of their revenue-generating operations and as a method of control of access to resources.

The operations of the State and of the market economy are generally more easily recognized by us in the archaeological record than are other forms of exploitation. They undoubtedly played an important part in creating the economic formations of late Roman Britain. But we run the risk of over-emphasizing them precisely because they are so visible to us. For the bulk of the population, their experience of economic activity may have been very different, consisting largely in socially mediated access to and disposal of resources, with only the occasional 'trip to market' to connect them to the other economic systems. This, of course, has important implications for the fifth century. The State and the market crumbled, but did this spell the end of all economic activity?

Religion

The study of religion in fourth-century Britain has also been a field where concentration on certain highly visible elements has distracted attention from much else, which might tell a rather different story. The master narrative of religion in fourth-century Britain has been the advance of Christianity and the corresponding retreat of paganism (cf. Watts 1991). All that was to be discussed was the strength and speed of that advance and the stages of the retreat. The place of Christianity as the dominant religion of Britain and Europe over the last millennium and a half always meant that Christian origins in Britain were going to be a major object of inquiry. The documentary evidence of the presence of bishops from Britain at the ecclesiastical councils of Arles in 314 and Arminium in 360 showed that a Church hierarchy had been established in Britain, as elsewhere. The activities of the British heresiarch Pelagius in the early fifth century showed a continuing British Christianity. Excavation of possible churches at Silchester and Richborough, mosaics at Hinton St Mary villa or wall-painting at Lullingstone villa, finds of silver plate and other objects bearing Christian symbols at places such as Water Newton, all attested archaeologically to the spread of the new religion, at least amongst the élite and the town-dwellers. The fact that by the end of the fourth century many pagan temples had been abandoned or were smaller or less well maintained than formerly seemed to betoken the corresponding loss of power and devotees by the traditional religions. Nevertheless, the subject-matter of many fourth-century mosaics showed that the ruling classes could retain a sophisticated knowledge of the old religions, presumably expressions of devotion. But ultimately, even the postulated pagan revival in Britain under the pagan emperor Julian (360–3) (historical fiction if ever there was) had failed to stem the tide of the victorious Nazarene. But while Christianity was undoubtedly present in fourth-century Britain, reducing all religious experience and expression ultimately to a battle between Christian and pagan is to over-simplify far too much. Also, our structure of Romano-British religion is driven by literary and epigraphic evidence, and is thus much concerned with deities. But religion is also to do with cosmology, eschatology, ritual and worship, rites of passage. All of these have been shown to have archaeological correlates, and may be more fruitful ways of analysing the archaeological record. More fruitful too will be a return to looking at major classes of archaeological manifestations of religion: buildings; votive behaviour and use and significance of objects; burial.

Numerically, the first half of the fourth century sees a peak in the number of known temples (principally in the south and east), with a steepening decline through the second half of the century. Since this pattern matches that for towns and villas, this probably says less about the highs and lows of religious enthusiasm or the advance of Christianity than it does about the temporal patterning of architecture on the provincial Roman model. The study of temple buildings themselves has come to something of a dead end, since they seldom reveal anything other than their plan. More profitable is the relating of temples to their immediate and wider contexts. The fourth century sees some of the most elaborate temple complexes, such as Uley and Lydney (both in Gloucestershire), where there is a suite of buildings ancillary to the temple and also a range of objects (e.g. coins, curse tablets) whose study augments the traditional plan-based study. The recovery of as much as possible both of the temenos of a temple and of the material therefrom is beginning to give us new directions to work in. The use of GIS techniques to examine the placing of temples within their landscapes may also be another avenue to understanding their significance and functions.

Much more interest has recently been shown in patterns of votive behaviour, particularly hoard deposition. It used to be assumed that hoarding, be it of coins or of plate or jewellery, was a response to threat. Numismatists have shown that there are other reasons why coin is hoarded (e.g. political instability, monetary reform), including as votive offerings. Similar arguments can be advanced for other value-hoards, particularly in our period the great hoards of silver plate and other objects whose deposition dates seem to cluster around the turn of the fourth and fifth centuries. Following the lead of prehistorians, some workers have begun to posit religious or ritual motives to the deposition of material in places such as pits and wells, and even in features such as boundaries. Some of the material composing these deposits is also regularly found in burial contexts and also overlaps with material from temple complexes

Burial was long the poor relation in Romano-British archaeology. Over the last quarter-century this has changed, with the excavation and publication of major cemetery excavations, largely of the fourth century (cf. Philpott 1991). Such consideration of burials as there was tended to subsume them into the Christian:pagan opposition, with the proposed identification of Christian burial practice and even

Christian cemeteries. In fact, the notion of Christian burial, as we understand it, in the fourth century is almost certainly an anachronism, projecting back a seventh-century attitude. Nor is it at all clear that Christians were exclusive in their burial places in the fourth century. What is more striking is the large number of burials and cemeteries of the fourth century relative to earlier years. As always, archaeologically visible burial remains a feature of the south and east of Britain, of towns more than the countryside and of adult males more than females or juveniles. But the appearance of large, mainly urban, cemeteries must be telling us something about perceptions of the dead, and may again relate to changing perceptions of the (dead) body. It may also be telling us about towns as religious and/or social foci. Even the smaller, rural burial-groups and isolated burials may have something to tell us through their location in the landscape. Most fourth-century burials have no grave goods, but those that do offer possibilities for analysis of various types. One well-known example is the identification of probable ethnic differences from burial rites and use of objects in the fourth-century cemetery at Lankhills, Winchester. This was also related to gender and age differences, more standard issues in funerary analysis.

This brief discussion has been conventional in being structured by division by site-type. But as with élite residences, this fragmentation may be masking wider unities. Temples and sacred sites, votive deposition, burial are all religious and ritual manifestations of one sort or another. It is clear from looking at the sorts of objects found in these contexts that there is a regularity in what is used (animal remains, coins, curses, pottery). Also, such material can be found in probably religious or ritual contexts at towns, villas, forts, temples, rural sites. It thus helps unify many disparate types of settlement. It is thus widespread in and distinctive of the fourth century in Britain. Its survival or disappearance in the fifth century should thus be a powerful indicator of stability or change in religion and ritual, a central preoccupation of all sectors of Roman and post-Roman society.

Decline

Mention of the fifth century brings us to the last things, and the approaching end of the Roman period in Britain. What can a chapter on the fourth century contribute as a preface to the momentous changes of the fifth? The obvious answer is a discussion of the evidence for a 'decline' in the second half of the fourth century, and of the whole notion of 'decline'.

In looking at several of the classes of site and material considered above, it was noted that the second half of the fourth century saw a decline. One must be more precise: what is often meant is a numerical or quantitative decline. This is the case with the number of buildings at the 'large' towns, the numbers of villas, the numbers of temples. Sometimes it is a qualitative decline, for instance, the progressive abandonment of urban public buildings, or the stagnation of pottery forms and decoration, or the care taken over burial, or the building of hearths on villa mosaics ('squatter' occupation). It is, of course, very easy and very seductive to equate quantitative decline with some sort of systemic decline: there are fewer villas, so the villa system is in decline; there are fewer coins and counterfeits, so the economy is in decline. The risk is that one is lumping together a range of evidence types and thus producing a unilinear phenomenon, susceptible of a monocausal explanation. I plead guilty to this: in its time and place it had its uses (Esmonde Cleary 1989). Clearly now we must move on and attempt more multivariate explanations. To do this we must unbundle the various phenomena. For instance, in the discussion of the 'decline' of urban public buildings it was noted that what was happening to administrative buildings might have had different causes from what happened to public baths, which again differed from theatres. Likewise, the 'stagnation' or decline in the pottery industry risks homogenizing a wide range of different trajectories. In discussing pottery above, it was proposed that some observable distribution patterns respond to largely economic force: the requirements and requisitions of the State, or a version of the market economy. Clearly, analyses relating to the collapse of the State and/or the failure of market exchange will be relevant here. But it was equally noted that not all pottery distributions respond to this economic explanation. Some may respond to distribution networks and mechanisms which bypassed the State and the towns and related to estates, or kinship or local community identities. Identifying trajectories for the disappearance of this level of production and consumption will be a very different matter.

Nevertheless, it remains the case that between AD 350 and AD 450 a huge range of highly visible archaeological sites and material cease to exist. Individual sites, site-types or object-types may have had their particular stories, but it can be no coincidence that so many of these go into 'decline' at about the same time in the second half of the fourth century. What is noticeable about them is that they tend to be the aspects of the archaeology which are at the same time the most visible to us and the most expressive of a 'Roman' identity: towns, villas, mosaics, pottery. Traditionally (albeit implicitly) explanations have tended to be about a progressive cessation of production. The State was producing and supplying fewer coins; fewer houses were being built; there were fewer mosaicists to create mosaics; there were decreasing numbers and levels of skills of potters. Perhaps a more useful way round would be to look at it as a progressive cessation of consumption. What progressively seems to be ceasing to be consumed is late Roman provincial culture. This is particularly the culture of the élite, with their urban and rural residences, movables and materials. Why this should be happening is still hard to fathom. Was it purely a rejection of one set of cultural identities through choice? But in that case, what replaced these symbols of power and status? Was there an economic aspect, with decline in the outward trappings reflecting a decline in the ability to extract surplus? But on the other hand, we have no evidence for a decline in the ability of the State to extract surplus and use its coercive powers until the opening decades of the fifth century. But within the fourth century we are dealing only with decline; we must not allow the fifth century and hindsight to cloud our vision too much. What we seem to be seeing in the second half of the fourth century is a crisis of the élite. It is their archaeology which, for a multiplicity of interlocking reasons, is declining both quantitatively and qualitatively. It is they who are unable or unwilling to maintain the traditional means of status display. Add to that the crisis of the State in the early fifth century and the 'end of Roman Britain' supervenes. To contemporaries it was a failure of political authority and military power, to us it is a failure of a very distinctively 'Roman' complex of archaeological evidence: settlements, shrines, burials, objects.

Envoi

At the start of this paper the question was posed whether the aleatory division into centuries bequeathed us by Dionysius Exiguus actually responded to observable unities in the development of Roman Britain. I think that in some measure the answer must be yes. To begin at the ending: the collapse of Roman-style material culture early in the fifth century provides a terminus close in time to AD 400. The fact that so many and so varied types of evidence decease at the same time suggests that in life they were closely bound together. One hundred years or so earlier, the late third- to early fourth-century efflorescence of towns, villas, mosaics, that is, of markers of élite Roman culture, succeeded to the paucity of such markers in the mid-third century. The fourth century comprehended important chronological and regional variations, yet nevertheless it is distinct from what came before and what came after, and taken as a whole, its social, economic, religious and other formations have more in common with each other than with the third or the fifth centuries.

REFERENCES

Arnold, B. 1984. *Roman Britain to Saxon England*. London.
Burnham, B. and Wacher, J. S. 1990. *The 'Small Towns' of Roman Britain*. London.
Casey, J. C. (ed.) 1979. *The End of Roman Britain*. BAR (British Series) 71. Oxford.
Collingwood, R. G. and Myres, J. N. L. 1936. *Roman Britain and the English Settlements*. The Oxford History of England, volume 1. Oxford.
Dark, K. 2000. *Britain and the End of the Roman Empire*. Stroud.
Dobney, K. 2001. A place at the table: the role of vertebrate zooarchaeology within a Roman research agenda for Roman Britain. In S. James and M. Millett (eds), *Britons and Romans: Advancing an Archaeological Agenda*. CBA Research Report 125. York.
Esmonde Cleary, A. S. 1989. *The Ending of Roman Britain*. London.
Faulkner, N. 2000. *The Decline and Fall of Roman Britain*. Stroud.
Frere, S. S. 1987. *Britannia: A History of Roman Britain*, 3rd edn. London. [First published in 1967.]
Haverfield, F. 1905. *The Romanization of Roman Britain*. Oxford.
Hawkes, S. C. and Dunning, G. C. 1965. Soldiers and settlers in Britain, fourth to fifth century. *Medieval Archaeology*, 5, 1–70.
Higham, N. 1992. *Rome, Britain and the Anglo-Saxons*. London.
Hingley, R. 1989. *Rural Settlement in Roman Britain*. London.
Ireland, S. 1986. *Roman Britain: A Sourcebook*. London.
Johnson, S. 1980. *The Later Roman Empire*. London.
Jones, A. H. M. 1964. *The Later Roman Empire, 284–602*. Oxford.
Perring, D. 2002. *The Roman House in Britain*. London.
Philpott, R. 1991. *Burial Practices in Roman Britain: A Survey of Grave Treatment and Furnishing, A.D. 43–410*. BAR (British Series) 219. Oxford.
Reece, R. M. 1980. Town and country: the end of Roman Britain. *World Archaeology*, 12, 77–92.
——2002. *The Coinage of Roman Britain*. Stroud.
Richmond, I. A. 1955. *Roman Britain*. London.
Robertson, A. S. 2000. *An Inventory of Romano-British Coin Hoards*. Royal Numismatic Society Special Publication 20. London.

Smith, J. T. 1997. *Roman Villas: A Study in Social Structure*. London.

Thomas, C. 1986. *Celtic Britain*. London.

Tyers, P. 1996. *Roman Pottery in Britain*. London.

Watts, D. 1991. *Christians and Pagans in Roman Britain*. London.

Wheeler, R. E. M. and Wheeler, T. V. 1936. *Verulamium: A Belgic and Two Roman Cities*. Oxford.

CHAPTER TWENTY-THREE

The Final Phase

IAN WOOD

The end of Roman Britain has long been a subject of intense debate, not least because it is an age of legend as much as one of hard-headed scholarship. Occasionally scholars have tried to bring the two together, approaching the period as an 'Age of Arthur' (Morris 1973). Yet even leaving aside the arguments which have raged over the historical nature of otherwise of Arthur (James 2001: 101–2), interpretations have varied widely, depending on the extent to which archaeological or literary sources are emphasized, and indeed on the differing readings of those sources. Further, although recent years have seen a number of important archaeological excavations relevant to the period, the interpretation of those sites has not been lacking in controversy.

Much of the difficulty can be associated with problems of chronology. Those written sources which ought to provide the basis for a narrative account of the period are largely lacking in dates: even the dates of composition of the major written texts are themselves open to question. Patrick's death, which is the chief determinant of the date at which he wrote his letters, has been placed in the 460s and the 490s: every decade from the 490s to the 540s has been claimed for the composition of the *De Excidio Britanniae* by Gildas. As a result, however much progress has been made on the interpretation of these texts, there remain questions as to which part of the fifth and early sixth centuries they illuminate.

Of late other written texts, the inscriptions to be found on the standing stones of the south-west, of west Wales and of Galloway, have also attracted attention (Dark 1994: Thomas 1994: Handley 2001). Potentially, these inscriptions shed light on Christian developments in western parts of Britain, and on the élites of these areas. In particular they are central to our understanding of Irish settlement, notably in *Demetia*, and the subsequent establishment of kingdoms in south Wales. Unfortunately the majority of these monuments cannot be associated with individuals named in our narrative sources: a possible exception is Vortipor, one of five kings attacked by Gildas, who may be the individual commemorated on a standing stone from Castell Dwyran in Carmarthenshire.

Study of the standing stones has marked an advance in consideration of British material. More work has been done on both Roman and Anglo-Saxon sites. In the case of the former, the last phases of Roman occupation and the question of the subsequent fate of sites have attracted archaeologists less than the earlier phases of building and occupation. There have, however, been some important developments in this respect. A number of sites where particular attention has been paid to the upper archaeological levels have yielded important material relating to the late and sub-Roman periods, notably Wroxeter, Birdoswald and the Minster excavations at York. These sites have opened up the possibility of radical new readings of the fifth century. On the other hand, the fact that the upper levels at previously excavated sites were less carefully dug means that as yet we do not know if these new cases are the exception or the rule. At the same time, the notorious absence of coin-issues dating from later than the first decade of the fifth century has made it impossible to provide firm dates for these later phases even where they have been found.

The archaeology relating to the earliest phases of the Anglo-Saxon migration is also problematical. There is some evidence, literary and archaeological, for Germanic soldiers stationed in Britain in the fourth century (Todd 2001: 85). For the migration period itself the vast majority of the material comes from grave-finds. Certain types of burial (especially cremation burial) are diagnostic of Germanic settlers: so too are certain types of brooch and weapon – although few would now accept a simple correlation of objects and the ethnic identification of the person with whom they were buried. Moreover, once again there is a chronological problem. The dating of most of the artefacts in question is at best approximate, and some of the objects which have been regarded as crucial for the chronology of Germanic settlement have been redated over recent years (Dark 2000: 48–9). Thus what is regarded as the earliest Anglo-Saxon metalwork has been shifted from the first to the second quarter of the fifth century, while inhumation burials with weapons, which are usually thought indicative of Germanic settlers, have been moved from the middle to the third quarter of the fifth century.

Given the problems, any history of fifth-century Britain is bound to be uncertain. Nevertheless, the archaeology does provide a context within which the written material has to be read, and the written material itself both elucidates the general context in which it was set down and also provides *aperçus* into specific episodes and developments, even if it offers no overriding narrative. I will, therefore, offer brief sketches of the archaeological and literary material, before attempting to offer any reconstruction of precise events in the last phase of Roman Britain.

The archaeology of sub-Roman Britain was effectively revolutionized by work carried out at Wroxeter from 1966 to 1994 (White and Barker 1998). Excavation apparently revealed continuing use of parts of the dilapidated baths basilica down to the end of the fifth century. Some timber constructions were set up within the site, and a bread-oven continued in use down to a date sometime in the period 490–550. Thereafter, possibly between 530 and 570, the basilica was largely levelled, and a new group of timber constructions set up. Wroxeter therefore suggested that, at least at one site in the West Midlands, some sort of run-down lifestyle continued through-out the fifth century, and that in the middle of the sixth century a local authority, perhaps a bishop, was able to impose a complete new plan on a segment of the old Roman city.

Discoveries at York provided an equally startling insight into the post-Roman period in the course of excavations undertaken between 1966 and 1973 during the restoration of the Minster. Here the site was identified as being the *principia* of the Roman legionary fortress, and the evidence it yielded has been described as 'crucial, not only for the York Minster story but for post-Roman European archaeology more generally' (Carver in Phillips and Heywood 1995: 188). The most important finds for the history of the sub-Roman period were those found under a layer comprised of the collapsed roof of the basilica of the *principia*, which the excavator argued remained standing until the ninth century. Subsequently a more cautious interpretation has suggested that the collapse took place between the fifth and seventh and eighth centuries, and that before the collapse the building had been used for storing animals. Whether or not the *principia* survived until the ninth century, it is clear that some, perhaps largely agricultural, activity took place at the site during the fifth century: 'a run-down ruralised town' would seem a plausible description of the material (Carver in Phillips and Heywood 1995: 194), and it is one which could reasonably be applied to other sites, such as Canterbury.

A third excavation which cast light on the sub-Roman period, but which has also raised problems of chronology, was that at Birdoswald, on Hadrian's Wall, which took place between 1987 and 1992 (Wilmott 2001). Here, the excavator concluded that timber buildings were set up within the Roman fort after the period 388–95, and that there was continuous occupation of the site until around 520. This would imply that a Roman fort developed directly into the dwelling of some petty chieftain who built his hall on the site of the former granary.

Birdoswald shows one type of élite site, developing within a Roman stronghold. In previous decades archaeologists had drawn attention to the emergence of another type of élite site, the hill-fort, of which a number have been the subject of major excavations from the 1960s. The best-known of these hill-forts, including Cadbury Congresbury and Dinas Powys (Dark 2000: 138), reveal activity from the fifth century. Among the finds, pottery from across the Channel, and indeed from as far afield as the Mediterranean, suggests the presence of an aristocracy with access to a surprising range of goods brought along the Atlantic sea-routes. More famous still is the great promontory of Tintagel, which boasted the largest haul of fragments of Mediterranean pottery, suggesting an élite centre of considerable importance. The evidence for Atlantic trade provided by the pottery, which has become vital for a dating of these sites, has now been set in a long history of contacts between the British Isles, Brittany and Spain (Cunliffe 2001: 439–46, 456–65).

Wroxeter, York and Birdoswald have been only the most eye-catching of those sites which have indicated some sorts of continuity, alongside change, stretching from the fourth into the fifth century if not later – although one should also note the extent to which archaeologists have pointed to a decline in Romano-British towns already in the last years of the fourth century (Esmonde Cleary 1989: 131). Excavations at a number of villas have similarly indicated occupation into the fifth and even sixth centuries, though usually involving considerable change of use. For the most part, occupation seems to have been that of squatters rather than anyone intent on upholding some form of Roman lifestyle (Dark 2000: 113–17). Sometimes villas were used for burial, implying anything but continuity of living. At the same time, there is some indication that villas could survive as ecclesiastical centres, perhaps even as monasteries (Dark 2000: 124), much as they did in a number of places on the Continent, most famously at Martin's monastic centre of Ligugé.

The most important ecclesiastical excavation of recent years has been that carried out beyond Hadrian's Wall at Whithorn (Hill 1997). Although the excavator left open the date of the earliest phases of the site, it is clear that they can be placed in the late Roman period. Subsequently there was a good deal of activity, involving smelting of iron, no doubt related to the building of a church, perhaps that mentioned by Bede in his reference to Ninian's *Candida Casa*. Quite apart from Bede's reference, a number of inscribed stones from the fifth or sixth centuries reveal the presence of ecclesiastics at Whithorn and its immediate surroundings. The inscriptions, as well as the excavation, are a compelling reminder that by the last years of the Roman Empire, Latin Christian culture had moved beyond the boundaries of the Empire itself, and that a centre of Roman religious culture could be established beyond the *limes*.

This is a general point of unquestionable importance when one turns from the archaeology to the evidence of the literary texts, and to their authors, for the earliest of our authors, Patrick, spent almost all his career outside the Roman world, in Ireland. Yet he is a witness of considerable significance when it comes to assessing the culture of the last phase of Roman Britain. First, he reveals something of provincial life. The son of the deacon and decurion, Calpornius, and the grandson of a priest, Potitus, he was brought up in the small, unidentified *vicus* of *Bannavem Taberniae*. The fact of his father's being both a deacon and a decurion has been used to suggest that Patrick must have been born in the last decade of the fourth century or the first decade of the fifth (Hanson 1968: 178–9), but in truth it provides no firm chronology. Rather it simply tells us what was possible during Patrick's childhood, whenever that was. Recent scholarship had tended to place the saint's death in 493, with the result that the world of his childhood, to which he refers, would seem to be that of western Britain in the second quarter of the fifth century (Dumville 1993). By his own account he was not diligent at school, and indeed he regretted this later. Nevertheless, despite this idleness and his subsequent captivity in Ireland, his writings reveal a carefully structured pattern of thought, and while his culture is largely that of the Bible, other influences have been alleged.

Just as important is what Patrick reveals of Britain in his later years. He refers to an ecclesiastical structure, dominated by bishops, which clearly survived the end of secular Roman control in Britain. He also launches an attack on his critics within the Church, describing them with the odd phrase *dominicati rethorici*. Exactly what this means has been the subject of some debate, but it is clear that he associates them with rhetoric in some form or other. In other words, Britain in the fifth century could boast a literary culture.

That this was the case is also apparent from the other major source to have been written in Britain in the fifth and sixth centuries: the *De Excidio Britanniae* of Gildas. Again, Gildas' learning is dominated by the Bible, above all the Old Testament, whose literary structures he seems to have mastered (Howlett 1995: 72–81). Indeed, Gildas' prose is that of a master of rhetoric – something which must presuppose considerable intellectual training. Where he might have obtained this is an open question: even in Gaul secular schools were rare in the late fifth century. Later tradition has it that he was educated at the monastic school of Saint Illtud at Llantwit Major. The tradition may or may not be accurate, but it does raise the possibility of a high level of literary education within a British monastery in the late fifth or early sixth century. Unfortunately, our earliest evidence for Llantwit Major comes from the seventh- or possibly eighth-century *Life of St Samson*, although that text is at least evidence for the high regard in which Illtud and his monastery were held in eastern Brittany at the time of the work's composition.

The other major literary figures of the fourth and fifth centuries who can plausibly be identified as British are Pelagius and Faustus of Riez. There is, of course, nothing to suggest that the ideas of either were derived from their homeland. What is known of the former's career is associated entirely with the city of Rome in the closing decades of the fourth and opening decades of the fifth century. Faustus' ideas can be traced no further than the monastic world of Lérins. Nor have attempts to attribute various Pelagian letters to Britain been successful. Nevertheless Fastidius, who was once presented as the author of those letters, is attested as having been a British bishop, and is known to have been a theologian of some note, writing apparently in the first half of the fifth century (Hanson 1968: 40–1). Equally, although there is nothing to prove that the Pelagian letters were written by Britons, at least one of them was circulating in Britain during the lifetime of Gildas, who indeed described the author as being 'one of us', *quidam nostrum*. What this indicates is that there was considerable intellectual life in Britain in the fifth century – and this is a point of some significance, given that a number of the episodes dating to the fifth century that are well attested in the sources are concerned with the spread of heresy on the island. That there was intellectual life in Britain may also be indicated by the fact that Victricius of Rouen paid a visit to deal with problems within the Church at some point before 396. As a keen supporter of St Martin, he may also have brought with him news of Martinian monasticism. With the archaeological and literary sources sketched out, it is time to turn to what can be made of the chronology of the last phase of Roman Britain.

The beginning of the end of Roman rule in Britain can reasonably be linked to the series of revolts which culminated in the elevation of Constantine III as emperor. According to Orosius, the Roman troops in Britain elevated first Marcus, then Gratian, who appears to have been a civilian, and finally Constantine to the imperial throne. The last, we are told by the Byzantine ecclesiastic Sozomen, was chosen because his name was redolent of that of Constantine I, who had himself been raised to the purple in Britain. The date of the revolt is important in that it appears to have taken place in 406, that is, before the crossing of the Rhine by the Vandals, Sueves and Alans, which, according to one source, occurred on 31 December of the same year. The dating is important in that it indicates that the action of the British army was not prompted by the collapse of the Rhine frontier, but by more general dissatis-faction with the government in Ravenna. Constantine's actions are also important in that they show that whatever the original reason for the rebellion, it was not a desire to opt out of the Roman State. In 406 he crossed the Channel and marched south. The rest of his career was to be spent in Gaul and Italy. For the moment Constantine had some success, and in 409 Honorius recognized his authority, appointing him joint consul. Immediately afterwards, however, he faced a revolt from his right-hand man, Gerontius. He surrendered to Honorius' forces in 411 and was executed.

Meanwhile in Britain, some deeply puzzling events had taken place. According to Zosimus, Constantine's failure to protect the Empire against barbarians, who had been incited to invade by Gerontius, led the Britons and some Celts to throw off Roman rule. Having done so, they drove out the Saxons who had invaded. This prompted the Armoricans and some Gallo-Romans to follow suit, expelling their magistrates and setting themselves up as independent. The revolt and the defensive measures against the Saxons can be supported by a reference to the presence of the barbarians in Britain in the Gallic Chronicle of 452 under the year 411, although the problems of the Chronicle's chronology are such that no significance should be laid on that date. More important is the question of the nature of the British revolt and of that of the continentals who copied it. The Continental revolt has reasonably been linked with the Bacaudic uprisings, which caused problems through into the 430s. Less certainly, these revolts have been seen as peasant uprisings, and the whole has been cast as an episode of class struggle (Faulkner 2000: 174–80). Surviving evidence for the *bacaudae*, however, does not indicate that they were peasants, but rather backwoods opponents of the current regime (Wood 1984: 2–5). Further, the next evidence which appears to relate to Britain – Zosimus' account of Honorius' rescript sent telling the Britons to look to their own defence – implies that the islanders had appealed to the emperor for help. It has been doubted whether Zosimus is correct to identify the Britons as the recipients of the rescript. An account of an appeal and a similar response from the emperor is, however, to be found in Gildas. It looks, therefore, as if the British revolt was directed exclusively against Constantine's supporters. If it were a more general revolt, then a further change had taken place by 429, when some Britons were willing to accept Romans back to the island. Such a change is not impossible: later on in the century the history of Britain would be dominated by faction-fighting. Whether factions were already emerging is, however, unknown. In all this, the success against the Saxons should not be forgotten. At the turn of the first decade of the fifth century Britons were able to counter a Saxon attack.

Whether or not the Britons had revolted against Roman authority in general, they effectively existed without imperial guidance from 410 until 429. In the meantime, some significant theological changes had taken place. Pelagius and his heresy were condemned in 418, and the Empire and, somewhat grudgingly, the papacy turned against the heretics. According to Prosper of Aquitaine's annal for 429, Agricola, the son of a Pelagian bishop Severianus, corrupted the churches of Britain. It may well be that Britain's *de facto* independence from the Empire had made it a safe haven for Pelagians after 418. Whether Pelagius' ideas had reached his countrymen before then, we do not know. The visit of Victricius of Rouen to Britain to deal with some difficulty before 396 cannot have been concerned with Pelagianism, since at that date the ideas were not considered as heretical.

The success of Agricola in spreading heresy prompted the Church to act. According to Prosper the deacon, Palladius persuaded Pope Celestine to send Germanus of Auxerre to deal with the problem. According to the *Life of Germanus* by Constantius, an appeal was made to the bishops of Gaul by a British deputation. It may be possible to conflate the two accounts: Germanus seems to have received approval for his mission from Italy, but there may have been an initial request from Britons hostile to the Pelagians. As retold by Constantius, Germanus' visit is covered with a sheen of allegory. Germanus and Lupus of Troyes arrive in Britain, despite a demonic attempt to sink their ship: they defeat the Pelagians in debate: Germanus heals the daughter of a local tribune: he then makes a visit to the shrine of Alban, miraculously surviving a fire: finally, he goes to help the Britons counter a joint invasion of Picts and Saxons, first baptizing the army, and then instructing the troops to shout Alleluia at the enemy, who flee, many of them drowning in the process (Wood 1984).

The description of the defeat of the Picts and Saxons suggests an interesting revival of the sort of co-ordination of barbarian groups known from the *coniuratio barbarica* of 367. Whether we should make anything of Germanus' involvement in the repulse of such an invasion is questionable. Historians have ascribed to the saint a military career before his elevation to the episcopate on the grounds of one vague phrase, *ducatus culmen*, employed by Constantius. Since there is no other evidence that Germanus was a general before he became bishop, it may be better to see in the phrase an ambiguous reference to the administrative offices he is known to have held. More significant is Germanus' visit to the shrine of Alban. This is also attested in the earliest *Passio* of Alban, which probably dates from the sixth century, although it seems to have been based on an earlier version, which may well have been commissioned by Germanus himself. The *Passio* refers to the bishop's visit to the shrine, revealing that he had the tomb opened, took out some relics, and in their place left relics of saints which he had with him. We should probably see in the visit a deliberate policy of imposing the traditions of the continental Church onto the cult of the insular saint. Germanus may simultaneously have played a major role in the spread of the cult of Alban on the Continent.

This evidence for the cult of Alban can be set alongside other fragments of information on the development of the cult of saints within the British Isles. Gildas talks of the shrine of Alban and also of that of Julius and Aaron at Caerwent. Augustine of Canterbury later came across a cult of a martyr called Sixtus, which worried him because he knew nothing of the saint. The archaeological evidence from Whithorn may reflect the development of a shrine associated with relics of Martin, and subsequently with a cult of the community's founder, Ninian. Britain would not seem to be lagging far behind Gaul in the cult of the saints.

To the evidence for the first visit of Germanus to Britain, Prosper, writing in the *Contra Collatorem*, adds the interesting detail that it involved the exile of Pelagian heretics. This is a point which Constantius associates only with the saint's second visit to the island. That it was possible to exile heretics is a mark of how much Britain had come back into the Imperial fold. Here one should remember the extent of changes on the Continent since the crisis of 406–10. Constantius had re-established Ravenna's control over much of Gaul, prompting some even to talk of a political renaissance, an *ordo renascendi*. Although the deaths of Constantius and Honorius caused another crisis for the Theodosian dynasty, the sense of Imperial renewal continued under the usurping emperor John (423–5), who may well have drawn up the *Notitia Dignitatum* in its final form, with its optimistic entries on the military provision of Britain. John's failure provoked another crisis in Italy, and left a number of rivals fighting for control of the young emperor Valentinian. The eventual winner was Aetius, whose successes in the Rhineland against the Franks in about 428 may have had repercussions in Britain (Wood 1987: 252). The appeal of the British to the Gallic Church and the sending of Germanus to deal with the Pelagian crisis could have been influenced by Aetius' prior activities in provinces not far south of the Channel. The mission of Germanus may in turn have drawn the significance of a community of Christians in Ireland to the attention of Pope Celestine, while the success of the mission may have prompted the pope to send Palladius to those believers in 432. Certainly, these issues seem to have been associated in the mind of Prosper.

The first visit of Germanus to Britain is attested by both Constantius and Prosper. The second visit is not attested in any chronicle or work of theology, and that it ever took place has been doubted. The evidence of the *Vita Germani* is, however, supported in the *Life of Genovefa*, and there seems no reason to reject it (Wood 1984: 14). Exactly when Germanus returned, however, is a different matter. Constantius' narrative puts the second visit immediately before an appeal from the Armoricans to protect them against the Alan king Goar, who had been set on them by Aetius. The appeal in turn prompts Germanus to travel to Italy, where he dies: the punishment of the Armoricans went ahead because of the perfidy of their leader Tibatto. Assuming that Constantius' narrative is correct, the visit to Britain should have taken place shortly before the saint's death, which itself should be close in time to that of Tibatto. When the bishop died is unfortunately open to debate, but he did so thirty years after his predecessor, Amator. The latter's death-day is recorded as Wednesday, 1 May: in all probability this derives from a liturgical calendar, and is thus likely to be accurate. Possible years in which 1 May fell on a Wednesday are 407, 412, 418: this leaves 437, 442 and 448 as possible death-dates for Germanus (Wood 1984: 14–15). Each of these dates is unfortunately at odds with at least one piece of supplementary evidence, and one can do no more than look to a line of best fit. This appears to be provided by the account of the suppression of the Armorican rebels under Tibatto, which the Chronicle of 452 places in 437. The Chronicle's chronology, however, as already stated, is not above question. For the reign of Valentinian III its chronological systems are out of line, in part because of the insertion of an extra olympiad, with the result that the regnal dates are all four years earlier than the olympiad dates. Moreover, this is not the only problem with the Chronicle's chronology: where its dates can be compared with those of other chronicles they are often demonstrably wrong, and the chronicler seems to have had a tendency to arrange events into clusters, with the most important being placed as the culmination of the sequence (Wood 1987: 254–5). Nevertheless, the regnal dates do tend to be more accurate than the olympiads. The best that one can say is that Germanus' second visit to Britain should be placed alongside the revolt of Tibatto. This may be more than a chronological coincidence. The revolt and its suppression had much to do with Aetius' use of the Alans in northern Gaul. Just as Germanus' first visit can be set against Imperial activity in the Rhineland, so the second visit can be placed alongside activity to the north of the Loire. Germanus' visits to Britain point not just to ecclesiastical concerns, but also to the revival of Ravenna's authority in northern Gaul and beyond.

The Chronicle of 452 remains of importance in assessing the importance of the next set of events to plague Britain. Famously, the chronicler states that Britain, which had been the subject of various disasters, was handed over to Saxon jurisdiction. In the earliest manuscript, and at least two later ones, the entry runs over two years: 441–2 if one follows the regnal dating system of the chronicler, and 445–6 if one follows the olympiads. The event is placed four years after the suppression of Tibatto's revolt, which at least suggests a relative time-scale. It is also worth noting that another Chronicle, known as the Chronicle of 511, records the same catastrophe in

Britain, placing it in 440. In all probability the Saxons achieved a notable success in Britain about 440, three or four years after Germanus' last visit to Britain. What the nature of that success was is a problem, and it is one which needs to be considered in the light of Gildas' account of the same period.

According to Gildas, the Britons appealed to Aetius, consul for the third time, for help against the ravages of the Picts and Scots. The request fell on deaf ears. Driven to extremities, some Britons started to fight back and inflicted a defeat on the invaders. The council, however, decided to call in the help of Saxons. Following the invitation of the *superbus tyrannus*, the Saxons arrived in three boats. They established themselves in eastern Britain, but soon used the excuse that they were being given inadequate supplies and rebelled, causing devastation until the emergence of Ambrosius Aurelianus.

The difficulty here is a simple one to state, but an impossible one to solve without denying the accuracy of one or other of our sources. The Chronicle of 452, supported by that of 511, suggests that the Saxon successes should be dated to about 440: Gildas places the Saxon arrival and revolt after an appeal to Aetius during (or perhaps after) his third consulship, which he held in 446. In adjudicating between the two sources, it has to be said instantly that while the Chronicle's dates are suspect, Gildas' tirade is very carefully constructed on a model of recurrent cycles of sin, disaster, repentance and recovery, and it is perfectly possible that this pattern has interfered with the accurate narration of events.

Any solution involves the historian opting for an interpretation which seems to be compatible with what else is known of the period. Assuming that events on the Continent were still influential in this period, the following observations may be made. The period around the year 440 was marked by a startling number of concessions by the Empire. The Chronicle of 452 groups these concessions into a cluster: *agri deserti* around Valence were handed over to the Alans: Britain was given to the Saxons: *Gallia Ulterior*, which saw a further uprising subsequent to that of Tibatto, was subdued by the Alans: *Sapaudia* was given to the Burgundians and Carthage to the Vandals. The establishment of the Saxons in Britain should probably be interpreted alongside the other concessions listed in this group of Chronicle entries. This cluster of concessions is dated by the chronicler, following his regnal dating system, to the period from 440 to 444, with the cession of Carthage in the latter year. In fact, we know that Carthage was captured by the Vandals in 439 and officially ceded in 442 – and this is unfortunately the only event in this cluster that can be dated by reference to other sources. The chronology, therefore, is not beyond question. What is striking, though, is the grouping of these events, which seems to suggest the implementation of a particular policy: the use or acceptance of barbarians as federates. Such a policy may already have been employed in Britain some decades earlier (Todd 2001: 85–6). The council mentioned by Gildas can be seen as a remnant of Imperial government. In inviting the Saxons it was following a high-profile policy, and one which was being pursued by Aetius at exactly the same time. It even granted supplies (*epimenia*) to the federates. That the policy in Britain did not involve large numbers is suggested both by the small quantity of Anglo-Saxon finds from Britain dated to before 450, and by Gildas' overall narrative, which does not imply a large-scale migration: he talks of an initial three boats, perhaps a traditional figure, followed by a more substantial number of reinforcements.

It is possible that the invitation to the Saxons followed the appeal to Aetius, as stated by Gildas: it is equally possible that it took place closer to 440, and that the appeal was made in the aftermath of the Saxon uprising. Following this second reading, Gildas has misplaced the appeal and misidentified the enemy. Although Gildas is sometimes thought to be quoting the text of the appeal, it is notable that there is no indication of the identity of the enemy in the supposed quotation: they are merely barbarians. If it is Gildas' narrative, rather than the chronology of the chronicles, which is mistaken, the appeal may have been for help against the rebellious federates. Perhaps significantly, Aetius seems once again to have been active in the Rhineland in the mid-440s (Wood 1987: 256). Over these issues certainty is impossible, but it seems likely that we should set both the appeal and the use of Saxons within the framework of Aetius' policies.

The Chronicle entries on the presence of Saxons in Britain in the 440s are notoriously the last such entries relating to the island. Thereafter we are dependent on Gildas' narrative for the rest of the fifth century and beyond, although it is still possible to correlate events in Britain with those on the Continent. The Saxon revolt caused widespread destruction, and some fled abroad, but a resistance leader emerged in the person of Ambrosius Aurelianus. The flight of Britons abroad has sometimes been linked to the appearance of a number of British clerics on the Continent at this time. Mansuetus, described as bishop of the Britons, attended the Council of Tours in 461, while a priest and monk Riochatus is described as twice exiled in a letter of Sidonius Apollinaris of 471. Yet it is as well to remember that there were long-standing links between the Churches of Britain and Gaul, quite apart from those implied by the visits of Victricius and Germanus. Patrick, who may or may not have been to Gaul, comments on the Gallic habit of ransoming captives from the Franks, while Gildas tells of men in his own day crossing the sea for ordination. This would suggest that the would-be ordinands used the western seaways, whose importance can be traced in the archaeological record of items traded. There is no good reason to attribute the presence of Britons in Gaul solely to the temporary success of the Saxons. Similarly, the widespread destruction which Gildas claims was wrought on the cities of Britain has as yet found no obvious support in the archaeological record.

More interesting is what Gildas says of Ambrosius' parents, or perhaps relatives (*parentibus*), who were killed in the course of the Saxon wars. According to Gildas they had worn the purple, that is, they had held Imperial office. Since there is no evidence to suggest that Valentinian III or any of his successors had British links, this must indicate that Ambrosius' family had claimed the Imperial title within Britain. Further, unlike Constantine III, who instantly moved to the Continent, there is nothing to suggest that they had any interest in keeping Britain within the Roman Empire. If we take seriously Gildas' comments on the status of the parents of Ambrosius, it would seem that, while the council was trying to work together with Aetius, at least one faction within Britain was attempting to set up a British Empire beyond the authority of Rome.

Division within Britain is apparent in the evidence for the Pelagian crises of the 420s and 430s, when some appear to have appealed to outside help to get rid of the heretics. That not everyone agreed with Ambrosius is indicated by a much later source, the *Historia Brittonum* of 829, which talks of conflict between him and Vortigern, the *superbus tyrannus* of Gildas' narrative. Whether or not this reflects a genuine historical tradition, it is perfectly compatible with the earlier account. More-over, at least one Briton appears to have been so committed to the Roman Empire that, rather than remain in Britain at this time, he abandoned the island and took with him a sizeable military following. The story of Riothamus is told by the sixth-century historian Jordanes in his *Getica*. There the emperor Anthemius asked Riothamus, the king of the Britons, for help against the Goths. He crossed the ocean with 2000 men, sailed up the Loire and disembarked at Bourges. Before he could join up with the Romans, however, he was defeated and fled with his men to the Burgundians. Fortunately, this story can be amplified by the evidence of Sidonius Apollinaris, who had to deal with some of the fall-out of the settlement of Riothamus' men in the Lyons area, for they started to abduct the slaves of the established landowners. We need not accept the royal title conferred on Riothamus by Jordanes, nor need we believe that he had as many as 2000 men, but we can accept that a warlord left Britain about 470 to fight for the emperor Anthemius, with a following large enough to cause substantial problems in the neighbourhood of Lyons when it arrived there. The period is not one of known Saxon expansion, so there is no need to see Riothamus and his men as being driven from their homeland. It is worth remembering that at the very time that Sidonius was dealing with Riothamus, Constantius was writing his account of Germanus' visits to Britain, and claiming that Britain was still peaceful. Constantius, moreover, was a correspondent of Sidonius. It would seem, therefore, that the presence of Riothamus and his men was not occasioned by any Saxon expansion, but rather that it was the response of a group which did not want to abandon its allegiance to the emperor at the time of Ambrosius' successes.

How successful Ambrosius was is an unanswerable question. Gildas states that the defeated Saxons went home, but does so before describing the British revival. The home to which they returned was probably the territory in which they had been settled in eastern Britain. There is no gap in the archaeological evidence for Saxon settlement to suggest that they abandoned Britain altogether. It may well be that some territory which was officially ceded to Saxons as federates was held by them without interruption from the 440s. If this were the case, the earliest of the Saxon kingdoms would be comparable to those which emerged out of Aetius' grants on the Continent, and the structure of such a kingdom might well have been rather different from that of other kingdoms established subsequently as a result of conquest or even intermarriage.

The culmination of the revival begun by Ambrosius comes with the battle of Mount Badon. The passage in which Gildas tells of this is rather less easy to translate than most secondary accounts acknowledge. Bede states that the victory occurred forty-four years after the coming of the Saxons, while modern interpreters tend to place the forty-four years between Badon and Gildas' time of writing. Since Bede unquestionably saw a manuscript of Gildas older than any that survives, we would be wise to give careful consideration to his reading (Wood 1984: 23; James 2001: 95). If his reading is right, this must have implications for the date at which Gildas was writing. On the other hand, since Gildas held on to the initial draft of his text for ten years before completing it, the date of composition itself stretched over a good decade. Regardless of exact dates, Gildas claimed that the grandchildren of Ambrosius were active in his day. It may even be that one grandchild is the Aurelius Caninus who features among the five kings lampooned in the *De Excidio Britanniae*.

Gildas' five kings provide an interesting snapshot of power in his own day. At first sight they do not look Roman, yet there are interesting hints of some continuity with the past. Aurelius Caninus may have been a descendant of Ambrosius Aurelianus, and his name is Latin. What Gildas frowned on was his marital behaviour, which may have been little worse than that of a number of Christian Roman emperors, although there is a case for thinking that it reflected Celtic marriage practice. Constantine of *Dumnonia*, who also bore a good Imperial name, had been an abbot at the time he murdered his rivals to secure the throne. Roman emperors had ended up as church-men, but none had made the return journey from religious to secular power. Vorti-por, if he is to be associated with the memorial of Vorteporix *protector* from Castell Dwyran, had a title which might reflect some Roman military arrangement, but he himself seems to have been of Irish stock. The last two of Gildas' kings, Maglocunus and Cuneglasus, have been associated with the hill-forts of Deganwy and Dinarth in north Wales. Before condemning hill-forts as a reversion to a pre-Roman lifestyle, it is as well to remember that Vegetius urged their use, as did bishop Lupus of Troyes, Germanus' companion on his first visit to Britain. Moreover, the units over which these kings ruled may have had some basis in the tribal organization of Wales in the Roman period. There is a good case for seeing Vortipor's kingdom as being based on the Romano-British *Demetae* and Maglocunus' Gwynedd as deriving from the terri-tory of the *Ordovices* (Dark 1994: 112). That there was still some sense of citizenship in Gwynedd is attested by the remarkable sixth-century inscription to a *Venedos civis* from Penmachno, in the mountains of Snowdonia.

That the origins of such kingship lay firmly in the fifth century is also indicated by Patrick's comments on Coroticus. Although Patrick does not call him king, he de-scribes him ruling by tyranny (*per tyrannidem*), and he clearly has a war-band, his *milites*. Later sources call him king and even name his kingdom, though there is no telling whether the identification is based on fact. He might have been based in Wales, on the Clyde or even in Ireland itself. What is important is that he shows us the existence of a type of power which would evolve into kingship in the west at the time of the growing settlement of Anglo-Saxons in the east. Whoever controlled Birdoswald at the time of the revamping of the inside of the fort was probably a ruler of similar type.

It is scarcely possible to give a narrative for the last phase of Roman Britain. It is possible, however, to offer a number of general observations, especially if one keeps in mind the evidence for contemporary changes on the Continent (Wood 1987, 2000). Moreover, it is also possible to note a number of points of activity which suggest that there was anything but a simple collapse of Roman power occasioned by Con-tantine III's withdrawal of what is thought to have been a sizeable proportion of the troops of Britain. Despite the uprising which followed that withdrawal, as well as the failure of Honorius to provide help for Britain around the year 410, there is little to suggest that anyone saw this as marking a break in the island's association with the Roman Empire, at least not at the time. In the sixth century Procopius dated the end of Roman Britain to the revolt of Constantine, but he is the first known to have done so. If the uprising was in any sense a peasant revolt, which seems unlikely, the peasants were no longer in control a generation later. One group, however, does seem to have tried to exploit the absence of Roman officials: that, at least, would seem to be the implication of the spread of Pelagianism in the island. Other factions would emerge in the course of the next generation. That the Imperial court did not see Britain as drifting out of its orbit is suggested by the British entries in the *Notitia Dignitatum*. At the same time Constantius' statement that it was an appeal by the British which led to Germanus' mission in 429, and the comments, supported by Prosper, that the bishop was able to enforce a sentence of exile on the heretics, suggests that there were Britons who were equally keen to remain attached to Imperial power. Such Britons would seem to have been members of the council which appealed to Aetius for help in 446 or thereabouts. The appeal may have been prompted by the failure in Britain of the Imperial policy of using Germanic federates, or it may have led to the use of that policy. This loyalty to the Empire is all the more striking in that Imperial control of northern Gaul was by no means constant throughout this period. Indeed, there seems to be a correlation between British contact with the Imperial government and the activity of Aetius in the Rhineland or north of the Loire.

This association with the Empire is as apparent in the ecclesiastical as in the secular sphere. Certainly there were problems with heretics. As already mentioned, Pelagians appear to have exploited the weakness of Imperial control in Britain in the period after 418. Yet the journeys of Germanus suggest a willingness by a significant proportion of the British Church to work together with their Continental counter-parts, and even to accept the dictates of the pope in 429 and again in the 430s. Equally important, the debates over heresy are one indication that there was a thriving intellectual tradition within the British Church. The point is supported by Gennadius' reference to the works of Fastidius. British clergy, among them Mansue-tus and Riochatus, continued to have links with the Continent in the second half of the century. Similarly, Britons seem to have travelled to the Continent and returned in Gildas' day. By this time, however, there is firm evidence of clerics leaving Britain for good, among them Gildas himself. In the early years of the sixth century there is also Samson of Dol, although there is nothing in his *Vita* to suggest that the changing political situation in Britain had anything to do with his departure.

Contacts between Britain and the Continent may, however, have declined. In the middle of the fifth century one change in ecclesiastical practice failed to reach Britain. The tenth-century *Annales Cambriae* record the acceptance by Pope Leo of a new calculation for the date of Easter under the year 453, but there is no evidence to suggest that this change was noted in fifth-century Britain. By the time that August-ine reached Canterbury in 597 the British Church was definitely out of kilter with the Roman. Secular connections with the Empire seem to have failed at the same time, though here the cause was as much the failure of the Empire itself as any collapse within Britain. If, as suggested, Ambrosius was an isolationist figure, a section of the élite in Britain did opt out of contact with the Empire, though it did so not because it was overwhelmed by barbarians, but because the Empire had done little for its province for half a century. Britain in the 460s was coping better than many provinces with the barbarian threat. The success of the Anglo-Saxons was not to come until the sixth century.

FURTHER READING

The last phase of Roman Britain has become a growth area for research in recent years, and much of the latest work has been cited in the chapter dedicated to the subject. For the crucial excavations one should turn to the works listed in the bibliography by P. Hill, D. Phillips, R. White and P. Barker, and T. Wilmott. Among the more significant works of interpretation are the books by A. S. Esmonde Cleary and K. Dark. The articles by I. N. Wood have been concerned to set the literary sources for fifth-century Britain in a broad context stretching across the Channel. Some other texts deserve mention. The closing chapters of Peter Salway's *Roman Britain* (1981) offer a Romanist's view of the fifth century. E. A. Thompson's important articles on fifth-century Britain are unfortunately scattered through the pages of several journals, but the precision of his reading of texts can also be found in his *St Germanus of Auxerre and the End of Roman Britain* (1984), and *Who was St. Patrick?* (1985). Leslie Alcock's *Arthur's Britain: History and Archaeology AD 367–634* (1971) was seminal in drawing attention to the archaeology of the sub-Roman period, while Charles Thomas' *Christianity in Roman Britain to AD 500* (1981) was of equal importance in opening up the archaeology of early Christianity in Britain. Similarly classic is the volume edited by James Campbell, entitled simply *The Anglo Saxons* (1982). The first two chapters constitute a very clear reading of the late Roman period. Controversial, but important as a contribution to debate, has been the work of Nicholas Higham, in particular *Rome, Britain and the Anglo-Saxons* (1992). For Gildas, the volume edited by M. Lapidge and D. N. Dumville, *Gildas: New Approaches* (1984), is the obvious starting-point.

REFERENCES

Alcock, L. 1971. *Arthur's Britain: History and Archaeology AD 367–634.* Harmondsworth.

Campbell, J. 1982. *The Anglo-Saxons.* London.

Cunliffe, B. 2001. *Facing the Ocean: The Atlantic and its Peoples 8000 BC–AD 1500.* Oxford.

Dark, K. 1994. *Civitas to Kingdom: British Political Continuity 300–800.* Leicester.

——2000. *Britain and the End of the Roman Empire.* Stroud.

Dumville, D. N. 1993. *Saint Patrick A.D. 493–1993.* Woodbridge.

Esmonde Cleary, A. S. 1989. *The Ending of Roman Britain.* London.

Faulkner, N. 2000. *The Decline and Fall of Roman Britain.* Stroud.

Handley, M. A. 2001. The origins of Christian commemoration in Late Antique Britain. *Early Medieval Europe,* 10, 177–99.

Hanson, R. P. C. 1968. *Saint Patrick: His Origins and Career.* Oxford.

Higham, N. 1992. *Rome, Britain and the Anglo-Saxons.* London.

Hill, P. 1997. *Whithorn and St Ninian: The Excavation of a Monastic Town 1984–91.* Stroud.

Howlett, D. 1995. *The Celtic Latin Tradition of Biblical Style.* Dublin.

James, E. 2001. *Britain in the First Millennium.* London.

Lapidge, M. and Dumville, D. N. (eds) 1984. *Gildas: New Approaches.* Woodbridge.

Morris, J. 1973. *The Age of Arthur: A History of the British Isles from 350–650.* London.

Phillips, D. and Heywood, B. 1995. *Excavations at York Minster.* Volume 1. *From Roman Fortress to Norman Cathedral. Part 1. The Site.* London.

Salway, P. 1981. *Roman Britain.* Oxford.

Thomas, C. 1985. *Christianity in Roman Britain to AD 500.* London.

——1994. *And Shall These Mute Stones Speak?* Cardiff.

Thompson, E. A. 1984. *St Germanus of Auxerre and the End of Roman Britain.* Woodbridge.

——1985. *Who Was St Patrick?* Woodbridge.

Todd, M. 2001. *Migrants and Invaders: The Movement of Peoples in the Ancient World.* Stroud.

White, R. and Barker, P. 1998. *Wroxeter, Life and Death of a Roman City.* Stroud.

Wilmott, T. 2001. *Birdoswald Roman Fort. 1800 Years on Hadrian's Wall.* Stroud.

Wood, I. N. 1984. The end of Roman Britain: continental evidence and parallels. In M. Lapidge and D. N. Dumville (eds), *Gildas: New Approaches*. Woodbridge, 1–25.

—— 1987. The fall of the Western Empire and the end of Roman Britain. *Britannia*, 18, 251–62.

—— 2000. The north-western provinces. In A. Cameron, B. Ward-Perkins and M. Whitby (eds), *The Cambridge Ancient History*. Volume 14. *Late Antiquity: Empire and Successors A.D. 425–600*. Cambridge, 497–524.

CHAPTER TWENTY-FOUR

The Rediscovery of Roman Britain

MALCOLM TODD

The remote origins of interest in Roman Britain can be glimpsed in the work of the main chroniclers of the twelfth century: William of Malmesbury, Florence of Worcester and Henry of Huntingdon early on, Roger Hovenden and Gerald of Wales later. Geoffrey of Monmouth was a contemporary of the first three and a more successful populist, but a less substantial figure in scholarly history. William of Malmesbury was the first to record a Roman inscription in Britain, reading a text at Carlisle as MARII VICTORIAE (correctly MARTI ET VICTORIAE), set within a 'triclinium'. Unfortunately, William went on to see this as a monument recording a victory of Marius over the Cimbri, who then fled to Cumbria. Geoffrey of Monmouth was no more reliable a guide. As Francis Haverfield wrote: 'the pages of Geoffrey contain no new "fact" about Roman Britain which is also true.' His claim that he had access to 'a very ancient book in the British tongue' inspires not an atom of confidence. Nor do his comments on the significance of places like Silchester (a place where British princes were crowned) and Caerleon (the seat of a Roman archbishopric). Henry of Huntingdon contributed other errors and figments. He attempted to identify the twenty-eight cities of Britain listed by Gildas, with complete lack of success. He was equally inventive on the main Roman roads of Britannia, Ermine Street, Icknield Street, Watling Street and the Fosse Way, and their legacy to Saxon England.

Study of the Roman past of Britain was slow to emerge from the medieval traditions of British history. The cult of Arthur, supported at times by royal interest, impeded a purge of the credulity and sheer guesswork of writers down to the early sixteenth century. Renaissance writing elsewhere had virtually no impact on this field of enquiry in Britain. Even when Hector Boece wrote on the antiquities of Scotland in his *Scotorum Historia* of 1527, his account rested on embellishment of a range of arrant forgeries, possibly augmented by inventions of his own. The most generous judgment on Boece is that he did his best to make sense of the limited and inadequate material available to him. But this first Principal of Aberdeen University was on very shaky ground when he argued that Julius Caesar had advanced into Stirlingshire, building there the monument known as Arthur's O'on (see p. 446), that Caratacus was a king of the Scots and Boudicca was his grand-daughter, that the Silures lay in Ayrshire and that the Brigantes were based in Galloway. There is no hint in Boece's work of any recognition that the Roman occupation of Scotland had left any visible mark on the land, and no sites or antiquities seem to have come to his attention, with the exception of Arthur's O'on. It is no surprise that much of the basis of Boece's work was roundly rejected by the Englishman John Leland and the Welshman Humphrey Lluyd. Throughout much of the sixteenth century a fierce and often acrimonious struggle continued between the beleaguered defenders of the medieval tradition and the lively proponents of Renaissance learning. There was still little comment on sites, but artefacts began to figure more prominently.

Travel became easier and scholars were beginning to record their travels, as John Leland had done early in the century and William Lambarde had attempted in his *Perambulation of Kent* of 1576. But the age of observation in the field was only just beginning to dawn. Matters were not significantly advanced by the writings of George Buchanan in the *Rerum Scoticarum Historia* of 1582. Buchanan served as tutor to Mary Stuart and the young James VI. His knowledge of the Classical texts was impressive and he was aware of the value of evidence derived from inscriptions. He knew of the two great mural frontiers in northern Britain. That in England he assigned to Hadrian, that in Scotland to Septimius Severus. His subsequent conclusions are of no worth, though he had virtually nothing to go on. His contemporary Timothy Pont, an accomplished cartographer and mathematician, made much greater progress in mapping Roman sites in Scotland, notably on the Antonine Wall. Unfortunately, Pont's field-drawings have not survived, though several of the sites noted by him have been rediscovered in the past century. Pont may have been a worthy predecessor of the major field-workers of the eighteenth century, but few took up the burden in Scotland. Curiously, one of the early prospections for the collection of information was made by two or more German scholars about 1600. They recorded three inscriptions from the Antonine Wall, later published by Scaliger in the *Thesaurus Temporum Eusebii* of 1606.

From Camden to Horsley

The concept of Britannia, Britain as part of the Roman world, can be attributed to the publication of a single small book. This was the *Britannia* of William Camden, first published in Latin in 1586. Camden was born in London in 1551, the son of a painter, and educated at St Paul's School and Oxford. He did not take a degree as a result of his involvement in religious disputes, and he left Oxford in 1571, spending the next three years in travels around England. In 1575 he was appointed Second Master at Westminster School. His interest in antiquities, generously interpreted, brought him to the attention of several influential figures, including the leading European topographer and geographer Abraham Ortelius, who persuaded Camden to bring his collected material into the form of a book. The result was the *Britannia*. The roots of this epoch-making book lay not in medieval British scholarship but in Renaissance studies centred on Italy but pursued by scholars from several countries. For the first time, Camden tried to reconstruct the province of Britannia within a Roman context. His preface to the English edition of 1610 is eloquent.

Truly it was my project and purpose to seeke, rake out, and free from darknesse such places as Caesar, Tacitus, Ptolemee, Antonine the Emperor, Notitia Provinciarum and other antique writers have specified and time hath overcast with mist and darknesse by extinguishing, altering and corrupting their old true names.

The emphasis upon the ancient sources and the named places of Britain informed successive editions of the *Britannia*, but Camden introduced much else. He recorded a substantial number of Roman inscriptions, eighty by the 1607 edition. He included an eye-witness account of Hadrian's Wall and, in the 1600 edition, a pioneering study of Iron Age coinage. These laid foundations for later studies. Still more far-reaching was the reconstruction of the underlying tribal structure as revealed by Graeco-Roman geographers. The early editions of the *Britannia* thus provided a secure framework for further study and pointed out paths for the future. The influence of the work continued over two centuries. The editions of the seventeenth century were increasingly subject to the growth of practical fieldwork; in other words, they moved from the late Renaissance world to one in which antiquarian pursuits were rooted in more local soil. Towards the end of the century a greatly enlarged and revised edition was drawn up and issued in 1695. It was, astonishingly, the work of a 26-year-old man, Edmund Gibson, later in life successively Bishop of Lincoln and London, though an impressive team of about thirty contributors was also assembled, including Samuel Pepys, John Aubrey, John Evelyn, Ralph Thoresby and Robert Plot.

Collection of Romano-British antiquities began in earnest in the sixteenth century, mainly by men of substance and aristocratic figures. Lord Burghley assembled a fine library and a collection of Roman coins in the later sixteenth century, and was himself mentioned with respect by Camden. The Earl of Pembroke also collected over a wide range. These figures made less impact than Sir Robert Cotton, who had met Camden as a schoolboy at Westminster School and began collecting books and antiquities in his twenties. Cotton was more than a rich and discriminating collector. He was fully conversant with the sources for ancient Britain and saw how further studies might proceed. His magnificent library was later to form one of the founding collections of the British Museum (later the British Library). In 1599, Cotton toured northern England with his old schoolmaster Camden, with benefit to later editions of the *Britannia*.

Not all the collectors were men of means. Rene Wolfe gathered objects found in London. John Twyne collected Roman finds in Canterbury, and Thomas Wells brought together material in Somerset and Dorset. The collectors of the seventeenth century were obviously influenced by the activities of aristocratic figures in the Mediterranean world, especially the Earl of Arundel, the Duke of Buckingham and Sir Kenelm Digby. The sculpture collection known as the Arundel marbles, now in the Ashmolean Museum, stimulated interest in Classical art and indirectly in Roman remains in Britain.

Advances in knowledge were modest in most of the seventeenth century. Camden's *Britannia* continued to dominate the subject, and the county histories which appeared after the Civil War gave little impetus to local studies of the remote past. The pace of discovery and reporting quickened markedly after 1700. Improved communications were one factor but equally important was the foundation of the Society of Antiquaries of London in 1707 and its revival in 1717; for the first time, a major forum for the reporting of discoveries and informed discussion was in being. But the path forward was not to be smooth. London was by no means the only major focus. Some of the most important work of the earlier eighteenth century was carried out in Scotland and northern England.

The early decades of the eighteenth century saw the most significant advances in knowledge of Roman Britain, which were to place the study of the province upon a new and more secure footing. Several of the instigators of the work were active in Scotland and northern England. The leading figures were Sir Robert Sibbald, Sir John Clerk and Alexander Gordon, all Scots, and the Northumbrian John Horsley. Observation and publication also began to make great strides in the south, but the major publications issued from the northerners. Sibbald produced a slight but important volume, *Historical Inquiries*, in 1707, which established archaeological method as the only way in which knowledge could be advanced. Alexander Gordon came to study of Roman Britain via Classical studies at Aberdeen and a Grand Tour. In 1726 he published his important *Itinerarium Septentrionale*, which presented many sites and artefacts in the north, many of them illustrated by his own drawings. Gordon's methods and procedures were not above reproach, but his overall account of Roman Scotland, and especially of the Antonine Wall, provided a base-line for later scholars. Sir John Clerk of Penicuik was more of a catalyst than a direct contributor. Educated at Glasgow and later at Leiden, where he heard lectures on Classical archaeology, he toured Italy in 1697, an experience which coloured the rest of his life. After 1720 he developed an interest in the Roman past of Scotland and joined the circle of Ralph Thoresby, Alexander Gordon, the Gale brothers and William Stukeley. Like other landowners of the time, he collected antiquities, including sixteen altars and other inscriptions which were later donated to the museum of the Society of Antiquaries of Scotland. Clerk travelled with Gordon to Hadrian's Wall, and some of the results were incorporated in the *Itinerarium Septentrionale*. Clerk published virtually nothing himself, but he was a benign and supportive influence within the loose circle of Scottish antiquaries. In 1751, for example, Captain (later Lieutenant General) Robert Melville paid a visit to Clerk at Penicuik and was inspired by him to expand knowledge of Roman Scotland. He made an extensive tour in 1754, which revealed new forts and temporary camps. There was an even more significant and far-reaching result. Melville counted William Roy (see p. 447) among his proselytes as a student of Roman military works.

Very few roofed buildings survived from Roman Britain to be recorded by antiquaries. The most intriguing and probably the most complete was Arthur's O'on near Camelon in Stirlingshire. This was a remarkable circular domed building, over 6 metres high, with a single doorway. Although almost certainly a temple, the O'on probably was also a victory monument, dedicated to the goddess Victoria and erected either late in the first or mid-second century. The building was well recorded in 1720 by Stukeley, relying upon drawings by the architect Andrews Jelfe, but was sadly demolished in 1743. A full-size replica can still be seen on the stables at Penicuik House, where it was erected by Sir James Clerk.

Exploring the North

The study of Roman Britain was directed into new and productive paths by the Presbyterian minister and Morpeth schoolmaster John Horsley, an Edinburgh graduate who gave lectures on the natural sciences at Newcastle. When his professional and pastoral duties allowed, he travelled widely in England and Scotland, recording sites, sculptures and inscriptions with a mixture of accuracy and naiveté. His great work was the *Britannia Romana*, issued shortly before his death in 1732, one of the earliest detailed studies of a part of the Roman world published before 1900. His treatment of the northern frontiers was of outstanding value, based as it was on close personal knowledge. Whereas Camden's *Britannia* was a work of late Renaissance scholarship, John Horsley's book should have opened a new era. It did not, and study of the British past made little progress for a generation (Horsley 1732).

The finest and most original publication based on original fieldwork in this period was delivered by the Scot William Roy, who served on the staff of the Deputy Quartermaster-General as a military surveyor in northern Britain after the rebellion of 1745. Roy's own observation and well-founded archaeological knowledge were formative, and he made good use of reports submitted by Captain Robert Melville. But it was Roy's excellent knowledge of Roman campaigns in the north that provided the essential fabric for his *Military Antiquities of the Romans in Britain*, published in 1793, but incorporating work carried out nearly forty years earlier. More than fifty Roman forts and camps in northern England and Scotland were portrayed in a fine series of plates, along with a map of the Antonine Wall. Roy's surveys were the finest produced to that time and they were not surpassed for over half a century (Roy 1793).

At a time when the study of Roman Britain could have made major advances, progress was impeded and distorted by the sustained activity of a talented forger. Charles Bertram was born in London in 1723 to a family headed by a dyer of silk. In 1743 the family migrated to Copenhagen and joined the circle of the Danish princess Louisa, who later married the Crown Prince, and the later King Frederick V. In 1748 Bertram began a career as a teacher of English at the Marine Academy, where he compiled works on English and Danish grammar. Before the summer of 1747 he had created a forged manuscript on the history of Roman Britain, purported to be the work of a medieval scholar, Richard of Cirencester. His motive is not obvious, but it was not pecuniary. Bertram chose his target well. In June 1747 he wrote to William Stukeley, referring to the manuscript. Correspondence followed, in which Stukeley pressed Bertram to acquire the text and send a transcript. Nine years later Stukeley delivered a paper to the Society of Antiquaries, published in 1757 under the title 'An Account of Richard of Cirencester', including a discussion of the itinerary which it contained and a map. Early in 1758, Bertram himself published an edition, along with the texts of Gildas and Nennius. Mixing the false with the genuine has long been a favoured ploy of the forger.

Stukeley swallowed the forgery whole and never seems to have tried to relate the 'evidence' relayed by Bertram to the established ancient record. He should not be judged too harshly, for he was confronted by a very cunning correspondent.

Nevertheless, he was culpable in embracing Bertram's inventions with enthusiasm, even suggesting that the supposed author, a Westminster monk, was originally from Cirencester. Richard of Cirencester thus emerged and was accepted by most authorities as a prime source for Britannia for the next seventy years. But as early as 1795, Thomas Reynolds, later to edit the text of the Antonine Itinerary, condemned the document as a fake. Its supporters, however, were an impressive array, including Hutchins, Roy and Richard Colt Hoare. Even Gibbon accepted the list of Roman cities in the manuscript, though he was cautious about the work as a whole and found its evidence 'feeble'. After Reynolds, the next definitive judgment on Richard of Cirencester was delivered by the Northumberland scholar John Hodgson in 1827, and over the next twenty years the searching criticism of German scholars effectively destroyed any remaining credibility in Bertram's text. The *coup de grâce* was delivered by Bernard Woodward after 1847 and by J. E. B. Mayor in 1869. Even after this, Richard of Cirencester lingered in the memory, though Bertram's text no longer figured in any serious account of Roman Britain. Bertram himself was long dead. He died at the age of 42 in 1765 in straitened circumstances. His forgery brought him no advantage and he was compelled to sell his library to clear his debts. His fieldwork in Denmark was not without distinction, but may not have satisfied him. Bertram must not be underestimated. He was well versed in the ancient sources and displayed ingenuity in his bogus reconstruction of the map of Roman Britain. Although his motivation remains obscure, he may have been frustrated in the limited life offered by the court at Copenhagen. Bertram may have attempted to shape a career which was otherwise blocked by the creation of a great discovery. He failed, and in his failure retarded research on Roman Britain for over half a century.

Villas and Mosaics

The remains and ornaments of villas excited great interest in the eighteenth century, as landed families began to discern links between their own experience of rising prosperity and that of the Romano-British élite. From mid-century it was almost *de rigueur* to excavate a villa which lay on your estate; if visible remains such as mosaics resulted, then so much the better. Several sites were either destroyed or damaged in this way; a few others made a more permanent contribution. Great mosaics like those at Horkstow (Lincolnshire), Littlecote Park (Wiltshire) and Stonesfield (Oxfordshire) attracted much attention, the last-named being the first large mosaic in Britain to be uncovered in full and discussed in detail, in 1712. Large-scale and intelligent excavation of villas, however, made little headway until late in the century. The lead was provided by Samuel Lysons, the son of a Gloucestershire clergyman and Director and Vice-President of the Society of Antiquaries in 1798. Lysons placed the study of villas on a new footing by his excavation of several sites. His early work was carried out in his native Gloucestershire, at Withington, Great Witcombe and Woodchester. His publication of the palatial residence at Woodchester in 1797, dedicated to George III and with a text in both English and French (why?), is a magnificent volume, beautifully adorned with drawings, plans and illustrations of selected finds. The huge Orpheus mosaic on the floor of the great hall was a major find, but its evident splendour should not be allowed to dominate Lysons' achievement in revealing a coherent plan of a large part of the villa. At Bignor (Sussex) he was able to excavate more widely still and produced an excellent plan of this courtyard villa, as well as illustrating the mosaics with charming coloured drawings. Lysons cast an even wider net for his sumptuous *Reliquiae Britannico-Romanae*, issued in three folio volumes between 1801 and 1817. So splendid were these that only fifty copies were printed, at a cost to Lysons of 6,000 pounds but to subscribers of only 48 pounds and 6 shillings. Contemporary with Lysons' work was that of William Fowler in north Lincolnshire, though his interest was centred on the mosaics. The North Leigh (Oxfordshire) villa came in for attention about the same time, and Henry Hakewill published an account of this large country house in 1826. Other major sites were beginning to appear in the early nineteenth century. In 1805 a black and white mosaic was found by workmen at Fishbourne (Sussex), the first glimpse of the great Neronian and Flavian palace excavated from 1961.

Many locally based antiquaries were active in the mid and late eighteenth century; Roman villas and temples, real or imaginary, were popular targets for their efforts. Typical of these figures is Hayman Rooke, who settled near Mansfield after service in the army. In the 1770s and 1780s he worked on and recorded several sites in mid-Nottinghamshire, having already described the earthworks adjacent to the temple complex at Lydney. His interests centred on the Romans, and he tended to assign major earthworks to them without distinction. He excavated as well as surveying surface remains. From 1786 he exposed a large part of a villa at Mansfield Wood-house, by rudimentary measures and with no grasp of stratigraphy, though the published plan makes reasonable sense. Buildings were erected over the mosaic floors, but these were ruinous twenty years later. Rooke's main achievement lay in his good scale plans of earthworks. If he had been in contact with the leading surveyors of the day, notably William Roy (see p. 447), his legacy would have been richer.

Villas and mosaics continued to exert their attraction well into the nineteenth century, without contributing to a major advance in technical excavation. This is well illustrated by the excavation of the villa at Brading on the Isle of Wight from the 1860s to 1880. The supervising committee was as distinguished as it could be, including Sir John Lubbock, Sir Augustus Franks, Augustus Pitt-Rivers and Charles Roach Smith, but this did not guarantee the quality of the enterprise. The mosaic floors were handsomely reproduced in colour but the plan of the villa marked little progress on the previous century. Study of Roman Britain was marking time.

Other rural complexes were coming to light in the eighteenth century, but few were well recorded. The temple, baths and *mansio* at Lydney survived well above ground to the 1770s and were subjected to progressive destruction at that time. In 1805 Charles Bathurst, of the family which owned the estate, cleared the site and excavated several of its buildings. His plans and records were among the best of their day, but were not published until 1879. Bathurst's workmen did not penetrate the latest surfaces that they encountered, so that much was left intact for Mortimer Wheeler to excavate in 1928 (Bathurst and King 1879).

Improved opportunities for travel in northern England encouraged exploration and recording of Hadrian's Wall and the associated sites. Before 1702, Christopher Hunter toured Dere Street to Risingham and High Rochester, and the line of the Wall westward to Chesterholm and Housesteads. Hunter was positive in assigning the frontier to Hadrian, in correction of Camden's dating of the stone barrier to the late Roman period. Hunter's account was followed in 1716 by John Warburton's map of

Northumberland, which gave an important new outline of the Roman road network, along with identification of the Roman names for forts on the basis of inscriptions. Later in life, however, Warburton shamelessly plagiarized the work of John Horsley after the latter's death. The best that can be said about this sorry episode is that Warburton's plagiarism was a compliment to the most important single volume published on Britannia between Camden in 1586 and Roy in 1793.

Mapping the Frontiers

The later eighteenth century saw a marked increase in visitors to the frontier regions, especially after 1745, but little in the way of original investigation, Roy's great work always excepted. John Hodgson's survey of the mural works from 1810 onward, with due reference to Horsley but with emphasis upon more recent observation, provided a firm basis for the Hadrianic case, but controversy still raged over the question: who built Hadrian's Wall? Hodgson's excavations at Housesteads and those of the Revd Anthony Hedley at Chesterholm yielded strong evidence for a unity of design which had eluded Horsley and which firmly buttressed the case for Hadrianic construction, already pointed to by Hadrianic building records at Chesterholm and Milecastle 38. Hodgson appears to have been the first to consider the frontier-works as a whole and to reconstruct a frontier-system in which Wall, forts, milecastles, turrets and Vallum were all accommodated. By mid-century another Hadrianic building inscription had been found, at Milecastle 42, and the Hadrianic case was given wide currency by the large monograph of John Collingwood Bruce, *The Roman Wall* (1851; later editions in 1853 and 1867). Collingwood Bruce's views did not go unchallenged. There were still those who held that Septimius Severus had built the stone wall in replacement of the turf wall of Hadrian. This controversy resounded after 1900. As late as 1903, Francis Haverfield, then the leading light of Romano-British studies, could still argue for a Hadrianic turf barrier across the isthmus, replaced by a stone wall by Septimius Severus, despite the scepticism of local scholars.

There is no doubt that the fieldwork instigated and largely funded by John Clayton from his base at Chesters, and the support given by the fourth Duke of Northumberland, Algernon Percy, placed the study of Hadrian's Wall on its firmest foundation to that date. Clayton owned several forts in the central sector of the Wall and centred his work on Chesters, Carrawburgh and Housesteads, and the milecastles and turrets between them, in the period 1843 to 1870. But he left his friend and protégé Bruce to present his major results to a wider public. Clayton sought no fame for himself and his work should have been more widely recognized. By his publications, Collingwood Bruce dominated the dissemination of information about Hadrian's Wall, without himself contributing much in the way of original research. His guidebooks to the Wall in their successive editions from 1863 onward catered to the needs of the mounting number of visitors. Bruce's major works, *The Roman Wall* and *Lapidarium Septentrionale* (1875) provided a basis for further work on the frontier. After a brief pause, a major phase of excavation opened in the 1880s and continued to the First World War. This phase saw the extension of excavation to the outpost forts, to the hinterland, and renewed work in Scotland. These studies included digging at Hardknott in Cumbria and at Birrens from 1895, and a major series of excavations along the Antonine Wall from 1890 to 1893. Extensive work at Housesteads in the 1890s, at Ardoch in

1896–7 and at Camelon in 1899–1900 revealed the potential of these sites, not only for the history of the northern frontier but also for the organization of the Roman army in the late first and second centuries. Excavation of the forts in Scotland presented insuperable problems in that their internal buildings in timber were not always recognized by the investigators of the day. Nevertheless, there were advances in the study of timber structures, at Ardoch and Inchtuthil for example, while at Bar Hill the preservation of wooden posts provided valuable information and encouraged excavators to seek less obvious remains represented by foundation trenches and post impressions. The results of work at Birrens yielded a plan of an auxiliary fort as complete as any uncovered to that date. The principal buildings were clearly identified, along with granaries, officers' quarters, barracks and even ovens on the intervallum. The Birrens plan was soon followed by Bosanquet's plan of Housesteads (1898), Ward's plan of Gellygaer (1903) and Conway's plan of Melandra Castle (1906). Large-scale work at Corbridge from 1906 revealed the long history of the site, most importantly demonstrating the Flavian origins of the sequence of forts. Another of the important sites in northern Britain, Inchtuthil, was examined to a high standard by Lord Abercromby at the end of the nineteenth century, but the work was curtailed by a quarrel between the excavators and the Society of Antiquaries of Scotland.

Below Towns

The long-held legionary fortresses did not figure prominently among the sites which contributed substantially to the rediscovery of Britannia. Roman York was studied by a variety of people, but collectors greatly outnumbered scholars who could relate Eboracum to the wider world. Among the earliest recorders was Ralph Thoresby, a Leeds wool merchant, who collected many Roman objects from a cemetery between Bootham and the Ouse at the end of the seventeenth century. His collection was eventually sold off in London after the death of his son in 1764. The York surgeon Francis Drake drew up a detailed description of antiquities found in York and lodged in local collections. These formed the basis for his *Eboracum* of 1736. The first attempt at a reasoned synthesis of information on York did not appear until a century later, when the Revd Charles Wellbeloved published his *Eburacum or York under the Romans* in 1842. This excellent monograph contained detailed records of the defences of the fortress and of buildings revealed in the *colonia*. It was further distinguished by the accurate drawings of John Browne, historian of York Minster. Collection of material continued in the later nineteenth century. The Yorkshire Museum was founded and its collections steadily grew. These were well curated by the Revd James Raine until 1896, but purposeful excavation had to wait until the mid-1920s.

Chester did not have the benefit of an effective local antiquary in the eighteenth and early nineteenth centuries. In the 1880s the north wall of the fortress and the later city required extensive repair. A section west of the Northgate produced a few Roman facing-blocks and a tombstone. In 1887 the eastern stretch of the north wall was taken apart. Behind massive ashlar blocks lay many reused inscribed and sculptured stones. Three years later, further excavation in the western sector yielded another mass of inscriptions and sculptures. In all, over 150 inscribed stones, mainly tombstones, and sculpted pieces were recovered and installed in the recently founded Grosvenor Museum (Wright and Richmond 1955: 4–5).

Ten miles to the south of Chester lay the legionary works depot at Holt. This site had first been mentioned early in the seventeenth century, when the landowner found Roman masonry on his land. It was not forgotten thereafter but little further information was gathered until the early twentieth century, when kilns producing tiles and pottery vessels were revealed.

Unlike York and Chester, the legionary fortress at Caerleon lay largely clear of later settlement, but there was little study of its remains before the nineteenth century. The site was well known to medieval antiquaries, but accumulated legends rather than reliable information. King Arthur's Round Table was the descendant of the amphitheatre. The walled site was endowed with an ecclesiastical status which it had not enjoyed in the late Roman world. Excavation of a desultory sort proceeded in the mid-nineteenth century, but records were poor. The artefacts were gathered by J. E. Lee in 1862 and published as a catalogue: *Isca Silurum: An Illustrated Catalogue of the Museum of Antiquities at Caerleon*, with a supplement issued in 1868. The record of inscriptions was good, and was supported by reasonable drawings of samian ware and stamped tiles. Study of the fortress as a whole had to wait another sixty years.

The visible remains of Saxon Shore forts naturally received attention in the post-Roman centuries, notably at Richborough, Pevensey, Portchester, Reculver, Bradwell and Burgh Castle, though little investigative work was attempted. These impressive sites did not require rediscovery: they were prominent features of the landscape which housed churches or monastic sites, as at Reculver, Bradwell and Portchester, or castles, as at Portchester and Pevensey. Richborough enjoyed the reputation of being the landing-point of St Augustine in 597; and an Anglo-Saxon chapel existed here until the seventeenth century. A small Saxon church was inserted into one of the Roman gates at Bradwell, and at Reculver a large church was sited within the Roman fort. The first effort to treat the Saxon Shore as a whole was that of Charles Roach Smith, who recorded sites in Kent and Sussex in his *Antiquities of Richborough, Reculver and Lympne*. Several assaults had been mounted on the site of Richborough from the late eighteenth century. The massive platform of the triumphal quadrifons was probed in 1792 and again in 1826. Tunnels were resorted to in the examination of the huge concrete mass below the monument. Further tunnelling was attempted in 1843 and 1865, and trenching around the foundation produced fragments of the original cladding. Roach Smith had meanwhile turned his attention to Lympne, on which he issued a monograph in 1852. It is not now possible to assess the quality of his excavations as these were only sketchily described. The most interesting and useful feature of the monograph is the inclusion of plans and woodcuts of gates and towers on the defences, which had been in a state of collapse for some time. Very few finds were illustrated, though there were fairly good drawings of coins of Carausius and Allectus. The most innovative single illustration is a drawing of tile-stamps of the *classis Britannica*, one of the earliest illustrations of these objects.

Relatively few of the Roman forts of Wales were studied by travellers and antiquaries before the nineteenth century. Segontium, Caernarvon, is a notable exception. Its fame in the post-Roman period sprang from its supposed connection with Magnus Maximus (Maxen Wledig) but no observation on the ground is recorded before Camden's visit in 1590 and his insertion of a reference to the Roman site here in the fourth edition of the *Britannia* in 1594. The fort at Y Gaer, near Brecon, appears in a Norman charter of about 1100 as a *vasta civitas*, implying that there were extensive visible remains at that date. Records of finds began in 1684, when Thomas Dineley referred to an inscription and stamped tiles. Similarly vague notices followed in the eighteenth century.

Study and deliberate examination of the cities of Britain was slow to make progress before the nineteenth century. The antiquaries of the seventeenth and eighteenth centuries were incurious about the Roman origins of cities, probably because the lower levels of these sites were left largely undisturbed and thus there were few opportunities to record major structures. It was also the case that few active antiquaries were based in or near historic cities. Medieval curiosity about the Roman past of cities usually centred on Christian links, specifically with martyrs and relics. Inevitably, Verulamium enjoyed the greatest *réclame* of any early city. St Alban and his city came in for attention as early as the late eighth century and the reign of Offa of Mercia, when the king was advised in a vision to unearth the body of the saint and to place his relics in a worthy shrine. This clearly suggests a hiatus in observance of the martyrium between late Roman Britain and the late eighth century. By the eleventh century, the remains of the Roman city had become a quarry for Saxo-Norman builders, as Matthew Paris recorded. One of the particular targets was the mass of brick and tile in the city wall and substantial buildings, as can still be seen in the Norman abbey. The diggers for building materials found, as well as the foundations of buildings, pottery vessels and glass containers holding cremations. There are also mentions of altars, columns and many coins. Less credible is the report of books and rolls in a wall-recess, some of them in Latin. One was a history of St Alban, no doubt a timely discovery. The spoliation of the ancient city continued throughout the medieval centuries and was still proceeding in the sixteenth century. John Leland tells us that the road-surface of Watling Street was quarried for the repair of public roads, and refers to baked tiles which he thought were parts of an aqueduct, but may have been roof-tiles. Two hundred years later, Stukeley encountered hundreds of cart-loads of Roman bricks torn from Roman buildings and destined for road repairs. A century later the destruction of Verulamium still continued (Leland 1774: IV.168; Stukeley 1776: 116).

Bath can fairly claim to be the first Roman site to be commented on after the end of Roman rule. The Anglo-Saxon poem of the eighth century, *The Ruin*, admires and mourns the wreck of a great building in which there were thermal baths and thus was most probably inspired by the remains of the temple and baths of *Aquae Sulis*. The curative qualities of the Bath spring were appreciated in the Saxon and Norman periods, but not until John Leland arrived in Bath late in the 1530s did recording begin. Leland's notes on sculptural remains in particular were important and were exploited by Camden half a century later. Inscriptions and sculptures continued to emerge over the next 200 years, but the great boost to the rediscovery of Roman Bath came when the city became the most fashionable place of resort in England. The rebuilding of central Bath from the mid-eighteenth century began to reveal the kind of buildings and sculptures which educated minds of the day expected of a centre of Roman culture. A foretaste had been provided by the discovery of the gilded bronze head of Minerva in 1727. A golden age of recovery of the Roman past began when the Pump Room was replaced in 1790.

A mass of Roman masonry and sculpted blocks was exposed above a virtually intact Roman pavement four metres below the modern surface. The finds aroused immense interest, especially the sculpted pieces. These were brought together in an exemplary fashion by Samuel Lysons in the first volume of *Reliquiae Romano-Britannicae* of 1813 and reconstructed as the front elevation of a temple in the Corinthian order, the temple of Sulis Minerva. Matters rested there on the temple until the mid-nineteenth century. In 1867–9 the podium of the temple was identified but greater discoveries were made a decade later. The sacred spring and the adjacent reservoir were revealed in building works in 1879. The reservoir was partially emptied and many offerings recovered, though most of the deposit remained in place until the excavations of the 1970s.

The rediscovery of the great baths had begun in 1755 with the exposure of the eastern end of the complex by the builders of the Duke of Kingston's baths. This provoked huge local interest, and subsequent finds enabled the outline of the baths to be established, though much detail remained unclear. Not until 1867 was there significant progress and this was due to James Irvine, Clerk of Works in Bath from 1864 to 1871, not a trained archaeologist but an outstanding observer, investigator and recorder. He had earlier done much to reveal the temple podium. Now he turned his attention to the area south of the Duke of Kingston's Bath. Over the years 1867–9 he recorded much detail in the baths, adding to earlier records by drawing sections across the accumulated deposits in the building. But he was not in control of the work as a whole. That role was assumed by Major Davis, an energetic but far from sensitive investigator and recorder. Davis was as much concerned with practical problems as with the dispassionate record of the ancient structures. Davis' performance in dealing with the remains of the Great Bath was close to a disaster. The removal of rubble and earth went forward without record; even the remains of the vaulted roof were largely removed without study of their position. Matters went from bad to worse as the clearance continued. The Roman circular bath was exposed in 1883–5, and the heated baths in the west range were cleared and then immediately covered by a modern building. Archaeological opinion was outraged, with good reason. The Society of Antiquaries directed its local representative to inspect the results of Davis' work. The resultant report was far from encouraging. It was followed by a deputation later in 1885, which expressed deeper unease. Some of the issues debated were to recur sixty years later: the sealing off of ancient deposits; the preservation of Roman structures beneath or within modern buildings; the character of buildings erected over major Roman remains. The end result in Bath was not as bad as it seemed at the time. Deposits were sealed off rather than destroyed, enabling recovery of much vital information in the 1960s and 1970s. In many respects the rediscovery of Roman Bath anticipated controversies of the mid and late twentieth century (Davis 1884; Cunliffe 1984).

One of the most successful monographs devoted to a single city was the volume produced by Professor Buckman and C. H. Newmarch, *Illustrations of the Remains of Roman Art in Cirencester, the Site of Antient Corinium*, published in 1850. The florid title does not do justice to the contents of the book. It includes a reasonable discussion of the context of Roman Cirencester, its road-system, and the monuments then visible and recently recorded. The mosaics in town-houses are the most prominent single feature of the volume, and these are excellently illustrated in colour. The authors went beyond aesthetic assessment and examined the materials used in the mosaics and the methods of their construction. This was a new departure, and Buckman and Newmarch broke further fresh ground by publishing finds of pottery, glass and metal objects. The study of the samian pottery is especially impressive. The figured pieces were represented by full-size drawings, and potters' stamps were reproduced by accurate copies. Equally notable is a careful record of the coins from the city, mainly lodged in local collections. No other single study of a Roman city in Britain came close to this volume in the mid-nineteenth century or for some decades afterwards.

Of the few main Roman cities not covered by medieval and modern communities, Silchester was the most fruitfully explored. The site had been firmly recognized as Calleva by Horsley before 1732. Fieldwork on the city was begun by a remarkable local investigator, John Stair, a man of humble origins and limited means. In the 1730s and 1740s he uncovered remains of streets and houses, along with pottery and other objects. More ambitiously, he attempted to draw up an overall plan of the city, the first such effort in Britain. His records seem to have been limited, but in 1741 he submitted a plan of Silchester to John Collet and John Ward, the latter of Gresham College, London. Ward, with Stair in attendance, employed a surveyor to draw up a revised plan which was completed in 1742, sadly with Stair's name omitted. Ironically, an estate map of 1653 had already portrayed the defensive perimeter with a fair degree of accuracy. Stair continued his field observation but no further publications ensued. The next significant phase did not begin until a century later.

The second Duke of Wellington took a much closer interest than his illustrious father in the ancient city on his estate. In 1864 the supervision of renewed investigation was entrusted to the Revd J. G. Joyce, who held a living nearby but had no previous experience of excavation. The choice of excavator proved to be inspired. With a small team of labourers, Joyce examined the gates of the amphitheatre, the forum-basilica, a temple and a number of town-houses. He foresaw the possibility of dating structures by the associated objects, well before this principle was widely appreciated but also before a sound basis for dating existed. Charles Roach Smith could write a study of samian ware in 1849, but was unable to supply a scheme of dates. A substantial part of Joyce's achievement lies in his richly illustrated journal and sketchbook, as well as his three papers in *Archaeologia*. Sadly, increasing ill-health limited his work and the excavations slowly petered out before ending in 1884. Six years later they were resumed under the auspices of the Society of Antiquaries.

For a decade after 1890 extensive excavations, insula by insula, continued under the direction of G. E. Fox and W. H. St John Hope, the published record appearing in *Archaeologia*. The reports included good plans of houses and the public baths, and many coloured drawings of mosaics. The quality of excavation came in for severe criticism from some later commentators. Mortimer Wheeler referred to Silchester as having been 'dug like potatoes'. This was a harsh judgment and was based on anachronism. Inevitably, the excavations were a product of their time; and the techniques employed were no better, but certainly little worse, than those applied elsewhere in Britain at the time. A more relevant criticism might have targeted the treatment of the finds, especially those with commercial value. Animal remains were also poorly treated, as were the remains of insects and seeds. The yawning gap in the enterprise was the absence of a stratigraphical sequence, as Francis Haverfield and others were shortly to point out. It must be made clear that the excavators of the late nineteenth century did not penetrate far below the deposits of the later Roman period, so that their record could fairly present an overall picture of a Romano–British city at its peak. After the end of their work Silchester was not again disturbed until the late 1930s (Boon 1974: 22–7 in general).

Cities in which there was no local archaeological group, or which failed to attract the interest of a national body like the Society of Antiquaries, did not figure to any extent in the early studies of urban archaeology. One such case is Exeter where, aside from the records of Captain W. T. P. Shortt, published in 1841 as *Sylva Antiqua Iscana* and *Collectanea curiosa antiqua Dumnonia*, little was done until the late nineteenth century; organized excavation within the city did not begin until the 1930s.

Necessary changes in certain nineteenth-century cities led to discovery of their Roman past. At Lincoln the Roman system of sewers continued to function until the mid-nineteenth century, when they were surveyed by the health officer in the wake of the cholera outbreaks of the 1830s and 1840s and replaced by a modern network.

Many of the county historians of the later eighteenth century were not well equipped to record and develop knowledge of the Roman past. Philip Morant produced a massive compilation of local history and antiquities for Essex, but his reports represented little forward movement. This is also true of John Hutchins in Dorset and John Thorsby in Leicestershire. Far more important was the activity of Richard Colt Hoare and his associates in Wiltshire. and the work of the Lysons brothers in several southern English counties (Colt Hoare 1819; Lysons 1813, 1817a, b).

Towards the Modern Era

Not surprisingly, lesser rural sites received little attention before the late nineteenth century except at a local level. The most important excavations were those conducted by Augustus Pitt-Rivers on his estate in Cranborne Chase, Dorset and Wiltshire. This retired general with long-standing interests in the techniques of artillery and rifle design had conducted fieldwork at intervals during his military service, but his main interests in the mid-nineteenth century lay in evolutionary studies and in what we would now call typology. From the late 1860s, he engaged in fieldwork and excavation, in Yorkshire, Sussex, London and Ireland. In 1880 he inherited the 28,000-acre estate of Cranborne, which provided him with a substantial fortune and an ample stage for original fieldwork. His excavations at Woodcuts, Rotherly and Iwerne were not only the first extensive explorations of Late Iron Age and Roman rural settlements, but also provided the fullest publication of such sites and their associated artefacts to that date and for many years to come. The standard of Pitt-Rivers' excavations must not be overestimated. He left much to his foremen and was not in constant attendance. He did, however, exercise a controlling hand and ensured that the record of stratigraphy and finds was as full as it could be. The world of the Romano-British rural dweller in single farmsteads was fully revealed, though Pitt-Rivers believed he was uncovering small villages. Unfortunately, his work was not replicated elsewhere, and this aspect of Roman Britain languished for the next thirty years. Not until the advent of air photography in the 1920s did the rural landscape and settlement of Britain begin fully to emerge (Pitt-Rivers 1898).

Interest in the smaller objects from Roman sites quickened after about 1850, especially in southern Britain, where finds of pottery, bronzes, coins and glass were now turning up in quantity. Roach Smith, resident first in London and later in Kent, was one of the most assiduous recorders of lesser finds. He was particularly interested in pottery and was one of the first to recognize the significance of the samian ware factories of central and eastern Gaul for the dating of sites in Britain. His best work was achieved between 1850 and 1870; in 1856 he sold his collection of antiquities to the British Museum. Local finds were increasingly of interest and were finding their way into local collections.

One of the most important sources for the history and culture of Roman Britain was and is the corpus of inscriptions on stone and other materials. The first attempt at a comprehensive publication of this vital source was instigated by Theodor Mommsen and the Academy of Berlin. Emil Huebner, a more than competent epigrapher, undertook this work, which was published as volume VII of the *Corpus Inscriptionum Latinarum* in 1873. It was a remarkable achievement in the conditions of the time. It is difficult to point to a British scholar of the day who could have done better. Huebner made major topographical errors, but his work represented major progress; three supplements followed from his pen. By 1887 a suitably equipped British scholar had emerged and Mommsen entrusted the further record of Romano-British inscriptions to Francis Haverfield. Fresh discoveries were noted in the Supplements to *Ephemeris Epigraphica* in 1889 and 1913. Haverfield later took on the task of producing a new *Corpus* after the death in action of his pupil G. L. Cheesman in 1915, in concert with other Oxford scholars. But four years later Haverfield himself was dead and responsibility for the prosecution of the project passed to R. G. Collingwood, later joined by R. P. Wright. In 1965 the first volume of the *Corpus* appeared, followed more recently by fascicules devoted to individual categories of text. More than a century after Huebener the work continues.

By the later nineteenth century, British archaeology was slowly receiving official recognition and a rudimentary national structure. The 1860s saw important advances at both local and national level. There were greatly increased opportunities for active field-workers to meet and discuss discoveries and debate issues. The world of Lysons and Colt Hoare was left behind. Progress was still gradual but inexorable. The protection of ancient monuments was an increasing concern and was furthered by legislation in 1882, as a result of which Pitt–Rivers was appointed Inspector of Ancient Monuments in January 1883. This was an important step forward, but it did guarantee security for all remains of the Roman past. Parts of Hadrian's Wall, for example, were still being despoiled until well into the twentieth century, while the early phases of many historic cities were still vulnerable to piecemeal development. Nevertheless the origins of professional approaches were palpable in the late decades of the nineteenth century as a few scholars based in universities, notably Francis Haverfield at Oxford, engaged in the promotion of Romano-British studies. Although the war of 1914–18 put a brake on these developments, not everything came to a halt; there was still the basis for a resumption of work after 1920 in another world.

FURTHER READING

This subject has not yet been extensively treated by a recent scholar. Among the most important general studies there may be noted F. Haverfield, *The Roman Occupation of Britain* (1924), edited by G. Macdonald, especially pp. 59–88; T. D. Kendrick, *British Antiquity* (1950); S. Piggott, *William Stukeley* (revised edition 1985); E. Birley, *Research on Hadrian's Wall* (1961). The major contributions from the Tudor period onward are: W. Camden, *Britannia* (1586 and later editions); T. Gale, *Antonini Iter Britanniarum* (1709); R. Thoresby, *Musaeum Thoresbyanum* (1713); A. Gordon, *Itinerarium Septentrionale* (1727); J. Horsley, *Britannia Romana* (1732); W. Stukeley, *Itinerarium Curiosum* (second edition 1776); W. Roy, *Military Antiquities of the Romans in Britain* (1793); S. Lysons, *Reliquiae Britannico-Romanae* I (1813), II (1817), III (1817); W. Fowler, *Engravings of the Principal Mosaic Pavements* (1796–1818); R. Colt Hoare, *The History of Ancient Wiltshire* II (Roman Aera, 1819); R. Stuart, *Caledonia Romana* (1845); C. Roach Smith, *Collectanea Antiqua* I (1848); J. Collingwood Bruce, *The Roman Wall* (1851; second edition, 1853; third edition, 1867); *The Wallet-Book of the Roman Wall* (1863); *Lapidarium Septentrionale* (1875); A. Pitt-Rivers, *Excavations in Cranborne Chase* I (1887); R. Hingley, *Roman Officers and English Gentlemen* (2000) for the late nineteenth and early twentieth centuries.

REFERENCES

Bathurst, W. H. and King, C. W. 1879. *Roman Antiquities at Lydney Park, Gloucestershire.* London.

Birley, E. 1961. *Research on Hadrian's Wall.* Kendal.

Boon, G. C. 1974. *Silchester. The Roman Town of Calleva.* Newton Abbot.

Camden, W. 1789. *Britannia,* ed. R. Gough. London. [First published in 1586.]

Collingwood Bruce, J. 1863. *The Wallet-Book of the Roman Wall.* London.

—— 1867. *The Roman Wall,* 3rd edn. London. [First published in 1851.]

—— 1875. *Lapidarium Septentrionale; or, A Description of the Monuments of Roman Rule in the North of England.* London.

Colt Hoare, R. 1812–21. *Ancient History of North and South Wiltshire.* 2 vols. London.

—— 1822–44. *History of Modern Wiltshire.* 6 vols. London.

Cunliffe, B. 1984. *Roman Bath Discovered.* London.

Davis, C. 1884. *The Excavations of the Roman Baths at Bath.* Bath.

Fowler, W. 1796–1818. *Engravings of the Principal Mosaic Pavements.* Winterton.

Gale, T. 1709. *Antonini Iter Britanniarum.* London.

Gordon, A. 1727. *Itinerarium Septentrionale; or, A Journey thro' most of the Counties of Scotland, and those in the North of England.* London.

Haverfield, F. 1924. *The Roman Occupation of Britain,* ed. G. Macdonald. Oxford.

Hingley, R. 2000. *Roman Officers and English Gentlemen: The Imperial Origins of Roman Archaeology.* London.

Horsley, J. 1732. *Britannia Romana; or The Roman Antiquities of Britain.* London.

Kendrick, T. D. 1950. *British Antiquity.* London.

Leland, J. 1774. *Collectanea.* London.

Lysons, D. and Lysons, S. 1806–22. *Magna Britannia, being a Concise Topographical Account of the Several Counties of Great Britain.* 6 vols. London.

Lysons, S. 1813–17. *Reliquiae Britannico-Romanae.* 3 vols. London.

—— 1815. *An Account of the Remains of a Roman Villa Discovered in the County of Sussex.* London.

Piggott, S. 1985. *William Stukeley*, rev. edn. London.

Pitt-Rivers, A. L. F. 1887. *Excavations in Cranborne Chase I*. London.

——1898. *Excavations in Cranborne Chase IV*. London.

Roach Smith, C. 1848. *Collectanea Antiqua I*. London.

Roy, W. 1793. *The Military Antiquities of the Romans in Britain*. London.

Stuart, R. 1845. *Caledonia Romana*. Edinburgh and London.

Stukeley, W. 1776. *Itinerarium Curiosum*, 2nd edn. London.

Thoresby, R. 1713. *Musaeum Thoresbyanum*. London.

Wright, R. P. and Richmond, I. A. 1955. *The Roman Inscribed and Sculptured Stones in the Grosvenor Museum, Chester*. Chester.

Bibliography

Abramson, P. 1995. A late Iron Age settlement at Scotch Corner, North Yorkshire. *Durham Archaeological Journal*, 11, 7–18.

Alcock, J. P. 2001. *Food in Roman Britain*. Stroud.

Alcock, L. 1971. *Arthur's Britain: History and Archaeology AD 367–634*. Harmondsworth.

Aldhouse-Green, M. J. 2000. *Seeing the Wood for the Trees: The Symbolism of Trees and Wood in Ancient Gaul and Britain*. Centre for Advanced Welsh & Celtic Studies Research Paper 17. Aberystwyth.

——2001a. Alternative iconographies: metaphors of resistance in Romano-British cult-imagery. In *VII Internationales Colloquium über Probleme des Provinzialrömischen Kunstschaffens*. Cologne.

——2001b. *Dying for the Gods: Human Sacrifice in Ancient Europe*. Stroud.

Aldhouse-Green, M. J. and Raybould, M. 1999. Deities with Gallo-British names recorded in inscriptions from Roman Britain. *Studia Celtica*, 33, 91–135.

Alexander, D. 2000. Later prehistoric settlement in west central Scotland. In J. Harding (ed.) *Northern Parts*. BAR (British Series) 302. Oxford, 157–65.

Allason-Jones, L. 1989. *Ear-rings in Roman Britain*. BAR (British Series) 144. Oxford.

——1989. *Women of Roman Britain*. London.

——1991. Roman and native interaction in Northumberland. In V. A. Maxfield and M. J. Dobson (eds), *Roman Frontier Studies 1989*. Exeter, 1–5.

——1996. *Roman Jet in the Yorkshire Museum*. York.

——1999. Women and the Roman army in Britain. In A. Galsworthy and I. Haynes (eds), *The Roman Army as a Community*. London, 41–51.

Allason-Jones, L. and McKay, B. 1985. *Coventina's Well*. Chester.

Allen, D. F. 1975. Cunobelin's Gold. *Britannia*, 6, 1–19.

Allen, J. R. L. and Fulford, M. G. 1999. Fort building and military supply along Britain's Eastern Channel and North Sea coasts: the later second and third centuries. *Britannia*, 30, 163–84.

——1987. Romano-British settlement and industry on the wetlands of the Severn Estuary. *Antiquaries Journal*, 62, 237–89.

——1996. The distribution of south-east Dorset black-burnished Category 1 pottery in south-west Britain. *Britannia*, 27, 223–81.

Allen, T. G. 1990. *An Iron Age and Romano-British Enclosed Settlement at Watkins Farm, Northmoor, Oxon*. Oxford.

Allen, T. G., Darvill, T., Green, S. and Jones, M. 1993. *Excavations at Roughground Farm, Lechlade, Gloucestershire: A Prehistoric and Roman Landscape.* Oxford.

Allison, P. M. 1997. Roman households: an archaeological perspective. In H. M. Parkins (ed.), *Roman Urbanism.* London, 112–46.

Andrews, C. 2001. Romanisation: a Kentish perspective. *Archaeologia Cantiana,* 121, 25–42.

Appleton-Fox, N. 1992. Excavations at a Romano-British round; Reawla, Gwinear, Cornwall. *Cornish Archaeology,* 31, 69–123.

Armit, I. 1997a. *Celtic Scotland.* London.

—— 1997b. Cultural landscapes and identities: a case study in the Scottish Iron Age. In A. Gwilt and C. C. Haselgrove (eds), *Reconstructing Iron Age Societies.* Oxford, 248–53.

—— 1999. Life after Hownam: the Iron Age in south-east Scotland. In B. Bevan (ed.), *Northern Exposure.* Leicester, 65–79.

—— 1999. The abandonment of souterrains. *Proceedings of the Society of Antiquaries of Scotland,* 129, 577–96.

Armit, I. and Ralston, I. B. M. 1997. The Iron Age. In K. J. Edwards and I. B. M. Ralston (eds), *Scotland: Environment and Archaeology, 8000 BC–AD 1000.* Chichester, 169–94.

Armitage, P. 1979. Roman mules. *London Archaeologist,* 3, 339–46.

Arnold, B. 1984. *Roman Britain to Saxon England.* London.

—— 2001. Power drinking in Iron Age Europe. *British Archaeology,* 57 (February), 14–19.

Arnold, C. and Davies, J. L. 2000. *Roman and Early Medieval Wales.* Stroud.

Ashbee, P. 1996. Halangy Down, St Mary's, Isles of Scilly, excavations 1964–1977. *Cornish Archaeology,* 35, *passim.*

Audoin-Rouzeau, F. 1994. *La Taille du cheval en Europe de l'Antiquité aux Temps Modernes.* Juan-les-Pins.

Aufderheide, A. and Rodríguez Martin, C. 1998. *Cambridge Encyclopedia of Human Paleopathology.* Cambridge.

Aurelius Victor. 1975. *De Caesaribus,* ed. P. Dufraigne. Paris.

Ayres, K. 1995. *Analysis of animal bones from Piddington Roman villa, Northamptonshire.* Unpublished thesis, School of Archaeological Studies, University of Leicester.

Bagnall Smith, J. 1999. Votive objects and objects of votive significance from Great Walsingham, Norfolk. *Britannia,* 30, 21–56.

Bailey, G. B. 1994. The provision of fort annexes on the Antonine Wall. *Proceedings of the Society of Antiquaries of Scotland,* 124, 299–314.

Ballantyne, C. and Dawson, A. 1997. Geomorphology and landscape change. In K. Edwards and I. Ralston (eds), *Scotland: Environment and Archaeology, 8000 BC–AD 1000.* Chichester, 23–44.

Barber, B. and Bowsher, D. 2000. *The Eastern Cemetery of Roman London: Excavations 1983–90.* Museum of London Archaeological Service, Monograph 4. London.

Barker, P. A., Haldon, R. and Jenks, W. 1991. Excavations on Sharpstones Hill near Shrewsbury, 1965–71. *Transactions of the Shropshire Archaeological and Historical Society,* 67, 15–57.

Barker, P. and White, R. 1998. *Wroxeter: The Life and Death of a City.* Stroud.

Barker, P., White, R., Pretty, K., Bird, H. and Corbishley, M. 1997. *The Baths Basilica Wroxeter. Excavations 1966–90.* London.

Barnes, I., Butterworth, C. A., Hawkes, J. W. and Smith, L. 1997. *Excavations at Thames Valley Park, Reading, 1986–88.* Wessex Archaeology Monograph 14. Salisbury.

Barrett, J., Fitzpatrick, A. and Macinnes, L. (eds) 1989. *Barbarians and Romans in North-West Europe.* BAR (International Series) 471. Oxford.

Bateman, N. and Locker, A. 1982. The sauce of the Thames. *London Archaeologist,* 4, 204–7.

Bateson, J. D. and Holmes, N. M. McQ. 1997. Roman and medieval coins found in Scotland, 1988–95. *Proceedings of the Society of Antiquaries of Scotland,* 127, 527–61.

Bathurst, W. H. and King, C. W. 1879. *Roman Antiquities at Lydney Park, Gloucestershire.* London.

Bauchhenss, G. and Nölke, P. 1981. *Die Iupitersaülen in den germanischen Provinzen.* Cologne and Bonn.

Bell, L. and Piper, L. 2000. An introduction to palaeohistology. In M. Cox and S. Mays (eds), *Human Osteology in Archaeology and Forensic Science.* London, 255–74.

Bennett, J. 2001. *Trajan: Optimus Princeps.* London.

Bennion, E. 1986. *Antique Dental Instruments.* London.

Bevan, B. (ed.) 1999. *Northern Exposure: Interpretative Devolution and the Iron Ages in Britain.* Leicester Archaeology Monograph 4. Leicester

Bewley, B. 1994. *Prehistoric and Romano-British Settlement on the Solway Plain.* Oxbow Monograph 17. Oxford.

Bidwell, P. 1997. *Roman Forts in Britain.* London.

Bidwell, P. (ed) 1999. *Hadrian's Wall 1989–1999: A Summary of Recent Excavations and Research.* Kendal.

Bidwell, P. T. 1979. *The Legionary Bath-House and Forum and Basilica at Exeter.* Exeter.

——1991. Late Roman barracks in Britain. In V. A. Maxfield and M. J. Dobson (eds), *Roman Frontier Studies 1989.* Exeter, 9–15.

Biggins, J. A., Biggins, J. et al. 1997. Survey of the prehistoric settlement at Gardener's House Farm, Dinnington. *Durham Archaeological Journal,* 13, 43–53.

Bird, D. G. 1987. The Romano-British period in Surrey. In J. Bird and D. G. Bird (eds), *The Archaeology of Surrey to 1540.* Guildford, 165–96.

Bird, J., Hassall, M. W. C. and Sheldon, H. (eds) 1996. *Interpreting Roman London: Papers in Memory of Hugh Chapman.* Oxford.

Birley, A. R. 1979. *The People of Roman Britain.* London.

——1981. *The Fasti of Roman Britain.* Oxford.

——1988. *The People of Roman Britain.* London. [First published in 1979.]

——1997. *Hadrian: The Restless Emperor.* London.

——2001. The Anavionenses. In N. J. Higham (ed.), *Archaeology of the Roman Empire: A Tribute to the Life and Works of Professor Barri Jones.* BAR (International Series) 940. Oxford, 15–24.

——2002. *Garrison Life at Vindolanda: A Band of Brothers.* Stroud.

Birley, E. 1961. *Research on Hadrian's Wall.* Kendal.

——1986. The deities of Roman Britain. In W. Haase (ed.), *Principat.* vol. 18. *Religion. Aufstieg und Niedergang der Römischen Welt.* Berlin, 3–112.

Birley, R. 1990. *The Roman Documents from Vindolanda.* Newcastle upon Tyne.

Bishop, M. (ed.) 2002. *Roman Inveresk: Past, Present and Future.* Duns.

Bishop, M. C. 1991. Soldiers and military equipment in the towns of Roman Britain. In V. A. Maxfield and M. J. Dobson (eds), *Roman Frontier Studies 1989.* Exeter, 21–7.

Bishop, M. C. and Coulston, J. C. N. 1989. *Roman Military Equipment.* Princes Risborough.

——1993. *Roman Military Equipment.* London.

Black, E. W. 1986. Romano-British burial customs and religious beliefs in south-east England. *Archaeological Journal,* 143, 203–4.

——1987. *The Roman Villas of South-East England.* BAR (British Series) 171. Oxford.

Blagg, T. F. C. 1982. Roman Kent. In P. Leach (ed.), *Archaeology in Kent to AD 1500.* CBA Research Report 48. London, 51–60.

——1989. Art and Architecture. In M. Todd (ed.), *Research on Roman Britain 1960–89.* Britannia Monograph Series 11. London, 203–18.

——1991. Buildings. In R. F. J. Jones (ed.), *The Defences of the Lower City.* Archaeology of Lincoln 7.2. Lincoln, 3–14.

——2001. *Roman Architectural Ornament in Britain.* BAR (British Series) 329. Oxford.

Blockley, K., Ashmore F. and Ashmore, P. J. 1993. Excavations on the Roman Fort at Abergavenny, Orchard Site, 1972–73. *Archaeological Journal*, 150, 169–242.

Bloemers, T. 1989. Acculturation in the Rhine/Meuse Basin in the Roman period. In J. Barrett, A. Fitzpatrick and L. Macinnes (eds), *Barbarians and Romans in North-West Europe*. BAR (International Series) 471. Oxford, 175–97.

Bogaers, J. E. 1979. King Cogidubnus in Chichester: another reading of RIB 91. *Britannia*, 10, 243–54.

Böhme, Astrid. 1985. Tracht und Bestattungssitten in den germanischen Provinzen und der Belgica. In H. Temporini and W. Haase (eds), *Aufstieg und Niedergang der Römischen Welt*, vol. II, 12, 3. Berlin and New York, 423–55.

Böhme-Schönberger, Astrid. 1997. *Kleidung und Schmuck in Rom und den Provinzen*. Aalen.

Boon, G. C. 1972. *Isca: The Roman Legionary Fortress at Caerleon, Monmouthshire*. Cardiff.

—— 1974. *Silchester. The Roman Town of Calleva*. Newton Abbot.

—— 1977. A Graeco-Roman anchor stock from North Wales. *Antiquaries Journal*, 57, 10–30.

—— 1987. *The Legionary Fortress of Caerleon-Isca*. Cardiff.

Booth, P. 1996. Warwickshire in the Roman period: a review of recent work. *Transactions of the Birmingham and Warwickshire Archaeological Society*, 100, 25–58.

Boudet, R. 1988. Iberian type brooches [from Mount Batten, Plymouth]. In B. Cunliffe, *Mount Batten, Plymouth*. Oxford, 64.

Bourn, R., Hunn, J. R. and Symonds, J. 2000. Besthorpe Quarry, Collingham, Nottinghamshire: a multi-period occupation site. In R. Zeepvat (ed.), *Three Iron Age and Romano-British Settlements on English Gravels*. BAR (British Series) 312. Oxford, 71–117.

Bowden, M. 1996. Recent archaeological fieldwork in the Howgill Fells. *Transactions of the Cumberland and Westmorland Antiquarian and Archaeological Society*, 86, 1–11.

Bowen, H. C. and Fowler, P. J. 1966. Romano-British rural settlements in Dorset and Wiltshire. In C. Thomas (ed.), *Rural Settlement in Roman Britain*. London, 43–67.

Bowman, A. K. 1994. *Life and Letters on the Roman Frontier: Vindolanda and its People*. London.

—— 1998. *Life and Letters on Hadrian's Wall*. London.

Bowman, A. K. and Thomas, J. D. 1983. *Vindolanda: The Latin Writing Tablets*. Britannia Monograph 4. London.

—— 1991. A military strength report from Vindolanda. *Journal of Roman Studies*, 81, 62–73.

—— 1994. *The Vindolanda Writing-Tablets (Tabulae Vindolandenses II)*. London.

—— 1996. New writing tablets from Vindolanda. *Britannia*, 27, 299–328.

Boyd, W. E. 1984. Environmental change and Iron Age land management in the area of the Antonine Wall. *Glasgow Archaeological Journal*, 11, 75–81.

—— 1988. Cereals in Scottish antiquity. *Circaea*, 5.2, 101–10.

Boylston, A. and Roberts, C. A. 2000. The Roman inhumations. In M. Dawson, *Archaeology in the Bedford Region*. Bedfordshire Archaeological Monograph 4. Bedford, 309–36.

Branigan, K. 1971. *Latimer: Belgic, Roman, Dark Age and Early Modern Farm*. Bristol.

—— 1976a. *The Roman Villa in South-West England*. Bradford-on-Avon.

—— 1976b. Villa settlement in the West Country. In K. Branigan and P. Fowler (eds), *The Roman West Country: Classical Culture and Celtic Society*. London, 120–41.

—— 1977. *Gatcombe Roman Villa*. BAR (British Series) 44. Oxford.

—— 1985. *The Catuvellauni*. Gloucester.

—— 1989. Villas in the North. In K. Branigan (ed.), *Rome and the Brigantes: The Impact of Rome on Northern England*. Sheffield, 18–27.

Branigan, K. and Dearne, M. 1992. *Romano-British Cavemen*. Oxbow Monograph 19. Oxford.

Branigan, K. and Fowler, P. (eds) 1976. *The Roman West Country*. Newton Abbot.

Branigan, K. and Miles, D. (eds) 1988. *The Economies of Romano-British Villas*. Sheffield.

Breeze, D. J. 1981. Agricola the Builder. In J. Kenworthy (ed.), *Agricola's Campaigns in Scotland*. Scottish Archaeological Forum 127. Edinburgh, 14–24.

—— 1989 The impact of the Roman army on north Britain. In J. C. Barrett, A. P. Fitzpatrick and L. Macinnes (eds), *Barbarians and Romans in North-west Europe from the Later Republic to Late Antiquity*. BAR (International Series) 471. Oxford, 227–34.

—— 1989. *The Second Augustan Legion in North Britain. The Second Annual Caerleon Lecture*. Cardiff.

—— 1990. The impact of the Roman army on the native peoples of northern Britain. In H. Vetters and M. Kandler (eds), *Der Römische Limes in Österreich*. Akten des 14 Internationalen Limeskongresses 1986 in Carnuntum 1986. Vienna, 85–97.

—— 1996. *Roman Scotland*. London.

—— 1997. The regiments stationed at Maryport and their commanders. In R. J. A. Wilson (ed.), *Roman Maryport and its Setting: Essays in Memory of Michael G. Jarrett*. Maryport, 67–9.

—— 2001. The edge of the world: the imperial frontier and beyond. In P. Salway (ed.), *The Short Oxford History of the British Isles: The Roman Era*. Oxford, 173–202.

Breeze, D. J. and Dobson, B. 1985. Roman military deployment in northern England. *Britannia*, 16, 1–20.

—— 2000. *Hadrian's Wall*, 4th edn. London.

Breeze, D. J. and Hill, P. R. 2002. Hadrian's Wall began here. *Archaeologia Aeliana*, 5th ser. 29, 1–2.

Breeze, D. J. and Ritchie, J. N. G. 1980. A Roman burial at High Torrs, Luce Sands, Wigtownshire. *Transactions of the Dumfriesshire and Galloway Natural History and Archaeological Society*, 55, 77–85.

Breeze, D. J., Close-Brooks, J. and Ritchie, J. N. G. 1976. Soldiers' burials at Camelon, Stirlingshire. *Britannia*, 7, 73–95.

Brewer, R. J. 1993. *Caerwent Roman Town*. Cardiff.

—— 1993. Venta Silurum: a civitas capital. In S. J. Greep (ed.), *Roman Towns: The Wheeler Inheritance*. London, 56–65.

—— 2000. Caerleon and the archaeologists: changing ideas on the Roman fortress. *Monmouthshire Antiquary*, 17, 9–33.

Brewer, R. J. and Guest, P. 2001. Caerwent: *Venta Silurum*. *Current Archaeology*, 174, 232–40.

Brigham, T. 1990. The late Roman waterfront in London. *Britannia*, 21, 99–183.

—— 1998. The port of Roman London. In B. Watson, *Roman London: Recent Archaeological Work*. Portsmouth, 23–34.

Britnell, J. E., Cool, H. E. M., Davies, J. L., Manning, W. H. and Walters, M. J. 1999. Recent discoveries in the vicinity of Castell Collen Roman Fort, Radnorshire. *Studia Celtica*, 33, 33–90.

Brothwell, D. R. and Blake, M. L. 1966. The human remains from the Fussell's Lodge long barrow: their morphology, discontinuous traits and pathology. In P. Ashbee, Fussell's Lodge long barrow excavations 1957. *Archaeologia*, 100, 48–63.

Brown, J. 1999. *Romano-British Villa Complex: Chapel House Farm, Dalton on Tees, North Yorkshire*. York.

Brown, S. and Holbrook, N. 1989. A Roman site at Otterton Point. *Proceedings of the Devon Archaeological Society*, 47, 29–42.

Browne, D. M. 1977. *Roman Cambridgeshire*. Cambridge.

Brück, J. and Goodman, M. 1999. Introduction: themes for a critical archaeology of prehistoric settlement. In J. Brück and M. Goodman (eds), *Making Places in the Prehistoric World: Themes in Settlement Archaeology*. London, 1–19.

Brunt, P. A. 1963 Review of H. D. Meyer, *Die Aussenpolitik des Augustus und die augusteische Dichtung* (Cologne 1961). *Journal of Roman Studies*, 53, 170–6.

Buikstra, J. E. and Ubelaker, D. (eds) 1994. *Standards for Data Recording from Human Skeletal Remains*. Archeological Survey Research Seminar Series 44. Fayetteville, AR.

Burgers, A. 2001. *The Water Supplies and Related Structures of Roman Britain*. BAR (British Series) 324. Oxford.

Burleigh, G. 1984. Excavations at Baldock. *Herts Past*, 12, 1–18.

Burley, E. 1956. A catalogue and survey of the metal-work from Traprain Law. *Proceedings of the Society of Antiquaries of Scotland*, 89, 118–226.

Burnham, B. C. 1997. Roman mining at Dolaucothi: the implications of the 1991–3 excavations near the Carreg Pumsaint. *Britannia*, 28, 325–36.

Burnham, B. C. and Wacher, J. 1990. *The 'Small Towns' of Roman Britain*. London.

Burnham, B. C., Collis, J., Dobinson, C., Haselgrove, C. and Jones, M. J. 2001. Themes for urban research, *c*.100 BC to AD 200. In S. James and M. Millett (eds), *Britains and Romans*. CBA Research Report 125. London, 67–76.

Butler, S. 1989. Pollen analysis from the west rampart. In S. S. Frere and J. J. Wilkes, *Strageath: Excavations within the Roman Fort*. London, 272–4.

Camden, W. 1789. *Britannia*, ed. R. Gough. London. [First published in 1586.]

Cameron, A. 1985. *Procopius and the Sixth Century*. London.

Campbell, J. 1982. *The Anglo-Saxons*. London.

Carroll, M. 2001. *Romans, Celts and Germans: The German Provinces of Rome*. Stroud.

Carter, G. A. 1998. Excavations at the Orsett 'Cock' enclosure, Essex, 1976. *East Anglian Archaeology*, 86.

Caruana, I. 1989. Fieldwalking in the Solway Plain, 1983–84. *Transactions of the Cumberland and Westmorland Antiquarian and Archaeological Society*, 89, 51–68.

—— 1997. Maryport and the Flavian conquest of North Britian. In R. J. A. Wilson, *Roman Maryport and its Setting: Essays in Memory of Michael G. Jarrett*. Carlisle, 40–51.

Casey, J. 1994. *Carausius and Allectus*. London.

Casey, J. C. (ed.) 1979. *The End of Roman Britain*. BAR (British Series) 71. Oxford.

Casey, P. J. and Davies, J. L., with Evans, J. 1993. *Excavations at Segontium (Caernarfon) Roman Fort, 1975–79*. London.

Casey, P. J. and Hoffmann, B. 1995. Excavations at Alstone Cottage, Caerleon, 1970. *Britannia*, 26, 63–106.

Cassius Dio. 1898–1931. *Cassius Dio*. ed. U. P. Boissevin. 5 vols. Berlin.

Champion, T. 1995. Power, politics and status. In M. J. Green (ed.), *The Celtic World*. London, 85–94.

Champion, T. C. and Collis, J. R. (eds) 1996. *The Iron Age in Britain and Ireland: Recent Trends*. Sheffield.

Chaplin, R. E. and Barnetson, L. P. 1980. Animal bones. In I. M. Stead (ed.), *Rudston Roman Villa*. York, 149–55.

Chaplin, R. E. and McCormick, F. 1998. The animal bones. In I. M. Stead and V. Rigby (eds), *Baldock: The Excavation of a Roman and Pre-Roman Settlement 1968–72*. London, 396–415.

Chapman, J. and Smith, S. 1988. Finds from a Roman well in Staines. *London Archaeologist*, 16, 3–6.

Christie, P. M. 1978. The excavation of an Iron Age souterrain and settlement at Carn Euny, Sancreed, Cornwall. *Proceedings of the Prehistoric Society*, 44, 309–433.

Clarke, A. and Fulford, M. 2002. Silchester, a crowded late Roman city. *Current Archaeology*, 177, 364–9.

Clarke, D. L. 1972. A provisional model of an Iron Age society and its settlement system. In D. L. Clarke (ed.), *Models in Archaeology*. London, 801–69.

Clarke, S. 1999. Contact, architectural symbolism and the negotiation of cultural identity in the military zone. In P. Barker, C. Forcey, S. Jundi and R. Witcher (eds), *TRAC 98*. Oxford, 36–45.

Clarke, S. and Wise, A. 1998. *Liliesleaf North 1998. Interim report.* [Privately published.]

Clarke, S., Jackson, R. and Jackson, P. 1992. Archaeological evidence for Monmouth's Roman and early medieval defences. *Archaeology in Wales*, 32, 1–2.

Clauss, M. 2000. *The Roman Cult of Mithras: The God and his Mysteries.* Edinburgh.

Cleere, H. 1989. The Classis Britannica. In V. A. Maxfield (ed.), *The Saxon Shore.* Exeter, 18–22.

Cleere, H. and Crossley, D. 1986. *The Iron Industry of the Weald.* Leicester.

Coles, J. M. and Minnitt, S. 1995. *Industrious and Fairly Civilised: The Glastonbury Lake Village.* Taunton.

Collens, J. 1999. Flying on the edge: aerial photography and settlement patterns in Cheshire and Merseyside. In M. Nevell (ed.), *Living on the Edge of Empire.* Manchester, 36–40.

Collingwood, R. G. and Myres, J. N. L. 1936. *Roman Britain and the English Settlements.* The Oxford History of England, volume 1. Oxford.

Collingwood, R. G. and Wright, R. (eds) 1965. *Roman Inscriptions in Britain I: Inscriptions on Stone.* Oxford.

Collingwood Bruce, J. 1863. *The Wallet-Book of the Roman Wall.* London.

—— *The Roman Wall*, 3rd edn. London. [First published in 1851.]

—— 1875. *Lapidarium Septentrionale: or, A Description of the Monuments of Roman Rule in the North of England.* London.

Collis, J. R. 1994. The Iron Age. In B. Vyner (ed.), *Building the Past.* London, 123–48.

—— 1994: The Iron Age and Roman cemetery at Owslebury, Hampshire. In A. P. Fitzpatrick and E. Morris (eds), *The Iron Age in Wessex: Recent Work.* Salisbury, 106–8.

—— 1996. Hillforts, enclosures and boundaries. In T. C. Champion and J. R. Collis (eds), *The Iron Age in Britain and Ireland.* Sheffield, 87–94.

Colt Hoare, R. 1812–21. *Ancient History of North and South Wiltshire.* 2 vols. London.

—— 1822–44. *History of Modern Wiltshire.* 6 vols. London.

Conheeney, J. 2000. The inhumation burials. In B. E. Barber and D. Bowsher, *The Eastern Roman Cemetery of Roman London: Excavations 1983–1990.* Museum of London Archaeological Services Monograph 4. London, 277–96.

Cooke, C. and Rowbotham, T. C. 1958. A craniometric and dental investigation of 301 Romano-British skulls and jaws circa AD 150. *Journal of Dental Research*, 37, 753.

Cool, H. E. M. 2000a. The parts left over: material culture into the fifth century. In T. Wilmott and P. Wilson (eds), *The Late Roman Transition in the North.* BAR (British Series) 299. Oxford.

—— 2000b. The significance of snake jewellery hoards. *Britannia*, 31, 29–40.

Corbier, M. 1989. The ambiguous status of meat in ancient Rome. *Food and Foodways*, 3, 223–64.

Corney, M. 2000. Characterising the landscape of Roman Britain: a review of the study of Roman Britain 1975–2000. In D. Hooke (ed.), *Landscape, The Richest Historical Record.* Amesbury.

Cosh, S. R. 2001. Seasonal dining-rooms in Romano-British houses. *Britannia*, 32, 219–42.

Cotterill, J. 1993. Saxon raiding and the role of the Late Roman coastal forts of Britain. *Britannia*, 24, 227–39.

Cotton, J., Mills, J. and Clegg, G. 1986. *Archaeology in West Middlesex.* Uxbridge.

Cox, M. 2000. Ageing adults from the skeleton. In M. Cox and S. Mays (eds), *Human Osteology in Archaeology and Forensic Science.* London, 61–81.

Cox, P. W. and Hearne, C. M. 1991. *Redeemed from the Heath: The Archaeology of the Wytch Farm Oilfield 1987–90.* Dorchester.

Crawford Adams, J. 1983. *Outline of Fractures.* Edinburgh.

Creighton, J. 2000. *Coins and Power in Late Iron Age Britain.* Cambridge.

Creighton, J. D. and Wilson, R. J. A. (eds) 1999. *Roman Germany: Studies in Cultural Interaction*. Journal of Roman Archaeology, Supplementary Series 32. Portsmouth, RI.

Croom, A. T. 1994. Small finds. In M. E. Snape, An excavation in the Roman cemetery at South Shields. *Archaeologia Aeliana*, 5th ser. 22, 43–66.

—— 2000. *Roman Clothing and Fashion*. Stroud.

Crow, J. G. 1986. The function of Hadrian's Wall and the comparative evidence of late Roman long walls. In *Studien zur Militärgrenzen Roms III (13 Internationaler Limes Kongress Aalen 1983)*. Stuttgart, 724–9.

—— 1991. A review of current research on the turrets and curtain of Hadrian's Wall. *Britannia*, 22, 51–63.

—— 1995. *English Heritage Book of Housesteads*. London.

Crummy, P. J. 1985. Colchester: the mechanics of laying out a town. In F. Grew and B. Hobley (eds), *Roman Urban Topography in Britain and the Western Empire*. CBA Research Report 59. London, 78–85.

—— 1995. Late Iron Age burials at Stanway, Colchester. In J. Swaddling, S. Walker, and P. Roberts (eds), *Italy and Europe: Economic Relations 700 BC–AD 50*. British Museum Occasional Paper 97. London, 264–6.

—— 1997. *City of Victory: The Story of Colchester – Britain's First Roman Town*. Colchester.

—— 1999. Colchester: making towns out of fortresses and the first urban fortifications in Britain. In H. R. Hurst (ed.), *The* Coloniae *of Roman Britain*. Journal of Roman Archaeology, Supplementary Series 36. Portsmouth, RI, 88–100.

Cunliffe, B. 1972. The Late Iron Age metalwork from Bulbury, Dorset. *Antiquaries Journal*, 52, 293–308.

—— 1973. *The Regni*. London.

—— 1977. The Romano-British village at Chalton, Hants. *Proceedings of the Hampshire Field Club and Archaeological Society*, 33, 45–67.

—— 1982. Britain, the Veneti and beyond. *Oxford Journal of Archaeology*, 1, 39–68.

—— 1984. Relations between Britain and Gaul in the first century BC and early first century AD. In S. Macready and F. H.Thompson (eds), *Cross-Channel Trade*. London, 3–23.

—— 1984. *Roman Bath Discovered*. London.

—— 1984. Iron Age Wessex: continuity and change. In B. Cunliffe and D. Miles (eds), *Aspects of the Iron Age in Central Southern Britain*. Oxford University Committee for Archaeology Monograph 2. Oxford, 12–45.

—— 1987a. *Hengistbury Head, Dorset*. Volume 1. *The Prehistoric and Roman Settlement, 3500 BC–AD 500*. Oxford.

—— 1987b. The Iron Age fineware import [from Poundbury, Dorset]. In C. S. Green, *Excavations at Poundbury*. Volume 1. *The Settlements*. Dorchester, 117, mf B13–14.

—— 1988. *Mount Batten, Plymouth: A Prehistoric and Roman Port*. Oxford.

—— 1988. *The Temple of Sulis Minerva at Bath. 2. The Finds from the Sacred Spring*. Oxford University Committee for Archaeology 16. Oxford.

—— 1988. Romney Marsh in the Roman period. In J. Eddison and C. Green (eds), *Romney Marsh: Evolution, Occupation, Reclamation*. Oxford University Committee for Archaeology Monograph 24. Oxford, 83–7.

—— 1990. Social and economic contacts between Western France and Britain in the Early and Middle La Tène Period. In *La Bretagne et l'Europe préhistorique (Revue Archéologique de l'Ouest: Supplément 2)*, 245–51.

—— 1991. *Iron Age Communities in Britain: An Account of England, Scotland and Wales from the Seventh Century BC until the Roman Conquest*, 3rd edn. London and New York.

—— 1993. *Wessex to AD 1000*. Harlow.

Cunliffe, B. 1994. *The Danebury Environs Project, 6. Houghton Down: Excavation 1994, Interim Report.* Oxford.

—— 1995. *Roman Bath.* London.

—— 1996. Guernsey and the Channel Islands in the first millennium BC. In B. Burns, B. Cunliffe and H. Sebire, *Guernsey: An Island Community of the Atlantic Iron Age.* Oxford, 125–7.

—— 1997. Armorica and Britain: the ceramic evidence. In B. Cunliffe and P. de Jersey, *Armorica and Britain.* Oxford, 2–71.

—— 2000. *Roman Bath Discovered.* 2nd edn. Stroud.

—— 2001. *Facing the Ocean: The Atlantic and its Peoples 8000 BC–AD 1500.* Oxford.

—— 2001. *The Extraordinary Voyage of Pytheas the Greek.* London.

Cunliffe, B. W. (ed.) 1968. *Fifth Report on the Excavations of the Roman Fort at Richborough, Kent.* Oxford

—— 1971. *Excavations at Fishbourne, 1961–9.* Society of Antiquaries Research Report 26. Leeds.

Cunliffe, B. and Davenport, P. 1985. *The Temple of Sulis Minerva at Bath. I. The Site.* Oxford University Committee for Archaeology 7. Oxford.

Cunliffe, B. and de Jersey, P. 1997. *Armorica and Britain: Cross-Channel Relationships in the Late First Millennium BC.* Oxford.

Cuppage, J. et al. 1986. *Archaeological Survey of the Dingle Peninsula.* Ballyferiter.

Curle, J. 1911. *A Roman Frontier Post and its People: The Fort of Newstead in the Parish of Melrose.* Glasgow.

Daniels, C. M. 1978. *Handbook to the Roman Wall,* 13th edn. Newcastle upon Tyne.

Dark, K. 1994. *Civitas to Kingdom: British Political Continuity 300–800.* Leicester.

—— 2000. *Britain and the End of the Roman Empire.* Stroud.

Dark, K. and Dark, P. 1997. *The Landscape of Roman Britain.* Stroud.

Dark, P. 1999. Pollen evidence for the environment of Roman Britain. *Britannia,* 30, 247–72.

—— 2000. *The Environment of Britain in the First Millennium AD.* London.

Darling, M. J. with Gurney, D. 1993. *Caister-on-Sea: Excavations by Charles Green 1951–1955.* East Anglian Archaeology 60. Dereham.

Darling, M. J. and Jones, M. J. 1988. Early settlement at Lincoln. *Britannia,* 19, 1–57.

Darvill, T. 1987. *Prehistoric Britain.* London.

Davidson, D. and Carter, S. 1997. Soils and their evolution. In K. Edwards and I. Ralston (eds), *Scotland: Environment and Archaeology, 8000 BC–AD 1000.* Chichester, 45–62.

Davies, J. A. 1996. Where eagles dare: the Iron Age of Norfolk. *Proceedings of the Prehistoric Society,* 62, 63–92.

Davies, J. L. 1986. Carreg y Bwci: a Roman watch-tower? *Archaeologia Cambrensis,* 135, 147–53.

—— 1990. Military *vici*: recent research and its significance. In B. C. Burnham and J. L. Davies (eds), *Conquest, Coexistence and Change: Recent Work in Roman Wales.* Trivium 25. Lampeter, 65–74.

—— 1991. Roman military deployment in Wales and the Marches from Pius to Theodosius I. In V. A. Maxfield and M. J. Dobson (eds), *Roman Frontier Studies 1989. Proceedings of the XVth International Congress of Roman Frontier Studies.* Exeter, 52–7.

—— 1994. The Roman period. In J. L. Davies and D. P. Kirby (eds), *Cardiganshire County History.* Volume I. Cardiff, 275–317.

—— 1997. Native producers and Roman consumers: the mechanisms of military supply in Wales from Claudius to Theodosius. In W. Groenman-van Waateringe, B. L. van Beek, W. J. H. Willems and S. L. Wynia (eds), *Roman Frontier Studies 1995. Proceedings of the XVIth International Congress of Roman Frontier Studies.* Oxford, 267–72.

Davies, J. L. and Jones, R. H. (forthcoming). Recent research on Roman camps in Wales. In *Roman Frontier Studies 2001*. Papers presented to the 18th International Congress of Roman Frontier Studies.

Davies, R. W. 1971. The Roman military diet. *Britannia*, 2, 122–42.

—— 1989. *Service in the Roman Army*. Edinburgh.

Davis, C. 1884. *The Excavations of the Roman Baths at Bath*. Bath.

Davis, S. 1987. *The Archaeology of Animals*. London.

Dawson, M. 2000a. The Ouse Valley in the Iron Age and Roman periods: a landscape in transition. In M. Dawson (ed.), *Prehistoric, Roman and Post-Roman Landscapes of the Great Ouse Valley*. CBA Research Report 119. York, 107–30.

—— 2000b. *Iron Age and Roman Settlement on the Stagsden Bypass*. Bedfordshire Archaeological Monograph 3. Bedford.

de Jersey, P. 1997. Armorica and Britain: the numismatic evidence. In B. Cunliffe and P. de Jersey, *Armorica and Britain*. Oxford, 72–103.

de la Bedoyère, G. 1992. *Roman Towns in Britain*. London.

—— 1993. *Roman Villas and the Countryside*. London.

—— 1999. *The Golden Age of Roman Britain*. Stroud.

Delaine, J. and Johnston, D. E. (eds) 1999. *Roman Baths and Bathing*. Journal of Roman Archaeology, Supplementary Series 37. Portsmouth, RI.

Derks, Ton. 1998. *Gods, Temples and Ritual Practices*. Amsterdam.

Dessau, H. (ed.) 1892–1916. *Inscriptiones Latinae Selectae*. 3 vols. Berlin.

Detsicas, A. 1983. *The Cantiaci*. Gloucester.

Dixon, S. 1988. *The Roman Mother*. London.

Dobney, K. M. 2001. A place at the table; the role of vertebrate zooarchaeology within a Roman research agenda. In S. James and M. Millett (eds), *Britons and Romans: Advancing an Archaeological Agenda*. CBA Research Report 125. York, 36–45.

Dobney, K. M., Hall, A. and Kenward, H. 1999. It's all garbage . . . A review of bioarchaeology in the four English *colonia* towns. In H. R. Hurst (ed.), *The* Coloniae *of Roman Britain*. Journal of Roman Archaeology, Supplementary Series 36. Portsmouth, RI, 15–35.

Dobney, K. M. and Jaques, S. D. 1996. The mammal bone. In R. J. Williams, P. J. Hart and A. T. L. Williams (eds), *Wavedon Gate: A Late Iron Age and Roman Rural Settlement in Milton Keynes*, Buckinghamshire Archaeological Society, Monograph Series 10. Aylesbury, 203–33.

Dobney, K. M., Jaques, S. D. and Irving, B. G. 1996. *Of Butchers and Breeds: Report on Vertebrate Remains from Various Sites in the City of Lincoln*. Lincoln Archaeological Studies 5. Lincoln.

Downey, R., King, A. and Soffe, G. 1980. The Hayling Island temple and religious connections across the Channel. In W. Rodwell (ed.), *Temples, Churches and Religion in Roman Britain*. BAR (British Series) 77. Oxford, 289–304.

Drewett, P., Rudling, D. and Gardiner, M. 1988. *The South East to AD 1000*. Harlow.

Drinkwater, J. F. 1983. *Roman Gaul*. London.

—— 1987. Urbanisation in Italy and the Western Empire. In J. S. Wacher (ed.), *The Roman World*. London, 345–87.

—— 2000. Review of Ton Derks, *Gods, Temples and Ritual Practices. The Transformation of Religious Ideas and Values in Roman Gaul*, 1998. *Britannia*, 31, 458–9.

Driscoll, S. T. and Yeoman, P. A. 1997. *Excavation within Edinburgh Castle in 1988–91*. Society of Antiquaries Monograph 12. Edinburgh.

Drury, P. J. and Rodwell, W. 1980. Settlement in the Later Iron Age and Roman periods. In D. G. Buckley (ed.), *Archaeology in Essex to AD 1500*. CBA Research Report 34. London.

Dryden, H. 1845. Roman and Romano-British remains at and near Shefford, Co. Beds. *Proceedings of the Cambridgeshire Antiquaries' Society*, 1, no. 8.

Dumayne, L. 1994. The effect of the Roman occupation on the environment of Hadrian's Wall: a pollen diagram from Fozy Moss, Northumbria. *Britannia*, 25, 217–24.

Dumayne-Peaty, L. 1998. Human impact on the environment during the Iron Age and Romano-British times: palynological evidence from three sites near the Antonine Wall, Great Britain. *Journal of Archaeological Science*, 25, 203–14.

Dumville, D. N. 1993. *Saint Patrick A.D. 493–1993*. Woodbridge.

Dungworth, D. 1997. Copper metallurgy in Iron Age Britain: some recent research. In A. Gwilt and C. C. Haselgrove (eds), *Reconstructing Iron Age Societies: New Approaches to the British Iron Age*. Oxford, 46–50.

Dunnett, R. 1975. *The Trinovantes*. London.

Dunning, G., Hooley, W. and Tildesley, M. 1929. Excavation of an Early Iron Age village on Worthy Down, Winchester. *Proceedings of the Hampshire Field Club and Archaeological Society*, 10, 178–92.

Dunwell, A. 1999. Edin's Hall fort, broch and settlement, Berwickshire (Scottish Borders). *Proceedings of the Society of Antiquaries of Scotland*, 129, 303–58.

Durham University. 2000. *Quarry Farm, Ingleby Barwick, Stockton-on-Tees*. Archaeological Services, University of Durham.

Duval, P.-M. 1976. *Les Dieux de la Gaule*. Paris.

Edwards, K. and Whittington, G. 1997. Vegetational changes. In K. Edwards and I. Ralston (eds), *Scotland: Environment and Archaeology, 8000 BC–AD 1000*. Chichester, 63–82.

Edwards, K. J. and Ralston, I. (eds) 1997. *Scotland: Environment and Archaeology, 8000 BC–AD 1000*. Chichester.

Ehrenberg, M. 1989. *Women in Prehistory*. London.

Ellis, S. 2000. *Roman Housing*. London.

Emery, G. T. 1963. Dental pathology and archaeology. *Antiquity*, 37, 274–81.

Entwhistle, R., Fulford, M. and Raymond, F. 1993. *Salisbury Plain Project 1992–93 Interim Report*. Reading.

Erdrich, M., Giannotta, K. M. and Hanson, W. S. 2000. Traprain Law: native and Roman on the northern frontier. *Proceedings of the Society of Antiquaries of Scotland*, 130, 441–56.

Esmonde Cleary, A. S. 1989. *The Ending of Roman Britain*. London.

—— 1999. Roman Britain: civilian and rural society. In J. R. Hunter and I. Ralston (eds), *Archaeology of Britain: An Introduction from the Upper Palaeolithic to the Industrial Revolution*. London, 157–75.

—— 2001. The Roman to medieval transition. In S. James and M. Millett (eds), *Britons and Romans*. CBA Research Report 125. London, 90–7.

Eutropius. 1999. *Breviarium*, ed. J. Mellegovarc'h. Paris.

Evans, A. J. 1890. On a Late-Celtic urn-field of Aylesford, Kent. *Archaeologia*, 52, 315–88.

Evans, D. R. and Metcalf, V. M. *Roman Gates at Caerleon*. Oxford.

Evans, E. 2000. *The Caerleon Canabae. Excavations in the Civil Settlement 1984–90*. London.

Evans, J. 2001. Material approaches to the identification of different Romano-British site types. In S. James and M. Millett (eds), *Britons and Romans*. CBA Research Report 125. London, 26–35.

Ezzati, M. and Kammen, D. 2001. Indoor air pollution from biomass combustion and acute respiratory disease in Kenya: an exposure-response study. *Lancet*, 358 (9282), 619–20.

Farwell, D. E., Molleson, T. and Ellison, A. 1993. *Poundbury. Volume 2. The Cemeteries*. Dorset Natural History and Archaeological Society, Monograph Series 11. Dorchester.

Fasham, P. 1985. *The Prehistoric Settlement at Winnall Down, Winchester*. Stroud.

Faulkner, N. 1996. Verulamium: interpreting decline. *Archaeological Journal*, 153, 79–103.

—— 2000 *The Decline and Fall of Roman Britain*. Stroud.

Ferrell, G. 1997. Space and society in the Iron Age of north-east England. In A. Gwilt and C. C. Haselgrove (eds), *Reconstructing Iron Age Societies*. Oxford, 228–38.

Fishwick, D. 1972. Templum Divo Claudio Constitutum. *Britannia*, 3, 164–81.

Fitts, R. L, Haselgrove, C., Lowther, P. C. and Willis, S. H. 1999. Melsonby reconsidered: survey and excavations 1992–5 at the site of the discovery of the 'Stanwick' North Yorkshire Hoard of 1843. *Durham Archaeological Journal*, 14–15, 1–52.

Fitzpatrick, A. P. 1985. The distribution of Dressel 1 amphorae in north-west Europe. *Oxford Journal of Archaeology*, 4, 305–40.

—— 1991. Poole harbour and Hengistbury Head. In P. W. Cox and C. M. Hearne, *Redeemed from the Heath*. Dorchester, 230–1.

—— 1991. Death in a material world. The Late Iron Age and early Romano-British cemetery at King Harry Lane cemetery, St Albans, Hertfordshire. *Britannia* 23, 323–7.

—— 1992. The roles of Celtic coinage in south-east England. In M. Mays (ed.), *Celtic Coinage: Britain and Beyond; The Eleventh Oxford Symposium on Coinage and Monetary History*. British Archaeological Reports 222. Oxford, 1–32.

—— 1997. Everyday life in Iron Age Wessex. In A. Gwilt and C. C. Haselgrove (eds), *Reconstructing Iron Age Societies*. Oxford, 73–86.

—— 1997a. *Archaeological Excavations on the Route of the A27, Westhampnett Bypass, West Sussex*. Volume 2. *The Cemeteries*. Wessex Archaeological Report 12. Salisbury.

—— 1997b. A 1st-century AD 'Durotrigian' inhumation burial with a decorated Iron Age mirror from Portesham, Dorset. *Proceedings of the Dorset Natural History and Archaeological Society*, 118, 51–70.

—— 2000. Ritual, sequence and structure in Late Iron Age mortuary practices in north-west Europe. In J. Pearce, M. Millett and M. Struck (eds), *Burial, Society and Context in the Roman World*. Oxford, 15–29.

Fitzpatrick, A. P., Butterworth, C. and Grove, J. 1999. *Prehistoric and Roman Sites in East Devon: The A30 Honiton to Exeter Improvement DBFO, 1996–9* Volume 2. *Romano-British Sites*. Wessex Archaeology Monograph 16. Salisbury.

Forcey, C. 1998. Whatever happened to the heroes? In *Theoretical Roman Archaeology Conference Proceedings 1997*. Oxford, 87–98.

Foster, J. 1986. *The Lexden Tumulus*. BAR (British Series) 156. Oxford.

Foster, S. 1989. Analysis of spatial patterns in buildings (gamma analysis) as an insight into social structure: examples from the Scottish Atlantic Iron Age. *Antiquity*, 63, 40–50.

Fowler, E. 1960. The origins and development of the penannular brooch in Europe. *Proceedings of the Prehistoric Society*, 26, 149–77.

Fowler, P. 1976. Farms and fields in the Roman West Country. In K. Branigan and P. Fowler (eds), *The Roman West Country*. Newton Abbot, 162–82.

Fowler, W. 1796–1818. *Engravings of the Principal Mosaic Pavements*. Winterton.

Fox, A. 1997. Tin ingots from Bigbury Bay. *Proceedings of the Devon Archaeological Society*, 53, 11–24.

Fox, A. and Ravenhill, W. 1972. The Roman Fort at Nanstallon, Cornwall. *Britannia*, 3, 56–111.

Frayn, J. 1995. The Roman meat trade. In J. Wilkins, D. Harvey and M. Dobson (eds), *Food in Antiquity*. Exeter, 107–14.

Freeth, C. M. 1999. *Dental Health in Cultural Biocultural perspective. The Prevalence, Pattern and Distribution of the Dental Diseases in British Archaeological Populations from Geographic, Demographic and Temporal Viewpoints*. Unpublished PhD thesis, University of Bradford.

Frere, S. S. 1977. Roman Britain in 1976. I. Sites explored. *Britannia*, 8, 356–425.

—— 1983. *Verulamium Excavations II*. London.

—— 1987a. *Britannia: A History of Roman Britain*, 3rd edn. London. [First published in 1967.]

—— 1987b. Brandon Camp, Herefordshire. *Britannia*, 19, 49–92.

—— 1987c. Roman Britain in 1986. I. Sites explored. *Britannia*, 18, 301–59.

Frere, S. S. 1988. Roman Britain in 1987. I. Sites explored. *Britannia*, 19, 416–84.

—— 1989. Roman Britain in 1988. I. Sites explored. *Britannia*, 20, 258–326.

—— 1991. Roman Britain in 1990. I. Sites explored. *Britannia*, 22, 222–92.

—— 1992. Roman Britain in 1991. I. Sites explored. *Britannia*, 23, 256–308.

Frere, S. S. and Fulford, M. 2001. The Roman invasion of AD 43. *Britannia*, 32, 45–56.

Frere, S. S. and St Joseph, J. K. S. 1974. The Roman fortress at Longthorpe. *Britannia*, 5, 1–129.

—— 1983. *Roman Britain from the Air.* Cambridge.

Frere, S. S. and Tomlin, R. S. O. (eds) 1992. *The Roman Inscriptions of Britain* II.4. Stroud.

Frere, S. S., Roxan, M. and Tomlin, R. S. O. (eds) 1990. *The Roman Inscriptions of Britain* II.1. Gloucester.

Friendship-Taylor, R. and Friendship-Taylor, D. (eds), 1997. *From Round House to Villa.* Hackleton.

Frodsham, P. 2000. Worlds without ends: towards a new prehistory for central Britain. In J. Harding and R. Johnston (eds), *Northern Pasts: Interpretations of the Later Prehistory of Northern England and Southern Scotland.* BAR (British Series) 302. Oxford, 15–31.

Fuentes, Nicholas. 1987. The Roman military tunic. In M. Dawson (ed.), *Roman Military Equipment: Proceedings of the 3rd Roman Military Equipment Research Seminar.* BAR S336. Oxford, 41–75.

Fulford, M. G. 1978. The interpretation of Britain's late Roman trade: the scope of medieval historical and archaeological analogy. In H. Cleere and J. du Plat Taylor (eds), *Roman Shipping and Trade: Britain and the Rhine Provinces.* London, 59–69.

—— 1982. Town and country in Roman Britain – a parasitical relationship? In D. Miles (ed.) *The Romano-British Countryside.* BAR (British Series) 103. Oxford, 403–19.

—— 1984. Demonstrating Britannia's economic independence in the first and second centuries. In T. F. C. Blagg and A. C. King (eds), *Military and Civilian in Roman Britain.* BAR (British Series) 136. Oxford, 129–42.

—— 1989. The economy of Roman Britain. In M. Todd (ed.), *Research on Roman Britain 1960–89.* Britannia Monograph 11. London, 175–201.

—— 1989. Roman and barbarian: the economy of Roman frontier systems. In J. C. Barrett, A. P. Fitzpatrick and L. Macinnes (eds), *Barbarians and Romans in North-west Europe from the Later Republic to Late Antiquity.* BAR (International Series) 471. Oxford, 81–95.

—— 1991. Britain and the Roman Empire: the evidence for regional and long distance trade. In R. F. J. Jones (ed.), *Roman Britain: Recent Trends.* Sheffield, 35–47.

—— 1992. Iron Age to Roman: a period of radical change on the gravels. In M. Fulford and E. Nichols (eds), *Developing Landscapes of Lowland Britain. The Archaeology of the British Gravels: A Review.* Society of Antiquaries Occasional Paper 14. London, 23–38.

—— 1999. Veteran settlement in late 1st-century Britain and the foundations of Gloucester and Lincoln. In H. Hurst (ed.) *The Coloniae of Roman Britain: New Studies and a Review.* Journal of Roman Archaeology, Supplementary Series 36. Portsmouth, RI, 177–80.

Fulford, M. G. and Allen, J. R. L. 1992. Iron-making at the Chesters Villa, Woolaston, Gloucestershire: survey and excavation 1987–91. *Britannia*, 23, 159–216.

Fulford, M. G. and Timby, J. 2000. *Late Iron Age and Roman Silchester: Excavations on the site of the Forum-Basilica 1977, 1980–86.* Britannia Monograph 15. London.

Gaffney, V. and Tingle, M. 1989. *The Maddle Farm Project.* BAR (British Series) 200. Oxford.

Gale, T. 1709. *Antonini Iter Britanniarum.* London.

Gallacher, D. B. and Clarke, A. 1993. Burials of possible Romano-British date from Inveresk, East Lothian. *Proceedings of the Society of Antiquaries of Scotland*, 123, 315–18.

Garbsch, J. G. 1965. *Die norisch-pannonische Frauentracht im 1. und 2. Jahrhundert.* Münchner Beiträge zur Vor- und Frühgeschichte 11. Munich.

Garbsch, J. G. 1985. Die norisch-pannonische Tracht. In H. Temporini and W. Haase (eds), *Aufstieg und Niedergang der Römischen Welt*, vol. II, 12, 3. Berlin and New York, 546–77.

Gardner, J. F. 1986. *Women in Roman Law and Society*. London.

Garwood, P., Jennings, D., Skeates, R. and Toms, J. (eds) 1991. *Sacred and Profane*. Oxford.

Gates, T. 1982. Farming on the frontier: Romano-British fields in Northumberland. In P. Clack and S. Haselgrove (eds), *Rural Settlement in the Roman North*. Durham, 21–42.

—— 1999. *The Hadrian's Wall Landscape from Chesters to Greenhead: An Air Photographic Survey*. Hexham.

Gee, R. 2001. *The Faunal Assemblage from Charterhouse on Mendip*. Unpublished thesis, Department of Archaeology, University of Durham.

Gidney, L. 1999. The animal bones. In A. Connor and R. Buckley (eds), *Roman and Medieval Occupation in Causeway Lane, Leicester*. Leicester, 310–29.

Giles, M. and Parker Pearson, M. 1999. Learning to live in the Iron Age; dwelling and praxis. In B. Bevan (ed.), *Northern Exposure*. Leicester, 217–31.

Gillam, J. P. 1974. The frontier after Hadrian: a history of the problem. *Archaeologia Aeliana*, 5th ser. 2, 1–12.

Goette, H. R. 1989. *Studien zu römischen Togadarstellungen*. Mainz.

Going, C. 1993. The Iron Age and the Roman period. In A. Clark *Excavations at Mucking*. Volume 1. *The Site Atlas*. English Heritage Archaeological Report 20. London, 19–21.

—— 1996. The Roman countryside. In O. Bedwin (ed.), *The Archaeology of Essex. Proceedings of the 1993 Writtle conference*. Chelmsford, 95–107.

Going, C. and Hunn, J. R. 1999. *Excavations at Boxfield Farm, Chells, Stevenage, Hertfordshire*. Hertfordshire Archaeology Trust Report 2. Hertford.

Goodburn, R. 1978. Roman Britain in 1977. I. Sites explored. *Britannia*, 9, 404–72.

—— 1978. Winterton: some villa problems. In M. Todd (ed.), *Studies in the Romano-British Villa*. Leicester, 93–101.

—— 1979. Roman Britain in 1978. I. Sites explored. *Britannia*, 10, 268–338.

Goodburn, R. and Bartholemew, P. (eds) 1976. *Aspects of the Notitia Dignitatum*. Oxford.

Goody, J. 1982. *Cooking, Cuisine and Class*. Cambridge.

Gordon, A. 1727. *Itinerarium Septentrionale: or, A Journey thro' most of the Counties of Scotland, and those in the North of England*. London.

Granger-Taylor, Hero. 1982. Weaving clothes to shape in the ancient world: the tunic and toga of the Arringatore. *Textile History*, 13, 3–25.

Grant, A. 1971. The animal bones. In B. W. Cunliffe (ed.), *Excavations at Fishbourne*. Volume II. *The Finds*. London, 377–88.

—— 1975. The animal bones. In B. W. Cunliffe (ed.), *Excavations at Portchester Castle*. Volume I. *Roman*. London, 378–408.

—— 1981. The significance of deer remains at occupation sites of the Iron Age to the Anglo-Saxon period. In M. Jones and G. Dimbleby (eds), *The Environment of Man, the Iron Age to the Anglo-Saxon Period*. BAR 87. Oxford, 205–13.

—— 1982. The use of toothwear as a guide to the age of domestic ungulates. In B. Wilson, C. Grigson and S. Payne (eds), *Ageing and Sexing Animal Bones from Archaeological Sites*. BAR (British Series) 109. Oxford, 91–108.

—— 1984a. The animal husbandry. In B. W. Cunliffe (ed.), *Danebury: An Iron Age Hillfort in Hampshire*. Volume 2. *The Excavations 1969–1978: The Finds*. London, 496–548.

—— 1984b. Survival or sacrifice: a critical appraisal of animal burials in Britain in the Iron Age. In J. Clutton-Brock and C. Grigson (eds), *Animals and Archaeology. 4. Husbandry in Europe*. BAR (International Series) 227. Oxford, 221–7.

—— 1989. Animals in Roman Britian. In M. Todd, (ed.), *Research on Roman Britain 1960–89*. London, 135–46.

Grant, A. 1991. The animal husbandry. In B. Cunliffe and C. Poole (eds), *Danebury: An Iron Age Hillfort in Hampshire*. Volume 5. *The Excavations 1979–1988: The Finds*. London, 447–87.

—— 2000. Diet, economy and ritual: evidence from the faunal remains. In M. Fulford (ed.), *Iron Age and Roman Silchester, Excavations on the Site of the Forum-Basilica at Silchester 1977, 1980–86*. London, 423–80.

—— 2001. Preliminary note on the animal bone remains from Alchester. In E. Sauer, Alchester, a Claudian 'vexillation fortress' near the western boundary of the Catuvellauni: new light on the Roman invasion of Britain. *Archaeological Journal*, 157, 63.

—— 2002. Scales of reference: approaches to the study of behaviours and change. In K. Dobney and T. P. O'Connor (eds), *Bones and the Man: Studies in Honour of Don Brothwell*. York. Proceedings of York Bioarchaeology Research Forum.

Grant, N. 1995. The use of hillforts in Devon during the late Roman and post-Roman periods. *Proceedings of the Devon Archaeological Society*, 53, 97–108.

Green, M. 1992. *Animals in Celtic Life and Myth*. London.

Green, M. J. 1976. *A Corpus of Religious Material from the Civilian Areas of Roman Britain*. British Archaeological Reports 24.

—— 1984. *The Wheel as a Cult-Symbol in the Romano-Celtic World*. Brussels.

—— 1986. *The Gods of the Celts*. Gloucester.

—— 1991. *Sun Gods and Symbols of Ancient Europe*. London.

—— 1995. *Celtic Goddesses. Warriors, Virgins & Mothers*. London.

—— 1997. *Exploring the World of the Druids*. London.

—— 1998a. God in Man's image: thoughts on the genesis and affiliations of some Romano-British cult-imagery. *Britannia*, 29, 17–30.

—— 1998b. Humans as ritual victims in the later prehistory of Western Europe. *Oxford Journal of Archaeology*, 17, 169–89.

—— 1999. *Pilgrims in Stone: Images from the Gallo-Roman Sanctuary of Fontes Sequanae*. BAR (International Series) 754. Oxford.

Green, M. J. and Howell, R. 1997. *Celtic Wales*. Cardiff.

Greep, S. J. 1995. The worked bone, antler and ivory. In K. Blockley, M. Blockley, P. Blockley, S. S. Frere and S. Stow, *Excavations in the Marlowe Car-park and Surrounding Areas*. Part II. *The Finds*, 1112–70.

Greep, S. J. (ed.) 1993. *Roman Towns: The Wheeler Inheritance: A Review of 50 years' Research*. CBA Research Report 93. London.

Gregory, A. K. 1991: *Excavations at Thetford, 1980–82, Fisons Way*. East Anglian Archaeological Report 53. Norwich.

Gregory, T. 1982. Romano-British settlement in West Norfolk and on the Norfolk Fen edge. In D. Miles (ed.), *The Romano-British Countryside*. BAR (British Series) 103. Oxford, 351–76.

Gregson, M. 1988. The villa as private property. In K. Branigan and D. Miles (eds), *The Economics of Romano-British Villas*. Sheffield, 21–33.

Grew, F. and Hobley, B. (eds) 1985. *Roman Urban Topography in Britain and the Western Empire*. CBA Research Report 59. London.

Griffin, J. 1984. Augustus and the poets: Caesar qui cogere posset. In F. Millar and E. Segal (eds), *Caesar Augustus. Seven Aspects*. Oxford, 189–218.

Griffith, F. M. 1984. Roman military sites in Devon: some recent discoveries. *Proceedings of the Devon Archaeological Society*, 42, 11–32.

—— 1988. *Devon's Past: An Aerial View*. Exeter.

—— 1994. Changing perceptions of the context of prehistoric Dartmoor. *Proceedings of the Devon Archaeological Society*, 52, 85–99.

Grimes, W. F. 1930. *Holt, Denbighshire: The Works Depot of the Twentieth Legion at Castle Lyons*. London.

Grinsell, L. V. 1958. *The Archaeology of Wessex.* London.

Groenmann-van Waateringe, W. 1980. Urbanisation and the north-west frontier of the Roman empire. In W. Hanson and L. Keppie (eds), *Roman Frontier Studies 1979.* BAR 71. Oxford, 1037–44.

Guido, M. 1978. *The Glass Beads of the Prehistoric and Roman Periods in Britain and Ireland.* London.

—— 1979. Glass beads and catalogue. In G. Clarke, *Pre-Roman and Roman Winchester.* Part II: *The Roman Cemetery at Lankhills.* Oxford, 292–300.

—— 1999. *The Glass Beads of Anglo-Saxon England c. AD 400–700.* Woodbridge.

Guido, M. and Mills, J. M. 1993. Beads (jet, glass, crystal and coral). In D. E. Farwell and T. I. Molleson, *Poundbury.* Volume 2. *The Cemeteries.* Dorchester, 100–2.

Gurney, D. (ed.) 1986. *Settlement, Religion and Industry on the Fen Edge: Three Romano-British Settlements in Norfolk.* East Anglian Archaeology 31. Norwich.

Gwilt, A. and Haselgrove, C. C. (eds) 1997. *Reconstructing Iron Age Societies: New Approaches to the British Iron Age.* Oxbow Monograph 71. Oxford.

Hadman, J. 1978. Aisled buildings in Roman Britain. In M. Todd (ed.), *Studies in the Romano-British Villa.* Leicester, 187–95.

Haffner, A. and Schnurbein, S. von. 1996. Kelten, Germanen, Römer im Mittelgebirgsraum zwischen Luxemburg und Thüringen. *Archäologisches Nachrichtenblatt,* 1, 70–7.

Hald, Margrethe. 1980. *Ancient Danish Textiles from Bogs and Burials.* Copenhagen.

Halkon, P. and Millett, M. 1999. *Rural Settlement and Industry: Studies in the Iron Age and Roman Archaeology of Lowland East Yorkshire.* Otley.

Hall, D. and Coles, J. 1994. *Fenland Survey: An Essay in Landscape and Persistence.* London.

Hamshaw-Thomas, J. F. and N. Bermingham 1993. Analysis of faunal remains. In A. R. Hands (ed.), *The Romano-British Roadside Settlement at Wilcote, Oxfordshire I, Excavations 1990–92.* BAR (British Series) 232. Oxford.

Handley, M. A. 2001. The origins of Christian commemoration in Late Antique Britain. *Early Medieval Europe,* 10, 177–99.

Hanley, R. 1987. *Villages in Roman Britain.* Princes Risborough.

Hanson, R. P. C. 1968. *Saint Patrick: His Origins and Career.* Oxford.

Hanson, W. S. 1978. Roman campaigns north of the Forth–Clyde isthmus: the evidence of the temporary camps. *Proceedings of the Society of Antiquaries of Scotland,* 109, 140–50.

—— 1987. *Agricola and the Conquest of the North.* London.

—— 1996. Forest clearance and the Roman army. *Britannia,* 27, 354–8.

—— 1997. The Roman presence: brief interludes. In K. J. Edwards and I. B. M. Ralston (eds), *Scotland: Environment and Archaeology, 8000 BC–1000 AD.* Chichester, 195–216.

Hanson, W. S. and Breeze, D. 1991. The future of Roman Scotland. In W. Hanson and L. Slater (eds), *Scottish Archaeology: New Perceptions.* Aberdeen.

Hanson, W. S. and Macinnes, L. 1991. Soldiers and settlement in Wales and Scotland. In R. F. J. Jones (ed.), *Roman Britain: Recent Trends.* Sheffield, 85–92.

Hanson, W. S. and Maxwell, G. S. 1986. *Rome's North-west frontier: The Antonine Wall,* 2nd edn. Edinburgh.

Harding, D. 1984. *Holme House, Piercebridge.* Edinburgh.

Harding, D. W. (ed.) 1982. *Later Prehistoric Settlement in South-east Scotland.* Edinburgh.

Harding, J. (ed.) 2000. *Northern Pasts: Interpretations of the Later Prehistory of Northern England and Southern Scotland.* BAR (British Series) 302. Oxford.

Harman, M. 1996. Mammalian bones. In J. May (ed.), *Dragonby: Report on Excavations at an Iron Age and Romano-British Settlement in North Lincolnshire.* Oxford, 141–61.

Harrison, P. 2000. Where can you breathe easy? *Times Higher Educational Supplement* (24 November), 26.

Hartley, B. and Fitts, L. 1988. *The Brigantes*. Gloucester.

Hartley, B. R. 1972. The Roman occupation of Scotland: the evidence of samian ware. *Britannia*, 3, 4–15.

Haselgrove, C. C. 1987. *Iron Age Coinage in South-east England: The Archaeological Context*. BAR (British Series) 174. Oxford.

—— 1989. The later Iron Age in Southern Britain and beyond. In M. Todd (ed.), *Research on Roman Britain 1960–89*. Britannia Monograph Series 11. London, 1–18.

—— 1996. The Iron Age. In R. Newman (ed.), *The Archaeology of Lancashire: Present State and Future Priorities*. Lancaster, 61–73.

—— 1997. Iron Age brooch deposition and chronology. In A. Gwilt and C. C. Haselgrove (eds), *Reconstructing Iron Age Societies*. Oxbow Monographs 71. Oxford, 51–72.

—— 1999. Iron Age societies in Central Britain: retrospect and prospect. In B. Bevan (ed.), *Northern Exposure: Interpretation, Devolution and the Iron Ages in Britain*. Leicester Archaeology Monographs 4. Leicester, 253–78.

—— 1999. The Iron Age. In J. Hunter and I. Ralston (eds), *The Archaeology of Britain*. London, 113–34.

—— 2001. Iron Age Britain and its European setting. In J. R. Collis (ed.), *Society and Settlement in Iron Age Europe: Actes du XVIIIe Colloque de l'AFEAF, Winchester*. Sheffield Archaeological Monograph 11. Sheffield, 37–72.

—— 2002. The later Bronze Age and the Iron Age in the lowlands. In C. Brooks, R. Daniels and A. Harding (eds), *Past, Present and Future: The Archaeology of Northern England*. Architectural and Archaeological Society of Durham and Northumberland Research Report 5. Durham, 49–69.

Haselgrove, C. C. and McCullagh, R. 2000. *An Iron Age Coastal Community in East Lothian: The Excavation of Two Later Prehistoric Enclosure Complexes at Fisher Road, Port Seaton, 1994–5*. Edinburgh.

Haselgrove, C. C., Armit, I., Champion, T. C., Creighton, J., Gwilt, A., Hill, J. D., Hunter, F. and Woodward, A. 2001. *Understanding the British Iron Age: An Agenda for Action*. Salisbury.

Haselgrove, C. C., Ferrell, G., Henley, E. and Turnbull, P. 1988. *The Durham Archaeological Survey 1983–87*. Durham.

Hassall, M. 1983. The internal planning of Roman auxiliary forts. In B. Hartley and J. Wacher (eds), *Rome and her Northern Provinces*. Gloucester, 96–131.

—— 2000. Pre-Hadrianic legionary dispositions in Britain. In R. J. Brewer (ed.), *Roman Fortresses and their Legions*. London, 51–67.

Hassall, M. W. C. 1976. Britain in the Notitia. In R. Goodburn and P. Bartholomew (eds), *Aspects of the Notitia Dignitatum*. Oxford, 103–17.

Hassall, M. W. C. and Tomlin, R. S. O. 1979. Roman Britain in 1978: II. Inscriptions. *Britannia*, 10, 339–56.

—— 1983. Inscriptions. *Britannia*, 14, 336–41.

Hattatt, R. 2000. *A Visual Catalogue of Richard Hattatt's Ancient Brooches*. Oxford.

Haverfield, F. 1905. The Romanization of Roman Britain. *Proceedings of the British Academy*, 2, 185–217.

—— 1924. *The Roman Occupation of Britain*, ed. G. Macdonald. Oxford.

Hawkes, C. F. C. and Crummy, P. 1995. *Camulodunum 2*. Colchester.

Hawkes, G. 1999. Beyond Romanisation: the creolisation of food. A framework for the study of faunal remains from Roman sites. *Papers from the Institute of Archaeology*, 10, 89–96.

Hawkes, S. C. and Dunning, G. C. 1965. Soldiers and settlers in Britain, fourth to fifth century. *Medieval Archaeology*, 5, 1–70.

Henig, M. 1978. *A Corpus of Roman Engraved Gemstones from British Sites*. BAR (British Series) 8. Oxford. [First published in 1974.]

—— 1984. *Religion in Roman Britain*. London.

—— 1993. *Roman Sculpture from the Cotswold Region*. CSIR I.7. Oxford.

—— 1995. *The Art of Roman Britain*. London.

—— 1998. Togidubnus and the Roman liberation. *British Archaeology*, 37 (September) 8–9.

—— 1999. A new star shining over Bath. *Oxford Journal of Archaeology*, 18, 419–25.

—— 2002. *The Heirs of King Verica: Culture and Politics in Roman Britain*. Stroud.

Henig M. and Booth, P. 2000. *Roman Oxfordshire*. Stroud.

Henig, M. and Cannon, P. 2000. A sceptre-head for the matres cult and other objects from West Berkshire. *Britannia*, 31, 358–61.

Henig, M. and King, A. 1986. *Pagan Gods and Shrines of the Roman Empire*. Oxford University Committee for Archaeology 8. Oxford.

Henig, M. and Soffe, G. 1993. The Thruxton Roman villa and its mosaic pavement. *Journal of the British Archaeological Association*, 146, 1–28.

Heslop, D. H. 1987. *The Excavation of an Iron Age Settlement at Thorpe Thewles*. London.

Higham, N. J. 1986. *The Northern Counties to AD 1000*. London.

—— 1989. Roman and native in England north of the Tees: acculturation and its limitations. In J. C. Barrett, A. P. Fitzpatrick and L. Macinnes (eds), *Barbarians and Romans in North-west Europe from the Later Republic to Late Antiquity*. BAR (International Series) 471. Oxford, 153–74.

—— 1992. *Rome, Britain and the Anglo-Saxons*. London.

Higham, N. J. and Jones, B. 1985. *The Carvetii*. Gloucester.

Hill, J. D. 1995. *Ritual and Rubbish in the Iron Age of Wessex*. BAR (British Series) 242. Oxford.

—— 1995. The Iron Age in Britain and Ireland (*c.*800 BC–AD 100). *Journal of World Prehistory*, 9, 47–98.

—— 1996. Hillforts and the Iron Age of Wessex. In T. C. Champion and J. R. Collis (eds), *The Iron Age in Britain and Ireland*. Sheffield, 95–116.

—— 1997. 'The end of one kind of body and the beginning of another kind of body?' Toilet instruments and 'Romanization' in southern England during the first century AD. In A. Gwilt and C. C. Haselgrove (eds), *Reconstructing Iron Age Societies*. Oxford, 96–107.

—— 2002. Just about the potter's wheel: using, making and depositing Middle and Later Iron Age pots in East Anglia. In A. Woodward and J. D. Hill (eds), *Prehistoric Britain: The Ceramic Basis*. Oxford, 143–60.

—— (forthcoming). Was the core really a periphery? Indigenous changes in late Iron Age eastern England. In C. Haselgrove and T. Moore (eds), *The Later Iron Age in Britain and Beyond*. Oxford.

Hill, P. 1982a. Broxmouth hillfort excavations 1977–78. In D. W. Harding (ed.), *Later Prehistoric Settlement in South-east Scotland*. Edinburgh, 141–88.

—— 1982b. Settlement and chronology. In D. W. Harding (ed.), *Later Prehistoric Settlement in South-east Scotland*. Edinburgh, 4–43.

—— 1987. Traprain Law: the Votadini and the Romans. *Scottish Archaeological Review*, 4.2, 85–91.

—— 1997. *Whithorn and St Ninian: The Excavation of a Monastic Town 1984–91*. Stroud.

—— 1997. The stone wall turrets of Hadrian's Wall. *Archaeologia Aeliana*, 5th ser. 25, 27–49.

Hill, P. R. and Dobson, B. 1992. The design of Hadrian's Wall and its implications. *Archaeologia Aeliana*, 5th ser. 20, 27–52.

Hillson, S. 1986. *Teeth*. Cambridge.

Hind, J. G. F. 1989. The invasion of Britain in AD 43 – an alternative strategy. *Britannia*, 20, 1–21.

Hingley, R. 1989. *Rural Settlement in Roman Britain*. London.

Hingley, R. 1991. The Romano-British countryside: the significance of rural settlement forms. In R. F. J. Jones (ed.), *Roman Britain: Recent Trends*. Sheffield, 75–80.

—— 1992. Society in Scotland from 700 BC to AD 200. *Proceedings of the Society of Antiquaries of Scotland*, 122, 7–53.

—— 1997. Resistance and domination: social change in Roman Britain. In D. J. Mattingly, (ed.), *Dialogues in Roman Imperialism: Power, Discourse, and Discrepant Experience in the Roman Empire*. Journal of Roman Archaeology, Supplementary Series no. 23. Portsmouth, RI, 81–100.

—— 1999. The creation of later prehistoric landscapes and the context of reuse of Neolithic and early Bronze Age monuments in Britain and Ireland. In B. Bevan (ed.), *Northern Exposure*. Leicester, 233–51.

—— 2000. *Roman Officers and English Gentlemen. The Imperial Origins of Roman Archaeology.* London and New York.

—— (forthcoming). Iron Age 'currency bars' in Britain: items of exchange in liminal contexts? In C. Haselgrove and D. Wigg (eds), *Ritual and Iron Age Coinage*. Studien zu Fundmünzen der Antike. Mainz.

Hingley, R. and Miles, D. 2001. The human impact on the landscape. In P. Salway (ed.), *The Short Oxford History of the British Isles: The Roman Era*. Oxford, 141–72.

Hingley, R., Moore, H., Triscott, J. E. and Wilson, G. 1997. The excavation of two later Iron Age fortified homesteads at Aldclune, Blair Atholl, Perth & Kinross. *Proceedings of the Society of Antiquaries of Scotland*, 127, 407–66.

Hobley, A. S. 1989. The numismatic evidence for the post-Agricolan abandonment of the Roman frontier in northern Scotland. *Britannia*, 20, 69–74.

Hodder, I. and Millett, M. 1980. Romano-British villas and towns: a systematic analysis. *World Archaeology*, 12, 69–76.

Hodgson, N. 1991. The Notitia Dignitatum and the later Roman garrison of Britain. In V. A. Maxfield and M. J. Dobson (eds), *Roman Frontier Studies 1989*. Exeter, 84–92.

—— 1995. Were there two Antonine occupations of Scotland? *Britannia*, 26, 29–49.

Hodgson, N., Stobbs, G. and Van der Veen, M. 2001. An Iron Age settlement of earlier prehistoric date beneath South Shields Roman fort. *Archaeological Journal*, 158, 62–160.

Hogg, A. H. A. 1966. Native settlement in Wales. In C. Thomas (ed.), *Rural Settlement in Roman Britain*. London, 28–38.

—— 1968. Pen Llystyn: a Roman fort and other remains. *Archaeological Journal*, 125, 101–92.

Holbrook, N. (ed.), 1998. *Cirencester: The Roman Town-defences, Public Buildings and Shops (Cirencester Excavations V)*. Cirencester.

Holbrook, N. and Bidwell, P. T. 1991. *Roman Finds from Exeter*. Exeter

Holmes, N. M. McQ. and Hunter, F. 1997. Edston, Peeblesshire. In R. Bland and J. Ornstein (eds), *Coin Hoards from Roman Britain*. Volume 10. London, 149–68.

Horsley, J. 1732. *Britannia Romana: or, The Roman Antiquities of Britain*. London.

Howe, G. M. 1997. *People, Environment, Disease and Death*. Cardiff.

Howlett, D. 1995. *The Celtic Latin Tradition of Biblical Style*. Dublin.

Hughes, C., Heylings, D. J. A. and Power, C. 1996. Transverse (Harris) lines in Irish archaeological remains. *American Journal of Physical Anthropology*, 101, 115–31.

Hull, M. R. 1958. *Roman Colchester*. Society of Antiquaries Research Report XX. Oxford.

Hunn, J. R. 1995. The Romano-British landscape of the Chiltern dipslope: a study of settlement around Verulamium. In R. Holgate (ed.), *Chiltern Archaeology: Recent Work*. Dunstable, 76–91.

Huan, J. R. 2000. Hay Farm, Eardington, Shropshire: an Iron Age and Romano-British enclosure. In R. Zeepvat (ed.), *Three Iron Age and Romano-British Rural Settlements on English Gravels*. BAR (British Series) 312. Oxford, 119–44.

Hunter, Fraser. 1996. Recent Roman iron age metalwork finds from Fife and Tayside. *Tayside and Fife Archaeological Journal*, 2, 113–25.

—— 1997. Iron Age hoarding in Scotland and northern England. In A. Gwilt and C. C. Haselgrove (eds), *Reconstructing Iron Age Societies*. Oxford, 108–33.

—— 2001a. Roman and native in Scotland: new approaches. *Journal of Roman Archaeology*, 14, 289–309.

—— 2001b. *Excavations at Birnie, Moray 2000*. Edinburgh.

Huntley, J. P. 2000. The charred and waterlogged plant remains. In C. Haselgrove and R. McCullagh, *An Iron Age Coastal Community in East Lothian: The Excavation of Two Later Prehistoric Enclosure Complexes at Fishers Road, Port Seton, 1994–5*. Edinburgh, 157–70.

Hurst, H. R. 1985. *Kingsholm, Gloucester*. Cambridge.

—— 1987. Excavations at Box Roman villa, 1967–8. *Wiltshire Archaeological and Natural History Magazine*, 81, 19–51.

—— 1988. Gloucester (*Glevum*). In G. Webster, *Fortress into City*. London.

—— 1999. Topography and identity in *Glevum colonia*. In H. R. Hurst (ed.), *The* Coloniae *of Roman Britain*. Journal of Roman Archaeology, Supplementary Series 36. Portsmouth, RI, 113–35.

Hurst, H. R. (ed.) 1999. *The* Coloniae *of Roman Britain: New Studies and a Review*. Journal of Roman Archaeology, Supplementary Series 36. Portsmouth, RI.

Hutcheson, A. R. J. 1997. Ironwork hoards in northern Britain. In K. Meadows, C. Lemke and J. Heron (eds.), *TRAC 96: Proceedings of the Sixth Annual Theoretical Roman Archaeology Conference, Sheffield 1996*. Oxford, 65–72.

Hyland, A. 1990. *Equus. The Horse in the Roman World*. London.

Inman, R., Brown, D., Goddard, R. E. and Spratt, D. A. 1985. Roxby Iron Age settlement and the Iron Age in north-east Yorkshire. *Proceedings of the Prehistoric Society*, 51, 181–214.

Irby-Massie, G. 1999. *Military Religion in Roman Britain*. Leiden.

Ireland, S. 1986. *Roman Britain: A Sourcebook*. London.

Jackson, D. A. and Ambrose, T. 1978. Excavations at Wakerley, Northants, 1972–75. *Britannia*, 9, 115–242.

Jackson, R. 1988. *Doctors and Diseases in the Roman Empire*. London.

Jackson, R. P. J. and Potter, T. W. 1996. *Excavations at Stonea, Cambridgeshire, 1980–85*. London.

James, E. 2001. *Britain in the First Millennium*. London.

James, H. 1992. Excavations in Roman Carmarthen 1978–1990. *Carmarthenshire Antiquary*, 37, 5–36.

James, H. and Williams, G. 1982. Rural settlement in Dyfed. In D. Miles (ed.) *The Romano-British Countryside*. BAR (British Series) 103. Oxford, 289–312.

James, S. and Millett, M. (eds) 2001 *Britons and Romans: Advancing an Archaeological Agenda*. CBA Research Report 125. London.

James, S. T. 1984. Britain and the late Roman Army. In T. F. C. Blagg and A. C. King (eds), *Military and Civilian in Roman Britain*. BAR (British Series) 136. Oxford, 161–86.

—— 1999. *The Atlantic Celts. Ancient People or Modern Invention?* London.

Jarrett, M. G. 1976. An unnecessary war. *Britannia*, 7, 145–51.

—— 1994a. *Early Roman Campaigns in Wales. The Seventh Annual Caerleon Lecture*. Cardiff.

—— 1994b. Non-legionary troops in Roman Britain: Part 1: the units. *Britannia*, 25, 35–78.

Jarrett, M. G. and Mann, J. C. 1969. The tribes of Wales. *Welsh History Review*, 4, 161–71.

Jarrett, M. G. and Wrathmell, S. 1981. *Whitton: An Iron Age and Roman Farmstead in South Glamorgan*. Cardiff.

Jessup, R. F. 1954. The excavation of a Roman barrow at Holborough, Snodland. *Archaeologia Cantiana*, 68, 1–61.

Jobey, G. 1959. Excavations at the native settlement at Huckhoe, Northumberland, 1955–7. *Archaeologia Aeliana*, 4th ser. 37, 217–78.

Jobey, G. 1974a. Notes on some population problems in the area between the two Roman walls I. *Archaeologia Aeliana*, 5th ser. 2, 17–26.

—— 1974b. Excavations at Boonies, Westerkirk, and the nature of Romano-British settlement in eastern Dumfriesshire. *Proceedings of the Society of Antiquaries of Scotland*, 105, 119–40.

—— 1978. Iron age and Romano-British settlements on Kennel Hall Knowe, North Tynedale, Northumberland (1976). *Archaeologia Aeliana*, 5th ser. 6, 1–28.

Johns, C. M. 1996a. *The Jewellery of Roman Britain*. London.

—— 1996b. The classification and interpretation of Romano-British treasures. *Britannia*, 27, 1–16.

—— 1971. A Roman bronze statuette of Epona. *British Museum Quarterly*, 36, 37–41.

Johns, C. M. and Potter, T. 1983. *The Thetford Treasure*. London.

Johnson, A. 1983. *Roman Forts of the 1st and 2nd Centuries AD in Britain and the German Provinces*. London.

Johnson, C. and Albarella, U. 2002. *The Iron Age and Romano-British Mammal and Bird Assemblage from Elms Farm, Heybridge, Essex*. (Site Code, HYEF93–95.) Portsmouth.

Johnson, N. and Rose, P. 1982. Defended settlement in Cornwall – an illustrated discussion. In D. Miles (ed.), *The Romano-British Countryside*. BAR (British Series) 103. Oxford, 151–207.

Johnson, P. 1993. Town mosaics and urban *officinae*. In S. J. Greep (ed.), *Roman Towns*. CBA Research Report 93. London, 147–65.

Johnson, P. and Haynes, I. (eds) 1996. *Architecture in Roman Britain*. CBA Research Report 94. London.

Johnson, S. 1976. Channel commands in the Notitia. In R. Goodburn and P. Bartholomew (eds), *Aspects of the Notitia Dignitatum*. Oxford, 81–102.

—— 1980. *The Later Roman Empire*. London.

—— 1989. Architecture of the Saxon Shore forts. In V. A. Maxfield (ed.), *The Saxon Shore*. Exeter, 30–44.

Johnston, D. 1978. Villas of Hampshire and the Isle of Wight. In M. Todd (ed.), *Studies in the Romano-British Villa*. Leicester, 71–92.

Johnston, D. A. 1994. Carronbridge, Dumfries and Galloway: the excavation of Bronze Age cremations, Iron Age settlements and a Roman camp. *Proceedings of the Society of Antiquaries of Scotland*, 124, 233–91.

Johnston, D. A. (ed.) 1977. *The Saxon Shore*. London.

Jones, A. H. M. 1964. *The Later Roman Empire, 284–602*. Oxford.

Jones, A. J. K. 1988. Fish bones from excavations in the cemetery of St Mary Bishophill Junior. In T. P. O'Connor, *Bones from the General Accident Site, Tanner Row*. The Archaeology of York, 15 (2), 126–31.

Jones, G. B. D. and Webster, P. V. 1968. Mediolanum: excavations at Whitchurch 1965–6. *Archaeological Journal*, 125, 193–254.

Jones, G. B. D. and Wooliscroft, D. 2001. *Hadrian's Wall from the Air*. Stroud.

Jones, M. 2000. The plant remains. In M. Fulford and J. Timby, *Late Iron and Roman Silchester*. Britannia Monograph 15. London, 505–12.

Jones, M. E. 1996. *The End of Roman Britain*. Ithaca, NY.

Jones, M. J. 1980. *The Defences of the Upper Roman Enclosure*. Archaeology of Lincoln, 7.1. Lincoln.

—— 1999a. Roman Lincoln: changing perspectives. In H. R. Hurst (ed.), *The Coloniae of Roman Britain*. Portsmouth, RI, 101–12.

—— 1999b. Lincoln and the British fora in context. In H. R. Hurst (ed.), *The Coloniae of Roman Britain*. Portsmouth, RI, 167–74.

Jones, M. J. (ed.) 1999. *The Defences of the Lower City.* Archaeology of Lincoln, 7.2. Lincoln.

Jones, M. K. 1991. Food production and consumption – plants. In R. F. J. Jones (ed.), *Britain in the Roman Period.* Sheffield, 29–34.

Jones, N. W. 1993. Caersws Roman fort and *vicus*, Montgomeryshire, Powys, 1984–92. *Montgomeryshire Collections*, 81, 15–96.

Jones, R. F. J. 1975. The Romano-British farmstead and its cemetery at Lynch Farm, near Peterborough. *Northamptonshire Archaeology*, 10, 94–137.

—— 1991a. The urbanisation of Roman Britain. In R. F. J. Jones (ed.), *Britain in the Roman Period.* Sheffield, 53–66.

—— 1991b. Cultural change in Roman Britain. In R. F. J. Jones (ed.), *Britain in the Roman Period.* Sheffield, 115–20.

Jones, R. F. J. (ed.) 1991. *Britain in the Roman Period: Recent Trends.* Sheffield.

Jørgensen, Lise Bender. 1992. *North European Textiles until AD 1000.* Aarhus.

Josephus. 1980. *Bellum Judaicum*, ed. A. Pelletier. Paris.

Jurmain, R. D. 1999. *Stories from the Skeleton: Behavioral Reconstruction in Human Osteology.* Amsterdam.

Keevil, G. 1996. The reconstruction of the Romano-British villa at Redlands Farm, Northamptonshire. In P. Johnson (ed.), *Architecture in Roman Britain.* York, 44–55.

Keevil, G. and Booth, P. 1997. Settlement, sequence and structure: Romano-British stone-built roundhouses at Redlands Farm, Stanwick (Northants), and Alchester (Oxon). In R. and D. Friendship-Taylor (eds), *From Round House to Villa.* Hackleton, 19–45.

Kendal, R. 1996. Transport logistics associated with the building of Hadrian's Wall. *Britannia*, 27, 129–52.

Kendrick, T. D. 1950. *British Antiquity.* London.

Keppie, L. J. F. 1981. Excavation of a Roman bathhouse at Bothwellhaugh, 1975–76. *Glasgow Archaeological Journal*, 8, 46–94.

—— 1989. Beyond the northern frontier: Romans and natives in Scotland. In M. Todd (ed.), *Research on Roman Britain 1960–89.* Britannia Monograph 11. London, 61–74.

—— 1997. Roman Britain in 1996: Scotland. *Britannia*, 28, 405–14.

King, A. C. 1978. A comparative survey of bone assemblages from Roman sites in Britain. *Bulletin of the Institute of Archaeology*, 15, 207–32.

—— 1984. Animal bones and the dietary identity of military and civilian groups in Roman Britain, Germany and Gaul. In T. Blagg and A. King (eds), *Military and Civilian in Roman Britain.* BAR 137. Oxford, 187–217.

—— 1985. Excavations at Worthy Down, South Wonston, 1985. *Hampshire Field Club and Archaeological Society Newsletter*, NS 5, 16–17.

—— 1990. *Roman Gaul and Germany.* London.

—— 1991. Food production and consumption – meat. In R. F. J. Jones (ed.), *Britain in the Roman Period.* Sheffield, 21–8.

—— 1996. The south-east façade of Meonstoke aisled building. In P. Johnson (ed.), *Architecture in Roman Britain.* York, 56–69.

—— 1999a. Diet in the Roman world: a regional inter-site comparison of the mammal bones. *Journal of Roman Archaeology*, 12, 168–202.

—— 1999b. Animals and the Roman army: the evidence of animal bones. In A. Goldsworthy and I. Haynes (eds), *The Roman Army as a Community.* Journal of Roman Archaeology Supplementary Series 34. Portsmouth, RI, 139–49.

King, A. C. and Soffe, G. 1991. Hayling Island. In R. F. J. Jones (ed.), *Roman Britain: Recent Trends.* Sheffield, 111–13.

—— 1994. The Iron Age and Roman temple at Hayling Island. In A. P. Fitzpatrick and Morris (eds), *The Iron Age in Wessex: Recent Work.* Salisbury, 114–16.

King, A. C. and Soffe, G. 1999. L'Organisation interne et l'enfuissement des objets au temple de l'âge du fer à Hayling Island (Hampshire). In J. Collis (ed.), *Society and Settlement in Iron Age Europe; l'habitat et l'occupation du Sol en Europe. Actes du XVIIe Colloque de l'AFEAF, Winchester – Avril 1994.* Sheffield, 113–26.

Knight, D., Garton, D. and Leary, R. 1998. The Elmton fieldwalking survey: prehistoric and Romano-British artefact scatters. *Derbyshire Archaeological Journal*, 118, 69–85.

Knoch, J. T. 1997. *The Gododdin of Aneirin: Text and context from Dark Age Britain.* Cardiff.

Knusel, C., Roberts, C. A. and Boylston, A. 1996. When Adam delved . . . An activity-related lesion in three human skeletal populations. *American Journal of Physical Anthropology*, 100, 427–34.

Lamb, H. H. 1981. Climate from 1000 BC to 1000 AD. In M. Jones and G. Dimbleby (eds), *The Environment of Man: The Iron Age to the Anglo-Saxon Period.* BAR (British Series) 87. Oxford, 53–65.

Lambot, B., Fribulet, A. and Méniel, P. 1994. *Le site protohistorique d'Acy-Romance (Ardennes) II: Les necropoles dans leur contexte régional.* Mémoires de la Société Archéologique Champenoise 8. Reims.

Lapidge, M. and Dumville, D. N. (eds) 1984. *Gildas: New Approaches.* Woodbridge.

Larsen, C. S. 1995. Biological changes in human populations with agriculture. *Annual Review of Anthropology*, 24, 185–213.

Laver, P. G. 1927. The excavation of a tumulus at Lexden, Colchester. *Archaeologia*, 26, 241–54.

Leach, P. 1998. *Great Witcombe Roman Villa, Gloucestershire.* BAR (British Series) 266. Oxford.

Leech, R. H. 1976. Larger agricultural settlements in the West Country. In K. Branigan and P. Fowler (eds), *The Roman West Country.* Newton Abbot, 142–61.

—— 1982a. The Roman interlude in the south-west: the dynamics of economic and social change in Romano-British South Somerset and North Dorset. In D. Miles (ed.), *The Romano-British Countryside.* BAR (British Series) 103. Oxford, 209–67.

—— 1982b *Excavations at Catsgore 1970–1973.* Bristol.

Leech, R. H. and Leach, P. 1982. Roman town and countryside 43–450 AD. In M. Aston and I. Burrow (eds), *The Archaeology of Somerset: A Review to 1500 AD*: Bridgewater, 63–81.

Legge, A., Williams, J. and Williams, P. 1992. The determination of season of death from the mandibles and bones of the domestic sheep (*Ovis aries*). In R. Maggie, R. Nisbet and G. Barker (eds), *Archaeologia della Pastorizia nell'Europa Meridionale 2. Rivista di Studi Liguri*, A. 57 (1991), 49–65.

Leland, J. 1774. *Collectanea.* London.

Lenoir, M. 1979. *Pseudo-Hygin.* Paris.

Le Quesne, C. 1999. *Excavations at Chester. The Roman and Later Defences. Part I.* Chester.

Levick, B. 1990. *Claudius.* London.

Levitan, B. 1989. The vertebrate remains from Chichester Cattlemarket. In A. Down (ed.), *Chichester Excavations VI.* Chichester, 242–67.

—— 1993. Vertebrate remains. In A. D. Woodward and P. J. Leach (eds), *The Uley Shrines.* London, 257–345.

L'Hour, M. 1987. Un site sous-marin sur le côte de l'Armorique: l'épave de Ploumanac'h. *Revue Archéologique de l'Ouest*, 4, 113–31.

Ling, R. J. 1985. *Romano-British Wall-Painting.* Shire Archaeology 42. Princes Risborough.

—— 1993. Wall painting since Wheeler. In S. J. Greep (ed.), *Roman Towns.* CBA Research Report 93. London, 166–70.

—— 1997. Mosaics in Roman Britain: discoveries and research since 1945. *Britannia*, 28, 259–95.

Lobb, S. and Rose, P. 1996. *Archaeological Survey of the Lower Kennet Valley, Berkshire.* Wessex Archaeology Monograph 9. Salisbury.

Lucas, R. N. 1993. *The Romano-British Villa at Halstock, Dorset. Excavations 1967–1985.* Dorset Natural History and Archaeological Society Monograph 13. Dorchester.

Luff, R. M. 1992. The faunal remains. In N. P. Wickenden (ed.), *The Temple and Other Sites in the North-eastern Sector of Caesaromagus.* York, 116–24.

Lynch, F., Aldhouse-Green, S. and Davies, J. L. 2000. *Prehistoric Wales.* Stroud.

Lynn, C. J. 1997. Excavations at Navan Fort, 1961–71. In D. M. Waterman (ed.), *Excavations at Navan Fort.* Northern Ireland Archaeological Monographs 3. Belfast.

Lysons, D. and Lysons, S. 1806–22. *Magna Britannia, being a Concise Topographical Account of the Several Counties of Great Britain.* 6 vols. London.

Lysons, S. 1813–17. *Reliquiae Britannico-Romanae.* 3 vols. London.

—— 1815. *An Account of the Remains of a Roman Villa Discovered in the County of Sussex.* London.

McCarthy, M. 2002. *Roman Carlisle and Lands of the Solway.* London.

MacCullagh, R. 1992. *The Irish Currach Folk.* Dublin.

Macdonald, P. 1996. Llyn Cerrig Bach: an Iron Age votive assemblage. In S. Aldhouse-Green (ed.), *Art, Ritual and Death in Prehistory.* Cardiff, 32–3.

McElroy, A. and Townsend, P. K. 1996. *Medical Anthropology in Ecological Perspective.* Boulder, CO.

McGrail, S. 1983. Cross-Channel seamanship and navigation in the late 1st millennium BC. *Oxford Journal of Archaeology* 2, 299–337.

McGrail, S. 2001. *Boats of the World.* Oxford.

Macinnes, L. 1982. Pattern and purpose: the settlement evidence. In D. Harding (ed.), *Later Prehistoric Settlement in South-east Scotland.* Occasional Publication 8. Edinburgh, 57–74.

—— 1984. Brochs and the Roman occupation of Lowland Scotland, *Proceedings of the Society of Antiquaries of Scotland,* 114, 234–49.

—— 1989. Baubles, bangles and beads: trade and exchange in Roman Scotland. In J. C. Barrett, A. P. Fitzpatrick and L. Macinnes (eds), *Barbarians and Romans in North-west Europe from the Later Republic to Late Antiquity.* BAR (International Series) 471. Oxford, 108–16.

—— 1994. Brochs and the Roman occupation of Lowland Scotland. *Proceedings of the Society of Antiquaries of Scotland,* 114, 234–49.

Mackie, E. 1982. The Leckie broch, Stirlingshire: an interim report. *Glasgow Archaeological Journal,* 9, 60–72.

McKinley, J. 1993. *Human Skeletal Report from Baldock.* [Unpublished.]

—— 2000. The analysis of cremated bone. In M. Cox and S. Mays (eds), *Human Osteology in Archaeology and Forensic Science.* London, 403–21.

Mackreth, D. F. 1978. Orton Hall Farm, Peterborough: a Roman and Saxon settlement. In M. Todd (ed.), *Studies in the Romano-British Villa.* Leicester, 209–28.

Macready, S. and Thompson, F. H. (eds) 1984. *Cross-Channel Trade between Gaul and Britain in the Pre-Roman Iron Age.* London.

McWhirr, A. 1981. *Roman Gloucestershire.* Gloucester.

Main, L. 1998. Excavations of a timber round-house and broch at the Fairy Knowe, Buchlyvie, Stirlingshire, 1975–8. *Proceedings of the Society of Antiquaries of Scotland,* 128, 293–418.

Mallory, J. P. 1997. Emain Macha and Navan Fort. In D. M. Waterman (ed.), *Excavations at Navan Fort.* Belfast, 197–206

Maltby, M. 1979. *The Animal Bones from Exeter, 1971–1975.* Sheffield.

—— 1984a. The animal bones. In M. Fulford (ed.), *Silchester Defences: Excavations on the Defences 1974–80.* London, 199–215.

Maltby, M. 1984b. Animal bones and the Romano-British economy. In C. Grigson and J. Clutton-Brock (eds), *Animals and Archaeology 4: Husbandry in Europe*. BAR (International Series) 227. Oxford, 125–38.

—— 1989. Urban-rural variations in the butchering of cattle in Romano-British Hampshire. In D. T. W. Serjeantson (ed.), *Diet and Crafts in Towns: The Evidence of Animal Remains from the Roman to the Post-Medieval Period*. BAR (British Series) 199. Oxford, 75–106.

—— 1994. The meat supply in Roman Dorchester and Winchester. In A. R. Hall and H. K. Kenward (eds), *Urban-Rural Connections: Perspectives from Environmental Archaeology*. Oxford, 85–102.

—— 1998. The animal bones from Roman 'small towns' in the Cotswolds. In J. Timby (ed.), *Excavations at Kingscote and Wycomb, Gloucestershire*. Cirencester.

Manchester, K. 1991. Tuberculosis and leprosy: evidence for interaction of disease. In D. Ortner and A. C. Aufderheide (eds), *Human Paleopathology: Current Syntheses and Future Actions*. Washington, DC, 23–35.

Manchester, K. and Roberts, C. A. 1986. *Palaeopathological Evidence of Leprosy and Tuberculosis in Britain*. Unpublished SERC Report (Grant 337.367), University of Bradford.

Mann, J. C. 1974. The northern frontier after AD 369. *Glasgow Archaeological Journal*, 3, 34–42.

—— 1976. What was the Notitia Dignitatum for? In R. Goodburn and P. Bartholomew (eds), *Aspects of the Notitia Dignitatum*. Oxford, 1–10.

—— 1977a. Duces and Comites in the fourth century. In D. A. Johnston (ed.), *The Saxon Shore*. London, 11–15.

—— 1977b. The Reculver Inscription. In D. A. Johnston (ed.), *The Saxon Shore*. London, 15.

—— 1989. Historical development of the Saxon Shore. In V. A. Maxfield (ed.), *The Saxon Shore*. Exeter, 1–11.

—— 1992. Loca. *Archaeologia Aeliana*, 5th ser. 20, 53–5.

Manning, W. H. 1975. Economic influences on land use in the military areas of the highland zone during the Roman period. In J. G. Evans, S. Limbrey and H. Cleere (eds), *The Effect of Man on the Landscape: The Highland Zone*. London, 112–16.

—— 1976. The Conquest of the West Country. In K. Branigan and P. J. Fowler (eds), *The Roman West Country*. Newton Abbot, 15–41.

—— 1981. Native and Roman metalwork in northern Britain: a question of origins and influences. *Scottish Archaeological Forum*, 11, 52–61.

—— 1981. *Report on the Excavations at Usk 1965–1976: The Fortress Excavations 1968–1971*. Cardiff.

—— 1988. *Early Roman Campaigns in the South-West of Britain*. Cardiff.

—— 2001. *Roman Wales*. Cardiff.

Marsden, P. 1994. *Ships of the Port of London*. London.

Marvell, A. 1996. Excavations at Usk 1986–1988. *Britannia*, 27, 51–110.

Marvell, A. G. and Heywood, B. 1992. Excavations at Neath. *Bulletin of the Board of Celtic Studies*, 39, 171–298.

Marvell, A. G. and Owen-John, H. S. 1997. *Leucarum. Excavations at the Roman Auxiliary Fort at Loughor, West Glamorgan 1982–94 and 1987–88*. London.

Mason, D. J. P. 2000. *Excavations at Chester. The Elliptical Building*. Chester.

—— 2001. *Roman Chester: City of the Eagles*. Stroud.

Mattingly, D. 1997. Dialogues of power and experience in the Roman empire. In D. Mattingly (ed.), *Dialogues in Roman Imperialism: Power, Discourse and Discrepant Experiences in the Roman Empire*. Journal of Roman Archaeology, Supplementary Series 23. Portsmouth, RI, 7–24.

Mattingly, D. J. (ed.), 1997. *Dialogues in Roman Imperialism*. Journal of Roman Archaeology, Supplementary Series 23. Portsmouth, RI.

Mawer, C. F. 1995. *Evidence for Christianity in Roman Britain: The Small Finds.* BAR (British Series) 243. Oxford.

Maxfield, V. A. 1991. Tiverton Roman Fort (Bolham): Excavations 1981–86. *Proceedings of the Devon Archaeological Society,* 49, 25–98.

Maxfield, V. A. (ed.) 1989. *The Saxon Shore.* Exeter.

Maxfield, V. A. and Dobson, M. 1991. *Roman Frontier Studies 1989.* Exeter.

Maxwell, G. S. 1981. Agricola's campaigns: the evidence of the temporary camps. In J. Kenworthy (ed.), *Agricola's Campaigns in Scotland.* Scottish Archaeological Forum XII. Edinburgh, 25–54.

—— 1989. *The Romans in Scotland.* Edinburgh.

—— 1995. Map-making in Roman Scotland: from Marinus to the military survey. *Proceedings of the Society of Antiquaries of Scotland,* 125, 11–99.

—— 1998. *A Gathering of the Eagles: Scenes from Roman Scotland.* Edinburgh.

—— 2003. Size matters: a review of small camps and temporary camp annexes in Scotland and northern England. In G. B. Dannell (ed.), *Papers Presented to K. F. Hartley.*

Mays, S. 1993. Infanticide in Roman Britain. *Antiquity,* 67, 883–8.

—— 1995. Killing the unwanted child. *British Archaeology,* 2 (March), 8–9.

Mays, S., Taylor, G. M., Legge, A. J., Young, D. B. and Turner-Walker, G. 2001. Paleopathological and biomolecular study of tuberculosis in a Medieval skeletal collection from England. *American Journal of Physical Anthropology,* 114, 298–311.

Meadows, K. I. 1995. You are what you eat: diet, identity and Romanisation. In S. Cottam, C. D. Dungworth, S. Scott and J. Taylor (eds), *TRAC 1994: Proceedings of the Fourth Theoretical Roman Archaeology Conference, Durham.* Oxford, 133–40.

—— 1999. The appetites of households in early Roman Britain. In P. Allison (ed.), *The Archaeology of Household Activities.* London, 101–20.

Meates, G. W. 1979. *The Lullingstone Roman Villa, I.* Maidstone.

Merbs, C. F. 1989. Trauma. In M. Y. Iscan and K. A. R. Kennedy (eds), *Reconstruction of Life from the Skeleton.* New York, 161–89.

Mercer, R. J. and Tipping, R. 1994. The prehistory of soil erosion in the northern and eastern Cheviot hills, Anglo-Scottish borders. In S. Foster and T. C. Smout (eds), *The History of Soils and Field Systems.* Aberdeen, 1–25.

Metzler, J., Waringo, R., Bis, R. and Metzler-Zens, N. 1991. *Clemency et les tombes de l'aristocratie en Gaule-Belgique.* Dossiers d'Archéologie du Museé National d'Histoire et d'Art 1. Luxembourg.

Miket, R. and Burgess, C. (eds) 1984. *Between and Beyond the Walls: Essays on the Prehistory and History of North Britain in Honour of George Jobey.* Edinburgh.

Miles, D. 1982a. Confusion in the countryside: some comments on the Upper Thames region. In D. Miles (ed.), *The Romano-British Countryside.* Oxford, 53–79.

—— 1986. *Archaeology at Barton Court Farm, Abingdon, Oxon.* CBA Research Report 50. York.

—— 1988. Villas and variety: aspects of economy and society in the Upper Thames landscape. In K. Branigan and D. Miles (eds), *The Economies of Romano-British Villas.* Sheffield, 60–72.

Miles, D. (ed.) 1982b. *The Romano-British Countryside: Studies in Rural Settlement and Economy.* BAR (British Series) 103. Oxford.

Millett, M. 1990a. *The Romanization of Britain: An Essay in Archaeological Interpretation.* Cambridge.

—— 1990b. Iron Age and Romano-British settlement in the southern Vale of York and beyond. In S. Ellis and D. Crowther (eds), *Humber Perspectives: A Region through the Ages.* Hull, 347–56.

—— 1993. A cemetery in the age of transition; the King Harry Lane cemetery reconsidered. *Archäologische Schriften des Instituts für Vor- und Frühgeschichte der Johannes*

Gutenberg-Universität Mainz. Band 3. *Römerzeitliche Gräber als Quellen zu Religion, Be-völkerungsstruktur und Sozialgeschichte,* 255–82.

Millett, M. 1995. *Roman Britain.* London.

—— 2001. Approaches to urban societies. In S. James and M. Millett (eds), *Britons and Romans.* CBA Research Report 125. London, 60–6.

Milne, G. 1985. *The Port of Roman London.* London.

—— 1995. *Roman London.* London.

Mitchell, S. 1983. Cornish tin, Iulius Caesar and the invasion of Britain. *Studies in Latin Literature and Roman History.* Collection Latomus 180. Paris, 80–99.

Molleson, T. I. 1989. Social implications of mortality patterns of juveniles from Poundbury Camp Romano-British Cemetery. *Anthropologische Anzeiger* 47, 27–38.

Molleson, T. I. and Cox, M. 1988. A neonate with cut bones from Poundbury Camp, 4th century AD, England. *Bulletin de la Société Royale d'Anthropologie et de Préhistoire,* 99, 53–9.

Moore, I. E. 1988. *The Archaeology of Roman Suffolk.* Ipswich.

Morris, J. 1973. *The Age of Arthur: A History of the British Isles from 350–650.* London.

Muckelroy, K., Haselgrove, C. and Nash, D. 1978. Pre-Roman coin from Canterbury and the ship represented on it. *Proceedings of the Prehistoric Society,* 44, 439–44.

Munksgaard, Elisabeth. 1974. *Oldtidsdragter.* Copenhagen.

Murdoch, T. 1991. *Treasures and Trinkets.* London.

Musson, C. 1989. Air-photography and Roman forts, summer 1989. *Archaeology in Wales,* 29, 56.

Napoli, J. 1997. *Recherches sur les fortifications linéaires romaines.* Collection de l'École Français de Rome 229. Rome.

Nash, D. 1984. The basis of contact between Britain and Gaul in the late pre-Roman Iron Age. In S. Macready and F. H. Thompson (eds), *Cross-Channel Trade.* London, 92–107.

Nash-Williams, V. E. 1939. An Iron Age coastal camp, at Sudbrook near the Severn Tunnel, Monmouthshire. *Archaeologia Cambrensis,* 94, 42–79.

—— 1953. The Roman villa at Llantwit Major in Glamorgan. *Archaeologia Cambrensis,* 102, 89–163.

—— 1969. *The Roman Frontier in Wales,* rev. M. G. Jarrett. Cardiff.

Neal, D. S. 1978. The growth and decline of villas in the Verulamium area. In M. Todd (ed.), *Studies in the Romano-British Villa.* Leicester, 33–58.

—— 1989. The Stanwick villa, Northants: an interim report on the excavations of 1984–88. *Britannia,* 20, 149–68.

—— 1996. *Excavations on the Roman Villa at Beadlam, Yorkshire.* Leeds.

Neal, D. S. and Cosh, S. R. (forthcoming). *Roman Mosaics of Britain.* 4 vols.

Neal, D. S., Wardle, A. and Hunn, J. 1990. *Excavation of the Iron Age, Roman and Medieval Settlement at Gorhambury, St Albans.* English Heritage Archaeological Report 14. London.

Nevell, M. 1999. Iron Age and Romano-British rural settlement in north-west England: marginality, theory and settlement. In M. Nevell (ed.), *Living on the Edge of Empire.* Manchester, 9–12.

Nevell, M. (ed.) 1999. *Living on the Edge of Empire: Models, Methodology and Marginality.* Manchester.

Nevell, M. and Walker, J. 1999. Introduction: models, methodology and marginality in Roman archaeology. In M. Nevell (ed.), *Living on the Edge of Empire.* Manchester, 9–12.

Niblett, R. 1995. *Roman Hertfordshire.* Wimborne.

—— 1999. *The Excavation of a Ceremonial Site at Folly Lane, St Albans.* Britannia Monograph 14. London.

—— 2000. Funerary rites at Verulamium during the early Roman period. In J. Pearce, M. Millett and M. Struck (eds), *Burial, Society, and Context in the Provincial Roman World.* Oxford, 97–104.

Niblett, R. 2001. *Verulamium: The Roman City of St Albans*. Stroud.

Nixon, C. E. V. and Rodgers, B. S. 1994. *In Praise of Later Emperors: the Panegyrici Latini*. Berkeley, CA.

North, J. and Price, S. 1998. *Religions of Rome*. Cambridge.

Oakberg, K., Levy, T. and Smith, P. 2000. A method for skeletal arsenic analysis applied to the Chalcolithic copper smelting site of Shiqmina, Israel. *Journal of Archaeological Science*, 27, 895–901.

O'Connor, T. P. 1986. The animal bones. In P. Zienkiewicz (ed.), *The Legionary Fortress Baths at Caerleon. II. The Finds*. Cardiff, 224–48.

—— 2000. *The Archaeology of Animal Bones*. Stroud.

O'Connor, T. P. and van der Veen, M. 1998. The expansion of agricultural production in late Iron Age and Roman Britain. In J. Bayley, (ed.), *Science in Archaeology: an Agenda for the Future*. London, 127–43.

Ogilvie, R. M. 1969. *The Romans and their Gods*. London.

Oliver, M. and Applin, B. 1979. Excavation of an Iron Age and Romano-British settlement at Ructstalls Hill, Basingstoke, Hampshire, 1972–5. *Proceedings of the Hampshire Field Club and Archaeological Society*, 35, 41–92.

Orosius. 1990–1. *Historia adversus Paganos*, ed. M.-P. Arnaud-Lindet. Paris.

Ortner, D. J. and Ericksen, M. 1997. Bone changes in infancy in the human skull probably resulting from scurvy in infancy and childhood. *International Journal of Osteoarchaeology*, 7, 212–20.

Ortner, D. J. and Mays, S. 1998. Dry bone manifestations of rickets in infancy and childhood. *International Journal of Osteoarchaeology*, 8, 45–55.

Oswald, A. 1997. A doorway on the past: practical and mystic concerns in the orientation of roundhouse doorways. In A. Gwilt and C. C. Haselgrove (eds), *Reconstructing Iron Age Societies*. Oxford, 87–95.

Ottaway, P. 1993. *Roman York*. London.

—— 1997. Recent excavations of the late Roman signal station at Filey, North Yorkshire. In W. Groenmann-van Waateringe (ed.), *Roman Frontier Studies 1995*. Oxford, 135–41.

Owen, O. A. 1992. Eildon Hill North. In J. S. Rideout, O. A. Owen and E. Halpin (eds), *Hillforts of Southern Scotland*. Edinburgh, 21–71.

Owen-John, H. 1988. Llandough: the rescue excavation of a multi-period site near Cardiff, South Glamorgan. In D. M. Robinson (ed.), *Biglis, Caldicot and Llandough*. BAR (British Series) 188. Oxford, 123–77.

Painter, K. 1997. Silver hoards from Britain in their Late-Roman context. *Antiquité Tardive*, 5, 93–110.

—— 1999. The Water Newton Silver: votive or liturgical? *Journal of the British Archaeological Association*, 152, 1–23.

Palmer, S. C. 1999. Archaeological excavations in the Arrow Valley, Warwickshire. *Transactions of the Birmingham and Warwickshire Archaeological Society*, 103, 1–230.

Parfitt, K. 1995. *Iron Age Burials from Mill Hill, Kent*. London.

Parker, A. J. 1988. The birds of Roman Britain. *Oxford Journal of Archaeology*, 7, 197–226.

Parker Pearson, M. 1996. Food, fertility and front doors in the first millennium BC. In T. C. Champion and J. R. Collis (eds), *The Iron Age in Britain and Ireland*. Sheffield, 117–32.

—— 1999. Food, sex and death: cosmologies in the British Iron Age with particular reference to East Yorkshire. *Cambridge Archaeological Journal*, 9, 43–69.

—— 2000. Great sites: Llyn Cerrig Bach. *British Archaeology*, 53 (June), 8–11.

Parker Pearson, M. and Sharples, N. 1999. *Between Land and Sea: Excavations at Dun Vulan, South Uist*. Sheffield.

Parkhouse, J. 1988. Excavations at Biglis, South Glamorgan. In D. M. Robinson (ed.), *Biglis, Caldicot and Llandough*. BAR (British Series) 188. Oxford, 1–64.

Parkhouse, J. and Evans, E. 1996. *Excavations in Cowbridge, South Glamorgan, 1977–88.* Oxford.

Parkins, H. M. (ed.) 1997. *Roman Urbanism: Beyond the Consumer City.* London and New York.

Pearce, J., Millett, M. and Struck, M. (eds) 2000. *Burial, Society, and Context in the Provincial Roman World.* Oxford.

Pearson, A. 2002. *The Roman Shore Forts: Coastal Defences of Southern Britain.* Stroud.

Perring, D. 1991. *Roman London.* London.

Perring, D. and Brigham, T. 2000. Londinium and its hinterland: the Roman period. In Museum of London Archaeological Service, *The Archaeology of Greater London: An Assessment of Archaeological Evidence for Human Presence in the Area now covered by Greater London.* London, 119–70.

Perry, B. 1966. Some recent discoveries in Hampshire. In C. Thomas (ed.), *Rural Settlement in Roman Britain.* London, 39–42.

Petch, D. F. 1962. A Roman inscription, Nettleham. *Lincolnshire Architectural and Archaeological Society,* NS 9, 94–7.

Phillips, C. W. (ed.) 1970. *The Fenland in Roman Times.* London.

Phillips, D. and Heywood, B. 1995. *Excavations at York Minster.* Volume 1. *From Roman Fortress to Norman Cathedral. Part 1. The Site.* London.

Phillips, E. J. 1976. A workshop of Roman sculptors at Carlisle. *Britannia,* 7, 101–8.

Philpott, R. A. 1991. *Burial Practices in Roman Britain: A Survey of Grave Treatment and Furnishing AD 43–410.* BAR (British Series) 219. Oxford.

—— 1998. New evidence from aerial reconnaissance for Roman military sites in Cheshire. *Britannia,* 29, 341–53.

Philpott, R. A. and Adams, M. 1999. Excavation of an Iron Age and Romano-British settlement at Irby, Wirral, 1987–96. In M. Nevell (ed.), *Living on the Edge of Empire.* Manchester, 64–73.

Piggott, S. 1953. Three metalwork hoards of the Roman period from southern Scotland. *Proceedings of the Society of Antiquaries of Scotland,* 87, 1–50.

—— 1985. *William Stukeley,* rev. edn. London.

Pinter-Bellows, S. 1993. The human skeletons. In N. Crummy, P. Crummy and C. Crossan, *Excavations of Roman and Later Cemeteries, Churches and Monastic Sites in Colchester, 1971–1988.* Archaeological Report 9. Colchester Archaeological Trust, 62–92.

Pitt-Rivers, A. L. F. 1887. *Excavations in Cranborne Chase I.* London.

—— 1898. *Excavations in Cranborne Chase IV.* London.

Pitts, L. F. and St Joseph, J. K. S. 1985. *Inchtuthil.* Britannia Monograph Series 6. London.

Ponsford, M. 1999. Abergavenny, Castle Street Car Park. *Archaeology in Wales,* 39, 98–9.

Potter, T. W. 1981. The Roman occupation of the central Fenland. *Britannia,* 12, 79–133.

—— 1989. Recent work on the Roman Fens of eastern England and the question of imperial estates. *Journal of Roman Archaeology,* 2, 267–74.

—— 1997. *Roman Britain.* London.

Potter, T. W. and Potter C. F. 1982. *A Romano-British Village at Grandford, March, Cambridgeshire.* British Museum Occasional Paper 35. London.

Potter, T. W. and Trow, S. D. 1988. Puckeridge–Braughing, Herts.: The Ermine Street Excavations, 1971–1972. The Late Roman and Iron Age Settlement. *Hertfordshire Archaeology,* 10.

Pounds, N. J. G. 1994. *The Culture of the English People: Iron Age to the Industrial Revolution.* Cambridge.

Price, E. 2000. *Frocester: A Romano-British Settlement, its Antecedents and Successors.* Stonehouse.

Price, J. 1988. Romano-British glass bangles from eastern Yorkshire. In J. Price and P. R. Wilson (eds), *Recent Research in Roman Yorkshire.* BAR (British Series) 193. Oxford, 339–66.

Pritchard, F. A. 1986. Ornamental stonework from Roman London. *Britannia*, 17, 169–89.

Proudfoot, E. V. W. 1978. Camelon native site. *Proceedings of the Society of Antiquaries of Scotland*, 109, 112–28.

Ptolemy. 1881. *Geographia*, ed. C. F. A. Nobbe. Leipzig.

Putnam, B. 1984. *Roman Dorset*. Wimborne.

Quinnell, H. 1986. Cornwall in the Iron Age and the Roman period. *Cornish Archaeology*, 25, 111–34.

—— 1994. Becoming marginal? Dartmoor in later prehistory. *Proceedings of the Devon Archaeological Society*, 52, 75–83.

Rahtz, P., Hayfield, C. and Bateman, J. 1986. *Two Roman Villas at Wharram Le Street*. York.

Ramm, H. 1978. *The Parisi*. London.

Raoult, D., Aboudharam, G., Crubézy, E., Larrouy, G., Ludes, B. and Drancourt, M. 2000. Molecular identification by 'suicide PCR' of Yersinia pestis as the agent of medieval black death. *Proceedings of the National Academy of Sciences*, 97, 12800–3.

Raybould, M. 1999. *A Study of Inscribed Material from Roman Britain*. BAR 281. Oxford.

Reader, R. 1974. New evidence for the antiquity of leprosy in early Britain. *Journal of Archaeological Science*, 1, 205–7.

Reece, R. M. 1991. *Roman Coins from 140 Sites in Britain*. Oxford.

—— 1999. Colonia in context: Glevum and the civitas Dobunnorum. In H. R. Hurst (ed.), *The Coloniae of Roman Britain*. Portsmouth, RI, 73–85.

Reilly, K. 1996. The bird bones. In R. J. Williams, P. J. Hart and A. T. L. Williams (eds), *Wavedon Gate: A Late Iron Age and Roman Rural Settlement in Milton Keynes*. Buckinghamshire Archaeological Society, Monograph Series 10. Aylesbury, 230–3.

Reitz, E. J. and Wing, E. S. 1999. *Zooarchaeology*. Oxford.

Revell, L. 1999. Constructing Romanitas: Roman public architecture and the archaeology of practice. In P. Baker, C. Forcey, S. Jundi and R. Witcher (eds), *Theoretical Roman Archaeology Conference Proceedings 1998*. Oxford, 52–8.

Riccobono, S., Baviera, J., Ferrini, C., Furlani, J. and Arangio-Ruiz, V. (eds) 1940–3. *Fontes iuris Romani anteiustiniani*. 3 vols. Florence.

Richmond, I. A. 1937. Review of R. G. Collingwood and J. N. L. Myres, *Roman Britain and the English Settlements. Archaeologia Aeliana*, 4th ser. 14, 258–67.

—— 1943. Roman legionaries at Corbridge, their supply-base, temples and religious cults. *Archaeologia Aeliana*, 4th ser. 21, 127–224.

—— 1947. *Handbook to the Roman Wall*, 10th edn. Newcastle upon Tyne.

—— 1950. Hadrian's Wall 1939–49. *Journal of Roman Studies*, 40, 43–56.

—— 1961. A new building inscription from the Saxon-shore fort at Reculver, Kent. *Antiquaries Journal*, 41, 224–8.

—— 1968. *Hod Hill II*. London.

—— 1993. The four Roman camps of Cawthorn. *Archaeological Journal*, 89, 17–78.

Richmond, I. A. and McIntyre, J. 1934. The Roman camps at Rey Cross and Crackenthorpe. *Transactions of the Cumberland and Westmorland Antiquarian and Archaeological Society*, ser. 2, 34, 50–61.

Rigby, V. 1995. Italic imports in late Iron Age Britain: a summary of the evidence from 'chieftains' burials. In J. Swaddling, S. Walker, and P. Roberts (eds), *Italy and Europe: Economic Relations 700 BC–AD 50*. British Museum Occasional Paper 97. London, 235–64.

Rippon, S. 1996. *The Gwent Levels: The Evolution of a Wetland Landscape*. CBA Research Report 105. York.

—— 1997. *The Severn Estuary. Landscape Evolution and Wetland Reclamation*. London.

Rivet, A. L. F. (ed.) 1966. *The Iron Age in Northern Britain*. Edinburgh.

—— 1969. *The Roman Villa in Britain*. London.

Rivet, A. L. F. and Smith, C. 1979. *The Place-names of Roman Britain*. London.

Roach Smith, C. 1848. *Collectanea Antiqua I*.

Roberts, C. A. 1984. *The Human Skeletal Report from Baldock, Hertfordshire*. Calvin Wells Laboratory, University of Bradford. [Unpublished.]

—— 1985. An osteochondroma from Derby Racecourse Roman cemetery. *Paleopathology Association Newsletter*, 50, 7–8.

—— 1987. A possible case of pituitary dwarfism from the Roman period. *British Medical Journal*, 295, 1659–60.

—— 1989. *The Human Remains from 76 Kingsholm, Gloucester*. Calvin Wells Laboratory, University of Bradford. [Unpublished.]

—— 1996. The biological evidence or what the people say. In E. O'Brien and C. A. Roberts, Archaeological study of church cemeteries: past, present and future. In J. Blair and C. Pyrah (eds), *Church Archaeology: Research Directions for the Future*. CBA Research Report 104. York, 159–81.

—— 2000. Did they take sugar? The use of skeletal evidence in the study of disability in past populations. In J. Hubert (ed.), *Madness, Disability and Social Exclusion: The Archaeology and Anthropology of Difference*. London, 46–59.

Roberts, C. A. and Buikstra, J. E. (forthcoming). *Tuberculosis: Old Disease with New Awakenings*. Gainesville, FL.

Roberts, C. A. and Cox, M. (forthcoming). *Health and Disease in Britain: Prehistory to the Present Day*. Gloucester.

Roberts, C. A. and McKinley, J. (forthcoming). A review of British trepanations in antiquity, focusing on funerary context to explain their occurrence. In R. Arnott and S. Finger (eds), *Proceedings of the International Symposium on Trepanation in Antiquity, Birmingham*. Amsterdam.

Roberts, C. A., Lewis, M. E. and Boocock, P. 1998. Infectious disease, sex and gender: the complexity of it all. In A. Grauer and P. Stuart Macadam (eds), *Sex and Gender in Paleopathological Perspective*. Cambridge, 93–113.

Roberts, M. R. 1995. Excavations at Park Farm, Binfield, 1990: an Iron Age and Romano-British settlement and two Mesolithic flint scatters. In I. Barnes, C. A. Butterworth, J. W. Hawkes and L. Smith, *Early Settlement in Berkshire*. Wessex Archaeology Monograph 6. Salisbury, 93–132.

Robertson, A. S. 1978. The circulation of Roman coins in North Britain: the evidence of hoards and site finds from Scotland. In R. A. G. Carson and C. Kraay (eds), *Scripta Nummaria Romana*. London, 186–216.

Robinson, D. M. (ed.) 1988. *Biglis, Caldicot and Llandough. Three Late Iron Age and Romano-British Sites in South-east Wales, Excavations 1977–79*. BAR (British Series) 188. Oxford.

Roche-Bernard, Geneviève. 1992. *Costumes et textiles en Gaule romaine*. Paris.

Rodwell, W. J. and Rodwell K. A. 1986 and 1993. *Rivenhall: Investigations of a Villa, Church and Village 1950–1977*. CBA Research Reports 55 and 80. York.

Rogers, J. 1986. Mesomelic dwarfism in a Romano-British skeleton. *Paleopathology Association Newsletter*, 55, 6–10.

—— 1990. The human skeletal material. In A. Saville, *Hazleton North, Gloucestershire, 1979–1982. The Excavation of a Neolithic Long Cairn of the Cotswold-Severn Group*. English Heritage Archaeological Report 13. London, 182–98.

—— 2001. DISH and the monastic way of life. *International Journal of Osteoarchaeology*, 11, 357–65.

Rogers, J. and Waldron, T. 1995. *A Field Guide to Joint Disease in Archaeology*. Chichester.

Romeuf, A.-M. 2000. *Les ex-voto gallo-romains de Chamalières (Puy de Dóme)*. Paris.

Rook, T. 1997. The view from Hertfordshire. In D. and R. Friendship-Taylor (eds), *From Round House to Villa*. Hackleton, 53–7.

Roskams, S. 1999. The hinterlands of Roman York: present patterns and future strategies. In H. R. Hurst (ed.), *The* Coloniae *of Roman Britain*. Sheffield, 45–72.

Roskams, S. and Saunders, T. 2001. The poverty of empiricism and the tyranny of theory. In U. Albarella (ed.), *Environmental Archaeology: Meaning and Purpose*. Dordrecht, 61–74.

Roxan, M. M. 1981. The distribution of Roman military diplomas. *Epigraphic Studies*, 12, 265–86.

—— 1985. *Roman Military Diplomas, 1978–1984*. Institute of Archaeology Occasional Paper 9. London.

—— 1989. Women on the frontiers. In V. A. Maxfield and M. J. Dobson (eds), *Roman Frontier Studies 1989: Proceedings of the XV International Congress on Roman Frontier Studies*. Exeter, 462–7.

Roy, W. 1793. *The Military Antiquities of the Romans in Britain*. London.

Royal Commission on the Ancient and Historic Monuments of Scotland. 1978. *Lanarkshire: An Inventory of the Prehistoric and Roman Monuments*. Edinburgh.

—— 1990. *North-east Perth: An Archaeological Landscape*. London.

—— 1994. *South-east Perth: An Archaeological Landscape*. Edinburgh.

—— 1997. *Eastern Dumfriesshire: An Archaeological Landscape*. Edinburgh.

Royal Commission on Ancient and Historical Monuments in Wales. 1986. *An Inventory of the Ancient Monuments in Brecknock (Brycheiniog): The Prehistoric and Roman Monuments, Part II: Hill-forts and Roman Remains*. Cardiff.

Royal Commission on Historical Monuments (England). 1962. *Eboracum: Roman York*. London.

—— 1976. *An Inventory of Iron Age and Romano-British Monuments in the Gloucestershire Cotswolds*. London.

Roymans, N. 1990. *Tribal Societies in Northern Gaul*. Amsterdam.

—— 1999. Man, cattle and the supernatural in the Northwest European Plain. In C. Fabech and J. Ringtved (eds), *Settlement and Landscape: Proceedings of a Conference in Åarhus, Denmark, May 4–7 1998*. Mooesgård, 291–300.

Rudling, D. R. 1982. Rural settlement in Late Iron Age and Roman Sussex. In D. Miles (ed.), *The Romano-British Countryside*. BAR (British Series) 103. Oxford, 269–88.

—— 1997. Round 'house' to villa: the Beddingham and Watergate villas. In D. and R. Friendship-Taylor (eds), *From Round House to Villa*. Hackleton, 1–8.

—— 1998. The development of Roman villas in Sussex. *Sussex Archaeological Collections*, 136, 41–65.

Rule, M. and Monaghan, J. 1993. *Gallo-Roman Trading Vessel from Guernsey*. St Peter Port.

Sadler, P. 1997. Faunal remains. In A. G. Marvell and H. S. Owen-John (eds), *Leucarum: Excavations at the Roman Auxiliary Fort at Loughor, West Glamorgan 1982–4 and 1987–8*. London.

St Joseph, J. K. S. 1973. Air reconnaissance in Roman Britain, 1969–72. *Journal of Roman Studies*, 63, 214–46.

—— 1976. Air reconnaissance in Roman Scotland, 1939–75. *Glasgow Archaeological Journal*, 4, 1–28.

—— 1977. Air reconnaissance in Roman Britain, 1973–76. *Journal of Roman Studies*, 67, 125–61.

—— 1978. The camp at Durno and Mons Graupius. *Britannia*, 9, 271–88.

Salway, P. 1981. *Roman Britain*. Oxford.

Salway, P. (ed.) 2001. *The Short Oxford History of the British Isles: The Roman Era*. Oxford.

Sargent, A. 2002. The north–south divide revisited: thoughts on the character of Roman Britain. *Britannia*, 33, 219–26.

Sauer, E. 1999. The Augustan army spa at Bourbonne-les-Bains. In A. Goldsworthy and I. Haynes (eds), *The Roman Army as a Community.* Journal of Roman Archaeology Supplementary Series 34. Portsmouth, RI, 52–79.

—— 2000. Excavations at Alchester, Oxon. *Archaeological Journal.*

Scholz, B. I. 1992. *Untersuchungen zur Tracht der römischen Matrona*, Cologne.

Schultz, M. 1999. The role of tuberculosis in infancy and childhood in prehistoric and historic populations. In G. Pálfi, O. Dutour, J. Deák and I. Hutás (eds), *Tuberculosis, Past and Present.* Szeged and Budapest, 503–7.

—— 2001. Paleohistopathology of bone: a new approach to the study of ancient disease. *Yearbook of Physical Anthropology*, 44, 106–47.

Scott, E. 1991. Animal and infant burials in Romano-British villas: a revitalization movement. In P. Garwood, D. Jennings, R. Skeates and J. Toms (eds), *Sacred and Profane.* Oxford University Committee for Archaeology 32. Oxford, 115–21.

—— 1993. *A Gazetteer of Roman Villas in Britain.* Leicester.

Sealey, P. R. 1997. *The Boudican Revolt against Rome.* Princes Risborough.

Sebaste, J. L. and Bonfante, L. (eds) 1994. *The World of Roman Costume.* Madison, WI.

Sekulla, M. F. 1982 The Roman coins from Traprain Law. *Proceedings of the Society of Antiquaries of Scotland*, 112, 285–94.

Sellwood, L. 1987. The non-Durotrigian Celtic coins [from Hengistbury]. In B. Cunliffe, *Hengistbury Head.* Oxford, 138–40.

Sharples, N. M. 1991. *Maiden Castle: Excavation and Field Survey 1985–6.* English Heritage Archaeological Report 19. London.

Sharples, N. M. and Parker Pearson, M. 1997. Why were brochs built? Recent studies in the Iron Age of Atlantic Scotland. In A. Gwilt and C. C. Haselgrove (eds), *Reconstructing Iron Age Societies.* Oxford, 254–65.

Sheldon, H. and Schaaf, L. 1978. A survey of Roman sites in Greater London. In J. Bird, H. Chapman and J. Clark (eds), *Collectanea Londiniensia: Studies Presented to Ralph Merrifield.* London, 59–88.

Shepherd, J. 1998. *The Temple of Mithras, London: Excavations by W. F. Grimes and A. Williams at the Walbrook.* London.

Shirley, E. 2001. *Building a Roman Legionary Fortress.* Stroud.

Shotter, D. 1996. *The Roman Frontier in Britain.* Preston.

Silvester, R. 1981. Excavations at Honeyditches Roman villa, Seaton, in 1978. *Proceedings of the Devon Archaeological Society*, 39, 37–88.

Simco, A. 1984. *Survey of Bedfordshire: The Roman Period.* Bedford.

Simpson, F. G. and Richmond, I. A. 1937. The Roman fort on Hadrian's Wall at Halton. *Archaeologia Aeliana*, 4th ser. 19, 151–71.

Simpson, G. 1964. *Britons and the Roman Army.* London.

Simpson, S., Griffith, F. and Holbrook, N. 1989. The prehistoric, Roman and early post-Roman site at Hayes Farm, Clyst Honiton. *Proceedings of the Devon Archaeological Society*, 47, 1–28.

Simpson, W. G. 1966. Romano-British settlement on the Welland gravels. In C. Thomas (ed.), *Rural Settlement in Roman Britain.* London, 15–25.

Smith, A. 2001. *The Differential Use of Constructed Sacred Space in Southern Britain, from the Late Iron Age to the 4th Century AD.* BAR (British Series) 318. Oxford.

Smith, C. 1979. The historical development of the landscape in the parishes of Alrewas, Fisherwick and Whittington: a retrogressive analysis. *Transactions of the South Staffordshire Archaeological and Historical Society*, 20, 1–14.

Smith, J. T. 1978. Halls or yards? A problem of villa interpretation. *Britannia*, 9, 351–8.

—— 1978. Villas as a key to social structure. In M. Todd (ed.), *Studies in the Romano-British Villa*. Leicester, 149–85.

Smith, J. T. 1985. Barnsley Park villa: its interpretation and implications. *Oxford Journal of Archaeology*, 4, 341–51. [See also the reply by Webster, 6, 1987, 69–89.]

—— 1997. *Roman Villas: A Study in Social Structure*. London.

Smith, R. A. 1912. On Late Celtic antiquities discovered at Welwyn, Herts. *Archaeologia*, 63, 1–30.

Smout, T. C. (ed.) 1993. *Scotland since Prehistory: Natural Change and Human Impact*. Aberdeen.

Sommer, C. S. 1999. From conquered territory to Roman province: recent discoveries and debates on the Roman occupation of south-west Germany. In J. D. Creighton and R. J. A. Wilson (eds), *Roman Germany*. Portsmouth, RI, 160–98.

Soranus. 1956. *Gynecology*, trans. O. Temkin. Baltimore, MD.

Southern, P. and Dixon, K. 1996. *The Late Roman Army*. London.

Stallibrass, S. 1982. The faunal remains. In T. W. Potter and C. F. Potter (eds), *A Roman-British village at Grandford, March, Cambridgeshire*. London, 98–127.

Stanford, S. C. 1995. A Cornovian farm and Saxon cemetery at Bromfield, Shropshire. *Transactions of the Shropshire Archaeological and Historical Society*, 70, 95–141.

Stead, I. M. 1967. A La Tène burial at Welwyn Garden City. *Archaeologia*, 109, 1–63.

—— 1989. The earliest burials of the Aylesford Culture. In G. de G. Sieveking, I. M. Longworth and K. E. Wilson (eds), *Problems in Economic and Social Archaeology*. London, 401–16.

Stead, I. M. and Rigby, V. 1986. *Baldock: The Excavation of a Roman and Pre-Roman Settlement, 1968–73*. Britannia Monograph 7. London.

—— 1989. *Verulamium: The King Harry Lane Site*. English Heritage Archaeological Report 12. London.

Stead, I. M., Bourke, J. B. and Brothwell, D. 1986. *Lindow Man: The Body in the Bog*. London.

Stephens, G. R. 1985. Civic Aqueducts in Britain. *Britannia*, 16, 197–208.

Stevens, C. E. 1951. Britain between the Invasions (54 BC–AD 43). In W. F. Grimes (ed.), *Aspects of Archaeology, in Britain and Beyond*. London, 332–44.

Stevenson, R. B. K. 1976. Romano-British glass bangles. *Glasgow Archaeological Journal*, 4, 45–54.

Still, B., Vyner, B. and Benley, R. 1997. A decade of air survey in Cleveland and the Tees Valley hinterland and a strategy for air survey in County Durham. *Durham Archaeological Journal*, 5, 1–10.

Stini, W. A. 1990. Osteoporosis: etiologies, prevention and treatment. *Yearbook of Physical Anthropology*, 33, 151–94.

Stoertz, C. 1997. *Ancient Landscapes of the Yorkshire Wolds: Aerial Photographic Transcription and Analysis*. Swindon.

Stokes, P. 2000. A cut above the rest? Officers and men at South Shields Roman fort. In P. Rowley-Conwy (ed.), *Animal Bones, Human Societies*. Oxford, 145–51.

Stout, M. 1997. *The Irish Ringfort*. Dublin.

Straker, V. 1987. Carbonised cereal grain from first-century London: a summary of the evidence for importation and crop-processing. In P. Marsden (ed.), *The Roman Forum Site in London: Discoveries before 1985*. London, 151–5.

Stuart, R. 1845. *Caledonia Romana*. Edinburgh and London.

Stuart Macadam, P. 1991. Anaemia in Roman Britain. In H. Bush and M. Zvelebil (eds), *Health in Past Societies*. BAR (British Series) 567. Oxford, 101–13.

Stuart Macadam, P. and Kent, S. (eds) 1992. *Diet, Demography and Disease: Changing Perspectives on Anaemia*. New York.

Stukeley, W. 1776. *Itinerarium Curiosum*, 2nd edn. London.

Suetonius. 1927. *Divus Vespasianus*, ed. A. W. Braithwaite. Oxford.

—— 1959. *Divus Claudius*, ed. J. C. Rolfe. London and Cambridge, MA.

Suetonius. 1959. *Galba*, ed. J. C. Rolfe. London and Cambridge, MA.

Sumner, Graham. 2002. *Roman Military Clothing I: 100 BC–AD 100*. Oxford.

Swan, V. G. and Philpott, R. A. 2000. Legio XX VV and tile production at Tarbock, Mersey-side. *Britannia*, 31, 55–67.

Swift, E. 2000. *Regionality in Dress Accessories in the Late Roman West*. Montagnac.

Syme, R. 1958. *Tacitus*. Oxford.

Tacitus. 1967. *Historiarvm Libri*, ed. C. D. Fisher. Oxford.

—— 1967. *De Vita Agricolae*, ed. R. M. Ogilvie and I. A. Richmond. Oxford.

—— 1973. *Annalivm Libri*, ed. C. D. Fisher. Oxford.

Tate, J., Barnes, I. and MacSween, A. 1985. Analysis of massive bronze armlets. In T. Bryce and J. Tate (eds), *The Laboratories of the National Museum of Antiquities of Scotland*. Volume 2. Edinburgh, 89–94.

Taylor, D. J. A., Robinson, J. and Biggins, J. A. 2000. A report on a geophysical survey of the Roman fort and *vicus* at Halton Chesters. *Archaeologia Aeliana*, 5th ser. 28, 37–46.

Taylor, G. M., Rutland, P. and Molleson, T. 1997. A sensitive polymerase chain reaction method for the detection of *Plasmodium* species DNA in ancient human remains. *Ancient Biomolecules*, 1, 193–203.

Taylor, G. M., Widdison, S., Brown, I. N. and Young, D. 2000. A mediaeval case of lepromatous leprosy in 13th–14th century Orkney. *Journal of Archaeological Science*, 27, 1133–8.

Taylor, J. 2001. Rural society in Roman Britain. In S. James and M. Millett (eds), *Britons and Romans*. CBA Research Report 125. York, 46–59.

Thomas, C. 1966a. The character and origins of Roman Dumnonia. In C. Thomas (ed.), *Rural Settlement in Roman Britain*. London, 74–98.

—— 1985. *Christianity in Roman Britain to AD 500*. London.

—— 1994. *And Shall These Mute Stones Speak?* Cardiff.

Thomas, C. (ed.) 1966b. *Rural Settlement in Roman Britain*. London.

Thomas, W. G. and Walker, R. F 1959. Excavations at Trelissey, Pembrokeshire, 1950–1. *Bulletin of the Board of Celtic Studies*, 18, 295–303.

Thompson, E. A. 1984. *St Germanus of Auxerre and the End of Roman Britain*. Woodbridge.

—— 1985. *Who Was St Patrick?* Woodbridge.

Thoresby, R. 1713. *Musaeum Thoresbyanum*. London.

Timby, J. 1998. *Excavations at Kingscote and Wycomb, Gloucestershire*. Cirencester.

Tipping, R. 1994. The form and fate of Scotland's woodlands. *Proceedings of the Society of Antiquaries of Scotland*, 124, 1–54.

—— 1997. Pollen analysis and the impact of Rome on native agriculture around Hadrian's Wall. In A. Gwilt and C. C. Haselgrove (eds), *Reconstructing Iron Age Societies*. Oxford, 239–47.

—— 1999. Towards an environmental history of the Bowmont valley and the northern Cheviot hills. *Landscape History*, 20, 41–50.

Todd, M. 1968. *The Roman Fort at Great Casterton*. Oxford.

—— 1973. *The Coritani*. London.

—— 1985. Forum and Capitolium in the early Empire. In F. Grew and B. Hobley (eds), *Roman Urban Topography in Britain and the Western Empire*. CBA Research Report 59. London, 56–66.

—— 1985. Oppida and the Roman army. *Oxford Journal of Archaeology*, 4, 187–99.

—— 1987. *The South-West to AD 1000*. Harlow.

—— 1996. Pretia Victoriae? Roman lead and silver mining on the Mendip Hills, Somerset. *Münstersche Beitrage zur Antiken Handelsgeschichte*, 15, 1–18.

—— 1999. *Roman Britain*. Oxford.

—— 2001. *Migrants and Invaders: The Movement of Peoples in the Ancient World*. Stroud.

Todd, M. 2002. Mining, bullion and the balance of payments in the Roman West. *Laverna*, 13, 81–90.

Todd, M. (ed.) 1978. *Studies in the Romano-British Villa*. Leicester.

—— 1989. *Research on Roman Britain 1960–89*. Britannia Monograph Series 11. London.

Tolan-Smith, M. 1997. The Romano-British and later prehistoric landscape. In C. Tolan-Smith (ed.), *Landscape Archaeology in Tynedale*. Tyne-Solway Ancient and Historic Landscapes Research programme, Monograph 1. Newcastle-upon-Tyne, 69–78.

Tomalin, D. 1987. *Roman Wight: A Guide Catalogue*. Newport.

Tomlin, R. S. O. 1988. The curse tablets. In B. Cunliffe, *The Temple of Sulis Minerva at Bath. 2. The Finds from the Sacred Spring*. Oxford University Committee for Archaeology 16. Oxford, 59–277.

—— 1996. A five-acre wood in Roman Kent. In J. Bird, M. Hassall and H. Sheldon (eds), *Interpreting Roman London*. Oxford, 209–15.

—— 1996. The Vindolanda writing tablets. *Britannia*, 27, 459–63.

—— 2000. The Legions in the late Empire. In R. J. Brewer (ed), *Roman Fortresses and their Legions*. London, 159–78.

Topping, P. 1989. Early cultivation in Northumberland and the Borders. *Proceedings of the Prehistoric Society*, 55, 161–79.

Toynbee, J. M. C. 1973. *Animals in Roman Life and Art*. London.

Trow, S. and James, S. 1988. Ditches villa, North Cerney. An example of locational conservatism in the early Roman Cotswolds. In K. Branigan and D. Miles (eds), *The Economics of Romano-British Villas*. Sheffield, 83–7.

Tyers, P. 1996. *Roman Pottery in Britain*. London.

Tylecote, R. F. 1976. *A History of Metallurgy*. London.

van der Veen, M. 1992. *Crop Husbandry Regimes: An Archaeobotanical Study of Farming in Northern England 1000 BC–AD 500*. Sheffield Archaeological Monographs 3. Sheffield.

—— 1994. Reports on the biological remains. In P. Bidwell and S. Speak, *Excavations at South Shields Roman Fort* I. Newcastle, 243–69.

van Driel Murray, C. 1995. Gender in question. In P. Rash (ed.), *Theoretical Roman Archaeology: Second Conference Proceedings*. Aldershot, 3–21.

—— 2001. Vindolanda and the dating of Roman footwear. *Britannia*, 32, 185–97.

Vermaseren, M. J. 1977. *Cybele and Attis: The Myth and the Cult*. London.

Vigne, J.-D. 1992. The meat and offal (MOW) method and the relative proportions of ovicaprines in some ancient meat diets of the north-western Mediterranean. *Rivista di Studi Liguri*, A.57 (1991), 21–47.

Vyner, B. and Allen, D. W. 1988. A Romano-British settlement at Caldicot, Gwent. In D. M. Robinson (ed.), *Biglis, Caldicot and Llandough*. BAR (British Series) 188. Oxford, 65–122.

Wacher, J. S. 1979. *Roman Britain*. London.

—— 1995. *The Towns of Roman Britain*, rev. edn. London. [First published in 1975.]

Wacher, J. S. 1998. The dating of town walls in Roman Britain. In J. Bird (ed.), *Studies in Rome's Material Past in Honour of B. R. Hartley*. Oxford, 41–50.

—— 2000. *A Portrait of Roman Britain*. London.

Wacher, J. and McWhirr, A. 1982. *Early Roman Occupation at Cirencester*. Cirencester.

Wainwright, G. 1971. The excavation of a fortified settlement at Walesland Rath, Pembrokeshire. *Britannia*, 2, 48–108.

—— 1979. *Gussage All Saints: An Iron Age Settlement in Dorset*. Archaeological Report 10. London.

Waldron, T. 1982. Human bone lead concentrations. In A. McWhirr, L. Viner and C. Wells, *Romano-British Cemeteries at Cirencester*. Cirencester, 203–20.

—— 1983. On the post-mortem accumulation of lead by skeletal tissues. *Journal of Archaeological Science*, 10, 35–40.

Waldron, T. 1989. *The Human Remains from Alington Avenue*. Unpublished report.

—— 1994. *Counting the Dead: The Epidemiology of Skeletal Populations*. Chichester.

Walters, B. 1984. The 'Orpheus' mosaic in Littlecote Park, England. In R. Farioli Campanati (ed.), *III colloquio internazionale sul mosaico antico*. Ravenna, 433–42.

—— 1992. *The Archaeology and History of Ancient Dean and the Wye Valley*. Cheltenham.

—— 1996. 'Exotic' structures in 4th-century Britain. In P. Johnson (ed.), *Architecture in Roman Britain*. CBA Research Report 94. York, 152–62.

—— 2001. A perspective on the social order of Roman villas in Wiltshire. In P. Ellis (ed.), *Roman Wiltshire and After. Papers in honour of Ken Annable*. Devizes, 127–46.

Waterman, D. M. 1997. *Excavations at Navan Fort, 1961–71*. Northern Ireland Archaeology Monographs 3. Belfast.

Watkins, T. 1980. Excavation of a settlement and a souterrain at Newmill, near Bankfoot, Perthshire. *Proceedings of the Society of Antiquaries of Scotland*, 110, 165–208.

Watson, B. (ed.) 1998. *Roman London: Recent Archaeological Work*. Journal of Roman Archaeology, Supplementary Series 24. Portsmouth, RI.

Watts, L. and Leach, P. 1996. *Henley Wood, Temples and Cemetery Excavations 1962–69*. CBA Research Report 99. York.

Webster, G. 1960. The Roman military advance under Ostorius Scapula. *Archaeological Journal*, 115, 49–98.

—— 1970. Military situations in Britain A.D. 43–71. *Britannia*, 1, 179–97.

—— 1975. *The Cornovii*. London.

—— 1980. *The Roman Invasion of Britain*. London.

—— 1982. *Rome against Caratacus*. London.

—— 1993. *Boudica*, 2nd edn. London.

—— 1998. *The Roman Imperial Army*. Norman, OK.

Webster, G. (ed.) 1988. *Fortress into City: The Consolidation of Roman Britain, First Century AD*. London.

Webster, G., Fowler, P., Noddle, B. and Smith, L. 1981–5. The excavation of a Romano-British rural establishment at Barnsley Park, Gloucestershire, 1961–79. *Transactions of the Bristol and Gloucestershire Archaeological Society*, 99, 21–77; 100, 65–189; 103, 73–100.

Webster, J. 1995. Roman word-power and the Celtic gods. *Britannia*, 26, 153–61.

—— 1997. Necessary comparisons: a post-colonial approach to religious syncretism in the Roman provinces. *World Archaeology*, 28, 324–38.

—— 1998. Freedom fighters under a mystic cloak. *British Archaeology*, 39 (November), 18.

—— 1999. At the end of the world: druidic and other revitalization movements in post-conquest Gaul and Britain. *Britannia*, 30, 1–20.

—— 1999. Here be dragons! the continuing influence of Roman attitudes to northern Britain. In B. Bevan (ed.), *Northern Exposure*. Leicester. 21–31.

Webster, J. and Cooper, N. (eds) 1996. *Roman Imperialism: Post-colonial Perspectives*. Leicester Archaeology Monographs 3. Leicester.

Webster, P. V. 1990. The first Roman fort at Cardiff. In B. C. Burnham and J. L. Davies, *Conquest, Co-existence & Change: Recent Work in Roman Wales*. Trivium 25. Lampeter, 35–9.

Wedlake, W. J. 1982. *The Excavation of the Shrine of Apollo at Nettleton, Wiltshire 1956–1971*. London.

Welfare, H. and Swan, V. 1995. *Roman Camps in England: The Field Archaeology*. London.

Wells, C. 1982. The human burials. In A. McWhirr, L. Viner and C. Wells, *Romano-British Cemeteries at Cirencester*. Cirencester, 135–202.

Wells, C. and Woodhouse, N. 1975. Paget's disease in an Anglo-Saxon. *Medical History* 19, 396–400.

Wells, P. S. 2002. Perspectives on changes in early Roman Gaul. *Archaeological Dialogues*, 9, 47–51.

Wheeler, R. E. M. 1926. The Roman Fort at Brecon, *Y Cymmrodor*, 36.

Wheeler, R. E. M. and Wheeler, T. V. 1932. *Report on the Excavation of the Prehistoric, Roman and Post-Roman Site in Lydney Park, Gloucestershire*. Oxford.

—— 1936. *Verulamium: A Belgic and Two Roman Cities*. Oxford.

Whimster, R. 1981. *Burial Practices in Iron Age Britain*. BAR (British Series) 90. Oxford.

—— 1989. *The Emerging Past: Air Photography and the Buried Landscape*. London.

White, D. A. 1961. *Litus Saxonicum*. Madison, WI.

White, K. D. 1970. *Roman Farming*. London.

White, R. 1997. Summary of fieldwork carried out by the Wroxeter Hinterland Project 1994–7. *Transactions of the Shropshire Archaeological and Historical Society*, 72, 1–8.

White, R. and Barker, P. 1998. *Wroxeter, Life and Death of a Roman City*. Stroud.

Whittaker, C. R. 2000. Frontiers. In A. K. Bowman, P. Garnsey and D. Rathbone (eds), *The High Empire*, A.D. *70–192. The Cambridge Ancient History*, volume XI, 2nd edn. Cambridge, 223–82.

Whittaker, C. R. (ed.) 1988. *Pastoral Economies in Classical Antiquity*. Cambridge.

Whittington, G. and Edwards, K. J. 1993. *Ubi solitudinem faciunt, pacem appellant*: the Romans in Scotland, a palaeo-environmental contribution. *Britannia*, 24, 13–25.

—— 1997. Climate change. In K. Edwards and I. Ralston (eds), *Scotland: Environment and Archaeology, 8000 BC–AD 1000*. Chichester, 11–22.

Whitwell, J. B. 1970. *Roman Lincolnshire*. Lincoln.

Wigg, A. 1999. Confrontation and interaction: Celts, Germans and Romans in the Central German Highlands. In J. Creighton and R. J. A. Wilson (eds), *Roman Germany*. Journal of Roman Archaeology, Supplementary Series 32. Portsmouth, RI, 35–53.

Wild, J. P. 1968. Clothing in the north-west provinces of the Roman Empire. *Bonner Jahrbücher*, 168, 166–240.

—— 1970. Button and loop fasteners in the Roman provinces, *Britannia*, 1, 137–55.

—— 1970. *Textile Manufacture in the Northern Roman Provinces*. Cambridge.

—— 1978. Villas in the Lower Nene valley. In M. Todd (ed.), *Studies in the Romano-British Villa*. Leicester, 59–69.

—— 1985. The clothing of Britannia, Gallia Belgica and Germania Inferior. In H. Temporini and W. Haase (eds), *Aufstieg und Niedergang der Römischen Welt*, vol. II,12,3. Berlin and New York, 362–422.

—— 2002. The textile industries of Roman Britain. *Britannia*, 33, 1–42.

Wilkins, J., Harvey, D. and Dobson, M. (eds) 1995. *Food in Antiquity*. Exeter.

Willems, W. 1981 and 1984. Romans and Batavians: a regional study in the Dutch eastern river area. *Berichten Rijksdienst Oudheidkundig Bodemonderzoek*, 31, 5–201, and 32, 42–491.

Williams, D. 1987. Amphorae [from Hengistbury]. In B. Cunliffe, *Hengistbury Head*. Oxford, 271–5.

Williams, G. and Mytum, H. 1998. *Llawhaden, Dyfed: Excavations on a group of small defended enclosures, 1980–4*. BAR (British Series) 275. Oxford.

Williams, J. H. C. (forthcoming). Coin inscriptions and the origins of writing in pre-Roman Britain. *Numismatic Chronicle*.

Williams, R. J. and Zeepvat, R. 1994. *Bancroft: A Late Bronze Age/Iron Age Settlement, Roman Villa and Temple/Mausoleum*. Buckinghamshire Archaeological Society Monograph 7. Aylesbury.

Williams, R. J., Hart, P. and Williams, A. 1996. *Wavendon Gate: A Late Iron Age and Roman Settlement in Milton Keynes*. Buckinghamshire Archaeological Society Monograph 10. Aylesbury.

Willis, S. 1996. The Romanization of pottery assemblages in the east and north-east of England during the first century A.D.: a comparative analysis, *Britannia*, 27, 223–82.

Willis, S. 1999. Without and within: aspects of culture and community in the Iron Age of north-east England. In B. Bevan (ed.), *Northern Exposure*. Leicester, 81–110.

Wilmott, T. 2001. *Birdoswald Roman Fort. 1800 Years on Hadrian's Wall*. Stroud.

Wilson, B. 1986. Faunal remains: animal bones and shells. In, D. Miles, (ed.), *Archaeology at Barton Court Farm, Abingdon, Oxfordshire*. Oxford Archaeological Unit and the Council for British Archaeology, Fiche 8, A1–G14. Oxford.

Wilson, L. M. 1924. *The Roman Toga*. Baltimore, MD.

—— 1938. *The Clothing of the Ancient Romans*. Baltimore, MD.

Wilson, P. R. 1991. Aspects of the Yorkshire signal stations. In V. A. Maxfield and M. J. Dobson (eds), *Roman Frontier Studies 1989*. Exeter, 142–7.

—— 2002. *Roman Catterick and its Hinterland*. CBA Research Reports 128–9. London.

Wise, A. 2000. Late prehistoric settlement and society: recent research in the central Tweed valley. In J. Harding and R. Johnson (eds), *Northern Pasts: Interpretation in the Later Prehistory of Northern England and Southern Scotland*. BAR (British Series) 302. Oxford, 93–9.

Witt, R. E. 1971. *Isis in the Graeco-Roman World*. London.

Wood, I. N. 1984. The end of Roman Britain: continental evidence and parallels. In M. Lapidge and D. N. Dumville (eds), *Gildas: New Approaches*. Woodbridge, pp. 1–25.

—— 1987. The fall of the Western Empire and the end of Roman Britain. *Britannia*, 18, 251–62.

—— 2000. The north-western provinces. In A. Cameron, B. Ward-Perkins and M. Whitby (eds), *The Cambridge Ancient History*. Volume 14. *Late Antiquity: Empire and Successors A.D. 425–600*. Cambridge, 497–524.

Wood, J. E., Milner, G. R., Harpending, H. C. and Weiss, K. M. 1992. The osteological paradox: problems of inferring health from the skeletal samples. *Current Anthropology*, 33, 343–70.

Woodside, R. and Crow J. 1999. *Hadrian's Wall: An Historic Landscape*. London.

Woodward, A. 1992. *Shrines and Sacrifice*. London.

Woodward, A. and Leach, P. 1993. *The Uley Shrines: Excavation of a Ritual Complex on West Hill, Uley, Gloucestershire: 1977–9*. London.

Woolf, G. 1998. *Becoming Roman: The Origins of Provincial Civilization in Gaul*. Cambridge.

Worley, F. 2001. *Roman Cremated Animal Remains from Brougham, Cumbria*. Conference (Beyond Bones) Presentation at the Groningen Institute of Archaeology, February 16. [Unpublished.]

Wrathmell, S. and Nicholson, A. 1990. *Dalton Parlours: Iron Age Settlement and Roman Villa*. Yorkshire Archaeology 3. Bradford.

Wright, E. V., Hedges, R. E. M., Bayliss, A. and Van de Noort, R. 2001. New AMS radiocarbon dates for the North Ferriby boats – a contribution to dating prehistoric seafaring in north-western Europe. *Antiquity*, 75, 726–34.

Wright, R. P. 1964. Inscriptions. *Journal of Roman Studies*, 54, 177–85.

Wright, R. P. and Hassall, M. W. C. 1973. Inscriptions. *Britannia*, 4, 324–37.

Wright, R. P. and Richmond, I. A. 1955. *The Roman Inscribed and Sculptured Stones in the Grosvenor Museum, Chester*. Chester.

Zeepvat, R. 1987. Romano-British settlement in the Upper Ouse and Ouzel valleys. In D. Maynard (ed.), *Roman Milton Keynes. Excavations and Fieldwork, 1971–82*. Buckinghamshire Archaeological Society Monograph 1. Aylesbury.

Zeepvat, R. (ed.) 2000. *Three Iron Age and Romano-British Rural Settlements on English Gravels*. BAR (British Series) 312. Oxford.

Zienkiewicz, J. D. 1986. *The Legionary Fortress Baths at Caerleon*. Cardiff.

Index